Chablis

THE
WORLD ATLAS
OF WINE

FOURTH EDITION

This edition is dedicated to the memory of
three men who changed the world of wine:
Julio Gallo,
Baron Philippe de Rothschild,
Max Schubert

Hugh Johnson

THE
WORLD ATLAS
OF WINE

FOURTH EDITION
COMPLETELY REVISED

MAISON FONDÉE
MITCHELL
BEAZLEY
EN 1969

Contents

THE WORLD ATLAS OF WINE
Hugh Johnson

The World Atlas of Wine © 1971, 1977, 1985, 1994
Mitchell Beazley International Limited
Text © 1971, 1977, 1985, 1994 Hugh Johnson
Maps and graphics © 1971, 1977, 1985, 1994
Mitchell Beazley International Limited

Published in Great Britain in 1994
by Mitchell Beazley
an imprint of Reed Consumer Books Ltd
Michelin House
81 Fulham Road
London SW3 6RB
and Auckland, Melbourne, Singapore and Toronto

Senior Editor: Stephanie Horner
Senior Art Editor: Paul Drayson
Cartographic Editor: Zöe Goodwin
Editors: Diane Pengelly, Anthea Snow
Designers: Mike Moule, Paul Tilby, Keith Williams
Fulfilment Manager: Barbara Hind

Index: Lyn Greenwood
Gazetteer: Sally Chorley
Production: Michelle Thomas

Executive Editor: Anne Ryland
Art Director: Tim Foster

Revisions and new cartography for the fourth edition:
Thames Cartographic Services
Original cartography: Clyde Surveys Limited

Colour reproduction: Mandarin Singapore
Produced by Mandarin Offset
Printed in China.

A CIP catalogue record for this book is available from
the British Library

ISBN 1–85732–268–1

All comparative statistics are taken from the Office International
de la Vigne et du Vin (OIV) booklet, The State of Vitiviniculture in
the World and the Statistical Information in 1991, by R Tinlot and
M Rousseau, published Nov/Dec 1992.

How the maps work

The maps in this Atlas vary considerably in scale, the
level of detail depending on the complexity of the area
mapped. There is a scale bar with each map. Contour
intervals vary from map to map and are shown in each
map key. In general, Roman type on the maps indicates
names and places connected with wine; italic type mainly
shows other information.

Each map page has a grid with letters down the side
and numbers across the bottom. To locate a château,
winery, etc, look up the name in the Gazetteer (pages
306–19) which gives the page number followed by the
grid reference.

Every effort has been made to make the maps in this
Atlas as complete and up to date as possible. In order
that future editions may be kept up to this standard, the
publishers will be grateful for information about changes
of boundaries or names which should be recorded.

1 INTRODUCTION

Foreword 7
Introduction 8
The World of Wine 10
The Ancient World 12
The Middle Ages 14
The Evolution of Modern Wine 16
The Vine 18
Designing a Vineyard 20
Terroir 22
The Choice of a Grape: 1 24
The Choice of a Grape: 2 26
Wine and the Weather 28
A Winemaker's Calendar 30
How Wine is Made 32
The Art of the Winemaker 34
Anatomy of a Château 36
Anatomy of a Winery 38
Wine and Time 40
Tasting and Talking about Wine 42
Taking Notes and Giving Scores 44
Looking After Wine 46
Serving Wine 48
Serving Wine: Temperature 50

2 FRANCE

Introduction 52
Burgundy 54
The Côte d'Or: the Quality Factor 56
The Côte d'Or 58
The Côte de Beaune: Santenay 59
The Côte de Beaune: Meursault 60
The Côte de Beaune: Beaune 62
The Côte de Nuits: Nuits-St-Georges 64
The Côte de Nuits: Gevrey-
Chambertin 66
The Côte Chalonnaise 68
The Mâconnais 69
Beaujolais 70
The Crus of Beaujolais 72
Chablis 73
The Heart of Chablis 74
Champagne 76
The Heart of Champagne 78
Bordeaux: Introduction 80
Bordeaux: the Quality Factor 82
The Bas-Médoc 84
St-Estèphe 86
Pauillac 88
St-Julien 90
The Central Médoc 92
Margaux and the Southern Médoc 94
Graves and Entre-Deux-Mers 96
Pessac–Léognan 98
Sauternes and Barsac 100
The Libournais 102
St-Emilion 104
Pomerol 106
Bourg and Blaye 108
Bergerac 109
Cognac 110
Wines of the Southwest 112
The Loire Valley and Muscadet 114
Anjou 116
Chinon and Bourgueil 117
Vouvray 118
Pouilly and Sancerre 119
Alsace 120
The Heart of Alsace 122
The Rhône Valley: the North 124
Côte Rôtie and Condrieu 126
Hermitage 127
The Rhône Valley: the South 128
Châteauneuf-du-Pape 130
Roussillon, Corbières and Minervois 132
Languedoc – the Plains 134
Provence 136
Savoie and the Jura 137
Vins de Pays 138
Corsica 140

3 GERMANY

Introduction 142
The Quality Factor 144
The Saar 146
The Ruwer 148
The Middle Mosel: Piesport 150
The Middle Mosel: Bernkastel 152
The Nahe 154
The Rheingau: Rudesheim 156
The Rheingau: Eltville 158
The Pfalz 160
Rheinhessen 162
Baden-Württemberg 164
Franconia 166
Sachsen and Saale-Unstrut 167
German Wine Law and Labels 168

4 SOUTHERN AND EASTERN EUROPE AND THE MEDITERRANEAN

ITALY 170
Northwest Italy 172
Piemonte 174
Barbaresco and Barolo 176
Lombardy: Valtellina and Oltrepò Pavese 177
Northeast Italy 178
Veneto and Friuli-Venezia Giulia 180
Verona 182
Collio 183
Trentino 184
Alto Adige 185
Central Italy 186
Chianti 188
South Tuscany 190
Bolgheri 191
Umbria 192
The Castelli Romani 193
Southern Italy 194

SPAIN 196
Jerez de la Frontera 199
The Sherry Country 200
Rioja 202
Catalonia 204
Rueda and the Duero 206
Montilla, Málaga and the Canaries 207

PORTUGAL 208
Lisbon 209
Bairrada 210
Minho and Dão 211
The Alto Douro 212
The Port Lodges 214
Alentejo 215
Madeira 216

SWITZERLAND 218
Valais and Vaud 220

AUSTRIA 222
Vienna 224
Wachau 225

HUNGARY 226
Tokay 228

THE CZECH AND SLOVAK REPUBLICS 230
SLOVENIA 231
THE FORMER YUGOSLAVIA 232
BULGARIA 234
ROMANIA 236
GREECE 238
RUSSIA, CRIMEA 240
MOLDOVA 241
THE EASTERN MEDITERRANEAN 242
CYPRUS 244
NORTH AFRICA 245
ASIA 246
JAPAN 247

5 THE NEW WORLD

NORTH AMERICA 250
California 252
Sonoma Valley 254
North Sonoma 255
Mendocino and Lake County 256
Carneros 257
Napa Valley 258
Napa: the Quality Factor 261
South of the Bay 262
The South Central Coast 264
The Central Valley 266
The Southwest States and Mexico 268
The Pacific Northwest 270
Yakima 272
Willamette 273
New York, the Eastern States and Ontario 274

AUSTRALIA 276
New South Wales 278
Victoria 280
South Australia 1: Barossa, Clare 282
South Australia 2: Southern Vales, Coonawarra 284
Western Australia 286
Tasmania 287

NEW ZEALAND 288

SOUTH AFRICA 290
Paarl and Stellenbosch 292

SOUTH AMERICA 294
Chile 296

ENGLAND AND WALES 298

General Index 300
Gazetteer 306
Acknowledgments 320

'Wine tasting in London docks' by George Cruikshank, 1821

INSTITUT NATIONAL DES APPELLATIONS D'ORIGINE

138 Champs Elysées   75008 PARIS

Quel redoutable honneur que de préfacer cette quatrième édition de l'Atlas Mondial du Vin, car cet ouvrage remarquable de Monsieur Hugh Johnson est une institution; par ailleurs, le fait que cet atlas soit mondial confère au français que je suis une responsabilité particulière. Il me faut tenter de l'assumer.

Le vin est oecuménique par essence, et par nature. Fait de variété, sachant prendre de multiples facettes, le vin sait satisfaire une gamme très ouverte de consommateurs, issus des quatre coins de la planète. Il sait rassembler un monde divisé. Nos vignobles du monde nous viennent de l'histoire, de la culture; ils sont faits d'histoire et de culture. Les savoir-faire des hommes issus le plus souvent de la tradition, ont su extraire des entrailles de la terre des vins aux expressions d'une complexité si fantastique que tout amateur aspire en permanence à les découvrir. Comment ne pas rendre hommage à Hugh Johnson qui nous offre, avec cet ouvrage, le monde du vin, dans toute sa richesse et toute sa diversité.

Il est notamment une diversité qui nous est chère à l'I.N.A.O.; il s'agit de celle des terroirs. Le terroir est ce complexe fait de géographie, d'histoire, de géologie, de climatologie, de sociologie, d'ethnologie; il est constitué de la symbiose entre l'homme et son environnement.

L'empirisme a permis aux hommes de sélectionner le ou lés cepages qui savent révéler au mieux l'expression du terroir, au travers des vins élaborés dans notre monde viticole.

N'oublions jamais la part assumée par les terroirs dans l'expression de nos vins; ne banalisons pas ces terroirs en leur substituant des techniques standardisatrices. Car c'est d'eux que viennent la richesse et la diversité de nos vins, puisqu'ils sont eux même riches et divers.

Le marché du vin est mondial, la concurrence y est forte. Mais les consommateurs dans le monde expriment du Nord au Sud, de l'Est à l'Ouest des relations au vin différentes, auxquelles il nous faut obéir dans leur pluralité. Il s'agit là d'une grande richesse qui nous laisse beaucoup d'espoir. Encore faut-il que nous sachions l'entretenir en preservant une offre de vins respectueuse des diversités.

Un grand merci à Hugh Johnson qui avec ce bel ouvrage entretient la connaissance de nos vignobles; chacun nous montre sa spécificité, et de la mosaïque de ces vignobles nait la formidable palette de nos vins. Que de messages à puiser dans l'univers du vin pour notre monde à la fois perturbé et, malgré tout, toujours enclin à se réfugier dans la standardisation.

Paris, Février 1994

ALAIN BERGER

DIRECTEUR DE L'INSTITUT NATIONAL DES APPELLATIONS D'ORIGINE

Introduction

This Atlas was conceived in 1970 as a way of making the happily absorbing study of wine easier, clearer and more precise. To anyone who hopes to distinguish and remember among the bewildering thousands of the world's wines, maps are the logical, the vital, ally. With a map names are no longer isolated but part of a picture, distinctions and relationships become clearer, tastes begin to form a pattern which is much more memorable than individual impressions.

Revising and largely rewriting it for this fourth edition has made me reflect on 23 years of constantly accelerating change. The first edition was published in 1971, the second in 1977 and the third in 1986. Each new version gave me truckloads of new material and an increasing sense that the world of wine, far from being peacefully repetitive, a long afternoon of vines and vats, was expanding and advancing steadily, apparently towards a golden age of quality and plenty.

The fourth edition appears in a less certain climate. The 1990s began with Revolutions that have redrawn the political map of Europe; but parallel revolutions, too, in the way we question traditions, the way we collect and analyse data, and the world-wide spread of technology.

The end of the Cold War jolted the world's sense of stability. It also coincided with, or set off, a depression that threatened many well-found businesses and drove the affluent wine-drinking world to count its pennies.

These circumstances have caused stresses and found fault lines in the long-evolved world of wine. They have set off fundamental debates about how wines should be described, defined, judged and valued. To understand the situation now it is best to start where I did in 1970, in a world of accepted convention, if not of innocence.

The first appellations
In 1970 France was the only wine country with a comprehensive set of wine laws based on geography – the result of the foundation in the 1930s of the Institut National des Appellations d'Origine. The new appellations were beautifully mapped by Louis Larmat in the 1940s. Larmat's were the only detailed wine maps of any country until the first edition of this Atlas. Since that date, country after country and region after region has defined or redefined its vineyards and produced maps to prove it.

Italy started in the 1960s, Spain in 1970, Germany in 1971, Austria and South Africa in 1972. Since then Portugal, Greece, the former Yugoslavia, New Zealand, Argentina, Chile, Bulgaria and, since 1980, the United States have plotted, or started plotting, appellations, under whatever name or guise. By 1993 even Australia was scrambling to the finishing line with a list of countless wine regions – though still no maps. Now there is a pressing motive; the whip of the harmonization squad of the European Community.

The maps in this Atlas were originally based largely on informal sources, on usage rather than statute. Every year has brought more precise data, more appellations with the force of law, and more refinements of existing appellation systems – all grist to the map-maker's mill.

But while governments have been preparing to defend their traditions, or at least their markets, with the geographical weapons first devised by the French, the global village effect has been pulling in the opposite direction. The authorities who designate and control appellations, especially the French, approach the 21st century with a certain apprehension.

The system of appellations so successfully and elaborately constructed on local knowledge of *terroirs*, masterminded in Paris, has almost the force of a religion. In any religion, though, faith is necessary. Any heresy can be contagious. The 1980s saw the rise of a powerful heresy, not in France but in the New World countries that emulate and envy her. It is that only the grape variety really matters.

Name a grape
'Varietalism', to give it a name, is easy. No historical background is needed. The trick is to persuade consumers that the tastes and aromas of specific grapes are all that constitutes character and quality in wine.

Once you have shown that Chardonnay from Oregon, South Africa, no matter where, has a flavour in common with Chardonnay from Burgundy (and even more when you have added to it the expensive flavour of French-grown oak) you can begin to argue that that is all there is to it.

It is a seductive argument at first for anyone whose vineyards are outside the hallowed circle of the 'classics'. It tries to show the concept of privileged *terroirs* as hocus-pocus intended merely to defend established interests. It defeats itself, though, on two counts.

First and most important, because the differences between *terroirs* are facts. No one can seriously defend the view that valley and hillside, chalk and sand, north slope and south slope make no difference to the wine. This is the subject-matter of this Atlas: open it anywhere and see the evidence.

Second, the anti-*terroir* argument falls because it is against progress. If progress is about making better wine it is about choosing the best places to grow it: in other words discovering new excellent *terroirs*. This is the excitement of plotting the developing wine world. It is the very opposite of the dull varietal position. It explores the globe (as freelance oenologists increasingly do) for places that can add new forms of excellence for us all to choose from.

New regions to note
What are the new places that we should know about – regions that are exploring their own *terroirs*, either for the first time or with new urgency and resolve? Italy should probably have pride of place, because in 1992 her increasingly outmoded DOC laws were replaced with a completely new system that precisely embodies what I have described above: the acceptance, on conditions, of newly defined *terroirs*, and the rejection of appellations based primarily on grape varieties.

Spain and Portugal have certainly created many new regions – though here one feels it is sometimes more in anticipation than realization of great new discoveries. The same is true of Greece – and come to that of many of the AVAs that now so impressively carve up the USA.

France continues to evolve; especially in the heartland of her best-selling *vins de pays*, the Midi (one of the places, incidentally, where the varietal/*terroir* debate is most vividly seen in action). More space is also devoted in this edition to Alsace,

Beaujolais and Chablis. The German authorities, meanwhile, continue to miss every boat, bus and plane to a wine-law that its growers and the world can take seriously.

For lack of official German resolution this Atlas takes the initiative and maps for the first time what the authorities have sadly failed to recognize: the finest *terroirs* in the finest regions. Although this mapping is my own responsibility and must be considered provisional, I hope it will break the absurd log-jam that prevents the world from recognizing Germany's greatest wines. In the same way this edition plots for the first time the precise vineyards of the first-growths of Bordeaux – and also of Tokay, Eastern Europe's greatest wine region, now at last free again to make its unique great wine.

Other regions that have extra space and new maps in this edition, in recognition of their progress in defining their own potential, include the Northwest, Southwest and Northeast of the United States, parts of Australia and New Zealand, Chile, Slovenia, East Asia and the ex-USSR.

You, the consumer

The emphasis of this Atlas continues to be on the consumer's point of view. My priorities are those of a wine-lover of the Western world, unattached to any particular country or region except by the appeal of its produce.

There can be no question of finding one style or one set of criteria to apply to every map. No two regions have the same standards, or place emphasis on the same things. In Burgundy there is the most complex grading of fields ever attempted: each field, and even parts of fields, being classified in a hierarchy that is cut and dried. In areas of Bordeaux there is a formal grading of properties; not directly related to the land but to the estates on it. In Germany there is no official land classification at all, so I have attempted my own. In Champagne whole villages are classed, in Jerez soils of certain kinds, in Italy some of the best wine zones, but not others.

Behind all this tangle of nomenclature and classification lies the physical fact of the *terroir*, the hills and valleys where the vine grows. In each case I have tried to make it plain, so far as I have been able to discover, not only which corner of the countryside gives the best wine, but why; what happy accident of nature has led to the development of a classic taste which has become familiar – at least by name – to half the world.

There are reproductions of paintings; music has scores; poems are printed; architecture can be drawn – but wine is a fleeting moment. One cannot write about wine, and stumble among the borrowed words and phrases which have to serve to describe it,

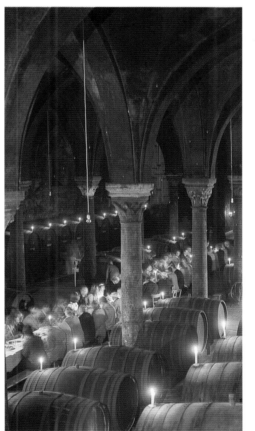

The cellar of the 12th-century Cistercian abbey of Eberbach in the Rheingau has sheltered the wines of the Steinberg for 700 years. Together with the Clos de Vougeot in Burgundy it symbolizes the crucial role of Christianity in the history of wine.

without wanting to put a glass in the reader's hand and say, 'Taste this'. For it is not every Nuits-St-Georges or Napa Cabernet that answers the glowing terms of a general description – the liquor shops of the world are awash with wines that bear little or no relation to the true character of the land.

This is the reason for giving the most direct form of reference available: the labels of more than 1,000 producers whose wines truly represent the subject matter of the Atlas. Among the many thousands who qualify to be included choice is almost impossible. As it stands it is partly personal, as anything to do with taste must be, and partly arbitrary, as the limitations of space ruthlessly cut out firm favourites.

Personal thanks

No book like this could be attempted without the generous help of authorities in all the countries it deals with. Their enthusiasm and painstaking care have made it possible. On page 320 there is a list of government and local offices, and some of the many growers, merchants and scholars, who have so kindly helped, and to whom I owe the great volume of information embodied both in the maps and the text. The facts are theirs; unless I quote a source, on the other hand, I must be held responsible for the opinions.

Apart from those named above and those whose help is acknowledged, this is the place to record my thanks to the team in the front line. Map-making is the most demanding form of draughtsmanship: I owe a great debt to Thames Cartographic and Bob Croser for the thousands of hours they have spent plotting and checking. Zoë Goodwin must be the world's most cheerful, as well as disciplined, supervisor of cartography, responsible for the research, briefing and correction of every map.

It falls to the editor to coordinate and make sense of every aspect of a book. Stephanie Horner combines understanding and resilience, patience, intuition and tact to a high degree. She has also beavered away as very few editors do on many aspects of research which ought, by rights, to be the author's.

Paul Drayson has now designed so many of my books that I am in danger of taking for granted the meticulous freshness and elegance of his work. Simon McMurtrie and Anne Ryland, in overall charge, kept us all relatively calm in a schedule with no respite, not only producing this English edition, but also coordinating German and French editions to appear simultaneously.

To all of them, to my wife Judy, who knows more than she wants about every detail, and to my secretary, Hanne Evans, I publicly acknowledge that the author of such a book as this gets far more than his fair share of the credit.

The World of Wine

The world today has some 20 million acres – 8.5 million hectares – of vineyards. They produce an annual crop of more than 25,000 million bottles of wine; enough, if there are 5,000 million people on earth, to give the world's entire population five bottles a year each.

Yet wine, food and comforter as it is, is very far from being a universal phenomenon. It is part of a cultural and agricultural pattern peculiar to the earth's temperate zones where Mediterranean, or 'Western', man has flourished. Wine-growing and wine-drinking are rooted in the most widespread, longest-lived civilization the earth has known. But they have never yet successfully or significantly colonized other cultures.

The map shows the distribution of vineyards and wine production around the world. Europe still accounts for over three-quarters of production. Many Eastern countries have considerable vineyards but produce no wine, or very little; table-grape acreage is included in the figures.

Italy and France remain far and away the biggest producers (with Spain now in third place) – but no longer the biggest consumers by their traditional massive margin. From 1968 to 1991 the French average consumption dropped by nearly two-thirds: from an annual 150 bottles per head to 67. Italian wine-drinking is dwindling almost as fast. Modern life has no place for the heroic quantities working people used to put away. A car-filled world inevitably means drinking much less – but also better. Expenditure on wine has risen as consumption has fallen.

The few countries that are increasing their consumption over the medium term (although not at a rate anything like fast enough to absorb the surplus) are those where wine is considered a luxury rather than a staple beverage: the USA, Britain, Japan (though these three have actually declined slightly with recession), Germany, Australia, Canada, South Africa, Belgium, Switzerland, the Netherlands and Scandinavia.

Spain, Portugal and Hungary are the exceptions: big producers who are also slightly increasing their consumption.

In the 1960s and 1970s the world's vineyard acreage was increasing fast, with the USSR and other communist-bloc countries, Argentina and the USA leading the way. It peaked in 1980 and has been steadily shrinking since. It is now lower than at any time since the 1950s. Greater productivity from a smaller acreage accounts for part of this decline: between 1950 and 1980 acreage increased by 13%, production by 35%. So does the reversal of Soviet agricultural policy in the 1980s. Most important, and pointing the way forward, is the increased emphasis on quality at the expense of quantity. Those who are drinking less are spending more. The new recruits in North America, northern Europe, Australasia are being trained to demand well-made wine.

Alas, for the poor traditional wine farmer the 'wine lake' will not go away. From time immemorial there has been a glut of third-rate wine. Never before, until the present age of scientific advance and technological control, has there been more than enough good wine to go round.

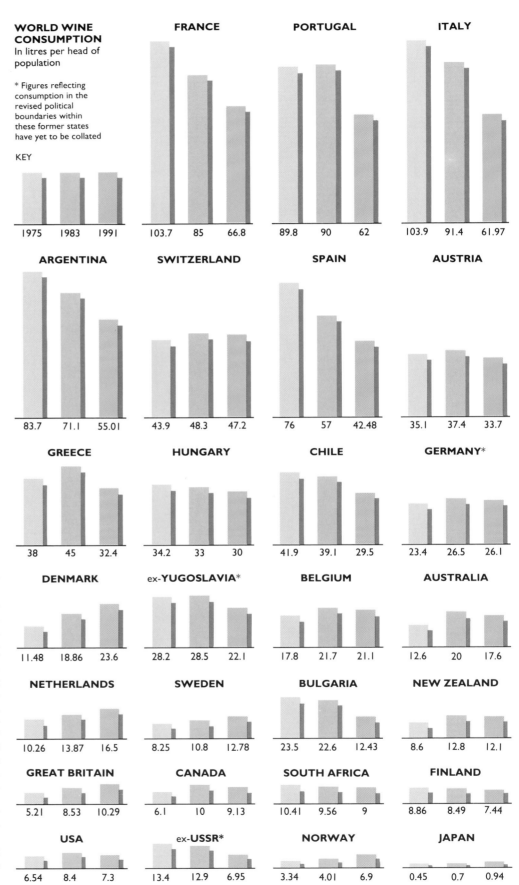

WORLD WINE CONSUMPTION
In litres per head of population

* Figures reflecting consumption in the revised political boundaries within these former states have yet to be collated

KEY

1975	1983	1991

FRANCE — 103.7 | 85 | 66.8
PORTUGAL — 89.8 | 90 | 62
ITALY — 103.9 | 91.4 | 61.97
ARGENTINA — 83.7 | 71.1 | 55.01
SWITZERLAND — 43.9 | 48.3 | 47.2
SPAIN — 76 | 57 | 42.48
AUSTRIA — 35.1 | 37.4 | 33.7
GREECE — 38 | 45 | 32.4
HUNGARY — 34.2 | 33 | 30
CHILE — 41.9 | 39.1 | 29.5
GERMANY* — 23.4 | 26.5 | 26.1
DENMARK — 11.48 | 18.86 | 23.6
ex-YUGOSLAVIA* — 28.2 | 28.5 | 22.1
BELGIUM — 17.8 | 21.7 | 21.1
AUSTRALIA — 12.6 | 20 | 17.6
NETHERLANDS — 10.26 | 13.87 | 16.5
SWEDEN — 8.25 | 10.8 | 12.78
BULGARIA — 23.5 | 22.6 | 12.43
NEW ZEALAND — 8.6 | 12.8 | 12.1
GREAT BRITAIN — 5.21 | 8.53 | 10.29
CANADA — 6.1 | 10 | 9.13
SOUTH AFRICA — 10.41 | 9.56 | 9
FINLAND — 8.86 | 8.49 | 7.44
USA — 6.54 | 8.4 | 7.3
ex-USSR* — 13.4 | 12.9 | 6.95
NORWAY — 3.34 | 4.01 | 6.9
JAPAN — 0.45 | 0.7 | 0.94

10

DISTRIBUTION OF THE WORLD'S VINEYARDS

In 1,000s hectares (1991 figures)

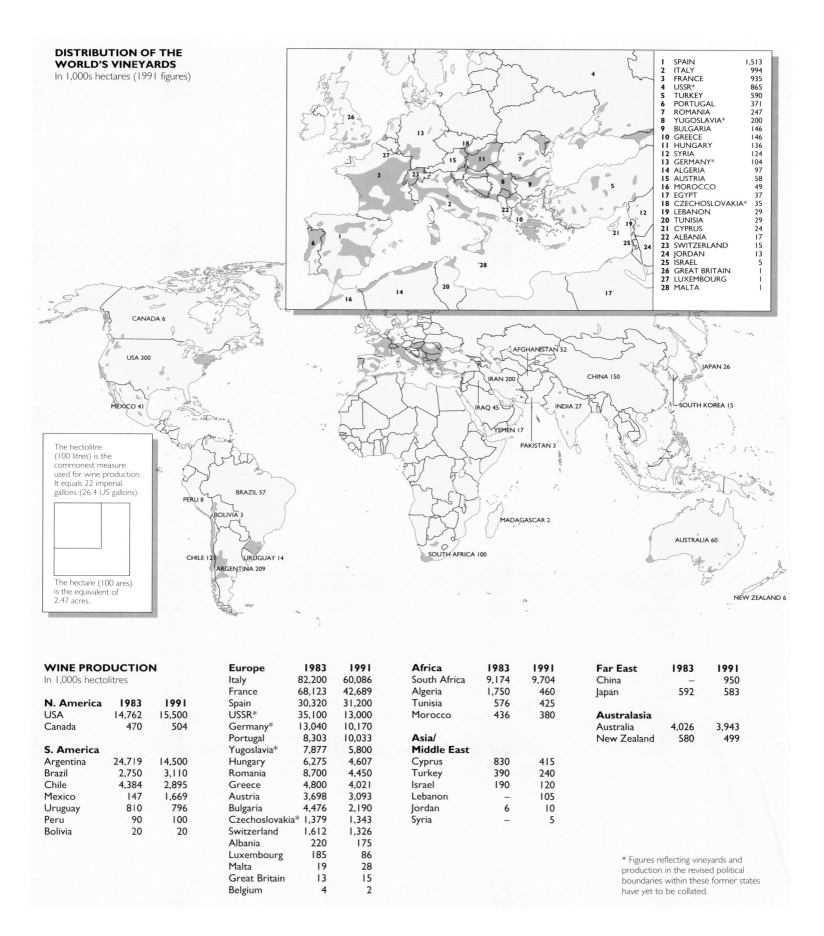

1	SPAIN	1,513
2	ITALY	994
3	FRANCE	935
4	USSR*	865
5	TURKEY	590
6	PORTUGAL	371
7	ROMANIA	247
8	YUGOSLAVIA*	200
9	BULGARIA	146
10	GREECE	146
11	HUNGARY	136
12	SYRIA	124
13	GERMANY*	104
14	ALGERIA	97
15	AUSTRIA	58
16	MOROCCO	49
17	EGYPT	37
18	CZECHOSLOVAKIA*	35
19	LEBANON	29
20	TUNISIA	29
21	CYPRUS	24
22	ALBANIA	17
23	SWITZERLAND	15
24	JORDAN	13
25	ISRAEL	5
26	GREAT BRITAIN	1
27	LUXEMBOURG	1
28	MALTA	1

Map labels:

CANADA 6
USA 300
MEXICO 41
PERU 8
BOLIVIA 3
BRAZIL 57
CHILE 121
URUGUAY 14
ARGENTINA 209
AFGHANISTAN 52
IRAN 200
IRAQ 45
YEMEN 17
PAKISTAN 3
INDIA 27
CHINA 150
JAPAN 26
SOUTH KOREA 15
MADAGASCAR 2
SOUTH AFRICA 100
AUSTRALIA 60
NEW ZEALAND 6

The hectolitre (100 litres) is the commonest measure used for wine production. It equals 22 imperial gallons (26.4 US gallons).

The hectare (100 ares) is the equivalent of 2.47 acres.

WINE PRODUCTION

In 1,000s hectolitres

N. America	1983	1991
USA	14,762	15,500
Canada	470	504

S. America	1983	1991
Argentina	24,719	14,500
Brazil	2,750	3,110
Chile	4,384	2,895
Mexico	147	1,669
Uruguay	810	796
Peru	90	100
Bolivia	20	20

Europe	1983	1991
Italy	82,200	60,086
France	68,123	42,689
Spain	30,320	31,200
USSR*	35,100	13,000
Germany*	13,040	10,170
Portugal	8,303	10,033
Yugoslavia*	7,877	5,800
Hungary	6,275	4,607
Romania	8,700	4,450
Greece	4,800	4,021
Austria	3,698	3,093
Bulgaria	4,476	2,190
Czechoslovakia*	1,379	1,343
Switzerland	1,612	1,326
Albania	220	175
Luxembourg	185	86
Malta	19	28
Great Britain	13	15
Belgium	4	2

Africa	1983	1991
South Africa	9,174	9,704
Algeria	1,750	460
Tunisia	576	425
Morocco	436	380

Asia/ Middle East		
Cyprus	830	415
Turkey	390	240
Israel	190	120
Lebanon	–	105
Jordan	6	10
Syria	–	5

Far East	1983	1991
China	–	950
Japan	592	583

Australasia		
Australia	4,026	3,943
New Zealand	580	499

* Figures reflecting vineyards and production in the revised political boundaries within these former states have yet to be collated.

11

The Ancient World

Wine is far older than recorded history. It emerges with civilization itself from the East. The evidence from tablets and papyri and Egyptian tombs fills volumes. Mankind, as we recognize ourselves, working, quarrelling, loving and worrying, comes on the scene with the support of a jug of wine.

Pharaonic wine, however vividly painted for us to see, is too remote to have any meaning. Our age of wine, with still-traceable roots, begins with the Greeks and Phoenicians who colonized the Mediterranean, starting about 1500 BC. It was then that wine first arrived where it was to make its real home: Italy, France and Spain. The Greeks called Italy the Land of Vines, just as the Vikings called America Vinland from the profusion of its native vines 2,000 years later. North Africa, southern Spain, Provence, Sicily, the Italian mainland and the Black Sea had their first vineyards in the time of the Greek and Phoenician Empires.

The wines of Greece herself, no great matter today, were lavishly praised and documented by her poets. There was even a fashionable after-dinner game in Athens which consisted of throwing the last few mouthfuls of wine in your cup into the air, to hit a delicately balanced dish on a pole. Smart young things took coaching in the finer points of 'kottabos'. But such treatment of the wine, and the knowledge that it was almost invariably drunk as what we would call 'a wine cup', flavoured with herbs, spices and honey and diluted with water (sometimes even seawater) seems to question its innate quality. That the wines of different islands of the Aegean were highly prized for their distinct characters is indisputable. Chios in particular was a supplier in constant demand. Whether the wines would appeal to us today we have no way of knowing.

Greeks industrialized winegrowing in southern Italy, Etruscans in Tuscany and further north, and Romans followed. So much was

Above: this ancient Egyptian painting shows grape-treaders under an arbour of vines. It comes from the tomb of Nakht, an official from Thebes who died in the 15th century BC.

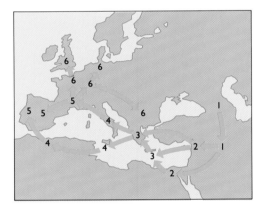

written about wine and winemaking in ancient Rome that it is possible to make a rough map (right) of the wines of the early Roman Empire. The greatest writers, even Virgil, wrote instructions to winegrowers. One sentence of his – 'Vines love an open hill' – is perhaps the best single piece of advice which can be given to a winegrower.

Others were much more calculating, discussing how much work a slave could do for how little food and sleep without losing condition. Roman winegrowing was on a very large scale, and business calculation was at the heart of it. It spread right across the Empire, so that Rome was eventually importing countless shiploads of amphoras from her colonies in Spain, North Africa – the entire Mediterranean.

How good was Roman wine? Some of it apparently had extraordinary powers of keeping, which in itself suggests that it was well made. It was frequently concentrated by heating, and even smoked to achieve what must have been a madeira-like effect. On the other hand Pliny, whose Natural History contains a complete text-book on wines and winemaking, recommends the boiling of concentration of must in vessels made of lead, 'to sweeten it'. The resulting lead oxide poisoning must have been excruciating. The cholics, and eventual blindness, insanity and death that resulted were never connected with their cause; pains were even put down to bad vintages.

Left: the early movements of the vine. Starting in Caucasia or Mesopotamia **1** in perhaps 6000 BC it was cultivated in Egypt and Phoenicia **2** in about 3000 BC. By 2000 BC it was in Greece **3** and by 1000 BC it was in Italy, Sicily and North Africa **4**. In the next 500 years it reached at least Spain, Portugal and the south of France **5** and probably southern Russia as well. Finally (see map on opposite page) it spread with the Romans into northern Europe **6**, getting as far as Britain.

Right: the ceremonial of wine-drinking is one of the favourite motifs of Greek painting. This wine-cup from about 500 BC illustrates the wine mixed in a *krater* being labelled, with due reverence, into a drinking-cup or *kylix*. A 'symposium' was simply an evening of wine-drinking.

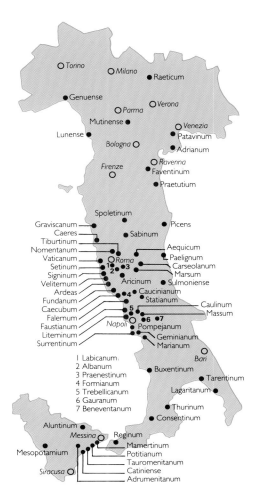

Above: barrels were used by the Romans. This one was found being used as the lining of a well at Silchester in southern England. *Left*: the Romans interpreted the graceful Greek wine god Dionysus as a more fleshly creature; in a mosaic from Pompeii, he rides his traditional mount, a lion, but boozes from a monstrous pot.

Above: the wines the Romans drank; a reconstruction of winegrowing Italy in AD 100. Names of modern cities are given in italics; wine names in roman type.

Rome's great vintages were discussed and even drunk for longer than seems possible; the famous Opimian – from the year of the consulship in Opimius, 121 BC – was being drunk when it was 125 years old.

Certainly the Romans had all that is necessary for ageing wine. They were not limited to earthenware amphoras like the Greeks – although they used them. They had barrels just like modern barrels and bottles not unlike modern bottles. The art of glass-making came to Rome from Syria. Most Italians of 2,000 years ago probably drank wine very like their descendants today; young, rather roughly made, sharp or strong according to the vintage. The quantities they drank, though, were prodigious; the Roman orgy is by no means a flight of later imagination. Even the Roman method of cultivation of the vine on trees, the festoons which became the friezes on classical buildings, is still practised here and there in the south of Italy and (especially) northern Portugal.

The Greeks – or perhaps the Etruscans from Tuscany – took wine north to southern Gaul.

The Romans domesticated it there. By the time they withdrew from what is now France in the fifth century they had laid the foundations for almost all the most famous vineyards of the modern world.

Starting in Provence, which had had Greek-planted vineyards already for centuries, they moved up the Rhône valley and into the Languedoc, the Provincia Narbonensis, and across (or by sea?) to Bordeaux in the time of Julius Caesar. All the early developments were in the river valleys, the natural lines of communication, which the Romans cleared of forest and cultivated, at first as a precaution against ambushes. Besides, boats were the best way of moving anything so heavy as wine. Bordeaux, Burgundy, Trier on the Moselle (where the museum preserves a fully laden and manned Roman wine-boat in stone) probably all started as merchant-centres for imported Italian or Greek wine, then planted their own vines and eventually surpassed the imported product.

By the second century there were vines in Burgundy; by the third on the Loire; and by the fourth at Paris (not such a good idea), in Champagne, and on the Moselle and the Rhine. The foundations had been dug for the French wine industry we still know.

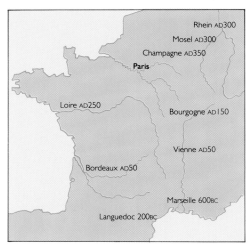

Above: the vineyards of France and Germany at the fall of the Roman Empire. The dates of their founding are mainly conjectural. Vineyards in the Languedoc and Marseille were founded by the Greeks; the rest by the Romans in the heyday of Roman Gaul.

The history of all these vineyards has been continuous; Alsace – which does not appear here – was probably founded in about AD 800.

The Middle Ages

Out of the Dark Ages which followed the fall of the Roman Empire we gradually emerge into the illumination of the medieval period, to see in its lovely painted pages an entirely familiar scene; winemaking methods that were not to change in their essentials until this century. The Church was the repository of the skills of civilization in the Dark Ages – indeed the continuation of Rome's Imperial administration under a new guise. The Emperor Charlemagne re-created an Imperial system – and took great and famous pains to legislate in favour of better wine.

As expansionist monasteries cleared hillsides and walled around fields of cuttings, and as dying winegrowers and departing crusaders bequeathed it their land, the Church came to be identified with wine – not only as the Blood of Christ, but as luxury and comfort in this world.

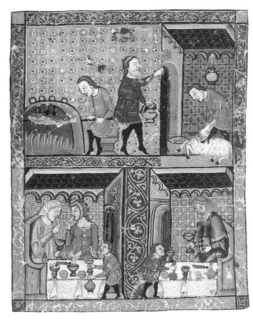

Right: wine had an important place in medieval life as part of both Jewish and Christian observance. This picture of a Jewish Passover is from an early 14th-century haggadah from northern Spain or Provence.

Cathedrals and churches, but above all the multiplying monasteries, owned or created most of the greatest vineyards of Europe.

The Benedictines, from their great mother-houses of Monte Cassino in Italy and Cluny in Burgundy, went out and cultivated the finest vineyards, until their way of life became notorious: 'rising from the table with their veins swollen with wine and their heads on fire'. Reaction came in 1112, when the young St Bernard split from the Benedictines and founded the ascetic order of the Cistercians, named for their new abbey of Cîteaux, within walking distance of the Côte d'Or. The Cistercian order was explosively successful, founding not only the great walled vineyards of the Clos de Vougeot in Burgundy and the Steinberg in the Rheingau, beside their abbey of Kloster Eberbach, but eventually magnificent monasteries all over Europe – and eventually, of course, becoming as notorious for their gluttony as the Benedictines.

The one important exception to domination by the Church was the thriving vineyard of

Bordeaux, where development was simply commercial with a single market in view. From 1153 to 1455 the great Duchy of Aquitaine, most of western France, was united by marriage to the crown of England and bent its efforts to filling great annual wine fleets with hogsheads of light claret, the *vin nouveau* the English loved.

But it was within the stable framework of the Church and the monasteries, in which tools and terms and techniques seemed to stand still, that the styles of wine and even some of the grape varieties now familiar to us slowly came into being.

Right: the most sumptuous of all the famous prayer books of the Middle Ages was the *Très Riches Heures* painted for Jean, Duc de Berry by Pol Limbourg and his brothers about 1416. The month of September is represented by the homely scene of the vintage, under the splendid battlements of Saumur.

Below: a late 15th-century tapestry in the Musée de Cluny in Paris shows the court happily obstructing the vintagers on the banks of the Loire.

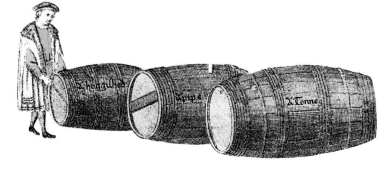

Right: in 1497 English wine measures included a hogshead (63 gallons), a pipe (two hogsheads) and a tonne (two pipes). The size of ships was measured by the number of tonnes they could carry.

The Evolution of Modern Wine

Up to the start of the 17th century wine was in the unique position of being the one and only wholesome and – up to a point – storable beverage. It had no challengers. Water was normally unsafe to drink, at least in cities. Ale without hops very quickly went bad. There were no spirits, nor any of the caffeine-containing drinks that appear essential to life today.

Europe drank wine on a scale it is difficult to conceive of; she must in fact have been in a perpetual fuddle. It is hard to have confidence in the descriptions of wine which survive from before about 1700. With the exception of Shakespeare's graphic tasting notes: 'a marvellous searching wine, and it perfumes the blood ere one can say "What's this?"', they tend to refer to royal recommendations or miraculous cures rather than to taste and characteristics.

In the 17th century all this changed; starting with chocolate from Central America, then coffee from Arabia and finally tea from China. At the same time the Dutch developed the art and commerce of distilling, turning huge tracts of western France into suppliers of cheap white wine for their stills; hops turned ale into more stable beer and great cities began to pipe the clean water they had lacked since the Romans.

The wine industry was threatened with catastrophe unless it developed new ideas. It is no coincidence that we date the creation of most of the wines we consider classics today from the second half of the 17th century. But these developments would never have succeeded without the timely invention of the glass wine bottle.

Since Roman times wine had spent all its life in a barrel. Bottles, or rather jugs, usually of pottery or leather, were used simply for bringing it to table. The early 17th century saw changes in glassmaking technology that made bottles stronger and cheaper to blow. At about the same time some unknown thinker brought together the bottle, the cork and the corkscrew.

Bit by bit it became clear that wine kept in a tightly corked bottle lasted far longer than wine kept in a barrel, which was likely to go off at any time after the barrel was broached. It also aged differently, acquiring a 'bouquet'. The *vin de garde* was created and with it the chance to double and treble the price of wines capable of ageing.

It was the owner of Château Haut-Brion who first picked up the idea of what we might

Above: Philippe Mercier's *Le Jeune Dégustateur*, painted in London in the 1740s, is one of the first illustrations of a corkscrew.

call 'reserve' wines; selected, later-picked, stronger, carefully made, and matured. In the 1660s he opened London's first restaurant under his own name, Pontac's Head, to publicize it.

In Champagne the great oenologist monk Dom Pérignon proceeded with the same idea, of perfecting by blending a drink so luxurious that the aristocracy would beg for it. By accident, or rather by the inherent nature of the wine of the region, once bottled it started to sparkle. The oenologist disapproved; the clientele did not.

In the early 18th century Burgundy changed its nature too. The most delicate wines, Volnay and Savigny, were once the most fashionable. Now these *vins de primeur* began to give way to the demand for long-fermented, dark-coloured *vins de garde*, especially from the Côte de Nuits.

The wine that benefited most from this treatment was the fiery port the English had started to drink in the late 17th century – not out of

choice but because the duty on their preferred French wine was raised to prohibitive levels by wars. They had doubts about it at first, but as the century, and their bottles, grew older, their opinion of it rose sharply. The trend is graphically illustrated by the way the port bottle changed shape within a hundred years. The old carafe model would not lie down, so its cork dried out. The slimmer bottle is easy to 'bin' horizontally in heaps. Before long the benefits of bottle-age were beginning to change the style of all the best wines of Europe.

In 1866 A Jullien published the figures for the alcoholic strengths of recent vintages. By today's standards the burgundies are formidable: Corton 1858, 15.6%; Montrachet 1858, 14.3%; Clos de Bèze 1858, 14.3%; Volnay 1859, 14.9%; Richebourg 1859, 14.3%. In contrast Bordeaux wines of the same two years ranged from 11.3% (St-Emilion Supérieur) to 8.9% (Château Lafite).

The low natural strength of the Bordeaux wines explains what seems today a curious habit of the old wine trade. Up to the mid-century the wines for England – which was most of the best

The evolution of the port bottle from 1708 when it was a carafe to 1812 when it had its modern proportions is a record of the emergence of vintage wine. With the discovery that bottled wine improved with keeping, bottles were designed to be 'laid down'.

| 1708 | 1719 | 1739 | 1741 | 1753 | 1780 | 1793 | 1807 | 1812 |

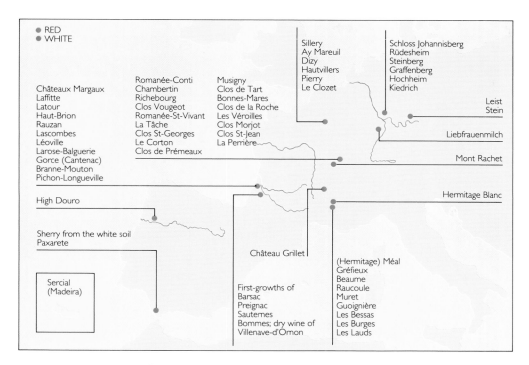

● RED
● WHITE

Châteaux Margaux
Laffitte
Latour
Haut-Brion
Rauzan
Lascombes
Léoville
Larose-Balguerie
Gorce (Cantenac)
Branne-Mouton
Pichon-Longueville

Romanée-Conti
Chambertin
Richebourg
Clos Vougeot
Romanée-St-Vivant
La Tâche
Clos St-Georges
Le Corton
Clos de Prémeaux

Musigny
Clos de Tart
Bonnes-Mares
Clos de la Roche
Les Véroilles
Clos Morjot
Clos St-Jean
La Perrière

Sillery
Ay Mareuil
Dizy
Hautvillers
Pierry
Le Clozet

Schloss Johannisberg
Rüdesheim
Steinberg
Graffenberg
Hochheim
Kiedrich

Leist
Stein

Liebfrauenmilch

Mont Rachet

High Douro

Sherry from the white soil
Paxarete

Sercial
(Madeira)

Château Grillet

First-growths of
Barsac
Preignac
Sauternes
Bommes; dry wine of
Villenave-d'Ornon

Hermitage Blanc

(Hermitage) Méal
Gréfieux
Beaume
Raucoule
Muret
Guoignière
Les Bessas
Les Burges
Les Lauds

of Bordeaux – were subjected to what was known as *le travail à l'anglaise*. One recipe called for 30 litres of Spanish wine (Alicante or Benicarlo), 2 litres of unfermented white must and a bottle of brandy to each barrel of claret. The summer after the vintage the wine was set to ferment again with these additives, then treated as other wines and kept several years in wood before shipping. The result was strong wine with a good flavour, but 'heady and not suitable for all stomachs'. It fetched more than natural wine.

Today's preoccupation with authenticity, even at the expense of quality, makes these practices seem abusive. But it is as if someone revealed as a shocking practice the addition of brandy to port. We like Douro wine with brandy in it; our ancestors liked Lafite with Alicante in it.

German wines of the last century would be scarcely more familiar to us. It is doubtful whether any of today's pale, intensely perfumed, rather sweet wines were made. Grapes picked earlier gave more acid wine, which needed to mature longer in cask. 'Old brown hock' was a recommendation.

Champagne was sweeter and fuller in colour and flavour – although otherwise very like it is today. Port and sherry had both been perfected. There was much more strong sweet wine: Malaga and Marsala were in their heydays. Madeira, Constantia and Tokay were as highly regarded as modern Trockenbeerenausleses.

The wine trade was booming. In the wine-growing countries an unhealthy amount of the economy rested on wine: in Italy in 1880 it was calculated that no less than 80% of the population more or less relied on wine for a living. This was the world phylloxera struck (see page 18). At the time, when it caused the pulling up of almost every vine in Europe and the New World it seemed like the end of the world of wine.

Above: It is interesting to compare A Jullien's 1866 classification of the world's great wines with our modern ideas. In his *Topographie de Tous les Vignobles Connus* his complete list named the vineyards shown on this map (in their original spelling). *Right*: Bordeaux's vineyard area and wine production in relation to wars, pests, diseases, slumps, booms and the weather, plotted by Philippe Roudié of Bordeaux University. Two great chemical aids, sulphur (against oidium mould) and Bordeaux mixture (copper sulphate and lime) against mildew had immediate effect. The prosperous 1980s saw a remarkable increase in crops.

The last 90 years have seen wine's Industrial Revolution. More particularly in the last 40 years the scientific background to winemaking has become so much clearer that many things which were thought impossible have become easy. Quality table wines from warm climates of the New World became possible in the 1940s, with refrigeration. The very lack of tradition and convention in Australia and California made these the places where wine science and experiment moved faster than ever. The modern winemaker is embarrassed by the number of options available. At the same time have come temptations to lower the standards of the best, to make more wine at the expense of quality. In due course the Old World began to learn new tricks. The pages of this Atlas seek to portray the wine world as it leaves the 20th century.

Today's great danger is the insidious trend towards using a limited palette of grapes to make familiar, safe wine, without local character, to please every taste. Winegrowers are anxious for a new market, and technology has shown them how to control what they make. It is essential for wine drinkers to demand individual wines with all their local character intact. It is up to us to see that the most enthralling thing about wine – its endless variety – survives.

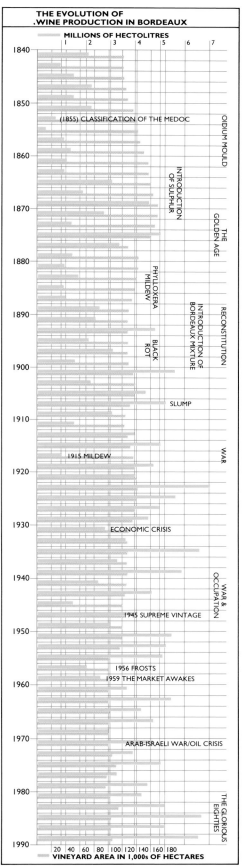

THE EVOLUTION OF WINE PRODUCTION IN BORDEAUX

MILLIONS OF HECTOLITRES
1   2   3   4   5   6   7

1840

1850
(1855) CLASSIFICATION OF THE MEDOC   OIDIUM MOULD

1860
                    INTRODUCTION OF SULPHUR

1870   THE GOLDEN AGE

1880
        PHYLLOXERA MILDEW

1890   INTRODUCTION OF BORDEAUX MIXTURE   RECONSTITUTION

1900   BLACK ROT

                    SLUMP
1910

        1915 MILDEW   WAR
1920

1930   ECONOMIC CRISIS

1940   WAR & OCCUPATION

        1945 SUPREME VINTAGE
1950

        1956 FROSTS
        1959 THE MARKET AWAKES
1960

1970   ARAB-ISRAELI WAR/OIL CRISIS

1980   THE GLORIOUS EIGHTIES

1990
20 40 60 80 100 120 140 160 180
VINEYARD AREA IN 1,000s OF HECTARES

The Vine

As early as the beginning of April in northern Europe (or September in the southern hemisphere) the gnarled wood of the vine sports tender shoots.

Within ten days of budding the stalk, leaves and tendrils are all obvious – and also vulnerable to nights of frost, which can come in late May.

In late May or early June the vine forms its flower buds, looking like tiny bunches of grapes in the place where the grapes will eventually be.

Early in June comes the vital flowering, which must go on for 10–14 days for good grapes to form. Heavy rain now is fatal to the vintage.

If the flowers escape rain and frost, their place is taken by baby grapes in June. In August the grapes 'set': turn from green to red or translucent yellow;

at this point the ripening process begins. From flowering to harvest in September or October is about 100 days (see the chart on page 28).

Wine is the juice of grapes. Every drop of wine you drink is rain recovered from the ground by the mechanism of the plant that bears grapes, the vine. For the first three or four years of its life a young vine is too busy creating a root system and building a strong woody stalk to bear more than a few grapes. Thereafter, left to nature, it would rampage away, bearing some fruit but spending much more of its energy on making new shoots and putting out long wandering branches of leafy wood, until it covered as much as an acre (nearly half a hectare) of ground, with new root systems forming wherever the branches touched the soil.

This natural form of reproduction, known as *provignage*, was used to make a vineyard in ancient times. To prevent the grapes rotting or the mice getting them, since they lay on the ground, little props were pushed under the stems to support each bunch. If the vine grew near trees, it used its tendrils to climb them to dizzy heights. The Romans planted elms especially for the purpose. Freelance labour was hired for the vintage: it was too dangerous to risk your own slaves.

Modern vines, of course, are not allowed to waste their precious sap on making long branches – however much they may try (see page 20). Better-quality grapes grow on a vine that is regularly cut back to a very limited number of buds. The annual pruning is done in mid-winter, when the dormant plant will lose least sap from its wounds.

Like most other plants, vines will reproduce from seed. Sowing grape pips would be much the easiest and cheapest way of getting new vines. But like most highly bred plants its seeds rarely turn out like their parents. Pips are used for experimenting with new crosses between different varieties. For planting a new vineyard, though, every vine has to be a cutting – either planted to take root on its own or grafted to a rooted cutting of another species.

Pests which threaten the vine include, top left, the grub of the cochylis moth, seen here eating the flower buds; top right, the tiny red spider, which sucks the sap from the undersides of leaves; lower left, mildew, which attacks anything green. Mildewed grapes never ripen properly and have a peculiar taste. Lower right: oidium, or powdery mildew, is often more serious; its attack on Madeira in 1852, just before phylloxera hit island, began the decline in Madeira's fortunes. It rots the stalks, shrivels the leaves and splits the grapes, ruining the wine and finally killing the vine.

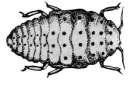

Left and below: the vine's deadliest enemy, *Phylloxera vastatrix*, in its root-eating form and its flying form. *Below right*: larvae and eggs. A century ago this American bug almost entirely destroyed the vineyards of Europe and some of the New World, too. In the current century phylloxera is now causing renewed concern in the USA – California in particular.

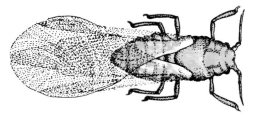

All European vines are now grafted on to American roots, which resist attack. Fierce debate raged as to whether the wine suffered, but few now remember pre-phylloxera wine.

Cuttings are only taken from plants that are healthy and free of virus. The little 'slips' are put in sand in a nursery for a season until they form roots. If there is any danger of virus infection 'meristem' culture uses only the virus-free growing-tip, which has to be nurtured in a laboratory to become a rooted plant. They then go out into rows, in traditional vineyards about three feet (one metre) apart, but more often today planted at one and a half, two or even three times that spacing. The total crop can be the same with half as many vines exploiting the same volume of soil.

As a vine grows older its principal roots penetrate deeper into the ground. While it is young and they are all near the surface they can be quickly affected by drought or floods, or even manure (which put on the land too liberally will taint the wine). A young vine shows its immaturity; its wine is always light and insubstantial. From about 12 to about 40 years a vine is in the prime of life.

The best soils (see right) drain quickly and deeply, drawing the roots down to great depths to find a stable water supply. At the same time the vine constantly grows new feeder roots near the surface. Where irrigation is needed the best method is slow dripping beside the stem to encourage deep rooting within a restricted area.

The vine has countless enemies, the worst of them diseases and pests introduced far too recently (mostly from America) for it to have developed any natural resistance. In the 19th century first downy mildew (not too serious), then powdery mildew or oidium (much worse) attacked Europe's vines – which includes European vines planted in the New World. Laborious remedies were discovered for these two maladies, though both still need treatment by spraying all too often.

One insect pest is disastrous: the phylloxera which lives on the roots of the vine and kills it. In the years after the 1870s it almost destroyed the entire European vineyard, until it was discovered that the roots of the native American vine (phylloxera came from America) are immune. Virtually every vine in Europe had to be pulled up and replaced with a European cutting grafted on to a rooted cutting from an American vine.

The bug was outmanoeuvred – or so it appeared. But experiments in California with hybrid rootstocks encouraged growers to use varieties whose resistance was not fully proven. Today the scourge is back, possibly in a more virulent form than ever. It is eating the vineyards of California (and also New Zealand) at a rate that spells disaster for many growers. No one can calculate the cost of the essential replanting on totally resistant roots.

The upper works of the vine are on the menu for a whole menagerie, too. Red spiders, the grubs of the cochylis and eudemis moths, various sorts of beetles, bugs and mites find it nutritious. Most of them, however, are taken care of by the various sprays to which the vine is subjected summer-long.

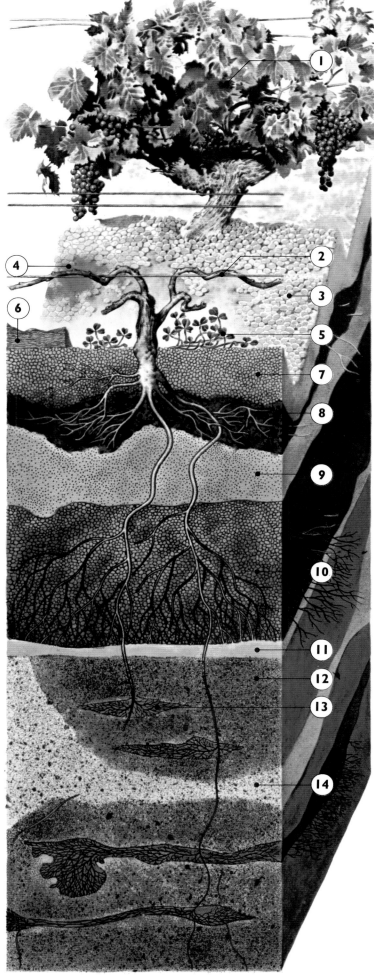

Wine has its origin as water in the soil. This cross-section of the vineyard of a riverside château in St-Julien in the Médoc shows how a vine finds enough moisture and food in poor soil by exploiting a deep and wide area. Gravel and sand are here plus factors for quality. They make the ground permeable to a great depth, let the rain run through, and encourage the vine to go deep. In the background a 50-year-old Cabernet vine **1**, trained on wires, bears fruit. In the foreground a 20-year-old vine **2** is in its winter state; pruned and with the earth banked up around it for protection. Pebbles **3** on the surface are stained with copper sulphate **4**. Clover **5** or other crops are often ploughed in as fertilizer. Pressed skins **6** (marc – see page 32) are also spread on the ground. The top 12 inches (30cm) of soil **7** is pebbly and sandy with few roots. Then comes a layer of marl **8,** brought from elsewhere and spread by hand years ago, possibly when the vines were planted. Roots and rootlets spread horizontally in it. The next layer **9** is sandy but compacted hard and has nothing to offer. There are no feeding rootlets but only main roots descending to another thicker layer **10** like the surface, gravelly and sandy, but slightly richer in organic matter (possibly from manuring years ago) where roots abound. These roots are again brought up short by a compacted layer **11** of sand at 4 feet (just over a metre) deep. Below this different colours of sand, rusty **12** and yellow **14,** lie in clearly defined layers, with odd horizontal patches of grey sand **13** among them. The grey is evidently where the water drains; it is filled with rootlets, which are no-where else in the area. A 50-year-old vine still has roots an inch (25-30mm) thick here, going down to deeper layers of grey sand and gravel. Roots can only find so much of the minerals they seek in a form they can use (ie in solution).

The more grapes a vine bears, therefore, the less of these flavouring elements there will be per grape; the argument for restricting the crop to achieve maximum intensity of flavour. In St-Julien one vine produces enough juice for only half a bottle of wine.

Based on investigations by Gérard Seguin published in his *Étude de Quelques Profils de Sols du Vignoble Bordelais* (Bordeaux 1965)

Designing a Vineyard

To a winegrower whose birthright is a slaty slope perched above the Mosel, or a gravel bank in the Médoc, the concept of 'designing' his vineyard would be an absurdity.

But it was not to his forebears, who worked out over generations the best way to arrange their vines on their peculiar *terroir*. The ideal distance between the vines, how best to train them, the height of the posts (and, later, wires), the number of buds to keep when pruning, whether to cultivate between the rows or leave grass to grow, whether to ignore the sprawling shoots of summer or to trim them off … the solutions to these puzzles, which may not have been consciously thought about, have created the world's best vineyards, and produced qualities of wine that growers all over the world aspire to.

Starting from scratch, growers in new regions in the past have usually had two priorities. Grape variety was (or should have been) the first; the second was making the wine. In the 1950s all aspirations centred on controlling fermentation temperatures. It was the vat room that was being designed. In the 1970s and 80s they focused on more abstruse manoeuvres, the use of oak for flavouring and conditioning the wine being the most obvious.

In the 1990s the design department has gone right back to the vineyard. Baffled by aspects of winemaking which were expensive but not necessarily efficacious, the winegrower today is realizing that the quality of the grapes is the most important factor in determining his relative success or failure.

Looking at his accounts he is faced with a simple dilemma (simple at first sight, at any rate): the question of more or better. The graph that measures number of bottles against price per bottle is always in his mind's eye. With the spirit of a pioneer, untrammeled by law or custom, a grower in the New World wants (and probably needs if he is to ensure solvency) perfect grapes in improbable quantities. Proudly he defies the wisdom of the French who equate high quality with low quantity (but who can be flexible about this, too). His axiom must be that if the vine is working at full efficiency it can produce good grapes, and lots of them.

The basis of faith in small crops is vague at best. Certain famous vintages in the past have seemed to gain their quality from concentration, derived, logic says, from small yields. Logic goes on to say, then, that there is a certain amount of potential flavour in a vine, or a vineyard, and the more liquid passes through it, the more the flavour will be diluted. This makes a vintage like 1970 in Bordeaux hard to explain. It was very big, and very good. And so were 1982 and 1990.

The last few years have seen the study of viticulture, the science of growing grapes for wine, advance in great strides. Until recently planting was mainly a question of replacing old vineyards in the same fashion as before. The quantity of wine was increasing but the world's vineyard area was contracting: healthier plants and greater use of fertilizers accounted for the bigger yield.

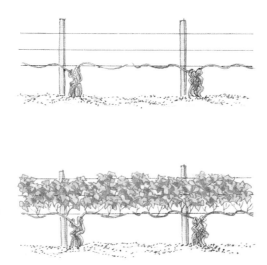

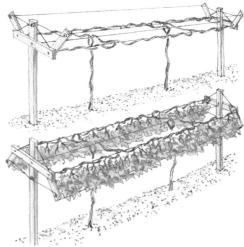

Double Guyot: the standard training system of Bordeaux, Burgundy and most northerly vineyards. The vine is pruned to two fruiting canes and trained along the bottom one of two or three wires. The upper wires support new growth and heavy foliage, fruit hangs from the lower one.

Geneva Double Curtain: many trellising systems are devised for vigorous widely spaced vines in fertile soils. In this system an outer wire on a pivoting arm supports young growth and can then be tilted downwards, which discourages further growth and lets sun into the centre.

Right: the illustrations show a theoretically ideal vineyard in the Rheingau, where warmth is at a premium (see main text) in late September, the crucial ripening season. It lies on a western slope, with a windbreak to the east to prevent the prevailing summer wind from blowing out warm air trapped between the vines. The rows run north–south to allow maximum sunshine to reach the soil. In the morning (top picture) mist shrouds the vines – the low sun with long shadows does little good – but at noon (below) when the mist clears the sun at its height floods the vines with warmth.

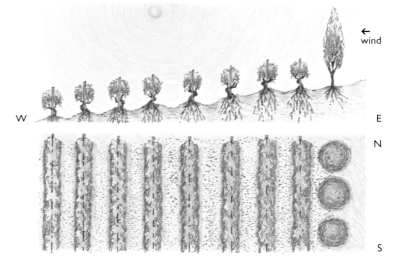

But in the 1970s and 1980s the demand for more and better wine started a planting boom, and at the same time set winegrowers to questioning the traditional forms of vineyard. The questions they now ask are not just 'what vines?', but 'on what roots?', 'how far apart?', 'trained high or low?', 'up the slope or across it?' New vineyards (and there are a lot in this Atlas) embody the latest thinking about what makes grapes ripen in good health.

The basic needs of the vine are easy to grasp. In nature it is a climber of lowland woods in the Mediterranean region. As such it needs a great deal of light (its reason for climbing), a warm climate, plenty of water (it is confined in nature to low land with a relatively high water table) and relatively humid air.

The immediately interesting thing is that the last two points clash with the classic formula for successful winegrowing: Virgil's 'vines love an open hill'. High-quality wine seems to come from dry (certainly well-drained) ground where humidity is relatively low. What is good for the plant, in other words, is quite possibly bad for its crop. The grower's task is not just to keep the vine happy, but to persuade it to ripen as many grapes as possible. How he does this depends on his climate and his soil: the factors are inextricably interwoven.

A famous study undertaken in the Rheingau in the 1970s by Dr G Horney concluded that in this northern zone the vine is well-supplied with everything it needs except warmth. It has enough moisture, enough sunlight for photosynthesis, but temperature is crucial. Growth and every other function of the plant is linked to ground temperatures above 50°F (10°C). Assimilation and transpiration (ie the process of drawing up moisture and nourishment from the ground and 'breathing' through the leaves) proceeds more efficiently with rising temperatures up to a certain point. But at 82°F (28°C) evaporation exceeds assimilation: the vine demands more of its roots than they can draw from the ground; growth and ripening rates slow and stop. There is therefore an optimum temperature in the region of 77–82°F (25–28°C). Anything higher reduces a vine's efficiency.

In the Rheingau temperatures rarely reach that optimum range – or indeed rises above 68°F (20°C) – for very long. Therefore the ability of a site to heat up and stay warm must be a crucial factor for quality. 'Local climates' in vineyards are created above all by shelter from the wind: the vines sheltering each other, or a hedge or a hill sheltering the vineyard. For vines in the cool north mutual shelter is therefore vital.

In Mediterranean climates, on the other hand, where it is frequently too hot, the determining factor is the water supply: hence the widely spaced, 'goblet-trained', bushes in southern vineyards. They also survive the summer winds much better.

Dr Horney concluded that a northern vineyard can be given the best chance of being warmer than the ambient temperature by planting the rows across the wind that prevails

in the warmest weather – in the Rheingau, the east wind. Rows planted north–south will avoid having their precious microclimate blown away – while the ground in the north–south alleys is warmed by the midday sun. These conclusions, in favour of close rows of vines running north–south, and preferably sheltered by wind-

breaks, are of course only a recipe for the Rheingau and similar areas.

Today far more vineyards are being planted in hot regions than cool, often on fertile virgin soil which threatens to oversupply the vine with nutrients. In many hot areas irrigation is essential to the life of the vine – compounding the problem, which is grossly excessive vigour. Long shoots with big leaves smother the centre of the plant, and its fruit, in deep shade.

The most recent detailed experiments in designing an efficient vineyard have been led by an Australian scientist, Dr Richard Smart, who is regularly faced with lush top-heavy vines ('California sprawl' is one term), which however healthy they look produce mediocre crops of under-ripe grapes.

Dr Smart's analysis of the situation is simple. He starts with the success of Europe's best vineyards, always on poor (he calls it 'low-potential') soil. Vine vigour here is naturally low. Vines are planted close together; in Bordeaux and Burgundy the standard density is 10,000 plants per hectare, which means spaced one metre apart in both directions. This is the regional answer to the need for as many ripe grapes as possible. It is right because each vine is small (and kept strictly within bounds by clipping off any straggling mid-summer growth).

European growers have learnt to keep their vines from growing too leafy, to allow sun and air to reach the fruit and shoots, as a precaution against rot after rain. Incidentally a light 'canopy' also allows the sun to reach and warm the soil.

Most New World vineyards, argues Dr Smart, are planted on 'high potential' soil – and with the rows up to 10 feet (3 metres) apart, which economizes on plants and makes cultivation and mechanical harvesting easy. The resulting problem is excessive vigour. Vines throw up huge shoots almost impossible to control: the more you lop them off the more you invigorate the plant until it becomes a jungle, burying its own fruit in deep shade. Not only, then, do the grapes not ripen, but the wood which will carry the next year's crop does not ripen either. The embryo buds on the cane need exposure to the sun to make them fruitful. Too many layers of leaves thus start a vicious spiral of smaller crops and more foliage year by year.

The illustrations opposite show some of the ingenious training systems devised to spread out a vigorous canopy to allow the sunlight in. Several make use of the principle that a shoot forced to grow downwards is 'de-vigorated'. But the right training system also depends on the variety of vine. Cabernet and Sauvignon, for example, grow lustily upward. Riesling droops. The peculiar heart-shaped loop-training used on the Mosel has evolved to keep the grape bunches from trailing, while each independent plant (they are not wired together) benefits from all the sunlight available. Perhaps even more important, it allows the poor mountaineering vigneron to move across the slope as well as up and down it.

Terroir

English has no precise translation for the French word *terroir*. Terrain comes nearest, but has a less specific, let alone emotive, connotation. Perhaps this is why many Anglo-Saxons mistrust it as a Gallic fancy; a conveniently mystical way of asserting the superiority of French soil and landscape and the unknowable peculiarities that give French wines special qualities.

Yet there is no mystery about *terroir*. Everyone – or at least every place – has one. Your garden and mine have *terroirs*; probably several. The front and back of your house almost certainly offer different growing conditions for plants. That is all *terroir* means.

At its most restrictive the word means soil. By extension, and in common use, it means much more. It embraces the dirt itself, the subsoil beneath it, its physical properties and how they relate to the local climate – for example how quickly it drains, whether it reflects sunlight or absorbs its heat. It embraces the lie of the land: its degree of slope, its orientation to the sun, and the tricks of microclimate that spring from its location and its surroundings.

Thus if the foot of a slope is frost-prone, the fact is an aspect of the *terroir*. Warmth or mist arising from nearby water is another – mist that can, for example, encourage botrytis and make golden sweet wines possible. An east slope that catches the morning sun may have identical soil to a west slope that warms up later and holds the evening rays: its *terroir* is different – and its grapes will be subtly different too.

Château Latour, seen here from the west, has the most privileged *terroir* in the Médoc. The courtyard of *chais* occupies the site of a medieval fort commanding the Gironde, surrounded by stony soils that slope directly to the broad estuary. Frost damage is rare here, drainage good and ripening steady.

So are two plots of soil that nature made identical, but one of which has been pampered and the other neglected. Investment in cultivation has a marked effect on *terroir*; whence partly the price of Grand Cru land. It was the best situated in the first place; then nurtured for centuries.

An extension of this aspect of *terroir* is the view held by some organic winegrowers that the term should also apply to all the flora and fauna of the land, whether visible or microscopic. Nicolas Joly, owner of the great Coulée de Serrant in Anjou, goes further and says that chemical treatments which kill microfauna denature the *terroir*. He would go so far as to deny appellations to growers who use chemical treatment on their land. One such aspect of *terroir* which has had little study is its indigenous yeasts, which certainly count among the microfauna of a vineyard and which almost certainly impart their territorial character to the wine.

Distinctions between wines can have many causes. When the ancient Greeks preferred the wine of Chios to the wine of Naxos who knows how much was due to *terroir*, how much to competence, tradition, or indeed fashion?

The first methodical identification and definition of different *terroirs* we know about (and still profit from) was done by monks in the Middle Ages, most famously by the fanatical Cistercians in Burgundy, who are said to have 'tasted the soil' in their efforts to understand its secrets. Their efforts were not just directed at making the best wine. They were obsessed with the consistent differences between plot and plot. To make wines that were as distinctive, as recognizably unalike as possible was their passion – handed down to us in the jigsaw pattern of crus that makes the Côte d'Or so perplexing.

Even where the object was to make one consistent winegrowers became acutely aware of the *terroir(s)* at their disposal. The recently published archives of Château Latour (unique in their completeness over 300 years) give glimpses of how in the 17th and 18th centuries this especially privileged *terroir* revealed itself to its stewards. Its 100-odd acres at the time were divided into 19 plots, from 3.5 to 13 acres (1.4 to 5.2 hectares) in size, according to their soil (particularly the size of the big pebbles that cover the surface), their drainage, their orientation and their performance.

Latour, like the other first-growths, habitually divided its crop into Grand Vin and Second Vin, just as it does today. The second wine always came from the less privileged *terroirs*; the base of the slopes, with more clay and smallaer stones, and poorer drainage of both water and cold air.

It was soon discovered, and has been confirmed regularly ever since, that the site of

Latour as a whole has unique qualities. Its bank of pebbles sloping almost to the edge of the broad Gironde is the least frost-prone site in the Médoc. Undoubtedly the unceasing ebb and flow of the tide in the estuary contributes by keeping the air constantly in motion, however slightly. Even hail storms for some unexplained reason seem to avoid the Enclos, as the exposed riverside hillock is called.

The same records also reveal, however, exactly how much money the owners spent on keeping their vineyard on peak form. One regular task was to collect all available soil from ditches and roadways and spread it on the soil (which was only manured once in every 20 years). In the early 19th century it seems that the vineyard was flagging; monoculture was taking its toll. For 13 years no less than 1,000 wagonloads of fresh soil were brought in from adjacent fields every year to be spread among the vines. It is a theological question whether or not this altered the *terroir*.

Modern winegrowers, and especially winegrowers in the New World, work on a different scale. Until the 1980s they scarcely referred to their soil at all, unless, like the terra rossa of South Australia's Coonawarra, it was too obviously peculiar to ignore. The word *terroir* did not enter their (censored) vocabulary. They could not avoid being aware of what you might call macro-*terroirs*: fertile but frosty bottom-land in the Napa Valley, for example, as compared to the shallow soils with good air-drainage in the hills.

But their preoccupation was and remains essentially with climate. Probably because the whole object of growing Chardonnay, for instance, and flavouring it with French oak, was to achieve the much-desired characteristics of another country, the last thing most winemakers did was the 'taste the soil' of their own.

This is changing rapidly today. Two motives are making growers think in terms of *terroir*. One is increased confidence. They believe they have gone as far as cellar technology will take them. The other is increased competition. The moment has finally come when Another Chardonnay, however beautifully dressed and painfully expounded on its back-label, has to draw credibility – and more important character – from something more than varietal flavour and nicely judged oak maturation.

California has added about as much value as it can with its not-exactly-specific appellations. What is the next logical step but out into the vineyard to do what the Cistercians did?

'Growing a wine' is the catch-phrase of those who have moved their quest from the cellar to the soil. They have some encouraging examples to follow. The Cabernet Joseph Heitz made from Martha's Vineyard in the Napa Valley from the 1960s was the most recognizable, and soon became the most expensive, in California. You recognized it by its balsamic smell, like eucalyptus trees. Like the eucalyptus trees, in fact, that stand round the vineyard. *Terroir* is the sum of many things. It need not be terrifying at all.

Above: the *terroir* of Côte Rôtie in the northern Rhône Valley is essentially artificial. This 'roasted slope' has had to be built on a complex of terraces to retain any soil. Each vine is individually staked, its grapes almost literally cooked in summer, while the folds of the cliff break the force of the destructive spring Mistral.

Below: vineyards around Auckland in New Zealand suffer from rainfall towards vintage-time. Waiheke Island, just offshore, offers a distinctive *terroir*, with much lower rainfall and more even temperatures, coupled with excellent drainage. The result is some of New Zealand's ripest and most harmonious Cabernet and Merlot.

The Choice of a Grape: 1

The wine vine is only one species of one genus of a vast family of plants, which ranges from a huge decorative Japanese climber to the familiar Virginia creeper.

The species is *Vitis vinifera*. Its varieties can be numbered in thousands – as many as 5,000 are named. Most wine-lovers, however, are concerned with about 50, of which we show 25 on these and the next two pages. These are the varieties whose names identify their wines, or rather identify them in every region except the ones that originally selected and perfected them.

All over the Old World, the natural selection of the variety that does best, and gives the best quality combined with reasonable quantity and a reasonable resistance to disease, has taken place gradually over centuries. The Pinot Noir (also the Gamay) appeared in Burgundy in the 14th century; Riesling in Germany not much later, but Cabernet Sauvignon in Bordeaux not until the 18th century. In many places (eg the port country, Chianti, Bordeaux, Champagne, Châteauneuf-du-Pape) no one variety provides exactly what is needed: the tradition is either to grow a number together, or to grow them separately and blend the resulting wines.

So in the classic districts of the Old World it is not the practice to specify a grape variety. It is assumed. Indeed it is enforced by law. The exceptions are such regions as Alsace, which have traditionally grown a choice of varieties.

The longer a wine has been traded the more likely it is to be known by its place of origin. To say 'Chablis Chardonnay' or 'Beaune Pinot Noir' is tautologous. 'Bordeaux Cabernet' is almost as redundant. True, Bordeaux is made of a blend of grapes with Cabernet Sauvignon dominant in one area, Cabernet Franc or Merlot in another. But to specify would be absurdly pedantic: the name Bordeaux means a kind of wine made from grapes of a certain group in certain vineyards, with familiar and wonderful results.

Thus there are many important grapes only winemakers normally talk about: the Palomino and the Pedro Ximénez of sherry; the Tintas of port; the Furmint of Tokay; the Airén of southern Spain, which covers more acres than any other variety in Europe, the Rkatsiteli of Russia and Eastern Europe, which in acreage is not far behind (and in quality considerably ahead); the Bonarda or Garganega of northern Italy; the Schiava of the Adige; the Sangiovese of Chianti; the Melon of Muscadet; the Folle Blanche and Ugni Blanc of Cognac; the Chasselas of Switzerland; the Malbec and Petit Verdot of Bordeaux; the Tempranillo of Rioja; the Savagnin of the Jura; the Arinto and Alvarinho of Portugal.

Wine-lovers develop their knowledge and appreciation by learning the attributes and aromas of these grapes. Winemakers look longer and harder at them as they sense the world growing a trifle weary of a diet of Chardonnay and Cabernet. Indeed one of the most satisfying trends of the last decade of the 20th century is the willingness of growers in the New World to experiment with varieties whose names are known to only a fraction of the market-place.

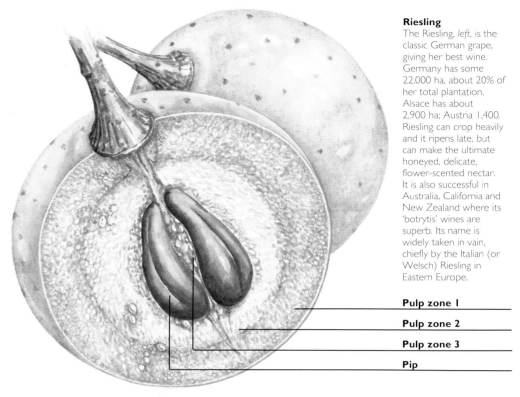

Riesling

The Riesling, *left*, is the classic German grape, giving her best wine. Germany has some 22,000 ha, about 20% of her total plantation. Alsace has about 2,900 ha; Austria 1,400. Riesling can crop heavily and it ripens late, but can make the ultimate honeyed, delicate, flower-scented nectar. It is also successful in Australia, California and New Zealand where its 'botrytis' wines are superb. Its name is widely taken in vain, chiefly by the Italian (or Welsch) Riesling in Eastern Europe.

Pulp zone 1

Pulp zone 2

Pulp zone 3

Pip

Above: an enlargement of a Riesling grape one month before the vintage. It is still green, and about half its final size. Ripening, it grows translucent gold with dark speckles on the skin. The stalk is normally torn off before the grapes are pressed in modern winemaking. The pulp divides naturally into three zones. Zone 2 gives up its juice in the press first, before the zones in contact with pips and skin. The first juice from the press has long been held to make the best wine; perhaps for this reason.

Ampelography, the study of grapes, is one of the most delicate and difficult studies connected with wine. Experts often disagree about the identities of grapes: their relationships remain far beyond lay comment. That many grapes have synonyms in other languages (often in their own, too) makes the study all the more confusing. To find out how much it can add to your appreciation of wine there is a standard text that complements this Atlas perfectly. The book is Jancis Robinson's *Vines, Grapes and Wines*.

The distribution of ten important grape varieties in France

Red		White	
○ Cabernet Sauvignon	● Gamay	○ Chardonnay	● Chenin Blanc
● Carignan	● Grenache	● Sauvignon Blanc	● Riesling
	● Pinot Noir		● Ugni Blanc

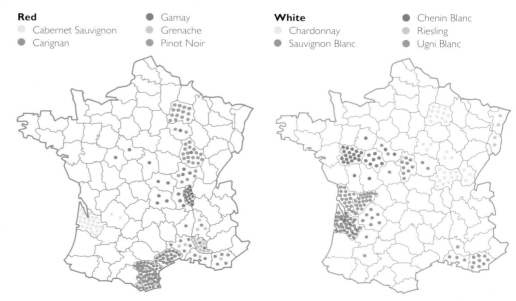

Gamay

Only makes first-class wine on the granite hills of Beaujolais, with their sandy soil. In the rest of Burgundy it is an inferior variety, although adequate in certain other parts of France (the Loire, Auvergne and Ardèche), and Switzerland. At its best Gamay produces wine that is incomparably light, fruity and gulpable, pale red, or, exceptionally, a dark wine ageing well for six or seven years.
In Burgundy a mixture of Gamay and Pinot Noir is called Passe-Tout-Grains.

Chardonnay

The grape of white burgundy (Chablis, Montrachet, Meursault, Pouilly-Fuissé) and Champagne. It gives firm, full, strong wine with scent and character, on chalky soils becoming almost luscious without being sweet. Ages well, with or without oak flavouring by fermentation and/or maturing in barrel.
Easy to grow and to like. Now planted almost universally, with best results in parts of California, Australia, Italy, South Africa and New Zealand.

Muscat

Several varieties, all easy to recognize by aromas like hothouse table grapes. Can be black or white. The best is Muscat Blanc à Petits Grains. It spread from the Aegean with civilization, to the Crimea, Sicily, Italy, etc. Most muscat, except in Alsace, Bulgaria and a little from Australia, is sweet – often intensely so. The best in France comes from Beaumes de Venise. Muscats or muscatels are made all over the world and once included South Africa's Constantia. Australia's 'liqueur muscats' are its modern equivalent.

Sémillon

This grape has the great gift, shared with the Riesling, of rotting nobly. Under certain conditions of warmth and humidity a fungus (*Botrytis cinerea*) softens the skin and lets the juice evaporate, concentrating the sugar and flavour to make luscious creamy wine. The great golden wines of Sauternes are made like this, with a proportion of Sauvignon. Sémillon is also important for dry wines in the Graves and is the speciality of Australia's Hunter Valley, whose Sémillons can age for decades.

Cabernet Sauvignon

Small, tough-skinned grape that gives tannin, body and aroma to the red wines of Bordeaux, although always blended with Merlot and/or Cabernet Franc. The best Médoc vineyards have up to 80% of this Cabernet, but in St-Emilion and Pomerol the Cabernet Franc is used. Now almost universal, with great success in California, where its best wine needs long ageing, in Australia, South Africa, Chile, Argentina, Bulgaria, etc. All Cabernet wines gain by age in bottle as well as wood.

Sauvignon Blanc

The chief white Bordeaux grape, used with Sémillon and a little Muscadelle to make dry Graves and sweet Sauternes. Very aromatic and smoky, or like gooseberries, at Pouilly and Sancerre on the upper Loire and throughout Touraine; in the Dordogne, near Chablis; in northeast Italy, in Chile and in the coastal valleys of California. New Zealand can bring out wild pungency; Australia and South Africa riper flavours, though its wine is never better than very good.

Chenin Blanc

The white grape of Anjou and Touraine on the Loire gives nervy, intense wine, honey-like when very ripe but always with high acidity, so it ages well – at its best, almost indefinitely. Its finest wines are Vouvray, Coteaux du Layon, Savennières; at Vouvray and Saumur it also makes sparkling wine. The grape is often called Pineau de la Loire. A form called Steen is South Africa's favourite white grape. Chenin can also be admirable in California.

Pinot Noir

The single red grape of the Côte d'Or in Burgundy, ie the world's best red-wine grape, in the right place. In Champagne it is pressed before fermentation to make white wine, a vital ingredient of the best champagnes. At its best the scent, flavour, body, texture of its wine are all profound pleasures. It makes light wines in Germany and Eastern Europe. Coastal California, Oregon, Victoria, Tasmania, New Zealand and the Cape are all gradually learning to grow it.

Grenache

A sweet grape making strong wine with character but not much colour, used in a blend to make Châteauneuf-du-Pape and on its own to make Tavel, the best rosé of the Rhône. Known as Garnacha in Spain, where it is the most planted red variety. Used for dessert wines at Banyuls near the Franco-Spanish frontier. Known in Sardinia as Cannonau. Used for port, rosé and blending in California and for blending in Australia. There is also a white variety.

The Choice of a Grape: 2

The wine world has become steadily more grape-variety-conscious over the last three decades. The process began when California started labelling its better wines by their 'varietal' names. In such regions as Alsace and much of central and eastern Europe it was already common practice, but it was California that methodically introduced its more ambitious wines to new consumers through the names of their grapes.

Thus New World new wine-drinkers were reared on a mixture of complex Old World appellations and snappy one-grape designations. It is no surprise that the grape-name system caught on.

Wine grapes can be broadly divided into five categories. The largest (in volume grown) is of grapes with no special flavour or character. These are mainly grapes of the Mediterranean basin: the Garnacha Tinta of Spain (Grenache of the south of France) is one; it is possibly the most widely planted red grape of all, but no one (or no lay person) would recognize it. The wine of these grapes is not necessarily either good or bad; it simply has no clearly distinctive aroma or taste. For certain purposes this can be an advantage. The Swiss say each Chasselas (to take a non-Mediterranean grape) is a 'picture post-card' of where it is grown – being so neutral in itself. But the most significant trend today is a rapid fall in demand for masses of daily wine without character in favour of better and distinctive wines – even at twice the price.

The second category is the rising one: grapes with recognizable flavours whose homes tend to be the cooler vineyards of northern Europe. They include all those whose names appear on varietal labels, from Cabernet Sauvignon to Riesling. Muscat grapes have a category of their own, so different is the muscat taste.

The fourth category comprises the wild vines of North America and their descendants, which all taste more or less 'foxy' (see pages 250–51). The fifth is the growing field of hybrids between species of *Vitis* and crosses between varieties of *V. vinifera*. Breeders are constantly trying to find new varieties to improve on the old.

The original object of crossing French vines with American was to achieve a plant with resistance to phylloxera (which American vines have) but with European-tasting grapes. These French-American hybrids, first developed in France by such breeders as Seyve-Villard and Seibel, are scorned in their native land, referred to as PDs (*producteurs directs*, since they are not grafted) and banned from all appellation contrôlée areas – although still often grown outside them. But they have been welcomed in many other countries for their hardiness and apparent potential for good, if not fine, wine. They are most used in the eastern USA, Canada and in England.

German breeders have been at work on the Riesling for a century, trying to tame its temperament and advance its ripening without losing its hardiness and balance of flavours. Dr Müller of Thurgau made the first famous cross between the early and prolific Silvaner and the light-cropping, late-ripening Riesling. There is now a growing catalogue of crosses of crosses, often between two or more selected clones of Riesling – even red Rieslings have been produced.

Among the better ones are the Reichensteiner (it too has French blood), the Ehrenfelser (another, improved Riesling x Silvaner), Kerner (Riesling x pale red Trollinger, giving fragrant and tasty wine), Bacchus and Optima (both Riesling x Silvaner x Müller-Thurgau).

Meanwhile at Davis Dr H Olmo developed several promising new vines, aiming to combine mass-production with flavour. His Emerald Riesling and Ruby Cabernet were introduced in 1948 to give good balancing acidity in the hot San Joaquin Valley. But none proved as original and useful as one bred in South Africa in 1925 by crossing Pinot Noir and Cinsaut: the Pinotage.

The search for ideal grapes continues. At Montpellier the Institut National de Récherche Agricole is tackling the problem of ever-bigger crops (from healthier vines in more fertile soils) which take ever longer to ripen, with consequent risks of autumn rain and rot. INRA has successfully crossed – among many others – Chardonnay and Listan (Palomino) to produce Chasan, Cabernet and Sauvignon and the Tannat of Madiran to produce Ekigaïna, and Cabernet Sauvignon and Grenache to produce Marselan; three new varieties specifically designed for commercial crops of good quality in the Midi.

It is easy to forget that a variety like the Pinot Noir or the Riesling, which has been in cultivation for centuries, has already naturally divided into many different 'clones'; some with more vigour, some ripening earlier; some with more flavour and aroma. When a winegrower goes to a nurseryman, therefore, for new plants, a good deal of the quality of his eventual wine is decided by the particular clone he chooses.

Cloning is as emotive a subject in the wine world as anywhere. Proponents of genetic diversity have good reasons against it; to others it seems foolish not to select and propagate only the plants that show particularly desirable characteristics.

The most successful clonal development has probably been that of the Riesling in Germany, where its productivity has been increased many times without demonstrable loss of flavour. The open question is the ageing potential of vigorous clones. It worries few people, though, since most modern German wine is bottled early for drinking young. The least successful have been Pinot Noirs that are all vigour and juice and no flavour, and Cabernets with thick skins that will not rot, nor ripen either.

MEASUREMENTS OF SUGAR-CONTENT

SPECIFIC GRAVITY	1.060	1.065	1.070	1.075	1.080	1.085	1.090	1.095	1.100	1.105	1.110	1.115	1.120	1.125
°OECHSLE	60	65	70	75	80	85	90	95	100	105	110	115	120	125
BAUMÉ	8.2	8.8	9.4	10.1	10.7	11.3	11.9	12.5	13.1	13.7	14.3	14.9	15.5	16.0
BRIX	14.7	15.8	17.0	18.1	19.3	20.4	21.5	22.5	23.7	24.8	25.8	26.9	28.0	29.0
% POTENTIAL ALCOHOL V/V	7.5	8.1	8.8	9.4	10.0	10.6	11.3	11.9	12.5	13.1	13.8	14.4	15.0	15.6

Each country has its own system for measuring the sugar content or ripeness of grapes, known as the 'must weight'. This chart relates the three principal ones: German (°Oechsle), French (Baumé) and American (Brix) to each other, to specific gravity and to the potential alcohol by volume (v/v) of the resulting wine if all the sugar is fermented out.

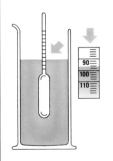

The grape's content of sugar and 'extract' measured by a hydrometer, left, is the first decisive factor for wine quality. A hydrometer is a float calibrated to show the specific gravity of a sugar and water solution at a certain temperature. (On page 163 a Rheinhessen grower is shown measuring the sugar content of the must with a hydrometer.)

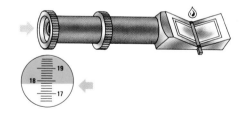

The ripeness of grapes is often measured with a refractometer. Light passing through a drop of juice held between two prisms bends at a different angle according to its sugar content. A scale, read through the eyepiece, gives the % of sugar in the juice.

WATER	70–85%
EXTRACT	15–30%
CARBOHYDRATES	12–27%
PECTINS	0.01–0.10%
PENTOSANS	0.01–0.05%
INOSITAL	0.02–0.08%
ACIDS, TOTAL	0.3–1.5%
MALIC	0.1–0.8%
TARTARIC	0.2–1.0%
CITRIC	0.01–0.05%
TANNIN	0.0–0.2%
NITROGEN	0.01–0.20%
ASH	0.2–0.6%

This chart (adapted from 'Table Wines' by Amerine and Jocelyn) shows the proportions of different constituents of grape juice and the possible variations among more or less ripe grapes. Sugar and acid are the most important to a winemaker, but 'extract' – other soluble solids – is also vital: the more the better. An ideal sugar/acid balance, according to a German rule of thumb, is 1 gram per 1,000 of acidity for each 10° Oechsle, e.g. sweet Auslesen at 90° would need 0.9% acidity for perfect balance.

 **Silvaner** (or Sylvaner) Germany's third grape after Müller-Thurgau and Riesling. Ripens early with big crops but only slight flavour, lacking Riesling's fruity acidity. At its best Franconia, where it can be superb. Also grown in Alsace, northern Italy, the Valais and eastern Europe.

 **Sangiovese** (or Sangioveto) is the principal red grape of Tuscany, hence of Chianti. Only a moderate producer, rather late to ripen and without deep colour, but with good acid balance and pleasant flavour. One strain, the Brunello, is used alone to make the legendary Brunello di Montalcino, which ages, it seems, almost for ever.

 **Müller-Thurgau** Historic forerunner of many crosses of Riesling with other grapes (here the Silvaner) and still the most planted German variety. Now the chief grape in Rheinhessen, the Pfalz, the Nahe, Baden and Franken. Its plentiful wine is highly aromatic, rather soft for lack of acid, never of Riesling standard, at its best when sweet.

 **Syrah** (or Sérine) is the best red grape of the Rhône, making dark, tannic, long-lived Hermitage and Côte Rôtie. As Shiraz it succeeds admirably in Australia, which has the largest planting – over 15,000 acres (6,140 ha) – and uses it for both table and dessert wines, blended or alone. Some of California's Petite Syrah may be the same, in which case it should have a great future.

 **Pinot Blanc** A white variant of Pinot Noir, unrelated to Chardonnay but making similar wine with less substance and aroma. Much grown in northern Italy (where it makes the best dry sparkling wine), Alsace and central Europe. Its cousin Pinot Gris (Ruländer in Germany) has more personality, giving low-acid, blunt but sometimes pungent wine.

 **Merlot** The noble cousin of the Cabernet grown in St-Emilion and Pomerol, ripening earlier than the Cabernet and giving softer, fleshier wine which matures sooner. Used in the Médoc in a blend (with Cabernet and other grapes). Makes good light wine in north east Italy and Italian Switzerland. Can be very fine in cooler California regions and in Australia and South Africa.

 **Gewürztraminer** is the spicy speciality of Alsace (where it occupies 20% of the vineyard). The most pungent wine grape, with rather small crops ripening early in the season tending to potent fatness, but at best irresistibly perfumed. Germany has a little, central Europe more. Gewürztraminer can be excellent in California, Oregon and especially New Zealand.

 **Palomino** (or Listan) The great sherry grape, gives big quantities of rather neutral wine with low acidity which oxidizes easily. It is widely grown in Australia, South Africa (where it is called White French) and California for sherrymaking, as well as in Jerez (where it occupies 90% of the vineyard).

 **Nebbiolo** The late-ripening source of Barolo and Barbaresco, the great red wines of Piedmont. Its wines are brilliantly sharp-etched with formidable tannins framing flavours of fabulous finesse. Long maturing is mandatory. Also known in northern Italy as Spanna and Chiavennasca, but scarcely planted at all elsewhere until recent rather successful trials in California and, remarkably, Mexico.

 **Zinfandel** Excellent red-wine grape peculiar to California, although it may be the same as the Primitivo of Puglia. Makes good lively fruity wine for drinking young, and can make top-quality, highly concentrated wine for long ageing, which at 50 years can taste like great Bordeaux. Likes a dry climate and gives best quality in cool areas such as northern Sonoma.

 **Welschriesling** (or Walschriesling, or Italian Riesling) The 'Riesling' of Austria, Slovenia, northern Italy and central Europe, giving good standard wine but never approaching real Riesling in quality. An early ripener and moderate cropper. The curious name 'Welsch' means 'foreign'. Since 1981 EC law has banned the name 'Riesling', unqualified, for its wine.

 **Carignan** By far the most common grape in France, where there are 412,000 acres (167,000 ha), largely in the Midi. Makes huge quantities of harmless but dull red wine, low in acidity, extract and tannin, but useful for blending. Rots easily in wet weather, but much planted in Algeria, Spain and California. 'Ruby Cabernet' is a Carignan x Cabernet cross.

 **Kerner** One of the new generation of German grapes produced by the Wine School at Geisenheim, a cross between Riesling and red Trollinger. Makes spicy, very fruity wine with good acidity, a bit blatant beside Riesling but a healthy reliable vine, increasingly used in Rheinhessen to make more exciting wine than the usual Müller-Thurgau.

 **Seyval Blanc** (alias Seyve-Villard 5/276) One of the most successful of hybrids between French and American vines made by the French breeder Seyve-Villard. The vine is very hardy and the wine attractively fruity, without a 'foxy' flavour. Banned from French appellation areas, but winning converts to hybrids both in the eastern States, Canada and England.

 **Catawba** Perhaps the most famous native American wine-grape, a chance cross of *V. labrusca*, giving an abundance of fruity, but strongly 'foxy', white or pale red wine. The mainstay of the mid-19th-century Ohio industry, whose sparkling Catawba was world famous. Still popular in New York for sparkling wine; only the infamous Concord is more widely planted.

Wine and the Weather

The weather is the great variable in wine-growing. Every other major influence, including the climate – the expected, or averaged, regional weather – is more or less constant and known in advance. But in the end it is the weather from budbreak to harvest that makes or breaks a vintage.

The vine is dormant (in the northern hemisphere) from November to March. Only an abnormally deep frost, say below about 5°F (−15°C) can harm it then. But from the time it buds to the vintage in September or October every drop of rain, hour of sunshine and degree of heat has its eventual effect on the quality and character of the crop.

The finest wines of northern Europe are those most affected by irregular weather. In the south and in most wine regions of the New World vintages tend to be a little more consistent. On these pages we look at some of the factors affecting France.

The chart at the foot of this page shows the chief events in a vine's life cycle over 15 years in Bordeaux. There is a 38-day maximum variation in the starting and finishing of this cycle, and infinite variations in between, as the weather hurries it on or holds it back.

On the opposite page are isopleth graphs showing the average rainfall, temperature and sunshine for four wine regions of France. While they prove nothing, but they provide a fascinating field of calculation as to just what weather in what moment in a vine's cycle will result in a good or great vintage.

A thoroughgoing study of this question in Burgundy was done by Rolande Gadille in her great book *Le Vignoble de la Côte Bourguignonne*, to which this Atlas owes a great debt. The two lower graphs opposite show her plotting of the difference in reality over 17 years between good vintages, mediocre and the average; just where the weather changed to the benefit or detriment of the wine. They are worth study.

Above: a New World answer to the threat to young vines of severe frost is to keep the air circulating in the vineyard with giant wind machines.

Above: in Champagne frost in May is a real danger. One solution is to light braziers in the vineyard – which sometimes need tending throughout the night.

Sunshine in May and especially June, affecting the timing and success of flowering, seems particularly important; the temperature surprisingly less so. This is because rain on the flowers prevents proper pollination. Another surprising fact is that good vintages seem to have consistently more sunshine from February to November, while May and October temperatures, oddly, seem not to matter so much.

Frost in late spring and hail at any time are the grower's nightmares. Hail tends to be localized; one reason why growers like to have little holdings scattered all over the parish. A bad storm will not only wreck a vintage, but bruise the wood of the vine so as to affect the following year's wine.

The determining factor for the quality of a northern vintage (in Burgundy, for instance, or Bordeaux) is the ripeness of the grapes. They should all be equally ripe. Hence the importance of sunshine at flowering; rain causes *millerandage*, a proportion of the grapes remaining green and acid right up the harvest. As a grape ripens its acidity decreases and its sugar increases. The right moment to pick is when the two are in balance; the sugar as high as it will go without the acidity dropping too far. In the past the danger of a change in the weather (September rain bringing rot) made growers often pick too soon, whereas today they can usually fight rot with fungicides and wait for ideal ripeness.

It almost goes without saying that dry years are normally best. But the exact balance of importance between rain, sun, temperature and humidity has never been determined. What gives character to each individual vintage is the interaction between them: bright sunlight causing early ripening; overcast skies slowing growth but sometimes enriching the grapes with minerals which give the wine long life and complexity; high temperatures reducing acidity.

Even given exactly the same ripeness at picking, grapes reflect the year they have been through: scorching by sun or wind; too much vegetation (leaves and stems) or too little; mould resulting from damp ground or bruises from hail. No two years are ever the same.

Below: frost is one of the most serious sudden weather hazards for growers. Dramatic methods to combat it include giant flame throwers to heat the frosty night air.

The annual cycle of a Cabernet vine at Château Latour, Pauillac			
(figures in brackets represent quarters of the month)			
Year	**Budbreak**	**Flowering**	**Vintage**
1978 ■	March (4)	June (1 → 3)	October (2 → 3)
1979 ■	March (4)	June (3)	October (1 → 3)
1980 ▼	April (1)	June (1) → July (1)	October (2 → 3)
1981 ■	March (4)	June (2)	September (4) → October (2)
1982 ▲	March (4)	June (1)	September (3 → 4)
1983 ■	March (3)	June (2)	September (3) → October (2)
1984 ▼	April (2)	June (3 → 4)	October (1 → 2)
1985 ▲	April (1)	June (1 → 2)	September (4) → October (2)
1986 ▲	April (2)	June (3)	September (4) → October (3)
1987 ▼	April (2)	June (1 → 4)	October (1 → 3)
1988 ▲	April (1)	June (2 → 3)	September (4) → October (2)
1989 ▲	March (4)	May (4)	August (4) → September (3)
1990 ▲	March (1)	May (4) → June (2)	September (2) → October (1)
1991 ▼	March (4)	June (1 → 3)	September (4) → October (2)
1992 ■	March (4)	June (1)	September (3) → October (2)
1993 ■	March (3)	June (1)	September (4) → October (1)

▼ difficult   ■ good   ▲ excellent

Left: the annual cycle of a Bordeaux Cabernet vine over 16 years. In late March to early April the buds break; between late May and mid-June the vines flower; between mid-July and mid-August the grapes 'set' – change from green to red. The grapes should be ripe 100 days after flowering. But the chart shows how the dates can vary. All the best vintages (1982, '89, '90 especially) were picked early. Such growth patterns account for variations of vintage style: no two are quite the same.

A winegrower can give a fair guess at vintage time at what the quality of his wine is likely to be, weighing its ripeness against past experience. But there is inevitably a chance that weather factors he is unaware of have played their part. Tasting in the spring after vintage can still bring him a surprise.

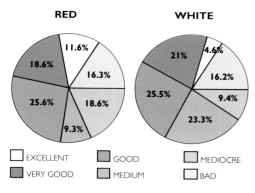

RED

11.6%
18.6%
25.6%
9.3%
18.6%
16.3%

WHITE

21%
4.6%
16.2%
9.4%
23.3%
25.5%

☐ EXCELLENT   ▨ GOOD   ▨ MEDIOCRE
▨ VERY GOOD   ▨ MEDIUM   ☐ BAD

Above: white burgundy seems less affected by weather than red. Out of 43 vintages the white wines were outstandingly good or bad in only half; the reds divided almost equally into outstandingly good, bad or medium.

Below: the temperature and sunshine month by month in Burgundy are shown in relation to good, average and bad vintages. The important differences seem to be in mid-summer temperature and spring sunshine. Bad vintages suffer cold at flowering time and never catch up.

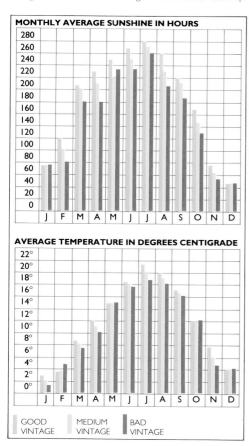

MONTHLY AVERAGE SUNSHINE IN HOURS

280 260 240 220 200 180 160 140 120 100 80 60 40 20 0

J F M A M J J A S O N D

AVERAGE TEMPERATURE IN DEGREES CENTIGRADE

22° 20° 18° 16° 14° 12° 10° 8° 6° 4° 2° 0°

J F M A M J J A S O N D

▨ GOOD VINTAGE   ▨ MEDIUM VINTAGE   ▨ BAD VINTAGE

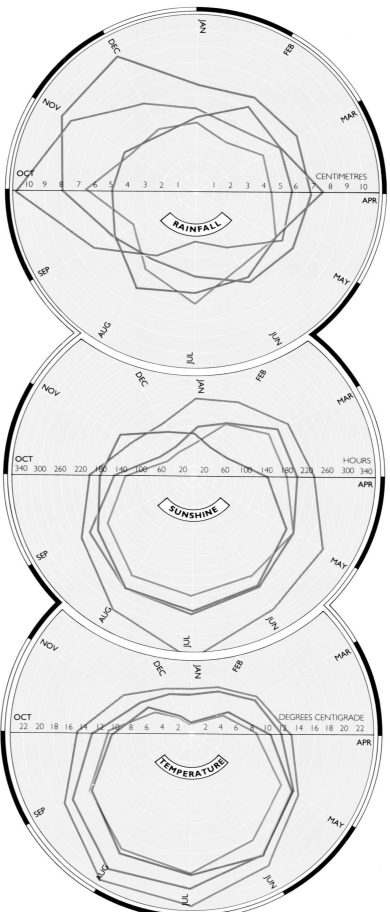

—— CHAMPAGNE
—— BORDEAUX
—— MONTPELLIER
—— BURGUNDY

Left: isopleth graphs show the year's weather as a continuous process in the four French wine regions marked on the map above.

Rainfall (*top graph*): sunshine and temperature come to a peak everywhere in mid-summer; rainfall is more unpredictable. Bordeaux has a very wet winter, a comparatively rainy spring (flowering is in late May), but a long dry summer, growing wetter again, unfortunately for the vintage, in late September. Burgundy is dry in spring, wetter in summer but as dry as Bordeaux in early September. Champagne is wet in July but dry at vintage time.

Sunshine (*left*): all the regions get their maximum sunshine in July: the south by far the most all the year round. Bordeaux and Burgundy have curiously similar summer patterns from May to August, then Bordeaux has a distinctly sunnier end of season. Champagne has a good May, useful for the flowering of the vines.

Temperature (*left*): latitude is the chief factor. Only in June is Burgundy as warm as Bordeaux. By September it is getting cool in Champagne; by November both Burgundy and Champagne are really cold. Bordeaux stays almost as mild as the south all the winter. Regional temperature averages are the least accurate for any particular vineyard, since local altitude and exposure make wide variations, known as microclimates.

A Winemaker's Calendar

There is a job indoors in the cellar, and a job outdoors in the vines, for every day of a winemaker's year. Each district has different methods, and a different timetable, besides modern innovations. But this is the life of a typical traditional vigneron, somewhere in the heart of France . . .

JANUARY

Pruning Traditionally pruning started on St Vincent's Day, 22 January. Nowadays it starts in December. If there is no snow the ground is often frozen. Vines will survive temperatures down to about –18°C (–0.4°F).

Barrels of new wine must be kept full to the top and their bungs wiped every other day with a solution of sulphur dioxide. In fine, dry weather, bottling of older wine can be done. Labelling and packing in boxes ready for shipment to customers.

FEBRUARY

Finish pruning and take cuttings for grafting. Make grafts onto rootstock and put them in sand indoors. Prepare machines for the outdoor work of the new season. Order copper sulphate for spraying.

Racking: in fine weather with a new moon and a north wind (that is, when there is high atmospheric pressure), start 'racking' the new wine into clean barrels to clear it. 'Assemble' the new wine in a vat to equalize the casks.

MARCH

Ploughing About mid-month the vine begins to emerge from dormancy; sap begins to rise; brown sheaths on buds fall off. Finish pruning. First working of the soil, deeply, to aerate it and uncover the bases of the vines.

Finish first racking before the end of the month. Some mysterious sympathy between vine and wine is supposed to start the second fermentation when the sap rises. Keep the casks topped up. Finish bottling.

JULY

Spray vines regularly with Bordeaux mixture. Third cultivation of the soil against weeds. Trim long shoots so that vines spend their energy on making fruit.

No shipping in hot weather. All efforts to keep cellar cool, in heatwaves, when close weather makes it necessary to shut doors at night, burn a sulphur candle. Vine growth slows down; bottling can start again when there is a spare moment.

AUGUST

Keep vineyards weeded and the vines trimmed. Black grapes turn colour. General upkeep and preparation of equipment which will be needed for the vintage.

Inspect and clean vats and casks to be used for the vintage. Vine growth (and fermentation) starts again about mid-month so bottling must stop. Low strength wine (being less stable) can turn in warm weather, so it must be carefully watched.

SEPTEMBER

Vintage Keep small boys and birds out of the vineyard. Keep vines trimmed, pray for sunshine. About the third week the grapes are ripe; the vintage begins. Activate your family.

Before the vintage scour out the *cuvier* where the wine will be made. Put anti-rust varnish on all metal parts of the presses, etc. Fill fermenting vats with water to swell the wood and make them perfectly tight.

APRIL

Finish ploughing Clear up vineyard, burning any remaining prunings and replacing any rotten stakes. Plant one-year-old cuttings from the nursery. Pray for late vegetation, as frosts are frequent and hail (the grower's nightmare) possible.

Topping up must still go on. There must never be any ullage (empty space) in the cask. About 5% of the wine evaporates through the wooden sides of the barrel every year ('the angels' share').

MAY

Frost danger at its height. On clear nights stoves may be needed among the vines, which means sitting up to fuel them. Second working of the soil to kill weeds. Spray against oidium and mildew. Every ten days remove any suckers to encourage the sap to rise in the vines.

Send off orders to customers. Towards the end of May, just before vines flower, begin the second racking off the lees into clean barrels.

JUNE

The vines flower at the beginning of June when the temperature reaches 18–20°C (65–68°F). Weather conditions are critical: the warmer and calmer the better. After flowering, thin shoots, tying the best ones to the wires. Spray for oidium with powdered sulphur.

Finish second racking of new wine and rack all old wines in the cellar. Evaporation is naturally accelerated by the warm weather; check all the casks for any weeping from between the staves.

OCTOBER

The vintage continues (see pages 36–37) for perhaps two weeks. When it is over, spread manure (pressed grape skins are good) and fertilizer over the vineyard. Deep-plough the land for new plantations.

New wine is fermenting. Year-old wine should be given a final racking, the barrels bunged tightly and rolled a quarter-turn so the bung is at the side. Move barrels to the second-year cellar to make room for the new wine.

NOVEMBER

Cut off long vine shoots and collect them for fuel. Finish manuring. Plough the vineyard to move soil over the bases of the vines to protect them from frost.

Bottling Rack and 'fine' (filter by pouring in whisked egg white which sinks to the bottom, taking any particles with it) wine to be bottled. In rich and ripe vintages rack new wine now; in poor ones leave it on the lees for a further month.

DECEMBER

If soil has been washed down slopes by rain it must be carried back up and redistributed throughout the vineyard. Pruning the vines can start before Christmas, usually about 15 December.

Casks must be topped up frequently. Cellar temp-erature must be kept even to see the fermentation right through to its finish. More bottling of older wine can be done. Start tasting new wine with old friends.

How Wine is Made

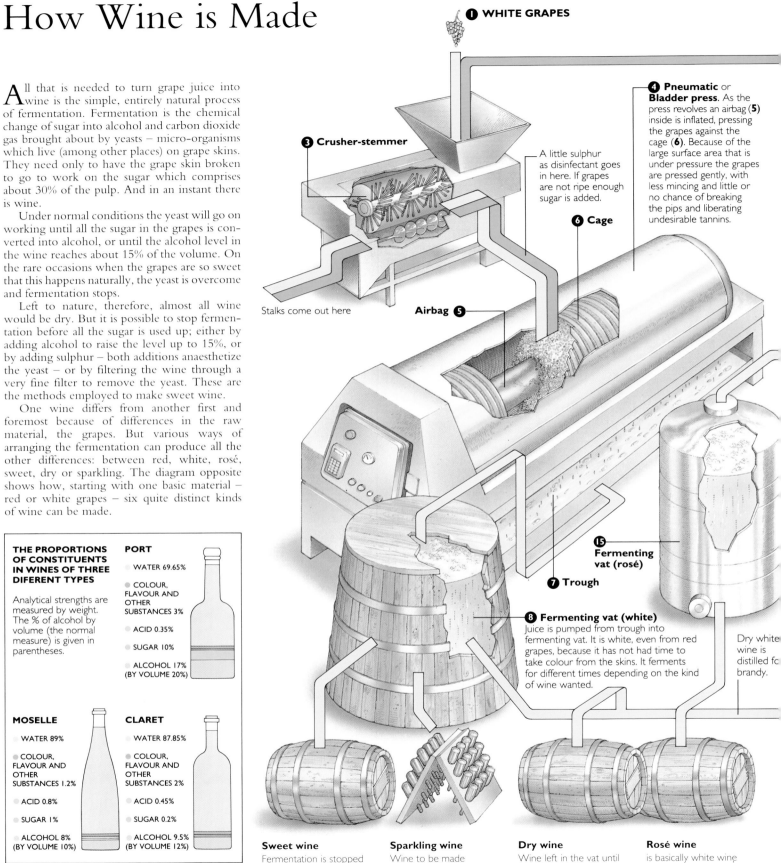

① WHITE GRAPES

All that is needed to turn grape juice into wine is the simple, entirely natural process of fermentation. Fermentation is the chemical change of sugar into alcohol and carbon dioxide gas brought about by yeasts – micro-organisms which live (among other places) on grape skins. They need only to have the grape skin broken to go to work on the sugar which comprises about 30% of the pulp. And in an instant there is wine.

Under normal conditions the yeast will go on working until all the sugar in the grapes is converted into alcohol, or until the alcohol level in the wine reaches about 15% of the volume. On the rare occasions when the grapes are so sweet that this happens naturally, the yeast is overcome and fermentation stops.

Left to nature, therefore, almost all wine would be dry. But it is possible to stop fermentation before all the sugar is used up; either by adding alcohol to raise the level up to 15%, or by adding sulphur – both additions anaesthetize the yeast – or by filtering the wine through a very fine filter to remove the yeast. These are the methods employed to make sweet wine.

One wine differs from another first and foremost because of differences in the raw material, the grapes. But various ways of arranging the fermentation can produce all the other differences: between red, white, rosé, sweet, dry or sparkling. The diagram opposite shows how, starting with one basic material – red or white grapes – six quite distinct kinds of wine can be made.

③ Crusher-stemmer

Stalks come out here

A little sulphur as disinfectant goes in here. If grapes are not ripe enough sugar is added.

④ Pneumatic or **Bladder press**. As the press revolves an airbag (**5**) inside is inflated, pressing the grapes against the cage (**6**). Because of the large surface area that is under pressure the grapes are pressed gently, with less mincing and little or no chance of breaking the pips and liberating undesirable tannins.

⑥ Cage

Airbag ⑤

⑮ Fermenting vat (rosé)

⑦ Trough

⑧ Fermenting vat (white) Juice is pumped from trough into fermenting vat. It is white, even from red grapes, because it has not had time to take colour from the skins. It ferments for different times depending on the kind of wine wanted.

Dry white wine is distilled fo[r] brandy.

THE PROPORTIONS OF CONSTITUENTS IN WINES OF THREE DIFERENT TYPES

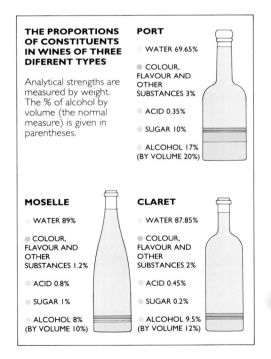

Analytical strengths are measured by weight. The % of alcohol by volume (the normal measure) is given in parentheses.

PORT

- WATER 69.65%
- COLOUR, FLAVOUR AND OTHER SUBSTANCES 3%
- ACID 0.35%
- SUGAR 10%
- ALCOHOL 17% (BY VOLUME 20%)

MOSELLE

- WATER 89%
- COLOUR, FLAVOUR AND OTHER SUBSTANCES 1.2%
- ACID 0.8%
- SUGAR 1%
- ALCOHOL 8% (BY VOLUME 10%)

CLARET

- WATER 87.85%
- COLOUR, FLAVOUR AND OTHER SUBSTANCES 2%
- ACID 0.45%
- SUGAR 0.2%
- ALCOHOL 9.5% (BY VOLUME 12%)

Above: the proportions of constituents in wines of three different types. The Moselle is an almost-dry white wine; a little sugar has been kept in it, probably by filtering the yeast out. The claret is a totally natural red wine. Adding brandy to the port has increased its strength to 17°.

Sweet wine
Fermentation is stopped while some sugar remains by adding sulphur or by fine filtration. Dry wine can be sweetened with unfermented grape juice.

Sparkling wine
Wine to be made sparkling is taken from the vat and bottled before fermentation is completely finished. It continues in bottle.

Dry wine
Wine left in the vat until it is fully fermented has all sugar converted to alcohol, leaving the wine quite dry.

Rosé wine
is basically white wine made from red grapes and given a little colour and flavour by being left a short time with the skins.

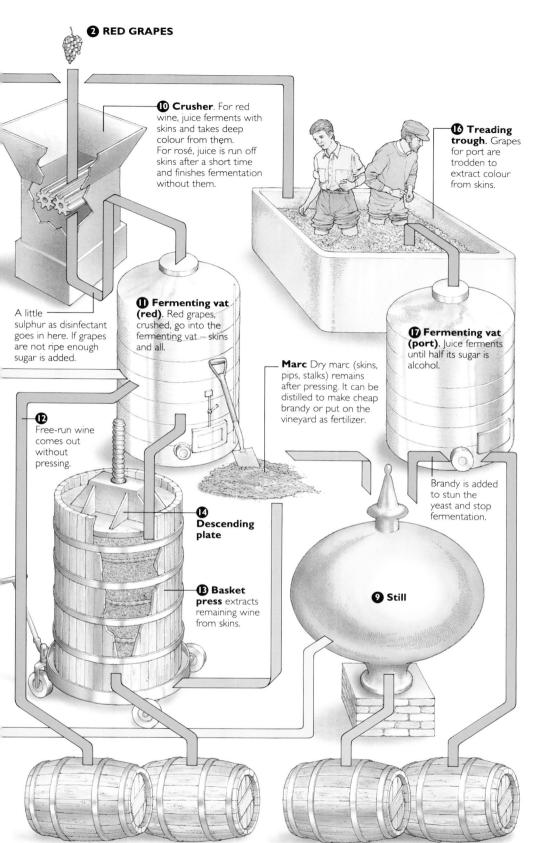

2 RED GRAPES

10 Crusher. For red wine, juice ferments with skins and takes deep colour from them. For rosé, juice is run off skins after a short time and finishes fermentation without them.

16 Treading trough. Grapes for port are trodden to extract colour from skins.

A little sulphur as disinfectant goes in here. If grapes are not ripe enough sugar is added.

11 Fermenting vat (red). Red grapes, crushed, go into the fermenting vat – skins and all.

Marc Dry marc (skins, pips, stalks) remains after pressing. It can be distilled to make cheap brandy or put on the vineyard as fertilizer.

17 Fermenting vat (port). Juice ferments until half its sugar is alcohol.

12 Free-run wine comes out without pressing.

14 Descending plate

13 Basket press extracts remaining wine from skins.

Brandy is added to stun the yeast and stop fermentation.

9 Still

In this diagram the processes of making all the basic types of wine are shown schematically. The flow of white wine is shown in yellow; of rosé in pink, of red in magenta and of fortified wines in amber. Fermentation is indicated by a spiral. Numbers refer to the text below, describing the process in detail. At the foot of this diagram the end products are shown flowing into barrels.

White
Either white **1** or red **2** grapes are fed into a crusher-stemmer (or *égrappoir*) **3** which tears off the stalks and pumps the broken grapes into a pneumatic press **4**. The press revolves and an airbag inside is inflated, pressing the grapes against the cage, **6**. The marc (skins) is left behind as the must (fresh juice) falls into a trough, **7** from which it is pumped into a fermenting vat, **8**, after which there are several courses open to it. It may be made into sweet wine by having its fermentation stopped while it still contains sugar, or be bottled before fermentation is finished, to make sparkling wine. Or it may be fermented until all its sugar is used up, to make dry wine. And finally, the dry wine may be distilled **9** to make brandy.

Red
Red grapes **2** are fed through a crusher **10** (or often a crusher-stemmer **3**) and pumped into a vat **11** where they ferment in contact with their skins. Traditionally the stalks go in too but they are usually removed today. The wine gradually draws out the colour and tannin from the skin. Fermentation is allowed to go on until all sugar is gone (up to 14 days). Then the tap is opened and the 'free-run' wine **13** is run off. For lighter, quicker-maturing wine the modern practice is to take the wine off the skins after a few days to finish fermentation separately. The skins are traditionally pressed in a hydraulic basket press **13** by a descending plate **14** which forces the juice out through slatted sides. Layers of matting help the juice to run out. This press wine (*vin de presse*), deeply coloured and tannic, is not usually mixed with the free-run wine. The marc left in the press is either used as fertilizer or distilled to make cheap brandy.

Rosé
Red grapes **2** are fed through a crusher **10** and straight into a vat **11** complete with their skins to begin fermentation. The juice for rosé wine takes on a light pink colour from the skins but it is run off almost immediately into another vat **15** to ferment on its own. Normally it is allowed to finish its fermentation naturally, and is thus completely dry.

Port
(traditional method) Red grapes **2** are put in a stone trough **16** and continuously trodden with bare feet for 12 hours to make the juice take the colour of the skins. The juice is run into a vat **17** to ferment until half its sugar is converted to alcohol, when it is mixed with brandy from the still **9** to raise the alcohol level to above 15%. This stuns the yeast and stops fermentation, so that the wine is both strong and sweet.

Free-run wine
Vin de goutte (about four-fifths of total) runs out of the vat without needing pressing, and goes straight into barrels.

Press wine
Vin de presse is very dark, harsh and unpalatable. It is sometimes mixed with free-run wine to increase tannin and colour.

Brandy
The product of distilling wine is brandy. If grape skins (marc) are distilled the product is called marc (or grappa).

Port
and most fortified wines and 'vins doux naturels' have their fermentation arrested with alcohol. They need ageing to 'marry' their different elements.

33

The Art of the Winemaker

The previous two pages showed the simple steps that are common to all winemaking. Thirty years ago there was not much else to be done: you made your wine, more or less carefully and skilfully with better or worse grapes, and then waited to see how it would turn out.

The best wines of the classic French and German regions are still, on the whole, made in the same spirit. One of the reasons for the emergence of these very regions is that natural conditions (low autumn and winter temperatures, for example) provide natural controls. Here the winemaker is more midwife than creator.

Growers and winemakers in warmer regions have to take a different approach. They cannot merely watch; they must control. Technology supplies them with a vast range of alternatives. And as they control, so at every stage of the process they must decide.

The decisions start with the fruit in the vineyard. When to pick it —and how; by hand or machine. Hazards of weather apart, as the fruit ripens its balance of sugar, acids, extracts and water alters daily. *Force majeure* will often oblige winemakers to take grapes when they can (especially if they buy them as the alternative to growing them). But a winemaker in full control can take the idea of the wine he wants to make into the vineyard with him, analyse the grapes hanging on the vine and calculate how the wine will be if the crop is harvested today – or tomorrow.

Having chosen the moment to pick (early-morning or night-time picking in hot weather gets the grapes into the vat cooler, which can make a difference to freshness and aroma), the winemaker will inspect the grapes as they come in. If many of them are underripe, overripe or rotten he must decide whether to include them or throw them out (an expensive decision).

For white wine the winemaker may believe in separating the juice from the skins immediately; may think it is better to let them separate gently and naturally; or want to leave them in contact for a while, at a low temperature to prevent premature fermentation.

In the first case the grapes can be pressed straight away (with or without their stalks; the stalks make pressing easier but can give the wine a stalky flavour) and then use a centrifuge, which separates the clear liquid from the remaining suspended solids instantly, expensively; some say too violently.

In the second case he can again crush the (cooled) grapes but not press them, leave them in a vat with a draining vent at the bottom while the liquid runs out naturally, before the remaining solids are pressed. According to some, this 'free-run' wine is always better. Certainly it is

Right: this photograph of naked men breaking up the 'cap' of skins in a fermenting vat (from the Musée des Arts et Traditions Populaires in Paris) was taken in Burgundy as recently as the 1950s. Today the task is usually done mechanically, but in small family cellars like this one, often the only change has been a tendency to wear more clothes.

lighter, more limpid, and quicker maturing.

A third method is traditional in hot areas where the grapes lack acid: by macerating in the juice (even in some places briefly fermenting in the juice) the skins give tannin and aroma to wine that would otherwise be too soft and oxidize too easily. The question of whether to protect the must from oxygen entirely or allow some oxidation is another decision with implications for the final character of the wine.

The next stage is fermentation. Traditionally, for certain strong, high-flavoured wines (white burgundy, for example) this is done in small oak barrels, which give a noticeable taste of oak to the wine. The usual (and much less expensive) practice is to ferment in stainless steel or glass-

or tile-lined, or even plain concrete vats. The first decision here is which yeast to use. New World winemakers almost always prevent any 'wild' yeasts on the grapes from starting the fermentation (a strong dose of sulphur dioxide, wine's all-purpose antiseptic, does this). Instead they choose a pure yeast culture. The vineyards of Europe generally have a sufficient natural population of benevolent yeasts to start the fermentation without help. Besides, indigenous yeasts are part of the precious individuality of the vineyard.

The second decision is whether to ferment warm, cool or cold. In a warm climate, without control, the fermenting wine will get hotter and hotter until the yeasts can no longer multiply

Right: computer control now allows one man to operate a whole winery simply by pressing buttons. The panel displays the fermentation temperature of every vat and the whereabouts of every batch of wine. This is the degree of change that has overtaken winemaking in the past 30–40 years.

Bladder press

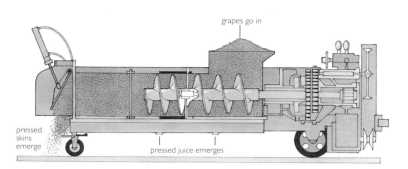

bag empty for filling press   bag inflated

trough for pressed juice

Continuous press

grapes go in

pressed skins emerge   pressed juice emerges

and the fermentation 'sticks' – which can easily lead to vinegar. New World practice is to ferment white wine very cool (at between 10 and 15°C, or 50–60°F). Cold fermentation takes a long time – four to six weeks and longer. Some winemakers take it faster and warmer, others even slower. In old cellars in northern Europe the cellar itself decides.

If the winemaker wants a very delicate, grapey wine he will take every precaution to keep oxygen away from it at every stage. For example, he will fill a tank with carbon dioxide gas before he pumps in the wine and a 'blanket' of the gas will be maintained in the space at the head of the vat all the time. This has the added advantage of preventing the natural carbon dioxide, dissolved in the wine after fermentation, from escaping into the air. A little carbon dioxide gives white wine a pleasant freshness, a faint prickle on the tongue, which is especially valuable when it is low in acid.

It is common practice today to adjust the acidity in warm areas by adding either tartaric acid before fermentation or citric acid after. It would be nice if it were not necessary, but since both these acids are natural components of wine no one can object to their being boosted. Sugar, after all, is routinely added in France.

When fermentation is finished the wine must be syphoned or 'racked' off the lees – the dead yeast cells and other solids at the bottom of the container – although some winemakers prefer to leave it in contact (*sur lie*) for a while to gain extra flavour. There is a natural tendency in most wines to start fermenting again soon after. This secondary (or malolactic) fermentation is in fact the action of bacteria which feed on the malic (apple) acid and convert it to lactic (milk) acid, which is less sharp to taste. In cool areas with acid wines, malolactic fermentation is a boon: it softens the sharpness of the wine, and contributes in ways which are not fully understood to its general complexity and distinction.

Hot-country, low-acid wines, however, need to keep all the acidity they have, and the winemaker must decide whether he requires secondary fermentation or not. If not, he can stop it by keeping the sulphur dioxide level in the wine high (it constantly drops as the SO_2 combines with other elements and needs

Above: how the grapes are pressed affects both the quality and quantity of the wine. The bladder press (*above left*), in which a huge balloon is inflated, squeezing the grapes against the slatted sides of a cylinder, is gentle but slow. The quality is high, but each batch must be filled and emptied by hand. The continuous press (*above right*) is faster but can be brutal, grinding skins and crushing pips, unless it is run slowly and at low pressure.

Right: good wine 'falls bright' (ie clarifies itself) naturally. The traditional way of giving it a final polish is by 'fining' and 'racking'. Fining consists of pouring beaten egg white, ox blood or isinglass into the barrel; as it sinks it carries all suspended solids with it. The clear wine is then 'racked' off the residue at the bottom. The modern method of separating solids is to use a centrifuge.

replenishing) and by frequent racking (or rapid sterile bottling).

Does the winemaker want a freshly grapey, pale wine? If so, he must keep it protected from the air until it is bottled. Does the wine have the strength and potential to mature into something rich and deep? He has a choice of containers to keep the wine in, allowing just enough interaction with the air for it to mature. Winemakers have recently done extensive research into the different ways different oak barrels act on wine. They have tried oak of various French forests, traditionally used in Bordeaux and Burgundy, as well as Balkan and American white oak. Each variety has a subtly different effect on the taste and texture of the wine. This is another way in which the winemaker can express preferences.

I have not mentioned the choice of whether the white wine is to be dry or sweet. If sweet wine is wanted, there is a choice of ways of stopping the fermentation from using all the sugar. There is also the alternative, commonly used in Germany, of adding sweet unfermented grape juice to a dry wine.

Nor have I discussed the similar range of alternatives in making red wine – of which perhaps the most crucial is the length of the fermentation of juice and skins together. The modern tendency is to try to get as much colour from the skins as possible with as little tannin. Tannin is the awkward element, the natural preservative which tastes hard and harsh itself but without which no red wine can keep long enough to mature.

Fining and racking

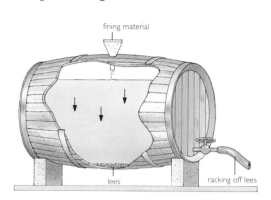

fining material

lees   racking off lees

Winemakers have experimented with fermentations on the skins as short as three days (often in a Vinomatic churning fermenter). But there is no shortcut to quality: two or three days may be long enough to give a fine red tint to the juice (there is even a 'heat treatment' practised to extract the colour quickly), but ten days' slow fermenting at about 24°C (about 75°F) is what is needed for deep colour and long-lasting, satisfying wine.

One alternative method of fermenting red wine which has long been practised in Beaujolais and is now widely practised – sometimes (eg in Burgundy) in conjunction with 'normal' fermentation. It is to put the whole bunches of grapes, uncrushed, stalks and all, into a closed vat full of carbon dioxide. A different sort of fermentation takes place inside the grapes, extracting the skin colour internally and eventually bursting the berry. This 'carbonic maceration', without further fermentation, makes well-coloured, very aromatic, soft-flavoured wine that needs drinking young.

Even when the wine is ready for bottling there are decisions to take. The safe course to ensure shining and brilliant wine is to strain it through a fine filter. But filters remove flavour as well as specks and motes. Ideal wine eventually 'falls bright' in the barrel without special treatment, or by simple 'fining' with beaten egg whites. At this stage, as at every other, the less the wine is manipulated the better. The ultimate art of the oenologist is to know when to do nothing.

Anatomy of a Château

The routine at a Bordeaux château provides a good example of the essential simplicity of winemaking when its object is only to express to the maximum the qualities of the *terroir*. The grapes are simply picked, destalked, crushed; the rest is nature ... but nature kept under careful watch, with discreet adjustments where necessary.

Château Langoa at St-Julien in the Médoc is the archetype of a great Bordeaux estate that has fulfilled the same function for two and a half centuries. It is also the only Médoc cru classé whose owners are the same family who owned and inhabited it at the time of the famous 1855 Bordeaux classification – and for 30 years before.

The first of the Barton family in Bordeaux arrived from Ireland in 1725. Within 50 years they were known as the most prosperous of all the wine-shipping family firms of the region. During the Revolution Hugh Barton had to flee France, leaving the business in the hands of his French partner, Daniel Guestier. He returned to even greater prosperity, in 1821 buying Château Langoa from the de Pontets and in 1825 the adjacent part of the great Léoville estate, whose mansion became Château Léoville-Poyferré.

Langoa retains its traditional buildings and vats, while using the prosperity of recent years to update its winemaking methods, mainly in terms of space, convenience, hygiene and precise control.

The time-honoured technique is simple. The wine is made in oak vats in the *cuvier*. It ferments for about ten days before it is run off the skins and the skins are pressed in a Vaslin hydraulic press, which is wheeled to each vat in turn. If the weather is too hot and the fermentation temperature rises above 86°F (30°C), the vats are cooled by submerged steel cooling plates. In the rare case when the weather is too cold the same plates can warm the fermentation.

The wine stays in a vat until the end of its gentle secondary or malolactic fermentation which rids it of malic acid, making it less harsh. Traditionally, secondary fermentation did not start until March, when the sap rises in the vines, but modern practice brings it forward. In November the wine is 'assembled' and pumped into *barriques* in the first-year *chai* (wine store). It stays here for a year, being constantly topped up and 'racked' every three months into a fresh barrel.

The following November the barrels are all moved into the second-year *chai*, bunged tight, and left to mature until the next summer. Bottling starts in late May or June and should be finished by July (August is the month of holidays, before getting ready for the next vintage).

Langoa has a unique complicating factor: it is two châteaux in one; the third-growth Langoa-Barton and the second-growth Léoville-Barton, a 90-acre (36-hectare) part of the Léoville estate. The two wines are always kept apart in separate *chais*, meaning that two first-year and two second-year *chais* are required. Both vineyards are planted with the same vines: 70% Cabernet Sauvignon. It is a mark of the uncanny accuracy of the old classification that the second-growth is almost invariably a superior, slightly more concentrated yet ultimately more harmonious wine.

Pickers use secateurs; they are often students and earn a net 220 francs a day plus food for about two weeks of very hard work. The grapes are collected from them in tubs on a trailer.

Trailers arrive in the courtyard **1** where the grapes are carried by a conveyor-belt to the *fouloir-égrappoir*, to be crushed and stripped of their stalks, then pumped into the vat.

The *cuvier* **2** is a magnificent sight, with 26 vats, each of which holds 20,000 litres, forming a great oak avenue. Many other châteaux have converted to stainless-steel tanks for fermentation, but those who have oak vats believe the extra maintenance is justified by a hallmark they give the wine.

The fermenting vat is filled four-fifths full to allow room for seething movement.

Remontage. Every morning and evening the fermenting wine is pumped up and sprayed over the floating 'cap' of skins. In fine years it is pumped via an open tub to allow aeration.

When fermentation is complete the 'free-run' wine is drained from the tank. Then a horizontal Vaslin press **3** is wheeled alongside and the residue of skins is pumped into it.

The hydraulic press **4** will press the skins to extract the remaining

one-fifth of the wine after the rest has been run off (see pages 32–33). The deeply coloured *vin de presse* is kept separately from the rest until the *assemblage* of the final wine.

The wine, 'free-run' or pressed, stays in the vat until its malolactic fermentation is over, usually by November. During the winter the different vats are tasted and the final selection is made for the *assemblage*, when the vats of different varieties (Cabernets, Merlot and Petit Verdot)

and different picking dates are blended (or rejected) to make the wines of the two different châteaux. At this stage the press wine is added, and the wine is 'assembled' in vats or the seven stainless steel 'overflow' tanks **5** which are a new addition to the château's amoury.

From the vats the two wines are then pumped into (Tronçais) oak

barriques in the first-year *chais*, **6** for Léoville-Barton and **7** for Langoa. Each year half the *barriques* are bought new. They are stoppered with loose glass bungs to make the task of regular topping up (*ouillage*) easy.

The second-year *chais*, **8** for Léoville, **9** for Langoa. *Barriques* (which each hold the equivalent of 24 dozen bottles) are

moved to these *chais* after a year by forklift truck to make room for the next vintage.

In its second winter the wine is fined with egg white to remove any fine matter in suspension. In May it is prepared for bottling by being moved to vats or stainless steel tanks to eliminate possible differences between barrels.

The bottling room **10**. Before bottling the wine is given the lightest possible filtration.

11 The *cuisine de vendange* Copious and delicious meals for the pickers are essential for morale in the hard slog of the vintage. Next door is the office of the *régisseur*, (manager) where the basics (sugar content, acidity, etc) of the new vintage are measured.

After bottling, wine at a château of this quality is immediately labelled and packed in wooden boxes of 12 bottles, 6 magnums or smaller numbers of bigger bottles. The tasting room **12** welcomes visitors, brokers and merchants who come to taste the new vintages.

About half the wine is usually sold in a first 'tranche' in the spring after the harvest. By the time it is bottled most has been sold and will be delivered to the buyer without delay.

Buildings across the road **13** include barns for the château's agricultural equipment, including the high tractors that straddle the vine rows. They also include the insulated warehouse where the bottled wines are kept before dispatch.

The cellar **14** under the house has examples of the château's and its neighbours' wines going back 50 years. Formerly it was used as a *chai* for barrels. The château is the most perfect unaltered example of an 18th-century *chartreuse* in the Médoc, consisting of a single line of three reception rooms on one floor joining two pavilions, one for the family, one for guests.

Anatomy of a Winery

There is no typical modern winery. They range from tiny 'boutiques' on the scale of a small Burgundy cellar, making a few thousand bottles, to great factories which look like oil refineries without chimneys. The majority, though, are conceived on a far bigger scale than traditional châteaux, and with the great difference that they produce not one wine but a range of different sorts.

This is the dominant principle of most contemporary wineries, especially in California: flexibility. They must be able to handle different grapes from different sources at the same time and turn them into different kinds of wine. Unlike the château on the preceding pages, which follows a single-minded course year after year, a winery may make a dozen different wines, reproducing the conditions (in European terms) of Bordeaux, Burgundy, Alsace, the Rhine and perhaps Spain or Portugal or Italy under one roof. Most wineries keep their options as open as possible to adapt to the market. The best limit themselves today to half a dozen wines or less. Specialization is on the increase.

The fairly typical medium-sized California winery illustrated here is based on Trefethen, the first important establishment that visitors to the Napa Valley see as they leave Napa city heading north. It is distinguished by its century-old wooden barn – said to be Napa's oldest – standing among its vineyards, supplemented today by other wooden structures in keeping. When it was built in 1886 the Eshcol winery (its original name, from the Old Testament valley that grew gigantic grapes) was 'state-of-the-art'. Its plan was almost identical to three others by the same architect (Inglenook, Far Niente and Greystone), based on the gravity-flow system so that grapes were hoisted to the top for crushing, must fermented on the middle floor and wine matured and bottled on the (coolest) ground floor. The three others are stone buildings; only Eshcol was built of timber.

Trefethen is also a family home with a much loved garden and the centre of a considerable vineyard estate: very close, in fact, to a New World 'château'.

Efficiency in a winery includes having the longest possible winemaking season, using its presses and fermenting vats continually from the arrival of 'precocious' grapes in early autumn to the latest ripeners, after the first frosts. Trefethen is an estate winery, growing all its own grapes (and also supplying grapes to such customers as Domaine Chandon, which made its first California sparkling wine in this building in 1973). Growing all its grapes it has maximum control over the timing and condition of the vintage – which is not to say that vintage-time is not frantic as grape lots are sorted and processed in order.

One of the new possibilities for high-tech wineries (not practised at Trefethen) is to chill and store the grapes at vintage, then ferment them in batches later. The electricity bill is high, but there is a big saving on fermentation capacity – always a point of stress at vintage time.

1 Grapes are delivered from the vineyard in boxes by tractor and trailer or heaped in a 'gondola' and weighed on the scales. Their condition and sugar content is checked here.

2 The grapes are tipped into a hopper and carried by Archimedean screw and conveyor belt either to (for white grapes) the crusher-rollers that just break their skins or (for red) to the crusher-destemmer **3** that separates the grapes from their stalks.

4 The stalks and pressed skins mount another conveyor to the pomace trailer for disposal.

5 The crushed white grapes go straight into a Bucher bladder press, from which the juice is piped directly into the temperature-controlled fermenting tanks in the next building **6**.

The crushed and destemmed red grapes are conveyed by 4-inch (10-cm) hose to tanks behind the presses to macerate, juice and skins together, for 7–10 days.

7 The red must is then pressed and the juice pumped to the battery of fermenting tanks outside, while their dry pomace is carted away for distilling or as fertilizer.

8 After fermentation red wines and certain whites (eg Chardonnay) may be given a few months to two years ageing in French or American oak barrels in the old barn (ground and upper floors), depending on the degree and type of oak fragrance desired in the wine. Many Chardonnays are also fermented in new French barrels. The Trefethen style, though, avoids

strong oak flavours by doing all fermenting in steel, and ageing only a proportion of Chardonnay in oak, of which only 15% is new. The result is fresh-tasting wine that matures slowly but wonderfully in the bottle.

9 In the laboratory the winemaker keeps a constant check on the progress of each lot of wine, including frequent chemical analysis.

Before bottling there is a choice of whether or not to filter. The

wine should be stable and clear enough for a very light filtration to be all it needs. The topic of whether filtration robs the wine of flavour often sparks debate. A little unfiltered wine is sometimes kept for those who value maximum flavour above perfect clarity.

10 The bottling line can handle up to 55 bottles a minute. Bottles arrive already in cartons, are

taken out, filled and put back, then stacked on palates ready for storage or dispatch **11**.

Reserve or 'Library' wines of good vintages are regularly stored here in perfect conditions for up to as much as six years before release.

12 Reception and tasting rooms for visitors, as well as a shady garden for them to stroll in, induce them to linger, taste and buy.

Computer records of different lots of wine from reception to dispatch are essential.

13 Stainless steel tanks can be used for both fermentation and when necessary storage, which increases the winery's capacity. A wide variety of tank sizes give flexibility in handling big or small lots and making different 'assemblages'.

Wine and Time

Some wines can hardly be drunk too soon after they are made. Others improve immeasurably by being kept for even as much as 50 years. As a general rule these *vins de garde* are the better. But why? And why is it that such a mystique attaches to an old bottle of wine?

Most white wines, rosés, simple low-price wines of any colour and such light-bodied, low-tannin reds as Beaujolais and Valpolicella are at their best young. The pleasure in them is a matter of freshness and what are termed primary scents and flavours, at one simple remove from their grapes.

The great white wines and most of the best reds, however, are grown to be as full of their own particular character as possible. When young they contain an unresolved complex of principles: of acids and sugars, minerals and pigments, phenols and tannins. Good wines have more of these things than ordinary wines, and great wines more than good wines. Which is why, in the end, they have more flavour. But it takes time for these elements, the primary grape-derived aromas and the secondary ones of fermentation, of yeasts and barrels, to resolve themselves into a harmonious whole and for the distinct scent of maturity, called (by analogy with flowers) the bouquet, to form. Time, and oxygen.

It was not until Louis Pasteur was asked by Napoleon III in 1863 to find out why so much wine went bad on its way to the consumer, to the great harm of the French trade, that the role of oxygen was discovered. Pasteur established that too much contact with the air allows the growth of vinegar bacteria. On the other hand he found that it was very slight amounts of oxygen that makes wine mature; that the oxygen's action is not 'brusque' but gradual, and that there is enough of it dissolved in a bottle of wine to account for an ageing process lasting for years. He showed, by sealing wine in test tubes, alternately full and half-full, that oxygen in the air of the half-full tube caused the same deposit in a few weeks as is found in very old bottles, and that it affected colour in exactly the same way as extreme old age.

In fact he immensely speeded up the process that happens in a bottle: the oxygen in the wine acts on its constituents to mature them, but beyond the period of maturity it continues to act; from then on the wine deteriorates.

Pasteur found that even wine that is carefully kept from the air has opportunities to absorb oxygen: first of all through the staves of its barrel (so that their thickness, whether or not they are encrusted with tartrate crystals, the capacity of the barrel, whether it stands in a draught, all become relevant); then when it is being racked from one barrel to another.

If wine in barrels is subject to gradual oxidation it also has the wood itself as an agent for change. It picks up certain elements – extra tannin, and vanillin, which gives a vanilla flavour, particularly to spirits – from the oak. Winemakers today choose the source of their barrel-staves, the very forest that grew them, to give

Louis Pasteur, born at Dôle in the Jura in 1822, was the first scientist to turn his mind to wine. He discovered that yeast causes fermentation, as well as other facts of enormous importance to winemakers.

In these hand-coloured illustrations from his *Etudes sur le Vin*, Pasteur recorded the effect of time and oxygen on red and white wine. *Left*: Pasteur found that red wine without air did not change colour. *Centre left*: with air, it faded. *Centre right*: white wine without air was unchanged. *Right*: with air it became brown.

specific aromas and flavours to their wine.

The maximum, sometimes overpowering, aromas come from fast-growing forests whose oak is more porous. American oak gives wine (eg Rioja) or whisky (eg Bourbon) great sweetness and spice. Of French regions the Limousin is the most aromatic; too much so for top-class wines. Tronçais, a single 25,000-acre (10,000-hectare) forest in the département of the Allier, is slow-growing and often considered best. Oak from the cold forests of the Baltic is excellent for low porosity and delicate aroma.

Left too long in a barrel a light wine fades rapidly: its colour goes, its fruitiness disappears, it starts to taste dry, flat and insipid. The same wine bottled after a year or less will keep its fruit, body and acidity, and last (and perhaps improve) for several more years. Historically many wines were aged in barrel much longer than necessary, often simply for lack of demand. In bottle they would have retained their flavour better – but a bottle is an extra cost.

The ageing that takes place in bottle is a totally different process. Almost the opposite in fact. Rather than absorbing oxygen the wine gradually loses it. The life of all its constituents is dependent on the very small amount in solution, and between the wine and the cork. Being used up the oxygen supply is steadily reduced – hence the term 'reductive ageing'.

In the bottle tannins interact with pigments and acids to form new compounds. Red wine pigments are destroyed and the wine loses colour (and gains complexity – and sediment). Tannins likewise become less astringent. At the same time acids and alcohol react with oxygen to form compounds called esters and aldehydes.

The equivalent process in white wines, which have very little tannin or phenols, is more complex, but results in a gradual darkening to gold as primary and secondary fruity and 'winey' aromas and crisp acids mellow into honeyed or nutty or oily complexities. If the main preservative of red wine is tannin, of white it is acidity. White wines with sufficient acidity (and sufficient substance to balance it) will mature as long as reds – or in the case of some German Rieslings and Loire Chenin Blancs, even longer.

The question on every winelover's lips is: 'when will this wine be at its best?' For the majority of the world's wines the answer is now. If freshness and fruitiness is a wine's charm – as it is with most modern wines – there is no object in keeping it – except to find out what takes the place of the freshness when it goes.

It would be a logical and desirable development to abandon the traditional cork for this class of wine and use screwstoppers, which suggest that there is nothing to wait for: the product is ready to be consumed. The air of permanence about a cork can be misleading. Since there is a world shortage of good cork, it should be kept for wines that need it.

There is no English equivalent to the French term *vins de garde* for wines that need 'laying down' to achieve their full potential. We know which they are by experience, tradition – and price: high price takes into account a long potential life span in which the asset can increase in value.

By far the most important body of true *vins de garde* are the crus classés of Bordeaux. A generation ago such wines were made to endure, on the assumption that they would be kept a minimum of seven or eight years, and more likely 15. Modern taste looks for softer, less astringent tannins that can be drunk after a mere five years or so. But much still depends on nature: the 1986 Bordeaux vintage, for example, is determinedly old-fashioned: a 10-year wine at least.

California's best Cabernets behave similarly – although some extremely tannic, 'over-extracted' wines lose their sweetness long before their black cloak of tannin yields. Australian Cabernets are far friendlier.

Red burgundy poses fewer problems because its tannins are rarely obtrusive enough to make patience essential. For this reason, though, some critics urge us to drink up in five years wine whose potential for weaving magic spells of fragrawill not be exhausted for 25. The same is true of the finest white burgundies, and even truer of the great Rieslings of the Mosel and Rheingau.

When to drink a wine is of course partly a matter of personal taste – even national taste. The British notoriously like to 'hang it till it drops'; the French frequently commit infanticide by drinking *vins de garde* before they have even started to mellow. Convention can only give the vaguest guidance: 'at its best between five and 15 years'. For awkward as it is, every wine and every vintage has its own time scale. The same red bordeaux of 1990 and 1992 will be at its best four years after the vintage (the '92) or (the '90) at perhaps 15.

The deciding factors are ripeness and concentration. Can they not be measured? They can, of course; yet even such measurement is no clear guide to the future. A *vin de garde* goes through a number of stages in its maturation. The duration of each stage is one of the most unpredictable things about wine.

A graph to express the improvement of flavour may climb steeply at first, then flatten out, climb and flatten out again . . . it may even dip at certain points over a number of years. The graph for another vintage of the same wine may climb very slowly, may take eight or nine years to reach a plateau, then hold a level or only edge imperceptibly upwards for another ten years. Even at 20 years the future is not certain. There are wines that keep an equilibrium for decades, and others that grow sharp or dry and dismal, losing their vitality and the sweet taste of fruit without warning after a long plateau of excellence.

With true *vins de garde* – above all the great wines of Bordeaux – the final verdict is never in until the last bottle has been opened.

Right: an astonishing survival: a full ancient Roman wine bottle, now in the Pfalz Historical Museum at Speyer. Air was kept from the wine by a layer of oil on top.

Principal sources of French oak

France could be called the mother-country of oak as well as wine. One-third of her surface is forested, and one-third of the entire forest is oak. The map shows the vast belt of intermittent oak-forest that crosses the country from s–w to n–e. Further south more forests are pine and the two top-quality oak species, *Quercus petraea* and *robur*, give way to mountain and Mediterranean kinds.

The highest-quality oak is the slow-grown *Q. petraea*, the sessile oak, from the Val de Loire, Centre and Burgundy. Close-grained, aromatic and low in tannin, it is ideal for top white wines.

The fame of the Limousin forests seems to come from their proximity to the two biggest consumers of barrels, Cognac and Bordeaux. Limousin oak is mainly *Q. robur*, relatively fast-grown, open-pored and tannic, better for red wine than white. The best comes from near Poitiers.

'Vosges' oak (from Champagne, Lorraine, Alsace) is also relatively tannic, the choice for red rather than white.

Just as vital as the origin of the oak is how much it is scorched, or 'toasted', by the barrelmaker – a taste often very evident, especially in Chardonnays.

1 Val de Loire
(includes Orne and Allier)
13% of French oak forest
only 18% of annual 'crop'
but 35% of France's top
quality for barrels, etc

2 Bourgogne
(includes Nièvre
and Franche Comté)
17% of French oak
forest 14% of annual
'crop' but only 8% of
top quality

3 Champagne, Alsace, Lorraine
19% of French oak forest
28% of annual 'crop'
22% of top quality

4 Limousin and Poitou
13% of French oak forest
14% of annual 'crop'
only 8% of top quality

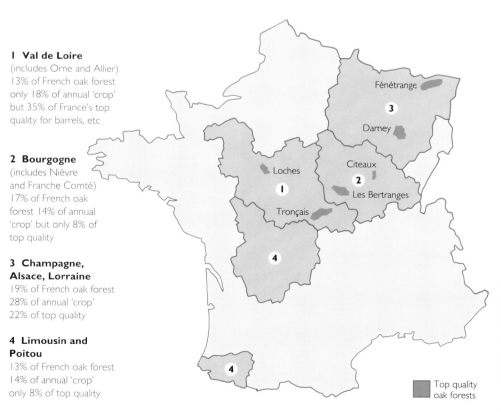

Top quality oak forests

Tasting and Talking about Wine

Most good, even most great wine is tasted. It flows over tongues and down throats of people who are not attuned to it; not receptive to what it has to offer. They are preoccupied or deep in conversation; they have just drunk whisky or gin which numb the sense of taste, or taken a mouthful of vinegary salad which overwhelms it; they have a cold; or they have simply never tuned in to the differences between mere wine and fine wine. Nothing the winemaker can do dispenses with the need for a sensitive and interested drinker.

If the sense of taste were located in the mouth (where our impulses tell us it is), anyone swallowing a mouthful of wine would get all the sensations it has to offer. But as this model of Bacchus shows, the nerves that receive anything more distinctive than the basic sensation of sweet, sour, salt and bitter are higher in the head and deeper in the brain.

In fact we smell tastes, rather than tasting them with our lips and tongues and palates. The real organ of discrimination is in the upper nasal cavity, where in normal breathing the air never goes. And the only sensations that can reach it are the vapours of volatile substances. To reach the brain the vapours of wine need to be inhaled (either through nose or mouth) into the upper part of the nasal cavity, where they are dissolved in moisture. From the moisture long thin nerve processes (vacilli) take the sensations to the olfactory bulb, above the nasal cavity and right in the brain.

It is often remarked how smells stir memories far more rapidly and vividly than the other sensations. From the position of the olfactory bulb, nearest neighbour to the temporal lobe where memories are stored, it seems that smell, the most primitive of our senses, has a privileged position of instant access to the memory-bank. Experienced tasters often rely on the immediate reaction of their memory to the first sniff of a wine. If they cannot relate it straight away to wines they have tasted in the past they must fall back on their powers of analysis, located in the parietal lobe. In the frontal lobe their judgment of the wine is formed (to be stored in turn in the temporal lobe for future reference).

The range of reference available is the great difference between an experienced taster and a beginner. There is little meaning in an isolated sensation – although it may be very pleasant. Where the real pleasures of winetasting lie are in the cross-references, the stirring of memories, the comparisons between similar and yet subtly different products of the same or neighbouring ground.

Wines differ from one another in terms of colour, texture, strength, structure, body and length, as well as smell and their complex of flavours. A taster takes all these into account.

What is much harder than appreciating wine is communicating its sensations. There is no notation of taste, as there is of sound or colour; apart from the words sweet, salt, sour and bitter every word in the language of taste is borrowed from the other senses. And yet words, by giving an identity to sensations, help to clarify them. Some of the most helpful of the great many words used by tasters are listed opposite.

Left: Michelangelo's head of Bacchus the wine god, has been remodelled to show the organs of taste and smell used in appreciating wine in their relation to the judgment and memory in the brain. The tongue perceives only whether the wine is sweet (at the tip **1A**), sour (at the sides **C**), salt (at the front sides **B**), or bitter (at the back **D**). But the volatile components of the wine (principally esters and aldehydes) rise as vapour through the nostrils and from behind the soft palate **2** into the upper part of the nasal cavity **3**. Moisture in the cavity dissolves the vapours and nerves carry them to the olfactory bulb **4** in the brain. Just behind the olfactory bulb is the temporal lobe **5**, the storehouse of memory. Sensations of smell easily awake memories. The experience is analysed in the parietal lobe **6**. In the frontal lobe **7** judgment is passed. The alcohol in wine at first releases the mechanism of the brain and facilitates the awakening of memories. But it rapidly goes too far and upsets the delicate balance of the brain's functions. Professional tasters, therefore, always spit out a wine after they have drawn from it all the information they need.

The colour of the wine at the rim of the glass, tipped against a white background, gives the taster his first information. Is it clear? Is it red-purplish (young) or turning to brick-red with age? Great wines have strikingly deep and fresh colour. Is white very light, touched with youthful green (chlorophyll), or turning to gold?

Almost everything about a wine is revealed by its scent. The taster inhales deeply. The first impression is the most telling. Is there any 'foreign' or 'wrong' smell? Does it smell of fresh grapes or have a complex 'bouquet' from age in barrel and bottle? Is the grape identifiable (as, for instance, Riesling, Pinot, Cabernet)?

The taste in the mouth confirms the information given by the nose. The taster takes a good mouthful, not a sip, and lets it reach every part of his mouth. The body, or wineyness, now makes its impact. Is it generous or meagre? Is it harsh with tannin as young reds should be? Is it soft and flat or well-balanced with acidity?

Holding the wine in his mouth, the taster draws air between his lips. The warmth of his mouth helps to volatilize the wine; a more positive impression of the taste materializes at the very back of the mouth as vapours rise to the nasal cavity from behind. After swallowing (or spitting) is the flavour short-lived or lingering?

The wine's appearance

Blue Red Wines often have a hint of blue when very young.
Brick-red Colour of mature claret
Brilliant Completely clear
Brown Except in sherry or madeira, brown wine is too old
Cloudy Something is wrong; all wine should be bright
Gris Very pale rosé, the same as 'blush' wine
Intensity A good sign; can be judged by trying to read print through a full glass.
Maderized Brown or going brown with the effect of oxygen.
Pelure d'oignon Onion skin: the tawny-pink of Provençal rosé or advanced signs of age in burgundy.
Pétillant 'Pearling' or *spritzig*; wine with natural fine bubbles which stick to the glass
Purple A young colour; translucent in young Beaujolais, deep in red wine which will take time to mature
Rosé Pink; neither red nor white; a term of abuse for red wine
Ruby (of port in particular) The full red of young wine
Tawny (of port in particular) The faded amber of old wine

The smell of wine

Acetic Wine that is 'pricked' or gone irredeemably sour through contact with the air smells of acetic acid or vinegar
Aroma The primary grape-and-ferment smell of young wine
Bouquet The complex smell arising with maturity in good wine
Complex Scents-within-scents; suggestions of many different fruits, flowers, etc
Corky The smell of the (rare) bottle that has had a mouldy cork
Foxy The smell of the native American grape; more like soap than foxes
Heady High in alcohol

Lively A self-explanatory good sign; a fresh, frank smell from wine that is young and will last
Musty Unpleasant smell, possibly from a barrel with a rotten stave
Rancio The smell of oxidized fortified wine, the speciality of southwest France and Catalonia
Sappy Translation of the French 'sève': the lively, forthright style of a fine young wine, especially burgundy
Sulphury The hot and nose-tickling smell often given by cheap white wine in which sulphur is used as a preservative. It will go off with age or when the wine gets enough air
Yeasty The smell of yeast can be attractive in young wine, although it usually means it is unstable. Yeast is an essential element in the scent of champagne

Describing wine

Many words are borrowed to invoke the qualities of their originals: aromas or flavours that can be described in no other way, appearing in wine in traces of the same chemical constituents as the fruit (or whatever) cited. A schematic system appears on page 45. The following list covers some of the commonest/simplest terms:

Apples Derives from malic acid which is common in young whites. In Mosels it can be very apparent.
Blackcurrants Smell and flavour in many red wines, esp. Cabernets
Earthy A virtue or fault depending on the context. Complimentary in eg red Graves
Flowery Used generally for an attractive and forthcoming scent
Grapey A great wine has more than grapiness, but a fresh-grape smell is always a good sign
Gunflint Scent of flint sparks in some white wine, eg Pouilly Fumé

Honey Associated particularly with botrytis or noble rot in great sweet wines, but can be an element in reds or other whites, eg Chablis
Nuts Nuttiness is usually found in mature wines – eg Meursaults. It is very marked in old sherry.
Oak An aroma and flavour given to wine by the barrel. Important and attractive as it is, it should not be strong enough to overwhelm the fruit
Peaches Associated with a certain fruity acidity, eg in some Loire wines
Petroleum Smell found, often in association with lemons, in mature Rieslings.
Raspberries A common flavour in very good reds, particularly of Bordeaux and the Rhône.
Smoke Smokiness is claimed for many white wines, eg Bernkastels
Spice Very pronounced in Gewürztraminer
Stalks A green-wood smell which can arise in an under-ripe vintage
Truffles The most elusive of all scents, found by burgundians in burgundy, Barolans in Barolo, hermits in Hermitage
Vanilla Scent given to wine and (much more) brandy by a component of the oak of the cask
Violets A distinctive 'high-pitched' scent, especially in fine burgundies
Volatile Acidity apparent to the nose. A technical fault, although within reason it can be excitingly piquant

The list can be much extended: many tasters play the free-association game and jot down 'rubber', 'pear-drops', 'wool', etc

General terms of appreciation

Acid Tartaric acid is the prime refreshing and preserving factor in white wines. 'Fruity-acid' is the highest compliment in Germany. But acid should be in balance with other components

Astringence An effect of tannin, but part of the character of eg Chianti
Balance Essential quality: the right proportions of elements
Baked Flavour resulting from too hot sun on grapes
Body The 'volume' of a wine, partly due to alcoholic strength
Breed Balance of qualities in very fine wine due to grapes, soil and skill
Clean Free from defects, fresh
Coarse Tasting crudely made
Dry The opposite of sweet, but in an old wine can be a sign of the wine's cracking up
Dumb Not offering its full quality (wine is too young or too cold)
Elegant As of a woman, indefinable
Fat As of a man, well-fleshed. Not a desirable characteristic in itself
Fiery A good quality in moderation
Finesse Literally, fine-ness
Finish Aftertaste; in great wine the whole flavour lingers in the mouth for a considerable time after swallowing
Firm Young with a decisive style
Flat The opposite of firm
Fruity Ripe-tasting
Hard Tannin makes young wines hard. Acidity in whites can be hard, too
Long What the finish should be
Nervy Vigorous and fine; good in wine as in horses
Noble The ultimate accolade: breed, body, maturity in harmony. Use with care
Racy From French *race*, meaning breed; or vital and exciting
Rough Poor, cheap, badly made
Short What the finish should not be
Silky Accurate word for a certain texture (found in fine Beaujolais)
Stiff Similar to dumb
Supple Opposite of hard, but not pejorative as soft would be
Unresolved Not old enough for all the components to have harmonized
Vigorous Young at heart and lively; much to be desired

Taking Notes and Giving Scores

From talking about wine to writing about it is but a step – which few wine-drinkers ever take. Yet there is a strong case for keeping notes on what you drink or taste in a more or less organized way.

In the first place, having to commit something to paper makes you concentrate; the prime requirement for being able to taste wine properly at all. In the second it makes you analyse and pin labels on the sensations passing across your palate. In the third it is an aide-mémoire: when somebody asks you what a wine is like you can look it up and say something definite. In the fourth it allows you to extend comparison between wines over time – either the same wine a year later, or different but related wines on different occasions.

In short, keeping tasting notes is like keeping a diary: obviously a good idea, but hard to get off the ground.

With this in mind I asked Michael Broadbent, Director of the Wine Department of Christie's, London, whose book *Wine Tasting* is the standard work on the subject, to collaborate with me in compiling a suitable tasting card for keen amateurs to use.

There have been many studies (notably the one opposite from the University of California) of what they call Sensory Methods of Evaluating Wine. Most depend on a scoring system of points (for clarity, colour, aroma and the rest) which lends a slightly inappropriate air of indoor games to what is really an analytical exercise.

The Broadbent–Johnson card, reproduced below, does encompass a conventional way of scoring with points if this is what you want to do. But it can be used perfectly adequately without them.

The notes at the bottom right of the card explain its use. The left-hand column divides each of the three basic aspects of wine (sight, smell and taste) into facets that can be isolated and examined. One of the descriptions of these facets in the first column should fit every wine.

The centre column is simply a list of suggested adjectives for what you may find in the glass before you. These are words (see page 43) that are commonly used even by laypeople when discussing wine. None of them may apply to any given wine – which is the purpose of the right-hand column: this is to record your own impressions, again analytically, by sight, smell and taste. The Aroma Wheel opposite is an excellent source of inspiration.

After the analysis, the judgment. The space for Overall Quality allows your general feelings of pleasure or dislike to override your objective assessment, as in the end it will, and should, do, whether or not you find it helpful to turn your judgment into a numerical score .

Are numerical scores appropriate for judging wine? Under some circumstances, such as professional competitions or shows, they are unavoidable – or almost. In my 30 years as a wine commentator I have found myself obliged to use them only on a handful of occasions.

Above: a pre-auction tasting at Christie's auction rooms in St James's, London. Concentration is difficult at crowded tastings: note-taking is essential.

Below: a consistent analytical approach is the best way to learn about, judge and remember wine. Scoring is not compulsory, but forces you to decide.

Name of Wine Vintage District/type		Date purchased Merchant/bottler Price	
SIGHT Score (max. 3) ☐			**Comments**
CLARITY cloudy, bitty, dull, clear, brilliant DEPTH OF COLOUR watery, pale, medium, deep, dark COLOUR (whites) green tinge, pale yellow, yellow, gold, brown; (reds) purple, purple/red, red, red/brown VISCOSITY slight sparkle, watery, normal, heavy, oily		starbright, hazy, tuilé, straw, amber, tawny, ruby, garnet	
SMELL Score (max. 6) ☐			
GENERAL APPEAL neutral, clean, attractive, outstanding, off (eg yeasty, acetic, oxidized, woody, etc) FRUIT AROMA none, slight, positive, identifiable eg Riesling BOUQUET none, pleasant, complex, powerful		corky, sulphury, woody, cedarwood, dumb, flowery, smoky, honeyed, lemony, spicy, peardrops	HOW TO USE THIS CHART Wine appeals to three senses: sight, smell and taste. This card is a guide to analysing its appeal and an aide-mémoire on each wine you taste. Tick one word for each factor in the left-hand column and any of the descriptive terms that fit your impressions. Then award points according to the pleasure the wine gives you. Use the right-hand column for your comments.
TASTE Score (max. 8) ☐			
SWEETNESS (whites) bone-dry, dry, medium-dry, medium-sweet, very sweet TANNIN (reds) astringent, hard, dry, soft ACIDITY flat, refreshing, marked, tart BODY very light and thin, light, medium, full-bodied, heavy LENGTH short, acceptable, extended, lingering BALANCE unbalanced, good, very well-balanced, perfect		appley, bitter, burning, blackcurrants, caramel, earthy, fat, flinty, green, heady, flabby, mellow, metallic, nutty, salty, sappy, silky, spicy, fleshy, woody, watery	
OVERALL QUALITY Score (max. 3) ☐		supple, finesse, breed, elegance, harmonious, rich, delicate	
Coarse, poor, acceptable, fine, outstanding			
SCORING Total score (out of 20) ☐		DATE OF TASTING	

Theoretically it looks simple, and should be accurate. The 20-point score on the card illustrated provides an example. Let us suppose the wine is the appropriate colour and brilliantly clear. It will score three points for Sight. The smell is clean and attractive, clearly identifiable but a simple fruit smell – not a complex or developed bouquet. It would be reasonable to give it half the possible maximum for Smell: another three points: total score so far 6. It is dry with marked acidity, medium-bodied with acceptable length and good balance. Again, half the possible marks is appropriate. The total score is now 10.

What is your feeling about its overall quality? It is not fine, but it is certainly acceptable – if it were less you would give it no score here, so you add one to the total: 11/20. Quite possibly you think this looks a bit mean so you add a point for luck: 12/20.

Has scoring helped you to judge the wine? It has made you think, at least. In practice many tasters judging a group of wines are much less objective. They decide on the wines they prefer and give them scores to reflect their order of preference, rather than the other way round. Moments of doubt or indecision often result in half-points – so the total possible in reality is 40 different marks.

Many professionals argue that the more restricted a score-card is the more accurately it reflects their judgment; or strictly speaking the more it concentrates their powers of discrimination. One can argue for a 5-, a 7- or a 10-point system on this basis. All are regularly used.

The least appropriate or reliable system curiously is the one widely used in the USA and heavily publicized: the 100-point system. Of these 100 points the wine scores 50 just by being there, as candidates do in American high-school examinations. More accurately, therefore, it should be called a 50-point system (and is thus very close to the ditherer's 40-point version of the one above).

The much-vaunted advantage of this high-numbers approach is greater accuracy. Its very real disadvantage is that this apparent accuracy is almost certainly spurious – or at least not subject to any kind of scientific check.

A single taster, such as Robert Parker, who popularized the 100-point system and whose personal preferences become known to his public (and to winemakers), can perform a useful service by publishing such detailed scores. It is doubtful, to say the least, that on a second tasting of the same wines the same niceties of judgment would reappear. But they record one skilled appraisal as accurately as possible (and the reader can make allowance for the taster's known preferences).

A far less satisfactory situation arises when the scores of several tasters are averaged. In this case the apparent pinpoint accuracy is completely misleading. This may be among the reasons why fashion seems to be moving away from scoring wines and towards describing them – often with arpeggios of epithets that make the Aroma Wheel seem a positively constipated phrase-book.

The Aroma Wheel

showing first, second and third tier terms, after Noble *et al.*
(© American Society of Enologists and Viticulturists)

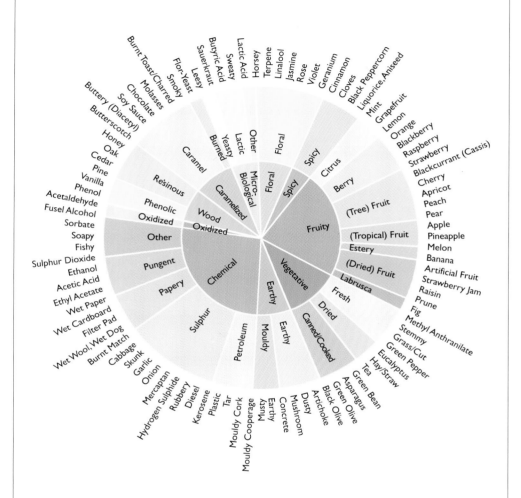

The Department of Viticulture and Enology of the University of California, at Davis, near Sacramento, has done more to organize our perceptions of the aromas of wine than any other institution. Dr Ann Noble and her colleagues at Davis developed the Aroma Wheel, on the analogy of the famous Colour Wheel of the French scientist Chevreul.

In the centre of the wheel are such broad groups of aromas as Fruity and Earthy (but also the specific character of, for example, oxidation, which is so dominant it cannot be ignored). In the next circle are less broad groupings. 'Fruity' for example is divided into citrus, berry, tree fruit, tropical fruit, estery, dried fruit and *labrusca* (the foxy American grape).

The circumference then particularizes even further, breaking down berry fruits into blackberry, raspberry, strawberry, and blackcurrant.

The aroma wheel works the other way too – and probably more often. In practice it is just as likely that a taster will begin on the circumference, by instantly recognizing a specific smell, than in the middle with the general notion of a wine's fruitiness. Spatial relationships around and within the shape of the wheel are therefore not the essence of the system. Nevertheless, their arrangement in this apparently logical way can be extremely helpful in an attempt to analyse or pin down an aroma that remains elusive to description.

Looking after Wine

To buy good wine and not to look after it properly is like hanging a masterpiece in a dark corner, or not exercising a racehorse, or not polishing your Rolls-Royce. If good wine is worth paying extra for it is worth keeping, and above all serving, in good condition.

There is nothing mysterious or difficult about handling wine. But doing it well can add vastly to the pleasure of drinking it – and doing it badly can turn nectar into sludge.

Wine only asks for two things: to be kept lying quietly in a dark, cool place and to be served generously, not hurriedly, with plenty of time and room to breathe the air.

Storage is a problem to almost everyone. Cellars like the one opposite, the perfect place for keeping a collection, are rarely built today. Most people have to make shift with a cupboard. But even a cupboard can have the simple requirements of darkness, freedom from vibration, and – if not the ideal coolness – at least an even temperature. Wine is not overfussy: anything from 7–21°C (45–70°F) will do. What matters more is that it stays the same. No wine will stand alternate boiling and freezing. In high temperatures it will age quicker. And there is the danger of it seeping around the cork; if there is any sign of this, drink it immediately. But if coolness is impractical, steady moderate warmth will do.

No special equipment is needed in cellar or cupboard. Bottles should always be kept lying down to prevent the cork from drying and shrinking and letting in air. They can be stacked in a pile if they are all the same; but as they are more likely to be all different it is better to keep them in a rack so that bottles can easily be taken from the bottom.

Given the space, there is a good argument for buying certain wines young, at their opening price, and 'laying them down' in cellar or cupboard until they reach perfect maturity. Wine

Finest Bordeaux served the English way: decanted into a claret jug over a candle flame – one of wine's best established rites, but one that still arouses controversy.

merchants are now slow to point out that they may appreciate in monetary, as well as gastronomic, value. While at the very top end of the market with First Growths there is a reasonable prospect of this, with more modest wines the only object is to be able to drink them in good condition when they have matured to suit your taste.

It was Pasteur who discovered (see pages 40–41) the effects on wine of exposing it to the air. The same effects lie behind the custom of decanting, or pouring wine from its original bottle into another – more often a glass carafe – before serving it. Decanting is much discussed but little understood, largely because its effect on

a given wine is unpredictable. There is a mistaken idea that it is something you only do to ancient bottles with lots of sediment - a mere precautionary measure to get a clean glass of wine. But experience shows that it is usually young wines that benefit most. The oxygen they contain has had little chance to take effect. But the air in the decanter works rapidly and effectively. In a matter of a few hours it can often induce the opening of what was a closed bud. This can mean literally twice as much of the scent and flavour that you paid for. Some strong young wines can benefit by even as much as 24 hours in a decanter. An hour makes all the difference to others.

Surprisingly little study has been done on the effects of aeration on different wines. For one example, fine mature Beaujolais *crus* can seem dead in the bottle when they are first opened, but spring to scented, succulent life half an hour after decanting. The French rarely decant at all. They miss a great deal.

The technique of decanting is illustrated below. The only essential equipment is a carafe and a corkscrew. But a cradle is the best way of keeping the bottle in almost the same position as in the rack where it was lying, so that any sediment remains along the lower side. And a corkscrew such as the Screwpull that pushes against the mouth of the bottle makes it easy to avoid jerking.

Cut the capsule and take it off completely. Take the cork out gently. Wipe the lip of the bottle. Hold the bottle (best done without the basket) in one hand and the decanter in the other, and pour steadily until you see the sediment (if any) moving into the lower neck of the bottle. Then stop. Having a flashlight behind or below the neck of the bottle makes it easier to see when the dregs start to move – although a candle is more in keeping with the pleasantly sensuous ritual.

A wine-basket should never be used for pouring at table. Its purpose is to hold the bottle steady for opening before decanting in a position as near to horizontal as possible.

A Screwpull corkscrew gives a strong and steady pull by pushing against the lip of the bottle. Its worm is coated with Teflon for drawing the cork with a smooth single screwing action.

A lighted candle below the neck of the bottle makes it easier to see when the sediment in the wine forms a dark line moving towards the neck: this is the point at which to stop pouring.

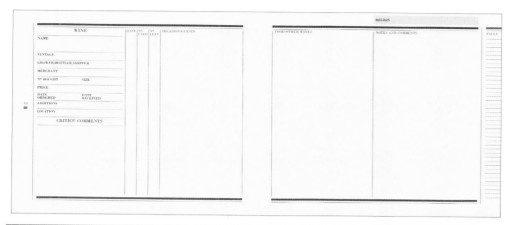

Above: wine paraphernalia for the 21st century: the Leverpull is the world's fastest corkscrew, the silver 'Champagne Star' grips tough champagne corks, and the bizarre Impitoyable tasting glass intensifies the aromas of wines to the point of caricature.

Above right: a cellar book is intended to provide an orderly biography of each wine you buy. It provides a record of wines bought, stored and eventually consumed. It has space for details about the vintage, vineyard, merchant, price, and meals when it is drunk. It is helpful to record the company, the food and of course how the wine tasted. Finally, notes on a particular wine help you to calculate when a vintage will peak – or when it is time to drink the last bottles.

Right: the cellar of an old English country house has brick 'bins' along the wall, originally built to hold the whole contents of one barrel each. Today thay are filled with racks, two bottles deep, that give each bin a maximum capacity of about 150 bottles, but of any number of different wines, readily accessible and easy to catalogue. The rack on the end wall can hold a further twelve dozen bottles, while space on the floor is used for storing cases before unpacking.

An alternative to pouring straight into the decanter: a silver funnel with a perforated strainer and its spout curved sideways to make the wine run down the side of the decanter without splashing.

Serving Wine

The care we take in serving wine and the little customs and courtesies of the table cannot do much to change its virtues or vices. But they can add tenfold to its enjoyment. If there are different glasses, decanters, even rituals for different wines, it is not out of any physical necessity but as an expression of the varying sensuous pleasures they give. In helping to emphasize the different characters of wine – and reminding us of their origins – they add to the experience and make it memorable.

These pages show some of the most practical, and prettiest, forms of glasses which have been evolved to put each kind of wine in its best light. What they have in common are the essentials of reasonably generous but not exaggerated or pretentious size (so that a good measure fills them only a third- to half-full), clear uncoloured glass so that the colour of the wine is undimmed, and a rim that cups in slightly towards the top, which makes it possible to swirl the wine in the glass to release its scent without spilling it. The glass should be thin without feeling perilously fragile.

The only cut glass in the picture is one for German wine. Some purists scorn all cut glass, but there is no doubt that the Treviris glass used on the Mosel reflects flashes of light into the pale green wine and gives it brilliance. Nor does it seem inappropriate to gaze at your Rhine wine through etched bunches of grapes.

It may seem too obvious to mention, but wine glasses should be clean, ie polished and untainted with smells of detergents or cupboards. They should be rinsed with hot water and polished by hand. They are much easier to polish while they are still hot. No wisps of towel should stick to

1 The 'official' tasting glass of the International Standards Organization is a model of function and form. It is designed for sampling, therefore for a small amount of wine, to expand its aroma and funnel them to the nose. In fact it is very close to a sherry copita (**6**) enlarged.

2 A Burgundian silver *tastevin*. Professional tasters in Burgundy keep one in their pockets. Its gleam through the wine in a dark cellar is a surer judge of colour and clarity than a glass, and it is unbreakable.

3 Decanter for claret, port, sherry or madeira. This three-ring decanter of 1800 is from the classic period for English glass.

4 Silver or gold labels for decanters are a practical old custom that has been revived. A London firm made the reproduction of a delicate vineleaf in the picture. They are suitable for any wine or spirit that is served or kept in a decanter.

5 An English lead crystal baluster wine-glass dating from the early 18th-century. This is one of the classic designs, very satisfying to handle, but its flared rim dissipates the wine's aroma.

6 A handmade cognac glass in Swedish crystal. Balloon glasses are never used by experts in Cognac.

7 The sherry copita: one of the best-designed tasting glasses, funnelling the scent of the wine to the nostrils. The perfect size for drinking sherry, filled two-thirds full.

8 Silver decanting funnels are collectors' items. This English model, dated 1790, is unusual in being scaled-up to magnum size. Its perforated insert catches any cork or sediment.

9 A 20th-century magnum decanter decorated with elegant copper-wheel engraving. A magnum is better than a bottle for maturing fine wines slowly to perfection; it ensures that up to 12 guests taste the same bottle.

10 Conventionally red burgundy is served in rotund glasses that maximize the surface area of the wine – and hence its bouquet.

11 Restaurants often use (and 1980s fashion demanded) oversize wine glasses. A quarter of a bottle of wine at a time seems a normal portion.

12 A red-wine glass ideal for burgundy or Bordeaux, based on the classic Bordeaux model. Big enough to be filled only a third full – the perfect amount for appreciating the wine.

13 It is customary to serve white wine in slightly smaller glasses than red. A matching set is ideal for fine wines at a dinner party.

them. Cupboard smells usually come from keeping glasses upside down. This may be necessary on open shelves, but it is better to keep them right way up in a clean dry airy cupboard. Sniff them before putting them on the table.

Some of the attentions paid to wine are frivolous. Others (notably decanting, see page 46) can make all the difference between mere satisfaction and real delight.

Any good wine benefits by comparison with another. It is no affectation, but simply making the most of a good thing, to serve more than one wine at a meal. A young wine served first shows off the qualities of an older one; a white wine (usually) shows off a red one; a light wine a massive one; a dry wine a sweet one. But any of these combinations played the other way round would be a disaster for the second wine. In the same way a really good wine puts in the shade a lesser wine served after it, and the same thing happens to a dry white wine served after a red.

The question of how much to serve is more difficult. There are six good glasses of wine (which means generous glasses filled one-third full, not small ones filled to the brim) in a normal bottle. At a light lunch one glass a person might be enough, whereas at a long dinner, five or six might not be too much. A total of half a bottle a person (perhaps one glass of white wine and two of red) is a reasonable average for most people and occasions – but the circumstances and mood of the meal, and above all how long it goes on, are the deciding factors. A bottle each is certainly not too much for a long evening. There is a golden rule for hosts: be generous but never pressing. And offer water, too.

14 The first patent corkscrew design, and still a very efficient model, is the 'Henshall'. Its ridged 'button' prevents the cork from twisting and makes it easy to draw.

15 Today's most fashionable shaped champagne glass. It displays the bubbles perfectly and is easier to polish inside than its neighbour.

16 The flute: the traditional and most beautiful sparkling-wine glass. Slow to fill, as the bubbles rise like a rocket. 'Tulips' are also good for champagne; flat shallow glasses are not.

17 Champagne or any white wine is at its best thoroughly cooled. The ideal way is in a deep ice bucket full of cold water, with ice cubes in the water. The ice bucket in

the picture is unusual in being so deep; most designs are too shallow, so it is necessary to stand the bottle on its head in them for a few minutes to cool the top of the bottle as well as the bottom.

18 The traditional Rhine-wine or hock glass has a stout knobbed stem of brown glass, to reflect the desired colour into the wine. Although today the fashion is for pale wine, its use continues.

19 The pretty engraved Trier or Treviris glass for Mosel. Even cafés on the Mosel use this graceful glass to make their pale white wine catch the light and seem more inviting than ever.

20 Stands for decanters of bottles to prevent them from making rings on the table are known as coasters. They can be made of silver or gold, or wood or papier mâché. The coaster on the far left is in painted 'Toleware', the magnum one is 18th-century English silver.

21 A wooden 'port cradle' is a useful implement for pulling corks without standing the bottle up and disturbing the sediment.

49

Serving Wine: Temperature

Nothing makes more difference to enjoying wine than its temperature. Stone-cold claret and lukewarm Rhine wines are abominations. And there are several good reasons why this should be so.

Our sense of smell (and hence the greater part of our sense of taste) is only susceptible to vapours. Red wine has a higher molecular weight – and is thus less volatile – than white. The object of serving red wine at room temperature, or *chambré*, is to warm it to the point where its aromatic elements begin to vaporize – which is at a progressively higher temperature for more solid and substantial wines. A light Beaujolais can be treated as a white wine; even cold, its volatility is almost overwhelming. On the other hand, a full-scale red wine needs the warmth of the room, of the cupped hand around the glass, and of the mouth itself to volatilize its complex constituents.

As an apparent exception to this rule the French tend to serve red burgundy cooler than red Bordeaux. Some grapes make wine that is inherently more volatile than others: for example, Pinot Noir is one of the 'showy' grapes – the reason why young red burgundy is much more attractive than young Bordeaux.

Cold is also necessary to provide a sense of balance to the richness of very sweet wines, even if in doing so it masks some of their flavours. On the chart opposite, all the sweetest white wines are entered at the coldest point. It is a good idea to pour them very cold and let them warm up slightly while you sip them: the process seems to release all their aroma and bouquet. Extreme cold has also been used to make over-aged white wine presentable.

The chart also sets out in some detail the wide range of temperatures that brings out the best in different wines. It is based on personal experience, often modified in discussions (not to mention arguments) with many wine-lovers. Personal taste and habits vary widely from in-dividual to individual; and indeed from country to country. But it is worth remembering that when the term *chambré* was invented the prevailing temperature in French dining-rooms was unlikely to have been above 15–16°C (60°F).

It is easier to serve white wine at the right temperature than red: a refrigerator can make the necessary adjustments so simply. The fastest way to cool a bottle is to put it in a bucket of ice and water (not ice alone). In a very warm room (and especially a hot garden) it is a good idea to keep the bottle in the bucket between pourings, even if it means pouring the wine a bit too cold; it warms up all too quickly in the glass. A useful tip for large quantities (several bottles in a big bucket) is to make a monster block of ice by putting a polythene bag of water in the deep-freeze: the bigger the block the slower it thaws. Tall German bottles should be put in the water upside-down for a few minutes first to cool the wine in the neck.

Persuading a red wine to reach the right temperature is harder. If it starts at cellar temperature it takes several hours in a normal room to raise it 10 or 12 degrees. The kitchen is the logical place – but many kitchens are well over 18°C (64°F), especially while dinner is cooking. At this sort of temperature any red wine is thrown out of balance; the alcohol starts to vaporize and produces a heady smell, which masks its character. The most practical way of warming red wine in a hurry is first to decant it, then to stand the decanter in water at about 21°C (70°F). It does not harm to heat the decanter (within reason) first.

Right: A selection of containers for lowering the temperature of wine. A large Chinese fish bowl is as good as any for mass-cooling bottles. Use lumps of ice topped up with water rather than ice only. The earthenware cooler uses evaporation to lower the temperature and the transparent, vacuum-filled cooler is handy to keep a ready-chilled bottle cool.

The chart below suggests ideal temperature for serving a wide range of wines. 'Room temperature' is low by modern standards: all the better for fine wine.

DOMESTIC FRIDGE TEMP.		CELLAR TEMPERATURE ▼ THE IDEAL CELLAR			ROOM TEMP. ▶
SWEET WHITES	DRY WHITES	LIGHT REDS	FULL SCALE REDS		

C° 4   5   6   7   8   9   10   11   12   13   14   15   16   17   18
F° 39 41 43 45 46 48 50   52   54   55   57   59   61   63   64

Wine	Approx. position
MUSCADET	6–7°C
CHABLIS	8°C
MACON	8–9°C
BORDEAUX BLANC	8–9°C
CHINON	10–11°C
BEST WHITE BURGUNDIES AND GRAVES	12–13°C
RED BURGUNDY	15–16°C
SAUTERNES	6–7°C
GEWURTZTRAMINER	6–7°C
BEAUJOLAIS NOUVEAU	10–11°C
BEAUJOLAIS CRUS	12–13°C
COTES DU RHONE (RED)	12–13°C
TOP RED RHONE	15–16°C
SANCERRE/POUILLY	6–7°C
VINTAGE PORT	16–17°C
GROS PLANT	5°C
ALSACE/RIESLING	7–8°C
MIDI REDS: CORBIERES, ETC	12–13°C
MUSCATS	5°C
SYLVANER	6–7°C
ORDINARY RED BORDEAUX	14–15°C
ALIGOTE	5°C
FINO SHERRY	9°C
TAWNY PORT	11°C
CREAM SHERRY	13°C
TOKAY	5°C
NON-VINTAGE CHAMPAGNE	7–8°C
AMONTILLADO	11°C
MADEIRA	13°C
CAHORS	14–15°C
FINE RED BORDEAUX	16–17°C
MONTLLA	10–11°C
MADIRAN	15°C
SPARKLING WINE (SEKT, CAVA ETC)	5–6°C
VIN JAUNE	11°C
BANDOL	16°C
BEST CHAMPAGNE	7–8°C
EISWEIN	5°C
GOOD GERMAN & AUSTRIAN WINES	9°C
BEST DRY GERMAN WINES	11°C
BEST SWEET GERMAN WINES	13°C
CHIANTI RESERVAS	15°C
LIEBFRAUMILCH	5°C
SWEET LOIRE CHENIN BLANCS	5–6°C
FRASCATI	7°C
VALPOLICELLA	11–12°C
ORVIETO	7°C
FIASCO CHIANTI	13°C
RIOJA RESERVAS	15°C
SOAVE	8°C
SICILIAN REDS	13°C
BEST PORTUGUESE REDS	17°C
VERDICCHIO	8°C
HUNGARIAN WHITES	11°C
BARBERA	13°C
BAROLO	16°C
VINHO VERDE	6°C
FENDANT	7°C
VALDEPENAS	11°C
CHILEAN CABERNET	15°C
DOLE	11°C
LAMBRUSCO	7°C
LIGHT ZINFANDELS	13°C
RETSINA	4°C
YUGOSLAV REISLING	7°C
S.A. CHENIN BLANC	7°C
CALIFORNIA/AUSTRALIAN/OREGON PINOT NOIR	15–16°C
CHARDONNAY	8°C
TOP CALIFORNIA/AUSTRALIAN CHARDONNAYS	11–12°C
LIGHT MUSCATS	5°C
N.Z. SAUVIGNON	7°C
CALIFORNIA SAUVIGNON BLANC	9°C
BEST CALIFORNIA CABERNETS & ZINFANDELS	16–17°C
JOHANNISBERG RIESLING	6–7°C
BAROSSA RIESLING	7°C
LIQUEUR MUSCATS	11°C
OLD HUNTER VALLEY WHITES	13°C
VIN ROSE	7°C
TOP AUSTRALIAN CABERNET/SHIRAZ	17°C

France

France

Left: new Tronçais oak *barriques* in the second-year *chai* at Château Margaux in the Médoc await filling. Tronçais oak from the Allier in central France is the most prized of all oaks used for barrels.

When the last raindrop has been counted, and no geological stone is left unturned, there will still remain the imponderable question of national character which makes France the undisputed mistress of the vine; the originator and producer of more and more varied great wines than all the rest of the world.

France is not only sensuous and painstaking; France is methodical. She not only has good vineyards; she defines, classifies and controls them. The listing, in order, of the best sites has been going on for 200 years. In the last 70 or so it has been codified in ever-increasing detail as the law of the land in every sense.

It started with the Appellation d'Origine Contrôlée which restricted the use of the name Roquefort to cheese made and matured in a certain area, by a certain method, from ewes' milk. The same principle applies to each wine appellation: restriction of area, of method and of grape variety or varieties. The law also stipulates the maximum crop per hectare and minimum strength. AOCs (or ACs for short) are adminis-

tered by the Institut National des Appellations d'Origine (INAO).

Since its inception in 1973 the second most important category of French wines has been Vins de Pays; a well-conceived and highly successful scheme to encourage local pride and aspirations in what was formerly plain vin de table, sold on strength and price alone. Vins de Pays may choose between looser and stricter definitions (see pages 138–39), but as a group they constitute the selection pool for future possible appellations. Between the two comes the much less numerous category of Vins Délimités de Qualité Supérieure (VDQS). In practice this is the proving ground for wines (often promoted from Vins de Pays) aspiring to AC status. It should be said that not all do, or ever will. There are good growers who prefer more freedom of manoeuvre than an AC would ever allow.

This atlas does not attempt to reproduce the boundaries set by law to every French wine region. It has the wine-drinker rather than the lawyer in mind.

Below: France imports almost half as much wine as she exports. Most imports are blending wine.

Left: France produced 65.4 million hectolitres of wine in 1992, of which nearly 60% was red and 36% was AOC. Of the total amount exported almost one-third was AOC wine, both still and sparkling, which represented more than 80% of the total value of French wine exports. The biggest earners are champagne and Bordeaux.

French Wine Exports by Volume (%)

Germany	24%
Great Britain	18%
Belgium/Lux	12%
Netherlands	9%
USA	5%
Switzerland	5%

Above: Exports total about 12 million hectolitres a year. Germany is by far the biggest consumer in volume terms, followed by Britain, but the USA is the largest in value.

Total French Wine Exports and Imports by Volume

Exports	12 million hectolitres
Imports	5.4 million hectolitres

—— · —— International boundary

— — — — Département boundary

○   Chief town of département

●   Centre of VDQS area

Côte Roannaise   VDQS name – a guide to VDQS wines not mapped elsewhere appears on pages 138-39

   Champagne (page 76)
   Loire Valley (pages 114-15)
   Burgundy (page 55)
   Savoie and Jura (page 137)
   Rhône (pages 125 and 129)
   Southwest (pages 112-13)
   Cognac (pages 110-11)
   Bergerac (page 109)
   Bordeaux (page 80)
   Midi (pages 133-35)
   Provence (page 136)
   Alsace (page 120)
   Other wine-producing areas

Proportional symbols

44   Area of vineyard per département in thousands of hectares

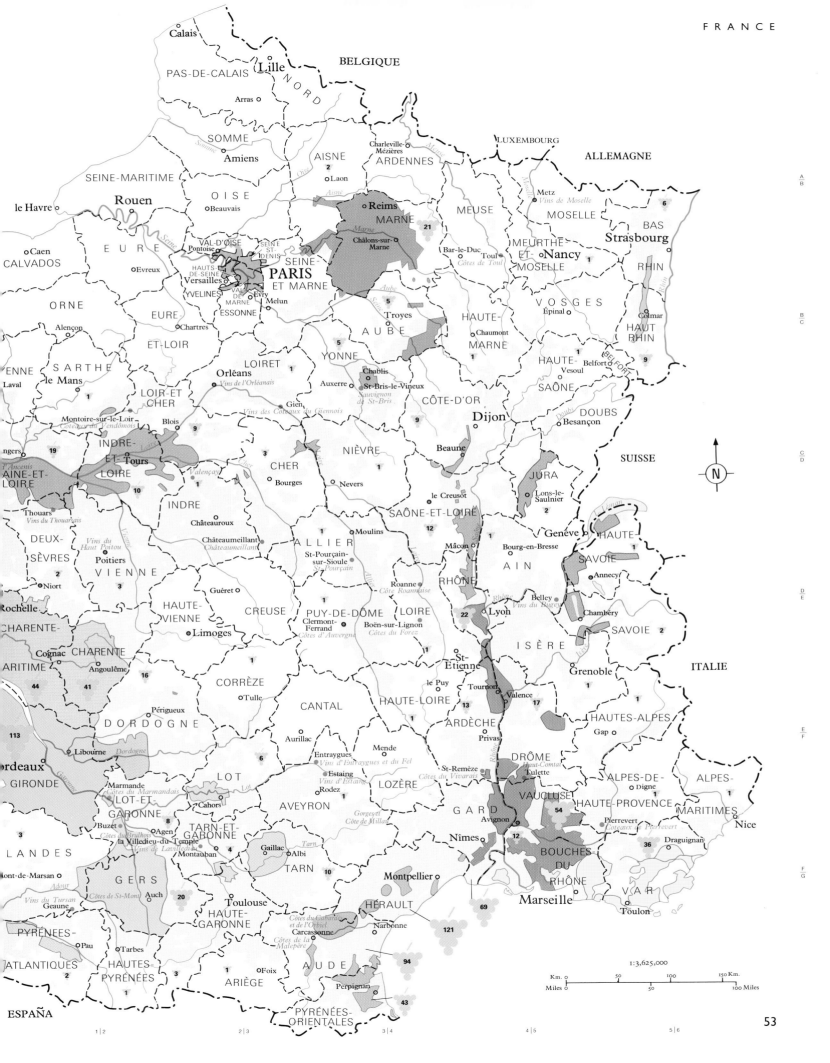

Burgundy

The very name of Burgundy has a sonorous ring. Is it the chapel- or the dinner-bell? Let Paris be France's head, Champagne her soul; Burgundy is her stomach. It is a land of long meals, well supplied with the best materials (Charolais beef to the west, Bresse chickens to the east, fish in the rivers and snails on the vines). It was the richest of the ancient duchies of France. But even before France became Christian it was famous for its wine.

Burgundy is not one big vineyard, but the name of a province which contains at least three of France's best. By far the richest and most important of its regions is the Côte d'Or, in the centre, composed of the Côte de Beaune and the Côte de Nuits. But Chablis, Beaujolais and the Mâconnais have old reputations which owe nothing to their richer brother's.

For all the ancient fame and riches, Burgundy still feels simple and rustic. There is hardly a grand house from end to end of the Côte d'Or – none of the elegant country estates which stamp, say, the Médoc as a creation of leisure and wealth in the 18th and 19th centuries. Most of the few big holdings of land, those of the

The old road from Monthélie to Volnay runs between stone walls through the Premier Cru Taillepieds. The vines on the left belong to the Hospices de Beaune; their wine is the Cuvée Blondeau.

Below: In 1991 Burgundy and Beaujolais produced almost 2.4 million hectolitres of wine, over 75% of which was red. Exports accounted for almost 42% of the total: just under 1 million hectolitres.

Ten years ago Switzerland and the USA took over half Burgundy's total exports between them. Since then, Germany and the USA have virtually exchanged places.

Exports of Burgundy (including Beaujolais) by Volume

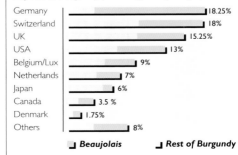

Germany	18.25%
Switzerland	18%
UK	15.25%
USA	13%
Belgium/Lux	9%
Netherlands	7%
Japan	6%
Canada	3.5 %
Denmark	1.75%
Others	8%

Beaujolais   *Rest of Burgundy*

Church, were broken up by Napoleon. It is now one of the most fragmented of the important winegrowing districts of France. The average grower owns a mere 10 acres (4 hectares).

The fragmentation of Burgundy is the cause of the single great drawback of its wine: its unpredictability. From the geographer's point of view the human factor is unmappable, and in Burgundy, more than in most places, it needs to be given the limelight. For even having pinned down a wine to one particular *climat* (field of vines) in one particular commune in one particular year, it could still, in many cases, have been made by any one of six or seven people owning small parcels of the land, and reared in any one of six or seven cellars. 'Monopoles', or whole vineyards in the hands of one grower, are rare exceptions. Even the smallest grower has parcels in two or three vineyards. Bigger ones may own a total of 50–100 acres (20–40 hectares) spread in small lots in a score of vineyards from one end of the Côte to the other. The Clos de Vougeot has 80 growers in its 125 acres (50 hectares).

For this very reason about 65% of burgundy is still bought in barrel from the grower when it is new by négociants (or shippers), who blend it with other wines from the same area to achieve marketable quantities of a standard wine. This is offered to the world not as the product of a specific grower, whose production of that particular wine may be only a cask or two, but as the wine of a given district (be it as specific as a vineyard or as vague as a village) élevé – literally, educated – by the shipper.

The reputations of these négociants-éleveurs (most of whom are also growers themselves) vary from being the touchstone of the finest burgundy to something much more earthy.

What is certain is that all the very finest wine goes to market (as everywhere in the world) with the most detailed possible description of its antecedents on its label, almost always including the vineyard proprietor's name and the fact that the wine is bottled in the proprietor's cellars.

The map on this page shows the whole of winegrowing Burgundy, the relative sizes and positions of the big southern areas of Beaujolais and the Mâconnais, Chablis in the north, the much smaller Côte Chalonnaise and the narrow strip of the Côte d'Or and its little-known hinterland, the Hautes Côtes de Beaune and the Hautes Côtes de Nuits (shown in detail on pages 59–67). The key is an index to the detailed large-scale maps of the areas which follow.

There is a total of some 200 ACs in Burgundy. Most refer to geographical areas and appear on the next 20 pages. Built into these geographical appellations is a quality classification which is practically a work of art in itself (explained on page 58). However, the appellations Bourgogne, Bourgogne Aligoté (for white wine), Bourgogne Passe-Tout-Grains and Bourgogne Grand Ordinaire can be used for wine from the appropriate grapes coming from any part of Burgundy, including vineyards within famous communes whose soil and situation are below par.

THE LANGUAGE OF THE LABEL

Climat Vineyard (individual field)

Commune or **Finage** Parish

Grand Cru One of the very few élite vineyards with its own Appellation Contrôlée

Mise dans nos caves Bottled in our cellars (not necessarily those of the grower)

Mise (or **Mise en bouteilles**) **du** (or **au**) **Domaine** (or **à la propriété**) Bottled at the property where it is made

Mise par le propriétaire Bottled by the grower

Monopole The whole of the vineyard named belongs to the same proprietor

Négociant-Eleveur A merchant who buys wine from the grower in its first year and 'brings it up' in his own cellars

Premier Cru The second class of burgundy vineyard (below Grand Cru)

Propriétaire-Récoltant Owner-manager

Récolte Vintage

-Village Wine with the simple 'appellation communale' of the commune named

-Villages From selected parishes within the region named

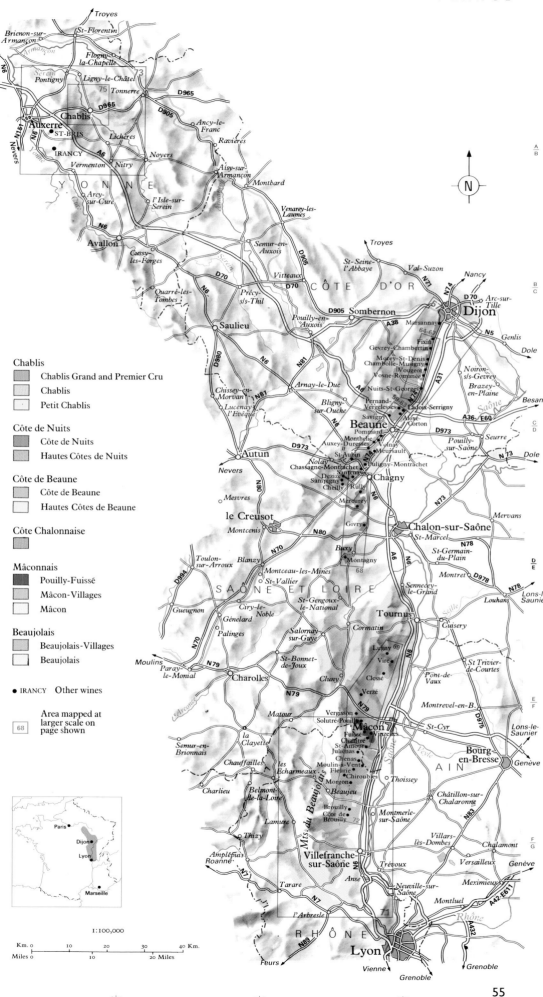

Chablis
- Chablis Grand and Premier Cru
- Chablis
- Petit Chablis

Côte de Nuits
- Côte de Nuits
- Hautes Côtes de Nuits

Côte de Beaune
- Côte de Beaune
- Hautes Côtes de Beaune

Côte Chalonnaise

Mâconnais
- Pouilly-Fuissé
- Mâcon-Villages
- Mâcon

Beaujolais
- Beaujolais-Villages
- Beaujolais

● IRANCY Other wines

68 Area mapped at larger scale on page shown

1:100,000

Km. 0   10   20   30   40 Km.
Miles 0   10   20 Miles

The Côte d'Or: the Quality Factor

A Burgundian understandably feels a certain reverence towards the rather commonplace-looking ridge of the Côte d'Or, like the Athenians towards an unknown god. One is bound to wonder at the fact that a few small parcels of land on this hill give superlative wine, each with its own positive personality, and that others do not. Surely one can discover the factors that distinguish one parcel from another – giving to some grapes more sugar, thicker skins, a pulp more rich in minerals?

One can. And one cannot. Soil and subsoil have been analysed time and again. Temperature and humidity and wind direction have been recorded; wines have been analysed by gas chromatography . . . yet the central mystery remains. One can only put down certain physical facts, and place beside them the reputations of the great wines. No one can prove how the two are connected.

Burgundy is the northernmost area in the world which produces great red wine. Its climate pattern in summer is curiously like that of Bordeaux – the continental influence making up to some extent for its position further north. Yet total failure of the vintage is a more frequent problem here. No overriding climatic consideration can explain the excellence of the wine – or even why a vineyard was established here in the first place.

The general pattern is simple enough. The Côte lies along an important geological fault line where the seabed deposits of several different geological epochs, each rich in calcium from defunct shellfish, are exposed like a sliced layer-cake. Exposure has weathered their rocks into soils of different ages and textures; the varying degrees of slope have mixed them in different proportions. Minor local fault lines which lie at right angles to the Côte add variations to the *macédoine*.

The altitude of the mid-slope is roughly constant at about 820 feet (250 metres). Higher, on the thinly soiled hard rock cap of the hill, the climate is harsher; grapes ripen later. Lower, where the soil is more alluvial, valley mists and untimely frosts are more common.

The Côte faces east with a bias to the south, locally skewed (especially in the Côte de Beaune) to full south and even west exposure.

The Côte de Nuits is a sharper slope than the Côte de Beaune. Along its lower part, generally about a third of the way up, runs a narrow outcrop of marlstone, making limy clay soil. Marl by itself would be too rich a soil for the highest quality wine, but in combination with the stones and scree washed down from the hard limestone higher up it is perfect. Erosion continues the blend below the actual outcrop, the distance depending on the angle of incline.

In the Côte de Beaune the marly outcrop (Argovien) is wider and higher on the hill; instead of a narrow strip of vineyard under a beetling brow of limestone there is a broad and gentle slope vineyards can climb. The vines almost reach the scrubby peak in places.

On the dramatic isolated hill of Corton the soil formed from the marlstone is the best part of the vineyard, with only a little wood-covered cap of hard limestone above it.

In Meursault the limestone reappearing below the marl on the slope forms a second and lower shoulder to the hill, limy and very stony; excellent for white wine.

Such illustrations are only random examples

For location of cross-sections see map opposite

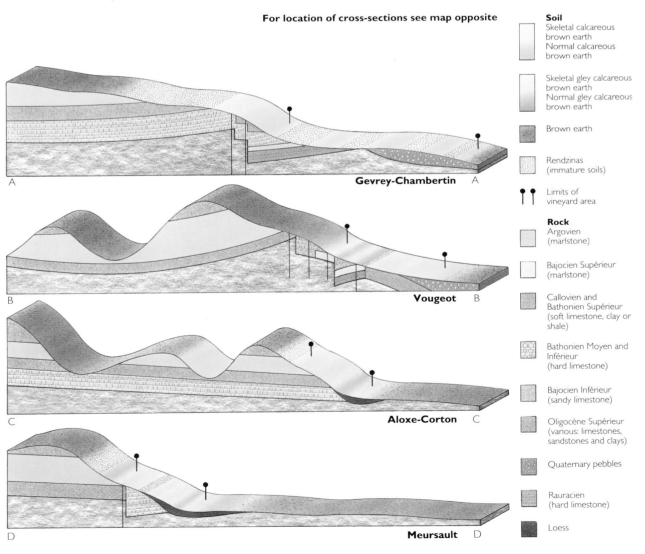

Soil

Skeletal calcareous brown earth
Normal calcareous brown earth

Skeletal gley calcareous brown earth
Normal gley calcareous brown earth

Brown earth

Rendzinas (immature soils)

Limits of vineyard area

Rock

Argovien (marlstone)

Bajocien Supérieur (marlstone)

Callovien and Bathonien Supérieur (soft limestone, clay or shale)

Bathonien Moyen and Inférieur (hard limestone)

Bajocien Inférieur (sandy limestone)

Oligocène Supérieur (various: limestones, sandstones and clays)

Quaternary pebbles

Rauracien (hard limestone)

Loess

Gevrey-Chambertin

Vougeot

Aloxe-Corton

Meursault

Left: a cross-section of the Côte d'Or through four great vineyards. The surface (soil) derives from the rock both under it and higher up the hill. In Gevrey-Chambertin immature soil or rendzinas (indicated by dots: see key) persists low down until the layer of marlstone. On and below the marlstone is good calcareous brown earth on limestone in a well-sheltered position (Chambertin). A mixture of soils continues into the valley, giving good vineyard land.

At Vougeot the marlstone outcrops twice. Below the top outcrop is Grands Echézeaux; on and below the second Clos de Vougeot.

The hill of Corton has a broad band of marlstone almost to the top; the best vineyards are on it. But on this steep gradient growers constantly have to collect soil from the bottom and carry it back up the slope. Where limestone debris falls from above white wine is grown (Corton-Charlemagne). At Meursault the marlstone is again high and broad but its benefit is felt lower where it forms stony soil on a limestone outcrop. The best vineyards are on this convex ramp.

of the varied structure of the Côte. And with each change of soil comes a change in drainage, in the soil's temperature – in any one of a hundred factors which will affect the vine.

Probably it is the microclimate which, in combination with the physical structure, has the most decisive effect. The best vineyards of the Côte face due east; it is the morning sun they want, to warm the ground gradually all day. They are sheltered from the southwest, from the moist rainbearing wind – but not so sheltered as to be frost pockets on still nights. It is fascinating to speculate on what other details of their position count in the thousands of hours that the grapes are hanging on the vines.

The other, unmappable, quality factor is the grower's choice of vines and the way they are pruned and fertilized. There are more or less vigorous 'clones' of the classic varieties, and a grower who chooses the most productive, prunes inadequately or overfeeds the soil, inevitably compromises quality. Much disappointing short-lived wine is made this way.

The reasons why the Côte d'Or needs mapping in more detail than any other wine region arise both from its singular pattern of soils and microclimates and from its unique history.

Of all regions it is the one where wine quality has been studied for longest – certainly in unbroken succession since the 12th century when Cistercian and Benedictine monks got to work in earnest. It is said that they 'tasted the soil' – so eager were they to explore its potential and distinguish one 'cru' from another. The word cru means both the land and the wine, defined as an entity distinct from the next cru on the hill. Where to draw the lines was the whole aim of the monks' passionate enquiry.

The great Dukes of Burgundy of the house of Valois in the 14th and 15th centuries did everything possible to encourage and profit by the wines that gave them unique standing among regional potentates. Every generation

since has added to the sum of local knowledge that is expressed in the climats and crus of the hills from Dijon to Chagny.

The map on this page gives the essential overview. The top of the not-very-impressive hills is a broken plateau with abrupt scarps where geological fault-lines protrude: the Hautes Côtes, divided into those of Beaune and those of Nuits, rising to over 1,300 feet (400 metres) and subject to cold and exposure which puts their crop a week behind the pampered Côtes below.

This is not to say that in their more sheltered east- and south-facing combes the Pinot Noir and Chardonnay cannot produce lightish wines of true Côte d'Or character. The best communes

in the Hautes Côtes de Beaune, where the Chardonnay is dominant, include Nantoux, Echevronne, La Rochepot, and Meloisey. In the Hautes Côtes de Nuits, where red wines dominate, Marey-les-Fussey, Magny-les-Villers, Villers-Fontaine and Bévy. The Hautes Côtes de Beaune conclude in the south with a recent appellation, Maranges, covering the three communes just west of Santenay.

The sheltered vineyards of the two Côtes are densely concentrated in the north, where they face east on a more or less consistent and unbroken slope. South of Nuits the communes of Comblanchien and Corgoloin slice marble from the hills; an abrupt change from the ranks of vines. Then vines spread out south and west from the oval hill of Corton in a more sprawling landscape with more southern slopes. The Côte de Beaune produces more than twice as much wine as the Côte de Nuits, almost half of it white. The Côte de Nuits concentrates on one thing only: the Pinot Noir.

Key:
- – · – · – Département boundary
- Wine-producing areas
- 59 Area mapped at larger scale on page shown
- A——A Cross-section (see opposite page)

1:220,000

Km. 0 1 2 3 4 5 Km.
Km. 0 1 2 3 Miles

The Côte d'Or

The Côte d'Or – the Côte de Beaune and the Côte de Nuits, separated only by a few miles where vines give way to marble quarries – is an irregular escarpment some 30 miles (50 kilometres) long. Its top is a wooded plateau; its bottom the beginning of the plain-like valley of the River Saône. The width of the slope varies from a mile and a half to a few hundred yards – but all the good vineyards lie in this narrow strip.

The classification of the qualities of the land in this strip is the most elaborate on earth. As it stands it is the work of the Institut National des Appellations d'Origine (INAO), based on classifications going back more than 100 years but only finally perfected and mapped in 1984. It divides the vineyards into four classes, and stipulates the precise labelling of each wine accordingly. Grands Crus are the first class. There are 32 of them. Each has its own appellation. Grands Crus do not normally mention the name of their commune on their labels. The single, simple vineyard name – Musigny, Corton, Montrachet or Chambertin (sometimes prefixed by 'Le') – is the patent of Burgundy's highest nobility.

Premiers Crus, the next rank, use the name of their commune, followed by the name of their vineyard (or, if the wine comes from more than one Premier Cru vineyard, the commune name plus the words Premier Cru).

Appellation Communale is the third rank; that is, with the right to use the commune name. Such wines are often referred to as (eg) Meursault-Villages. A vineyard name is permitted – though rarely used; if it is the letters are printed much smaller than the commune name. A few such vineyards, often called Clos de …, while not officially Premiers Crus, belong to a single good grower and can be considered in the same class.

Fourth, there are inferior vineyards, even within some famous communes, which have only the right to call their wine Bourgogne.

There remains a class of vineyard which the system does not specifically recognize, but which could be called superior Premiers Crus. For only in the Côte de Nuits and five communes of the Côte de Beaune are there any Grands Crus; all the rest of the finest vineyards are Premiers Crus, despite the fact that, particularly in communes such as Pommard and Volnay, some consistently give much better wine than the others.

The INAO also lays down the regulations which control quality, demanding that only the classic grapes be used (Pinot Noir for red wine, Chardonnay for white); that only so much wine (from 40 hectolitres per hectare for the best, to 60 or so for the more ordinary) be made; that it achieve a certain natural strength (from 12% alcohol for the best white and 11.5 for the best red down to 10% for the most ordinary red).

The consumer must remember to distinguish the name of a vineyard from that of a commune. Many villages (Vosne, Chassagne, Gevrey, etc) have hyphenated their name to that of their best vineyard. The difference between Chevalier Montrachet (from one famous vineyard) and a Chassagne-Montrachet (from anywhere in a big commune) is not obvious; but it is vital.

The city of Beaune has one of the most famous hospitals in the world. The Hospices was built in the mid-15th century and is still busily in practice, tending the sick of Beaune without charge. It was founded by Nicolas Rolin, Chancellor of the Duke of Burgundy, and his third wife, Guigone de Salin, in 1443, and endowed with vineyards in the surrounding countryside. Since then winegrowers have continued to bequeath their land to the hospital (or Hôtel-Dieu).

The proceeds of the annual sale of its wine maintains the Hospices with all the modern equipment it requires.

Left: a Victorian engraving of the founder and his wife.
Above: the city of Beaune is seen above the famous roofs of the Hospices. In the background like the vineyards of the Côte de Beaune.

The wine merchants of Beaune

Beaune still keeps its town walls; their turrets are often used as cellars. Many of the best merchants of Burgundy work within the old city.

 1 Chanson Père & Fils
 2 Bouchard Aîné & Fils
 3 Patriarche Père & Fils
 4 Caves de la Reine Pédauque
 5 Calvet
 6 Albert Morot
 7 Jaffelin
 8 Joseph Drouhin
 9 Les Cordeliers
10 Léon Violland
11 Louis Latour
12 Remoissenet Père & Fils
13 Bouchard Père & Fils
14 Louis Jadot

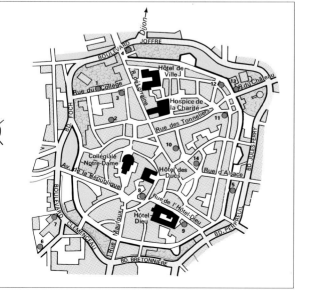

The Côte de Beaune: Santenay

The maps on this and the following eight pages represent the conclusion of the first complete official survey and classification of the vineyards of the Côte d'Or by the authorities, the INAO. They trace the vineyards of the Côte from south to north. The orientation of the maps has been turned through approximately 90 degrees so that what appears to be south is east-southeast.

The Côte de Beaune starts without a great explosion of famous names. It leads in gradually, from the obscure villages of Sampigny, Dézize and Cheilly, which share the one well-known cru of Les Maranges (all beyond the limits of this map; see page 57), into the commune of Santenay. After the hamlet of Haut-Santenay and the little town of Santenay (a spa frequented by local gamblers and good livers) the Côte half turns to take up its characteristic slope to the east.

This southern end of the Côte de Beaune is the most confused geologically and in many ways is atypical of the Côte as a whole. Complex faults in the structure of the hills make radical changes of soil and subsoil in Santenay. Part of the commune is analogous to parts of the Côte de Nuits, giving deep, if not exquisitely fine, red wine with a long life. Other parts give light wine more typical of the Côte de Beaune. Some of the highest vineyards have proved too stony to pay their way.

Les Gravières (the name draws attention to the stony ground, as the name Graves does in Bordeaux) and La Comme are the best *climats* of Santenay. As we move into Chassagne-Montrachet the quality of these excellent red-wine vineyards is confirmed. The name of Montrachet is so firmly associated with white wine that few people expect to find red here at all. But almost all the vineyards from the village of Chassagne south grow at least some red wine: Morgeot, La Boudriotte and (on page 62) Clos St-Jean are the most famous. Their wines are solid, long-lived and deep-coloured, coming closer in character to Gevrey-Chambertin than to, say, Volnay.

Indeed, no one really knows why white-winegrowing took over in this district. Visiting at around the time of the French Revolution Thomas Jefferson reported that white-wine-growers here had to eat hard rye bread while red-wine men could afford it soft and white. Perhaps the local growers were emulating the success of Le Montrachet (which had been famous for white wine since the 16th century). The Chardonnay is a more accommodating vine in stony soil – which it certainly finds in Meursault. Whatever the answer, Chassagne-Montrachet is known to the world chiefly for its dry but succulent, golden, flower-scented white wine.

The southern end of the Côte de Beaune is known principally for its robust red wines from Santenay, and full-bodied whites from Chassagne-Montrachet. Maranges is a new appellation just west of Santenay; Hautes-Côtes de Beaune for the hills above.

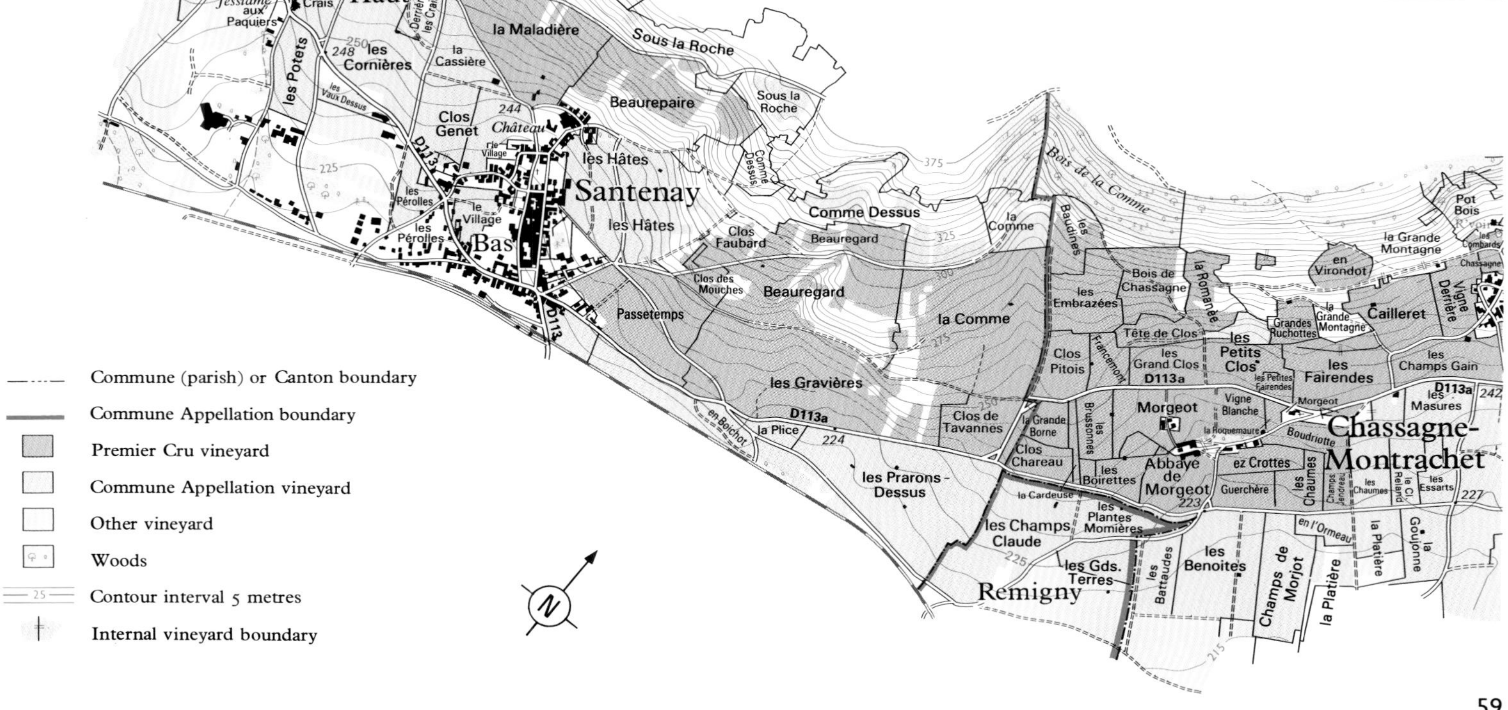

1:25,000

Km. 0 — 1 Km.
Miles 0 — ½ Mile

- – - – Commune (parish) or Canton boundary
- —— Commune Appellation boundary
- ▓ Premier Cru vineyard
- � Commune Appellation vineyard
- □ Other vineyard
- Woods
- 25 Contour interval 5 metres
- Internal vineyard boundary

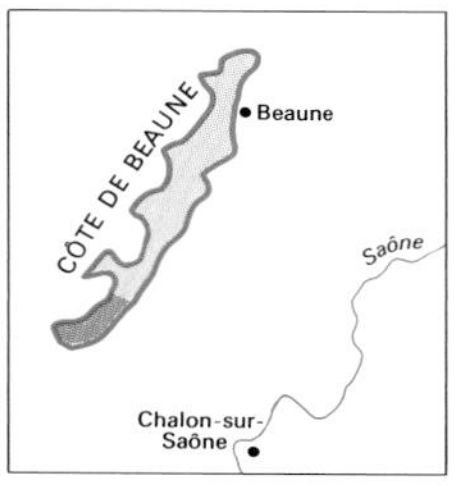

The Côte de Beaune: Meursault

A side valley in the hills just north of Chassagne, leading up to the hamlet of Gamay (which gave its name to the Beaujolais grape in the bad old days before the Pinot came into its own), divides the vineyards of the commune in two. South of it there is excellent white wine but the emphasis is on red. North, on the border of Puligny, there is the best white wine in Burgundy, if not the world.

The Grand Cru Montrachet earns its fame by an almost unbelievable concentration of the qualities of white burgundy. It has (given ten years) more scent, a brighter gold, a longer flavour, more succulence and yet more definition; everything about it is intensified – the mark of truly great wine. Perfect exposure to the east, yet an angle which means the sun is still flooding down the rows at nine on a summer evening, a sudden streak of very limy soil, are factors giving it an edge over its neighbours. For

Chassagne-Montrachet's fame owes to its share of the Grand Cru Montrachet, yet most of its wines are red. Puligny has a little Pinot Noir, too.

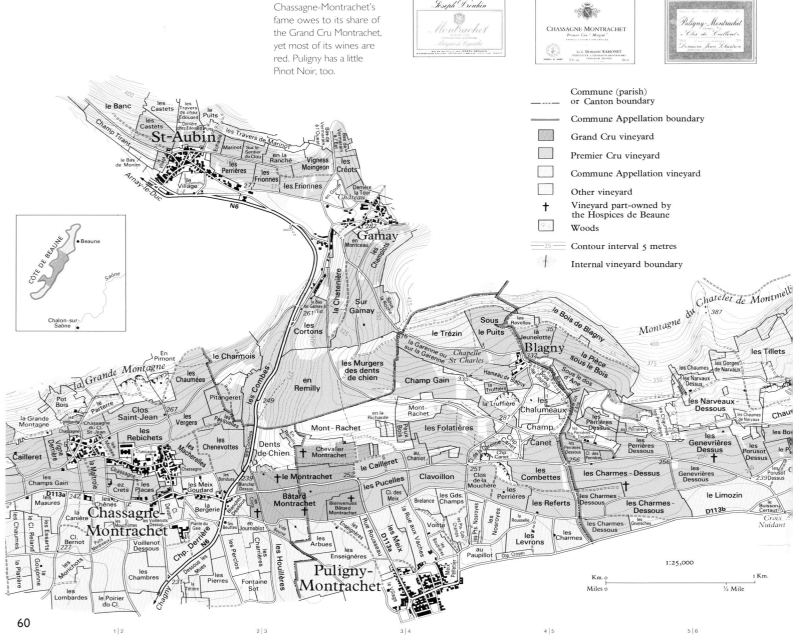

Commune (parish) or Canton boundary

Commune Appellation boundary

Grand Cru vineyard

Premier Cru vineyard

Commune Appellation vineyard

Other vineyard

Vineyard part-owned by the Hospices de Beaune

Woods

Contour interval 5 metres

Internal vineyard boundary

1:25,000

the other Grands Crus grouped about it come near but rarely excel it. Chevalier Montrachet tends to have less depth (its soil is stonier; the best has been used for renewing Le Montrachet). Bâtard- lies on heavier ground and often fails to achieve quite the same finesse, though it can take as long to age. Les Criots (in Chassagne) and Bienvenues belong in the same class – as at their best do the Puligny Premiers Crus Les Pucelles, Les Combettes, Les Folatières and Le Cailleret (and the best of Meursault's Les Perrières).

There is a distinction between Puligny-Montrachet and Meursault, quite clear to those who know them well but very hard to define – and to account for. The vineyards of the one flow without a break into the other's. In fact the hamlet of Blagny – making excellent wine high up on stony soil – is in both, with a classically complicated appellation: Premier Cru in Meursault, Blagny Premier Cru in Puligny-Montrachet,

AC Blagny when (which is rare) the wine is red.

Meursault is a slightly softer, richer but less vividly fine, lively and fruity wine than Puligny-Montrachet. The words 'nutty' and 'mealy' are used of it, whereas Puligny, with higher, more nervous acidity, is more a matter of apples and peaches. Overall Meursault has less brilliant distinction (and no Grand Cru) but a very high and generally even standard over a large area. The upper parts of Les Perrières, Les Genevrières and Les Charmes offer the most Puligny-like wines; Poruzots and Goutte d'Or a nuttier, broader, mainstream Meursault experience. Narvaux and Tillets, even higher *climats*, while not Premiers Crus, can also make intense, age-worthy wines.

The big busy village lies across another dip in the hills where roads lead up to Auxey-Duresses and Monthélie, both sources of very good red and a little white which are less highly valued (being shorter-lived) than Volnay, and therefore

frequently bargains. Behind them (see the map on page 57) lies the often-forgotten St-Romain, a promoted former Hautes Côtes village for light but sterling red and white.

Meursault in turn flows into Volnay. Much red wine is grown on this side of the commune, but it is called Volnay-Santenots rather than Meursault. Conversely, Volnay white is called Meursault. Volnay and Meursault sometimes draw as near together as red and white can without being rosé: both soft-textured, very fragrant, the red rather pale yet with great personality and a long, perfumed aftertaste.

If Volnay makes the Côte's lightest wine it can also be the most brilliant. Its lifespan is relatively short – perhaps ten years, though more for Clos des Chênes and Caillerets, the great names here. Champans, La Bousse d'Or and Taille Pied are close behind, while the steep little Clos des Ducs is the best *climat* on the north side of the village.

Left: a handful of the dozens of famous growers of this part of the Côtes. St-Romain is not mapped here, lying back in the hills behind Auxey-Duresses.

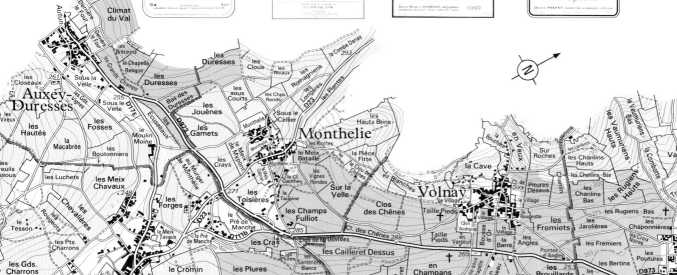

The Côte de Beaune: Beaune

Logically you would expect the Pommard vineyards bordering Volnay (mapped on the previous page) to give the most Volnay-like, fragrant and ethereal wines. But far from it. The commune boundary marks a soil change that makes Les Rugiens (ruddy as its name suggests with iron-rich earth) Pommard's standard-bearer for a different style entirely: dark, heady and tannic. It is Pommard's misfortune that while much of its wine (especially from the Villages vineyards that make up 80% of the commune) is dark and heady, little has any grace or distinction. With the exception of two or three Premiers Crus – above all Rugiens and Epenots – and four or five fine growers, Pommard is the dull patch between the high points of Volnay and Beaune. But remember that in Burgundy the grower counts as much as the vineyard; the saying goes 'there are no great wines; only great bottles of wine'.

Pommard's most prestigious vineyard is the lower part of Les Rugiens (map page 61), above the village. One of the best *cuvées* of the Hospices de Beaune, Dames de la Charité, is made from Rugiens and Epenots combined. The Clos de la Commaraine and the wines of the growers Courcel, Armand, Gaunoux and de Montille are Pommard's finest; sturdy wines that need ten years to develop the lovely savoury character of the best burgundy.

In the line of famous vineyards which occupy what the Burgundians call 'the kidney of the slope', at about the 800-feet (250-metre) line above Beaune, a large proportion belongs to the city's négociants: Drouhin, Jadot, Bouchard Père et Fils, Chanson and Patriarche among them. The late Maurice Drouhin was one of the more recent of the centuries-old list of donors to the Hospices de Beaune. His firm's part of the Clos des Mouches is celebrated; it makes a succulent white Beaune as well as a superb red one. A part of Grèves, belonging to Bouchard Père et Fils, is known as the Vigne de l'Enfant Jésus, and makes another marvellous wine. No Beaune is a Grand Cru, perhaps because it was impossible to choose among the Premiers. Beaune is usually gentle wine, lasting well but not demanding to be kept ten years or more, as a Romanée or a Chambertin would.

After Beaune the road crosses a plain and the hills and vineyards retreat. Ahead looms the prow of Corton, the one isolated hill of the whole Côte d'Or, with a dark cap of woods. Corton breaks the spell which prevents the Côte de Beaune from having a red Grand Cru. Its massive smooth slide of hill, vineyard to the top, presents faces to the east, south and west; all excellent. Indeed, it has not one but two Grand Cru appellations: for white wine and red,

covering most of the hill. The white, Corton-Charlemagne, is grown on the upper slopes to the south and west, where debris from the limestone top is washed down, whitening the brown marly soil. What is truly strange is that only in the last century or so has Charlemagne been planted with Chardonnay. This massive, often superlative white, at best a rival to Montrachet, is a recent conversion.

The big tannic red is grown in a broad band all round – too broad on the east-facing slopes, where some of the lower Grand Cru land is frankly inferior. Top red Cortons only come from Le Corton itself, Bressandes, Le Clos du Roi and Les Renardes. Confusingly the part marked Corton-Charlemagne on the map grows both white wine (above) and red Corton (below). There is a slight Alice in Wonderland air about the legalities, but none whatsoever about the wine.

The most celebrated grower of Corton is Louis Latour, whose noble presshouse, known as Château Grancey, stands in an old quarry in Les Perrières. Aloxe-Corton is the appellation of the lesser wines (red or white) grown below the hill.

If Savigny and Pernand are slightly in the background it is only because the foreground is so imposing. The best growers of both make wines up to the highest Beaune standard: Savigny sometimes a marvel of finesse. Part of Pernand has the appellations Corton and Corton-Charlemagne.

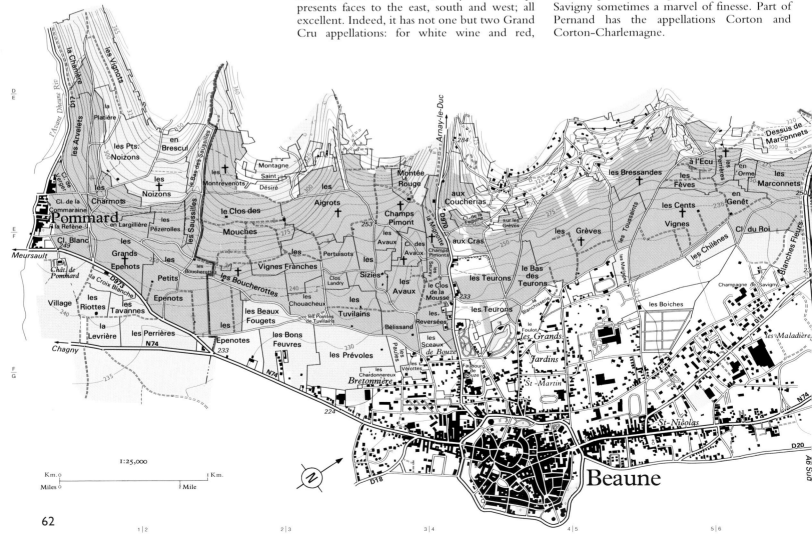

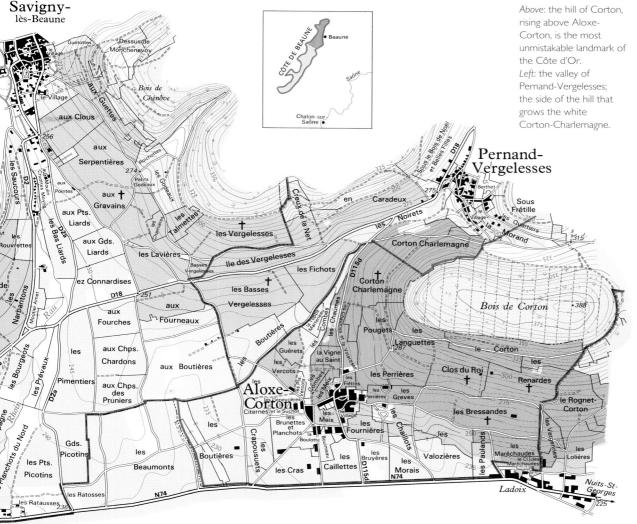

Savigny-
lès-Beaune

CÔTE DE BEAUNE
• Beaune
Saône

Chalon-sur-
Saône

Pernand-
Vergelesses

Above: the hill of Corton,
rising above Aloxe-
Corton, is the most
unmistakable landmark of
the Côte d'Or.
Left: the valley of
Pernand-Vergelesses;
the side of the hill that
grows the white
Corton-Charlemagne.

Guétottes
Dessus de Monchenevoy
le Village
aux Guettes
le Village
aux Clous
256
Bois de Chênôve
aux Serpentières
Rochottes
les Godeaux
274
Petits Godeaux
Sous le Bois de Noël et Belles Filles
Cl. Berthet
Sous Frétille
les Godeaux
aux Gravains
les Talmettes
Creux de la Net
en Caradeux
la Morand
Village
Sous les Quartiers
275
aux Pts. Liards
les Charmerottes
les Noirets
315
aux Gds. Liards
les Vergelesses
les Lavières
les Fichots
Corton Charlemagne
325
Basses Vergelesses
Ile des Vergelesses
les Basses Vergelesses
Corton Charlemagne
Bois de Corton · 388
ez Connardises
D18 251
aux Fourches
aux Fourneaux
les Combes
les Pougets
375
les Languettes
287
le Corton
aux Chps. Chardons
Boutières
les Guérets
la Vigne au Saint
300
les
les Vercots
aux Chps. des Pruniers
aux Boutières
Clos du Roi
Renardes
les Perrières
350
les Perrières
les Greves
300
Aloxe-Corton
Citernes et le Suchot
les Meix
Village
les Fiètres
les Bressandes
le Rognet-Corton
275
Gds. Picotins
les Brunettes et Planchots
Boutolle
les Fournières
les Challiots
Valozières
les Maréchaudes
le Cl. des Maréchaudes
les Lolières
les Pts. Picotins
les Crapousuets
Boutières
les Bruyères
les Caillettes
les Morais
N74
les Paulands
les Cras
Nuits-St-Georges
les Beaumonts
Ladoix
225
les Ratosses
N74
les Ratausses
236

Legend

—·—·— Commune (parish) or Canton boundary

———— Commune Appellation boundary

Grand Cru vineyard

Premier Cru vineyard

Commune Appellation vineyard

Other vineyard

† Vineyard part-owned by the Hospices de Beaune

Woods

—300— Contour interval 5 metres

✝ Internal vineyard boundary

Right: the top label is
the design for Hospices
de Beaune *cuvées*. The
others include Beaune's
most illustrious merchant-
growers and the leading
domaines of Corton-
Charlemagne.

The Côte de Nuits: Nuits-St-Georges

More 'stuffing', longer lie, deeper colour are the signs of a Côte de Nuits wine compared with a Volnay or Beaune. This is red wine country: white is a rarity.

The line of Premiers Crus, wriggling its way along the hill, is threaded with clutches of Grands Crus. These are the wines that express with most intensity the inimitable sappy richness of the Pinot Noir. The line follows the outcrop of marlstone below the hard limestone hilltop, but it is where the soil has a mixture of silt and scree over the marl that the quality really peaks. Happily, this corresponds time and again with the best shelter and most sun.

The wines of Prémeaux go to market under the name of Nuits-St-Georges. The quality is very high and consistent: big strong wines which almost approach the style of Chambertin at their best. Clos de la Maréchale is the monopole of the excellent house of Faiveley, Clos Arlot another monopole: both impeccable, though the quality climax is probably reached just over the commune boundary in Les St-Georges and Vaucrains; Grands Crus in all but name with tense, positive flavours demanding long bottle-age – something that cannot be said of most Nuits 'Villages'.

Nuits is divided by its little river. North of its valley the Premiers Crus leading into Vosne-Romanée are a worthy introduction to that extraordinary parish.

Unlike bustling Beaune, Nuits is a one-restaurant town, but it is the home of a number of négociants, some of whom make sparkling red burgundy out of the year's unsuccessful wine. By all means try it.

Vosne-Romanée is a modest little village. There is nothing here to suggest that the world's most expensive wine lies beneath your feet. It stands below a long incline of reddish earth, looking up severely trimmed rows of vines, each ending with a stout post and a taut guy.

Nearest the village is Romanée-St-Vivant. The soil is deep, rich in clay and lime. Mid-slope is Romanée-Conti: poorer, shallower soil. Higher up, La Romanée tilts steeper; it seems drier and less clayey. On the right the big vineyard of Les Richebourgs curves around to face east-northeast. Up the left flank runs the narrow strip of La Grande Rue, and beside it the long slope of La Tâche. These are among the most highly prized of all burgundies. Romanée-Conti, La Tâche, Richebourgs and Romanée-St-Vivant are all owned or managed wholly or in part by the Domaine de la Romanée-Conti. For the finesse, the velvety warmth combined with a suggestion of spice and the almost oriental opulence of their wines the market will seemingly stand any price. Romanée-Conti is the most perfect of all, but the whole group has a family likeness: the result of small crops, old vines, late picking and great care.

Clearly one can look among their neighbours for wines of similar character at less stupendous prices. All the other named vineyards of Vosne-Romanée are splendid. One of the old textbooks on Burgundy remarks drily: 'There are no common wines in Vosne.'

The big 75-acre (30-hectare) *climat* of Echézeaux and the smaller Grands Echézeaux are really in the commune of Flagey, a village over the railway to the south which has been absorbed (at least oenologically) into Vosne. Some very fine growers have property here, and make beautiful, delicate, so-called 'lacy' wines. They are often a bargain – because the name looks hard to pronounce? Grands Echézeaux has more regularity, more of the lingering intensity which marks the very great burgundies; certainly higher prices.

One high stone wall surrounds the 125 acres (50 hectares) of the Clos de Vougeot; the sure sign of a monastic vineyard. Today it is so subdivided that it is anything but a reliable label on a bottle. But it is the *climat* as a whole which is a Grand Cru. The Cistercians used to blend wine of the top, middle and sometimes bottom slopes to make what we must believe was one of the best burgundies of all … and one of the most consistent, since in dry years the wine from lower down would have an advantage, in wet years the top slopes. There are wines from near the top – La Perrière in particular (just outside the Clos) – that can be almost as great as Musigny. The name of the grower must be your guide.

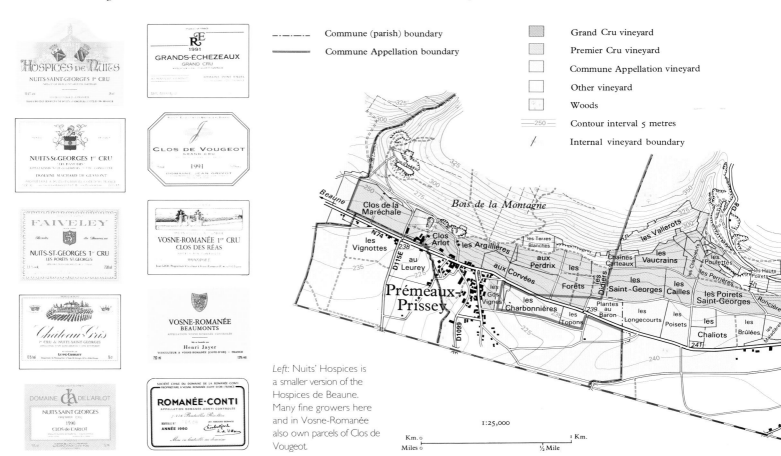

Grand Cru vineyard

Premier Cru vineyard

Commune Appellation vineyard

Other vineyard

Woods

Contour interval 5 metres

Internal vineyard boundary

Commune (parish) boundary

Commune Appellation boundary

Left: Nuits' Hospices is a smaller version of the Hospices de Beaune. Many fine growers here and in Vosne-Romanée also own parcels of Clos de Vougeot.

The viticultural landscape changes dramatically in the space of a few kilometres, from the impeccable monotony of the Grand Cru Romanée-Conti (*above*) to the pretty jumble of vines and woods in the Hautes-Côtes de Nuits near the village of Arcenant (*left*) to the west.

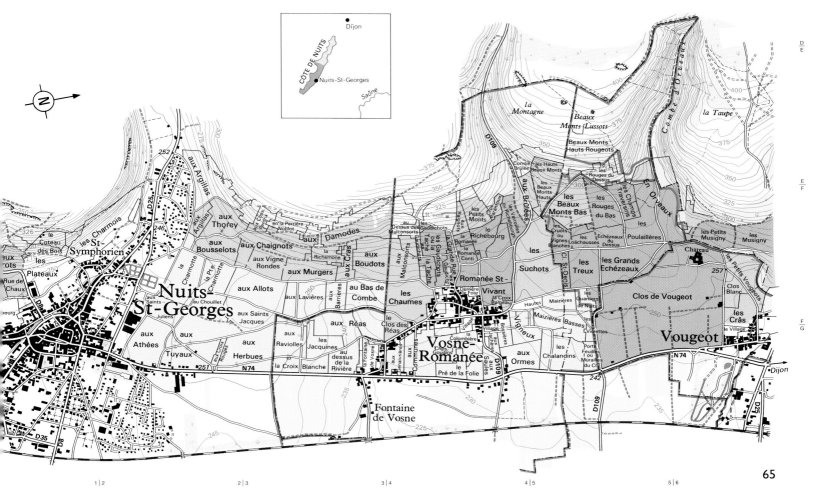

The Côte de Nuits: Gevrey-Chambertin

Left: the spirited goings-on of the Confrérie des Chevaliers du Tastevin are notorious. This famous wine fraternity meets at the Château du Clos de Vougeot for banquets with up to 600 guests from around the world. The Confrérie's own label (*top*) may be used for wines which have been approved by its regular tasting committee.

Here, at the northern end of the Côte d'Or, the firmest, longest-living, eventually most velvety red burgundies are made. Nature adds rich soil to the perfect combination of shelter and exposure provided by the hills. The narrow marlstone outcrop, overlaid with silt and scree, follows the lower slopes. From it Chambertin and the Grands Crus of Morey and Chambolle draw their power: wines of weight and muscle, unyielding when young, but eventually offering more complexity and depth of flavour than any.

The Grand Cru Musigny stands apart, squeezed in under the barren limestone crest, obviously related to the top of the Clos de Vougeot. The slope is steep enough to mean the vignerons must carry the brown limy clay, heavy with pebbles, back up the hill when it collects at the bottom. This and the permeable limestone subsoil allow excellent drainage. Conditions are right for a wine with plenty of 'stuffing'.

The glory of Musigny is that it covers its undoubted power with a lovely haunting delicacy of perfume; a uniquely sensuous savour. A great Musigny makes what is so well described

1:25,000

Km. 0   1 Km.

Miles 0   ½ Mile

— · — · — Commune (parish) boundary

———— Commune Appellation boundary

Grand Cru vineyard

Premier Cru vineyard

Commune Appellation vineyard

Other vineyard

Woods

Contour interval 5 metres

Internal vineyard boundary

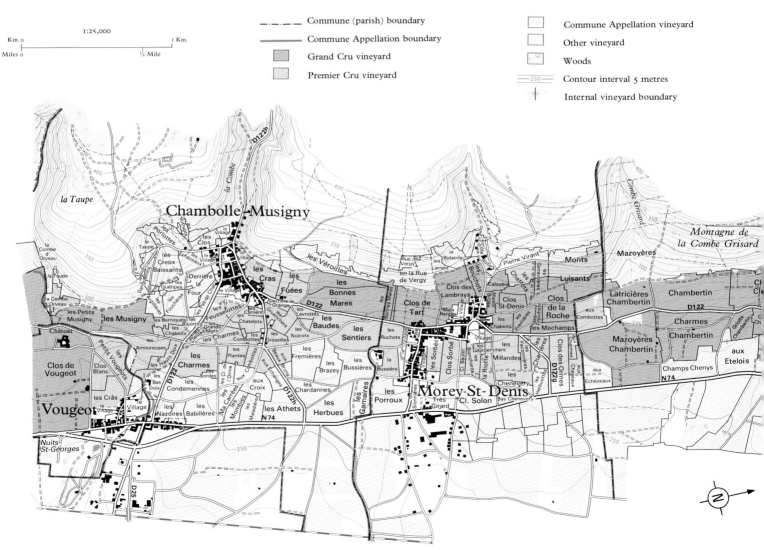

as a 'peacock's tail' in your mouth, opening to reveal ever more ravishing patterns of flavour. It is not so strong as Chambertin, not so spicy as Romanée-Conti – but whoever called it 'feminine' must have been a great respecter of women. It needs 10 or 15 years' ageing. Les Bonnes-Mares is the other Grand Cru of Chambolle. It starts as a tougher wine than Musigny, and ages perhaps a little slower, never quite achieving the tender grace of its neighbour.

Les Amoureuses and Les Charmes – their names perfectly expressive of their wine – are among the best Premiers Crus of Burgundy. But any Chambolle-Musigny is likely to be very good.

The commune of Morey is overshadowed in renown by its five Grands Crus. Clos de la Roche, with little Clos St-Denis (which gave its name to the village), like Chambertin, are wines of great staying power, strength and depth, fed by lime-rich soil. The Clos des Lambrays is a 'monopole' promoted to Grand Cru rank in 1981; a wine to wait for. Clos de Tart, the monopole of the house of Mommessin, is consistently fine, intense but not weighty.

Morey has more than 20 tiny Premiers Crus, few of whose names are well known but whose general standard is very high. The vineyards climb the hill, finding soil higher up than anywhere else in this area. The lofty, stony Monts-Luisants is even used for white wine.

Gevrey-Chambertin has a vast amount of good land. Vineyard soil stretches further out from the hill here than elsewhere; even beyond the main road is appellation Gevrey-Chambertin, rather than plain Bourgogne. Its two greatest vineyards, Chambertin and Clos de Bèze, lie under the woods on a more gentle slope. They were acknowledged Grands Crus at a time when the citizens of Gevrey were quarrelling with the worthies of Beaune who were handing out the honours. Otherwise their constellation of vineyards – Mazis, Latricières and the rest – would likely have been Grands Crus in their own right, too. Instead they have an in-between status, with the right to add -Chambertin after their names, but not (like Clos de Bèze) before. The Premier Cru Combottes deserves the same rank. French wine law can be more subtle than theology.

The commune also has a higher slope with a superb southeast exposure. Its Premiers Crus, Cazetiers, Lavaut, Clos St-Jacques and Les Varoilles, are arguably peers of the Grands Crus.

There are more famous individual vineyards in this village than in any other in Burgundy. To some the forceful red wine they make *is* burgundy. Hilaire Belloc told a story about his youth, and ended dreamily: 'I forget the name of the place; I forget the name of the girl; but the wine … was Chambertin.'

The slopes to the north, once called the Côte de Dijon, were until the last century considered among the best. But growers were tempted to grow bulk wine for the city and planted the 'disloyal' Gamay. Brochon became known as a 'well of wine'. Today its southern edge is included in Gevrey-Chambertin; the rest has only the right to the name Côte de Nuits-Villages.

Fixin, however, has a tradition of quality. The Premiers Crus Perrière, Hervelets and Clos du Chapitre are up to Gevrey standards – and notable value for money. Marsannay, just off the map, specializes in delicious Pinot Noir rosé.

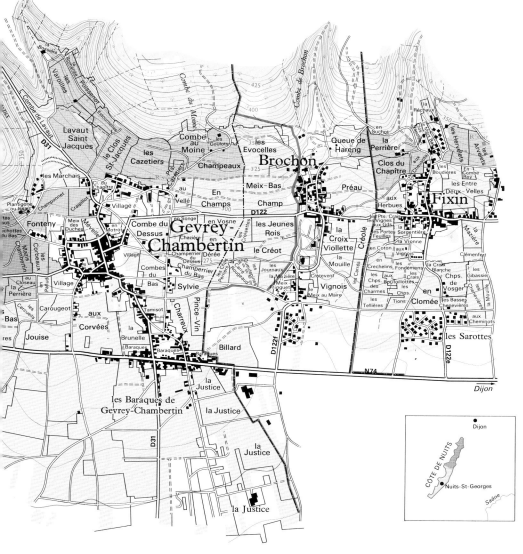

Above: Gevrey-Chambertin is a big commune with more than 1,200 acres (almost 500 hectares) of vines, nearly a fifth of which are Grands Crus. Many famous growers have holdings here. Marsannay (last label), just off the map to the east, specializes in delicate Pinot Noir rosé.

The Côte Chalonnaise

The hills south of Chagny are in many ways a continuation of the Côte de Beaune, although the regular ridge is replaced here by a jumble of limestone slopes on which vineyards appear among orchards and pasture. The altitude of these vineyards rises to 160 feet (50 metres) and more – higher than the Côte de Beaune, giving a slightly later vintage and less full ripeness. The 'Côte Chalonnaise' was named for its port of Chalon-sur-Saône to the east. Today most locals say the 'Région de Mercurey'.

The map shows the east- and south-facing slopes of the Côte, with the four major communes which have appellations: Rully, Mercurey, Givry and Montagny, and some of their better-known vineyards.

Mercurey is much the biggest producer, and 90% of its wine is red; Pinot Noir at least on a par with a minor Côte de Beaune: firm, solid, almost rough when young but ageing well, and steadily being improved as demand increases. The négociants Rodet and Faiveley are among the important producers. Its neighbour Givry is almost as dedicated to red; often lighter, easier and more enjoyable young than Mercurey.

Rully to the north makes slightly more white than red; the white brisk, high in acid, ideal material for sparkling Crémant de Bourgogne, and in good vintages much better than that: lively, apple-fresh and exceptional value. Rully reds tend to leanness – but not without class.

Montagny to the south is the one all white-wine appellation, and benefits from a unique rule that wine over 11.5° natural alcohol can be labelled Premier Cru. Neighbouring Buxy is included. The whites here are fuller and can be more like minor Côte de Beaune wines than the leaner Rully. On the other hand they can be rather heavy and obvious like many Mâcon-Villages. The firm of Louis Latour long ago discovered what good value they can be.

Meanwhile in 1979 Bouzeron was granted the only appellation for a single-village Aligoté white in Burgundy; a reward for perfectionist winemaking by, among others, the co-owner of the Domaine de la Romanée-Conti.

The whole area, Bouzeron included, is a good source of plain Bourgogne Rouge which, at two or three years, can be marvellous drinking. But perhaps its most welcome speciality is its sparkling Crémant; a revelation even to hardened champagne drinkers.

----- -----	Canton boundary
-- -- --	Commune (parish) boundary
☐	Vineyards
☐	Woods
—400—	Contour interval 20 metres

1:100,000

Km. 0 1 2 3 4 5 Km.
Miles 0 1 2 3 Miles

Above: the singular profile of Pouilly-Fuissé country. The rock of Solutré rears like a wave above the village. Pre-historic hunters used to drive their quarry over the edge: deer bones form a layer below the soil at the bottom of the hill.

Below, left: Côte Chalonnaise labels (red and white) and *right:* a selection from the prolific Mâconnais, Burgundy's great well of steady, ripe whites, reaching its climax in the richness of Pouilly-Fuissé.

The Mâconnais

The town of Mâcon on the Saône, 35 miles (55 kilometres) south of Chalon, gives its name to a wide, hilly and profoundly rural area which in general has neither the distinction of its neighbour to the north nor of Beaujolais to the south. Mâcon (mainly Gamay) red ·is just recognizably burgundian in character, the white definitely burgundy, but without frills.

On the Beaujolais border, however, there is a pocket of white-winegrowing with distinction of a different order. The Pouilly-Fuissé district is a sudden tempest of wave-shaped limestone hills, rich in the alkaline clay the Chardonnay loves. The map shows how the four Pouilly-Fuissé villages – Vergisson, Solutré-Pouilly, Fuissé and Chaintré – shelter on the lower slopes.

The best Pouilly-Fuissé is both mild and heady, without the scent of a Meursault or the style of a fine Chablis, but full to the point of richness and capable of sumptuous succulence with time. Perhaps a dozen small growers make wine which frequently reaches these heights; above all the Château de Fuissé. Unfortunately most others are merely bland in comparison – though not reticent in their pricing.

Pouilly-Vinzelles and Pouilly-Loché are theoretical alternatives, but are in very short supply. In practice the appellation St-Véran, which applies to similar white wines from a handful of villages north and south of Pouilly-Fuissé, is best value, though Mâcon-Prissé can be very similar.

All over the Mâconnais, cooperatives are the dominant producers, and extremely well run – though tending to overproduce. That at Chaintré is much the biggest producer of Pouilly-Fuissé. Others further north (notably at Viré, Lugny and Clessé) offer wines of similar sterling character. For reds the best zone is in sandy soil just west of Pouilly-Fuissé, centring around Pierreclos. The coop at Igé is a popular source.

The way to buy white Mâcon is to look for the name of a particular village on the label. Failing '-Prissé' or '-Clessé', look for the suffix '-Villages'. Few modest wines anywhere are as reliably fresh and wholesome.

-·-·-	Département boundary
-·-·-	Canton boundary
	Appellation Contrôlée boundary
AZÉ	A C Mâcon-Villages
CHÂNES	Commune entitled to A C St-Véran
POUILLY-FUISSÉ	Other Appellation Contrôlée
	Vineyards
	Woods
—200—	Contour interval 20 metres

1:130,000

Km. 0   1   2   3   4   5 Km.
Miles 0   1   2   3 Miles

Beaujolais

Each November for a few weeks the new vintage of Beaujolais becomes the world's favourite drink; a sort of worldwide vintage festival, as though folk-memory were reviving the ancient Bacchanalia. Such rapid cash-flow is something all winemakers would like, yet only Beaujolais can generate. In one of the marriages of grape and ground the French regard as mystical, in Beaujolais the Gamay, growing in sandy clay over granite, gives uniquely fresh, vivid, light but fruity, fairly strong but infinitely swallowable wine.

The Beaujolais region covers a 34-mile (55-kilometre) long stretch of mainly granite hills south of Mâcon in south Burgundy. Two-thirds of all burgundy comes from this most profitable spring. But the region is far from being homogeneous. Its soil divides it sharply, around the valley of the little River Nizerand, just north of Villefranche, the regional capital. South of here, in 'Bas' Beaujolais, the soil is clay, the wine plain Beaujolais. Its villages remain obscure: the highest their wine can aspire to is the extra degree of alcohol to qualify as Beaujolais Supérieur. From this deep well a million hectolitres of wine a year are drawn – and rapidly drunk.

Very fresh and new (and natural) it can be the ultimate bistro wine, drunk by the barrel in Lyon just down the road. Far more often it is over-chaptalized, losing its racy, almost stinging fragrance and easy-flowing lightness to become merely raw and heady. Plain 'Bas' Beaujolais rarely keeps well, even in a good vintage: its clay soil is too cold to ripen full flavours in the Gamay.

The northern part of the region, 'Haut' Beaujolais, is granite-based, with a variously sandy topsoil that drains, warms and ripens the Gamay, often to perfection. Thirty-nine of its villages have the right to the appellation Beaujolais-Villages. It is almost always worth paying more for a -Villages wine, even *en primeur*, for its extra concentration. On the other hand -Villages wines are scarcely ever at their best by late November. They demand and deserve at least three months in bottle. The 39 villages are distinguished on the map – although only individual growers who bottle (very much the minority) often use their names. Most Beaujolais is sold by merchants, who blend a generalized 'Villages' to their clients' tastes.

Ten of the villages use their own names and are expected to show distinct characteristics of their own. These are the Grands Crus, mapped on page 72. The group lies just south of the Mâconnais, adjacent to Pouilly-Fuissé. In this northern region a small amount of Beaujolais Blanc is also made.

The Grands Crus villages lie on spurs, outlying volcanic knolls and on the Beaujolais mountains themselves. This is much more seriously hilly country than the Côte d'Or. The road climbs and twists and climbs until vines and farms are left behind, woods thicken and upland streams tumble by. Looking behind and below,

Beaujolais-Villages vineyards climb the wooded mountains to the west to heights above 1,480 ft (450m). Each Gamay vine in Beaujolais is staked individually, without trellising.

the broad band of vineyards dwindles and an immense view of the plain of the Saône expands: in clear weather Mont Blanc hangs in the far distance to the east.

The country is owned or 'share-cropped' mostly by small farmers who sell their wine through négociants, but there are a few big estates. Their wine is the grandest of Beaujolais and is often bottled on the property; but this does not change its basic nature of being a delicious easy-going drink rather than a Grand Vin.

The Gamay is in its element here. Its plants are almost like people, leading independent lives: after ten years they are no longer trained, but merely tied up in summer with an osier to stand free. A Gamay vine will live as long as a human.

Beaujolais is traditionally made by carbonic maceration (see page 33), in which the whole bunches go into the vat unbroken and the grapes begin fermenting internally – a low-key fermentation that emphasizes the characteristic smell and flavour of the fruit and minimizes tannins and malic acid. After three or four days of maceration the grapes are pressed and the fermentation finished in a vat without skins – again minimizing tannin. Within a month of harvest the wine is made, ready to be pasteurized (or, better, sterile filtered), bottled, shipped and drunk.

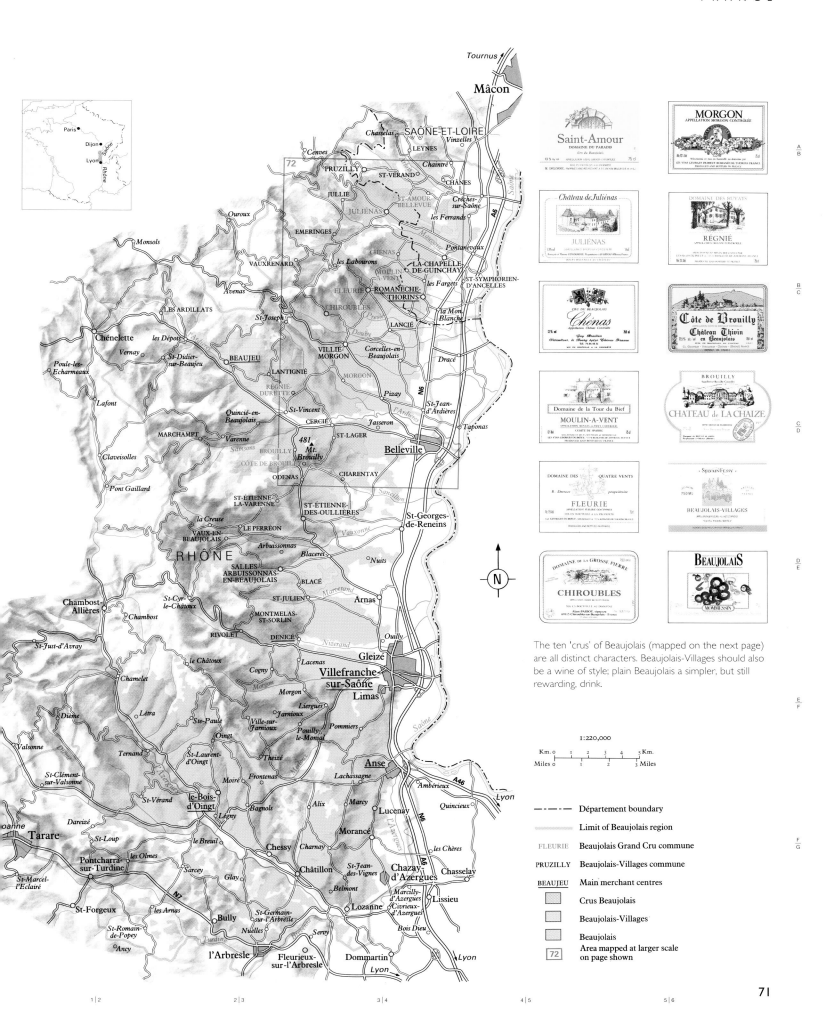

The ten 'crus' of Beaujolais (mapped on the next page) are all distinct characters. Beaujolais-Villages should also be a wine of style; plain Beaujolais a simpler, but still rewarding, drink.

1:220,000

Km. 0   1   2   3   4   5 Km.

Miles 0   1   2   3 Miles

– · – · –   Département boundary

Limit of Beaujolais region

FLEURIE   Beaujolais Grand Cru commune

PRUZILLY   Beaujolais-Villages commune

BEAUJEU   Main merchant centres

Crus Beaujolais

Beaujolais-Villages

Beaujolais

72   Area mapped at larger scale on page shown

The Crus of Beaujolais

The ten Crus of Beaujolais are all contained within this zone of steep hills, wooded on their heights, and almost continuous vines. Its whole extent is 15 miles (24 kilometres) by half as much. And yet the wines at their best display to perfection the effects of *terroir* on a single grape, the Gamay. Each Cru has a personality which good growers explore and express with as much vigour as the vintage allows. They range from crisply fragrant wines to drink young to rich brooding bottles that need several years for their heady pungency to evolve.

All the Cru vineyards are sited sufficiently high for frost damage to be relatively rare; the best on east and south slopes, sheltered from the lively westerlies. Soils range from decomposing slate (in Morgon) to limestone (in parts of St-Amour). Underlying it all is the granite of ancient volcanoes – obviously so in the stump of Mont Brouilly – with its acid sandy soils.

Brouilly is the largest of the Crus, its 3,000 acres (1,200 hectares) of vines filling most of the southern quarter of the map. With a production at times approaching one million cases it can best be described as variable. Good examples (such as Château de la Chaize) are perhaps more drinkable than memorable. The Côtes de Brouilly on the slopes of Mont Brouilly can reach appropriately greater heights; especially wines from the southeastern slopes (eg Château Thivin).

Morgon, the second largest of the Crus, is one of the most distinctive in terms of soil and savour. It centres on the Mont du Py, on a rock formation of crumbling slate that gives more colour, breadth and substance than any other Cru except Moulin à Vent. There is also less exciting low-ground Morgon. As usual, Georges Duboeuf's selections are among the best.

Régnié to the west has only had Cru status since 1988. Its image is still unclear, tending towards Morgon on that flank, and to the north towards the paler, more fragrant style of Chiroubles (sometimes called 'ladies' Beaujolais'). Without disrespect, Chiroubles is Beaujolais at its prettiest, both as wine and village.

Fleurie is central in every way. Good young Fleurie epitomizes the spirit of the region: the scent is strong, the wine fruity and silky, limpid; a joy to swallow. The transition to the severity of Moulin à Vent is a tale of *terroir* writ large. Here the soil is rich in iron and manganese, probably but unprovably implicated in the concentration, dumbness even, of its young wines and their ability to age ten years. Then their rich bouquet and flavour seems to express the Côte d'Or or the northern Rhône more than the instant good cheer of Beaujolais.

Chénas, the smallest Cru, has lost most of its best land to Moulin à Vent. Château Bonnet shows its sturdy transitional character well. The transition is to Juliénas: Fleurie-like in youth but at best fatter, fleshier and spicier with the backbone to keep it going five years. Juliénas is steep, ideally sheltered and drained. No Cru has a higher overall standard. St-Amour provides a final stage – from Beaujolais to St-Véran and the Mâconnais.

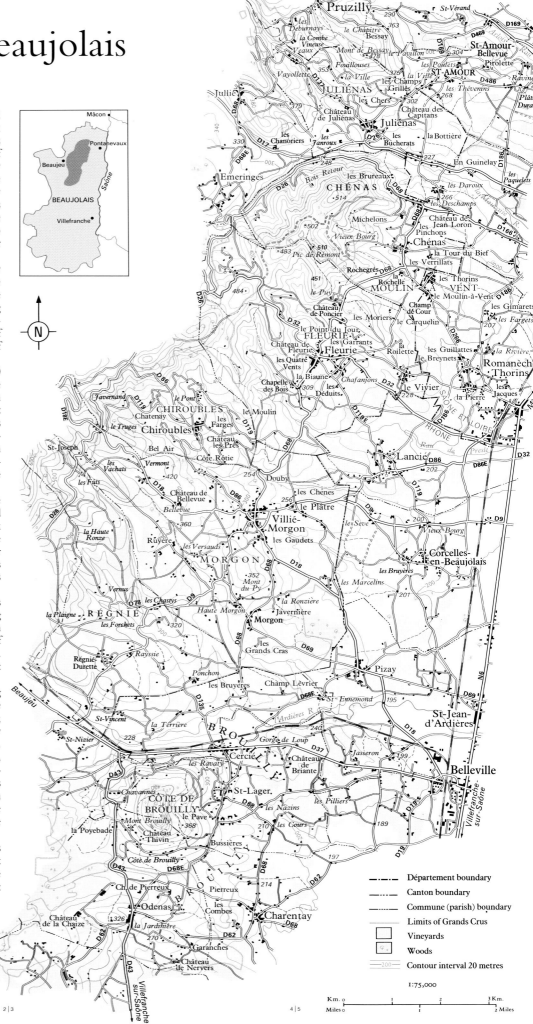

	Département boundary
	Canton boundary
	Commune (parish) boundary
	Limits of Grands Crus
	Vineyards
	Woods
	Contour interval 20 metres

1:75,000

Km. 0   1   2   3 Km.
Miles 0   1   2 Miles

Chablis

Chablis is almost the sole survivor of what was once a vast winegrowing region; the main supplier to Paris, only 60 miles (100 kilometres) away to the northwest. A century ago the *département* of the Yonne had 120,000 acres (50,000 hectares) of vines – mainly red – and filled the rôle of the Midi in more recent times. Its waterways flowing into the River Seine were thronged with wine-barges, except in spring when they were cleared for the massive *flottage* of firewood to the capital from every upstream forest.

First phylloxera crushed, then the railways bypassed, the winegrowers of the Yonne, leaving it one of France's poorest agricultural regions. By 1945 Chablis had a mere 1,000 or so acres (470 hectares) of vines left. Its trickle of wine was dwarfed by the flood from Spain, California, Australia and around the world that kept its fame alive by abusing its name. 'Chablis' became shorthand for any white wine, even while the region appeared to be dying.

The second half of the century has seen a great renaissance: the retreat (still not complete) of those who stole the name and a new justification for its renown. For Chablis is one of the great inimitable originals. Chardonnay responds to its cold *terroir* of limestone clay with flavours no-one can reproduce in easier (or any other) winegrowing conditions.

Chablis sends one rummaging for descriptive phrases even more desperately than most wines. There is something there one can so nearly put a finger on. It is hard but not harsh, reminiscent of stones and minerals, but at the same time of green hay; when it is young it actually looks green, which many wines are supposed to. Grand Cru Chablis tastes important, strong, almost immortal. And indeed it does last a remarkably long time; a strange and delicious sort of sour taste enters into it when it reaches about ten years of age, and its golden-green eye flashes meaningfully.

Cool-climate vineyards need exceptional conditions to succeed. Chablis lies 100 miles (160 kilometres) north of Beaune – and is therefore nearer to Champagne than to the rest of Burgundy. Geology is its secret: the outcrop of the rim of a great submerged basin of limestone. The far rim, across the English Channel in Dorset, gives its name, Kimmeridge, to this unique pudding of prehistoric oyster-shells. Oysters and Chablis, it seems, have been related since creation.

There are two other regions, one in France and one in Germany, where similar soils give wine of unique quality. They are quite unrelated, and yet their wines are each the world's best of their different grape varieties, despite (or perhaps because of) their cold growing conditions. Sancerre is one, where the Sauvignon Blanc reaches aromatic perfection on chalky clay. The other is the region of Franconia where the Silvaner, on 'Musselkalk', achieves quality and longevity unknown elsewhere.

These three white wines share qualities of flowing freshness, of firmness and of clear-etched character that transcend their different grapes – attributes which must, in other words, be the product of their pale soils and the rigour of their climates.

The hardy Chardonnay (known here as the Beaunois – the vine from Beaune) is the only vine. Where the slopes of Kimmeridgian clay face the sun it ripens excellently. But Chablis is not the only appellation of the Yonne. There remains a rump of the once-huge Auxerre vineyard in reasonable heart at Irancy, where Pinot Noir is stiffened by the local César. Coulanges-la-Vineuse is another, while St-Bris-le-Vineux and Chitry-le-Fort grow both the old Auxerre red varieties, a little Chardonnay and Aligoté and Sauvignon Blanc (VDQS Sauvignon de St-Bris) with some success. Tonnerre also has a remnant vineyard; unripe grapes find their way into Crémant de Bourgogne.

The green gleam in a glass of good Chablis is as individual as its limpid, dry, deeply satisfying flavour. I took this photograph in 1965: it still makes me thirsty.

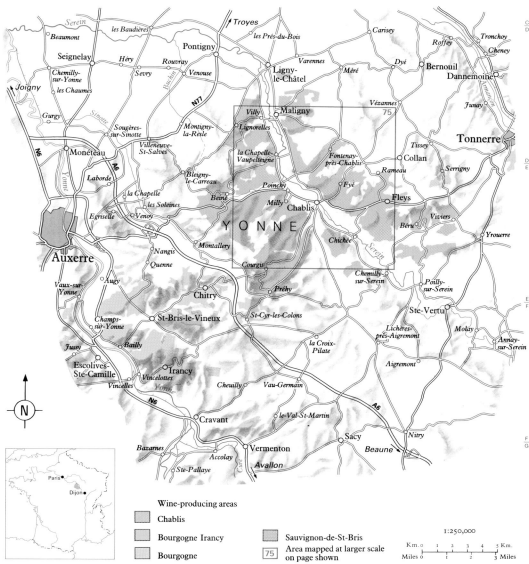

Wine-producing areas

Chablis

Bourgogne Irancy

Bourgogne

Sauvignon-de-St-Bris

75   Area mapped at larger scale on page shown

1:250,000

The Heart of Chablis

Left: looking up in winter and, *above*, down in summer at the Grands Crus vineyards spilling southwest down towards the little town of Chablis. The main slope in the picture is Valmur and Les Clos. In the foreground is the excellent Premier Cru Vaillons.

The classification of Chablis into four grades is one of the clearest demonstrations anywhere of the importance of southern slopes: Grand Cru wines always taste richer than the Premiers Crus, Premiers Crus than plain Chablis, and Chablis than Petit Chablis – an appellation that might well be allowed to disappear entirely.

All the Grands Crus lie in a single block looking south and west over the village and the river. Each of the seven has its own style. Many regard Les Clos and Vaudésir as best of all. Certainly they tend to be the biggest in flavour. But more important is what all have in common: intense, highly charged flavour on the scale of the best whites of the Côte de Beaune but with more of a leading edge – which, with age, leads to noble complexity.

Les Clos is the biggest, with 61 acres (24 hectares), and best-known; many would also say the first in flavour, strength and lasting-power. Fine vintages of Les Clos can develop almost a Sauternes-like perfume in time. Les Preuses should be very ripe, round and perhaps the least stony in character, while Blanchot and Les Grenouilles should be highly aromatic. Valmur is some critics' ideal: rich and fragrant; others prefer the definition and finesse of Vaudésir. Bougros comes last in most accounts – but the

handwriting of the producer is often more distinctive than that of the precise corner of this relatively homogeneous slope.

There used to be many more named Premiers Crus, but the lesser-known ones have long since been permitted to go to market under the names of the dozen best-known. The map shows both the old names and the new ones in common use. They vary considerably in southern exposure and gradient; certainly those on the north bank of the River Serein, flanking the Grands Crus to northwest (eg Fourchaume) and east (eg Montée de Tonnerre, Mont de Milieu), have the advantage.

A Premier Cru Chablis will have at least half a degree of alcohol less than a Grand Cru, and be correspondingly less impressive and intense in scent and flavour. Nonetheless, it should still be a very stylish wine. Its principal fault, these days, is likely to be dilution as a result of over-production.

The 1970s and 1980s saw a very substantial increase in the Chablis vineyards – the cause of continuing controversy among growers. The issue that divides them is the soil. Conservatives credit the Kimmeridgian limestone with unique properties; their opponents claim the same properties for the closely related Portlandian that crops up much more widely in the area. The

INAO has favoured the latter, thus allowing expansion – but still not to anything like the Chablis acreage of past times.

The area of vines producing Chablis Premier Cru has increased by 50 percent in the last ten years. That for Chablis has almost doubled. In 1960 there was more Premier Cru than Chablis. Today there is twice as much Chablis as Premier Cru (and five times as much Premier Cru as Grand Cru).

Some say the quality has suffered. It remains, as it always will do, very uneven from year to year as well as variable (particularly in style) from grower to grower. Most growers today favour tank-fermented fresh wines with no barrels. A few traditionalists continue to show that oak (but rarely new oak) has special properties to offer. The introduction of malolactic fermentation has softened the acidity; tending to age the wines more quickly. But on balance good Chablis is as good as ever – and maybe better.

Far more unpredictable is the quantity of each harvest – still perilously subject to frost damage – and hence the price. While prices see-saw precariously, the market remains uneasy. In truth, it shouldn't be. Grand Cru Chablis remains even now only about half the price of Corton-Charlemagne. Parity would be closer to justice.

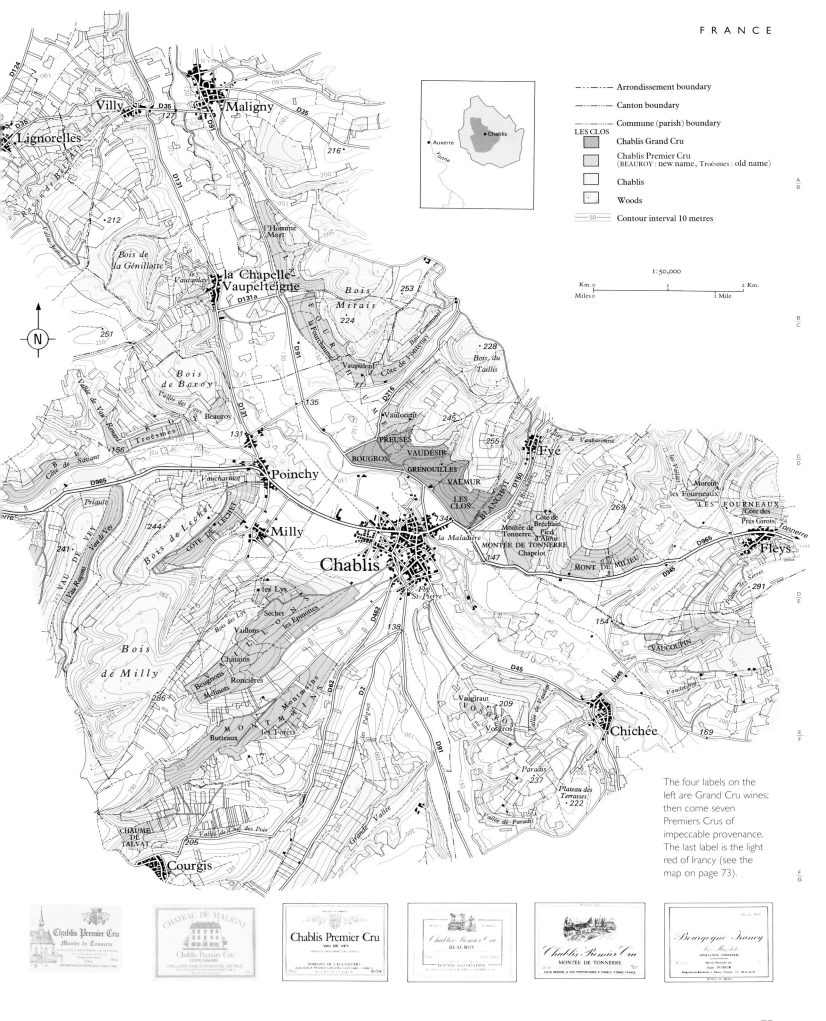

Villy
Maligny
Lignorelles

l'Homme Mort

la Chapelle-Vaupelteigne

Bois de la Génillotte

le Vautanlay

Bois Mitais

Bois du Taillis

Bois de Boroy

Vaupulent

Côte de Fontenay

Bois Communal

Beauroy

BEAUROY

Troësmes

Côte de Savant

Poinchy

Vaucharmot

Vaulorent

PREUSES

BOUGROS
VAUDÉSIR
GRENOUILLES
VALMUR
LES CLOS

Fyé

Vallée de Vaubarousse

Morein
les Fourneaux
LES FOURNEAUX
Côte des Prés Girots

Milly

Priault

Côte de Léchet

Bois de Léchet

Vaudevey

Vau de Vey

Vau Ragons

la Maladière

MONTÉE DE TONNERRE

Côte de Bréchain
Pied d'Aloue

Chapelot

Montée de Tonnerre

BLANCHOT

MONT DE MILIEU

Chablis

Fbg St-Pierre

les Lys

Séchet
les Epinottes

Vaillons

Châtains

Beugnons
Mélinots
Roncières

MONTMAINS

les Forêts

Butteaux

Bois de Milly

VAUCOUPIN

Fleys

D965

Vaugiraut
VOSGROS
Vosgros

Chichée

Paradis

Plateau des Terrasses

Vallée de Paradis

CHAUME DE TALVAT

Vallée de Chef des Prés

Grande Vallée

Courgis

The four labels on the left are Grand Cru wines; then come seven Premiers Crus of impeccable provenance. The last label is the light red of Irancy (see the map on page 73).

Arrondissement boundary
Canton boundary
Commune (parish) boundary

LES CLOS   Chablis Grand Cru

Chablis Premier Cru
(BEAUROY : new name, Troësmes : old name)

Chablis

Woods

50   Contour interval 10 metres

Auxerre   Chablis
Yonne

1:50,000

Km. 0   1   2 Km.
Miles 0   1 Mile

Chablis Premier Cru
Montée de Tonnerre

Château de Maligny
Chablis Premier Cru
Fourchaume

Chablis Premier Cru
VAU DE VEY
DOMAINE DE L'ÉGLANTIÈRE

Chablis Premier Cru
BEAUROY
DOMAINE Alain GEOFFROY

Chablis Premier Cru
MONTÉE DE TONNERRE
LOUIS MICHEL & FILS PROPRIETAIRES A CHABLIS (YONNE) FRANCE

Bourgogne Irancy
Les Mazelots
APPELLATION CONTROLÉE
Jean PODOR

Champagne

The name of champagne is limited not only to a defined area but to a process, through which every drop of wine must go before it can claim the name. A few countries outside Europe use the name as though it only meant the process. But the process simply makes it fizzy; the place is what makes it unique.

It would be claiming too much to say that all champagne is better than any other sparkling wine. There are champagnes and champagnes. But good champagne has a combination of freshness, richness, delicacy and raciness, and a gently stimulating strength, which no other wine ever quite achieves.

The region whose soil and climate have so much to offer is only 90 miles (145 kilometres) northeast of Paris, centred on a small range of hills rising from a plain of chalk and carved in two by the River Marne. Within this area the names of the villages do not directly concern the customer. For the essence of champagne is that it is a blended wine, known by the name of the maker, not the vineyard. The map on pages 78–79 shows the heart of Champagne.

The whole region encompasses parts of five *départements*. Only a tiny proportion of it has the right to the appellation Champagne, and that on very specific soils in privileged sites. Three-quarters of the vineyards are in the *département* of the Marne, but there are substantial minorities in the Aube to the south (15%) and the Aisne to the north (about 10%). So Champagne stretches from near Chablis to not far from Belgium; space for a very wide range of qualities and styles.

There are 68,000 acres (27,500 hectares) in Champagne, with 19,000 proprietors. Only 10% belongs to the great exporting firms responsible for the worldwide reputation of champagne. The country is owned not by great landowners but by thousands of growers, often part-time. There are 8,000 holdings of a hectare or less, and more than half of the 20,000 who work in the vineyards own at least some vines.

The trend in recent years has been for more and more of these small growers to process and sell their own wine, whereas they used to sell their grapes to the prestigious 'Maisons'.

What happens in the cellars of Champagne concerns us just as much as what happens in the vineyards. The champagne-making process has only just begun when the grapes are picked and pressed, in presses unique to the area that squeeze the juice very gently from four tons at a time.

The juice ferments lustily at first, but as it slows down the doors are thrown open to let in the autumnal chill. In the cold (today, of course, air-conditioned), fermentation stops. The wine spends a chilly winter, still with the potential of more fermentation latent in it.

So it used to be shipped. England in the 17th century was an eager customer for barrels of this delicate, rather sharp wine. The English bottled

The Grandes Marques are the makers who developed the styles, the quality and the name of champagne, and still lead the industry. *Top right*: the speciality of Les Riceys in the Aube, located at the bottom of the map.

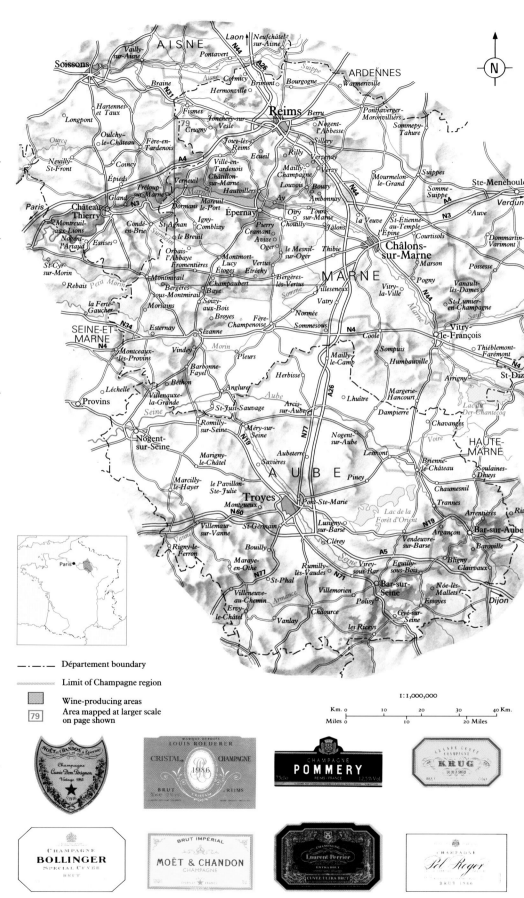

- — - — - Département boundary

Limit of Champagne region

Wine-producing areas

79 Area mapped at larger scale on page shown

1:1,000,000

Km. 0   10   20   30   40 Km.
Miles 0   10   20 Miles

it on arrival, in bottles that were stronger than any known in France. It re-fermented in spring: the corks went pop and the beau monde found that they had created a sparkling wine.

Whether or not it was the English who did it first, premature bottling is vital to the process which changed Paris's favourite local wine into the prima donna of the world.

For the wine continued to ferment in the bottle and the gas given off by the fermentation dissolved in the wine. If the natural effect was encouraged by a little more sugar, a little more yeast, what had been a pretty but very light wine was found to improve immeasurably, gaining strength and character over a period of two years or more. Above all, the inexhaustible bubbles gave it a miraculous liveliness.

Dom Pérignon, cellar-master of the Abbey of Hautvillers at the end of the 17th century, is wrongly credited with the next round of developments: the cork tied down with string,

The champagne caves of Reims were cut by the Romans as quarries. The Clicquot cellars have since been decorated with reliefs carved in the soft chalk walls, and filled with wine.

stronger bottles (although still not strong enough; half the wine was lost through bottles bursting). In fact Dom Pérignon took every precaution to avoid bubbles; the contribution that brought him such honour was the art of blending wines from different parts of the district to achieve the best possible flavour.

The chief difference between champagne brands lies in this making of the *cuvée*, as the blend is called. Everything depends on experience in assembling the young wines – and on how much the house is prepared to spend on raw materials. In general the more different components the finer the result: a grower using grapes solely from one vineyard can only make a simplistic champagne. Low-price champagnes sold by *récoltant-manipulants* nearly all fall into this category.

The reputation of an established house is based on its non-vintage wines, blended so that no difference is noticeable from year to year. Styles vary from the challenging concentration of a Krug or Bollinger to the seductive delicacy of a Taittinger, with Pol Roger, Clicquot and Roederer as models of classical balance.

The industrialization of champagne began with the widow Clicquot in the early 19th century. Her achievement was a way of cleaning the wine of its sediment (unavoidable when it re-ferments in bottle) without losing the bubbles. She invented a wooden 'desk' pierced with holes in which the mature bottles of wine could be stuck upside down (*sur point*). Her cellarmen gave each bottle a gentle shake and twist (*remuage*) every day until all the sediment had dislodged from the glass and settled on the cork. Then they released the cork, let the eggcupful of wine containing the sediment escape (*dégorgement*), topped up the bottle with sweetened wine and put in a new cork. To make disgorging easier today, the neck of the bottle is frozen first: a plug of murky ice shoots out when the bottle is opened, leaving perfectly clear wine behind.

The sweetness or dryness of the brand is determined at *dégorgement*. After the second fermentation the wine is naturally totally dry – too dry for most tastes. A little wine plus sugar is therefore added: less than 2% for champagne labelled Brut; 1.5–2.5% for Extra Dry; 2–4% for Sec; 4–6% for Demi-Sec; more than 6% for Doux. The last two are properly dessert wines; Brut is emphatically not.

THE LANGUAGE OF THE LABEL

Vintage (eg 1976, 1979): The wines of one good year only

Non-vintage (without a date): A blend of the wines of several years

Cuvée Blend: all champagne is blended

Blanc de Blancs Made from the juice of white grapes only

Crémant Half-sparkling, or 'creaming'

Rosé Pink champagne made by blending in a little red wine

Réserve Any wine can be called Réserve

Reserved for England Implies that the wine is dry, since the English like dry champagne

Récemment dégorgé Recently disgorged (of wine laid down to mature upside down and disgorged when considered ready to drink)

Brut Bone-dry

Extra Sec (or **Extra Dry**) Dry

Sec Slightly sweet

Demi-Sec Sweet

Doux Very sweet

Magnum 2 bottles in one

Jereboam 4 bottles in one

Rehoboam 6 bottles in one

Methuselah 8 bottles in one

Nebuchadnezzar 20 bottles in one

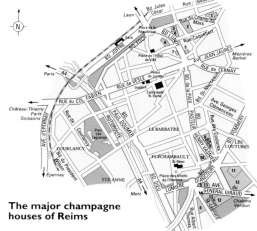

The major champagne houses of Reims

1	Heidsieck Monopole		
2	G H Mumm	8	Piper-Heidsieck
3	Irroy	9	Charles Heidsieck
4	Krug	10	Taittinger
5	Lanson	11	Ruinart
6	Veuve	12	Pommery
	Clicquot Ponsardin	13	Henriot
7	Louis Roederer	14	Abel Lepitre

The major champagne houses of Epernay

1	A Charbaut & Fils	3	Perrier-Jouët
2	Moët & Chandon	4	de Venoge
		5	Pol Roger
		6	de Castellane
		7	Mercier

The Heart of Champagne

The crystal scintillation of a frosty morning at Cramant on the Côte des Blancs seems the image of the character of its wines. Cramant grows exclusively Chardonnay grapes to make champagne of the ultimate brilliance and finesse.

Long before the wines of Champagne were made to sparkle they were highly prized in Paris under the names of '*vins de la rivière*' and '*vins de la montagne*'. The river was the Marne, the 'mountain' the wooded eminence, at best rising to less than 1,000 feet (300 metres), that separates it from the sacred city of Reims where France's kings were crowned. Most prized of all were the wines of Ay, with its propitious south-facing slope down to the river opposite Epernay.

All the vineyards are on deep chalk soils, uniquely rich in a rare fossil called belemnite. Chalk drains excellently; it reflects the sunlight (a relatively rare commodity in this climate) onto the vines, but needs constant top-dressing with organic fertilizer. In this marginal climate full ripeness is the exception, and slight variations of slope and aspect are crucial. Dom Pérignon made the discovery that no single site, nor grape variety, was ideal. In his day a dozen varieties were grown. (He preferred the Pinot Noir.)

Today three grapes dominate. First in acreage, with about 40%, comes Pinot Meunier, a cousin of the Pinot Noir, which is easier to grow and ripen, if not quite so fine. This is the base wine for all but the very finest champagnes. Pinot Noir is responsible for about a third of the total acreage, and Chardonnay for about a quarter.

The master plan for great champagne is to combine the qualities of the best grapes from the distinct parts of the region – of which, broadly speaking, there are three.

The Montagne de Reims is planted with Pinot Noir and (to a lesser extent) Pinot Meunier, both of whose black grapes have to be pressed very rapidly to give white wine without a trace of colour. No one has quite explained how in this most northern vineyard a north slope, which some of the best of the Montagne is, can give such good wine. The theory is that the air heats up on the plain below, and flows encouragingly up through the vines… Montagne wines contribute to the bouquet, the headiness and, with their firm acidity, to what the French call the 'carpentry' – the backbone of the blend.

The Vallée de la Marne has a succession of south-facing slopes which trap the sun and make these the fullest, roundest and ripest wines, with plenty of aroma. These too are predominantly black-grape vineyards, famous for Pinot Noir, but now increasingly invaded by Chardonnay. The village of Bouzy makes a small quantity of still red wine which the Champenois jealously keep for themselves. It can be like rather faint but exquisite burgundy.

The east-facing slope south of Epernay (topographically not unlike the Côte de Beaune) is the Côte des Blancs, planted with Chardonnay that gives freshness and finesse to the blend and encourages the sparkle. Wine from here is frequently sold as Blanc de Blancs, without the traditional proportion of Pinot Noir. Cramant, Avize and Le Mesnil are three villages with long-respected names for their (unblended)

wine. The first (and still the best) brand of Blanc de Blancs was Salon, from Le Mesnil.

These (and all Champagne-appellation) vineyards have what you might call a concealed classification – concealed because it is never mentioned on labels. The '*échelle*' (ladder) *des crus* gives the grapes of every commune a percentage rating. Whatever grape-price is decided on for the vintage as a whole (and there have been numerous changes in how this is achieved) a grower in one of the Grand Cru communes will be paid 100%. Premiers Crus receive between 99 and 90%, according to their place on the ladder, and so on down to 80% for some of the outlying areas.

The map indicates the *échelle* ratings of the heart of the region, where almost all the finer wines are grown. Such super-luxury 'prestige' brands as Dom Pérignon, Krug, Pol Roger's Sir Winston Churchill, Roederer Cristal, Perrier-Jouët's Belle Epoque, Clicquot's La Grande Dame or Taittinger's Comtes de Champagne naturally have the highest average *échelle* rating in their constituent wines.

Such wines should never be served very cold: certainly not icy. Nor should they be served too young. Great champagnes can mature for 20 years or more, gaining unsuspected depths of flavour. Most vintage wines are at their best between 8 and 15 years old. Even a non-vintage from a good house will improve for four or five years. Cheap champagnes, alas, have little to offer at any stage.

Reims

Tinqueux

Cité Charbonneaux

A26 · A4 · RD380 · D26

Janvry · Gueux · Ormes

Treslon · Bouleuse · Méry-Prémecy · Coulommes-la-Montagne · Vrigny

St-Euphraise-et-Clairizet · PARGNY-LES-REIMS · JOUY-LES-REIMS · LES MESNEUX · BEZANNES · CORMONTREUIL

Poilly · Sarcy · Aubilly · VILLE-DOMMANGE · Mont Benoît 121 · VILLERS-AUX-NOEUDS · Champfleury · TROIS-PUITS · TAISSY

Ville-en-Tardenois · Chambrecy · Bligny · Bouilly · Courmas · le Bois de la Fosse · ÉCUEIL · SACY · Chemin de la Barbarie · Mont Trouilly · MONTBRE · Mont de la Cuche 88 · SILLERY · PUISIEULX · BEAUMONT-SUR-VESLE

Chaumuzy · Marfaux · les Pâtis d'Écueil · CHAMERY · Sermiers · RILLY-LA-MONTAGNE · CHIGNY-LES-ROSES · Chemin de la Barbarie · VERZENAY · VERZY

Champlat-et-Boujacourt · Bois de Reims · Pourcy · les Pâtis de Sermiers · VILLERS-ALLERAND · LUDES · Mailly-Champagne · MAILLY 283 · VILLERS-MARMERY

la Neuville-aux-Larris · Belval-sous-Châtillon · Courtagnon · le Bois de St-Rémy · FORÊT DE LA MONTAGNE DE REIMS · Ville-en-Selve · TRÉPAIL · Mont Tournant · BILLY-LE-GRAND

Cuchery · Bois de Nanteuil · Nanteuil-la-Forêt · Bois de St-Quentin · Bois de Notre Dame · Germaine · Bois du Mont St-Hubn · LOUVOIS · Bois des Dames · VAUDEMANGES

Villers-sous-Châtillon · Bois du Roi · Bois de Fleury · Fleury-la-Rivière · Cormoyeux · Romery · St-Imoges · Bois du Gouffre · Mont Hurlet 234 · TAUXIÈRES-MUTRY · BOUZY · AMBONNAY

Vénteuil · Bois de St-Marc · HAUTVILLERS · CHAMPILLON · Bois de Charlefontaine · MUTIGNY · Fontaine-sur-Ay · Mt Ecouve · Mt des Plantes

Ch. de Boursault · Damery · CUMIÈRES · DIZY MAGENTA · AVENAY-VAL D'OR

Boursault · MARDEUIL · AY · MAREUIL-SUR-AY · BISSEUIL · Mont Charlier 131 · TOURS-SUR-MARNE · Condé-sur-Marne

Vauciennes · Étang d'Orléans · Étang Neuf · ÉPERNAY · CHOUILLY · OIRY · Châlons-sur-Marne

Forêt d'Épernay · PIERRY · Moussy · Vinay · Chavot-Courcourt · Monthelon · Mancy · CUIS · Butte de Saran · Ch. de Saran

Morangis · Moslins · GRAUVES · B. d'Avize · CRAMANT · AVIZE · OGER · LE MESNIL-SUR-OGER

Forêt d'Oger · Forêt du Mesnil · Gionges · VILLENEUVE-RENNEVILLE-CHEVIGNY

Forêt de Vertus · VERTUS · VOIPREUX · ÉTRÉCHY · BERGÈRES-LES-VERTUS · Châlons-sur-Marne

la Marne R. · Canal de l'Aisne · Canal Latéral

Legend

— · · —	Département boundary
— · —	Arrondissement boundary
— – —	Canton boundary
MAILLY	Commune (parish) with an average vineyard rating of 99% or more
MONTBRÉ	Commune (parish) with an average vineyard rating of 90-98%
	Other vineyard
	Woods
—200—	Contour interval 20 metres

1:157,000

Km. 0 1 2 3 4 5 6 Km.
Miles 0 1 2 3 4 Miles

Soissons · Reims · Châlons-sur-Marne · Épernay · CHAMPAGNE · Marne · Aisne · Seine · Aube · Troyes

79

Bordeaux

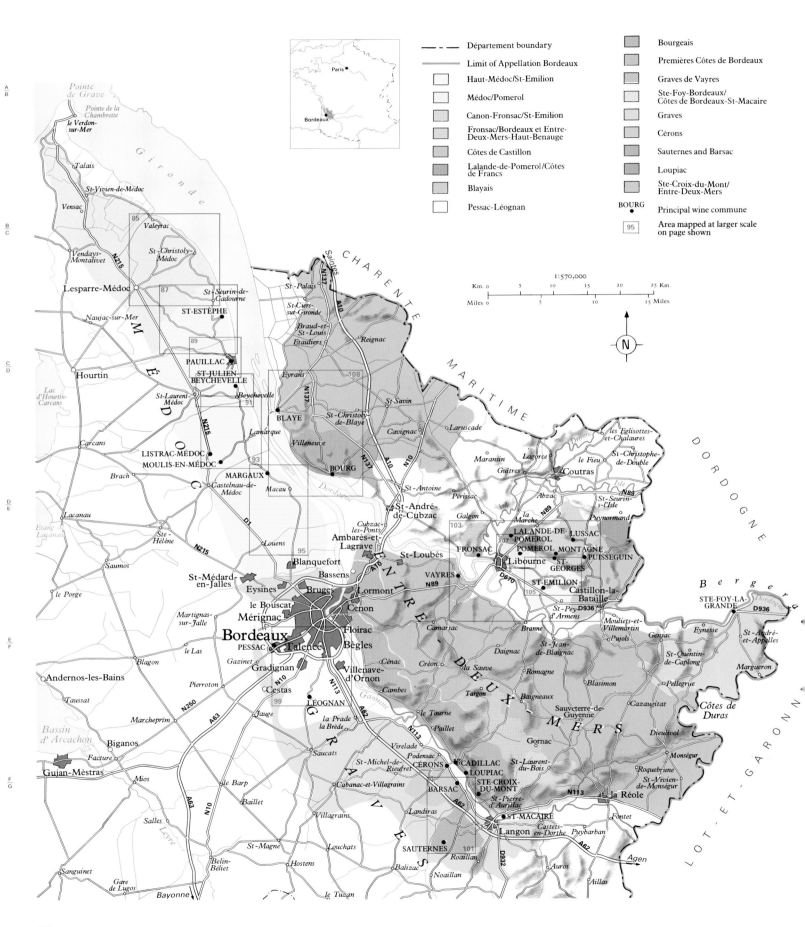

Département boundary

Limit of Appellation Bordeaux

Haut-Médoc/St-Emilion

Médoc/Pomerol

Canon-Fronsac/St-Emilion

Fronsac/Bordeaux et Entre-Deux-Mers-Haut-Benauge

Côtes de Castillon

Lalande-de-Pomerol/Côtes de Francs

Blayais

Pessac-Léognan

Bourgeais

Premières Côtes de Bordeaux

Graves de Vayres

Ste-Foy-Bordeaux/Côtes de Bordeaux-St-Macaire

Graves

Cérons

Sauternes and Barsac

Loupiac

Ste-Croix-du-Mont/Entre-Deux-Mers

BOURG   Principal wine commune

95   Area mapped at larger scale on page shown

1:570,000

Km. 0   5   10   15   20   25 Km.

Miles 0   5   10   15 Miles

N

If the name of Burgundy suggests richness and plenty, Bordeaux has more than a hint of elegance about it. In place of the plump prelate who seems to symbolize Burgundy, Bordeaux calls to mind a distinguished figure in a frock-coat. Picture him tasting pale red wine from a crystal glass. He has one thumb tucked into his waistcoat, while through the open door beyond him there is a glimpse of a turreted house, insubstantial in the pearly seaside light. He enters his moderate enthusiasms in a leather pocket book, observing the progress of beauty across his palate like moves in a game of chess.

Aspects of Bordeaux appeal to the aesthete, as Burgundy appeals to the sensualist. One is the nature of the wine: at its best indescribably subtle in nuance and complexity. Another is the sheer intellectual challenge of so many estates in so many regions and sub-regions that no one has mastered them all.

Bordeaux is the largest fine-wine district on earth. The whole *département* of the Gironde is dedicated to winegrowing. All its wine is Bordeaux. Its production dwarfs that of Burgundy: 7 million hectolitres in 1992.

Red wines outnumber white by four to one. The great red-wine areas lie to the north: the Médoc; the Graves immediately south of the city of Bordeaux; the country along the north bank of the Dordogne and facing the Médoc across the Gironde. The country between the two rivers is called Entre-Deux-Mers. Most of its wine is white, except for a fringe of villages which make red wine as well, facing Bordeaux and the Graves across the Garonne. This is the Premières Côtes de Bordeaux. The bottom third of the map is almost all white-wine country.

Bordeaux's great glories are its range of good to superlative red wines, the tiny production of very sweet golden wine of Sauternes, and a small but growing proportion of the dry Sauvignon/Sémillon whites of the Graves.

Compared with Burgundy the system of appellations in Bordeaux is simple. The map opposite shows them all. Within them it is the wine estates or châteaux which look after their own identification problem. On the other hand there is a form of classification by quality built into the system in Burgundy which is missing in Bordeaux. Here, in its place, is a variety of local classifications, unfortunately without a common standard.

By far the most famous of these is the classification of the châteaux of the Médoc – and one or two others – which was finalized in 1855, based on the prices the wines had fetched over the previous hundred years or more. Its first, second, third, fourth and fifth 'growths', to which were later added Crus Exceptionnels, Crus Bourgeois Supérieurs, Crus Bourgeois, Crus Artisans and Crus Paysans, are the most ambitious grading of the products of the soil ever attempted.

The overriding importance of situation in deciding quality is proved by the crus classés – which quite simply occupy the best soils. Where present standards depart from it there is usually

The city of Bordeaux glories in its grey stone architecture. *Top*: ships mount the Garonne to the old Pont de Pierre. *Left*: 18th-century merchants' houses on the Quai des Chartrons. *Right*: the medieval town gate.

an explanation (an industrious proprietor in 1855, and a lazy one now). Even more to the point, in many cases land has been added, or exchanged hands; the vineyard is not precisely the same.

In fact, more weight is placed today on the old classification than the system really justifies. The super-luxury first-growths regularly fetch twice the price of the second-growths, but thereafter a fifth-growth may fetch more, for example, than a second if it is better run. The relative qualities of different châteaux really need expressing in a more subtle way than by suggesting that one is always 'better' than another. The system adopted on the maps that follow is simply to distinguish between classed growths (in areas where they exist) and Crus Bourgeois.

Château is the word for a wine estate in Bordeaux. Its overtones of castle or stately home

are rarely justified. In most cases the biggest building at the château is the *chai* – the long sheds, often half underground, where the wine is stored – attached to the *cuvier* where it is made. (A Bordeaux château and its working routine is anatomized on pages 36–37.)

The vineyards of the château sometimes surround it in a neat plot. More often they are scattered and intermingled with their neighbours. They can produce annually anything from 10 to 1,000 barrels of wine, each holding 300 bottles. The best vineyards make a maximum of 5,000 litres from each hectare of vines, the less good ones considerably more. A hectare can have anything from 5,000 to 10,000 vines.

The *maître de chai* is an important figure at the château. At little properties it is the owner himself, at big ones an old retainer. It is he who welcomes visitors and lets them taste the new wine, cold and dark and unpalatable, from the casks in his care. Be knowing rather than enthusiastic; the wine will not be ready to drink for two years after it has been bottled at the very least – and maybe not for twenty.

Bordeaux: the Quality Factor

The advantages of the Bordeaux region for winegrowing can be listed quite simply. Its position near the sea and threaded with rivers gives it a moderate and stable climate. Europe's biggest forest, on the ocean side and to the south, protects it from strong salt winds and reduces the rainfall. The bedrock is well furnished with minerals, yet the topsoil in general is quite poor and often very deep.

The most earnest studies have been made to decide what it is that makes one piece of land superior to its neighbour. They all start by defining exactly the geological, pedological (ie soil) and climatological set-up for a very fine vineyard … and then tend to find that exactly the same

Left: the second wine of Cos d'Estournel is Château de Marbuzet. The château, at St-Estèphe in the north of the Médoc, embodies the lordly aspirations of late 19th-century proprietors in its giant neo-Palladian portico. Generally speaking, though, the quality of châteaux architecture lags far behind that of their wines.

considerations seem to apply next door, where the wine is not and never has been half so good.

In Bordeaux, however, there are more variables to help explain the differences. Instead of one constant grape variety, like the Pinot Noir for all red wine on the Côte d'Or, red Bordeaux is made from a mixture of three or four varieties, the proportions depending on the district and the taste of the proprietor. To jump to the conclusion that, let us say, the soil of Château Lafite gives lighter wine than that of Château Latour would be rash, unless you have taken into account that Lafite grows a good deal of Merlot while Latour is nearly all Cabernet Sauvignon. Another factor is the status of the vineyard. Success breeds success, meaning more money to spend on expensive care of the land – or on buying more. Differences that were originally marginal can thus increase over the years.

Furthermore the soil of the Médoc, to speak of only part of Bordeaux, is said to 'change at every step'. No one has yet been able to isolate

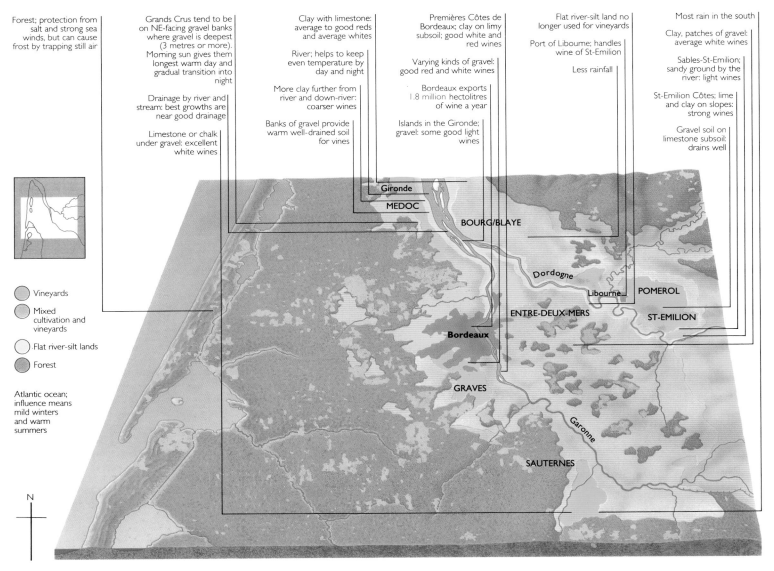

Forest; protection from salt and strong sea winds, but can cause frost by trapping still air

Grands Crus tend to be on NE-facing gravel banks where gravel is deepest (3 metres or more). Morning sun gives them longest warm day and gradual transition into night

Drainage by river and stream: best growths are near good drainage

Limestone or chalk under gravel: excellent white wines

Clay with limestone: average to good reds and average whites

River; helps to keep even temperature by day and night

More clay further from river and down-river: coarser wines

Banks of gravel provide warm well-drained soil for vines

Premières Côtes de Bordeaux; clay on limy subsoil; good white and red wines

Varying kinds of gravel: good red and white wines

Bordeaux exports 1.8 million hectolitres of wine a year

Islands in the Gironde; gravel: some good light wines

Flat river-silt land no longer used for vineyards

Port of Libourne; handles wine of St-Emilion

Less rainfall

Most rain in the south

Clay, patches of gravel: average white wines

Sables-St-Emilion; sandy ground by the river: light wines

St-Emilion Côtes; lime and clay on slopes: strong wines

Gravel soil on limestone subsoil: drains well

Vineyards

Mixed cultivation and vineyards

Flat river-silt lands

Forest

Atlantic ocean; influence means mild winters and warm summers

Gironde

MEDOC

BOURG/BLAYE

Dordogne

Libourne — POMEROL

ENTRE-DEUX-MERS

ST-EMILION

Bordeaux

GRAVES

Garonne

SAUTERNES

N

the wine made from a vine on one patch and compare it with that from two steps away. So nobody really knows what vines, on what kind of soil, give what kind of wine – except in the most general terms, and even then only with many reservations.

You would not expect this to prevent the University of Bordeaux from going on trying, however. The theory that finds widest support is that (contrary to traditional belief) geology is scarcely a factor at all in deciding quality, at least not in Bordeaux. A vine will find all the nourishment it needs almost anywhere; but the poorer the soil the deeper and wider the vine will root. Hence the paradox that poor soil makes good wine. Give a vine rich soil, or spread generous helpings of manure around it, and its roots will stay near the surface. But plant it in stony ground, give it only the bare necessities, and it will plunge metres deep to see what it can find. For the deeper the roots go, the more constant is their environment, and the less they

are subject to floods on the one hand, drought on the other, and fluctuations of food supply from manuring or lack of manuring. Then there can be a lake around it, or total drought can parch and crack the ground, and the vine will feed normally – provided only that the subsoil is well drained, so that the roots do not drown.

Enlarging on this idea, Dr Gérard Seguin of the University of Bordeaux has suggested that the nearer a vineyard is to an effective drain, the drier the subsoil will be and the deeper the roots will go; that the first-growths are vineyards nearest the drainage channels, the second-growths slightly further from them, and so on. There is an ancient Bordeaux saying that 'the vines should look at the river'. This theory explains it. It also explains why old vines give the best wine: their roots are deepest. The theory can be examined by studying the streams in the following maps in relation to the classed and other growths.

Hence, Dr Seguin continues, it is not the

chemical composition of the soil but its physical make-up that must be taken into account. Heavy clay or sand which drains badly are the least propitious components for wine: gravel and larger stones are best. Add to this the way stones store heat on the surface, and prevent rapid evaporation of moisture from under them, and it is easy to see that they are the best guarantee of stable conditions of both temperature and humidity that a vine can have.

In the Médoc it is the deep gravel beds that form gentle hills in Margaux, St-Julien and Pauillac which drain best. As you go north the proportion of clay increases, so that in St-Estèphe, despite steeper hills, drainage is less effective. This does not mean that all Margaux wines are first-growths and all St-Estèphe fifth – although there are many more classed growths in Margaux – but it does account for higher acidity, more tannin and colour, and less scent in St-Estèphe wines. It is, after all, not only a question of quality but also of character.

Left: some of the factors affecting the varying qualities and character of Bordeaux wine are shown in this diagram of the basin of the Gironde viewed from the south.

The Gironde is formed by the confluence of the rivers Dordogne (on the right) and the Garonne (on the left). Soil and subsoil have a bearing on the nature of the wine, but there is doubt about how important they are in determining its quality and character. Such factors as rainfall, and whether the sun reaches the vine in the morning or the after-noon, and above all the rapid drainage of the ground may play just as large a part.

The southern part of the area has most rainfall, the north the least. White wine is grown in the south, both red and white in the centre, and more red than white in the north. No positive link between the two facts can be proved, but it seems likely that the mists of the wetter southern area have been found helpful to white grapes over the years and have tended to cause rot in the red.

Right: A total of 37% of Bordeaux wine is exported – over 1.8 million hecto-litres a year. With 2% of the world's vineyards, Bordeaux represents 4% of the world wine exports by volume, and 10% by value.

Below: Bordeaux red-wine production exceeds Bordeaux white by 3:1.

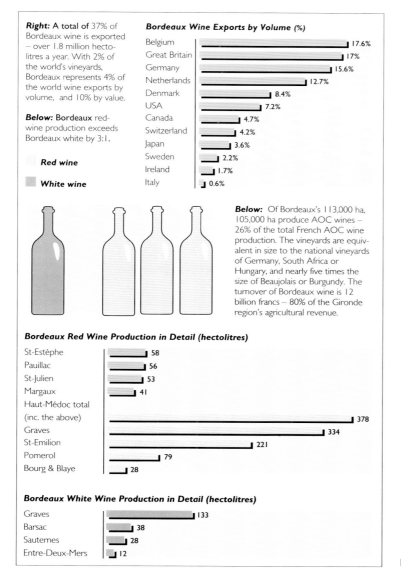

Bordeaux Wine Exports by Volume (%)

Belgium	17.6%
Great Britain	17%
Germany	15.6%
Netherlands	12.7%
Denmark	8.4%
USA	7.2%
Canada	4.7%
Switzerland	4.2%
Japan	3.6%
Sweden	2.2%
Ireland	1.7%
Italy	0.6%

Red wine

White wine

Below: Of Bordeaux's 113,000 ha, 105,000 ha produce AOC wines – 26% of the total French AOC wine production. The vineyards are equivalent in size to the national vineyards of Germany, South Africa or Hungary, and nearly five times the size of Beaujolais or Burgundy. The turnover of Bordeaux wine is 12 billion francs – 80% of the Gironde region's agricultural revenue.

Bordeaux Red Wine Production in Detail (hectolitres)

St-Estèphe	58
Pauillac	56
St-Julien	53
Margaux	41
Haut-Médoc total (inc. the above)	378
Graves	334
St-Emilion	221
Pomerol	79
Bourg & Blaye	28

Bordeaux White Wine Production in Detail (hectolitres)

Graves	133
Barsac	38
Sauternes	28
Entre-Deux-Mers	12

THE LANGUAGE OF THE LABEL

Négociant A shipping house which often buys wine from the château a few months old and keeps it (usually in Bordeaux) until it is ready to ship or bottle. Among the leading négociants today are Borie-Manoux, Cordier, Duclot, Dulong, Nathaniel Johnston, Alexis Lichine, de Luze, Mestrezat, Moueix, Quancard and Sichel

Château Estate

Récolte Vintage

Mis (or **Mise**) **en bouteille au château** Bottled at the property where it is made

Grand Vin Simply 'great wine', often to distinguish it from a 'second wine'

Cru Classé One of the first five official growths of the Médoc; also any classed growth of another district, however classified. The Médoc classifications are as follows – all go back to 1855:

Premier Cru	First-growth	
Deuxième Cru	Second-growth	rarely
Troisième Cru	Third-growth	appear on
Quatrième Cru	Fourth-growth	labels
Cinquième Cru	Fifth-growth	

Cru Exceptionnel In the Médoc, the second rank, below Cru Classé

Cru Bourgeois Supérieur The third rank (see below)

Cru Bourgeois The fourth rank – but often a very worthy wine – occasionally as good as most Crus Classés. The Cru Bourgeois categories are now strictly unofficial

Cru Artisan Rank below Cru Bourgeois

Cru Paysan Rank below Cru Artisan; these two terms are no longer used

Premier Grand Cru Classé The first rank of St-Emilion classed growths (1954 classification)

Grand Cru Classé The second rank of St-Emilion classed growths (1954 classification)

Supérieur (after the name of Graves or Bordeaux) Indicates wine with 1° of alcohol above the minimum allowed

Haut A mere verbal gesture, except as part of the name of Haut-Médoc

Propriétaire Owner

Société Anonyme Limited company

Société Civile Private company

Héritiers The heirs of . . .

The Bas-Médoc

Geographically, the Médoc is a great tongue of flat or barely undulating land isolated from the body of Aquitaine by the broad brown estuary of the Gironde.

In common usage its name is given to more fine wine than any other name in the world: Margaux, St-Julien, Pauillac, St-Estèphe and their surrounding villages are all 'Médoc' in location and in style. But the appellation Médoc is both more limited and less prestigious. It is more clearly understood under its former name of Bas- (meaning lower) Médoc. The term Bas was dropped for reasons of – shall we say? – delicacy. But the fact remains. The lower Médoc, the tip of the tongue, the farthest reaches of the region, has none of the high points, either physically or gastronomically, of the Haut-Médoc to its south.

The well-drained dunes of gravel give way to lower and heavier land north of St-Estèphe, with St-Seurin, the last commune of the Haut-Médoc, riding a characteristic hump between areas of channelled marsh.

North and west of here is fertile, long-settled land, with the bustling market town of Lesparre as its capital since the days of English rule six centuries ago.

Until recently, vineyards took their place here with pasture and orchard and woodland. Now they have spread to cover almost all the higher ground where gravel lightens the clay,

centring on the villages of St-Yzans, St-Christoly, Couquèques, By and Valeyrac along the banks of the Gironde, and covering much of the interior in St-Germain-d'Esteuil, Ordonnac, Blaignan and (the biggest) Bégadan.

There are no classed growths but an impressive number of worthy Crus Bourgeois. Twenty years ago the names of only three or four were known to the wider world. Much replanting and upgrading has happened since, and the lower Médoc now has an important place as a supplier of sound, solid reds. A dozen châteaux have built good reputations, using the expensive methods of the Haut-Médoc, and ageing their wines in new (or newish) barrels. Until recently these higher standards were signalled by promotion to Cru Bourgeois Supérieur. The European Community with typical obtuseness has banned this helpful distinction.

Clay suits Merlot better than Cabernet, giving the wine here a softer edge, even a passing resemblance to St-Emilion. The clearest way to see the difference between Médocs Haut and Bas is to compare one of the best of these wines with a Cru Bourgeois from St-Estèphe. Young, there may be little to distinguish them: both are vigorous, tannic, dry and 'très Bordeaux'. At five years, though, the Haut-Médoc is finding that fine-etched personality, that clean transparency of flavour, that will go on developing. The Bas-Médoc has begun to soften, but

remains a sturdy, rather rustic wine, often deep-coloured, satisfying and savoury rather than enlightening and inspiring. At ten years there has been more softening, but usually at the expense of 'structure'; not the refining of character that we find further south.

The châteaux with most established reputations (and in some cases considerable output) begin with Loudenne, the Gilbey's stronghold at St-Yzans by the river, which also makes a good dry white wine. Most prestigious are Château Potensac (which also uses the names Gallais-Bellevue, Cru Lassalle and others), with the same perfectionist owners as Château Léoville-Las Cases in St-Julien, and the (Lafite-) Rothschild-run Château La Cardonne on the same slight plateau.

Châteaux Livran at St-Germain, Greysac at St-Christoly and Laujac, west of Bégadan, all have well-established names, although today you can look for more modern-style wine, with more fruit and character, at Châteaux La Tour de By, La Clare, Monthil and Vieux-Château Landon in Bégadan, and Châteaux La Tour St-Bonnet and Les Ormes Sorbet in St-Christoly and Couquèques. Bégadan is the most important commune of the area as a producer: its growers' cooperative uses the grapes from 1,400 acres (560 hectares) to make 300,000 cases of very satisfactory wines annually under a number of labels.

Above: good-value reds, sturdy and full of flavour, typify the Bas-Médoc.
Right: Château Loudenne dominates the Gironde.

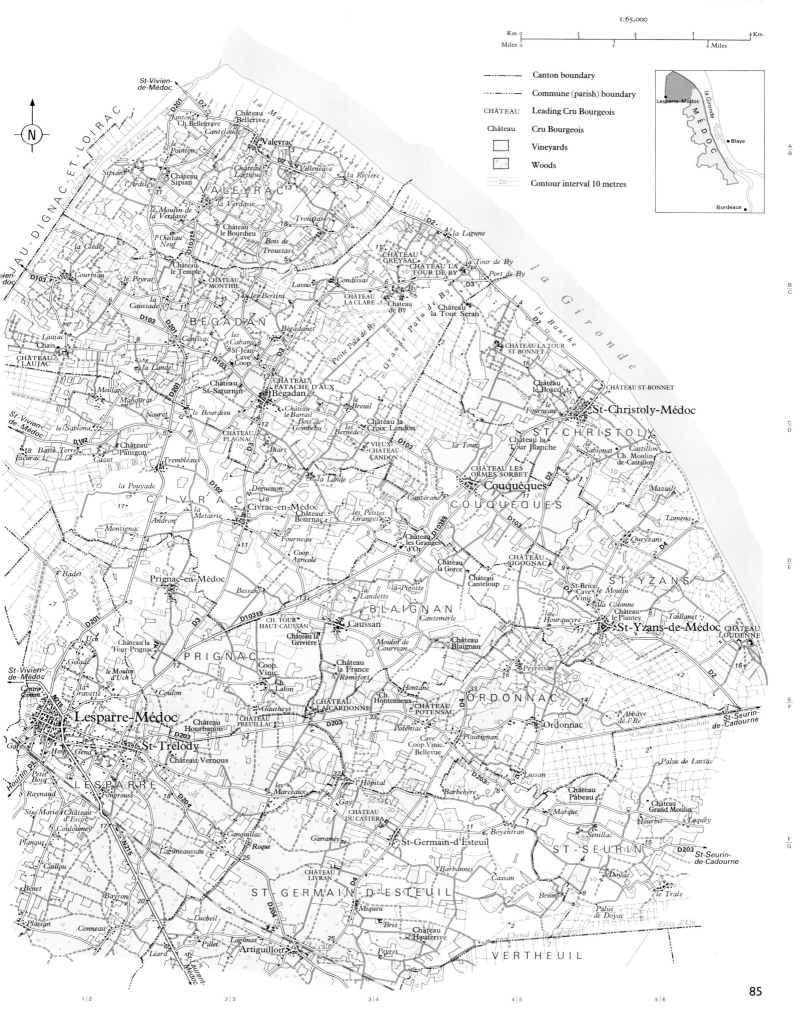

1:65,000

Km. 0   1   2   3   4 Km.

Miles 0   1   2 Miles

–·––·–·––·– Canton boundary

–··––··––··– Commune (parish) boundary

CHÂTEAU   Leading Cru Bourgeois

Château   Cru Bourgeois

Vineyards

Woods

——20—— Contour interval 10 metres

85

St-Estèphe

The gravel banks which give the Médoc and its wines their character and quality, stretching along the shore of the Gironde, sheltered from the ocean to the west by forest, begin to peter out at St-Estèphe. It is the northernmost of the four famous communes which are the heart of the Médoc. A *jalle* – the Médoc word for a stream – divides it from Pauillac, draining on the one hand the vineyards of Château Lafite, on the other three of the five classed growths of St-Estèphe: Châteaux Cos d'Estournel, Lafon-Rochet and Cos Labory.

There is a distinction between the soils of Pauillac and St-Estèphe: as the gravel washed down the Gironde diminishes there is a stronger mixture of clay found in it. Higher up, in Margaux, there is very little. In St-Estèphe it is heavier soil, which drains more slowly. The wines have more acidity, are fuller, more solid, often have less perfume but fairly fill your mouth with flavour. They are sturdy clarets which can become venerable without losing vigour.

Cos d'Estournel is the most spectacular of the classed growths. It has an eccentric Chinese-pagoda'd edifice, impressively crowning the steep slope up from the Pauillac boundary (with all too good a view of the Shell refinery below). Together with Château Montrose, overlooking the river, it makes the biggest and best of St-Estèphes; strong wines with a dark colour and a long life. 'Cos', as it is nearly always called, has been the leader in the commune in recent years, having a succulence and persistence of flavour (the result, perhaps, of a high proportion of Merlot in the vineyard) which is more seductive than that of its rival second-growth, Montrose. Montrose is an excellent château to visit to get an idea of a prosperous estate in the old-fashioned style. Its rather dark *chai*, heavily beamed, and its magnificent oak fermenting vats have the same air of permanence as its intense, tannic, deeply-flavoured wine. Classic Montrose vintages take 20 years to mature.

The other two classed growths near Cos,

Châteaux Lafon-Rochet and Cos Labory, have not distinguished themselves in recent years. Lafon-Rochet was bought and rebuilt by M Tesseron, a Cognac merchant, in the 1960s – the first Médoc château to be rebuilt in the 20th century. Yet its wine remains hard – possibly the result of too much Cabernet in a cold soil. Cos Labory is content to be full of fruity flavour at a fairly young age. Calon-Ségur, north of the village and the northernmost classed growth of the Médoc, comes somewhere between Cos d'Estournel and Montrose in style: firm and long-lived but not over-aggressive. Two hundred and fifty years ago the Marquis de Ségur, owner of both Lafite and Latour, reputedly said his heart was at Calon. It still is, on the label.

Above all, St-Estèphe is known for its Crus Bourgeois. There is an explosion of them on the plateau south and west of the village. Châteaux Phélan-Ségur and de Pez are both outstanding producers of very fine wine. Pez has an extraordinary historical record; as the property of the Pontacs of Haut-Brion its wine was sold as Pontac in London in the 17th century – possibly before any other growth of the Médoc.

Among the many worthy burgesses of the commune, Château Meyney, like a huge and immaculate farmyard without a farmhouse, is unusual in the Médoc for having monastic origins. Its situation by the river, neighbour to Montrose, might make one look for finer wine with more potential for development. In practice it is sturdy and reliable without notable finesse. More dashing wines, still in the hearty St-Estèphe style, are made at Les Ormes de Pez by the owner of Château Lynch-Bages in Pauillac. Châteaux Tronquoy-Lalande, Beau-Site and Capbern Gasqueton, south, west and east of the village, are all deserving of their good reputations. Château de Marbuzet is the name given to the second wine of Cos d'Estournel, while Châteaux Haut-Marbuzet, Chambert-Marbuzet and MacCarthy-Moula are all the property of an outstanding winemaker, Henri

Left: Cos d'Estournel has no château-residence, but gilded pagodaed *chais* which dominate the green valley north of Château Lafite.
Above and right: St-Estèphe has only five Crus Classés, but a dozen outstanding Crus Bourgeois. From its riverside situation Château Meyney might be expected to rank higher.

Duboscq, whose style is richly tasty and one of the surest things in the district. Andron Blanquet, Le Crock and Lavillotte continue the list of St-Estèphes that express the *terroir* with vigour and style, while Lilian-Ladouys is a new-comer that burst on the scene in the late 1980s with sumptuous new wines. The growers' cooperative, the 'Marquis de St-Estèphe', is also an important source of typical wine.

To the north of St-Estèphe the gravel bank diminishes to a promontory sticking out of the *palus* – the flat river-silted land on which no wine of quality grows. On top of the promontory the little village of St-Seurin-de-Cadourne has a dozen Crus Bourgeois. The gentle Château Coufran, the more tannic Verdignan, the full-blooded Sociando-Mallet and the admirable Bel Orme Tronquoy de Lalande are the leaders here, along with a big cooperative whose wine is sold as 'Canterayne'.

Where St-Seurin ends is the end of the Haut-Médoc: any wine grown beyond that point is only entitled to the appellation Médoc, plain and simple (see pages 84–85). The beautiful Château Loudenne, for more than a century owned by the British firm of Gilbey, occupies its first gravel knoll.

The country behind St-Estèphe, further from the river, has a scattering of Crus Bourgeois, few of them well known. Cissac and Vertheuil lie on stronger and less gravelly soil on the edge of the forest. Château Cissac is the outstanding growth: vigorous enough to be a Pauillac. At Cissac, Châteaux du Breuil and Hanteillan, and at Vertheuil Château Le Bourdieu and Le Meynieu are worth at least occasional investigation.

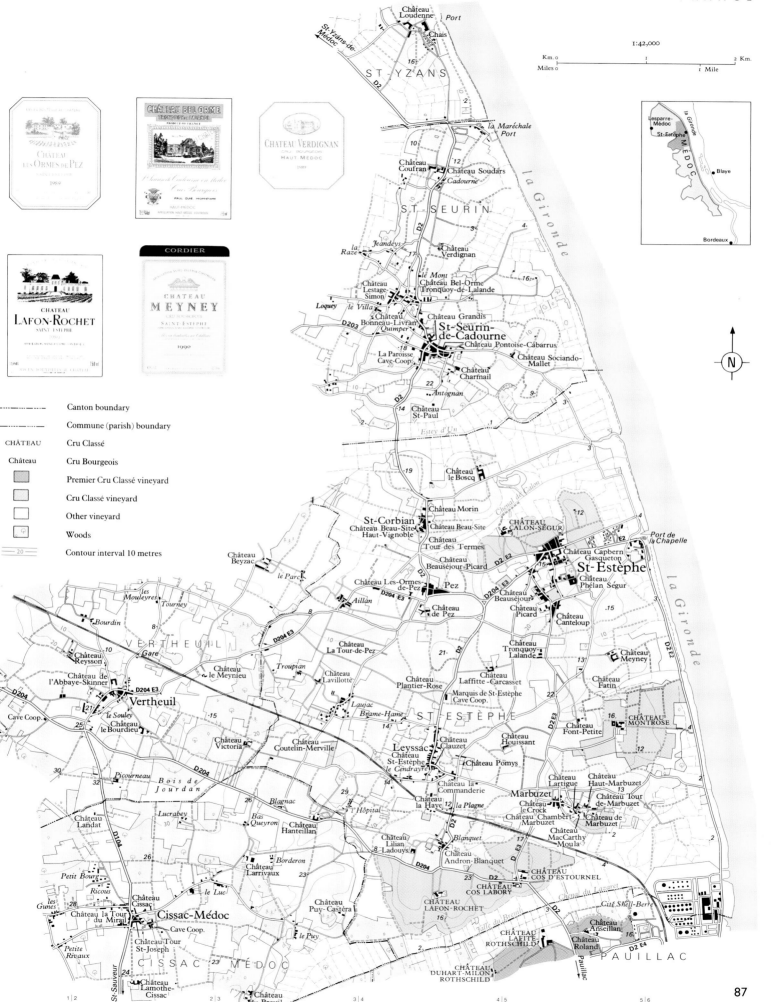

Pauillac

Pauillac Crus Classés have a sober approach to labelling. The one tearaway is Mouton Rothschild, which commissions a different artist every year.

If one had to single out one commune of Bordeaux to head the list, there would be no argument. It would be Pauillac. Châteaux Lafite, Latour and Mouton Rothschild, three out of the first five of the Médoc and Graves, are its obvious claim. But many claret-lovers would tell you that the wines of Pauillac have the quintessential flavour they look for in Bordeaux – a combination of fresh soft-fruit, oak, dryness, subtlety combined with substance, a touch of cigar-box, a suggestion of sweetness and, above all, vigour. Even the lesser growths approach their ideal claret.

At Pauillac the gravel *croupes* of the Médoc get as near as they ever do to being hills. The highest part, with Châteaux Mouton Rothschild and Pontet-Canet on its summit, reaches 100 feet (30 metres) – quite an achievement in this coastal area, where a mere swelling of the ground provides a lookout point.

The town of Pauillac is the biggest of the Médoc. Happily, its long-established oil refinery has ceased operation and become a mere (though colossal) depot. Its old quay has become a marina; a few restaurants have opened – yet it could still scarcely be called animated.

The vineyards of the châteaux of Pauillac are on the whole less subdivided than in most of the Médoc. Whereas in Margaux (for example) the châteaux are bunched together in the town, and their holdings in the surrounding countryside are inextricably mixed up – a row here, a couple of rows there – in Pauillac whole slopes, mounds and plateaux belong to a single proprietor. One would therefore expect greater variations in style derived from *terroir*. One is not disappointed.

The three great wines of Pauillac are all dramatically different. Châteaux Lafite-Rothschild and Latour stand at opposite ends of the parish; the first almost in St-Estèphe, the second almost in St-Julien. Oddly enough, though, their characters tend in quite the opposite direction: Lafite more towards the smoothness and finesse of a St-Julien, Latour more towards the emphatic firmness of a St-Estèphe.

Lafite, with 225 acres (90 hectares) one of the biggest vineyards in the Médoc, makes about 1,000 barrels of its fabulously expensive wine; a perfumed, polished, and quintessentially gentlemanly production. Its second label is Carruades.

The firmer and more solid Latour seems to spurn elegance, expressing its supremely privileged situation on the hill nearest the river in robust depths that take decades to reveal their complexity. Latour has the great merit of evenness over uneven vintages. Even the château's second wine, Les Forts de Latour, from separate parcels of land west of the main road (the D2), is considered and priced as a second Cru Classé. A junior selection, still often richly savoury, is sold simply as Pauillac.

The Baronne Philippine de Rothschild at Mouton makes a third kind of Pauillac: strong, dark, and full of the savour of ripe blackcurrants. Given the 10 or often even 20 years they need to mature (depending on the quality of the vintage), these wines reach into realms of perfection where they are rarely followed. But millionaires tend to be impatient: too much is drunk far too young.

Smelling the richness and feeling the force of Cabernet Sauvignon in these wines it is strange to think that it is a mere 200 years since it was recognized as the best vine for the Médoc. Up to that time even the first-growths had established the superiority of their *terroirs* with a mixture of inferior grape varieties – above all Malbec.

No visitor to Pauillac should miss the little museum of works of art connected with wine – old glass, paintings, tapestries – as well as the very fine *chais*, which make Château Mouton Rothschild the showplace of the whole Médoc.

The southern approach to Pauillac saw dramatic developments in the early 1990s. Ancient rivalry between the two halves of the historic Pichon estate, whose respective second-growth châteaux face each other across the road, took on a new dimension. For years Pichon-Lalande (as it is known for short) had the better name for its singularly rich and sensuous wine. Then the insurance group AXA bought 'Pichon-Baron' (as well as much else) and started what can best be described as an aggressive building programme, including a fort-like erection on each side of the road. In AXA's favour it must be said that its wine improved just as dramatically, orchestrated by the owner of Château Lynch-Bages, Jean-Michel Cazes.

Lynch-Bages, though 'only' a fifth-growth, has long been loved, particularly in England, for its richly fragrant wine – a sort of Mouton for non-millionaires. Now with the AXA-owned Cru Bourgeois Château Pibran and Château Haut-Bages-Averous, the second wine of Lynch-Bages, M Cazes directs a cast of model modern Pauillacs.

The mystery château meanwhile is Pontet-Canet, the biggest cru classé of all. Superbly sited as a neighbour to Mouton, it is however utterly different: tannic and lean where Mouton is opulent.

Château Duhart-Milon belongs to the Rothschilds of Lafite, and Château d'Armailhac (formerly Mouton-Baronne) to Mouton. Both clearly benefit from the wealth and technical knowledge of their proprietors and managers. The neighbouring classed growth Clerc Milon also belongs to the extensive (Mouton-) Rothschild stable.

Châteaux Batailley and Haut-Batailley lie back from the river in the fringe of the woods. (Haut-Batailley is related in ownership to the great Château Ducru-Beaucaillou in St-Julien.) La Couronne does duty as château and *chai*. One does not expect from them quite the same finesse as from the great wines made nearer the river, but both are consistently well made and good value. Haut-Batailley has the more finesse.

The two châteaux called Grand-Puy, Lacoste and Ducasse, both have high reputations, although the former is better known, consistently producing some of Pauillac's most vital

la Gironde

Chenal du Lazaret

St-Estèphe

CHÂTEAU COS
D'ESTOURNEL

CHÂTEAU
LAFON-ROCHET

CHÂTEAU
COS-LABORY

16

Cité Shell-Berre

ST - ESTÈPHE

16

D2

Raff. de
Pétrole

Château
Roland

Château Anseillan

3

CHÂTEAU
LAFITE-ROTHSCHILD

CHÂTEAU DUHART-
MILON ROTHSCHILD

Milon

26

13

18

Loubeyres

D2

E4

Mousset

CHÂTEAU la
Fleur-Milon

CHÂTEAU
MILON

CLERC

le Charite

Cissac-Médoc

9

D205

26

CHÂTEAU
MOUTON-ROTHSCHILD

Lhorte

21

3

Lescargean

les Carruades

14

le Pouyalet

Trompeloup

Château
Ramage la Batisse

la Garosse

CHÂTEAU D'ARMAILHAC

27

Padarnac

21

CHÂTEAU
PEDESCLAUX

Château
Bellerose

D104 E1

28

CARRUADES
DE LAFITE

D205

Château Tourteran

Guérin

24

Junlande

CHÂTEAU
PONTET-CANET

D2 E4

Canterayne
Cave Coop

Château Liversan

ST SAUVEUR

Béhéré

25

28

26

Pibran

16

Château la Tour Pibran

Château Pibran

Gare

D205

29

Labrousse

D104 E3

Château Peyrabon

30

31

PAUILLAC

la Rose-Pauillac
Cave Coop.

D2 E6

Château
le Fournas

Ste-Croix

le Fournas

Ch. le Fournas
Bernadotte

D104 E3

Pauillac

CHÂTEAU
GRAND-PUY-
DUCASSE
Port

27

la Naude

Château
Hourtin-Ducasse

20

27

Panneton

18

D206

D2 E4

Chai de Château
Duhart-Milon

la Verrerie

Château
Lieujan

30

CHÂTEAU HAUT-
BAGES-MONPELOU

Artigues

CHÂTEAU GRAND
PUY-LACOSTE

Grand Moussas

Bouhoubrun

Bages

CHÂTEAU
CROIZET-BAGES

Château Haut
Bages-Avérous

D104 E3

CHÂTEAU LYNCH-BAGES

Château
Haut-Madrac

CHÂTEAU
LYNCH-MOUSSAS

29

26

D206

23

Château
Cordeillan-
Bages

D2

les Gabarreys

4

Dauprat
Château
Bellegrave

St-Lambert

CHÂTEAU-HAUT-
BAGES-LIBÉRAL

Château Fonbadet

CHÂTEAU
BATAILLEY

23

Daubos

l'Enclos

14

Château
la Couronne

CH. PICHON-LONGUEVILLE
(BARON)

CHÂTEAU
LATOUR

CHÂTEAU
HAUT-BATAILLEY

CHÂTEAU PICHON-
LONGUEVILLE-COMTESSE-
DE-LALANDE

D2

29

25

D206

St-Julien-
Beychevelle

Juillac

LES FORTS
DE LATOUR

St-Laurent-
Médoc

St-Julien

ST - JULIEN

N

1:35,000

Km. 0   Km.
Miles 0   1 Mile

Lesparre-
Médoc

la Gironde

MÉDOC

Pauillac

Blaye

Bordeaux

Canton boundary

Commune (parish) boundary

CHÂTEAU   Cru Classé

Château   Cru Bourgeois

Premier Cru Classé vineyard

Cru Classé vineyard

Other vineyard

Woods

20   Contour interval 10 metres

and delicious wines. Lacoste is one fine continuous vineyard on high ground, surrounding its château, while the Ducasse property is scattered in three separate parcels to the north and west of Pauillac and its old château is on the quay in the town itself.

Of the remaining classed growths, Croizet-Bages is probably the best. Haut-Bages Libéral, its vineyards superbly sited in St-Lambert, has acquired new premises and a new lease of life recently. Lynch-Moussas, run in conjunction with Batailley, sells consistently good wine

at modest prices. Both Croizet-Bages and Pedesclaux are staunchly conservative – and none the worse for it.

Pauillac, having so many large estates, is not, like St-Estèphe, a warren of small-to-middling growers. Its one small Cru Exceptionnel, La Couronne, has already been mentioned. Of the Crus Bourgeois, Châteaux Pibran and Haut-Bages-Avérous are in more than capable hands, Fonbadet, screened from the road in St-Lambert by trees, has old vines and serious wine, and Haut-Bages Monpelou is co-owned

with Château Batailley. The local cooperative, under the name of La Rose-Pauillac, is also making creditable wine.

The map includes part of the next parish to the west, St-Sauveur. There are no wines of outstanding quality here; the Crus Bourgeois marked, however, are respectable and useful. Château Liversan (which includes Fonpiqueyre) belongs to the Polignac family; Château Peyrabon is a big, well-run vineyard and the wine of Ramage la Batisse is fragrant and stylish.

St-Julien

Château Beychevelle stands in formal magnificence behind iron grilles by the road entering St-Julien from the south. Behind it gardens and parkland stretch down over the flat *palus* (river-meadow) to the Gironde. *Palus* wine from rich soil was valued in the 17th century: today it is excluded even from the simplest Bordeaux appellation. All the character of the Médoc comes from its lean pebbly soil.

No other commune in Bordeaux has so high a proportion of classed growths as St-Julien. It is a small commune, with the smallest production of the famous four of the Médoc. Yet almost all of it is superlative winegrowing land: typical dunes of gravel, not as deep as in Pauillac (a cross-section of a St-Julien vine and its soil is shown on page 19), but all are either close to the river or sloping south to the considerable valley (considerable by Médoc standards) drained by the Jalle du Nord and the Chenal du Milieu.

Thus the great châteaux divide into two groups: the riverside estates epitomized by the Léovilles around the village of St-Julien itself and the southern group centred on the village of Beychevelle, led by Château Beychevelle and its neighbours and reaching back inland with Gruaud-Larose and Lagrange. Further inland in the next commune, St-Laurent, lie three more classed growths whose appellation is Haut-Médoc and whose style is altogether less finely tuned. Such few Crus Bourgeois as St-Julien can

find room for are grouped round Beychevelle – and led by the redoubtable Château Gloria.

If Pauillac makes the most striking and brilliant wine of the Médoc, and Margaux the most refined and exquisite, St-Julien forms the transition between the two. With one or two exceptions its châteaux make rather round and gentle wine – gentle, that is, when it is mature: it starts as tough and tannic in a good year as any.

The principal glory of the commune is the vast estate of Léoville, once the biggest in the Médoc, now divided into three. It lies on the Pauillac boundary, and it would be a brave man who would say that he could distinguish a Léoville from a Longueville every time (although he certainly should be able to distinguish a Château Latour, which lies equally close).

Château Léoville-Las-Cases has the biggest vineyards of the three, with over 200 acres (some 80 hectares), and for some years it has maintained a reputation as high as Château Pichon-Lalande in Pauillac for impeccable wine, although in a restrained, drier, more austere

St-Julien has a higher proportion of its land 'classé' than any other commune. No first-growth, but five seconds. Château Larose-Trintaudon, the Médoc's largest single property, lies just outside the commune of St-Julien in the appellation Haut-Médoc.

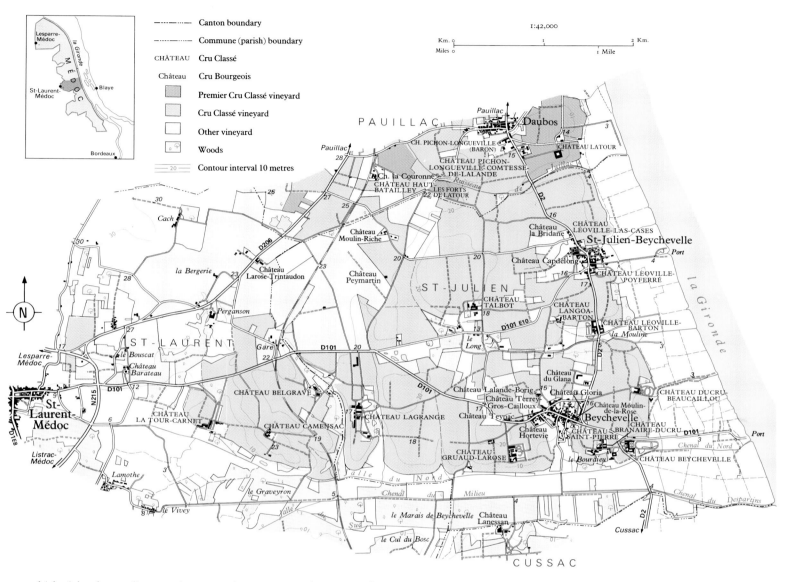

Canton boundary

Commune (parish) boundary

CHÂTEAU Cru Classé

Château Cru Bourgeois

Premier Cru Classé vineyard

Cru Classé vineyard

Other vineyard

Woods

Contour interval 10 metres

1:42,000

and 'classic' style, needing very long maturing.

Léoville-Barton runs it close. It belongs, together with the neighbouring Langoa Barton, to the old Irish family of Barton, who moved to Bordeaux as merchants early in the 18th century.

Anthony Barton lives in the beautiful 18th-century Château Langoa, and makes his two wines side by side in the same *chai*. Langoa is usually reckoned the slightly lesser wine of the two, being fuller and more tannic, but both are among the finest of clarets in a traditional manner and never less than good value, even in tricky years.

Léoville-Poyferré has had a much more patchy past, but in the 1980s it justified its great name with excellent forceful wines. What was the united Léoville like? It is hard to know how much of today's contrasts are due to diverging traditions and how much to the slightly varied *terroirs*. A different balance of Cabernet and Merlot will produce different barrels from the same vineyard. On the other hand, people who

taste the wines of several grape varieties from one vineyard before they have been 'assembled' in one barrel have often said that even while they tasted of the different grapes, each had the characteristic style of the estate.

South of the Léovilles Ducru-Beaucaillou with its Italianate mansion has established a style of its own, distinct in emphasizing finesse at a very high level, while its neighbour Branaire-Ducru is somehow more four-square. Château Beychevelle and its neighbour St-Pierre, on the other hand, convey finesse and elegance with an easy plumpness that is intensely seductive.

Château Gruaud-Larose begins the 'inland' section of St-Julien with wines whose richness and drive puts them in the very top rank. There is scarcely a more reliable château in Bordeaux than this, or indeed than its very big sister-château, Talbot, which occupies the central high ground of the commune. Talbot may be a shade less fine, but is consistently dense, smooth and savoury, perhaps owing almost as much to the skill of the Cordier family as to its site. Both

châteaux also make excellent second wines, respectively 'Sarget' and 'Connétable'.

Château du Glana, the large Cru Bourgeois next door, has not been as favoured recently as Hortevie, Moulin de la Rose, Terrey-Gros-Cailloux, and Lalande-Borie, a new creation of the owner of Ducru-Beaucaillou.

The last of the classed growths, Château Lagrange, used to be very highly regarded for its rich, substantial wine. A new (Japanese) régime since 1984 will undoubtedly bring it back into focus. It lies far back in the country in the sleepy hinterland on the border of St-Laurent (whose appellation is Haut-Médoc) and in a group with three other classed growths, all in different stages of resurrection. La Tour Carnet is most advanced; recently very attractive. Camensac was replanted a few years later by the owner of the huge and popular Cru Bourgeois Larose-Trintaudon. Its wine is gaining substance and recognition. Château Belgrave is the latest to be restored. Its first '80s promise future satisfaction.

The Central Médoc

This is the bridge passage of the Médoc, the mezzo forte between the andante of St-Julien and the allegro of Margaux. Four villages pass without a single classed growth; their appellation simply Haut-Médoc. Here the gravel dunes rise less proudly above the river. The commune of Cussac maintains some of the momentum of St-Julien with the outstanding Cru Bourgeois Château Lanessan, facing St-Julien across the canal that separates the parishes. Lanessan and its neighbour La Caronne Ste-Gemme (largely in neighbouring St-Laurent) are well-run properties whose owners can afford high standards.

Otherwise Cussac has little of the all-important gravel. The forest here comes close to the river. Château Beaumont occupies its best outcrop. Its wine is easy, fragrant, quick to mature. Oddly Château Tour du Haut-Moulin in Vieux Cussac is just the opposite: dark, old-fashioned, needing years – but worth it.

The riverside here is worth a visit to see the handsome 17th-century battlements of the Fort-Médoc – an anti-English precaution now turned to peaceful uses. At Lamarque an earlier fortress, the splendid Château de Lamarque, has established a name for carefully made, satisfyingly full-bodied wine with the true stamp of the Médoc on it. Lamarque is the Médoc's link with Blaye on the other side of the Gironde: a regular car-ferry service runs from the pier.

The fiddler on the press. A 50 year-old photograph catches the atmosphere of a past era. Yet such obsolete conditions sometimes produced wonderful wines.

A good deal of replanting has given the area a purposeful look which was lacking ten years ago. Château Malescasse was one of the first to be restored. And in the next commune south, Arcins, the big old properties of Château Barreyres and Château d'Arcins have been hugely replanted by the Castels, whose Castelvin is a staple of French diet. They, their well-managed neighbour Château Arnauld, and the cooperative 'Chevalier d'Ars' are steadily making Arcins better known. The food in the little Lion d'Or also helps.

It is not by the river, though, but west of Arcins that the gravel ridges rise and fan out inland, culminating at Grand Poujeaux (in the commune of Moulis) and at Listrac. These two communes are dignified with appellations of their own instead of the portmanteau 'Haut-Médoc'. In recent years Listrac and Moulis have risen steadily in estimation.

Quality rises with the gravel. Immediately over the parish boundary, Château Chasse-Spleen is one of the 'Exceptionnel' Bourgeois growths that can be considered as honorarily classified, almost as an honorary St-Julien, for its smoothness, its accessibility and yet its firm, oak-aged structure. Château Maucaillou can be just as fine. And Grand Poujeaux is surrounded by a knot of excellent Crus Bourgeois with 'Poujeaux' in their names: Theil, Gressier, Dutruch, La Closerie and more, all reliable for stout-hearted, long-lived red wines with the flavour that makes the Médoc unique.

Listrac has a higher plateau, chalk beneath its gravel, and a name for tough, tannic wines that

need time. The name here is Fourcas: the two châteaux that bear it, Hosten and Dupré, have long been outstanding. Much replanting and infilling has recently enlarged the vineyard considerably. Since 1973 Baron Edmond de Rothschild has created, with more than 300 acres (130 hectares), Château Clarke; the twin châteaux Fonréaud and Lestage have 230 acres (93 hectares) between them; Château Mauvezin has planted 150 acres (60 hectares). These re-developed estates temper the Listrac austerity and make rounder wines, which can only help to make the appellation better known.

Beyond the Jalle de Tiquetorte, in the south-east corner of the area, we enter the sphere of Margaux. The big Château Citran has begun a new era under Japanese ownership. It and the smaller Villegeorge (off this map, but a Cru Exceptionnel to watch) lie in the commune of Avensan. Both are well known, and approach Margaux in style.

Soussans is among the communes whose Appellation Contrôlée is not merely Haut-Médoc but Margaux. Its Château La Tour de Mons has made such fine wines in the past that critics have mooted promotion to classed growth. Tayac is another important Cru Bourgeois. Château Paveil de Luze was for a century the stylish country resort of one of the great merchant families of Bordeaux, making the kind of easy elegant wines the family liked.

Moulis, Listrac and Grand-Poujeaux between them count a score of far above-average Crus Bourgeois from gravel banks spreading inland.

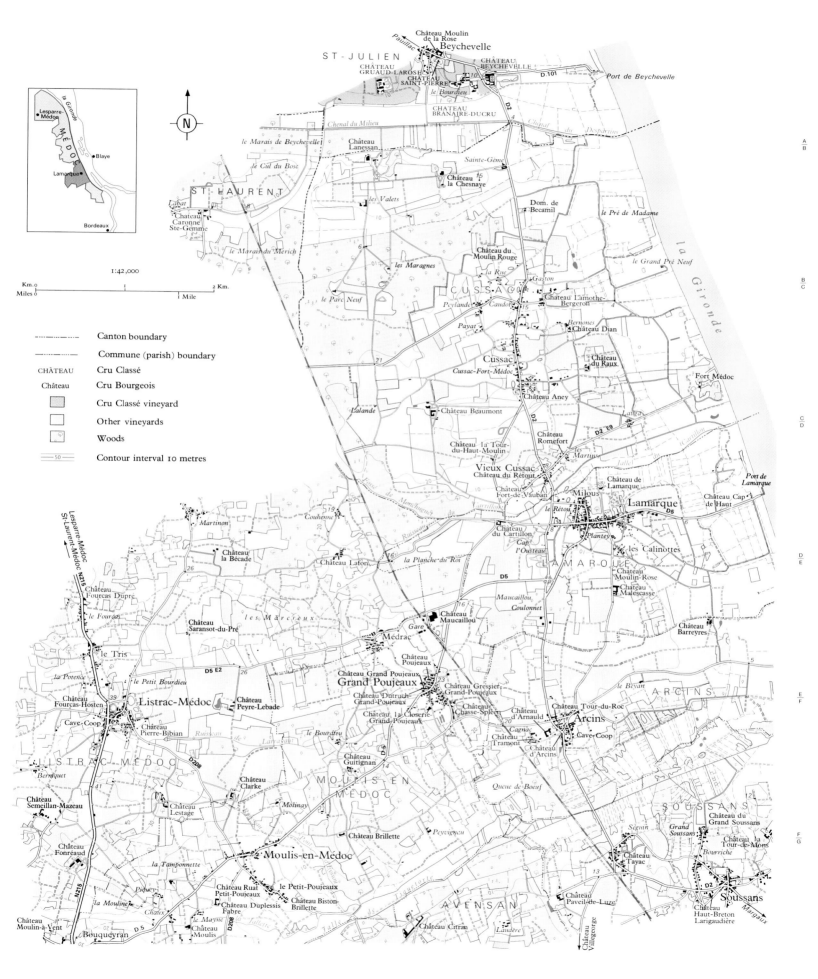

Km. 0   1   2 Km.
Miles 0   1 Mile

1:42,000

Canton boundary

Commune (parish) boundary

CHÂTEAU   Cru Classé

Château   Cru Bourgeois

Cru Classé vineyard

Other vineyards

Woods

—50—   Contour interval 10 metres

la Gironde

Lesparre-Médoc

MÉDOC

Blaye

Lamarque

Bordeaux

Château Moulin de la Rose

Beychevelle

ST-JULIEN

CHÂTEAU GRUAUD-LAROSE

CHÂTEAU SAINT-PIERRE

CHÂTEAU BEYCHEVELLE

D.101

Port de Beychevelle

le Bourdieu

CHÂTEAU BRANAIRE-DUCRU

D2

Chenal du Milieu

Chenal du Despartins

le Marais de Beychevelle

Château Lanessan

Sainte-Gème

Château la Chesnaye

les Valets

Dom. de Becamil

le Pré de Madame

ST-LAURENT

Labat

Château Caronne Ste-Gemme

le Cul du Bosc

le Marais du Merich

Château du Moulin Rouge

le Grand Pré Neuf

les Maragnes

la Rue

Gaston

le Parc Neuf

CUSSAGE

Peylande

Caudot

Château Lamothe-Bergeron

Payat

Bernones Château Dian

Château du Raux

Cussac

Cussac-Fort-Médoc

Château Aney

Fort Médoc

Lalande

Château Beaumont

Château Romefort

D2 E9

latga

Château la Tour-du-Haut-Moulin

les Martins

Vieux Cussac

Château du Rétout

Château Fort-de-Vauban

Milous

Château de Lamarque

Port de Lamarque

le Rétout

Lamarque

Château Cap de Haut

D5

Lesparre-Médoc
St-Laurent-Médoc

N215

Martinon

Couhenne

Château du Cartillon

Cap l'Ousteau

LAMARQUE

Château la Bécade

Château Lafon

la Planche-du-Roi

les Calinottes

Château Moulin-Rose

Château Fourcas Dupré

le Fourcas

les Marcieux

D5

Château Malescasse

Maucaillou

Coulonnet

Château Saransot-du-Pré

Gare

Médrac

Château Maucaillou

Château Barreyres

le Tris

la Potence

D5 E2

le Petit Bourdieu

Château Grand Poujeaux

Grand Poujeaux

Château Poujeaux

Château Gressier Grand-Poujeaux

le Beyan

ARCINS

Château Fourcas-Hosten

Listrac-Médoc

Château Dutruch Grand-Poujeaux

Château Chasse-Spleen

Château Tour-du-Roc

Cave-Coop

Château Pierre-Bibian

Château la Closerie Grand-Poujeaux

Château d'Arnauld

Cagnac

Arcins

Cave-Coop

Ruisseau de

Laraval

le Bourdieu

Château Tramont

Château d'Arcins

Château Guitignan

LISTRAC-MÉDOC

D208

Bernuquet

MOULIS-EN-MÉDOC

Queue de Boeuf

SOUSSANS

Château Semeillan-Mazeau

Château Clarke

Château Lestage

Mòlinay

Grand Soussans

Château du Grand Soussans

Château Fonréaud

la Tamponnette

Château Brillette

Peyvigneu

Séguin

Bourriche

Château la Tour-de-Mons

Château Tayac

N215

Moulis-en-Médoc

13

AVENSAN

Château Paveil-de-Luze

D2

Soussans

Château Moulin-à-Vent

D5

Piquey

Chaux

Château Ruat Petit-Poujeaux

le Petit-Poujeaux

Château Biston-Brillette

Château Haut-Breton Larigaudière

Margaux

Bouqueyran

la Mouline

Château Duplessis Fabre

le Mayne

Château Moulis

D208

Château Citran

Laudère

Château Villegeorge

Margaux and the Southern Médoc

Margaux and its 'satellites' are considered to make the Médoc's most polished and fragrant wine. Their historical record says so; their present is less consistent: there are more second- and third-growths here than anywhere, and most have sadly fallen from grace. The picking-up process is underway, but long overdue.

The map shows a rather different picture from Pauillac or St-Julien. Instead of the châteaux being spread out evenly over the land, they are huddled together in the village. An examination of the almost unliftable volumes of commune maps in the *mairie* shows a degree of intermingling of one estate with another which is far greater than in, say, Pauillac. One would therefore look to differences in technique and tradition more than changes of soil to try to explain the differences between châteaux.

In fact the soil of Margaux is the thinnest in the Médoc, with the highest proportion of rough gravel. It has the least to offer the vine in the way of nourishment but it drains well even in rainy years. The result is wines that start life comparatively 'supple', although in poor years they can turn out thin. In good and great years, however, all the stories about the virtues of gravel are justified: there is a delicacy about good Margaux, and a sweet haunting perfume, that can make it the most exquisite claret of all.

The wines of Châteaux Margaux and Palmer are the ones that most often reach such heights. Château Margaux is not only a first-growth of the Médoc, it is the one that most looks the part: a pediment at the end of an avenue; the air of a palace with *chais* to match. After over a decade in the doldrums new owners began to make superlative wine here again in 1978. Each vintage confirms its status. The third-growth Palmer, however, keeps up a formidable challenge.

Château Lascombes (which was restored and greatly enlarged by Alexis Lichine, and now belongs to the English brewers Bass Charrington) is a case where buying more land (there are now 235 acres (95 hectares)) diluted second-growth quality. Rather than carrying out strict selection the management opted to make vast quantities

of rosé; something hardly known in the Médoc. Since 1985, however, Lascombes has been serious again.

Of the famous pair which used to be the big Rausan estate, as famous in the 18th century as Léoville was in St-Julien, Rausan-Ségla is today much the better, having reformed in the 1980s. The smaller Rauzan-Gassies still lags far behind second-growth standards.

There are several distinguished pairs of châteaux in Margaux. The two second-growths Brane-Cantenac and Durfort-Vivens are jointly owned (by the ubiquitous Lurton family), yet make distinctly different wine: the Brane fragrant and almost melting, the Durfort much less generous. The little third-growth Desmirail has recently been resurrected to join them as a third bowstring. Pouget is the brother of Boyd-Cantenac. Ferrière is made at Lascombes. Malescot St-Exupéry (often miraculously scented and one of the best of Margaux) and the very small third-growth Château d'Alesme (formerly Marquis d'Alesme) belong to brothers.

Still in Margaux proper, Château Marquis de Terme, although rarely seen abroad, makes good rather old-fashioned wine, and Château d'Issan is perhaps the most beautiful house in the Médoc: a 17th-century manor within the complete moat of an old château-fort by the river. The admirable gentle slope of its vineyard to the road is one of the best situations in Margaux.

The Crus Bourgeois include a group on the theme of Labégorce: their names stick in the mind like a nursery rhyme. Of the three, the Belgian-owned Labégorce-Zédé is currently the best known, though Château Labégorce is giving it a hard run.

Our rather erratic path to and fro in Margaux becomes a little simpler as the châteaux thin out in Cantenac and farther south. Most of the land in the communes of Cantenac, Labarde and Arsac, as well as Soussans to the north, has been granted the appellation Margaux, making wines of very similar style and quality. If anything, Cantenac and hamlets further south make more powerful but less fragrant wines.

In Cantenac itself, the late Alexis Lichine's own château of Prieuré is deservedly famous for making some of Margaux's most consistent claret — and also for being the first to admit passers-by in a way which has only just become accepted practice. Château Kirwan was in eclipse until the 1980s, but has been restored and is beginning to shine.

Another tale of restoration and renewed quality has been the lonely Château du Tertre, isolated on high ground in Arsac, saved since the 1960s by the owner of Château Calon-Ségur. Recent vintages have been excellent.

Château Cantenac-Brown, which competes for the prize of ugliest Médoc château (it looks like a Victorian English school), flanks Brane-Cantenac. It was recently bought, like Pichon-Baron in Pauillac, by AXA insurance, which should ensure it a more prosperous future.

There are three more important classed growths before the Haut-Médoc vineyards come to an end: Giscours, whose half-timbered farm buildings in the overblown style of Le Touquet or Deauville face a most impressive sweep of vines and harbour dense, noble and concentrated wine; Cantemerle, a perfect Sleeping Beauty château, deep in a wood of huge trees and quiet pools, whose wine is more known for elegance; and the top-flight Château La Lagune, a neat 18th-century building just off the Bordeaux road (and the nearest classed growth of the Médoc to the city). La Lagune's style of wine is singularly rich and suave.

Dauzac, the fourth classed growth of this southern area, has recently raised its sights, although its nominally bourgeois neighbour Siran has long made better wine. Siran and Château d'Angludet, prettily situated by a stream and the home of one of Bordeaux's wisest heads, Peter Sichel, consistently make wine of classed-growth quality.

Below and right: a magnificent concentration of Crus Classés distinguishes Margaux and its area. They tend to emphasize their prestige with more gilded labels than the rest of the Médoc.

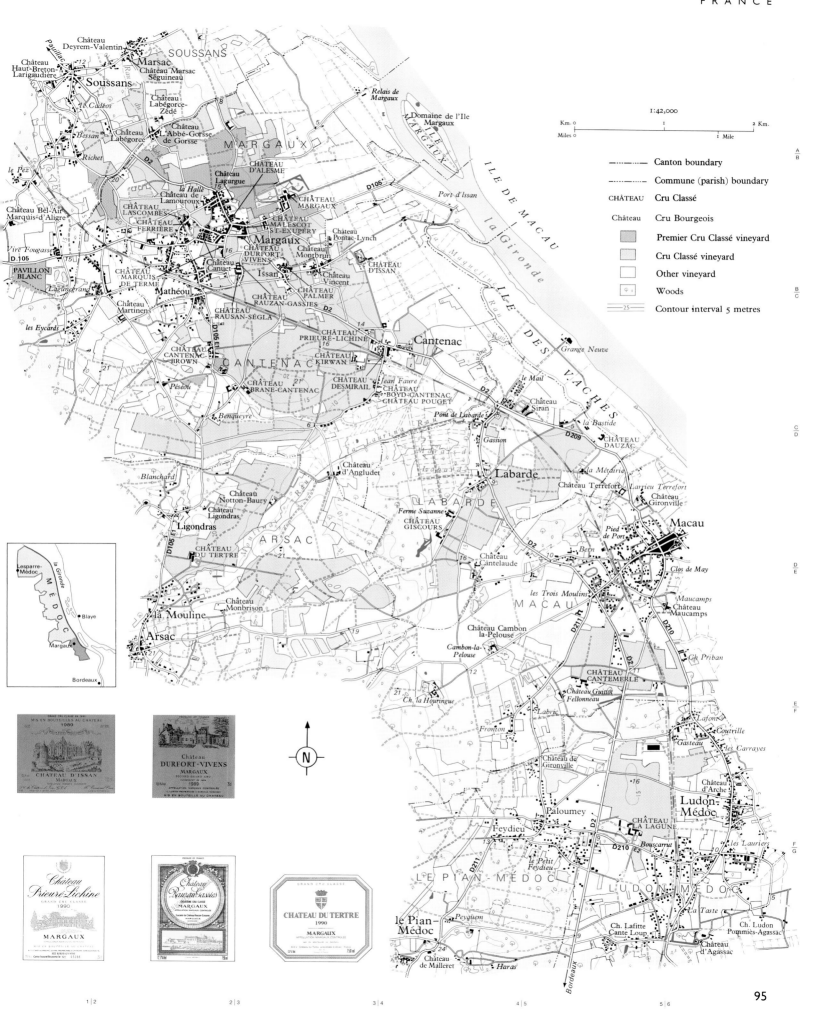

1:42,000

Km. 0 ——————— 1 ——————— 2 Km.
Miles 0 —————————————————— 1 Mile

- - - - - - - Canton boundary
- · - · - · - Commune (parish) boundary
CHÂTEAU Cru Classé
Château Cru Bourgeois
Premier Cru Classé vineyard
Cru Classé vineyard
Other vineyard
Woods
Contour interval 5 metres

Graves and Entre-Deux-Mers

As little as ten years ago there was no good reason for a detailed map of the southern half of the Bordeaux vineyard. All the interest lay to the north, in the red-wine country of the Médoc and St-Emilion–Pomerol – except for the few classified Graves properties on the outskirts of the city, now promoted to their own appellation of Pessac-Léognan (see pages 98 and 99), and the isolated concentration of Sauternes and Barsac (see pages 100 and 101).

There is much more to the Graves region than what you might call, by analogy with the Médoc, the Haut-Graves, but until recently it had not asserted itself. Entre-Deux-Mers, the lozenge of land between the rivers Garonne and Dordogne, was a generalized name for a harmless dry white. Few properties had established a name. The same was true of the hilly right bank of the Garonne opposite Graves, from Langon via Cadillac and Langoiran down to Bordeaux itself: the Premières Côtes de Bordeaux. The only names that made the knowing lick their lips were Ste-Croix-du-Mont and Loupiac. The occasional bottle of something remarkably like Sauternes kept their names alive.

Things have changed radically. The southern end of the Graves has come to life. Nondescript white has given place to fresh lively dry wines – and to a new wave of reds of deep fruit without hard tannins. Langon is now a regular resort of buyers looking for flavour and value. In central and southern Graves old properties, notably in the once-famous parishes of Portets, Landiras and St-Pierre-de-Mons, have new owners and new philosophies. And the Premières Côtes are delivering much better wine, abandoning a non-committal style of not-quite-dry white in favour of reds and clean modern whites.

It is too much to claim that the liquorous Ste-Croix-du-Mont has become a money-making proposition, as it once was, but three châteaux, Loubens, the tiny de Tastes and Lousteau-Vieil, make great efforts, and in neighbouring Loupiac Châteaux Loupiac-Gaudiet and Ricaud are ready to run the risks inherent in making truly sweet, rather than semi-sweet, wine.

Cérons, too, Barsac's northern neighbour in the Graves, a separate appellation long forgotten (it includes Illats and Podensac) has found new prosperity (eg at Château d'Archambeau) by making mainstream white and red under the Graves appellation, largely abandoning its tradition of a style midway between Graves and Barsac: softly rather than stickily sweet.

The ability of Graves soil to make red and white wine equally well is seen at Portets at Châteaux Rahoul and Chantegrive, and in properties dotted around Arbanats and Castres. It has also emerged in several small properties around Langon. One group (including Châteaux Chicane, Gaillat and others) is run by Langon négociant Pierre Coste, who makes fruity, slightly dusty, savoury red for drinking young. Another centres around Château Magence at St-Pierre-de-Mons, which vies with its neighbours Châteaux Respide, St-Pierre, Toumilon and others in making lively dry Sauvignon white and good sturdy red. Meanwhile in the forests just west of Sauternes the ancient Château de Landiras has come to life with densely fragrant Sémillon white and reds to age.

A number of Premières Côtes properties have distinguished themselves recently. Château Reynon at Béguey near Cadillac has succeeded with fresh Sauvignon white and very fruity red. The house of Cordier has an important position with 148 acres (60 hectares) of Châteaux Gardera and Tanesse. The Danish owners of Château de Haux have made thoroughly convincing modern red and white wines, while at Château Carsin the perfectionist new owners are Finns.

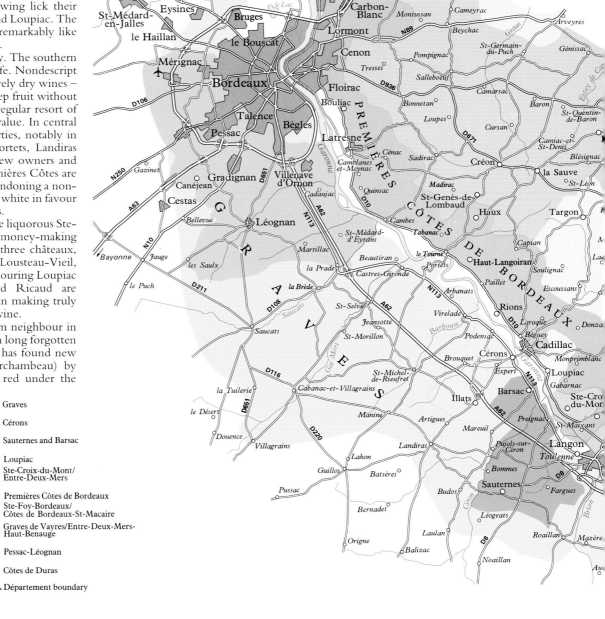

Graves

Cérons

Sauternes and Barsac

Loupiac

Ste-Croix-du-Mont/ Entre-Deux-Mers

Premières Côtes de Bordeaux

Ste-Foy-Bordeaux/ Côtes de Bordeaux-St-Macaire

Graves de Vayres/Entre-Deux-Mers-Haut-Benauge

Pessac-Léognan

Côtes de Duras

— · — · — Département boundary

Château Fayau at Cadillac is keeping up the local tradition of sweet fruity white.

By far the biggest territory is Entre-Deux-Mers – a name synonymous with reputable if unglamorous dry whites, but now one of the principal sources of red Bordeaux or Bordeaux Supérieur as well. A number of substantial châteaux have changed the aspect of the region, especially of the parishes in the north along the Dordogne Valley, from one of mixed farm and orchard to vinous monoculture. Some of the biggest are the Lurton family's excellent Château Bonnet at Grézillac, Launay at Soussac and Toutigeac in the little-used sub-appellation Haut-Benauge.

Above: Entre-Deux-Mers is gently rolling country, dotted with big pleasant country houses that produce middling-good wine. The vine-spacing in this vineyard is double the traditional width between rows to make mechanization and machine harvesting easier.

Right: the southern Graves and the appellation facing it across the Garonne are rising in estimation for both red and white wines.

Pessac-Léognan

It was here, in the southern outskirts of the city of Bordeaux, that the whole concept of great red Bordeaux was launched, in the 1660s, by the owner of Château Haut-Brion. Its arid sand and gravel had already supplied the region and its export market with its best red wine since at least 1300, when the archbishop who became Pope Clement V (of Avignon) planted what is now Château Pape Clément.

Pine trees have always been the main crop of the Graves. The vineyards are clearings, often isolated from one another in heavily forested country crossed by shallow river valleys. The map shows how the city and its oldest vineyards reach out into the forest, which continues (as the Landes) south and east from here to the Basque foothills of the Pyrenees.

Now the city has swallowed all the vineyards in its path except the superlative group on the deep gravel soils of Pessac: Haut-Brion and its neighbour and rival, La Mission Haut-Brion, the little Les Carmes Haut-Brion and, further out of town, the archi-episcopal Pape Clément.

Châteaux Haut-Brion and La Mission (with its former second wine, now smaller brother, La Tour Haut-Brion, and its incomparable little white vineyard, Laville Haut-Brion) are found on opposite sides of the old Arcachon road which runs through Pessac. Haut-Brion is every inch a first-growth, a suave equilibrium of force and finesse with the singularity of great Graves: hints of earth and fern, tobacco and caramel; a flavour not so high-toned but frequently more intriguing than even a Lafite or a Margaux. La Mission tastes denser, riper, more savage – and often just as splendid. In 1984 the American owners of Haut-Brion bought its old rival – not to unite the vineyards but to continue the match. Few pairings show so vividly what the *terroir*, the uniqueness of each piece of ground, means on this Bordeaux soil.

This map shows what has been termed 'Haut-Graves', but which in 1987 was given its own appellation: Pessac-Léognan. Most of the wine is red, as in the Médoc. Pessac-Léognan differs in producing a very little white of sometimes superlative quality, in most cases from châteaux also classified for their red wine. A very simple 'yes or no' classification, last reviewed in 1959, includes 15 châteaux, six for both red and white and two for white wine only. A revision is expected in 2000: it will certainly include châteaux beyond this map, in the wider Graves to the south which is busily upgrading and converting from the predominant white of old times to a healthy mix, with red dominant.

The commune of Léognan, well into the forest, is the hub of this map. Domaine de Chevalier is its outstanding property, despite its modest appearance. The domaine has never had a château. Although its *chais* and *cuvier* have been impeccably rebuilt and its vineyard expanded recently, it retains the air of a farm in a clearing in the pines. There is something almost Californian about the little winery with its two flavours . . . both of which turn out to be brilliant. Alas, there are only about 800 cases of

Above: the little Domaine de Chevalier in the west of Léognan prospered, expanded and rebuilt during the halcyon 1980s. The new circular *cuvier* epitomizes modern Bordeaux. In any new classification this property would be a second-growth.
Right: Crus Classés of Pessac and Léognan. Six are classified for red and white, Laville Haut Brion and Couhins for white only; the rest for reds.

the magnificent barrel-fermented Sauvignon/Sémillon white made each year.

Château Haut-Bailly is the other leading classed growth of Léognan; unusual in these parts for making only red wine, but deeply and persuasively. In recent vintages the restoration of Château de Fieuzal has given it a challenger and the world another very fine white – but, as is the way with the top Graves properties, only in exiguous amounts. Malartic-Lagravière is similar, though its wine has always seemed rather harder. It now belongs to Laurent-Perrier of Champagne. Château Carbonnieux is different. This old Benedictine establishment has always been more famous for its fine reliable white than for its red. And Château Olivier is known as another white-wine specialist.

No family is more active in the Graves today than the Lurtons, owners of châteaux all over Bordeaux, but in the Graves the driving force behind much of the recent renewal. Châteaux La Louvière, Rochemorin, Cruzeau, Bouscaut and part of Couhins are theirs; each contending for higher honours (Bouscaut, although classified, is not currently the best).

The commune of Martillac brings Pessac-Léognan to an end with two classed growths whose performance of late suggests they still need to prove themselves: the large (for the Graves) and largely red Smith Haut-Lafitte, and the less well-known La Tour-Martillac. As in the Graves as a whole, recent vintages show them tuning up for a distinctly brighter future.

Sauternes and Barsac

Left: Yquem is the hub of Sauternes and its Grand Cru *hors pair*, owned by the Lur Saluces family for two centuries. Yet even here there is land unfit for vines, badly drained and in danger of late spring frosts. *Above and right*: Sauternes labels match the glittering gold of the wine. A few châteaux make a strong dry wine as well as the famous sweet one, particularly in poor vintages.

All the other districts of Bordeaux mapped here make wines that can be compared with, and preferred to, one another. Sauternes is incomparable: a speciality which finds its only real rivals not in France but in Germany and in the legendary Hungarian Tokay. It depends on local conditions and on a very unusual wine-making technique. In great years the results can be sublime: a very sweet, rich-textured, flower-scented, glittering golden liquid. In other years it can frankly fail to be Sauternes (properly so-called) at all.

Above all it is only a few châteaux of Sauternes – and in this we include Barsac – that make such wine. Ordinary Sauternes, whether called 'Haut' or not makes no difference, is just sweet white wine.

The local conditions in this warm and fertile corner of Aquitaine include the mists which form along the little River Ciron on autumn evenings, lasting till after dawn. The special technique which only the considerable châteaux can afford to employ is to pick over the vineyard as many as eight or nine times, beginning in September and sometimes going on until November. This is to take full advantage of the peculiar form of mould (known as *Botrytis cinerea* to the scientist, or *pourriture noble* – 'noble rot' – to the poet) which forms on the grapes during the mild, misty nights, then multiplies in the heat of the day to reduce the grape skins to brown pulp.

Instead of affecting the blighted grapes with a flavour of rot, this botrytis engineers the escape of a proportion of the water in them, leaving the sugar and the flavouring elements in the juice more concentrated than ever. The result is wine with an intensity of taste and scent and a smooth, almost oil-like, texture which can be made no other way.

But it does mean picking the grapes as they shrivel, berry by berry – and the proprietors of little-known châteaux have no alternative but to pick the entire crop at once, and hope for as much botrytis as possible.

Production is absurdly low, since evaporation is actually encouraged. From each one of its 247 acres (100 hectares) Château d'Yquem, the most famous of the Sauternes producers, makes only about 7 hectolitres (933 bottles) of wine. A first-class Médoc vineyard would make five or six times as much.

The risk element is appalling, since bad weather in October can rob the grower of all chance of making sweet wine, and sometimes of any wine at all. Costs are correspondingly high, and the price of even the finest Sauternes (with the exception of Yquem), though rising recently, makes it one of the least profitable wines to the grower. Few drinkers realize what a bargain they are offered.

Sauternes was the only area outside the Médoc to be classed in 1855. Château d'Yquem was made a First Great Growth – a rank created for it alone in all Bordeaux. Strangely, for its dominant hill-top position, it has a 'perched', therefore unusually high, water-table that keeps its vines growing well even in drought.

Eleven other châteaux were made first-growths and 12 more were classed seconds. But the old ranks are out of date today. Dedication is what counts.

Five communes, including Sauternes itself, are entitled to use the name. Barsac, the biggest of them, has the alternative of calling its wine either Sauternes or Barsac, although its wine tends less to lusciousness, more to clean sweetness and finesse.

Styles of wine vary almost as much as standards. Château Suduiraut in Preignac (when on form) is lush and sumptuous; Château Rieussec (bought by the Rothschilds of Lafite in 1984) fine-drawn and elegant; Château Guiraud (recently restored) potentially a near-rival to Yquem. Lafaurie-Peyraguey, Sigalas-Rabaud, the Châteaux Fargues and Raymond-Lafon, Bastor Lamontagne and Gilette are the present names to conjure with in Sauternes. In Barsac, Coutet, Climens, Nairac and all three châteaux with the prefix Doisy- lead the field.

The economics of Sauternes are always knife-edge. For decades it could not be produced profitably at all: poor vintages persisted; demand dwindled. Vineyards were pulled up, or planted instead with red grapes, or used to make dry white wine – which cannot even be sold as Graves; its appellation is bare Bordeaux.

Happily the last ten years have seen a revival. The late 1970s and the 1980s saw a run of good vintages, new idealistic owners have appeared, and Sauternes is back in fashion. In France it is highly appreciated as a partner for *foie gras*. The Anglo-Saxon world, with Scandinavia and Germany, drinks it as the richest of endings to a rich meal.

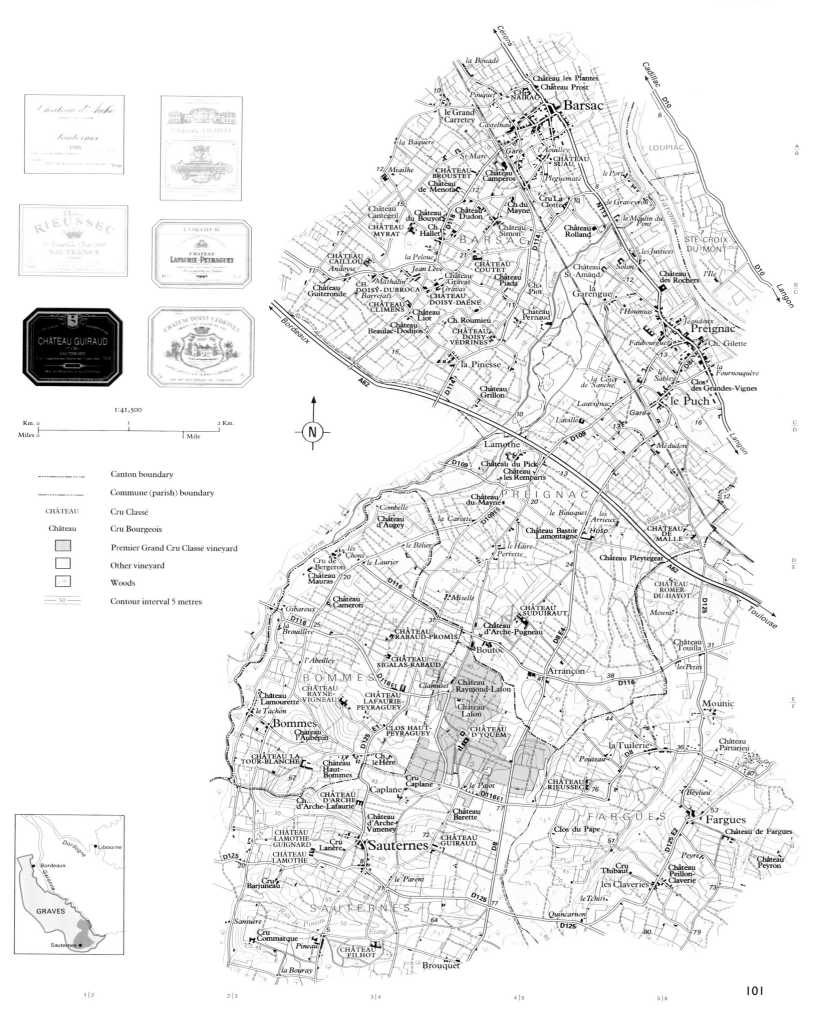

The Libournais

Left: Château St-Georges dominates the St-Emilion plateau from its hilltop in the neighbouring village of St-Georges. It was built in 1774 by Victor Louis, who also designed Bordeaux's theatre.

The French name for this region derives from its ancient capital, Libourne. Anglo-Saxons with Bordeaux in their blood call it 'the right bank' – of the river-system of the Garonne and the Dordogne, that is. (Though nobody seems to call the Médoc the left bank.)

Its most illustrious parishes are St-Emilion and Pomerol. But they are the heart of a much larger and more diffuse wine district. To the south and east seven small villages share the name of St-Emilion, and a further five to the northeast can add the name to their own. Pomerol adjoins the communes of Fronsac, Néac and Lalande.

With their mixture of vines, woods and pastures and their little hills and valleys, the villages to the east, north and west are more attractive than the monotonous vineyard of the plateau in the centre.

Even today they still seem remote and little-visited. It is hard even to identify the modest châteaux. Formerly a network of private contacts all over France, Belgium and the Low Countries was the principal market for their sound and solid red wine. Recently, though, they have considerably raised their profile (and their standards).

The châteaux shown on this map are most of the bigger and better known of the hinterland and of Fronsac, which holds a special position as a region in its own right. Fronsac wines are splendidly fruity and full of character, tannic when young, a touch rustic in style compared with the high gloss of, say, Pomerol, but improving year by year with investment in modernization. The investors include the leading négociant of Libourne, Jean-Pierre Moueix,

whose intervention is having a dramatic effect, especially in the limestone slopes along the river known as Canon-Fronsac.

North of Pomerol, Néac shares the appellation of Lalande-de-Pomerol: both are like Pomerol, unpolished. Châteaux de Bel-Air, des Annereaux and Siaurac provide polish.

The equivalent back-country châteaux to the north of St-Emilion are led in reputation by the splendid Château St-Georges, which overlooks the whole district from its hill. But many make excellent wine.

The vine is still dominant in this pretty, hilly landscape, even if there are no names to conjure with. Montagne makes excellent 'satellite' St-Emilion. So do Lussac and Puisseguin, often making up in satisfying solidity what they lack in finesse. Still further east the Côtes de Castillon and Francs keep up the family resemblance. Château Puygueraud is the outstanding property of the Côte des Francs, but the whole district is worth close scrutiny.

The cluster of villages east of St-Emilion is ranked higher. In St-Laurent, Château Larcis-Ducasse is a Grand Cru and rated among the top 25 or so wines of St-Emilion. Château Bellefont-Belcier in the same commune is also well known. To the north in St-Christophe, Château Haut-Sarpe is another Grand Cru, and Château Fombrauge has a high reputation. On the outcrop of the Côtes at St-Hippolyte, Château de Ferrand makes good wine and just to the east in St-Etienne Château Puy-Blanquet has a distinguished name. These châteaux and several others command prices comparable to St-Emilion Grands Crus from the central area mapped on page 105.

Above: labels from the eastern side of St-Emilion.
Right: labels from some of the top châteaux of Fronsac.

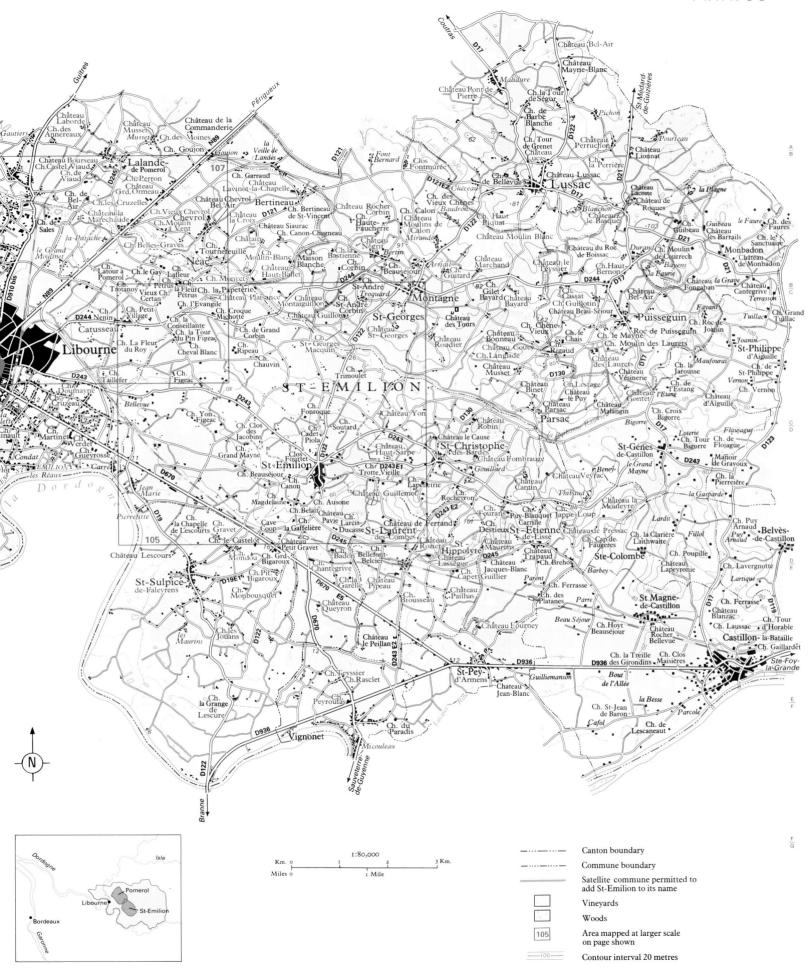

St-Emilion

The ancient and beautiful town of St-Emilion is propped in the corner of an escarpment above the Dordogne. Behind it on the plateau vines flow steadily on into Pomerol. Beside it along the ridge they swoop down into the plain. It is the little rural gem of the Bordelais – inland and upland in spirit, Roman in origin, hollow with cellars and heady with wine.

Even the church at St-Emilion is a cellar: cut, like them all, out of solid limestone. The hotel restaurant in the town square is actually on the church roof, and you sit beside the belfry to eat your lampreys stewed in red wine *à la Bordelaise*.

St-Emilion makes rich red wine. Before many people can really come to terms with the dryness and slight asperity of the Médoc they love the solid tastiness of St-Emilion. The best of them in ripe and sunny seasons grow almost sweet as they mature.

The grapes of St-Emilion are the Merlot and the Cabernet Franc. Cabernet Sauvignon, which ripens later, has problems ripening in this climate, slightly less tempered by the ocean. On the whole their wines here take less time to reach perfection than Médoc wines, if a little longer than Pomerols: say four years for the wine of a poor vintage; eight and upwards for a good one. Yet they can live as long.

There are two distinct districts of St-Emilion, not counting the lesser vineyards of the river plain and the parishes to the east and northeast which are allowed to use the name (described and mapped on pages 102–3).

One group of the inner châteaux lies on the border of Pomerol, on the sandy and gravelly plateau. The most famous of this group, and the whole of St-Emilion, is Cheval Blanc, a trim cream-painted house in a grove of trees which is far from suggesting the splendid red wine, some of the world's most full-blooded, which its vines produce.

Of Cheval Blanc's neighbours, it is the big Château Figeac which comes nearest to its level, but in a lighter, very fragrant style, from even more gravelly soil and with a proportion of Cabernet Sauvignon. Châteaux La Dominique, La Tour Figeac and Corbin are also outstanding.

The other, larger, group, the Côtes St-Emilion, occupies the escarpment around the town. At the abrupt edge of the plateau you can see that not very thick soil covers the soft but solid limestone in which the cellars are cut. At Château Ausone, the jewel of the Côtes, in one of the finest situations in all Bordeaux with the Dordogne Valley at your feet, you can

Above: the Jurade de St-Emilion, the district's ancient association of winegrowers, processes in scarlet robes through the streets of the town.
Below: Château Ausone commands a view of the Côtes to the east, and of the wide valley of the Dordogne.

walk into a cellar with vines, as it were, on the ground floor above you.

The Côtes wines may not be quite so fruity as the 'Graves' wines from the plateau (the name Graves is confusingly applied to them because of their gravel soil), but at their best they are some of the most perfumed and 'generous' wines of Bordeaux. They usually have 1% more alcohol than wine from the Médoc. The Côtes provide shelter from the north and west, an incline towards the sun, and relative immunity to frost. On the plateau around Cheval Blanc a slight dip in the ground acts as a sump in which freezing air can collect on cloudless winter nights. On one dreadful night in February 1956 the temperature went down to –11°F (–24°C). So many vines were killed that it took five or six years for production to pick up again.

Château Ausone is to the Côtes what Cheval Blanc is to the Graves. Château Belair, in the same ownership, is only a short step down. Châteaux Canon, Magdelaine, La Gaffelière, Pavie, l'Arrosée and Clos Fourtet would certainly be on a shortlist of the top Côtes wines: but the comfort of St-Emilion to the ordinary wine-lover is the number of other châteaux of moderate fame and consistently high standards which provide utterly enjoyable and relatively affordable wine.

St-Emilion is not classified as the Médoc is. It merely divides its châteaux (most recently in 1991) into Premiers Grands Crus Classés, Grands Crus Classés and plain Grands Crus. There are 11 of the first, headed by Cheval Blanc and Ausone in a separate category of two, and 63 of the second. The plain Grands Crus run into hundreds. Since 1984 all châteaux have had to meet certain objective criteria, including tasting by jury, to claim 'Classé' status. In practice the list has changed little.

The Grands Crus which normally fetch the highest prices are shown on the map in larger type than the others.

Most of St-Emilion's best
châteaux are clustered in
the 'Côtes' area around
the town. The great
exceptions are Cheval
Blanc and Figeac on the
plateau to the northwest.

Map labels:

POMEROL
Libourne
MONTAGNE
Montagne
ST-GEORGES
St-Christophe-des-Bardes

CHÂTEAU L'EVANGILE
CHÂTEAU LA CONSEILLANTE
Château Croque Michotte
la Croix Chante-Caille
Maillet
Guadet-Veyrat
Château la Grave Figeac
Ch. Grand Corbin Despagne
le Jura
Château Haut-Corbin
Château Carrie
Maison Neuve
Château la Tour du Pin Figeac
Château la Dominique
Ch. Corbin-Michotte
Château Corbin
Ch. Grand Corbin-Manuel
Château de Grand Corbin
CH. CHEVAL BLANC
Château Jean-Faure
Château Ripeau
Jean Voisin
Château
Toulifaut
Château la Tour-Figeac
Château Chauvin
Vachon
Clos Grand Faurie
la Grange Neuve
Fortin
Bézineau
le Fougueyrat
Château Trimoulet
Sarrensot
Château du Tailhas
CHÂTEAU FIGEAC
Petit-Montlabert
Château Montlabert
la Rose
Mérissac
Bellevue
Petit Figeac
la Croix Figeac
Château Moulin-de-Cadet
Ch. Cap-de-Mourlin
Château Dassault
Château Grand Barrail Lamarzelle Figeac (Hotel)
Château Lamarzelle
Balau
Pavillon-Cadet
Château Larmande
Château Clos de l'Oratoire Peyraud
Médoc
Château Yon-Figeac
Château Laniote
Château Fonroque
Château Faurie-de-Souchard
Magnan
le Cadet
Château Soutard
Château Petit Faurie de Soutard
Berthonneau
Château Laroze
Ch. Clos des Jacobins
Château la-Fleur-Pourret
Château Cadet-Piola
Château Cadet-Bon
Château Mauvezin
Jacquemeau
Château Grand-Mayne
Ch. Franc Mayne
Ch. Grand Pontet
Château Pontet-Clauzure
Ch. Guadet St-Julien
Ch. Balestard la-Tonnelle
Château Haut-Sarpe
le Rivalon
Château Coutet
Château Trois Moulins
Château Coutspaude
Château Sansonnet
Sarpe
Bord
Château Belleyue
Ch. Beau Séjour Bécot
Ch. Grandes-Murailles
Ch. la Carte et le Chatelet
CLOS FOURTET
Château Villemaurine
Château Couvent des Jacobins
Château Trotte Vieille
St-Christophe
Château Tour Fonrazade
Château Beauséjour Duffau Lagarosse
St-Martin
Château la Serre
le Barrail
Château l'Angelus
CHÂTEAU CANON
Ch. la Clotte
Château Bergat
la Barde
Fonrazade
Mazérat
St-Emilion
Ch. Chapelle Madeleine
Lapelletrie
Royllan
Château Matras
Ch. Curé Bon la Madeleine
Ch. Pavie-Macquin
Mondotte Belhle
Daugay
Pin de Fleur
Ch. Berliquet
CHÂTEAU MAGDELAINE
Ch. Moulin St-Georges
CHÂTEAU AUSONE
Ch. Troplong Mondot
Château Fonplegade
CHÂTEAU BELAIR
les Carrieres
St-Laurent
Château Tertre-Daugay
CHÂTEAU LA GAFFELIÈRE
St-Georges
Château St-Georges Côte Pavie
Château Pavie-Decesse
Goudeau
Château l'Arrosée
Cave Coop
Château Pavie-Macquin
Château la Clusière
CHÂTEAU PAVIE
Château Larcis-Ducasse
Château Bellefont-Belcier
St-Laurent-des-Combes
Château Canon-la-Gaffelière
l'Arsy
vers D670
Gueyrot

vers D670

N

Legend:

— — — Canton boundary
— · — Commune (parish) boundary
CHÂTEAU   Premier Grand Cru Classé (1991)
Château   Leading Grand Cru Classé
Château   Other Cru Classé
▨   Premier Grand Cru Classé vineyard
□   Other vineyard
⬚   Woods
══ 25 ══ Contour interval 5 metres

1:34,250

Km. 0 _____ 1 Km.
Miles 0 _____ 1 Mile

Wine labels (bottom):

Château CHEVAL BLANC — 1er Grand Cru Classé — St-Emilion Grand Cru — 1990

CHÂTEAU AUSONE — 1er GRAND CRU CLASSÉ — SAINT-EMILION GRAND CRU — 1983

CHATEAU BELAIR — 1er GRAND CRU CLASSÉ — SAINT-EMILION GRAND CRU — 1983

Château Canon — 1er Grand Cru Classé — 1990

Château BEAUSÉJOUR — SPECIMEN — Saint Emilion Grand Cru — 1990

Château LA DOMINIQUE — St Emilion Grand Cru Classé — 1986

Château LA GAFFELIÈRE — SAINT-EMILION — 1er GRAND CRU CLASSÉ — 1990

Château Pavie — 1er GRAND CRU CLASSÉ — SAINT-EMILION GRAND CRU — 1990 — VALETTE

CHATEAU-FIGEAC — PREMIER GRU CLASSÉ — St ÉMILION — 1990

CHÂTEAU MAGDELAINE — SAINT EMILION 1er GRAND CRU CLASSÉ — 1982

Clos Fourtet — 1er Grand Cru Classé — SAINT-EMILION GRAND CRU — 1989 — LURTON F.

CORDIER — CHÂTEAU Clos des Jacobins — Saint Emilion Grand Cru — 1990

105

1|2   2|3   3|4   4|5   5|6

Pomerol

Pomerol is, relatively speaking, the new star in the firmament of Bordeaux. You would think it had all been known for centuries. Yet although Romans had vineyards in Pomerol, a hundred years ago it was known only for 'good common wine' – much of it, surprisingly, white. Even 50 years ago it was not considered in the top flight. Yet today its best château fetches a far higher price than the first-growths of the Médoc, and an astonishing number of small properties, for an area no bigger than St-Julien, are generally agreed to be among the best in the whole of Bordeaux.

Pomerol is such a curious corner of the world that it is hard to get your bearings. There is no real village centre; every family makes wine, and every house stands apart among its vines. The landscape is evenly dotted with modest houses – each rejoicing in the name of château. The church stands oddly isolated too, like yet another little wine estate. And that is Pomerol; there is nothing more to see.

Pomerol is another big gravel bank, slightly rising and falling but remarkably flat overall. In the western and southern parts the soil tends to be sandy; to the east and north, where it meets St-Emilion, it is usually enriched with clay. Pomerol is entirely planted with vines, to the exclusion of all lesser plants. In the eastern part are the best growths, lying so cheek by jowl with St-Emilion that it is surprising to find any constant difference.

Nonetheless the consensus is that Pomerols are the gentlest, richest, and the more instantly appealing clarets. They have deep colour without the acidity and tannin that often go with it, a ripe-plummy, even creamy, smell, and sometimes great concentration of all their qualities: the striking essence of a great wine.

Pomerol is a democracy. It has no classification, and indeed it would be very hard to devise one. There is no long tradition of steady selling to build on. Châteaux are small family affairs and subject to change as individuals come and go. Nor is the complexity of the soil, as it switches from gravel to gravelly clay to clay with gravel, or from sandy gravel to gravelly sand, exactly reflected in vineyard boundaries.

There is a good deal of agreement, however, about which are the outstanding vineyards of Pomerol. Château Pétrus is allowed by all to come first. Trotanoy is perhaps runner-up – though Vieux-Château-Certan would contest this. Then in a bunch come La Fleur-Pétrus, La Conseillante, Lafleur, L'Evangile, Latour à Pomerol, Petit-Village and Certan-de-May. It would be wrong to distinguish one group from another too clearly. Clinet, L'Eglise-Clinet, Le Gay, Clos l'Eglise (how confusing these names are), La Croix-de-Gay, Clos-René, La Grave Trigant de Boisset, L'Enclos, each has extremely high standards. Châteaux de Sales, much the biggest property, with 115 acres (47 hectares), Rouget, Vraye-Croix-de-Gay (hints of jealousy!), Gazin, Lafleur-Gazin, La Pointe, Feytit-Clinet and Moulinet all make typical and desirable wines. The map distinguishes in larger

type the growths whose wines currently fetch the highest prices. The tight grouping of these châteaux on the clay soil is an indication of their character as well as quality. These properties generally make the densest, fleshiest and most opulent wines.

Before being overwhelmed by the complications of Pomerol it is worth knowing that the average standard here is very high. The village has a name for reliability. Bargains, on the other hand, are not often found.

The most potent influence in the district is the 'négoce', the merchant-houses, of Libourne, led with authority and style by the family firm of Jean-Pierre Moueix. They either own or manage a high proportion of the finest properties.

One advantage that has certainly helped the popularity of this little region is the fact that its wines are ready remarkably soon for Bordeaux. The chief grape here is not the tough-skinned Cabernet Sauvignon, whose wine has to live through a tannic youth; in Pomerol the Merlot, secondary in the Médoc, is the leading vine. Great growths have about 70–80% Merlot, with perhaps 20% Cabernet Franc, known here as Le Bouchet. The greatest Pomerol, Pétrus, is almost pure Merlot, growing in almost pure clay which limits its rooting range and depth – with astonishing results.

Even the best Pomerol has produced all its perfume and achieved its dazzling finesse within a dozen years or so, and most are already attractive at five years old.

Above: Pomerol has no village centre and no big properties. The little châteaux are scattered round the only landmark, the church spire. Yet the labels displayed on these two pages represent the greatest concentration of luxurious, voluptuous red wines in all Bordeaux.

St-Denis-de-Pile
Château des Annereaux
les Annereaux

Lalande-de-Pomerol
Château Castel Viaud
les Sables
le Perron
Château Perron
le Sablot
Château Bourseau
Viaud
Château de Viaud
le Moulin de Salles
Château de Bel-Air
Bel-Air
Canton-des-Chats
Château Grand Ormeau
St-Médard-de-Guizières
D245 E1
Château les Cruzelles
la Pignière
Château la Maréchaude
LALANDE-DE-LIBOURNE
N89
Château de Sales
le Petit Moulinet
Château Moulinet
Domaine de la Combe
Marchesseau
Château Vieux Chevrol
Château Moulin à Vent
D121 E3
Chevrol
Clos de la Combe
Château Patache
le Moulin de Lavaud
Lavaud
le Moulin
la Forêt
Barbanne
NÉAC
le Grand Garrouil
la Patache
CHÂTEAU LA GRAVE TRIGANT DE BOISSET
Château Belles Graves
le Moulin de Gazelis
Vieux Château Cloquet
CHÂTEAU ROUGET
Château Tournefeuille
Néac
Château Grand Moulinet
Château Rêve d'Or
CHÂTEAU L'ENCLOS
CHÂTEAU LATOUR À POMEROL
CLOS L'ÉGLISE
D245
Pignon
CHÂTEAU LE GAY
D121
la Chichonne
le Grand Moulinet
Château Feytit-Clinet
CHÂTEAU CLINET
Domaine de l'Église
Château la Croix-de-Gay
Château Lafleur-Gazin
René
CLOS RENÉ
Château Bellevue
Château Bel-Air
CH. L'ÉGLISE-CLINET
Château Vray-Croix-de-Gay
CHÂTEAU LAFLEUR
CHÂTEAU GAZIN
les Barrières
les Ormeaux
Château de Bourgueneuf
Château la Cabanne
Trochau
Château Lagrange
CHÂTEAU PÉTRUS
CHÂTEAU LA FLEUR-PÉTRUS
Château Franc-Maillet
Maillet
Château Mazeyres
Château Cantereau
Château de Grange-Neuve
COMMUNE
CHÂTEAU CERTAN GIRAUD
Château Haut-Maillet
Château Bourgneuf-Vayron
CHÂTEAU TROTANOY
Clos du Clocher
POMEROL
Château Le Bon Pasteur
Béquille
Château Gombaude-Guillot
D121 E4
CHÂTEAU CERTAN DE MAY
VIEUX CHÂTEAU CERTAN
CHÂTEAU L'ÉVANGILE
Château Croque Michotte
Château Clos Mazeyres
Beauséjour
DE
Château la Violette
CHÂTEAU L'ÉVANGILE
D244
Bonalgue
Château Bonalgue
Château Grate-Cap
D121
la Graviette
POMEROL
Montagne
Château la Pointe
CHÂTEAU LE PIN
Catusseau
Ch. la Croix St-Georges
CHÂTEAU PETIT-VILLAGE
CHÂTEAU LA CONSEILLANTE
Château Nenin
Château le Caillou
D245
Château la Tour du Pin Figeac
Château la Dominique
Château la Fleur du Roy
Château la Croix
Château Beauregard
CHÂTEAU CHEVAL BLANC
Château Plince
la Brandaude
ST-EMILION
Libourne
Château la Croix-du-Casse
Château Ferrand
les Grands Sillons
Toulifaut
Château la Tour-Figeac
Château la Commanderie
Ch. la Croix Taillefer
Rouilledinat
la Grange Neuve
la Bordette
la Lamberte
Château Taillefer
Faillas
Château du Tailhas
St-Emilion
D243
D243

1:25,000
Km. 0   1 Km.
Miles 0   ½ Mile

N

Dordogne
Isle
Libourne
Bordeaux
Garonne

Canton boundary
Commune (parish) boundary
CHÂTEAU   Top-quality château
Château   Other good château
First-growth vineyard
Other vineyard
Woods
Contour interval 5 metres

1990 CHÂTEAU GAZIN POMEROL

1989 CHÂTEAU LE GAY POMEROL

1985 Ch. Lafleur POMEROL

CLOS L'ÉGLISE POMEROL

Château Le Bon Pasteur POMEROL 1989

1988 CHÂTEAU DE SALES POMEROL LES HÉRITIERS A. DE LAAGE

Bourg and Blaye

History has not been kind to Bourg and Blaye, the productive little district opposite the Médoc across the Gironde. They were exporting wine long before the mighty Médoc was planted. The country is not flat like the Médoc; irregular hills make it much prettier. But silting-up robbed Bourg of its place as the first Gironde port before Bordeaux. Business went elsewhere.

In some respects the make-up of vines and soil here is closer to that of St-Emilion. In Bourg the predominantly red vineyards tend to be planted equally with Cabernet, Merlot and Malbec on soil that is largely clay over limestone. The wines are full of colour and meat, tannic enough to need keeping for three to six years, showing surprising differences in style from château to château on the various soils. They are altogether worth investigating.

Bourg and Blaye each have over 17,000 acres (about 7,000 hectares) under vine. Much of Blaye's is white. All the best, though, is red, under the appellation Premières Côtes de Blaye: comparable with that of Bourg but generally lighter. Both districts make sparkling wine in subterranean quarries like those of St-Emilion – the main source of building stone for Bordeaux.

The best châteaux, here as in the Médoc, lie close to the river. From the north, in Blaye, Châteaux Le Menaudat, Segonzac, Bourdieu, l'Escadre, and above all Barbé are the leading names. The Bourgeais district starts at the little River Brouillon. Château de Barbe is its most famous name, with Château de Thau at Gauriac, then, further south, La Croix-Millorit, Falfas, Eyquem, Mendoce, Caruel, Laurensanne, and, between Bourg and Tauriac, Brûlesécaille, du Bousquet, Guerry and Labarde. Further inland Châteaux Launay and Rousset are well reputed. Bourg's cooperative, La Vinifera, with 50 members, makes some pleasant rosé as well as red.

Bourg and Blaye are a reservoir for the kind of wines everyone wants: reliable, enjoyable and cheap. Their red wines are much better than their white.

Arrondissment boundary
Canton boundary
Commune (parish) boundary
Vineyards
Woods
Contour interval 10 metres

Bergerac

Bordeaux's very beautiful hinterland, the Dordogne, leading back into the maze of valleys cut in the stony upland of Périgord, was pre-eminent among the 'High Country' sources of wine once sold as Bordeaux. Being the wrong side of the *département* boundary of the Gironde it no longer has that privilege. But few could tell its better red and white wines from fringe Bordeaux, and the best are far better than that. Lightweight claret is an exactly apt description of Bergerac Rouge, made largely of Merlot and Cabernet Franc. Bergerac Rosé is proving to be particularly successful. And the range of whites is wide, if confusing, and worth exploring.

The whites start with crisp dry wines (Bergerac Sec) based on Sauvignon Blanc. They continue with off-dry to semi-sweet wines, softened with Sémillon and Muscadelle under a range of appellations which could well be rationalized. The wines of Saussignac are generally fuller-bodied dry whites; Montravel, Côtes de Montravel and Haut-Montravel are variably but unpredictably semi-dry to sweet. Rosette is too elusive to be certain. More importantly, all these wines are usually pleasant and good value.

Bergerac's most famous wine is Monbazillac, from the north-facing left bank of the valley. The tag of 'poor man's Sauternes' describes it too well to be avoided. It never reaches the unctuous richness and peachy balance of fine Sauternes, but ages in a different direction: to an amber, nutty sweetness – unless, that is, like most people you enjoy it young with your *foie gras*. Château Monbazillac, a handsome castle owned by the local cooperative, is the leader.

Superior red wine can use the appellation Côtes de Bergerac, but only the notably darker, deeper and firmer wines of an enclave on the right bank are entitled to use the excellent name of Pécharmant.

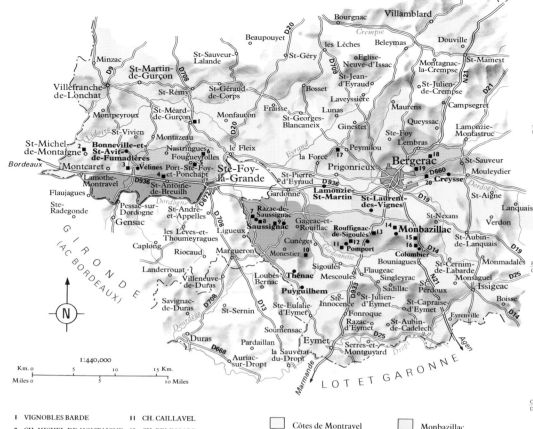

1:440,000
Km. 0   5   10   15 Km.
Miles 0   5   10 Miles

1	VIGNOBLES BARDE
2	CH. MICHEL-DE-MONTAIGNE
3	LES VIGNOBLES DE PAGNON
4	CH. LE BONDIEU
5	DOM. DE MAYAT
6	CH. PIQUE-SEGUE
7	CH. LE PAYNAL
8	CH. COURT LES MÛTS
9	CH. LES MIAUDOUX
10	CH. DE PANISSEAU
11	CH. CAILLAVEL
12	CH. BELINGARD
13	CH. LE CAILLOU
14	CH. DE MONBAZILLAC
15	CH. DE LA JAUBERTIE
16	DOM. DE L'ANCIENNE CURE
17	CH. COMBRILLAC
18	DOM. DU HAUT PÉCHARMANT
19	CLOS LES CÔTES
20	CH. DE TIREGAND

- ☐ Côtes de Montravel
- ☐ Haut-Montravel
- ☐ Montravel
- ☐ Bergerac
- ☐ Monbazillac
- ☐ Rosette
- ☐ Pécharmant
- ☐ Saussignac

- ■ BARDE — Leading producer
- ● Thénac — Leading wine commune
- — · — · — Département boundary

Below left: the Château de Monbazillac dominates the Dordogne Valley above Bergerac. Its liquorous golden wine (made by the local cooperative) is the Sauternes of the region. *Below right*: dry white and light Bordeaux-style reds from Bergerac châteaux have built up solid reputations for value.

Cognac

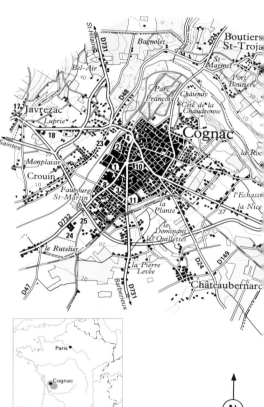

Tᴡo regions of France have wine industries based entirely on the distillation of the crop. Brandy can be made from any wine, but cognac and armagnac are as specific in their qualities, as firmly based on their *terroirs*, as Bordeaux or champagne.

The Appellation Contrôlée Cognac covers almost two entire *départements* just north of the Gironde estuary, the whole sparsely contoured basin of the River Charente, and even small islands offshore in the Bay of Biscay.

There is an uncanny fresh-grape sweetness about good cognac, as though the soul of the vine has been etherealized and condensed. It makes you think not just of wine but of great wine – it has the same elusive complexity; the same raciness and excitement.

And yet the wine it comes from has none of these qualities. The Charente vineyards, now given over exclusively to cognac, originally sold cheap wine to seamen from Britain and the Low Countries coming to buy salt. It was only in the 17th century that some of these immigrants began 'burning' the wine. But once the experiment had been made, the word got around. A Mr Martell came from the Channel Islands, a Mr Hennessy from Ireland and a Mr Hine from Dorset. Cognac had found its *métier*.

Above: one of Hennessy's several modern distilleries scattered round the region. Hundreds of farmers also distil their own wine before selling their new spirit to merchant houses. All Cognac is distilled twice in the characteristic Turkish cooking-pot still.

Some 15,000 farmers in this area grow white grapes, mainly Ugni Blanc (known locally as St-Emilion), for distillation. Its wine, capable of only about 7% alcohol and with as much as 10 grammes per litre of acidity, has few other possibilities. Indeed, the grapes have to be picked before they are fully ripe to ensure this acidity.

The quality of the cognac depends almost entirely on the soil. At its best, in the heart of the Charente (small map, page 111) it is as chalky as in Champagne. Hence the similarity of names between the two unrelated regions. Concentric bands of progressively less chalky and (for this purpose) inferior soils surround it. From a topsoil of 35% chalk, with 80–90% chalk less than a foot (20 centimetres) down, to 25%, to 15% is the progression from Grande Champagne to Petite Champagne to Borderies. The corresponding progression in the cognac is from maximum finesse to a more full-bodied and high-flavoured spirit – still excellent in its way. Beyond the small and central Borderies,

The cognac houses

▲ 1	Martell	
▲ 2	Hennessy	
▲ 3	Rémy Martin	
▲ 4	Otard-Dupuy	
▲ 5	Courvoisier	
● 6	Ricard-Bisquit Dubouché	
● 7	Hardy	
▲ 8	J G Monnet	
▲ 9	Camus	
▲ 10	Salignac	
▲ 11	Prince de Polignac	
● 12	Castillon	
▲ 13	Larsen	
▲ 14	Hine	
● 15	Tiffon	
▲ 16	Frapin	
● 17	Croizet-Eymard	
● 18	Dist. de Segonzac (Martell)
● 19	Dist. de Galienne (Martell)
● 20	Dist. de St-Martin (Martell)
● 21	Moulineuf (Martell)
▲ 22	Hennessy
● 23	Viticulteurs Réunis
▲ 24	Coop de Cognac et Vins Charentais
▲ 25	Hennessy
▲ 26	Hennessy
▲ 27	Martell
● 28	Hennessy
● 29	Hennessy
● 30	Hennessy
▲ 31	Delamain

● Distillery   ▲ Warehouse

however, the three Bois – Fins, Bons and Ordinaires – have yellower, richer soil which gives a distinct *gout de terroir* or earthiness.

Cognac is double-distilled in pot stills in the winter months as soon as possible after the wine has stopped fermenting. One barrel of cognac comes out for every ten of wine that went in.

Ageing in oak is as much part of the process as distillation. The forests of the Limousin or, better, Tronçais, in the centre of France, supply oak with a high porosity and rather low tannin content. Three years in barrel is the legal minimum for any cognac; in practice most good ones have three and VSOPs (Very Special Old Pale) have five or more. Airy *chais* where the barrels lie are scattered throughout the region, their roofs blackened with a fungus which lives on the fumes, for the rate of evaporation is daunting: as much cognac is lost into the air every year as is drunk in the whole of France.

Seven years is now the maximum age which the law allows a firm to claim on the label for its cognac, however old it may really be. The former practice of keeping unblended vintages has been outlawed as being impossible to control.

Cognac is normally diluted to 40% alcohol with distilled water. Sweetness and colour are adjusted with sugar and caramel. Each shipper has a house style and a secret way of achieving it, as well as reserves of very old cognac to draw on for premium and de luxe brands.

The large map shows the heart of Cognac: the country between Cognac, the prosperous little capital, Jarnac and Segonzac. The area south of the River Charente is in Grande Champagne, north is mainly Fins Bois and northwest, facing Cognac, is Borderies. The principal distilleries and warehouses are marked. In the well-tended but rather dull countryside the characteristic building is the *logis*: the old fortified farmhouse, high-walled and gated. Many have stills: the greater part of cognac is made by farmers and sold by them to be matured by shippers.

Armagnac, whose region is mapped on page 113, at its closest point is only 80 miles (130 kilometres) from the Charente. But the two brandies are poles apart in style and in the techniques used to make them.

The two areas of Armagnac areas that yield the best quality are Ténarèze and Bas-Armagnac – the latter might be called the Grande Champagne of the region, except that in place of chalk it has sandy soil.

Armagnac starts with a stronger flavour and scent than cognac. Comparisons of the two always categorize armagnac as 'rustic'. It has been compared with hand-woven tweed in contrast with worsted. But tweed is a rough cloth, and it is armagnac's special distinction to be velvety smooth. At the same time it is dry; sugar is not normally added. Armagnac has a more pungent smell, which stays in your mouth or even in an empty glass for a long while. Its spirity, fiery quality is very similar to cognac's. The one quality of the best cognacs it does not have is the brilliant, champagne-like finesse.

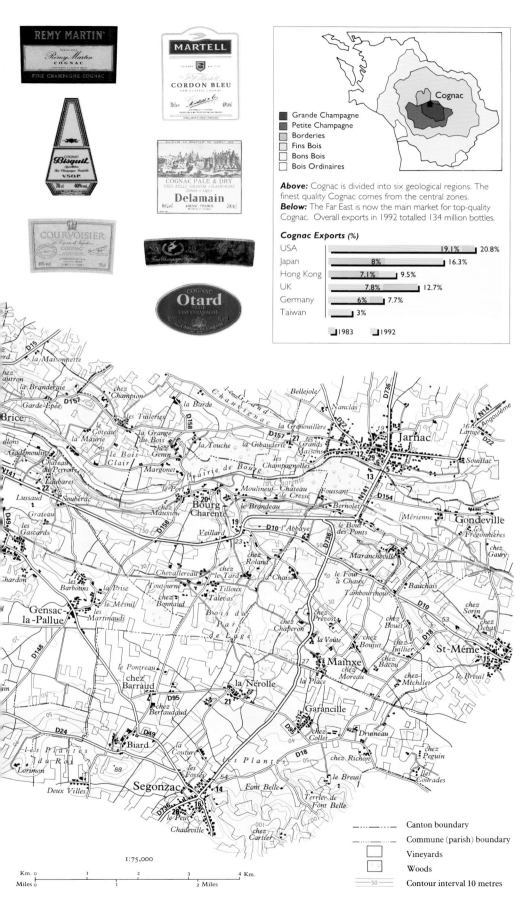

Above: Cognac is divided into six geological regions. The finest quality Cognac comes from the central zones.
Below: The Far East is now the main market for top-quality Cognac. Overall exports in 1992 totalled 134 million bottles.

Cognac Exports (%)

	1983	1992
USA	19.1%	20.8%
Japan	8%	16.3%
Hong Kong	7.1%	9.5%
UK	7.8%	12.7%
Germany	6%	7.7%
Taiwan	3%	

Grande Champagne
Petite Champagne
Borderies
Fins Bois
Bons Bois
Bois Ordinaires

Canton boundary
Commune (parish) boundary
Vineyards
Woods
Contour interval 10 metres

1:75,000

Km. 0   1   2   3   4 Km.
Miles 0   1   2 Miles

Wines of the Southwest

South of the great vineyard of Bordeaux, west of the Midi, and sheltered from the Atlantic by the forest of the Landes, the vine flourishes in scattered areas which have strong local traditions, each by a river – its old link to distant markets. This was the 'High Country' that the jealous merchants of Bordeaux excluded from the port until their local wine was sold.

Cahors is the senior wine of this part of France in reputation, though not in official recognition. Only in 1971 was it promoted to Appellation Contrôlée status. In Cahors they will tell you how, centuries ago, it was their wine, not meagre Médocs, that was most in demand among foreign buyers in Bordeaux.

Cahors has recently come back strongly into favour, not as the 'black' wine of legend (and fact: a generation ago its colour and tannin content well earned the epithet) but as a full-bodied, vigorous red with a definite bite in its youth, maturing fairly rapidly these days (four years is often enough) to a balance and complexity that would do credit to a St-Emilion.

The grape that Cahors uses, in large part, is the Malbec that formerly dominated Bordeaux, but here it is called the Auxerrois. Recent replanting has taken it from the alluvial gravel by the river up onto the rocky *causses*, where its wine is stronger, with more bite. Some of the best producers believe a blend of both is best. In fact, Cahors can be found in all shades and weights. Locally it is drunk rather cool.

The hill country around the River Tarn just below Albi, and below the magnificent gorge cut by the river into the Cévennes, is still lovely, with beautiful towns and villages. Seventy-three of them are contained within the appellation Gaillac, which is thus a very general name for any wine, red, white or rosé, made from a mixture of a fairly wide choice of grapes, including local and Bordeaux and Rhône reds, and the same white Mauzac that produces Blanquette de Limoux. Gaillac also has its Mousseux, traditionally made by the *méthode rurale*, the primitive

The wine regions of the southwest have almost returned from the dead since phylloxera crushed them. Today they are as closely followed as Bordeaux itself.

forerunner of the champagne method. Better known, however, is its slightly fizzy dry white Perlé; a simple thirst-quencher.

An inner-circle appellation, Premières Côtes de Gaillac, defends what is left of the local tradition of sweet (in reality semi-sweet) whites. But today most Gaillac is frankly unpretentious cooperative-made wine hard to characterize except by its ancient vine varieties.

To the west between the Tarn and Garonne the Côtes du Frontonnais is the local wine of Toulouse. But enterprise has moved in, led by Château Bellevue La Forêt, to make of its native Négrette grapes, mixed with Cabernet, Syrah and Gamay, a notable red; limpid and fruity. Fronton and Villaudric are the leading communes.

North of Armagnac, on the left bank of the Garonne, lies the appellation Buzet, whose production, from vineyards scattered over 27 communes of orchard and farm, is in the hands of one well-organized cooperative. Its top wine, Cuvée Napoléon, stands comparison with a quality Médoc. The Côtes du Marmandais, to the north, also has a very good cooperative (at Cocumont); so indeed does the Côtes de Duras, north again, whose largely Sauvignon white is comparable with Entre-Deux-Mers, although its red is more like that of its eastern neighbour, Bergerac. All these wines look to Bordeaux for either their market or their model, or both.

The remaining wine regions on this map lie in the Basque province of Béarn. A general appellation covers its red, white and rosé wines of a certain quality from vineyards outside its two celebrated wine centres, Madiran and Jurançon. These are the two true jewels of the southwest.

The Madiran vineyards lie on the hills along the left bank of the River Adour, just south of Bas Armagnac, the area that produces the finest of France's alternative spirit. A local red grape, the Tannat, is well named for its dark and tannic, tough and vigorous wines. Makers disagree on whether and how much to tame it with Cabernet. Twenty months is the minimum barrel-ageing period, and when the wines are bottled they are still harsh – especially if, as happens more and more, new barrels are used. But after seven or eight years fine Madiran is truly admirable,

aromatic, full of flavour, fluid and lively; of all the small-scale appellations the one that can hold its head up with fine Bordeaux. The robust spirit of Armagnac has also found a second string in its hugely popular white Vin de Pays des Côtes de Gascogne, made largely of Colombard.

Jurançon is a name to conjure with, although few people have ever tasted the reason why. These steep Pyrenean foothills once made France's best sweet wines, comparable to Sauternes or the rarities of the Loire. Today production is a fraction of what it was, and the high risk of picking grapes as late as November, necessary for *vin liquoreux*, has led most growers to make dry wine. The dry white still has richness of flavour allied to high acidity, but the rare *liquoreux* is sumptuous, like wildflower Sauternes.

The tiny appellation of Irouléguy is the final Basque bastion, doggedly making rosé, red and white wines of the local grapes, including the Tannat. The rosé label carries what might well be a Basque rallying cry – Hotx Hotxa Edan. Alas, it only means 'Chill before serving'.

Cahors is the senior south west wine in reputation; Armagnac its superlative spirit. Madiran, Jurançon, Gaillac have ancient roots, original grapes and a bright future.

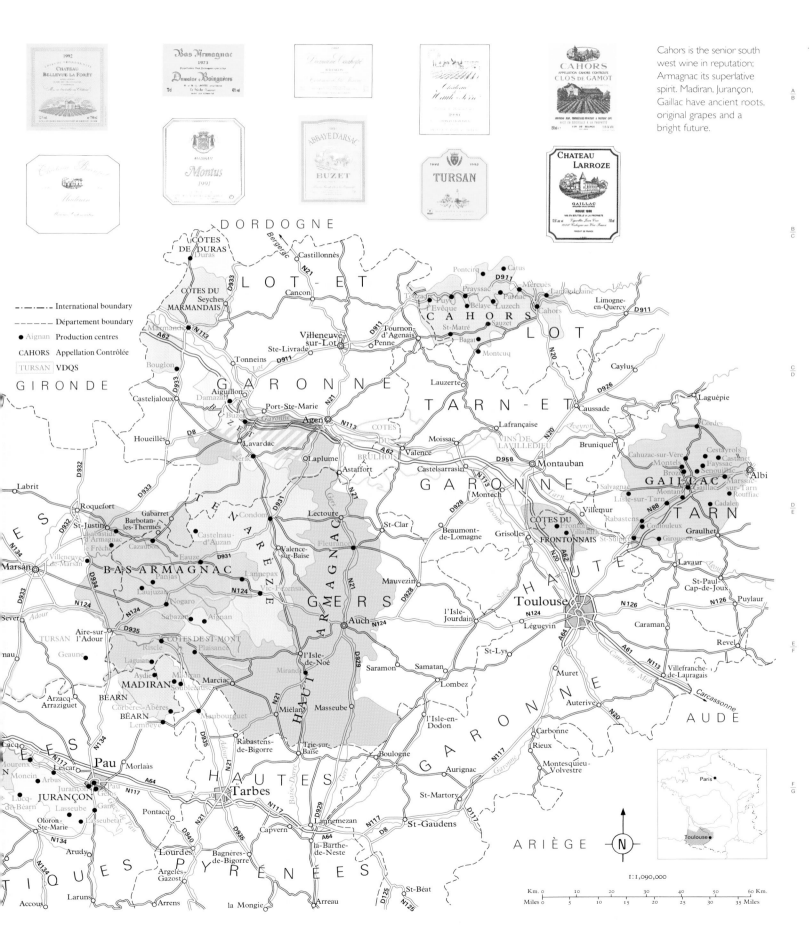

The Loire Valley and Muscadet

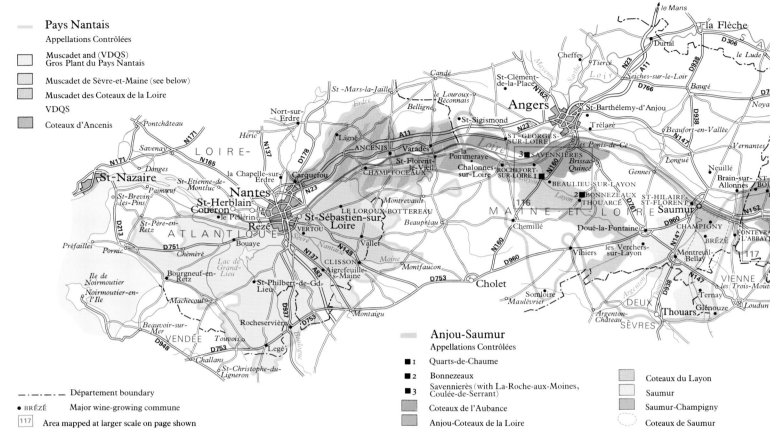

Pays Nantais

Appellations Contrôlées

☐ Muscadet and (VDQS)
  Gros Plant du Pays Nantais

☐ Muscadet de Sèvre-et-Maine (see below)

☐ Muscadet des Coteaux de la Loire

☐ VDQS

☐ Coteaux d'Ancenis

- ·—·—· Département boundary
- BRÉZÉ   Major wine-growing commune
- 117   Area mapped at larger scale on page shown

Anjou-Saumur

Appellations Contrôlées

■ 1   Quarts-de-Chaume

■ 2   Bonnezeaux

■ 3   Savennières (with La-Roche-aux-Moines,
         Coulée-de-Serrant)

☐ Coteaux de l'Aubance

☐ Anjou-Coteaux de la Loire

☐ Coteaux du Layon

☐ Saumur

☐ Saumur-Champigny

☐ Coteaux de Saumur

Complex as it is, the River Loire is worth mapping as a whole, with all its wines about it, for although they are so far-flung, with wide variations of climate, soil and tradition, and four or five important grape varieties, they do have a family likeness. They are light, with palpable acidity, grapey and refreshing. The classic word for them is charming.

In the main they are white. They divide clearly between the dry wines to the east (Sancerre and Pouilly) and west (Muscadet), and the sweeter wines of Touraine and Anjou in the middle, made from the Loire's own grape, the Chenin Blanc. Some of the wine of Touraine is red; the best a match for a top Beaujolais Cru. Much of the wine of Anjou is pink, and not remarkable. The best parts of the Loire are mapped on these and the next four pages.

The vineyard of Brittany – one might almost say Neptune's vineyard – is the Pays Nantais, the home of Muscadet. Muscadet was the first modern success story of the Loire. Forty-odd years ago it was an unknown *vin de pays*. Today it is the accepted drink with the glorious seafood of northern France. In the last 30 years the vineyard area has more than doubled. Muscadet is cheap, and yet perfect in context – very dry, but firm rather than acid: in fact in hot years it can lack acidity. 'It casts its pale golden glow', as one French critic has said, 'over the purple of lobsters and the pearl of oysters, the pink of shrimps and the red of mullet.'

Muscadet is the name of the wine, not of a place. The region of Sèvre-et-Maine (mapped

The River Loire cuts its great silvery swathe from the mountainous heart of France to the sea. The soft watery landscape of the Loire perfectly suggests the gentle spring-like quality of its wine.

on page 115) has 90% of the vineyards, densely planted on low sandy hills. The heart of the district lies around Vertou, Vallet, St-Fiacre and La Chapelle-Heulin; the area where the wines are ripest, liveliest and most scented. They are traditionally bottled *sur lie* – straight from the barrel, unracked – the lees contributing zest to the flavour (as in a different way they do in champagne).

The second wine of the region, Gros Plant, can be very pleasant – similar to Muscadet in style but with higher acidity. Some minor red wine is made around Ancenis from Gamay and Cabernet, but it cannot be compared with the often delicious Cabernet reds of Saumur-Champigny, just up-river in Anjou.

The wines of the Upper Loire are almost collectors' pieces, with the exception of Pouilly and Sancerre (see page 119). The historic vineyards of Quincy and Reuilly, and an expanding fragment at Menetou-Salon, make flinty, fruity Sauvignon Blancs and pale Pinot Noir to rival Sancerre. This area has a future. The Coteaux du Giennois probably has not. Orléans, once famous for vinegar, scarcely has a vineyard left. Cheverny makes sharp dry white from a grape not found elsewhere, the Romorantin.

Westwards, the broad appellation Touraine finds its best expression in the Oisly et Thésée cooperative near Contres. Its Sauvignon whites and Gamay and Cabernet reds are bargains. Amboise, Azay-le-Rideau, Mesland and Valençay use Chenin Blanc and other grapes; Jasnières and the Coteaux du Loir and the VDQS Coteaux du Vendômois make respectively Vouvray-style white and light red of the local Pineau d'Aunis.

Irregular quality dogs the growers in this northern area. Many Loire growths vary so widely from one year to another that they seem hardly the same wine. A fine autumn ripens grapes almost to raisins, but a wet one means a very acid product. Hence the importance of the sparkling-wine industry. The comparative failures of Vouvray or Saumur, fruity but acid, are ideal for transforming by the champagne method into sparkling Crémant de la Loire.

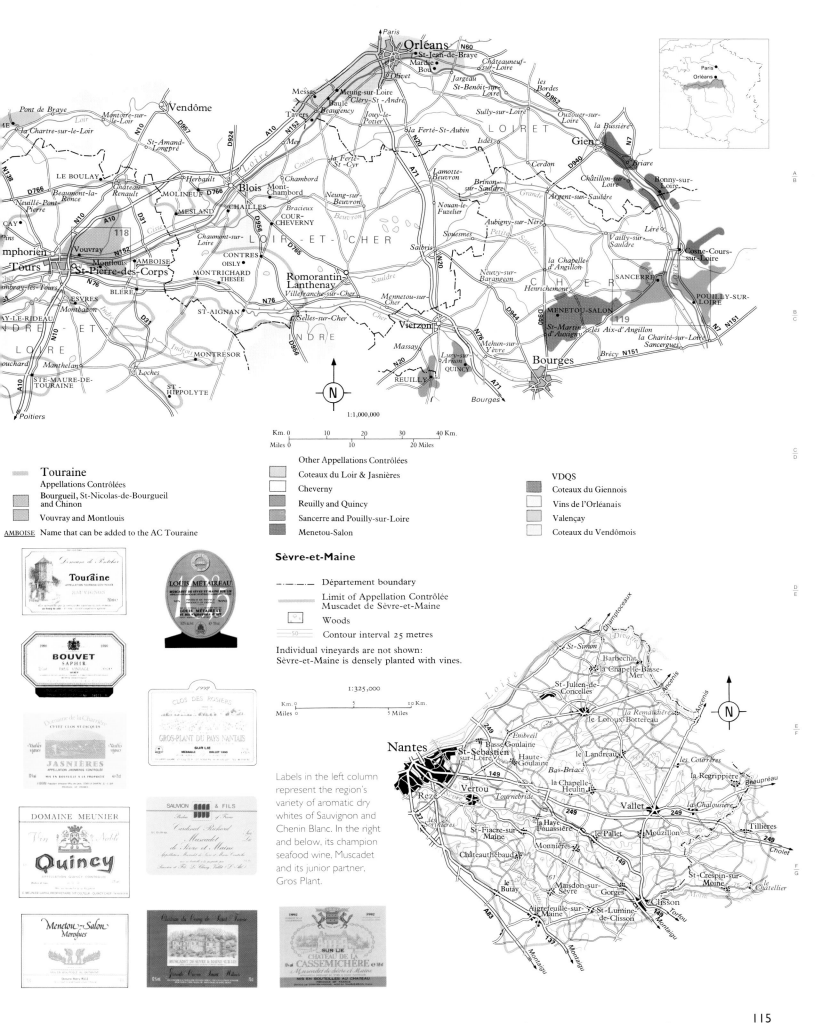

Túraine

Appellations Contrôlées

Bourgueil, St-Nicolas-de-Bourgueil and Chinon

Vouvray and Montlouis

AMBOISE Name that can be added to the AC Touraine

Other Appellations Contrôlées

Coteaux du Loir & Jasnières

Cheverny

Reuilly and Quincy

Sancerre and Pouilly-sur-Loire

Menetou-Salon

VDQS

Coteaux du Giennois

Vins de l'Orléanais

Valençay

Coteaux du Vendômois

Sèvre-et-Maine

—·—·— Département boundary

Limit of Appellation Contrôlée Muscadet de Sèvre-et-Maine

Woods

Contour interval 25 metres

Individual vineyards are not shown: Sèvre-et-Maine is densely planted with vines.

1:325,000

Km. 0 — 5 — 10 Km.

Miles 0 — 5 Miles

Labels in the left column represent the region's variety of aromatic dry whites of Sauvignon and Chenin Blanc. In the right and below, its champion seafood wine, Muscadet and its junior partner, Gros Plant.

1:1,000,000

Km. 0 — 10 — 20 — 30 — 40 Km.

Miles 0 — 10 — 20 Miles

Anjou

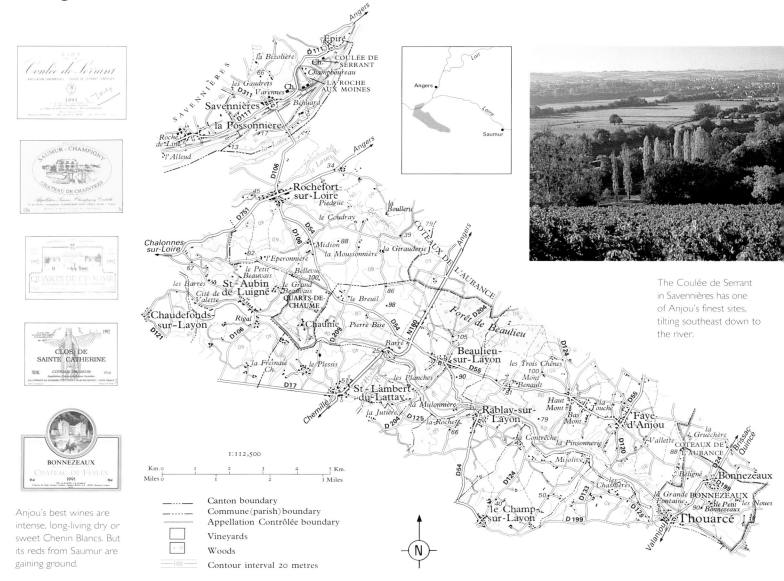

The Coulée de Serrant in Savennières has one of Anjou's finest sites, tilting southeast down to the river.

Canton boundary
Commune (parish) boundary
Appellation Contrôlée boundary
Vineyards
Woods
Contour interval 20 metres

1:112,500

The white wines of Anjou and Touraine have this in common with those of Germany: in their best vintages they achieve resplendent sweetness. At their very best they are dessert wines of velvet texture, smooth as glycerine, richly and yet freshly scented, tasting of grapes, peaches, apricots, hazelnuts, but with an underlying, elusive flintiness which prevents them cloying. This is after a long, warm autumn. Such wines go on improving for many years. But even in medium years they often have the balance of good German wines in which fruit and acid seem perfectly matched, making you want to sip and go on sipping.

The grape that gives us all this is the Chenin Blanc, called locally Pineau de la Loire. The area mapped here is where it reaches its ripest; where several geographical circumstances combine to give it the dry, open slopes, sheltered from north to east, which it needs. The River Layon, heading northwest to join the Loire, has cut a gully deep enough for its right bank to provide perfectly exposed but sheltered corners of hill.

A large part of its course has the appellation Coteaux du Layon, providing sweet (or *moelleux*) wines notably above the general Anjou standard. But Quarts de Chaume with only 120 acres (under 50 hectares) and Bonnezeaux (about double) are outstanding enough to have appellations of their own, like Grands Crus in Burgundy. Beaulieu, Rablay, Rochefort, St-Aubin, Faye and Thouarcé are communes with particularly good wines. The leading producer – by far – is the house of Touchais, based at Doué-la-Fontaine, south of Thouarcé. Moulin Touchais is a creamy-sweet legend.

The River Aubance, parallel with the Layon to the north, makes similar wines: both also grow Cabernet to make good light red wine, the famous delicate Cabernet Rosé d'Anjou and, paler still, *vin gris*, barely more than a blushing white.

Just south of Angers, and facing Rochefort, the north bank of the Loire has a series of small appellations of startling quality. Again it is the Chenin Blanc, although here – to confound all generalization – the wine at its best is dry. Savennières is the general appellation for this small region (which comes within the larger one of the Coteaux de la Loire). The law demands a savagely restricted crop; only 20 hectolitres per hectare. Within Savennières there are two Grands Crus – La Roche aux Moines with less than 70 acres (30 hectares) and La Coulée de Serrant with a mere 12 acres (5 hectares).

La Coulée de Serrant epitomizes the exceptional situation which makes outstanding wine: it faces southwest in a steep-sloping side-valley even more sheltered than the main river bank. Its old stone presshouse has an ecclesiastical air. The view over the Loire with its wooded and flowery islands is like the background to one of the medieval tapestries of Angers.

Savennières wine has a honey-and-flowers smell which makes its dryness surprising at first. Its impact is extraordinary: such concentration and mouth-filling flavour is rarely met with anywhere. Three or four years is the minimum age to drink it, and 20 sees it in full cry. Salmon is said to be its perfect partner, but there is such pleasure in its lingering flavour that it is a pity not to drink it on its own.

Chinon and Bourgueil

St-Nicolas-de-Bourgueil, Bourgueil and Chinon make Touraine's and the Loire's best red wines. Saumur-Champigny is the only one that comes close – and not often. On gravelly soil by the river, and on tufa on the higher slopes, Cabernet Franc – known here as Le Breton – makes a wine with the raspberry fruitiness of a very good Beaujolais. In an average year the purple wine is excellent within a few months of the vintage, drunk cool. In outstanding years such as 1990 it has the substance and structure to mature for a decade. For its quality and complete individuality it is absurdly undervalued.

Chinon makes the finest, most tender wine of the district; Bourgueil, with steeper slopes and more limestone, makes wine not unlike a light Médoc, which can improve for up to ten years in bottle. St-Nicolas-de-Bourgueil is very similar; more depends on the grower than the commune. Audebert, Lamé-Delille-Boucard, Marc Delaunay and the Clos de l'Abbaye are some of the names to look for in Bourgueil. Clos de la Contrie, Taluau, Jamet and again Audebert are leaders in St-Nicolas. In Chinon, Joguet, Couly and Raffault are all reliable producers.

A hundred years ago Chinon's wine was rated the equal of Margaux. In charm, if not in force or structure, it can come surprisingly close today. Production is expanding accordingly.

Chinon was the resort of Rabelais, who found the white wine of Ligré 'like taffeta'. Very little white wine is made there now, but some of the Loire's best rosé comes from the same grapes as are used to make the red.

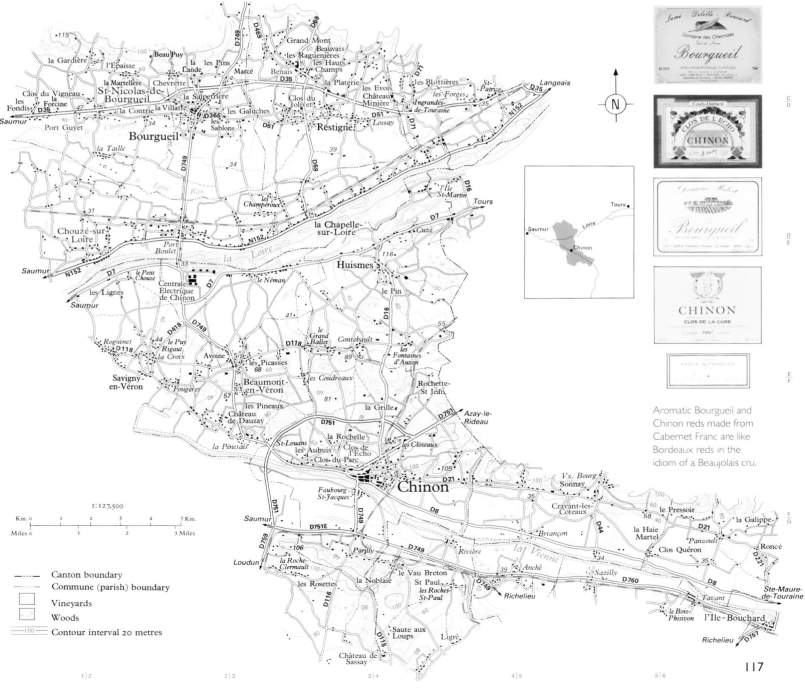

Aromatic Bourgueil and Chinon reds made from Cabernet Franc are like Bordeaux reds in the idiom of a Beaujolais cru.

1:127,500

Km. 0   1   2   3   4   5 Km.
Miles 0   1   2   3 Miles

--·-·- Canton boundary
------ Commune (parish) boundary
▢ Vineyards
▨ Woods
──100── Contour interval 20 metres

Vouvray

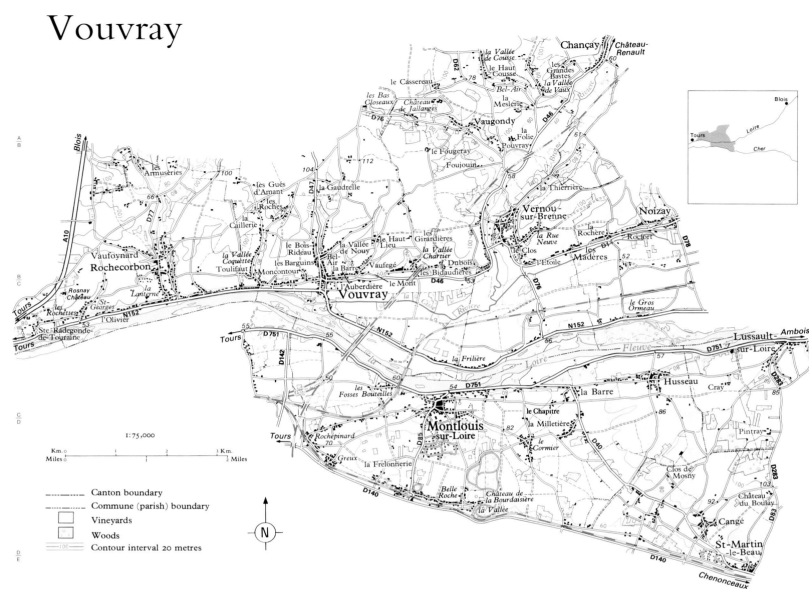

Canton boundary
Commune (parish) boundary
Vineyards
Woods
Contour interval 20 metres

1:75,000

Just as Savennières stands almost at the gates of Angers, Vouvray and Montlouis lie just outside Tours on the way to Amboise. Everything royal and romantic about France is summed up in this land of renaissance châteaux and ancient towns along the immense but gentle river.

Low hills of chalk flank the stream along the reach from Noizay to Rochecorbon. For centuries they have provided both cellars and cave-dwellings to the winegrowers of the district. The Chenin Blanc here, although often drier than in Anjou, at its best is honey-like and sweet. What distinguishes it more than anything, however, is its long life. For a comparatively light wine its longevity is astonishing. You may expect port to live for half a century, but in a pale, firm, rather delicate wine the ability to improve and go on improving for so long in bottle is matched only occasionally in Germany.

The first distinction in Vouvray is whether any given bottle is dry, semi-sweet, sweet (*moelleux*) or for that matter *pétillant* or fully sparkling: Vouvray alters character radically from vintage to vintage, and its natural tendency to re-ferment in the bottle has led to an industry in converting less successful vintages into very good sparkling wines. Normally only the richer vintages carry the name of one of the handful of famous *clos* on the best slopes. Best known is Le Haut-Lieu of Gaston Huet, mayor of the commune and its greatest spokesman. Huet also owns the Clos de Bourg and Le Mont. Prince Poniatowski owns Le Clos Baudoin, the Domaine Freslier the Quarts de Moncontour and the Allias family Le Clos du Petit Mont at the top of the Vallée Coquette. The biggest company in Vouvray, Marc Brédif, which is now owned by the Ladoucettes of Château du Nozet in Pouilly-sur-Loire, is a négociant with high standards. Montlouis has very similar soil and conditions to Vouvray, without the perfect situation of the first rank of Vouvray's vineyards along the Loire. Montlouis tends to be slightly softer and more gently sweet, and more Montlouis is destined for Mousseux.

About 25 miles (40 kilometres) from Montlouis up the River Cher lies the little town of Thésée, which with its neighbour Oisly gives its name to one of France's best-run cooperatives. Since the 1970s the Confrérie des Vignerons de Oisly et Thésée has stiffened what was formerly tart and pallid Touraine Sauvignon, Gamay and Cabernet into very attractive restaurant wines and has enormously enhanced the restricted reputation of Touraine.

A small band of growers make the great sweet wines of Vouvray and Montlouis in good years. Less good years provide base wine for *méthode traditionelle* sparkling.

Pouilly and Sancerre

The wines of Pouilly and Sancerre on the Upper Loire are perhaps the easiest to recognize in France. On these chalky hills, cut by the river, the Sauvignon Blanc can still make better wine than anywhere else in its worldwide plantations. Its character is often described as gunflint; it is smoky, slightly green, slightly spicy and appeals to most people intensely at first with its summery style. It may never achieve the depth and complexity that the Chenin Blanc of Anjou and Vouvray can reach with age. But Sancerre and Pouilly-Fumé can be wonderfully appetizing at table, particularly with shellfish. Sancerre's other passion is its pale Pinot Noir.

Pouilly-sur-Loire is the town; its wine is only called Pouilly-Fumé when made from the Sauvignon. Without the word Fumé, Pouilly-sur-Loire is a light café wine made from the mild Chasselas. (Neither has anything to do with Pouilly-Fuissé, the white wine of Mâcon.)

There is not much to choose between Pouilly-Fumé and Sancerre. The best of each are on the same level; the Sancerre perhaps slightly more obvious. In bad vintages, however, they can be very acid; their smell has been compared to wet wool and worse. Up to three years in bottle brings out the qualities of a good one, but they are not wines to lay down for much longer.

The village of Bué, its best vineyard the Clos du Chêne Marchand, makes the roundest, most solid wine of Sancerre. Chavignol (especially Les Monts Damnés) can be finer. Ménétréol gives steelier wine. In Pouilly the splendid Château du Nozet and Château de Tracy are the biggest and best-known estates.

The Loire meanders on a northwesterly route past the vineyards of Pouilly, on the right, towards the walled town of Sancerre on its abrupt hilltop in the distance. The Sancerre vineyards lie beyond, on a series of chalky ridges facing south and east.

Above: the best Sancerres come from Chavignol and Bué. Two big châteaux, de Nozet and de Tracy, dominate Pouilly. Only the best Pouillys are known as Fumé. Lesser (Chasselas) wines are called Pouilly-sur-Loire.

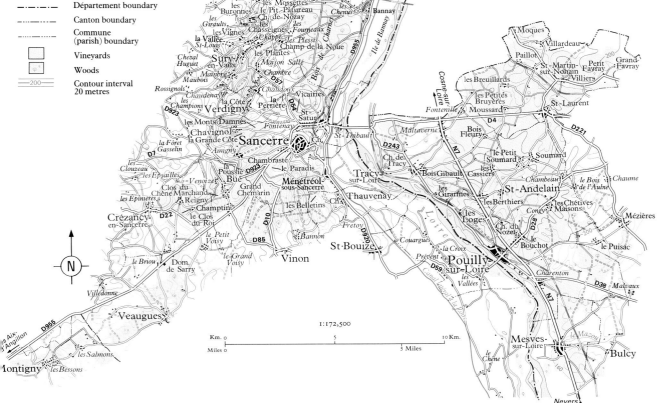

—··—··—	Département boundary
—·—·—·	Canton boundary
———————	Commune (parish) boundary
□	Vineyards
	Woods
=200=	Contour interval 20 metres

1:172,500

Km. 0 ... 5 ... 10 Km.

Miles 0 ... 5 Miles

Alsace

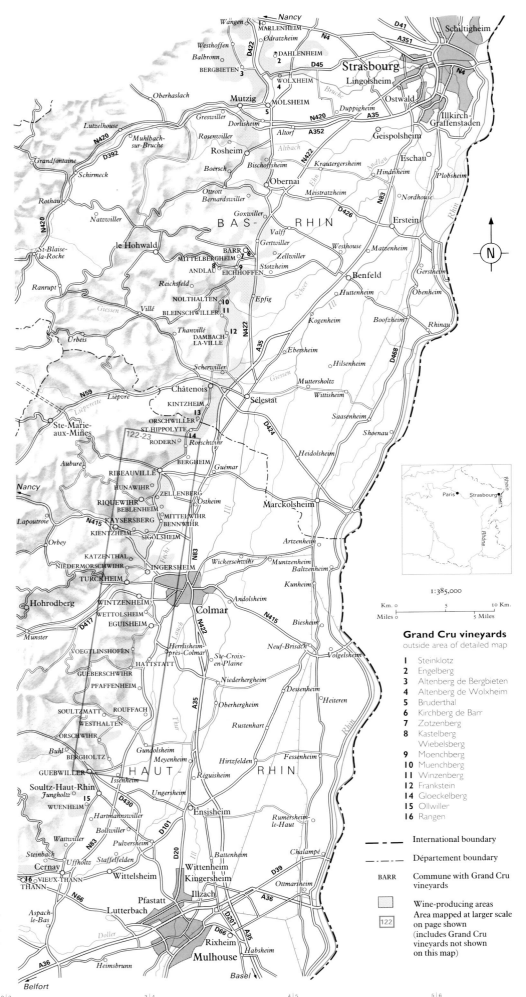

Alsace and the Midi are the two great regions of France which had lagged furthest behind in quality and yet have adapted most smartly to the demanding world of modern wine. For different reasons the 19th century was unkind to both; they had fallen into the rut of producing more quantity than quality. The appellation system more or less passed them by until the 1960s. They are both now making up for lost time.

The wine of Alsace reflects the ambivalent situation of a border province. There are two possible physical boundaries between France and Germany: the River Rhine and the crest of the Vosges, running parallel 15 miles (25 kilometres) to the west. The Rhine has been the political frontier through most of history, but the mountains have always been the line that makes the great climatic, stylistic, even linguistic difference. Alsace wine was historically classed as 'Rhenish' – of the Rhine. Its markets were in Germany, Switzerland, and in the parts of northern Europe reached by the Rhine and the North Sea.

Yet Alsace has never been German, except in periods of military occupation. Its language and its market may be, but its soul is entirely French. Alsace makes Germanic wine in the French way. The tone is set by the climate, the soil and the choice of grape varieties: all comparable with the vineyards of slightly further north, slightly further down the Rhine, which are in Germany. What does differ is the interpretation put on these things – because German and Alsatian wine-growers hold almost opposite views of what they want their wine to do and be.

The Germans prize natural balance above all. Their best wines, whether sweet or dry, are fine balancing acts between grape sugar and acidity, with alcohol almost incidental; certainly not boosted. German wine at its best is not necessarily for the table but for the drawing-room or the garden. Alsace wine is the great adjunct to one of France's most splendid cuisines. Alsace gives the flowery-scented grapes of Germany the body and authority of such table wines as white burgundy – proper accompaniments to strong and savoury food.

Instead of grape sugar lingering delicately in the wine, the grower likes a dry, firm, clean flavour, fermenting every ounce of the sugar which the long dry summers of Alsace give. This concentrates the essences of the fragrant German-style grapes into a sometimes overwhelming mouthful of flavour.

The grapes that give their names and special qualities to the wines of Alsace are the Riesling of the Rhine – responsible here and in Germany for the best wine of all – the Sylvaner, Muscat, Pinots Blanc and Gris, and the uniquely perfumed Gewürztraminer.

The Gewürztraminer is the perfect introduction to the province. You would not think that so fruity a scent could come from any wine so clean and dry. *Würze* means spice in German – although a more accurate description would make mention of rose petals, grapefruit and sometimes lychees.

Grand Cru vineyards
outside area of detailed map

1 Steinklotz
2 Engelberg
3 Altenberg de Bergbieten
4 Altenberg de Wolxheim
5 Bruderthal
6 Kirchberg de Barr
7 Zotzenberg
8 Kastelberg
   Wiebelsberg
9 Moenchberg
10 Muenchberg
11 Winzenberg
12 Frankstein
13 Gloeckelberg
14 Ollwiller
15 Rangen

– – – International boundary

– · – · – Département boundary

BARR Commune with Grand Cru vineyards

Wine-producing areas
Area mapped at larger scale on page shown (includes Grand Cru vineyards not shown on this map)

1:385,000

To the initiated, a wine with so marked a character can become dull after a while. It has its place with some of the richest of the very rich Alsatian dishes: goose or pork. But most Alsatians consider the Riesling their true *grand vin*. It offers something much more elusive: a balance of hard and gentle, flowery and strong, which leads you on and never surfeits.

These two, together with the Pinot Gris (traditionally, but no longer, called Tokay d'Alsace) and the Muscat, are classed as the noble grapes of Alsace. Only they can be grown in the 50 best-located vineyards which have been designated (25 of them in 1983, 25 in 1993) 'Alsace Grand Cru'.

The Grands Crus are slowly changing the way Alsace wines are perceived. They offer a higher quality level, with more restricted crops and increased levels of ripeness. They promote the wines from mere 'varietal' to enjoying appellation status in the fullest sense; the specific linkage of *terroir* and grape variety based on soil, situation and – up to a point – tradition.

For the present Alsace continues to be predominantly varietal in outlook. There is renewed interest today in the Pinot Gris, which makes the fullest-bodied but least perfumed wine of the region; it has an obvious place at table as an alternative to a 'big', and therefore expensive, white burgundy. The Muscat surprises everyone who knows the wine it makes anywhere else in the world, which is almost always sweet. In Alsace the Muscat keeps all its characteristic grapey scent, but makes a dry wine as clean as a whistle: a very good apéritif.

Much more important is the Pinot Blanc – a name used to cover both the nicely tart Pinot Blanc itself and the softer Pinot Auxerrois (the two are frequently blended). To keep matters complicated the Auxerrois is sometimes labelled Klevner. Formerly Pinot Blanc played a large part in the better 'Edelzwicker' blends; today its lightweight but lively wine is enormously appreciated as an apéritif. It is also often the base for sparkling Crémant d'Alsace made by the champagne method, and at its best a rival to the *crémants* of Burgundy and the Loire.

In a class above the common wines of the region, but only just reckoned noble, comes the Sylvaner. Alsace Sylvaner is light and sometimes nicely tart. Without the tartness it can be a little dull and coarse in flavour. It is often the

Above: the walled town of Riquewihr is the jewel of Alsace: an opera-set huddle of 16th-century buildings. The Grand Cru Schoenenbourg in the foreground slopes due south down to the ancient walls, a prime site for full-flavoured and long-lived Riesling.

first wine at an Alsatian dinner, to build up to the main wine, the Riesling.

The lesser grapes, the Chasselas and the Knipperlé (there are others), are not usually identified on the label. They are often the open wines of cafés. Very young, particularly in the summer after a good vintage, they are so good that visitors should not miss them by insisting on a smarter one with a name. The term Edelzwicker (noble mixture) is often applied to blends of more than one grape variety, noble or not. The ancient term *gentil* was much prettier.

What all these wines have in common is the Alsatian style of winemaking, which is almost fanatically concerned with naturalness. Alsatians like their wine to stabilize without fining, or anything that involves additions to the wine of any kind – except, alas, sugar: Alsace

is not immune from the French passion for chaptalization – adding sugar whether the wine needs it or not. Traditionalists keep it undisturbed in huge wooden casks, with minimum racking and filtering. They fill the bottle as full as possible and use a specially long cork – all to protect the wine from the air. These precautions achieve a remarkable balance of strength and freshness, fruit and acidity.

Nonetheless, when a really fine autumn comes on the heels of a good summer, and they find grapes ripening beautifully with no threat of bad weather, not even Alsatians, dedicated to clean dry table wines, can resist doing as the Germans do and getting the last drop of sugar out of their vines.

These late pickings used to be labelled with the German words Auslese and Beerenauslese. Today the phrase Vendange Tardive, meaning late harvest, is used. For the equivalent of a Beerenauslese, in which individual grapes are culled for their super-ripeness – sometimes with a degree of 'noble rot' – the term is 'Sélection des Grains Nobles'. Such wines can reach the same heights of lusciousness as great German dessert wines or Sauternes. A late-picked Gewürztraminer or Muscat has perhaps the most exotic smell of any wine in the world, and can at the same time keep a remarkable cleanness and finesse of flavour. It is not necessarily very sweet: 'intense' is a better word.

Alsace red wine is made from the Pinot Noir, but it rarely gets a much deeper colour than a rosé and never a very marked or distinguished flavour. Rouge d'Alsace, and sometimes *vin gris*, or very pale pink wine, will be found in brasseries (the word for a restaurant serving Alsatian food, traditionally to go with beer) in Paris and elsewhere.

Alsace itself has two of the best restaurants in France: Gaertner's Aux Armes de France at Ammerschwihr and Haeberlin's Auberge de l'Ill at Illhaeusern. *Foie gras frais* is one of the dishes worth travelling for. In general, Alsace cooking demonstrates what a French artist can do with German ideas. Sauerkraut becomes *choucroute*, and quite delicious. Dishes which look as though they are going to be heavy turn out to be rich but light. Quiches and onion tarts are almost miraculously edible. In Alsace no one looks beyond the range of white wines of the region to accompany this profusion of good things.

THE LANGUAGE OF THE LABEL

Cuvée Blend (normal practice in Alsace)
Grand Vin Wine with over 11% alcohol
Réserve Exceptionnelle, Grande Réserve (ditto)
Grand Cru The new appellation contrôlée for wines of the best varieties from the best, designated, vineyards
Mise d'Origine The law dictates that all Alsace wine is now bottled in Alsace
Vendange Tardive Late-picked wine, implying more strength and/or sweetness
Sélection des Grains Nobles Wine of hand-sorted over-ripe grapes, equivalent to a German Beerenauslese

In Alsace the producer's name and the grape have equal billing.

121

The Heart of Alsace

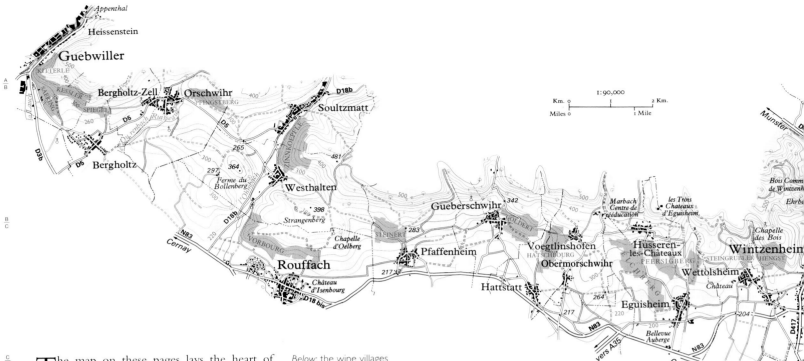

The map labels: Appenthal, Heissenstein, Guebwiller, Bergholtz-Zell, Orschwihr, Soultzmatt, D18b, Bergholtz, Westhalten, Gueberschwihr, Pfaffenheim, Voegtlinshofen, Obermorschwihr, Husseren-les-Châteaux, Wettolsheim, Wintzenheim, Hattstatt, Eguisheim, Rouffach, Château d'Isenbourg, Cernay, Colmar, les Trois Chateaux d'Eguisheim, Marbach Centre de rééducation, Chapelle des Bois, Bois Comm de Wintzenheim, Ehrbe, Chapelle d'Oelberg, Strangenberg, Ferme du Bollenberg, Munster.

Scale: 1:90,000. Km. 0 1 2 Km. Miles 0 1 Mile

The map on these pages lays the heart of the Alsace vineyard on its side, making it directly comparable to the maps of the Côte d'Or. The north lies to the right. As in so many of the great wine regions of Europe, a range of east-facing foothills provides an ideal environment for the vine. Spurs and re-entrants offer extra shelter and a privileged sunwards tilt in places where the vines face east, southeast or south. Every nuance of the unfolding landscape is echoed in the alignment of the vine rows to catch every minute of sunlight.

And Alsace is sunny. The high Vosges to the west are the secret of these vineyards, which lie along the mountain flank at an altitude of between 600 and 1,200 feet (180 and 360 metres), in a ribbon that is rarely more than a mile wide.

The higher the mountains are, the drier the land they shelter from moist west winds. In the north where they are lower their influence is not so marked; the wines of Bas-Rhin are often less richly ripe, although scarcely less fragrant and fine. ('Bas' has no connotation of being lower here – except in the sense of lower down the Rhine.) The map shows the central stretch of the Haut-Rhin vineyards, clustered to the north and south of the city of Colmar – where the mountains can keep the sky clear of clouds for weeks on end.

Ironically, the winegrowing conditions are so ideal that Alsace has been seen during long periods of its troubled history as a source of *vin ordinaire* or reliable blending material – rather as France once regarded Algeria. Hence the lack of a long-hatched hierarchy of the better and the best vineyards in the manner of the Côte d'Or.

The modern wine industry here developed through the enterprise of farmers, many of them working the same land since the 17th century, turning merchant and branding their own and their neighbours' wines, distinguishing them

Below: the wine villages of Alsace hug the eastern slopes around the 1,000-ft (300-m) contour line at the point where vineyards give way to woods: an uncanny echo of the Côte d'Or in Burgundy. This is Hunawihr, where the Rosacker vineyard slopes up to the church.

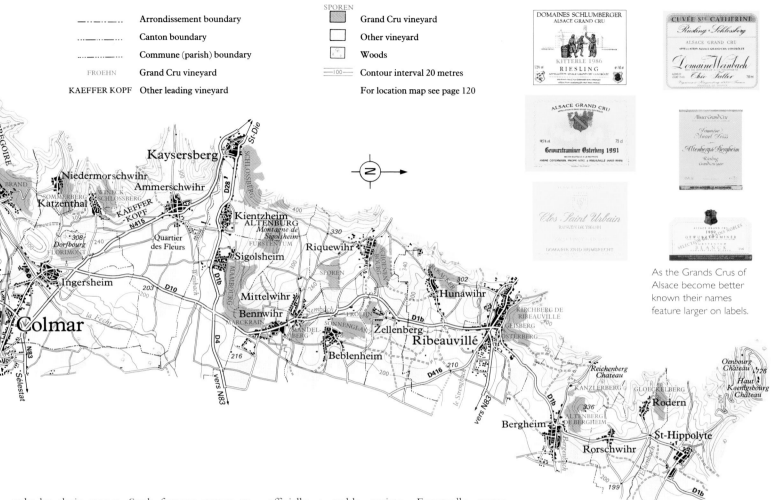

As the Grands Crus of Alsace become better known their names feature larger on labels.

only by their grapes. Such famous names as Hugel, Dopff, Trimbach, Humbrecht, Becker, Kuehn or Muré are the result. Alsace also had France's first cooperative cellar, in 1895, and such cooperatives as Eguisheim, Kientzheim, Beblenheim and Westhalten rank high among the quality producers today.

The new Grand Cru appellation (described on page 121) is a change in emphasis which is not without its problems. Over twenty years of gestation have witnessed some very lively discussions. First, the wine trade is organized to sell brands and varieties, not vineyards. The previous connotation of Grand Cru as some sort of 'reserve' status was extremely convenient, but merchants pointed out that, beyond their own small domaines, they had no way of confirming exactly where each wagon-load of grapes was picked. In other words the new Grands Crus tend to transfer the balance of power from merchants to growers.

Second, the decrees will eventually stipulate which of the noble wines each Grand Cru may grow. Some sites are deemed best for Riesling, others for Gewürztraminer or Pinot Gris. But any growers with a splendid patch of Sylvaner (for example in Zotzenberg, the Grand Cru of Mittelbergheim (see page 120), where it grows superbly) are excluded because Sylvaner is not

officially a noble variety. Eventually many growers will have to switch varieties to conform.

Some site/variety associations are already well in place. The Clos Ste-Hune of Trimbach, for example, is famous for its Riesling, Hugel's Sporen for its Gewürztraminer, Blanck's Schlossberg for its Riesling, Dopff & Irion's Clos des Amandiers for its Muscat, Zind-Humbrecht's Clos St-Urbain at Thann for its Riesling, and Willm's Clos Gaensbronnel at Barr for Gewürztraminer.

Other outstanding Grands Crus start in the extreme south with Rangen at Thann (see page 120). Riesling, Pinot Gris and Gewürztraminer all reach formidable ripeness on its volcanic soil. At Guebwiller the sandy Kitterlé is famous for its rich and luscious wines from the same three grape varieties, grown by the house of Schlumberger. At Westhalten Zinnkoepfle faces due south and makes fine Gewürztraminer, Riesling and Muscat.

Hatschbourg at Voegtlingshofen is a splendid limestone vineyard, ripening dense-textured Pinot Gris and Gewürztraminer. Eichberg at Eguisheim grows fine Gewürztraminer and Riesling. Brand and Hengst at Turckheim and Wintzenheim respectively are famous for the same varieties. At Riquewihr the sandy Schoenenbourg grows glorious Riesling and at

Bergheim Altenberg is a superb all-rounder.

But while the concept of the Grand Cru, and better still of the *clos*, the little self-contained vineyard inside a Grand Cru, appeals to many winemakers, others produce equally fine selections as 'Cuvées' of their best grapes.

A signposted Route des Vins takes visitors on a meandering course the whole length of the Alsace wine country. It calls on the way at some of the prettiest wine towns in the world. The richest possible operatic Gothick is the standard architecture here: overhanging gables, flower-filled courtyards, well-heads and cobbles and leaded lights and carved beams survive *en masse* in many of the villages. Riquewihr and Kaysersberg are the most beautiful. The city of Colmar, the capital of Alsace, has a magnificent collection of timber-frame houses which date from the 15th century.

Between the settlements the high-trained vines block out the view along the narrow lanes, until you reach a ridge and suddenly see the gleaming green sea rolling against the mountains before and behind, disappearing in a haze in the distance.

The Rhône Valley: the North

The valley of the Loire and the valley of the Rhône are two sides of the same coin. They contain respectively the best of northern and the best of southern French viticulture. Most Loire wine is white, most Rhône red. In each case there is a wide variety of styles of wine but a distinct family feeling.

Rhône red wines vary from the intensely concentrated and tannic, ruby-black or purple-black in youth, to some very wishy-washy productions. The best have depth, length and mature to lingering harmony comparable to the greatest wines of Bordeaux. They constitute the extremely limited output of the districts mapped in detail on the following pages. Everyday Côtes du Rhône is not the same sort of thing at all. The bulk comes from the wide southern area and needs choosing with great care. White wines are in the minority, tend to headiness but can be as notable as all but the best of the red.

In the course of the Rhône the country changes from oak forest, where the vine shares the fields with peach trees and nut trees, to the herbal scrub and olive groves of Provence. In the north the vine perches on terraced cliffs of crumbling granite wherever the best view of the sun can be found. In the south it lies baking

The grey Rhône sweeps past Condrieu and the stacked terraces of Château Grillet. This tiny estate constitutes a private appellation contrôlée – though few claim the wine is better than any other Viognier of Condrieu.

in broad terraces of smooth, round stones where the sun is everywhere.

The noble grape of the Rhône is the Syrah, alias (in Australia) Shiraz. The legend that it arrived in France from Shiraz in Persia via Greece and was brought by traders up the Rhône is neither impossible nor even improbable. In the south the dominant grape is the less noble but highly versatile Grenache.

Rhône wines are not as a rule made from one grape variety on its own, as burgundy is, but from a blend of anything from two to 13. It is common practice to add a little of a white variety to the very dark wine of the Syrah to add suppleness and finesse to Côte Rôtie and Hermitage. Châteauneuf-du-Pape is made from a whole roll-call of vines, both red and white.

The vineyards around the Rhône Valley fall naturally into two groups: the north, with a mere 5% of production, almost all fine wine, and the south, where fine wine is in a minority. The break comes at about Montélimar where

for a short stretch the vine is absent from the broad valley. The appellation Côtes du Rhône is a general one for the wine, red, white or rosé, of 150-odd communes, mainly in the south. But the separate appellation Côtes du Rhône-Villages is another matter. The 16 best communes in the southern zone have won the right to use their own names as appellations, together with the words Côtes du Rhône-Villages. A further 18 areas have their own separate appellations. With the exception of Châtillon-en-Diois and Die, all are shown on the map.

On the following pages the best areas of the northern and southern Rhône are mapped in detail. Côte Rôtie, Condrieu and Hermitage, the finest Rhône wines of all, all belong in the northern sector. Around them lie several others of strong local character, long traditions and spreading reputations. The best is Cornas, the country cousin to the noble Hermitage, made of the same Syrah grapes and with just as much authority, if less finesse. The appellation today is reduced to a mere 200 acres (81 hectares) of steep terraces, sheltered from the Mistral, but such is the fame of its incredibly vigorous blackstrap Syrah, far more truly a 'black' wine than anything made in Cahors, that the temptation to over-produce now threatens to kill the goose. Clape, de Barjac and Jaboulet make models of what the wine should be.

The temptation to stretch a good name to bursting point has already overtaken St-Joseph, the west-bank appellation to the north of Cornas. Until 1969 it was a group of six communes, of which Mauves was possibly the best. Since 1969 St-Joseph has been allowed to expand into a total of 45 communes, and to grow from 240 acres (97 hectares) to over 1,600 (648 hectares). From being a less formidable Cornas, a wine favourably compared with the better-known Crozes-Hermitage, much of St-Joseph today is merely a northern Côtes du Rhône, grown in the river valley instead of on its granite slopes. The names of the original six communes, Glun, Mauves, Tournon, St-Jean-de-Muzols, Lemps and Vion, remain a pointer to the best wines – along with the cooperative at St-Désirat. They are at their peak at five years or so. St-Joseph also makes one of the Rhône's least-known but most persuasive whites; often better than its red.

Champagne-method wines seem somehow out of place in this rustic, southern environment. But St-Péray, south of Cornas, has an old name for its heavy-grade, golden sparkling wine of the local Roussanne and Marsanne grapes (also made *tranquil*), while on the River Drôme to the east totally different grapes (Clairette and Muscat) make another sparkler, Clairette de Die, in the very opposite mode: featherweight and fragrant.

Meanwhile a relatively new appellation, started in 1974 southeast of Montélimar, has added to the supply of good, lively Rhône reds. The Coteaux du Tricastin uses a measure of Syrah to give its round red wine a satisfying backbone of flavour.

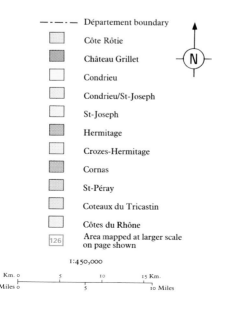

	Département boundary
	Côte Rôtie
	Château Grillet
	Condrieu
	Condrieu/St-Joseph
	St-Joseph
	Hermitage
	Crozes-Hermitage
	Cornas
	St-Péray
	Coteaux du Tricastin
	Côtes du Rhône
126	Area mapped at larger scale on page shown

1:450,000

Km. 0   5   10   15 Km.
Miles 0   5   10 Miles

For Southern Rhône map see page 129

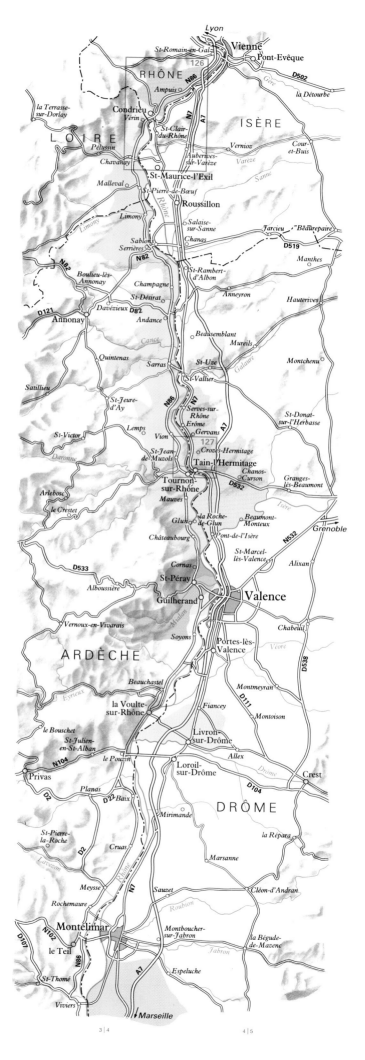

Cornas is the Rhône's best-kept secret; St-Joseph widely available; Die and St-Péray sparkling specialities. Ardèche vin de pays Chardonnay is first-rate.

Côte Rôtie and Condrieu

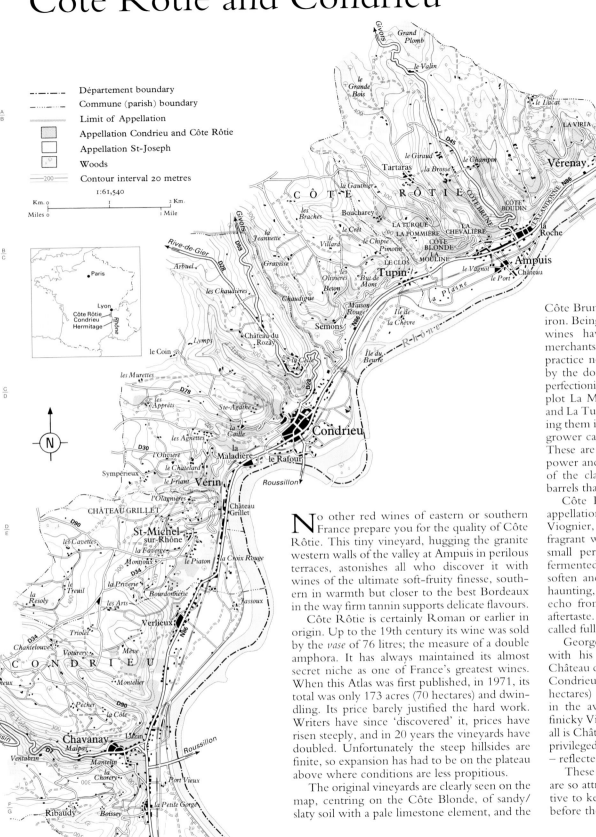

Côte Brune, whose heavier clay is darkened by iron. Being equal in quality but not in style their wines have in the past been blended by merchants to produce a unified Côte Rôtie; a practice now modified by several growers, led by the dominant figure in the appellation, the perfectionist Marcel Guigal. By bottling his single-plot La Mouline (Côte Blonde), La Landonne and La Turque (Côte Brune) separately and ageing them in new oak he has come as close as any grower can to creating a new Romanée-Conti. These are wines for millionaires, impressed by power and pungency, but not always for lovers of the classic gentle Côte Rôtie, matured in barrels that are themselves mature.

Côte Rôtie merges into the even smaller appellation of Condrieu, whose grape, the Viognier, gives lush, supple and magically fragrant white wine – in minute quantities. A small percentage of Viognier is traditionally fermented with the Syrah of Côte Rôtie to soften and perfume it. Alone, Viognier has a haunting, floral scent like a faint and disturbing echo from the Rhine and a very long, spicy aftertaste. The best examples are too rich to be called fully dry.

Georges Vernay is leader of the appellation with his Coteaux du Vernon, followed by Château du Rozay, Guigal and Pierre Dumazet. Condrieu, too, is growing, from 30 acres (12 hectares) to over 148 (60 hectares), not always in the awkward inaccessible spots where the finicky Viognier flourishes. Theoretically best of all is Château Grillet: 9.4 acres (3.8 hectares) in a privileged microclimate with its own appellation – reflected more in its price than its quality.

These precious but essentially fragile wines, are so attractive young that there is little incentive to keep them. Better to drink them young before the bloom goes off them.

No other red wines of eastern or southern France prepare you for the quality of Côte Rôtie. This tiny vineyard, hugging the granite western walls of the valley at Ampuis in perilous terraces, astonishes all who discover it with wines of the ultimate soft-fruity finesse, southern in warmth but closer to the best Bordeaux in the way firm tannin supports delicate flavours.

Côte Rôtie is certainly Roman or earlier in origin. Up to the 19th century its wine was sold by the *vase* of 76 litres; the measure of a double amphora. It has always maintained its almost secret niche as one of France's greatest wines. When this Atlas was first published, in 1971, its total was only 173 acres (70 hectares) and dwindling. Its price barely justified the hard work. Writers have since 'discovered' it, prices have risen steeply, and in 20 years the vineyards have doubled. Unfortunately the steep hillsides are finite, so expansion has had to be on the plateau above where conditions are less propitious.

The original vineyards are clearly seen on the map, centring on the Côte Blonde, of sandy/slaty soil with a pale limestone element, and the

Hermitage

France's main north–south artery, the Rhône, and its accompanying roads and railway, snakes by under the stacked terraces of the hill of Hermitage, making the vineyard's magnificent stance looking south down the river above Tain familiar to millions.

The south slopes of Hermitage amount to 311 acres (126 hectares) of terraced granite, not as steep as Côte Rôtie, covered with sandy soil containing some lime in the central and eastern parts away from the river. A hundred years ago its 'mas' – the local name for the individual vineyards – were named beside Château Lafite and Romanée-Conti as among the best red wines of the world. Writing in the 19th century the wine merchant A Jullien listed them in order of merit: Méal, Gréfieux, Beaume, Raucoule, Muret, Guoignière, Bessas, Burges and Lauds. Spellings have changed; the mas remain, but today few of their names are heard, and scarcely ever in the same breath as Château Lafite.

The adjective 'manly' has stuck to Hermitage ever since it was first applied to it. It has almost the qualities of port without the added brandy. Like vintage port it throws a heavy sediment in the bottle (it needs decanting) and improves for many years until its scent and flavour are almost overwhelming.

Young Hermitage of a good vintage is as closed and tannic as any young great red, but nothing can restrain its abounding perfume and the fistfuls of fruit that seem crammed into the glass. As it ages the immediacy of its impact does not diminish, but its youthful assault gives way to the sheer splendour of its mature presence. You could not drink it and not be impressed.

Like most great wines it has its shadow. Crozes-Hermitage is to the Grand Cru what a village Gevrey-Chambertin is to Le Chambertin. Crozes is the village at the back of the uprearing hill, and its appellation covers a very mixed bag of vineyards, both north and south of Tain and Hermitage itself. Only one Crozes wine, Paul Jaboulet's Domaine de Thalabert, is regularly comparable to a Hermitage. Most are full and fairly fruity without the classic bite and concentration. And others are very pallid.

Indeed some of the best Crozes-Hermitage is white, and the Hermitage hill is historically almost as famous for its white wine – now a quarter of its production – as its red. The red too can contain up to 15% of the white Marsanne.

Jullien named 'Raucoule' as the best white Hermitage. Today Chante-Alouette is the best known. Besides being a mas, it is a trademark of Chapoutier. The wine is golden, dry and full with a remarkably delicate, eventually nutty flavour, and matures like red Hermitage for a decade at least.

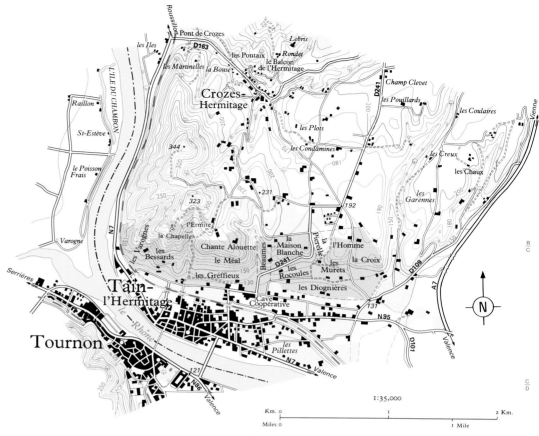

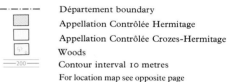

Département boundary
Appellation Contrôlée Hermitage
Appellation Contrôlée Crozes-Hermitage
Woods
Contour interval 10 metres
For location map see opposite page

The River Rhône washes the foot of the hill of Hermitage, skirting the city of Tain. The old hermitage chapel stills stands among the staked vines on top, in a patch giving some of the most potent wine.

Concentrations of quality and character in Côte Rôtie, Condrieu and Hermitage are formidable. Chante-Alouette (white) and La Chapelle (red) are the touchstones in Hermitage.

The Rhône Valley: the South

The funnel end of the Rhône Valley, where it releases its traffic to the Mediterranean, has a place in every traveller's affections. History and natural history combine to make it one of the richest regions of France for interest of every kind. Who cannot picture the vast engineering of the Romans, lizards alert on its slumbering stones, patches of early vegetables screened around against the wind, the pines and almonds yielding to olive groves as you go south – and always, on hillside or plain, sand or chalk, the cross-stitch of vines?

The heart of the region, the vineyard that sums up all its qualities, is Châteauneuf-du-Pape. History does not make so much of its neighbours. The huge appellation Côtes du Rhône, most of it on this map (with a little to the north) covers nearly 83,000 acres (33,500 hectares) in more than 100 communes north of Avignon. They form a rough circle straddling the low hills where the valley begins to widen.

The Côtes du Rhône crop can be three times as much as that of Beaujolais, and not very much less than all of Bordeaux. The great majority is red, soft, mildly fruity with a gentle warmth, much of it now made Beaujolais-style to accentuate its modest degree of flavour. It can rarely compete with standard Bordeaux for freshness and sapidity. It is wine for the easily satisfied.

Its central zone, where most of the superior -Villages communes lie, is mapped on pages 130–31. The two northernmost of the -Villages, Rousset-les-Vignes and St-Pantaléon-les-Vignes, used to sell their wines under the name Haut-Comtat, a name little seen today. Between here and the Rhône the up-and-coming appellation Coteaux du Tricastin is a parched Mistral-swept landscape better known in the past for its truffles that its wine. Even the best Tricastin wines, their flavour stiffened with Syrah, need no more than two or three years' ageing.

East of the -Villages lies another area of recent development, the (1973) AC Côtes du Ventoux. The tradition here is for light-coloured 'café' wines, lively when very young. The best-known *marque* is La Vieille Ferme, an outstation of the great Beaucastel of Châteauneuf (much more restaurant- than café-wine).

To their south the Montagne du Lubéron marks the northern boundary of Provence, with red wines comparable to the Côtes du Ventoux, surprisingly fresh whites and even a bargain sparkling wine from the *cave coopérative*.

The west bank of the Rhône has an even more varied range, starting in the north with the Coteaux d'Ardèche (see page 139), only a vin de pays but a celebrated success recently with wines as different as Syrah and Cabernet made as straight 'varietals' in the New World manner. Gamay, Chardonnay and Merlot have all found niches here too. This is certainly a corner of France to watch.

To the south comes the VDQS Côtes du Vivarais, rather like featherweight Côtes du Rhône, and further south again are the two excellent Côtes du Rhône-Villages of Chusclan and Laudun, both of which are known as well for their rosé (and white) wine as red.

Languedoc and Provence meet in the parched *causses* at Les Baux, whose famous restaurant serves some of Provence's best food and wine. The AC Les Baux-de-Provence (new in 1985) is led by the outstanding Domaine de Trévallon. To the west the Costières de Nîmes (formerly du Gard) is a big and busy appellation for (principally) red and rosé Côtes du Rhône-style, and a rather faint white formerly sold as Bellegarde. Here the Château de la Tuilerie is the clear local leader. Further west the isolated communes of the Coteaux du Languedoc should not be overlooked (see page 135).

Much the biggest producer of the region (and indeed of the whole of France) is the extra-ordinary 4,200 acres (1,700-hectare) Domaine Viticole des Salins du Midi, whose 'Listel' wines are grown on the very beaches along the seashore. Listel has learnt to use the sand as what a gardener would term a neutral growing medium, applying all the water and fertilizer the vines need, excluding the sea water with fresh-water dykes. Their wines are very clean, fruity, charming and well made: a most impressive achievement. All in all, few other wine regions contain so much variety as this, or so much promise.

The 'Villages' of the Côtes de Rhône cluster in the shelter of the hills of Montmirail and the Baronnies, often in a patchwork with orchards and olives.

Southern Rhône wines include Côtes du Rhône, more serious -Villages, Châteauneuf-du-Pape, sweet muscats and light 'sand wines' of Listel.

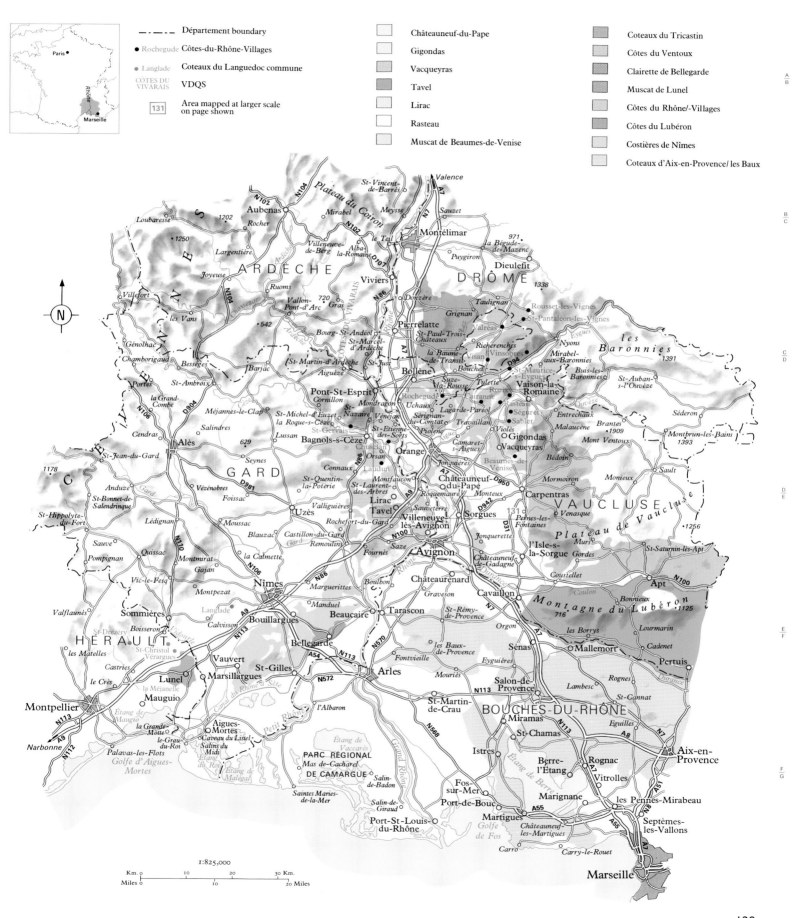

Légende / Legend:

- –·–·– Département boundary
- ● Rochegude Côtes-du-Rhône-Villages
- ● Langlade Coteaux du Languedoc commune
- CÔTES DU VIVARAIS VDQS
- 131 Area mapped at larger scale on page shown

- Châteauneuf-du-Pape
- Gigondas
- Vacqueyras
- Tavel
- Lirac
- Rasteau
- Muscat de Beaumes-de-Venise

- Coteaux du Tricastin
- Côtes du Ventoux
- Clairette de Bellegarde
- Muscat de Lunel
- Côtes du Rhône/-Villages
- Côtes du Lubéron
- Costières de Nîmes
- Coteaux d'Aix-en-Provence/ les Baux

1:825,000

Km. 0   10   20   30 Km.
Miles 0   10   20 Miles

Châteauneuf-du-Pape

The Avignon popes of the 14th century reigned from the château whose ruins now overlook the pebble-floored vineyards of Châteauneuf-du-Pape. A dozen grape varieties are grown, each vine an individual bush. Estates here are substantial châteaux, as they are in Lirac and in Tavel to the west.

Châteauneuf-du-Pape is the famous centre-piece of the Rhône, just north of Avignon: 8,151 acres (3,300 hectares) of vines on hills dominated by a ruined papal summer palace. Its vines are widely spaced; low bushes in a sea of smooth pink and beige glacier-worn stones with no earth to be seen. The deep red wine of Châteauneuf has the distinction not only of having the highest minimum strength of any French wine (12.5% alcohol) but of being the first to be so regulated. Its most famous grower, the late Baron Le Roy, initiated here what has become the national system of appellations contrôlées. Part of his original proposal, made in 1923, was that suitable land for fine Châteauneuf vines (there are 13 varieties) should be identified by the conjunction of lavender and thyme growing there. In addition, grape varieties, pruning, quantity and strength were to be controlled.

The Baron's foresight was rewarded by Châteauneuf-du-Pape emerging from obscurity to become one of the world's most famous wines.

Some 100,000 hectolitres of wine a year are made here, 97% of it red. Most of it is good to average; made relatively light (although not in alcohol) by increasing the proportion of Grenache grapes so that it can be drunk after a mere year or two. A number of big estates, like Bordeaux châteaux, are the producers of the classic dark and deep Châteauneuf, each using its own cock-tail of the 13 permitted varieties to make more or less spicy, more or less tannic or smooth, shorter- or longer-lived wine.

Modern winemaking methods have given new interest to what had become a somewhat disillusioned appellation. Today, such estates as the Châteaux Beaucastel, Fortia and Rayas, Le Vieux Télégraphe and La Nerthe have standards as high as the best in France. Their reds age to sumptuous, sometimes gamey, depths of flavour and their rare whites, succulent from youth, develop exotic scents, sometimes reminiscent of orange-peel, after seven or eight years. The principal estates use heavy embossed bottles of dark glass which help to identify their wines.

Châteauneuf-du-Pape is surrounded by more than a hundred communities that produce Côtes du Rhône. In the 1950s four of them, Gigondas and Cairanne to the northeast, and Chusclan and Laudun on the west bank of the Rhône, were singled out by the authorities as having the most potential, and directed to lower their productions and raise the strength and quality of their wines. Better prices proved them justified. In 1966 a new appellation, Côtes du Rhône-Villages, was decreed for these four along with a number of their neighbours, which has subsequently risen to 16.

Gigondas meanwhile raised its standards still further to become (in 1971) an appellation in its own right; a dark, deep red needing six or seven years' ageing, and a potential rival to Châteauneuf itself.

The Côtes du Rhône-Villages wines are all characters worthy of closer study. Cairanne and Vacqueyras are generally considered the best, and in 1990 Vacqueyras duly received its appellation accolade. They are both wines of firm structure (Vacqueyras has been described as 'a sort of rough-house Gigondas'), that need at least four years' ageing. Some others, such as Sablet, Valréas, St-Gervais and Rochegude, tend to be milder and sooner ready to drink. But growers (and cooperatives) vary as much as –Villages, particularly in the proportion of the tasty Syrah in relation to the merely strong Grenache in their wines. There are also individual producers outside the -Villages, such as the Château de Fonsalette at Lagarde-Paréol, well up to -Villages standards. It is always better to taste before buying.

Rosé is the historic speciality of Tavel and Lirac, the two southernmost of the true Rhône appellations. The potent dry Grenache rosé of Tavel, orange-tinted after a year or two, has its fervent admirers – though it is best drunk before the orange tint appears. Lirac, formerly also best known for rosé, inclines more today to softly fruity reds and well-made fresh whites.

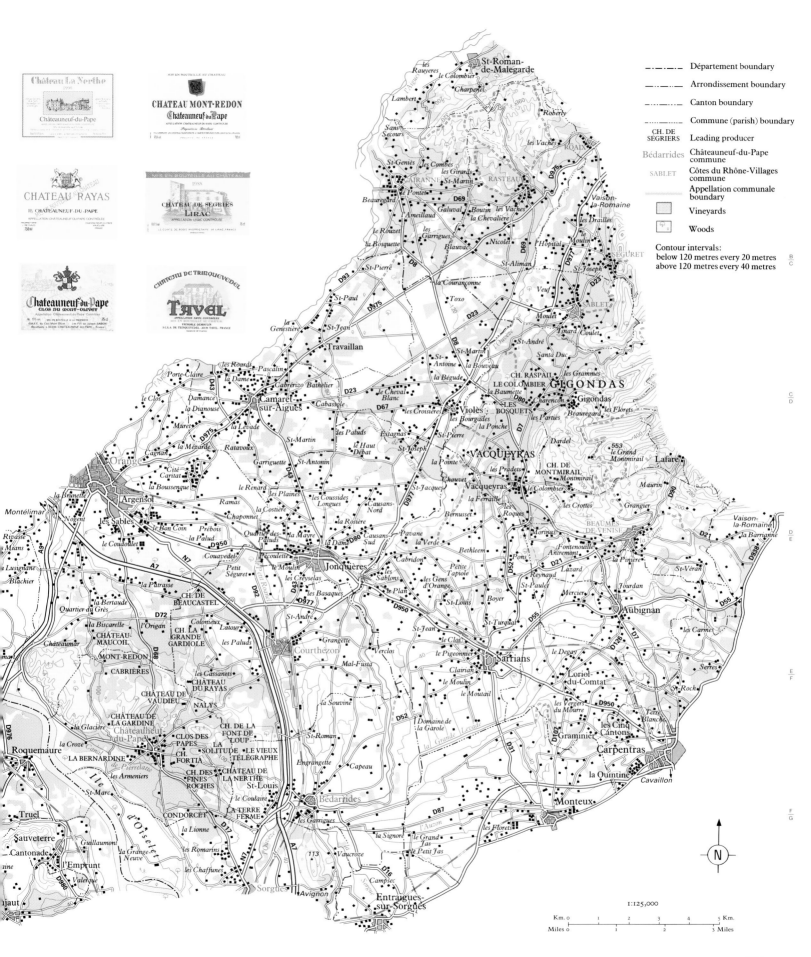

Roussillon, Corbières and Minervois

Previous editions of the Atlas mapped together the 120-mile (190-kilometre) sweep of the Languedoc and Roussillon coast and its hinterland, distinguishing only the hill regions as they emerged first as VDQS zones, later as full ACs. Here they feature at the scale they now deserve. For this is France's fastest-moving region.

More than a third of all French wine is grown in this area: the Midi. With over 865,000 acres (350,000 hectares) it is the biggest vineyard region in the world (Bordeaux has 100,000 hectares). The majority of its 60,000 growers take their grapes to no less than 550 *coopératives*. Two-thirds of the region's wine is made in these cellars, which vary from down-at-heel to startlingly modern. Of the vast production of the Midi almost all is red; perhaps 10–15% white or rosé. This is the traditional *vin ordinaire* territory: the *gros rouge* of the old-style French workman – plain reds, and strong sweet Vins Doux Naturels.

The sheer quantity of nameless wine produced (and the strikes provoked by the recurring glut) long obscured the quality of the best wines and the efforts which are improving them. Winegrowing started with the Romans. The vine flourished where nothing else would in the stony hills, and its produce was good. It was not until phylloxera crushed the hill-vignerons that the vine came down to the plain and the permanent crisis of overproduction began.

It is never easy to convince farmers that the way to prosperity is to grow less but better. But in the last 20 years the Midi has changed. The loss of Algeria, and the return of the *pieds noirs* who owned the vineyards, was perhaps the starting gun. France now has a New World of her own – and this is it. Two motors are at work here. The first is the revival and redevelopment of old hill vineyards, using traditional regional grapes to make *vins de terroir* typical enough to merit distinctive appellations. The second is the revolutionary (for France) introduction of *vins de cépage* – what Anglo-Saxons call varietal wines. Huge encouragement for both has been provided by the success of the concept of *vins de pays*, which is explained on pages 138–39.

The long curve of the coast pivots round the mouth of the Aude near Narbonne. The western arc mapped here is the more mountainous, the more traditional, tougher and more varied in its soils and climates. At its southern end the Pyrenees come down to the Mediterranean in a magnificent landscape; 1,600-foot (500-metre) peaks within sight of the sea.

This is Roussillon, the country of the oddly named Vins Doux Naturels – not naturally sweet wines, as the name infers, but strong wines stopped in their fermentation by adding alcohol; the same process as port, but with more wine and less spirit. Grand Roussillon is the general (but little-used) appellation for the 'VDNs'. The best areas have their own appellations.

Banyuls and Banyuls Grand Cru, on steep terraces of dark brown schist sloping to the sea just north of the Spanish frontier, are the southernmost vineyards of France. Their main grape is Grenache, sometimes blended with Carignan or even Syrah, all of which ripen to very high degrees, often shrivelling to raisins on the vine. For Grand Cru 30 months of barrel-ageing is mandatory. Formerly, the wines were kept in glass 'bonbons' exposed to the light which gave them a strong 'rancio' flavour. Today good Banyuls is dark amber, intense, highly fragrant but fresh and clean and long in the mouth.

The curious little appellation of Maury, on similar soils on the north bank of the River Agly, is considered almost the equal of Banyuls. The much bigger zone of Rivesaltes, between the two, offers a lighter and cheaper version of a Grenache-based VDN, most of it white. Far superior is the powerful white Muscat de Rivesaltes, seen in every bar in France.

The world outside France is more interested in the red table wines of Roussillon, which were already known and appreciated in north Europe in the 18th century. Côtes de Roussillon is the base level, made from Carignan, Grenache and Cinsault, the (better) standard Midi grapes, nowadays with a seasoning of *cépages améliorateurs*, flavour-boosters, which may be Syrah, Mourvèdre – even at a pinch Cabernet or Merlot.

Côtes de Roussillon-Villages are bolder, more positive wines, restricted to one-third of the area, to lower yields and higher strength. These were the first Midi reds to aspire to higher things in the 1960s by introducing carbonic maceration. They remain excellent value as firm, solid, age-worthy wines whose aromas come from the soil and their sheer vinosity rather than from fashionable aromatic grape varieties. They are produced in the valley of the Agly, one of three rivers (along with the Tet and the Tech) which sound as rugged as they are. Latour-de-France and Caramany are their best production centres.

The Corbières landscape is no less dramatic, a geological chaos of mountain and valley reaching from the sea 40 miles (60 kilometres) back into the Aude *département*. It is far less homogeneous even than Roussillon. Limestone alternates with schist, volcanic rock and sand; the influence of the Mediterranean with intermittent influence from the Atlantic, funnelling down the Aude Valley and over its western hills.

The region has recently been divided by its Syndicat de Défense into no fewer than 11 zones. Their full characters have yet to emerge. Previously four were recognized, broadly speaking increasing in quality potential as they went up into the hills, although up to 1985 the only appellation-rank Corbières was Fitou, a name for two groups of villages, one near the sea and one in central Corbières, introduced in 1948 *pour encourager*, one imagines, *les autres*. (The excellent little appellation Collioure in southern Roussillon might be similarly described.)

The quality of Fitou was based on small crops of Carignan, the workhorse grape of the Midi (which from old vines can be excellent) and Grenache, seasoned with Mourvèdre by the sea and Syrah in the hills. Carbonic maceration and standard vinification are both used to make wine with enough structure to age up to five years.

The extent of the cooling Atlantic influence here is most graphically seen in the region of Carcassonne. South of the fortified city Limoux gains notoriety year by year for its excellent sparkling Blanquette, based on the original Mauzac but now increasingly embellished with Chardonnay. A new AC stipulates stiff regulations for an oak-fermented Limoux Chardonnay without bubbles. More surprisingly Limoux is even making fine light Pinot Noir.

Limoux and its northern neighbour, the Côtes de la Malepère, are also busy proving that the Midi ends here and the southwest begins by growing very convincing Merlot and Malbec, Cabernet Sauvignon and Cabernet Franc.

The transition is even more evident across the Aude to the north, where the Côtes de Cabardès, clinging to the south flank of the Montagne Noire, seems to pay equal regard to the Mediterranean grapes of neighbouring Minervois and the Cabernet family blowing in from the west.

Minervois came to prominence, as prominence goes here, before Corbières, by making much the same sort of Carignan- and Grenache-based wines, spiced with Syrah and Mourvèdre, in a distinctive vein: firmer, fresher and more lively. How much of the difference is due to the *terroir* and how much to local motivation will be determined as the elaborate regional distinctions become better known and understood.

Southern Midi wines range from port-like Banyuls, to light sparkling Blanquette, via deep reds like Fitou or Collioure and piquant Minervois and Cabardès – even Chardonnay.

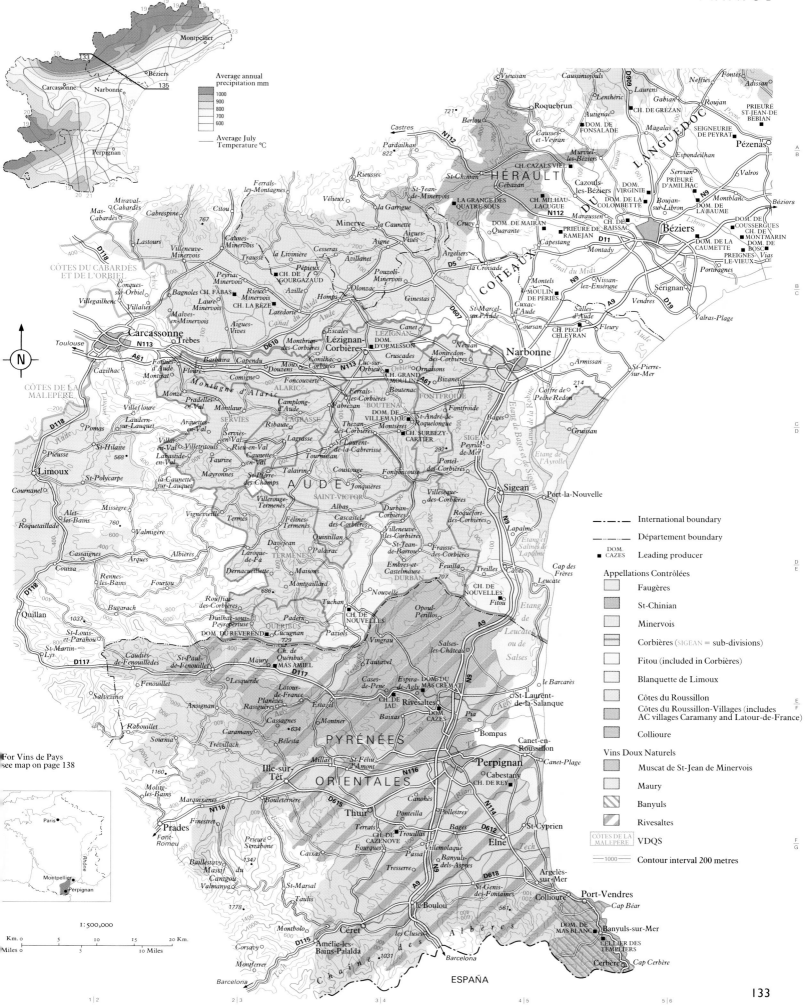

Average annual
precipitation mm

1000
900
800
700
600

Average July
Temperature °C

N

CÔTES DU CABARDÈS
ET DE L'ORBIEL

CÔTES DE LA
MALEPÈRE

For Vins de Pays
see map on page 138

International boundary

Département boundary

DOM.
CAZES   Leading producer

Appellations Contrôlées

Faugères

St-Chinian

Minervois

Corbières (SIGEAN = sub-divisions)

Fitou (included in Corbières)

Blanquette de Limoux

Côtes du Roussillon

Côtes du Roussillon-Villages (includes
AC villages Caramany and Latour-de-France)

Collioure

Vins Doux Naturels

Muscat de St-Jean de Minervois

Maury

Banyuls

Rivesaltes

CÔTES DE LA
MALEPÈRE   VDQS

——1000—— Contour interval 200 metres

Paris

Montpellier

Perpignan

1 : 500,000

Km. 0   5   10   15   20 Km.

Miles 0   5   10 Miles

ESPAÑA

Languedoc: the Plains

Mas de Daumas Gassac, northwest of Montpellier, symbolizes the change in the Languedoc in the 80s from quantity to quality. Its *terroir* gives wines of intense colour and high flavour. The Midi is set to be France's California.

Appellations, vins de pays, estates, brand names and 'varietals' all have equal standing in the Midi.

Twenty years ago it was hard to find anything positive to say about the Hérault, the *département* that covers most of this map, except that its eponymous river, crashing in gorges from the Cévennes, traverses some beautiful landscapes. Viticulturally the only glimmers were the very passable muscat Vins Doux Naturels of Frontignan and neighbouring Lunel and Mireval, and a few up-country producers of solid reds in the hills that continue intermittently eastwards from the Minervois.

The Minervois is eminently capable of clean and tasty reds of real personality, full and earthy (and a very little muscat, too, at St-Jean-de Minervois). The almost contiguous (but not so high) St-Chinian is no less so, particularly on the bizarre deep purple soil round the town, and big cooperative, of Berlou. The style here is softer, less structured than in Minervois; very good at about two years.

St-Chinian flows on into Faugères to the east, the next in the discontinuous group of the Coteaux du Languedoc and perhaps the most striking personality of the traditional Hérault hill wines. Faugères can be full, fresh and almost fiery, showing how well the often maligned Carignan, Cinsault and Grenache can do on dry schist with small crops. The Coteaux continue with Cabrières, St-Saturnin, Montpeyroux, Pic St Loup . . . the communes in a rough arc round the north of Montpellier and into the next *département*, the Gard. Excellent wine from old Cinsault and Carignan vines has also recently come from Villeveyrac, within smell of the sea.

An eccentric detached limestone massif on the coast, La Clape, an island in what was once the delta of the Aude, makes some of the Midi's best rosés and softer golden white from Malvasia. These, and the old white-wine appellations of Clairette du Languedoc (largely used for vermouth) and Picpoul de Pinet in the Hérault Valley, represent the fairly modest best of the old tradition. Carefully made these wines have characters which it would be a tragedy to lose: forthright, satisfying, well-balanced, based not on aromatic grapes but on the *terroir* – garrigue or gravel – sun-baked, windy and parched, that rears them. But they are no more the best the country can do than, for instance, Zinfandel represents the aspirations of California. Nor are the rigorous conditions of the Coteaux necessarily essential for more aromatic grape varieties.

In one simple step, therefore, the Midi is putting its past behind it. It is planting Cabernet, Merlot and Chardonnay, all the favourites of the international market, on the deep soils of the seaside plain where grapes that were dull or worse used to give undrinkable wine.

Sète has had a reputation since Roman times as a port where wine was 'trafficked' on an enormous scale. Béziers was synonymous with *gros rouge*. Now both are surrounded by substantial estates, the châteaux of the south, their huge all-purpose farm buildings filling up with stainless steel fermenters as their new *vins de cépages* turn the market on its head.

It is true that the Cinsault, Aramon and other bulk producers were largely planted on rich alluvial soils that should be growing corn. But the seaside plain has plenty of modest plateaux of well-drained shingle where good grapes have everything they need, without excess.

This is the paradox of modern Midi. Easy-to-sell varietal wines have only vin de pays status, while *vins de terroir*, bearing proud traditions and (admittedly newly granted) appellations have a

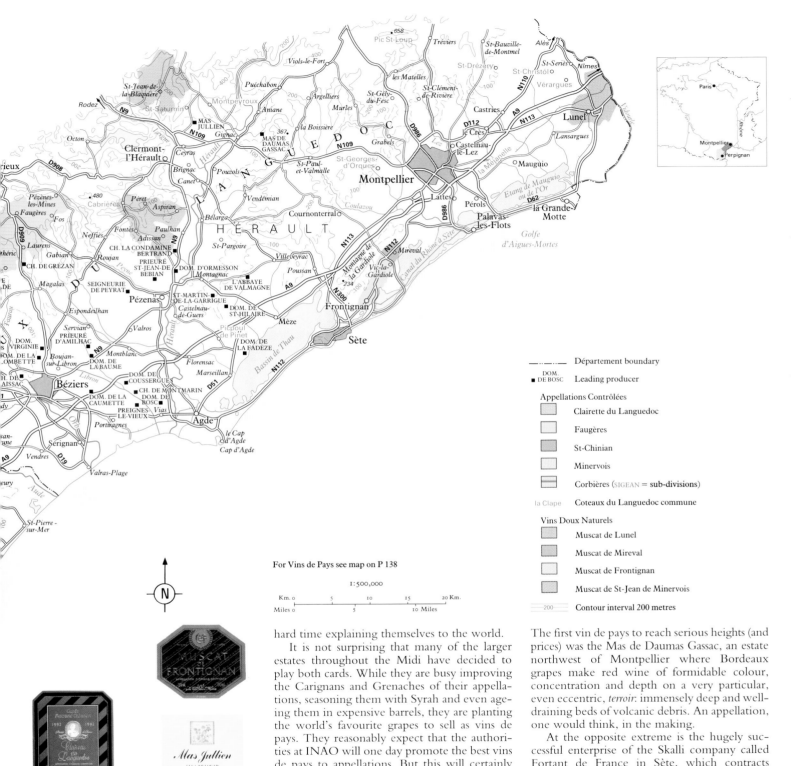

hard time explaining themselves to the world.

It is not surprising that many of the larger estates throughout the Midi have decided to play both cards. While they are busy improving the Carignans and Grenaches of their appellations, seasoning them with Syrah and even ageing them in expensive barrels, they are planting the world's favourite grapes to sell as vins de pays. They reasonably expect that the authorities at INAO will one day promote the best vins de pays to appellations. But this will certainly not happen until they are convinced about what they term 'the typicity' of the *terroir*.

The danger is not, as in Italy, that vins de pays will emerge better and at higher prices than AOC (in Italy DOC) wines. The danger is that with low land values a Chardonnay vin de pays d'Oc (the regional name) can drastically undercut a classic Burgundian Chardonnay, and that for the considerable saving the market will forgive it its lack of 'typicity'.

Not all Midi pacemakers have the same ideas.

The first vin de pays to reach serious heights (and prices) was the Mas de Daumas Gassac, an estate northwest of Montpellier where Bordeaux grapes make red wine of formidable colour, concentration and depth on a very particular, even eccentric, *terroir*: immensely deep and well-draining beds of volcanic debris. An appellation, one would think, in the making.

At the opposite extreme is the hugely successful enterprise of the Skalli company called Fortant de France in Sète, which contracts growers over a wide area to buy their Cabernet, Chardonnay and the other best-sellers. Hardys of Australia has a similar operation at the Domaine de la Baume near Béziers. (Australian technology is widely used, to the point of hiring itinerant Australian winemakers.) The idea is to produce the geographically neutral 'fruit-driven' wines which are anathema to the regulating authorities. Should the world ever be content with homogenized blends authors of wine atlases would join them among the unemployed.

Provence

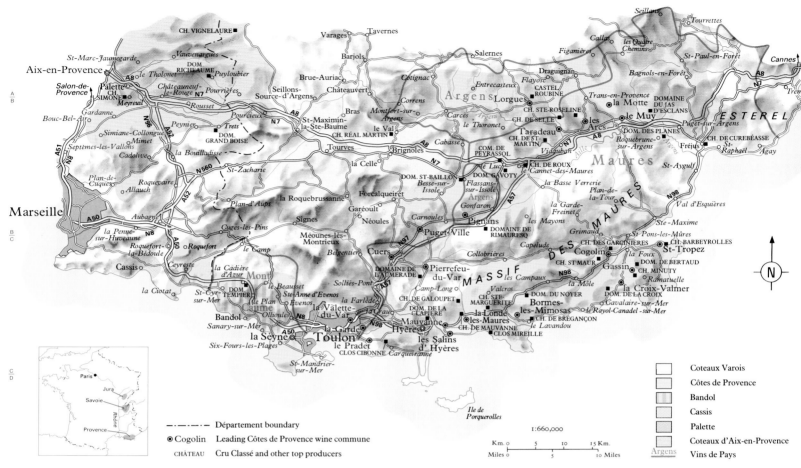

Coteaux Varois
Côtes de Provence
Bandol
Cassis
Palette
Coteaux d'Aix-en-Provence
Vins de Pays

There used to be only four small areas of fully fledged appellations contrôlées along the Mediterranean coast east of the Rhône. The longest-established are Cassis (no relation to the blackcurrant syrup), for full-bodied and lively white, and Bandol, for memorable, long-lived red based on an almost Syrah-like grape, the Mourvèdre. Palette near Aix was another tiny appellation for a patch of limestone soil exploited by one estate, Château Simone. Nice had its own high-priced reds, whites and rosés from tiny Bellet in the hills.

The wider appellation Côtes de Provence was created in 1977 for a far wider area, of great tourist fame but where fine wine was the exception. Over-strong and under-flavoured rosé was the staple. Since then standards have generally improved – in some cases dramatically. There are 400 properties now producing appellation wines, the majority still rosé, heady and orange-hued, or soft, rather pale reds of Grenache and Carignan; a fast-growing minority experimenting with such non-traditional grapes as Syrah and Cabernet to make some excellent wines with nerve and sinew. The term cru classé is allowed for the acknowledged best producers.

Descriptions of Provence wines always mention the sun-baked pines, thyme and rosemary and claim that the wine takes its character from them. One should add that hills of limestone or shale, and in some cases a cool breeze off the sea, can give considerable distinction to certain crus.

Upgrading goes on. The old VDQS Coteaux d'Aix en Provence and Coteaux des Baux became appellations in 1985 in recognition of the excellence òf such estates as Châteaux Vignelaure and Fonscolombe. Since 1992 the new AC Coteaux Varois covers the heart of the inland Var. Vins de Pays de Var include some good reds and the zonal Vin de Pays des Maures supplies St-Tropez with its daily needs. Further north the Côtes de Luberon (see page 129) and the Coteaux de Pierrevert (see page 139) are making increasingly good wines, in styles not remote from the southern Rhône.

The best wines of Provence are the fragrant, brisk but deep reds of the seaside appellation of Bandol, with Domaine Tempier and Château Vannières at their head. Cassis (*above*) is its white-wine opposite number. But Provence is seeing ever better wines from a wide scattering of substantial estates, led by Domaines Ott.

Savoie and the Jura

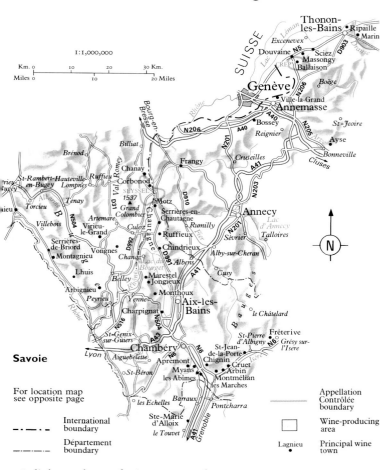

For location map
see opposite page

Savoie

International
boundary

Département
boundary

Appellation
Contrôlée
boundary

Wine-producing
area

Lagnieu • Principal wine
town

The wines of Savoie are
delicate, refreshing, alpine
in spirit.

The wine country of Savoie is diffuse and its produce hardly known. It epitomizes the 'little local wine' which travels only in legend: its cleanness and freshness are at one with the mountain air, the lakes and streams. Savoie wine is nearly all white, mostly from the Jacquère grape: dry and mild like ethereal Muscadet.

The AC Vin de Savoie applies to Jacquère wines of a certain strength. Of these, Ayse is the best-known commune for sparkling wine, Apremont, Abîmes and Chignin for still.

The best Savoie grape, though, is the Altesse or Roussette. Some claim it is the Furmint of Tokay. Altesse wine has weight and fragrance. It carries the AC Roussette de Savoie, best when qualified by such placenames as Monterminod, Frangy and (notably) Marestel.

The Swiss grape Chasselas, along with mild Jacquère and Molette, is the basis of sparkling Seyssel. It can be drier and more delicate than other sparkling wine – an intriguing alternative to champagne. The Seyssel district is the specialist. Still Seyssel, pure Chasselas, is even better.

Crépy lies just across the border from Switzerland; its grape is also the Chasselas and its whole nature more Swiss than French.

Although Gamay and Pinot Noir fetch a higher price, the best Savoyard red grape is the Mondeuse (in Italy the Refosco): smooth, fruity and tannic. Arbin, Montmélian and St-Jean-de-la-Porte are its best-known crus. Due west the VDQS vineyards of Bugey have shown that they can make, amongst other wines, smooth-scented Roussette in a blend with Chardonnay.

A little enclave of vines scattered among woodland and meadow in what seem like France's remotest hills… The Jura's production is a fraction of its former total; yet its wines are varied, good and wholly original. Its superior appellations, Arbois, Château-Chalon and l'Etoile, all count for something.

Jura wine is not only red, white and rosé, but yellow and grey. The best of it is 'yellow'; firm, strong white wine from the Savagnin grape which is kept for a minimum of six years in cask where it undergoes a transformation similar to that of sherry. The appellation Château-Chalon is limited to this odd but excellent wine, but good 'vin jaune' is also made at l'Etoile and Arbois.

The 'grey' wine is simply very pale rosé, rather sharp but extremely appetizing. The best Jura vin rosé, from Arbois, by contrast is more like pale red wine, unusually silky. Some of the white is made from the Chardonnay grape and compares well with minor white burgundies – especially that from the appellation l'Etoile. The red too can be interesting: soft, smooth and very satisfying with the local game.

A small amount of good sparkling wine is made at Arbois (and a large amount of the widely advertised Vin Fou, an inferior substitute). Liquorous vin de paille, made of loft-dried raisins, is very rare today. Like genuine hand-made Italian vin santo, it is worth its very high price. One final speciality is Macvin du Jura, now an appellation for a fragrant mixture of must and marc.

The pride of the Jura is its full-bodied vin jaune, aged (as Château-Chalon) into a sort of pale dry sherry. Reds and whites are soft and easy.

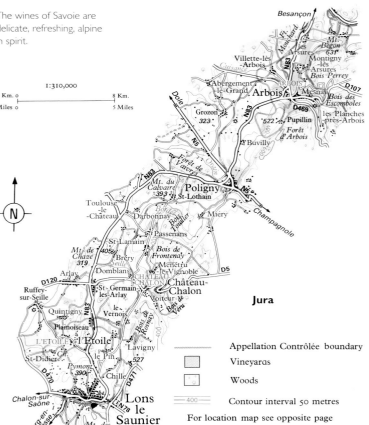

Jura

Appellation Contrôlée boundary

Vineyards

Woods

Contour interval 50 metres

For location map see opposite page

Vins de Pays

France has a way of producing, even in her remotest corners, wines that have more character and are more satisfying to drink than any but the best from the rest of Europe. She is intensely aware of her 'little' wines, and through the corps of inspectors of her Institut National des Appellations d'Origine is constantly feeling their pulses, rather like a coach keeping an eye on the colts team.

The appellation system evolved by degrees in the 1920s and 1930s. In 1949 it was followed by the creation of a second rank: Vins Délimités de Qualité Supérieure. VDQS wines have advanced steadily since their recognition. Most have already been promoted to AC. It is a fair bet that eventually all will.

Meanwhile there remained on the statute book an early version of the appellation laws known as appellation simple. Whereas the AC regulations stipulate not only the area and grape variety but also maximum qualities, minimum strengths, methods of pruning and much else besides, AS wines needed only to be grown from 'tolerated' varieties in recognized regions. Unpromoted they remained an unprofitable backwater.

The 1970s, though, saw a series of ordinances to give status and definition to the more identifiable of these 'table' wines. At the same time a new authority, ONIVIN, was created to look after them. In 1976 a list of 75 vins de pays appeared – a list that reads like poetry to anyone with a feeling for the French countryside: Vals, Coteaux and Monts, Gorges and Pays, Marches and Vicomtes, Baumes and Fiefs. Who could resist Vallée du Paradis, Cucugnan, L'Ile de Beauté, Mont Bouquet?

The list divides vins de pays into three categories: local, commune or district names, names of départements, and names of regions as vast as the whole of the Loire Valley.

The controls on quality are most stringent for district names, least for regional names. But all include a maximum crop (of between 70 and 90 hectolitres per hectare) and minimum natural alcohol levels, and lay down appropriate upper and lower limits for acidity and other analysable components. The wines have to be approved by a tasting panel, and they must be made from grape varieties officially recommended area by area. The 'noble' varieties that everyone wants, however, can be grown anywhere.

It is frankly admitted that some vins de pays have more validity than others. Some names have scarcely been used. But they are a challenge and a rallying point for growers to build on their local traditions. More spectacularly they are the golden opportunity for growers with heretical ideas to plant high-appellation 'noble' grapes in non-appellation areas. The first is a *vin de terroir*, the second a *vin de cépage*. The one crucial regulation is that no wine may be sold by a varietal name only; the label must show a vin de pays name – though it is odd how pale the printer's ink can become when a grower wants to sell a Chardonnay from no matter where. Some of the implications are discussed on page 135.

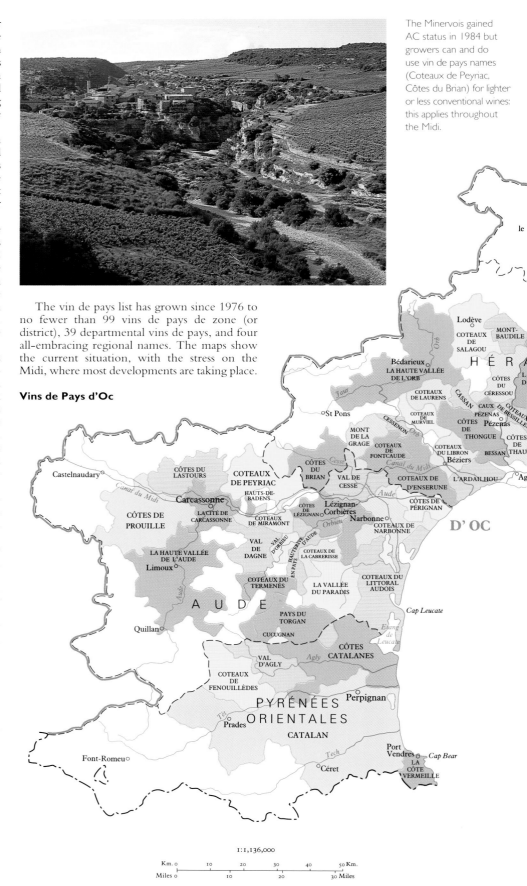

The Minervois gained AC status in 1984 but growers can and do use vin de pays names (Coteaux de Peyriac, Côtes du Brian) for lighter or less conventional wines: this applies throughout the Midi.

The vin de pays list has grown since 1976 to no fewer than 99 vins de pays de zone (or district), 39 departmental vins de pays, and four all-embracing regional names. The maps show the current situation, with the stress on the Midi, where most developments are taking place.

Vins de Pays d'Oc

1:1,136,000

Km. 0   10   20   30   40   50 Km.

Miles 0   10   20   30 Miles

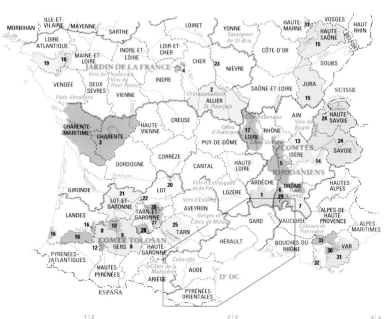

Vins de Pays

ARDÈCHE
1 Coteaux de l'Ardèche

ALLIER
2 Bourbonnais

CHARENTE/ CHARENTE-MARITIME
3 Charentais

CHER/INDRE
4 Coteaux du Cher et de l'Arnon

CORSICA
Ile de Beauté (not on map)

DRÔME
5 Collines Rhodaniennes (also in Ardèche, Isère, Loire, Rhône)
6 Comté de Grignan
7 Coteaux des Baronnies

GERS
8 Côtes de Gascogne (includes 9 and 10)
9 Côtes de Montestruc
10 Côtes du Condomois (also in Lot-et-Garonne)

HAUTE-MARNE
11 Coteaux de Coiffy

HAUTES-PYRÉNÉES
12 Bigorre

ISÈRE
13 Balmes Dauphinoises
14 Coteaux du Grésivaudan (also in Savoie)

JURA/HAUTE-SAÔNE
15 Franche-Comté

LANDES
16 Thézac-Perricard

LOIRE
17 Urfé

LOIRE-ATLANTIQUE
18 Marches de Bretagne (also in Maine-et-Loire and Vendée)
19 Retz

LOT
20 Coteaux de Glanes

LOT-ET-GARONNE
21 Agenais (includes 10; also in Gers and Tarn-et-Garonne)
22 Terroirs Landais

NIÈVRE
23 Coteaux Charitois

SAVOIE/ HAUTE-SAVOIE
24 Allobrogie

TARN
25 Côtes du Tarn

TARN-ET-GARONNE
26 Coteaux du Quercy (also in Lot)
27 Coteaux et Terrasses de Montauban
28 St-Sardos

VAUCLUSE
29 Principauté d'Orange (also in Drôme)

VAR
30 Argens
31 Maures
32 Mont-Caume
33 Verdon

Vins Délimités de Qualité Supérieure (VDQS)

France's *vins délimités de qualité supérieure* are marked on the map of France (page 53). Many are also on larger-scale maps. Those that do not appear in more detail elsewhere are shown on this map and listed below with their principal wines.

SAVOIE

Vins du Bugey: Roussette white, like Crépy, etc. Light red, locally good. (Bugey plus a village name indicates slightly higher strength and, theoretically, better quality.)

LOIRE VALLEY AND CENTRAL FRANCE

Châteaumeillant: grapey Gamay red, pale *vin gris*.
Côte Roannaise: light red of some character.
Côtes d'Auvergne: fresh Gamay red (Chanturgues) and rosé (Corent).
Côtes du Forez: Gamay red, like light Beaujolais.
Fiefs-Vendéens: white Muscadet alternatives, plus some red and rosé, from the Loire estuary.
St-Merd-la-Breuille: Promoted vin de pays from the remote Creuze. Chardonnay, Pinot Noir and Cabernet of character.
St-Pourçain-sur-Sioule: light Gamay rosé; improving red and white including Pinot Noir, Chardonnay, some Sauvignon and the local white grape Tresallier (known in north Burgundy as Sacy).
Vins du Thouarsais: sweetish white, light red and rosé.
Vins du Haut-Poitou: excellent dry whites, especially Sauvignon Blanc and Chardonnay, plus Gamay rosé.

LANGUEDOC-ROUSSILLON AND PROVENCE

Cabardès: emerging red and rosé of more southwestern than Midi character (also **Côtes du Cabardès et de l'Orbiel**).
Coteaux de Pierrevert: Provençal-type wines.
Côtes de la Malepère: above-average reds from Merlot, Malbec, Cabernets, Grenache and Syrah.

RHÔNE VALLEY

Haut-Comtat: Grenache red and rosé from the Drôme. In effect Côtes du Rhône.

SOUTHWEST

Gorges et Côtes de Millau: red, rosé and dry white from the banks of the Tarn.
Vins d'Entraygues et du Fel: very small area; light red and rosé, little white.

Two VDQS areas (both in Lorraine) appear only on the general map of France on page 53. These are: **Côtes de Toul** and **Vins de Moselle**: respectively very pale *vin gris* and rather acid red. The grapes of this region used to be taken to Champagne, where they disappeared.

--·--·-- International boundary

------ Département boundary

——— Boundary of regional Vins de Pays

Fiefs-Vendéens VDQS (see box opposite)

Vins de Pays areas are distinguished by colours

Corsica

The modern history of wine in Corsica, France's largest island and the most mountainous in the Mediterranean, starts in the 1960s, with the loss of Algeria to France, resulting in the migration of skilled growers, encouraged by de Gaulle, to the then-malarial east coast.

Within 12 years Corsica's vineyard area had quadrupled, covered almost entirely with bulk-producing vines. A great deal of this hasty planting has since been pulled out again, but 80% of Corsican wine is still destined for blending, with a maximum ambition of becoming a vin de pays and carrying the island's seductive *nom de verre*, L'Ile de Beauté.

The remaining 20%, however, has rediscovered its birthright in the hardy native grape varieties and the rocky hills where they grow best. The classic Corsican red grape is the Sciacarello, grown principally on the west coast around Ajaccio, the capital (and the birthplace of Napoleon), at Calvi and in the Sartènais region round Propriano, to make highly drinkable, soft yet spicy red and rosé which remains lively despite its high alcohol content.

The Niellucio, often cited as the other native Corsican grape, is in fact the Sangiovese of Tuscany, which seems to have come to the island relatively recently. Nonetheless it dominates the northern appellation of Patrimonio, inland from the port of Bastia. Patrimonio was the first full appellation to be created in Corsica and remains one of the best. Alone on the majestically craggy island it has limestone soil, which gives firm Rhônish reds, well-balanced whites and rich muscat Vins Doux Naturels of high quality. Sweet wines, of muscat or Vermentino ('Malvoisie de Corse'), are also the speciality of Cap Corse, the long north point of the island. Certain good judges rate the Muscatellu and Rappu of Rogliano, Cap Corse, as the finest of all French muscats, above Beaumes de Venise and Frontignan. Their appellation is Coteaux de Cap Corse. Vermentino also produces a much-appreciated, soft and golden dry white in the same area.

The appellation of Calvi in the northwest uses Sciacarello, Niellucio and Vermentino, as well as more 'modern' grapes, for heady table wines; Figari and Porto Vecchio do the same in the southeast. The Figari vineyards surround Bonifacio, the ferry port for Sardinia. It is thirsty country with wines that could scarcely be called thirst-quenching. Porto Vecchio seems to have come furthest in making wines, particularly whites, with a degree of modern, fruity crispness.

In comparison with these concentrated wines of traditional character, the regular Vin de Corse, and even most of the vin de pays, from around Aleria and Ghisonaccia on the eastern coastal plain are of no special interest.

In many ways Corsican wine can be compared with Provençal. The rosé in both cases is commonly the best. Each has found a new generation of growers eager to make the most of their *terroir*, and a market eager to find in their wines the elusive scents of the hot herbs of the *maquis*.

From the heights of Pozzo di Borgo above the capital, Ajaccio, the rugged interior of Corsica rises to snow-capped peaks in the centre. All the winegrowing regions lie in the coastal zones.

Corsica's best and most characterful wines come from the island's few indigenous grape varieties, plus muscats and light malmseys (called Vermentino) from the northeast cape.

PATRIMONIO **Appellation Contrôlée**

☐ Wine-producing area

1:1,585,000

Germany

Germany

Germany's best vineyards lie as far north as grapes can be persuaded to ripen. Many are on land unfit for normal agriculture: if there were no vines there would be forest and bare mountain. All in all their chances of giving the world's best white wine look slim. And yet on occasion they do, and stamp it with a style that no one, anywhere, can imitate.

Their secret is the balance of sugar against acidity. Sugar without acid would be flat; acid without sugar would be sharp. But in good years the two are so finely counterpoised that they have the inevitability of great art. They provide the stage for a mingling of essences from the grape and the ground, an ensemble customarily described in the single word 'breed'. It is more apparent in German wines than any others because they are far lower in alcohol. With less body in the background they are more trans parent to the tongue; nuances of flavour are brilliantly distinct; more often than not there is a great canopy of bouquet.

Great German wines are so full of character, charm and inherent fascination that they are best enjoyed, unlike most wines, alone in all their glory rather than with food. But rather than being seen as a merit, today this is a commercial handicap that has led growers to make their wines completely or almost completely dry and offer them as wines for the table like any others.

Since the vogue for 'trocken' wines began in the early 1980s the genre has advanced from thin productions (a fully dry Mosel Kabinett can be painfully tart) to wines of firm and convincing elegance; principally dry Spätlesen. Yet so far the world at large has not learned to love them. It is a challenge that a new generation of growers is facing vigorously with wines of thrilling vitality. The tragedy is that they are being undercut and demoralized by the ethos of bulk production which is, sadly, sanctioned by their government.

Since 1971 German wine law seems almost to have set out deliberately to confuse and even mislead the consumer. The laws are framed for the short-term advantage of growers who over-produce to sell at unsustainably low prices. The result, too much totally undistinguished wine, has been a critical and commercial disaster for German wine as a whole – but especially for the perfectionists (and there are many) who have dazzlingly good wines to offer.

The German wine label (see page 168), the most explicit on earth, is both cause and instrument of much of the industry's problems. Germany's vineyards lie along the River Rhine and its tributaries. They are scant in the extreme south and thickest in Rheinland-Pfalz near the French border. All the principal areas are mapped on the following pages.

The Riesling (see page 24) is the great grape of Germany. The great majority of Germany's best wines are made from it, and it is planted to the exclusion of almost everything else in the best sites of the Mosel-Saar-Ruwer, Rheingau, Nahe and Pfalz (the Palatinate). The price of quality in the Riesling is relatively limited

quantity, and the dangers inherent in a grape that ripens late. For larger and less risky production, Germany turned to the Müller-Thurgau, a supposed cross made a century ago between Riesling and Silvaner. Müller-Thurgau very rarely rises to heights of quality, except in late-harvested sweet wines. It lacks the lovely clean 'nerve', the backbone of fruity acidity (and the blossoming bouquet) of the Riesling. Nonetheless it covers some 62,000 acres (25,000 hectares) today, while Riesling is planted on only 52,000 acres (21,000 hectares). Standard cheap German wines with no mention of the grape on the label can be assumed to be made (at least mainly) from Müller-Thurgau.

Plantings of Silvaner have fallen far behind, to some 20,000 acres (8,000 hectares). But these include the best sites in Franconia, where it makes better wine than Riesling, and some excellent ones in Rheinhessen and Baden. A demanding variety, Silvaner can be excellent.

New varieties (see page 26) had a great vogue in the early 1980s, particularly in Rheinhessen and the Pfalz. Two factors have dampened the early enthusiasm for them: their strident, over-obvious flavours, and experience of very cold winters, when they have proved less hardy than the Riesling.

Pinot Noir (known as Spätburgunder – the 'late Burgundy'), the commoner Portugieser and, in Württemberg, the Trollinger are the main sources of red wine. Only the valley of the Ahr near Bonn cultivates more red than white.

German wine law makes no attempt to classify vineyards as the French do. Any vineyard in Germany can, in official theory, produce top-class wine. The law concerns itself instead only with ripeness: 'must weight', the measure of

sugar in the grapes at harvest time. The system is explained on page 26.

But nobody truly pretends that all German vineyards are equally well sited, with equally perfect soil. This additional failure in the wine law has at last led to unofficial classification of the best vineyards. In this edition the best vineyards are clearly indicated on maps for the first time. Germany's consortium of top-quality growers, the VDP (Verband Deutsches Prädikatsweingüter) has collaborated with local organizations and experts to help me produce this first mapping, which will be further elaborated in future editions until it (or something similar) becomes official.

The Quality Factor maps on the following pages outline some of the physical considerations. The detailed maps focus on those regions where millennia of experience have taught growers to plant the best varieties, and where premiums are paid for the names of specific sites. It is extremely rare for a first-class wine to emerge from an unexpected quarter.

Besides the labelling regulations explained on page 168, the following is essential information for understanding the keys to the German maps.

The individual vineyard (only in very rare cases less than about 12.5 acres – 5 hectares), is called an **Einzellage**. It is Einzellagen that are classified here. The 1971 law greatly enlarged many Einzellagen. Disputes about their 'real' boundaries therefore complicate their classification.

A **Grosslage** is a group of Einzellagen; an area formed by a number of neighbouring individual vineyards (whether or not adjacent, or in the same village) and deemed to be of equal quality. A Grosslage is usually given the name of what was formerly its most renowned Einzellage. The label does not (and is not allowed to) state whether the vineyard it specifies is an individual site (Einzellage) or collective one (Grosslage). This is a serious weakness of the German wine law, since very few people can be expected to remember which of several similar names is specific and which is not. The maps make it clear. Rarely is any top-quality wine sold under any name except that of its Einzellage. Many quality producers would like to see an end to Grosslagen altogether and will never use their names.

The geographical unit larger than a Grosslage is a **Bereich**. The whole of the Middle Mosel, for example, is called Bereich Bernkastel; the entire Rheingau, Bereich Johannisberg. The law can be criticized here too: most foreign customers probably think they are buying Bernkasteler or Johannisberger. Beware of the Bereich.

Larger than the Bereich is the **Lände**, a more recently introduced geographical concept that applies only to wines at a quality level just above the minimum. 'Landwein' is theoretically on the same level as a French vin de pays.

The largest unit is the **Gebiet**, which embraces the whole of a winegrowing region (Nahe, Mosel-Saar-Ruwer, Rheinhessen or Pfalz, for example) as shown on the map opposite.

Exports of German Wine by Volume

UK	56.4%
Holland	9%
USA	5.8%
Japan	4.8%
Denmark	4.5%
Sweden	4.3%
Canada	2.6 %
Belgium/Lux	2%
Finland	1.9%
Norway	1.8%
Others	8.4%

Above: Over half of the 2.7 million hectolitres Germany exports annually goes to the UK. The bulk of this is semi-sweet white cut-price 'quality' wine.

Below: Germany produces some 16 million hectolitres of wine a year – a quarter that of France. Nearly 84% of German vineyards are planted with white grapes.

German wine   French wine

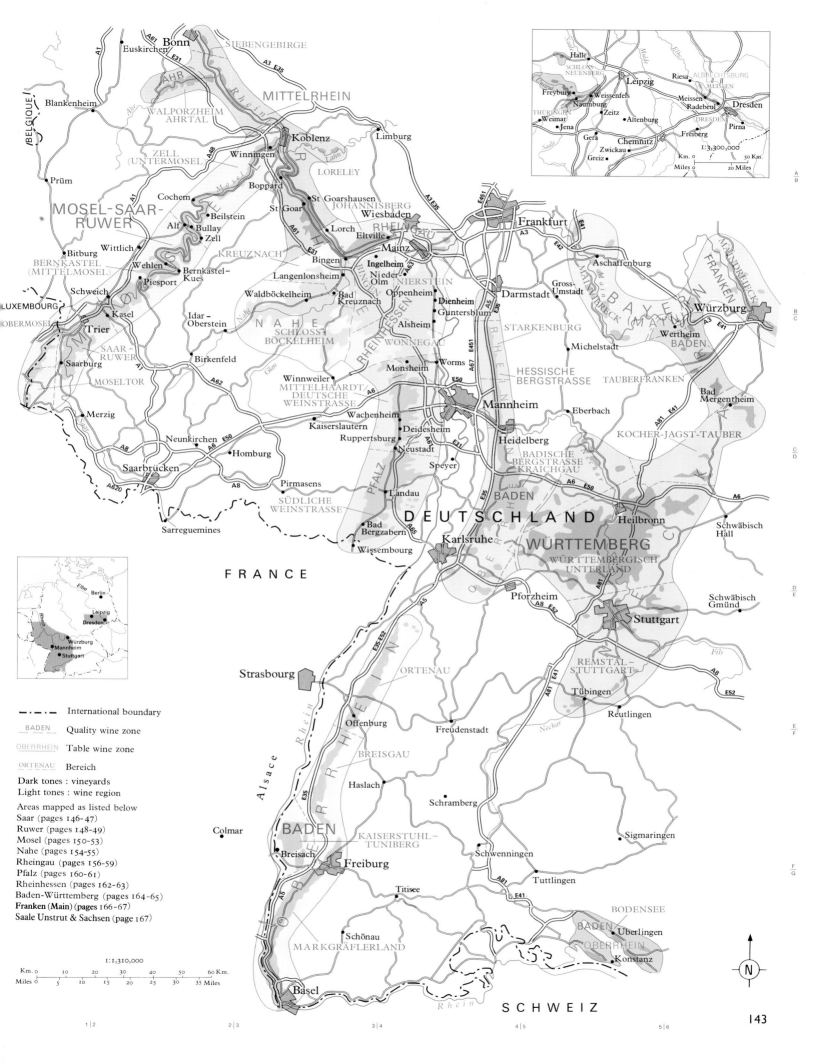

BELGIQUE

Bonn
Euskirchen
Blankenheim

SIEBENGEBIRGE
A3 E35

AHR
WALPORZHEIM
AHRTAL

MITTELRHEIN

Koblenz
Limburg

Prüm

ZELL
(UNTERMOSEL)
Winningen

LORELEY

Cochem
St Goarshausen
Boppard

MOSEL-SAAR-
RUWER

Alf
Beilstein
Bullay
Zell
St Goar
Lorch

JOHANNISBERG
Wiesbaden
Eltville
RHEINGAU

Bitburg
Wittlich

Aschaffenburg
Frankfurt

Wehlen
BERNKASTEL
(MITTELMOSEL)
Bernkastel-
Kues
Piesport

KREUZNACH

Bingen
Mainz
Ingelheim
Nieder-
Olm

Gross-
Umstadt

FRANKEN

LUXEMBOURG

Schweich

Langenlonsheim
NIERSTEIN
Oppenheim

Darmstadt

Würzburg

OBERMOSEL
Kasel

Waldböckelheim
Bad
Kreuzheim
Dienheim
Guntersblum

STARKENBURG

Wertheim
BADEN

Trier

NAHE
SCHLOSS
BÖCKELHEIM

RHEINHESSEN
WONNEGAU
Alsheim

Michelstadt

SAAR-
RUWER
Saarburg

Idar-
Oberstein

Worms

HESSISCHE
BERGSTRASSE

TAUBERFRANKEN

MOSELTOR

Birkenfeld

Monsheim

Bad
Mergentheim

Merzig

Winnweiler
MITTELHAARDT
DEUTSCHE
WEINSTRASSE

Mannheim
Eberbach

KOCHER-JAGST-TAUBER

Neunkirchen
Homburg

Kaiserslautern
Wachenheim
Deidesheim
Ruppertsburg
Neustadt

Heidelberg
BADISCHE
BERGSTRASSE
KRAICHGAU

Saarbrücken

Pirmasens
Speyer

Heilbronn
Schwäbisch
Hall

SÜDLICHE
WEINSTRASSE

PFALZ
Landau

BADEN

DEUTSCHLAND

WÜRTTEMBERG
WÜRTTEMBERGISCH
UNTERLAND

Sarreguemines

Bad
Bergzabern
Wissembourg

Karlsruhe

FRANCE

Pforzheim

Schwäbisch
Gmünd

Stuttgart

Strasbourg

ORTENAU

REMSTAL-
STUTTGART

Tübingen

Reutlingen

Offenburg
Freudenstadt

BREISGAU

Haslach

Schramberg

Sigmaringen

Colmar

BADEN

KAISERSTUHL-
TUNIBERG

Schwenningen

Tuttlingen

Breisach
Freiburg

BODENSEE

BADEN
OBERRHEIN
Überlingen

Titisee

Konstanz

Schönau

MARKGRÄFLERLAND

Basel

SCHWEIZ

Halle
SCHLOSS
NEUENBERG
Leipzig
Riesa
ALBRECHTSBURG
MEISSEN

Freyburg
Weissenfels
Naumburg
Zeitz
THÜRINGEN
Weimar
Jena
Altenburg
Meissen
Radebeul
Freiberg
Dresden
Pirna

Gera
Chemnitz
Zwickau
Greiz

1:3,300,000
Km. 0   50 Km.
Miles 0   20 Miles

Berlin
Elbe
Rhein
Leipzig
Dresden
Würzburg
Mannheim
Stuttgart

International boundary

BADEN   Quality wine zone

OBERRHEIN   Table wine zone

ORTENAU   Bereich

Dark tones : vineyards

Light tones : wine region

Areas mapped as listed below
Saar (pages 146-47)
Ruwer (pages 148-49)
Mosel (pages 150-53)
Nahe (pages 154-55)
Rheingau (pages 156-59)
Pfalz (pages 160-61)
Rheinhessen (pages 162-63)
Baden-Württemberg (pages 164-65)
Franken (Main) (pages 166-67)
Saale Unstrut & Sachsen (page 167)

1:1,310,000
Km. 0   10   20   30   40   50   60 Km.
Miles 0   5   10   15   20   25   30   35 Miles

N

143

Germany: the Quality Factor

If in Burgundy the emphasis for the study of quality is on the soil and the microclimate, and in Bordeaux on the physical makeup of the soil affecting drainage, in Germany it centres on the weather. Every conceivable aspect of weather is examined for its possible effect on the specific gravity of the grape juice – the 'must weight' – or the amount of sugar in the grapes.

The map below shows sunshine and rainfall during the growing season in the principal wine regions. Some of the findings of perhaps the most elaborate investigation ever mounted into wine quality are shown opposite. The government of Hesse has spent vast sums and many years studying the Rheingau – the state's best vineyard and one of the greatest in Germany.

They have recorded the soil (which changes abruptly and often) in great detail, and then the amounts of sunshine, wind, late frost (in May, which can interfere with flowering) and early frost (in September, which can kill the leaves and stop the grapes ripening: this map is not shown) that every spot of ground could expect. Finally, with a daring all too rare among scientists, they plotted the area where the wine should be best (the last map).

Certain sites do emerge with a distinctive tint in almost every map. The Rüdesheimer Berg at the western end of the Rheingau is the only one that achieves 'excellent' in the aptitude test (map 5). But a consistent string of vineyards at a certain altitude is noticeable on each map. They include most of the highest priced of the Rheingau. The Rüdesheimer Berg, Schloss Johannisberg, Schloss Vollrads, Steinberg, the southern slopes of Kiedrich and Rauenthal are among them. And the most consistently noticeable down by the river is the acknowledged first-growth Marcobrunn at Erbach.

Much can be learned by comparing these maps with those on pages 156–59. But each region, of course, has its own peculiar interaction of soil and climate.

What is hard is to explain is why, with such clear evidence of the naturally privileged sites before them, and such a long historical record of the finest wines by every possible measurement from highest must-weight to highest price, Germany has repeatedly shied away from the obvious step of grading, or classifying, vineyards into quality bands.

It may be argued that in different parts of Germany different criteria apply, or should apply. It may be argued that a bad winemaker can make bad wine from even the finest grapes. Even, though with much less evidence, that a good winemaker can make a vinous silk purse out of a viticultural sow's ear.

Regional classifications have occasionally been made. In 1868 the King of Prussia graded the vineyards of the Mosel-Saar-Ruwer into eight ranks for tax purposes, which certainly minimized aspiration to the top rank.

The government's reluctance to accept a classification today appears to stem from a mistaken notion of democracy: that to classify is to be elitist, anti-democratic. But quality is by its very nature elitist, and refusal to acknowledge this causes only misapprehension and confusion. It is in the hope of giving a lead towards an eventual complete classification, for the good of consumers of German wine and of the industry as a whole, that this Atlas clearly designates the best vineyards on each map.

Right: Germany's greatest wine area analysed: the Rheingau's soil, sunshine, frost and wind, all major factors affecting the quality of its wine, are recorded by the Hessische Landesamt für Bodenforschung, Wiesbaden. The maps are reproduced with their kind permission. Their significance is discussed in the text. The bottom map is the first attempt at classifying German winegrowing land, based on the findings in the four maps above it.

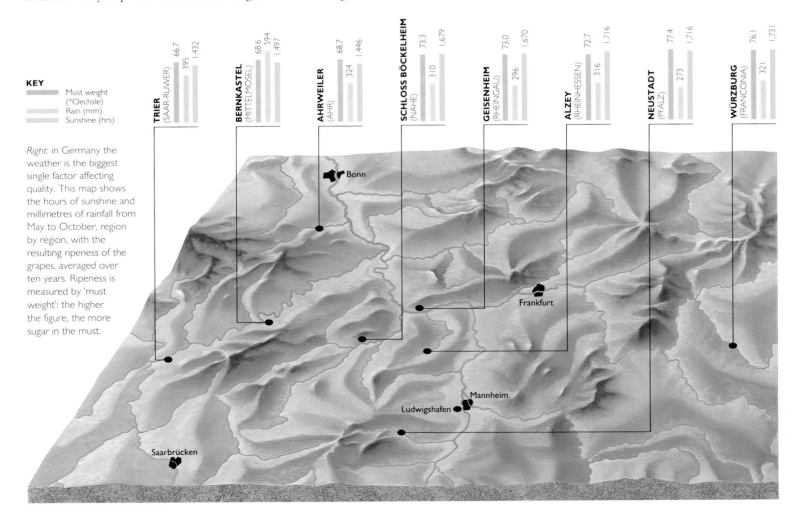

KEY

- Must weight (°Oechsle)
- Rain (mm)
- Sunshine (hrs)

Right: in Germany the weather is the biggest single factor affecting quality. This map shows the hours of sunshine and millimetres of rainfall from May to October, region by region, with the resulting ripeness of the grapes, averaged over ten years. Ripeness is measured by 'must weight': the higher the figure, the more sugar in the must.

TRIER (SAAR-RUWER) — 66.7 / 395 / 1,432

BERNKASTEL (MITTELMOSEL) — 68.6 / 594 / 1,497

AHRWEILER (AHR) — 68.7 / 324 / 1,446

SCHLOSS BÖCKELHEIM (NAHE) — 73.3 / 310 / 1,679

GEISENHEIM (RHEINGAU) — 73.0 / 296 / 1,670

ALZEY (RHEINHESSEN) — 72.7 / 316 / 1,716

NEUSTADT (PFALZ) — 77.4 / 273 / 1,716

WÜRZBURG (FRANCONIA) — 76.1 / 321 / 1,731

Bonn

Frankfurt

Mannheim

Ludwigshafen

Saarbrücken

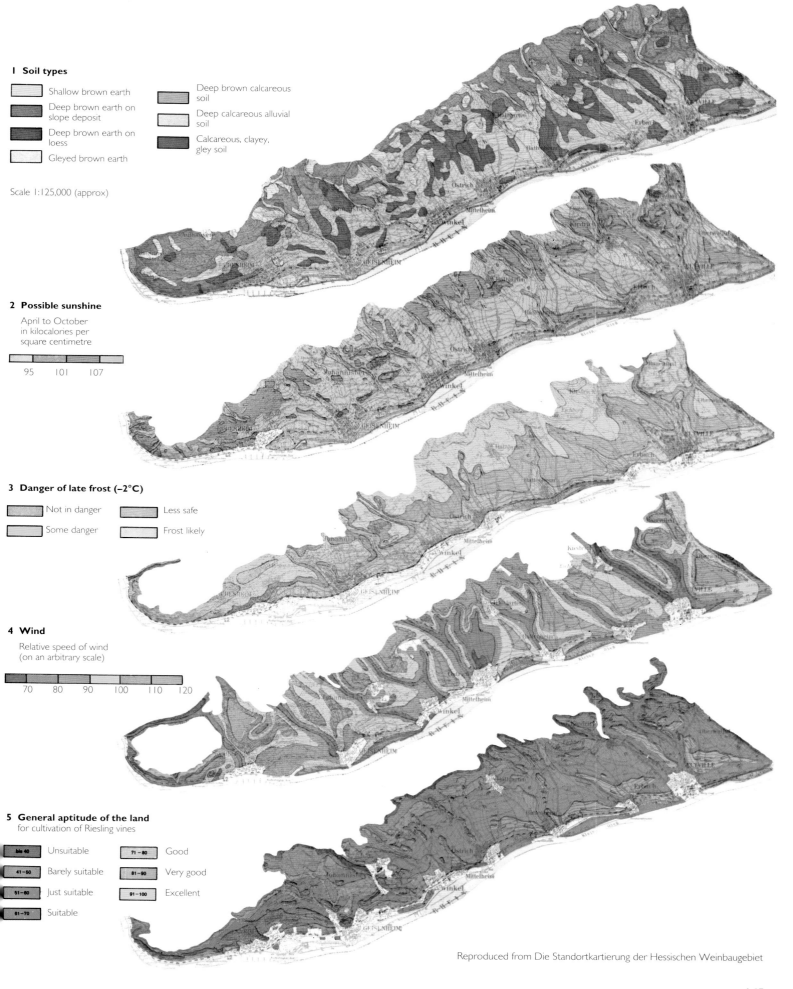

1 Soil types

Shallow brown earth

Deep brown earth on slope deposit

Deep brown earth on loess

Gleyed brown earth

Deep brown calcareous soil

Deep calcareous alluvial soil

Calcareous, clayey, gley soil

Scale 1:125,000 (approx)

2 Possible sunshine

April to October in kilocalories per square centimetre

95   101   107

3 Danger of late frost (−2°C)

Not in danger

Some danger

Less safe

Frost likely

4 Wind

Relative speed of wind (on an arbitrary scale)

70   80   90   100   110   120

5 General aptitude of the land
for cultivation of Riesling vines

bis 40   Unsuitable

41–50   Barely suitable

51–60   Just suitable

61–70   Suitable

71–80   Good

81–90   Very good

91–100   Excellent

Reproduced from Die Standortkartierung der Hessischen Weinbaugebiet

145

The Saar

The dignified old manor house of Egon Müller and the most famous estate of the Saar, Scharzhof stands at the foot of Wiltingen's Scharzhofberg. In its cellars lie some of the world's most exquisite steely-sweet Rieslings, its Scharzhofberger gold-capsule Ausleses.

German wine, its problems and its triumphs, is epitomized nowhere better than in the valley of the Mosel's tributary, the Saar. The battle for sugar in the grapes rages most fiercely in this cold corner of the country. It is won only perhaps three or four years in ten; (the sequence of the '88, '89, '90, and '92 was exceptional). Yet those years give one of the world's superlative white wines; every mouthful a cause for rejoicing and wonder.

A mere 1,500 acres (600 hectares) of vines share the valley with orchard and pasture. It is calm open agricultural country; impossible to believe that only just upstream the blast furnaces of the industrial Saar are at work.

The map shows more clearly than any other the way the south slopes – here nearly all on banks of hill sidling up to the river – offer winegrowers the chance of enough sunshine.

As in the best part of the Mosel, the soil is slate and the grape the Riesling. The qualities of Mosel wine: apple-like freshness and bite, a marvellous mingling of honey in the scent and steel in the finish, can find their apogee in Saar wine. If anything, the emphasis here is more on the steel than the honey.

Unsuccessful vintages make wine so sharp that even the best growers can sell their produce only to the makers of sparkling Sekt, who need high acidity in their raw material. But when the sun shines and the Riesling ripens and goes on ripening far into October, even November, the great bosomy smell of flowers and honey which it generates would be too lush were it not for the appley emphasis of acidity. Then the Saar comes into its own. It makes sweet wine that you can never tire of: the balance and depth make you sniff and sip and sniff again.

Superlative sites are few. Most are in the hands of rich and ancient estates that can afford to wait for good years and make the most of them. The labels of the principal ones – austere compared with the flowery creations of some parts of Germany – appear on these pages. One of the first State Domains operates here, with its headquarters in the nearby city of Trier. Its vineyards in Serrig are unusual in that, at the turn of the century they were created by the Prussian State from virgin woodland: an optimistic move since Serrig has even more uncertain weather than the rest of Saar. It takes a long golden autumn ... but then it justifies everything.

The most famous estate of the Saar is that of Egon Müller, whose house appears on the map as Scharzhof at the foot of the Scharzhofberg in Wiltingen. Among the other owners of parts of the Scharzhofberg is Trier Cathedral (Hohe Domkirche) which adds the word 'Dom' before

More dignified than dashing, the labels of some of the most illustrious estates of the Saar. Saar wines depend on a certain sweetness for balance; a dry Kabinett or Spätlese with such steely acidity would be too austere for pleasure.

the names of its vineyards. Egon Müller also manages the Le Gallais estate, with the famous Braune Kupp vineyard at the other end of Wiltingen. The top vineyards such as Ayler Kupp, Ockfener Bockstein and Herrenberg, Wawerner Herrenberger and the Falkensteiner Hofberg above Niedermennig are renowned ... for their good vintages. The Grosslage name for the whole of the Saar is Scharzberg – almost suspiciously easy to confuse with the great Scharzhofberg.

Many of the Mosel's vineyards, particularly in the Saar, belong to a group of religious and charitable bodies in Trier. The Friedrich-Wilhelm-Gymnasium (Karl Marx's old school); the Bischöfliches Konvikt (a Catholic boarding school); the Bischöfliches Priesterseminar (a college for priests); the Vereinigte Hospitien (an almshouse) and the cathedral are all important winegrowers. The two Bischöfliches and the cathedral operate their total of 260 acres (105 hectares) of vineyards, here and in the Middle Mosel, together as the Vereinigte Bischöfliches Weingut. In their deep damp Roman cellars in the city one has the feeling that wine is itself an act of charity rather than mere vulgar trade.

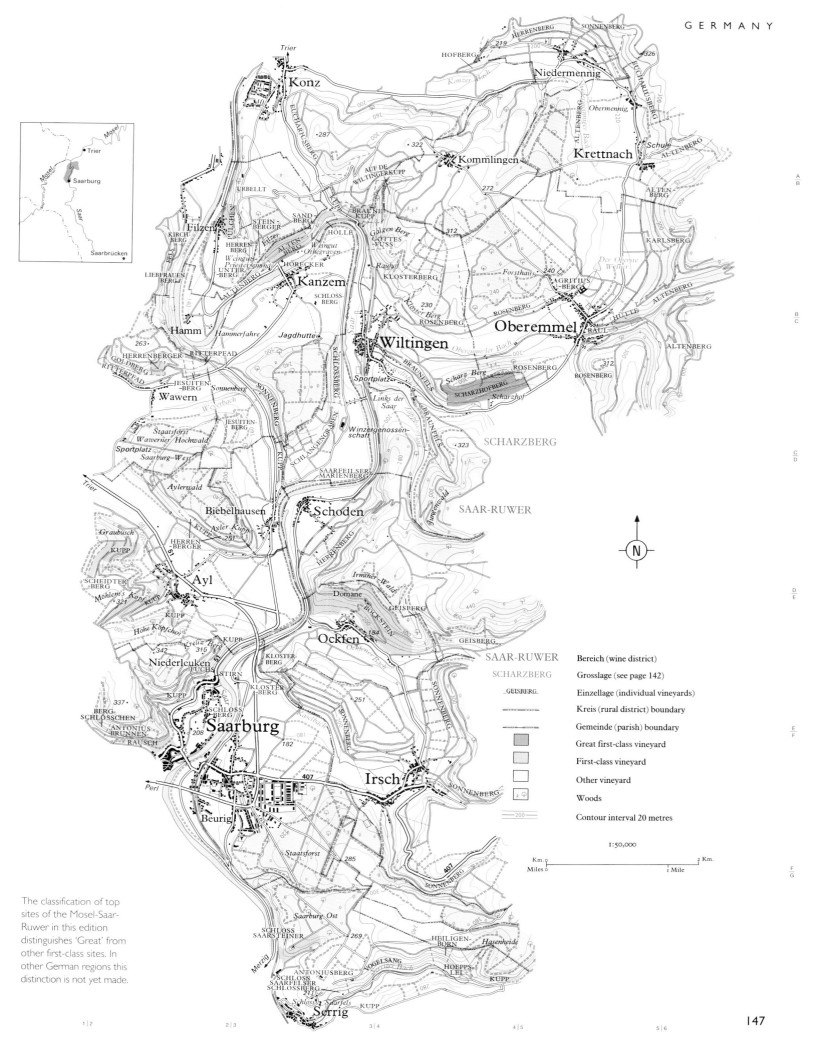

The classification of top sites of the Mosel-Saar-Ruwer in this edition distinguishes 'Great' from other first-class sites. In other German regions this distinction is not yet made.

Bereich (wine district)	
Grosslage (see page 142)	
Einzellage (individual vineyards)	
Kreis (rural district) boundary	
Gemeinde (parish) boundary	
Great first-class vineyard	
First-class vineyard	
Other vineyard	
Woods	
Contour interval 20 metres	

1:50,000

Mosel

Trier

Saarburg

Saar

Saarbrücken

Konz

Trier

Niedermennig

Krettnach

Obermennig

Kommlingen

Filzen

Kanzem

Hamm

Wawern

Wiltingen

Oberemmel

SCHARZBERG

SAAR-RUWER

Biebelhausen

Schoden

Ayl

Ockfen

Niederleuken

SAAR-RUWER

SCHARZBERG

GEISBERG

Saarburg

Irsch

Beurig

Serrig

N

147

The Ruwer

The Ruwer is a mere stream. Its vineyards add up to about half those of one Côte d'Or commune. There are years when most of its wine is unsatisfactory: faint and sharp. Yet like the Saar, when conditions are right it performs a miracle: its wines are Germany's most delicate; gentle yet infinitely fine and full of subtlety.

Waldrach, the first wine village, makes good light wine but rarely more. Kasel is far more important. The von Kesselstatt estate and the Bischöfliches Weingut of Trier have holdings here. There are great Kaselers in hot years.

Mertesdorf and Eitelsbach could not be called famous names, but each has one supreme vineyard, owned by one of the world's best winegrowers. Mertesdorf's Maximim Grünhaus stands obliquely to the left bank of the river with the manor house, formerly monastic property, at its foot. The greater part of its hill of vines is called Herrenberg; the top-quality part Abtsberg (for the abbot) and the less-well-sited part Bruderberg (for the brothers).

Across the stream Karthäuserhofberg echoes that situation, again with an old monastic building, now the manor house, below. The hill's subdivisions are marked on the map.

Trier, an important wine city with Roman origins, lies 5 miles (8 kilometres) away up the Mosel. Included in the city limits is the isolated clearing of Avelsbach, belonging to the State Domain and Trier Cathedral, and the famous old Thiergarten. Avelsbach wine is similar to that of the Ruwer: supremely delicate – sometimes even more perfumed and forthcoming.

Above: the beautiful old-fashioned label and (*below*) the manor of Maximin Grünhaus from its vineyard. In the background is Kasel and, beyond, Waldrach.

Above: the Eitelsbacher Karthäuserhofberg neck label is in place of a rectangular one on the bottle. *Right*: Ruwer estates include Trier Cathedral (*top right*). Avelsbach and Eitelsbach are officially both parts of Trier.

Kasel on the Ruwer, like all other German wine-villages, hangs out welcoming signs and offers its wines by the glass (*Weinprobe*).

Ruwer

MARIENHOLZ

MARIENHOLZ

Lambertysmühle
MAXIMINER

MARIENHOLZ

MAXIMINER

Karthhäuserhof

Eitelsbach

KARTHÄUSERHOFBERG

JOHANNISBERG

Neuenberg

MARIENHOLZ

KARTHÄUSERHOFBERG

Grüneberg

BRÜDERBERG

Mertesdorf

SAAR-
RUWER

RÖMERLAY

HERRENBERG

Friedrichshof

HERRENBERG

ABTSBERG

FELSLAY

Grünhaus

MÄUERCHEN

HERRENBERG

Langrets

HITZLAY

HERRENBERG

TIMPERT

KEHRNAGEL

Pauliner

Grunhäuser

NIES'CHEN

Kasel

DOMINI-
KANERBERG

*Standort
ubungsplatz* Wald

ALTENBERG HERRENBERG

PAULINSBERG

HERRENBERG

RÖMERLAY

KUPP

Abeler Wald

KEHRNAGEL

HAMMERSTEIN

KURFÜRSTENBERG

KRONE

JESUITENGARTEN

MEISENBERG

ROTLEI

DOKTORBERG

Avelsbach

DOKTORBERG
Falsemer Berg

N

Waldrach

SAAR-
RUWER

RÖMERLAY

ABTSBERG

Bereich
Grosslage
Einzellage
Gemeinde boundary
Great first-class vineyard
First-class vineyard
Other vineyard
Woods
Contour interval 20 metres

EHRENBERG

LAURENTIUSBERG

SONNENBERG
213

1:31,500

Km. 0   Km.
Miles 0   ½ Mile

Trier

Mosel

Saarburg

Saarbrücken

The Middle Mosel: Piesport

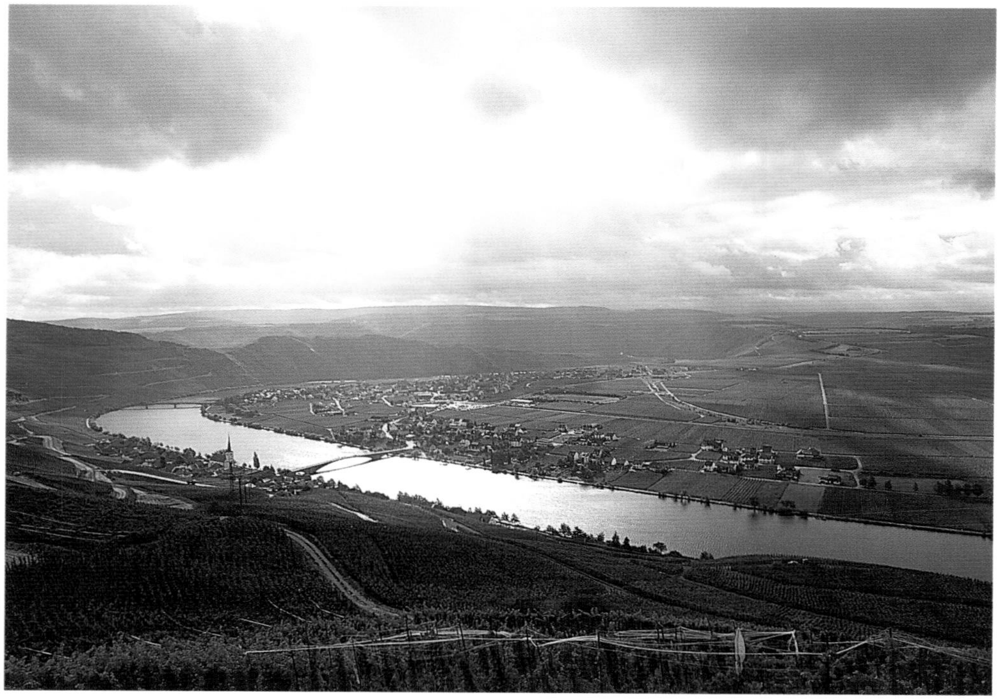

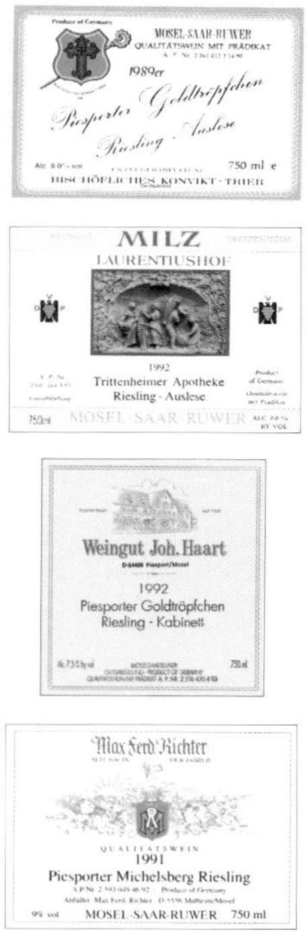

MOSEL-SAAR-RUWER
1989er
Piesporter Goldtröpfchen
Riesling Auslese
750 ml e
BISCHÖFLICHES KONVIKT · TRIER
MILZ
LAURENTIUSHOF
1992
Trittenheimer Apotheke
Riesling · Auslese
MOSEL-SAAR-RUWER
Weingut Joh. Haart
1992
Piesporter Goldtröpfchen
Riesling · Kabinett
Max Ferd. Richter
QUALITÄTSWEIN
1991
Piesporter Michelsberg Riesling
MOSEL-SAAR-RUWER 750 ml

Far left: the view east over Piesport from the western part of the Goldtröpfchen vineyard. Over the river the flat land is Piesporter Treppchen, whose wine (largely Müller-Thurgau) cannot be compared with the great Rieslings of the steep slopes.
Left: Piesport is the hub of this upper stretch of the Middle Mosel, giving its famous name to a large proportion of the wine of the area. The Grosslage name of Michelsberg is all too often seen. Growers with the confidence and pride to sell under the names of less-renowned villages (eg Trittenheim, Leiwen or Neumagen) often offer more interesting wine at better value for money.

The Mosel is acquainted with the reflections of vines all the way from its rising in the Vosges mountains to its union with the Rhine at Koblenz. Light wines of little consequence grow on the French Moselle; in Luxembourg considerable quantities of light, often fizzy and very refreshing wine is made mainly of Rivaner and Elbling. But only in the central part of the German Mosel do the spectacular river walls of slate, rising in places over 700 feet (200 metres) above its course, provide perfect conditions for the Riesling vine. In the central 40 miles (65 kilometres) of the river's snake-like meanderings – which take it only half that distance as the crow flies – the Mosel's great wine is made.

The wines of the river vary along its banks even more than, say, the wines of Burgundy vary along the Côte d'Or. Given south, southeast or southwest exposure, the steeper the bank the better the wine. It is only because the thin soil here is pure slate, through which rain runs as if through a sieve, that any of it stays in place on near-precipices. The coincidence of quickly drying, stable soil in vineyards that are held up to the sun like toast to a fire is the Mosel's secret.

There is no formal agreement on what constitutes the Middle Mosel. In the maps on these pages we have extended it beyond the central and most famous villages to include several whose wine is often underrated.

The first in this category is Klüsserath. The Bruderschaft vineyard is immediately typical of a fine Mosel site: a steep bank curving from south to southwest. Then the long tongue of land which ends in Trittenheim is almost a cliff where the village of Leiwen jumps the river to claim part of the vineyard of Laurentiuslay, flattening to only a gentle slope before the bend. Down to here the Grosslage name is St Michael.

The best-exposed sites of Trittenheim are Felsenkopf and Leiterchen (over the bridge). These are the first vineyards of the Mosel that make wine of real breed. It is always delicate, but not faint. In such a year as 1990, when the wines of the Saar and Ruwer were Germany's best, Trittenheimers come into their own.

The town of Neumagen, a Roman landing place, keeps in its little leafy square a remarkable Roman carving of a Mosel wine ship, laden with barrels and weary galley slaves. The wines of Dhron, its partner, are slightly better known. Here the Mosel banks fall back as gentle slopes. The tributary river Dhron has the steepest slopes and the best sites; above all Dhroner Hofberger, classified here as first growth.

Piesport has a standing far above its neighbours. It contains the ideal site: a steep amphitheatre facing due south. The name of the slopes flanking the village, Goldtröpfchen, is famous for gently honeyed wines, not with great power but with magical fragrance and breed. Half is classified as Great growth, half first growth. The vast plantation across the river known as Piesporter Treppchen is not close to the same class.

Michelsberg is the Grosslage name for this part of the river, from Trittenheim to Minheim. 'Piesporter Michelsberg', therefore, is not normally Piesporter at all – a typical example of how the law misleads the consumer.

Minheim, Wintrich and Kesten can all make fine wines. But there are no perfectly aligned slopes in this stretch, except for the beginning of the great ramp that rises to its full height opposite the village of Brauneberg. In Kesten it is called Paulinshofberger. In Brauneberg it is the Juffer, 100 years ago reckoned to be the greatest wine of the Mosel, perfectly satisfying the taste for wine that was full-bodied and golden.

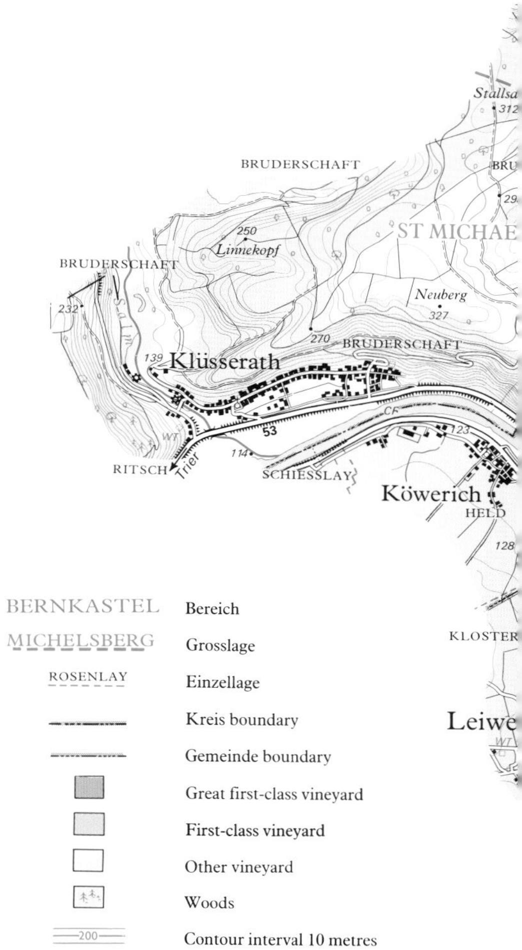

Stallsa
312
BRUDERSCHAFT
BRU
29
ST MICHAE
250
Linnekopf
BRUDERSCHAFT
232
Neuberg
327
270
BRUDERSCHAFT
139
Klüsserath
WT
53
RITSCH
Trier
114
SCHIESSLAY
Köwerich
HELD
128
KLOSTER
Leiwe
BERNKASTEL Bereich
MICHELSBERG Grosslage
ROSENLAY Einzellage
Kreis boundary
Gemeinde boundary
Great first-class vineyard
First-class vineyard
Other vineyard
Woods
200 Contour interval 10 metres

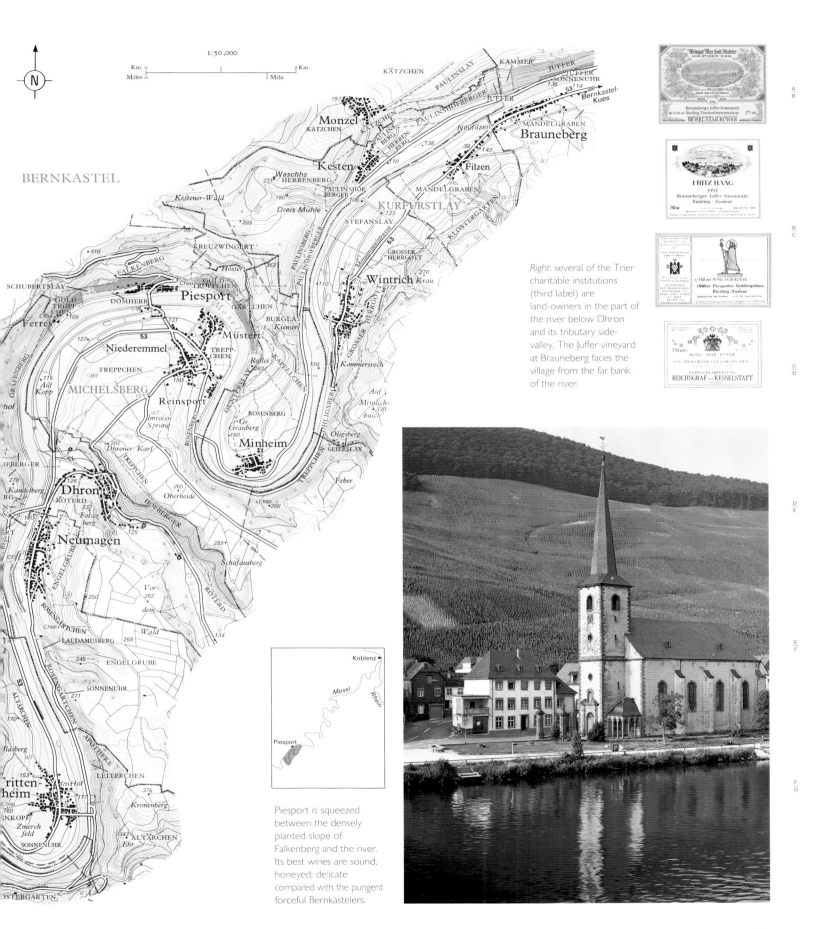

1:50,000

Km. 0   2 Km.
Miles 0   1 Mile

BERNKASTEL

Right: several of the Trier
charitable institutions
(third label) are
land-owners in the part of
the river below Dhron
and its tributary side-
valley. The Juffer vineyard
at Brauneberg faces the
village from the far bank
of the river.

Piesport is squeezed
between the densely
planted slope of
Falkenberg and the river.
Its best wines are sound,
honeyed; delicate
compared with the pungent
forceful Bernkastelers.

The Middle Mosel: Bernkastel

The view from the bridge at Bernkastel is of a green wall of vines 700 feet (200 metres) high and 5 miles (8 kilometres) long. Only the Douro, in the whole gazetteer of rivers to which the vine is wedded, has anything approaching a comparable sight.

From Brauneberg to the Bernkastel suburb of Kues the hills are relatively gentle. The Kirchberg in Veldenz (the village is just off the map) is one of those marginal vineyards which makes beautiful wine after a hot summer. Lieser is perhaps best known for the grim great mansion formerly owned by the von Schorlemer estate at the foot of the Rosenlay. In the Niederberg Helden it has a perfect full south slope.

The greatest vineyard of the Mosel starts abruptly, rising almost sheer above the gables of Bernkastel; dark slate frowning at slate. The butt of the hill, its one straight south elevation, is the Doctor – perhaps the most famous vineyard in Germany. From its flank the proudest names of the Mosel follow one another. Comparison of the first growths of Bernkastel with those of Graach and Wehlen, often with wines from the same growers in each place, is a fascinating game. The trademark of Bernkastel is a touch of flint. Wehleners are richer, Graachers softer.

The least of these wines should be something of very obvious personality: water-white with a gleam of green and dozens of little bubbles in the bottom of the glass, smelling almost aggressively of grapes, filling and seeming to coat the mouth with sharpness, sweetness and scent. The greatest of them, long-lived, pale gold, piquant, profound yet frivolous…are wines that beg to be compared with music and poetry.

But the name of Bernkastel is used for very much more wine than her slopes can grow. The law allows it without shame; Bereich Bernkastel is a possible name for any 'quality' wine from the Middle Mosel. And Bernkastel has two Grosslage names: Badstube (exclusive to its five best sites) and Kurfürstlay, available to vineyards as far off as Brauneberg and Wintrich. The law pretends to believe that such niceties are likely to be remembered.

Zeltingen brings the Great Wall to an end. It is the Mosel's biggest wine commune, and among its best. At Urzig, across the river, reddish clay mixed with slate, in rocky pockets

Bernkastel (foreground) and Kues seen from the Schlossberg. After the Bernkasteler Doctor slope come Graach, Wehlen and Zeltingen. All make intense Rieslings, some smoky, some earthy, some simply honeyed.

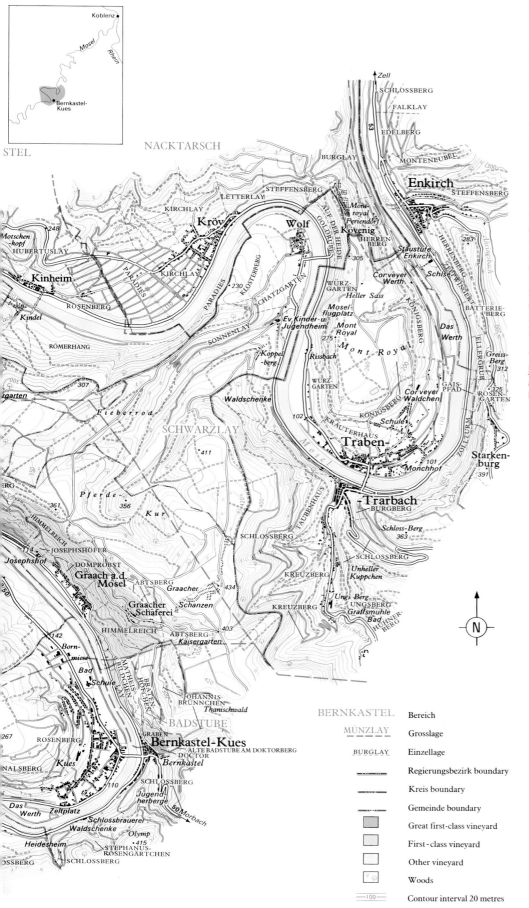

instead of a smooth bank, gives the Würzgarten (spice garden) wines a different flavour, more penetrating and 'racy' than Zeltingers. Erden at its best (in Treppchen) is in the same rank. Lösnich and Kinheim begin a decline.

Traben-Trarbach is one community. The wines of Trarbach are well known. Enkirch deserves to be. Its Batterieberg can offer round, light, slightly spicy wine with all the delicate complexity the Middle Mosel is famous for.

The Middle Mosel ends here. Downstream towards Koblenz the vineyard continues as the Untermosel, among operatic villages, one or two with famous names and some with outstanding vineyards, but the whole loses its concert pitch. Zell is the best-known town, for its (Grosslage) Schwarze Katz. Bullay has wine at least as good, and Neef (its best site the Frauenberg) rather better. The Untermosel has much better wines than tradition will admit, especially from Bremmer Calmont, Merler Fettgarten, and the Winningen vineyards of Brückstück and Röttgen.

The heart of the Middle Mosel has many first-class estates. J J Prüm (bottom left) is perhaps most respected of all. Bottom right: a label from the little-regarded Lower Mosel near Koblenz. Winningen is a name to look for.

BERNKASTEL	Bereich
MÜNZLAY	Grosslage
BURGLAY	Einzellage
	Regierungsbezirk boundary
	Kreis boundary
	Gemeinde boundary
	Great first-class vineyard
	First-class vineyard
	Other vineyard
	Woods
	Contour interval 20 metres

The Nahe

The Kupfergrube (copper mine) vineyard of the State Domain at Schlossböckelheim. Its Rieslings are the most intense yet delicate of the whole Nahe Valley.

The River Nahe, flowing north out of the Hunsrück hills to join the Rhine at Bingen, is surrounded by scattered outbreaks of wine-growing where either its own banks or its tributaries' face south. But at one point a sandstone barrier impedes the river's flow, a range of hills rears up along the north bank, and suddenly there are all the makings of a great vineyard.

Its wine seems to capture all the qualities best loved in German wine. It is very clean and grapey, with all the intensity of the Riesling, like a good Mosel or Saar wine. At the same time it has some of the full flavour that in the Rheingau evokes the alchemist's shop, as though rare minerals were dissolved in it, possibly gold itself.

Bad Kreuznach is the wine capital of the Nahe. It is a pleasant spa beneath hanging woods, with a casino and rows of strange brushwood erections down which salt water is poured to produce ozone for the benefit of convalescents.

Bad Kreuznach itself has some of the Nahe's best vineyards and the premises of some of the best growers. The Kahlenberg, Krötenpfuhl and Brückes sites, facing south over the town, can make exceptional wine. It also gives its name to the whole Bereich, or region, of the lower

KREUZNACH

BURGWEG

STEINBERG

Bereich

Grosslage

Einzellage

Kreis boundary

Gemeinde boundary

First-class vineyard

Other vineyard

Woods

Contour interval 20 metres

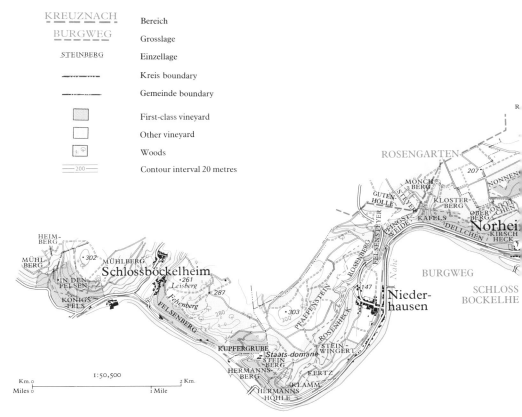

Left: the State Domain at Schlossböckelheim may be the Nahe's top single estate, but some forward-looking smaller properties cluster round the river and its tributaries. Schlossgut Diel at Burg Langen, Schloss Wallhausen and Kruger-Rumpf at Münster-Sarmsheim are all champions of the lower Nahe.

1:220,000

Km. 0   5   10 Km.
Miles 0   5 Miles

BURGWEG   Grosslage

ROXHEIM   Gemeinde (commune) with first-class vineyard

Nahe, down to the Rhine at Bingen. The upper Nahe is known as Bereich Schlossböckelheim and includes the Grosslage names Burgweg and (for Bad Kreuznach) Kronenberg.

The fireworks begin upstream at the Bad Münster bend. A red precipice, the Rotenfels, said to be the highest cliff in Europe north of the Alps, blocks the river's path. At the cliff-foot there is a bare 33 yards (30 metres) of fallen rubble, a short ramp of red earth. The vines are planted thick in the cramped space. They have ideal soil and enjoy a complete suntrap. This is the Rotenfelser (now called Traiser) Bastei. The degree of spice and fire in a Bastei of a good year is exceptional for such a northerly vineyard. It can be reminiscent of great Palatinate wine, with the freshness and finesse of the Saar thrown in.

From this bend on upstream there is a succession of fine slopes, through the villages of Norheim and Niederhausen, to the Nahe's most illustrious vineyard: the Kupfergrube (copper mine) on the eastern limit of the village of Schlossböckelheim.

The cellars where winemaking has at times reached its highest peak here, if not in the whole of Germany, face the Kupfergrube from the last slope of Niederhausen. The Nahe State Domain has holdings in several Niederhausen vineyards, including the excellent Hermannshöhle and Hermannsberg, and planted the Kupfergrube on the site of old copper diggings. Photographs still exist of the steep hill facing the cellars when it had no vines: it is easy to picture the director, observing the day-long sun on the mine workings, forming his plan.

Many find in this Domain everything they look for in white wine. The wines it made from the 1960s to 1990 are clean-tasting and fresh, fruity, racy and well balanced; very pale, with almost as much scent as a Bernkasteler and a long, lingering flavour in which sweetness and acidity are perfectly matched.

The State Domain also has vineyards on the lower Nahe, nearer to Bingen on the Rhine than Bad Kreuznach, in the parishes of Dorsheim and Münster-Sarmsheim in the Grosslage Schlosskapelle. Here, as at Langenlonsheim, an east-west-running shoulder of hill presents a south slope of stony loam at right angles to the river. The best of the Riesling grown here, above all that from the Einzellage Münsterer Dautenpflänzer, which has almost the beauty of the State Domain's upper Nahe wines, with more powerful and full-bodied flavours. Schloss Wallhausen in the valley has a similar privileged Riesling site. The wines of these lower Nahe villages are less famous than the Kreuznachers and Schlossböckelheimers, but stand equally far above the level of the surrounding countryside, among the élite of all Germany's wines.

The Rheingau: Rüdesheim

The Rheingau is the climax of the wine-growing Rhine. For almost all its length the river flows steadily northwest, except for the point just below Mainz where the high forested Taunus mountains stand in its way. It turns southwest for only 20 miles (32 kilometres) until it reaches the Rüdesheimer Berg. There, with a flurry of rocks and rapids, it forces a passage northwards again. But the influence of its broad waters in that space gives Germany its most magnificent vineyard.

The best part of the Rheingau is mapped on the page opposite and the following two pages. Opposite is the downstream end, where the Rüdesheimer Berg Schlossberg drops almost sheer to the river. This is the only part of the Rheingau that is so steep. Most of it consists of stiff slopes but no more.

The Riesling is the grape of the Rheingau, as it is of the Middle Mosel, but throughout the rest of the Rhine it appears only in the very best sites. The soil, described on page 144, is a great mixture, but is nearer in type to the soil of Burgundy than to that of Germany's other Riesling areas. The climate is comparatively dry and sunny. The river's presence makes for equable temperatures, promotes the mists that encourage 'noble rot' as the grapes ripen and, they say, gives extra sunlight by reflection off its surface. The river is more than half a mile (800 metres) wide here, a throbbing highway for slow strings of barges.

The Rheingau style of wine, at its best, is the noblest in Germany. It unites the flowery scent of the Riesling with a greater and more golden depth of flavour than the Mosel. Its character is bolder, more masculine. Soft and charming are words you should never hear in the Rheingau.

The westernmost town mapped opposite is Assmannshausen, around the corner from the main Rheingau and an exception to all its rules, being famous only for its red wine. The grape is the Pinot Noir. In spite of the fact that its wine is very pale here and lacks the power it should have, that made by the State Domain (among others) seems to be much sought after. Dry red Assmannshauser is the country's most famous red wine. Its pink Trockenbeerenauslesen, made only rarely, cost fortunes.

The Rüdesheimer Berg is distinguished from the rest of the parish by having the word Berg before each separate vineyard name. At their best (which is not always in the hottest years, since the drainage is too good at times) these are superlative wines, full of fruit and strength and yet delicate in nuance. In hotter years the vineyards behind the town come into their own.

Among the growers of the big parish is the wine school of Geisenheim, one of the most famous centres of wine learning in the world. Detailed soil and climate studies as well as new vine types developed here are of international importance (see pages 20–21).

The entire Rheingau was given the Bereich name of Johannisberg, its most famous single parish, in 1971. Thus might all the Médoc be allowed to use the name Margaux.

Schloss Vollrads has been the home of the Counts Greiffenclau since the 14th century. It produces dry austere wines designed to partner modern cuisine.

Schloss Johannisberg was granted in 1816 to Prince Metternich by Austria's Emperor. The present Fürst von Metternich makes consistently good wine.

The Rheingau has a longer and more consistent history than any great vineyard region in Europe, besides Burgundy. The distinction of having owned the same Rheingau vineyard for as much as (in one case) over six centuries is as great a patent of nobility as any in Europe.

As in Burgundy it was Benedictine and Cistercian brothers who laid the foundations. Kloster Eberbach (*below*: the press house) remains as witness to 700 years of more or less pious viticulture before Napoleon secularized the Church estates.

Among the great secular properties are those of the Princes of Hessen, Metternich and Löwenstein, Counts Greiffenclau and von Schönborn, the Barons Langwerth von Simmern and Ritter zu Groenesteyn.

Big estates outside this aristocratic circle include the

173-acre (70-ha) von Mumm estate at Johannisberg and the 136-acre (55-ha) Wegeler-Deinhard property at Winkel.

The dominating influence in the Rheingau today is the Charta association of growers dedicated to a conservative style of full-bodied dry Riesling.

Below: the magnificent 12th-century Kloster Eberbach in Hattenheim is the symbolic head-quarters of the German State Domain which has some 480 acres (195ha) in the Rheingau, including the great Steinberg, *left*.

Left: the Rheingau State Domain is the leading producer of Spätburgunder red wines in Assmannshausen.
Below: two of the many fine labels from the superlative sites of the Rüdesheimer Berg
Right: looking towards the Rhine from the slope of Schloss Johannisberg in winter. Legend has it that Charlemagne noticed the snow melted first on this slope.

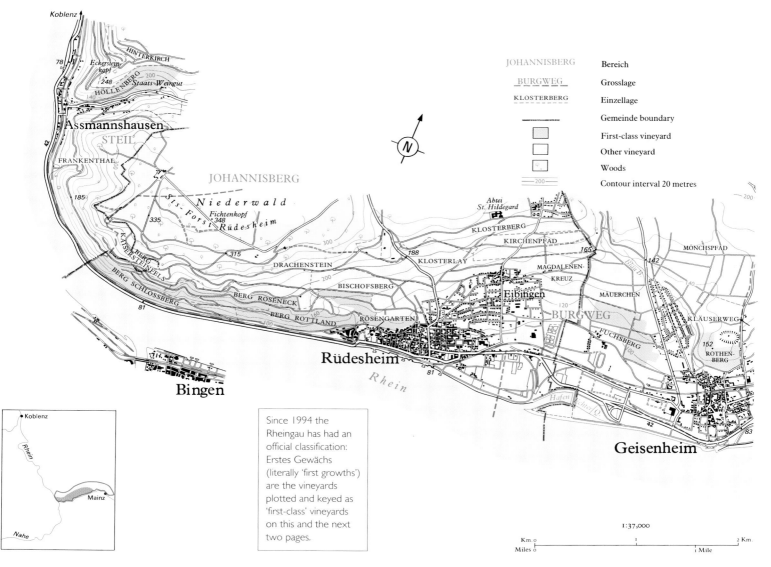

JOHANNISBERG	Bereich
BURGWEG	Grosslage
KLOSTERBERG	Einzellage
	Gemeinde boundary
	First-class vineyard
	Other vineyard
	Woods
200	Contour interval 20 metres

Since 1994 the Rheingau has had an official classification: Erstes Gewächs (literally 'first growths') are the vineyards plotted and keyed as 'first-class' vineyards on this and the next two pages.

1:37,000

Km. 0   1   2 Km.
Miles 0   1 Mile

The Rheingau: Eltville

Schloss Johannisberg, standing above a great apron of vines, dominates everything between Geisenheim and Winkel. The enormous prestige of its product, for which the winetaster's favourite term, 'elegant', might have been invented, tends to overshadow that of the rest of Johannisberg's excellent vineyards.

Schloss Vollrads (see page 156) stands more than a mile (2 kilometres) back from Winkel and leaves the name of the town off its label – unfortunately for Winkel, whose name would otherwise be better known than it is. Even its second-best vineyard, Hasensprung ('hare's leap'), is capable of producing rich aromatic wine with the endless nuances that put the Rheingau in a class by itself.

Mittelheim has little identity as distinct from the more important Winkel and Oestrich. Its name does not appear on any wine of special note. There are those who say the same about

Oestrich. Oestrichen have been criticized for lack of 'breed', but character and lusciousness they certainly have. Doosberg and Lenchen are not names to be dismissed.

In Hallgarten the Rheingau vineyards reach their highest point. Hendelberg is around 1,000 feet (300 metres) above sea level. There is less mist and less frost up here.

In the Würzgarten and Schönhell there is marly soil that gives strong wines of great lasting power and magnificent bouquet. No single vineyard makes the village name world famous.

The boundaries of Hattenheim stretch straight back into the hills to include the most illustrious of all the vineyards of the German state: the high ridge of the Steinberg, enclosed like the Clos de Vougeot with a Cistercian wall. Below in a wooded hollow stands the old monastery which might fairly be called the headquarters of German wine, Kloster Eberbach

(see page 156). The place, the astonishing wine and the implications of continuous industry and devotion to one idea of beauty going back 600 years make any comment seem trivial. Today Kloster Eberbach is the base of the German Wine Academy, which runs public courses.

Like Hallgarten, Hattenheim has marl in the soil. On its border with Erbach is the only vineyard that makes great wine right down by the river, in a situation that looks as though the drainage would be far from perfect. In Hattenheim this is called Mannberg; in Erbach it retains its ancient name Marcobrunn. Wine from either side of the parish boundary is very full flavoured, often rich, fruity, and spicy. Marcobrunn is every inch the Great growth.

The principal owner of Mannberg is Baron Langwerth von Simmern; of Marcobrunn Schloss Rheinhartshausen and Schloss Schönborn, the State Domain and the Knyphausen estate.

JOHANNISBERG   Bereich   ▢ First-class vineyard

GOTTESTHAL   Grosslage   ▢ Other vineyard

KLOSTERBERG   Einzellage   Woods

Gemeinde boundary   200 Contour interval 20 metres

For location map see page 157

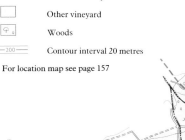

Erbacher Siegelsberg, which lies parallel with Marcobrunn, is next in quality. In Erbach the town's land goes back into the hills in a long narrow strip. These are good vineyards, but not the best. Steinmorgen, on the outskirts of the town, gives more powerful and memorable wine than Michelmark and Honigberg.

Kiedrich's beautiful Gothic church is the next landmark. The vineyards of the village make exceptionally well-balanced and delicately spicy wine. Dr Weil (which is now Japanese-owned) is the biggest Kiedrich-based estate. Gräfenberg is reckoned the best part of the vineyard, although Wasseros and Sandgrub are almost equally renowned.

Superlatives become tiring in an account of the Rheingau. Yet for drinkers of great white wine the peculiar sort of wine these growers make offers more to taste, consider and discuss than any other in the world.

The wines that fetch the high prices, and by which the vineyards are ultimately judged, have traditionally been the late-picked, sweet and intense ones which demand to be drunk with conscious attention, and on their own rather than with food. The leaders of the modern Rheingau, however, have deliberately moved away from this tradition: 62% of their wine is now made dry. The Charta organization of top growers leads the way with dry wines of Spätlese quality and rigorously low yields.

Rauenthal, the last of the hill villages and the furthest from the river, makes a different kind of superlative wine: the most expensive. The complex Rauenthalen are the Germans' German wine. The Auslesen of the State Domain and of two lordly growers, Baron Langwerth von Simmern and Count Schönborn, as well as those of several smaller growers on the Rauenthaler Berg, are prized for the combination of power and delicacy in their flowery scent and in their spicy aftertaste.

Eltville makes larger quantities of wine but without the supreme cachet. It is the headquarters of the State Domain (see page 156) as well as having the beautiful old mansions of the Eltz and von Simmern families, in a group of buildings of white plaster and rosy stone, draped with vines and roses, beside the river.

Without sharing the fame of their neighbours, the united Nieder- and Ober-Walluf and Martinsthal share much of their quality.

Some 15 miles (23 kilometres) further east, the Rheingau has an unexpected outpost: Hochheim. Hochheim vineyards (which gave us the word hock) lie on gently sloping land just north of the River Main, isolated in country that has no other vines. Good Hochheimers match the quality of the best Rheingauers with their own thrilling full-bodied earthiness.

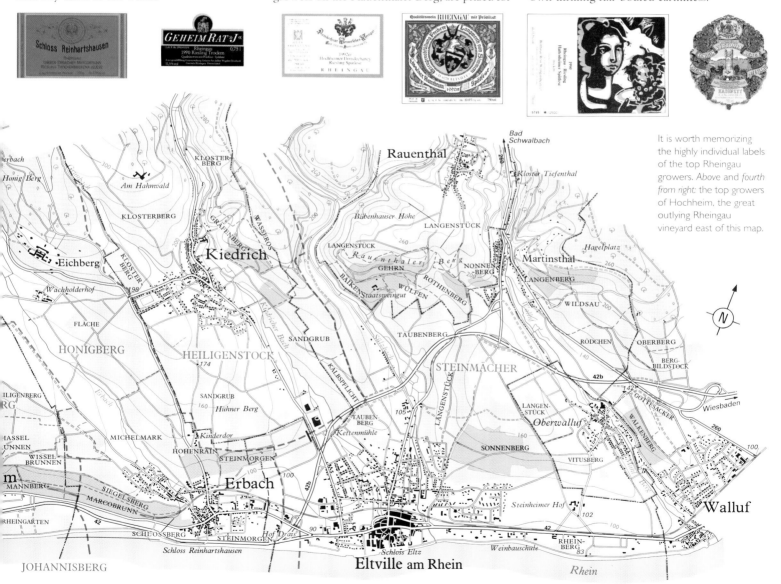

It is worth memorizing the highly individual labels of the top Rheingau growers. *Above* and *fourth from right:* the top growers of Hochheim, the great outlying Rheingau vineyard east of this map.

The Pfalz

Left: the southern Pfalz is a new centre of enterprise and excellence, little-known until the 1980s. Here the Haardt Mountains are lower and vineyards around Seibeldingen (*see smaller map, opposite*) and Birkweiler climb the lower slopes. Riesling shares the land with Grauburgunder, Weissburgunder and red Spätburgunder. *Above*: labels of the Mittelhaardt are much given to stately heraldry. Its finest wines are Rieslings that add succulence to finesse.

The Palatinate (German Pfalz) is Germany's biggest vineyard; a 50-mile (80-kilometre) stretch just north of Alsace, under the lee of the German continuation of the Vosges Mountains – the Haardt.

Like Alsace, it is the sunniest and driest part of its country, and has the never-failing charm of half-timbered villages among orchards, seeming part of a better, sunlit, half-fairytale world. A labyrinthine road, the Deutsche Weinstrasse, like the Alsatian Route du Vin, starts at the gates of Germany (literally: there is a massive gateway on the border at Schweigen) and winds northwards through unending vines and villages. A great part of the wine of the area (Südliche Weinstrasse is its Bereich name) is made by efficient cooperatives which have revolutionized casual old country methods and made the district famous as a source of good value wine.

There is little Riesling here; the style used to be sweetish and heavy with a preponderance of Müller-Thurgau and new grape varieties. Today it is Germany's workshop for a range of whites and reds of every complexion, including the whole Pinot family, with the emphasis on dry wines for the table, even using barrel-ageing in the modern style.

Most are still sold under Grosslage names, since few Einzellagen here have established reputations. But the top growers in half a dozen villages have now demonstrated the potential of their soil for wines that merit classification. These are indicated on the map opposite.

Neustadt an der Weinstrasse used to mark a sharp dividing line between 'country' wines of little pretension and a very different world: the Mittelhaardt, where some of Germany's biggest and most famous estates were well-established in the luxury and export markets. In the Mittelhaardt, the name given to the short string of little townships mapped in detail opposite, Riesling jumps from 5% to 75% of the plantation. Historically three famous producers have dominated this, the kernel of the Pfalz: Bürklin-Wolf, von Bassermann-Jordan and von Buhl. But any monopoly of quality they ever had has disappeared in a surge of ambitious and original winemaking on all sides. Today very fine wines come from as far south as Siebeldingen, especially from Gimmeldingen near Neustadt, and as far north as Grünstadt.

Mittelhaardt wine's special quality is succulent richness – even when, as often today, it is finished dry or 'half-dry'. It is far removed from the thrilling nervous acidity of, say, the Saar.

The Einzellagen on the hilly west side of the villages are the ones that most often attain the summits of succulence. Most of the best are within the Grosslage Forster Mariengarten.

In the south, Ruppertsberg officially begins the Mittelhaardt; its best sites (Linsenbusch, Hoheburg, Reiterpfad, Nussbien, Spiess) are all on moderate slopes, well exposed and largely Riesling. It is an anomaly that they should share the Grosslage name of Hofstück with inferior vineyards on the plain to the east. The hill slope sharpens at Deidesheim where the Grosslage Mariengarten begins. Deidesheim is generally reckoned the best village of the whole area, besides being one of the prettiest in Germany. Von Bassermann-Jordan and von Buhl have their cellars here. Hohenmorgen, Langenmorgen, Leinhöhle, Kalkofen, Kieselberg and Grainhübel are the top Lagen.

Forst has a reputation as the source of Germany's most succulent wine (not in mere sugar, it is frequently made as a dry Spätlese, but in style and character). A black basalt outcrop above the village provides dark warm soil, rich in potassium, which is quarried and spread on other vineyards, notably in Deidesheim. Forst's one street is the main road. The Jesuitengarten, its most famous vineyard, and the equally fine Kirchenstück lie just behind the church. Freundstück (largely von Buhl's) and, above it, part of Ungeheuer are in the same class.

The village of Wachenheim marks the end of

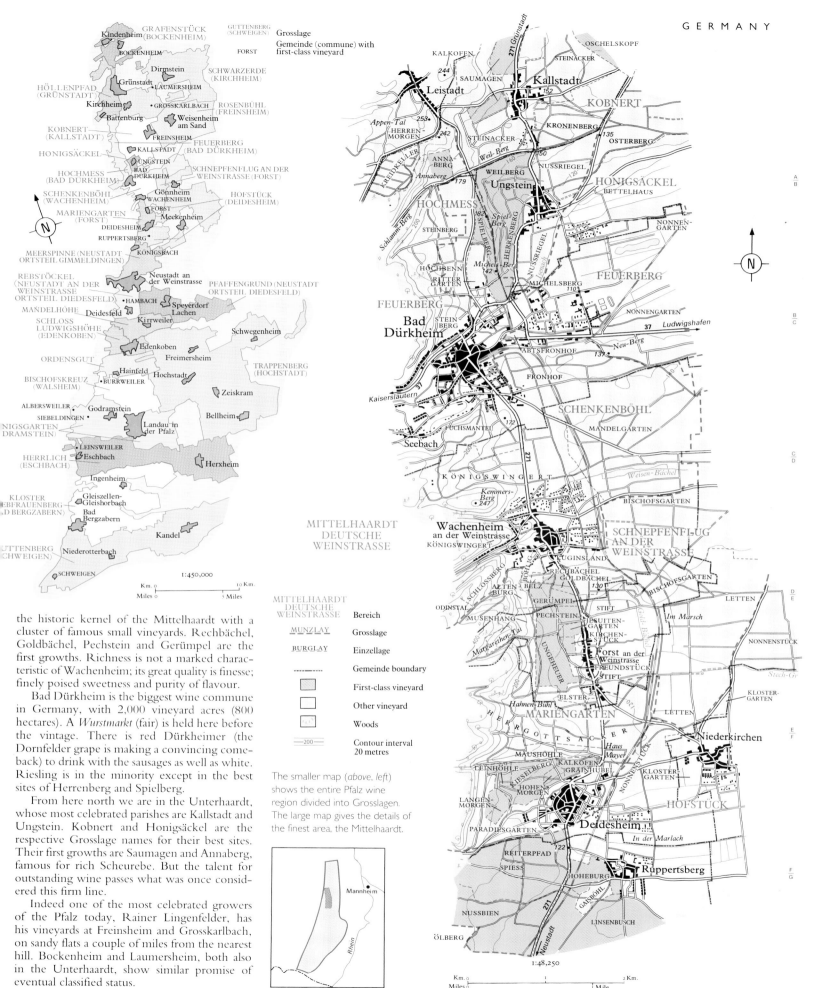

GRAFENSTÜCK
(BOCKENHEIM)
Kindenheim
GUTTENBERG
(SCHWEIGEN)
FORST
BOCKENHEIM
Dirmstein
SCHWARZERDE
(KIRCHHEIM)
HÖLLENPFAD
(GRÜNSTADT)
Grünstadt •LAUMERSHEIM
Kirchheim
ROSENBÜHL
(FREINSHEIM)
•GROSSKARLBACH
Battenburg
Weisenheim
am Sand
KOBNERT
(KALLSTADT)
FREINSHEIM
FEUERBERG
(BAD DÜRKHEIM)
HONIGSÄCKEL
•KALLSTADT
HOCHMESS
(BAD DÜRKHEIM)
UNGSTEIN
BAD
DÜRKHEIM
SCHNEPFENFLUG AN DER
WEINSTRASSE (FORST)
SCHENKENBÖHL
(WACHENHEIM)
Gönnheim
WACHENHEIM
FORST
Meckenheim
HOFSTÜCK
(DEIDESHEIM)
MARIENGARTEN
(FORST)
DEIDESHEIM
RUPPERTSBERG •
KÖNIGSBACH
MEERSPINNE (NEUSTADT
ORTSTEIL GIMMELDINGEN)
REBSTÖCKEL
(NEUSTADT AN DER
WEINSTRASSE
ORTSTEIL DIEDESFELD)
Neustadt an
der Weinstrasse
PFAFFENGRUND (NEUSTADT
ORTSTEIL DIEDESFELD)
MANDELHÖHE
•HAMBACH
Deidesfeld
Speyerdorf
Lachen
SCHLOSS
LUDWIGSHÖHE
(EDENKOBEN)
Kirrweiler
Schwegenheim
ORDENSGUT
Edenkoben
Freimersheim
BISCHOFSKREUZ
(WALSHEIM)
Hainfeld
•BURRWEILER
Hochstadt
TRAPPENBERG
(HOCHSTADT)
Zeiskram
ALBERSWEILER
SIEBELDINGEN •
Godramstein
Bellheim
NIGSGARTEN
DRAMSTEIN
Landau in
der Pfalz
HERRLICH
(ESCHBACH)
•LEINSWEILER
Eschbach
Herxheim
Ingenheim
KLOSTER
EBFRAUENBERG
D BERGZABERN)
Gleiszellen-
Gleishorbach
Bad
Bergzabern
Kandel
UTTENBERG
CHWEIGEN)
Niederotterbach
SCHWEIGEN

1:450,000
Km. 0 — 10 Km.
Miles 0 — 5 Miles

Grosslage
Gemeinde (commune) with
first-class vineyard

MITTELHAARDT
DEUTSCHE
WEINSTRASSE
MUNZLAY
BURGLAY

Bereich
Grosslage
Einzellage
Gemeinde boundary
First-class vineyard
Other vineyard
Woods
—200— Contour interval
20 metres

The smaller map (*above, left*)
shows the entire Pfalz wine
region divided into Grosslagen.
The large map gives the details of
the finest area, the Mittelhaardt.

MITTELHAARDT
DEUTSCHE
WEINSTRASSE

Mannheim
Rhein

the historic kernel of the Mittelhaardt with a
cluster of famous small vineyards. Rechbächel,
Goldbächel, Pechstein and Gerümpel are the
first growths. Richness is not a marked characteristic of Wachenheim; its great quality is finesse;
finely poised sweetness and purity of flavour.

Bad Dürkheim is the biggest wine commune
in Germany, with 2,000 vineyard acres (800
hectares). A *Wurstmarkt* (fair) is held here before
the vintage. There is red Dürkheimer (the
Dornfelder grape is making a convincing come-
back) to drink with the sausages as well as white.
Riesling is in the minority except in the best
sites of Herrenberg and Spielberg.

From here north we are in the Unterhaardt,
whose most celebrated parishes are Kallstadt and
Ungstein. Kobnert and Honigsäckel are the
respective Grosslage names for their best sites.
Their first growths are Saumagen and Annaberg,
famous for rich Scheurebe. But the talent for
outstanding wine passes what was once considered this firm line.

Indeed one of the most celebrated growers
of the Pfalz today, Rainer Lingenfelder, has
his vineyards at Freinsheim and Grosskarlbach,
on sandy flats a couple of miles from the nearest
hill. Bockenheim and Laumersheim, both also
in the Unterhaardt, show similar promise of
eventual classified status.

1:48,250
Km. 0 — 2 Km.
Miles 0 — 1 Mile

Rheinhessen

The Liebfrauenstift vineyard, origin of the name of Liebfraumilch (although long since divorced from it) lies around the Liebfrauenkirche in the city of Worms. Nylon netting protects the vines from birds.

Rheinhessen lies in the crook of the Rhine, hemmed in by the river on the east and north, the Nahe on the west and the Pfalz to the south. Its 150-odd villages, spaced out over an area 20 by 30 miles (30 by 50 kilometres), grow wine as part or all of their livelihood. It is dull, undulating, fertile country, without exceptional character except where the Rhine flows by.

The bulk of Rheinhessen wine, made from Müller-Thurgau or Silvaner, is equally unexceptional; light, soft, usually sweetish, sometimes earthy, rarely vigorous enough to claim attention. It finds its outlet as Liebfraumilch. This is now legally defined as a Qualitätswein (QbA) from Rheinhessen, Pfalz, Nahe or Rheingau; it contains at least 70% Riesling, Silvaner, Müller-Thurgau or Kerner and has a minimum of 18 grams per litre of residual sugar (the maximum for a 'halb-trocken' wine). Liebfraumilch can be expected to be mild and semi-sweet. But remember that Liebfraumilch is made for export. The locals are far more interested in dry wines, increasingly in dry Silvaners, which can be very satisfying.

The map on the facing page shows the whole of the winegrowing Rheinhessen with its Grosslage divisions: the names most commonly seen (apart from Liebfraumilch, that is) on its wine, which seldom assumes the distinction of an Einzellage name.

The vast majority of the growers have only a few acres of vines that are cultivated as part of a mixed-farming operation. Most of the wine is made by cooperatives.

Three Bereich names cover the whole region: Bingen the northwest, Nierstein the northeast, and Wonnegau the south, between the principal towns of Alzey and Worms. The town of Bingen, facing Rüdesheim across the

Nierstein has as many as 300 sizeable wine estates. Those of Guntrum and Balbach are among the biggest, Baron Heyl zu Hermsheim is another excellent grower. The last label is that of the most important estate at Bingen to the west (see map on facing page).

NIERSTEIN	Bereich
REHBACH	Grosslage
EBERSBERG	Einzellage
	Gemeinde boundary
	First-class vineyard
	Other vineyard
	Woods
	Contour interval 10 metres

1:37,500

Rhine, has excellent vineyards on the steep slopes of its first-growth Scharlachberg.

The Wonnegau has some respectable wines, Silvaners especially, round Alzey and to its southeast on chalky soil. But by far the best and most important vineyards of Rheinhessen are concentrated in the short stretch of the Rheinfront mapped on opposite.

The town of Nierstein has become as famous as Bernkastel. This is partly through its size and the number of its growers (about 300), partly because its name was widely and shamelessly borrowed (usually with the site name Domthal attached) before the 1971 wine laws, but mainly because of its superb vineyards.

The two towns that flank it, Oppenheim and Nackenheim, have vineyards as good as most of Nierstein, but none better than the sand-red roll of hill going north with the river at its foot. Hipping, Brudersberg, Pettenthal and Rothenberg (which is in Nackenheim) make wine as fragrant and full of character as the Rheingau, though they are a shade softer and more luxuriant. Oppenheim's first growths are comparable.

Any true Niersteiner will use one of the Lage names marked on the detailed map. The best will also specify that they are made from Riesling, although some interesting wines are being made from crosses such as Kerner, and Gewürztraminer grows well here.

Niersteiner Domtal was once the name on every tongue. It no longer exists. Niersteiner Gutes Domtal, on the other hand, is a Grosslage name available to 15 villages, but to only one part of Nierstein, and that the least distinguished. It is a name to avoid.

Outside the area of this map the best villages are those just north and south: Bodenheim, Guntersblum, Alsheim and Bechtheim.

Map legend:

DOMBLICK — Grosslage
ALSHEIM — Gemeinde (commune) with first-class vineyard

1:417,500

Km.0 — 10 — 20 Km.
Miles 0 — 5 — 10 Miles

Below: the best vineyards of Rheinhessen line the Rheinfront north and south of Nierstein on 300-ft (90-m) hills. Most of the Riesling in Rheinhessen is grown here.

Below: a Rheinhessen grower measures the sugar content of his must with a hydrometer. Fermentation in small barrels in a cool cellar is giving way to refrigerated vats in most districts.

Baden-Württemberg

The south of Germany, with its warmer climate, could be expected to be more of a wine region than parts further north. A hundred years ago it was. But the peculiar combinations of soil, climate and social structure that make quality winemaking possible and worthwhile in apparently unlikely spots on the Mosel and Rhine have only a few parallels in the huge state of Baden-Württemberg. The best of its wine is excellent, but it is so scattered and so keenly drunk in the region that the outside world rarely hears of it. Until recently, that is. Nowhere in Germany has the rationalization and modernization of the wine industry gone further and faster. Baden's vineyards have doubled in size and quadrupled in production. Only the Pfalz and Rheinhessen produce more.

The locomotive of this great surge forward has been the cooperatives. Ninety percent of the crop is handled by more than 100 of these establishments, and more than half of all this wine is marketed by the mammoth Badischer Winzerkeller at Breisach, the frontier town on the Rhine between Freiburg and Alsace. At the other end of the scale small producers have pioneered with imported ideas to add some exciting novelties to the region's repertoire.

One way to define Baden's style is to say that it is the opposite of the Mosel's. Ethereal floweriness is not so much to the point as substantial wineyness. Alsace lies just across the Rhine. Baden is a trifle damper and cloudier than the vineyards over the Rhine, umbrella'd by the Vosges. Its vineyards skirt the Black Forest, where mist and rain form part of some of Germany's loveliest pictures. The bulk of Baden's vineyards lie in a narrow 80-mile (130-kilometre) strip between the forest and the Rhine valley; the best of them either on privileged southern slopes in the forest massif or on the volcanic outcrops that form two distinct islands of high ground in the Rhine Valley: the Kaiserstuhl and Tuniberg.

No one grape variety is dominant. Müller-Thurgau forms one-third of the crop (the national average is closer to half). Spätburgunder (Pinot Noir) is the second variety, used for both middle-weight reds and pale Weissherbst. Pinot Gris goes by two names: Ruländer when it is made unctuous, Grauburgunder when (more often now) it is bottled as a full dry wine. Riesling makes classically elegant and long-lived wines, Weissburgunder (Pinot Blanc) smooth, soft wines, Gewürztraminer spicy ones, Silvaner (on the Kaiserstuhl) some wines almost as full of character as it makes in Franconia. The highly aromatic new varieties are little used. Badeners regard wine primarily as accompaniment to food. Few German wines fill the role better.

The Kaiserstuhl and Tuniberg furnish one-third of all Baden's wine. Their volcanic outcrops have been remodelled by earth-moving on a heroic scale to make modern vineyards out of old terraces and ledges. Red Spätburgunder is locally considered the best wine; Silvaner and Grauburgunder are sometimes splendid: stiff with flavour.

To the north, just south of the luxurious Black Forest spa of Baden-Baden, the Ortenau is a pocket of quality winegrowing with an emphasis on red wine. The lordly estates at Durbach, of the Margrave of Baden (Schloss Staufenberg) and of Count Wolff Metternich, make excellent Klingelberger (the local name for Riesling), Ruländer, Spätburgunder and Traminer. Much further north the Kraichgau and Badischer Bergstrasse form one Bereich, disparate as they are, with their best wines (at least in a visitor's opinion) made from the minority grapes, Riesling and Ruländer, grown in the best sites.

Far to the south, in the Markgräflerland, the corner of Germany between Freiburg and Basel, the favourite grape is the Gutedel, the local name for the Chasselas of Switzerland. It makes very refreshing, if rather reticent, wine. Its cross with Silvaner, the Nobling, is tastier. Weissherbst is popular here, too. Recent trials indicate that Chardonnay is also very much at home here.

The 'Seewein' (lake wine) of the southernmost area of all, around Meersburg on the Bodensee, is traditionally off-dry pink-tinted Weissherbst of Spätburgunder – almost a 'Blanc de Noir'. Müller-Thurgau is the principal white grape. The Margrave of Baden has another splendid estate here, Schloss Salem – even if it has no Riesling to match up to his noble Durbacher wine.

Württemberg, extensive though its vineyards are, remains better known to the world at large for its motorcars (at Stuttgart) than its wine. The region grows more red (or Weissherbst) wine than white, largely of its own varieties, the Trollinger, Lemberger and Schwarzriesling (or Pinot Meunier) as well as the universal Spätburgunder. The climate is not kind to winegrowers in Württemberg, so sites are chosen with care, lining the River Neckar and its tributaries. The Bereich to the north of the capital, the Württembergisch Unterland, has three-quarters of the region's vineyards.

Stuttgart and Heilbronn, in fact, almost bracket the whole industry. Visitors flock to taste its products: pale pink Schillerwein, Muskateller, Müller-Thurgau, Silvaner…a wide selection. The Traminer is good, but the Riesling, as almost everywhere in Germany, stands in a class apart.

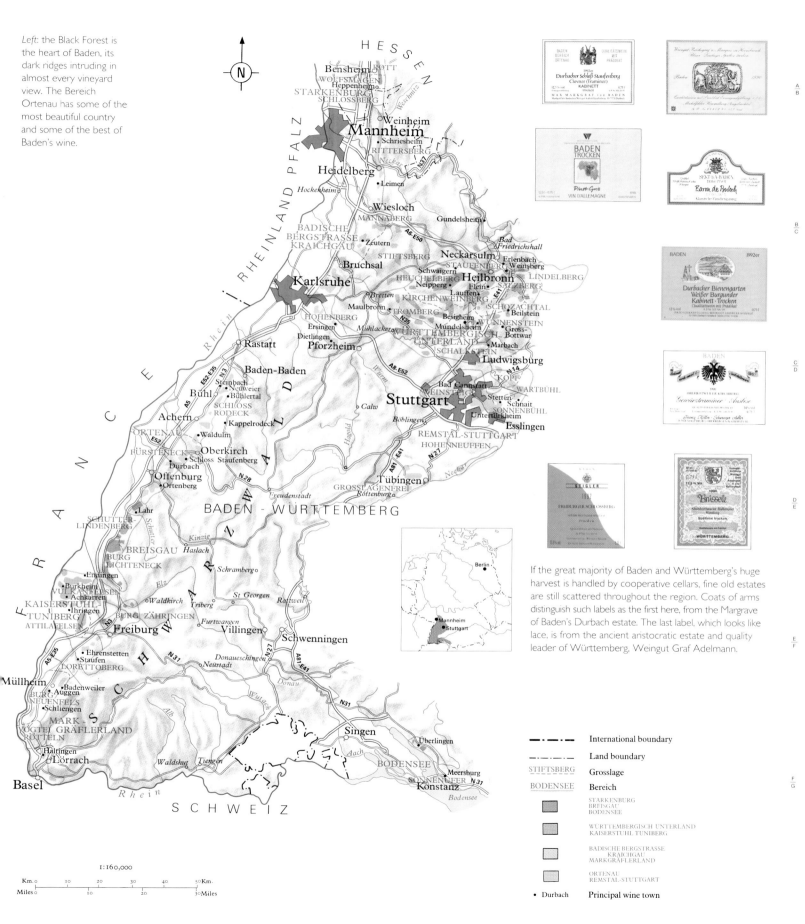

Left: the Black Forest is the heart of Baden, its dark ridges intruding in almost every vineyard view. The Bereich Ortenau has some of the most beautiful country and some of the best of Baden's wine.

If the great majority of Baden and Württemberg's huge harvest is handled by cooperative cellars, fine old estates are still scattered throughout the region. Coats of arms distinguish such labels as the first here, from the Margrave of Baden's Durbach estate. The last label, which looks like lace, is from the ancient aristocratic estate and quality leader of Württemberg, Weingut Graf Adelmann.

–·–·–·–	International boundary
––––––	Land boundary
STIFTSBERG	Grosslage
BODENSEE	Bereich
	STARKENBURG BREISGAU BODENSEE
	WÜRTTEMBERGISCH UNTERLAND KAISERSTUHL TUNIBERG
	BADISCHE BERGSTRASSE KRAICHGAU MARKGRÄFLERLAND
	ORTENAU REMSTAL-STUTTGART
• Durbach	Principal wine town

1:160,000

Km. 0   10   20   30   40   50 Km.
Miles 0   10   20   30 Miles

165

Franconia

Above: Franconia (Franken) is the one part of Germany that does not use the tall slim bottle. Its appetizing dry wines come in Bocksbeutels, a model protected by law for Franconia. *Below*: ancient casks in the candlelit cellars of the great baroque Residenz of the Prince-Bishop of Würzburg. Tiepolo painted the ceilings upstairs.

MAINDREIECK	**Bereich**
EWIG LABEN	**Grosslage**
HOMBURG	Gemeinde (commune) with first-class vineyard

Franconia is out of the mainstream of German wine both geographically and by its quite separate traditions. Politically it lies in the otherwise wineless former kingdom of Bavaria, which gives its State cellars a grandeur found nowhere else in Germany, and its consumers high expectations.

It makes the only German wine that does not come in flute bottles; it makes greater wines of Silvaner than of Riesling. And in savour and strength it draws away from the delicate sweetness of most German and nearer to some French wines, making it one of the best of German wines to drink with food.

The name Steinwein is loosely used for all Franconian wine. Stein is, in fact, the name of one of the two famous vineyards of the city of Würzburg on the Main, the capital of the district. The other is Leiste. Both distinguished themselves in the past by making wines that lasted incredibly long periods. A 16th-century Stein wine (of the great vintage of 1540) was still just drinkable in the 1960s.

Such wines were Beerenauslesen at least: immensely sweet. Franconia makes few such rarities today. The bulk of the wine in the characteristic flask-shaped *Bocksbeutel* is full-bodied and entirely dry, with something like the size and strength of white burgundy.

Franconia takes the vine further east and north than any other German region, into countryside whose climate is decidedly continental. In the Steigerwald, the easternmost of the three Franconian Bereichs, the vine looks almost a stranger in a setting of arable fields with forests of magnificent oaks crowning its sudden hills. The doll's-house princedom of Castell is a sort of unofficial capital of this Bereich, producing, with the parishes of Iphofen and Rödelsee, its finest wine.

This is the one part of Germany where the growing season is regularly too short for the Riesling to prosper. The Silvaner is the answer. In Franconia this normally second-division

Sachsen and Saale-Unstrut

grape gains first-division status – not for pyrotechnics of fragrance but for a combination of the subtle and forceful that commands respect. Making allowance for the flavours of quite different grapes, Premier or even Grand Cru Chablis are comparable wines.

But even in Franconia, unfortunately, Müller-Thurgau seems to offer a better return, at least on less-than-ideal sites. It has gained the upper hand in nearly half the 10,000 acres (4,000 hectares) of vineyard in the region. (For comparison, the Nahe has about the same total area of vines, the Rheingau two-thirds as much and the Pfalz five times.) A minority of Franconian wines are made of the super-aromatic varieties Bacchus and Kerner. The best innovation, though, is a late-ripening Riesling and Silvaner cross called Rieslaner.

The heart of winegrowing Franconia is all included in the Bereich Maindreieck, following the fuddled three-cornered meandering of the Main from Escherndorf (with its celebrated Einzellage, Lump) and Nordheim upstream of Würzburg, south to Frickenhausen, then north again through the capital to include all the next leg of the river and the outlying district around Hammelburg. What distinguishes all these scattered south-facing hillsides is the peculiar limestone known as Muschelkalk (whose origins are not so different from the Kimmeridgian clay of Chablis, or indeed of Sancerre). The much smaller Bereich Steigerwald, to the east of the Main, has heavier (although still alkaline) clay soil. The third Bereich, further downstream to the west, has lighter loam based on sandstone. This is the Mainviereck (see the map on page 143),which is of relatively small importance.

Where the legend 'Grosslagenfrei' appears on the map, it signifies that the wine villages are so scattered that they have not been grouped in Grosslagen. Their wines are sold under individual site names or the name of the Bereich. Most Franconian wine is made by cooperatives.

Würzburg is the essential visit: one of the great cities of the vine, with three magnificent estate cellars in its heart belonging respectively to the Bavarian State (Staatliche Hofkellerei), a church charity (Juliusspital) and a civic charity (Bürgerspital).

The Staatliche Hofkellerei lies under the gorgeous Residenz of the former prince-bishops, whose ceiling paintings by Tiepolo are reason enough to visit the city. There is also the noble Marienburg Castle on its hill of vines, the great baroque river bridge and the bustling *Weinstuben* (wine bars) belonging to these ancient foundations, where all their wines can be enjoyed with suitably savoury food.

The reunification of Germany reintroduces to the market the wines of two once-thriving little districts. Sachsen (Saxony in its English form) lies on the banks of the River Elbe between Meissen and Dresden. Thirty miles (50 kilometres) west, beyond Leipzig, the confluence of the rivers Saale and Unstrut gives its name to Germany's northernmost wine region – approximately on the latitude of London, but with a continental and far more extreme climate.

Together Sachsen and Saale-Unstrut amount to some 1,700 acres (700 hectares), with Müller-Thurgau as their principal vine, but with regional characters that can be worth pursuing.

Both districts make most of their wines dry, with late-picked bottlings rare in this cold area. Sachsen wines aim for fruity acidity and aromas. Weissburgunder, Traminer and a little red are grown. Sparkling wines are an old tradition here (and, according to legend, a century ago were shipped in bulk to Reims).

Saale-Unstrut has more in common with Franconia, its nearest neighbour to the south-west. It too has slopes of Muschelkalk, ideal limestone for soft, dry but pungent wines, on good south slopes to its rivers. It also has some splendid old cellars for fermenting. Silvaner, Weissburgunder and Gutedel are savoury; Morio-Muskat, Bacchus and Kerner are flowery. The red wines (largely Portugieser) are pale.

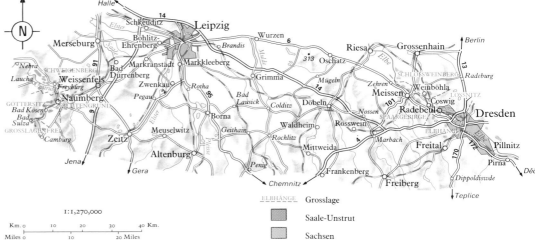

Left: Franconian labels are often round, like the faces of their bottles. Producers include two great charities.
Right: Saxon labels, and wines, are still unfamiliar outside the region.

German Wine Law and Labels

German wine laws do not classify vineyards as the French do. The land classifications in this Atlas have as yet no official standing. Instead, the law specifies exactly what degree of sugar (measured in degrees Oechsle) the must (crushed grapes) should contain to qualify for each quality grade.

The are four basic grades of quality, each with its own set of rules enshrined in the law, but, increasingly, the best producers are ignoring this cumbersome system and returning to much simpler, often older, appellations on the fringes of the law. They recognize that the German language with its long words, often printed in Gothic script, is incomprehensible to the great majority of foreigners. The sad result has been the proliferation of Liebfraumilch and a few market favourites such as 'Niersteiner Gutes Domtal', whose connection with Nierstein is a legal fiction.

The most popular simplified appellations are simply the commune name (eg Hochheimer, Deidesheimer) or even just the grape name linked to a brand, in New World style. In most cases the details required by law are included in small print or on a 'back' label. The object is that the wine identifies itself and its maker in the most succinct and recognizable manner.

The four grades of quality have precise limits to the amount and kind of information they can carry on their labels. The examples on this page, however, show how current labelling practice interprets the regulations fairly freely. It is no longer felt necessary to include all the formal information the law allows in the conventional way. The producer instead stresses what he considers to be the most important information to the consumer.

THE LANGUAGE OF THE LABEL

Amtliche Prüfungsnummer / AP Nr grapes' identifying quality test number
Bestimmtes Anbaugebiet specified region
Erzeugerabfüllung bottled by the producer (see Gutsabfüllung)
Flaschengärung bottle-fermented
Gemeinde wine commune
Gutsabfüllung bottled by producer (since 1993 used to replace 'Erzeugerabfüllung' if certain requirements are met)
Halbtrocken 'half dry', often an ideal balance for use at table, especially Kabinett wines
Oechsle scale for sugar content of grape juice
Perlwein slightly sparkling (carbonated) wine
Rotwein red wine
Schaumwein sparkling wine
Schillerwein pink wine made from mixed red and white grapes
Sekt sparkling wine, subject to quality controls
Trocken dry, often good with food in QbA and Spätlese categories, which have slightly more alcohol (about 10.5–11°) than wines with residual sugar
Weinbaugebiet wine region
Weinkellerei wine cellar or winery
Weissherbst pink wine from red grapes
Weisswein white wine
Winzergenossenschaft / Winzerverein wine-growers' cooperative

Deutscher Tafelwein

Ordinary table wine, which need attain only 5% natural alcohol (44° Oechsle) – 6% in some zones – before sugaring and must be made from approved varieties of grape. It may use the name of a region or subregion, but not the name of a village or a vineyard. If the label names a grape variety (eg Riesling) the Tafelwein must be at least 85% that variety. Tafelwein without the 'Deutscher' contains wine, or a blend of wines, from other European countries – usually Italy or Spain. On this label the stress is on the name of the (sufficiently famous) grower and the grape variety: Spätburgunder. Although it is an estate wine from the Lingenfelder estate at Grosskarlbach it may not legally refer to its vineyard. In this instance 'Tafelwein' does not mean low quality but it illustrates the grower's choice not to play by more exacting rules.

Landwein

In 1982 this category, which is theoretically superior to Tafelwein with slightly higher and more specific standards, was introduced to be the approximate equivalent of a French vin de pays.

Landwein must come from one of 15 designated regions, contain half a degree of natural alcohol more than Tafelwein, and not more than 18 grams per litre of residual sugar, which makes it relatively dry: at most a halbtrocken. On this label the growers' cooperative of Irsch-Ockfen on the Saar stresses the Landwein category. The other information (Müller-Thurgau grapes, 'half-dry' style) is useful, but not legally essential.

Qualitätswein bestimmter Anbaugebiete (QbA)

This is the misleading name of the large category of wine which has been chaptalized (to use the French term) with added sugar but is still deemed to have sufficient 'quality' to be able to specify its origins as fully as QmP (top category) wine. It must come from a specified region, be made only from certain permitted grape varieties, attain a certain must weight (with typical confusion this varies from area to area: Mosel-Saar-Ruwer QbA needs 51° Oechsle, for example, Pfalz QbA needs 60° Oechsle) and it must carry a test number. It can carry a vineyard name if at least 85% of the grapes were grown in that vineyard, a Grosslage or a Bereich name (see page 144) or the name of a village. This label proclaims the new philosophy of selling QbA wine without the complication of place names, giving only the general area (Rheinhessen), the grape (Silvaner) and the fact that it is dry (trocken). RS stands simply for Rheinhessen Silvaner. The estate is the highly regarded Villa Sachsen at Bingen.

Qualitätswein mit Prädikat (QmP)

Village of origin and vineyard	Riesling - grape variety
Defined Qba area	Spätlese - late gathered
	Trocken - dry
Name of estate,	(special attribute within Qmp grade)
producer & shipper	
	Vintage

Estate-bottled	Estate/producer address
Bottle contents	Analytical and tasting test number
Estate location	Degree of alcohol content

Qualitätswein mit Prädikat is the top category, which may not use sugar for the purpose of increasing the wine's alcohol content. In this category the precise vineyard and degree of ripeness can be specified, although in many cases (where the wine is Riesling) it is taken to be understood. The wine's natural must weight must be 67° Oechsle (the equivalent of 8.6% alcohol) or more depending on the region; the grapes must be of a certain variety; they must come from a particular area, be quality-tested and carry their identifying test number (AP Nr).

This highest grade is subdivided into five categories according to the ripeness of the grape (measured in ° Oechsle) although even these are subject to slight variation depending on area and grape variety.
Kabinett: minimum must weight about 73°
Spätlese: minimum must weight about 80°
Auslese: minimum must weight about 90°
Beerenauslese: minimum must weight about 120°.
Trockenbeerenauslese: minimum must weight about 150°.

Eiswein must be made of grapes that are frozen solid when picked (normally long after the rest of the harvest) and crushed while still frozen. The ice (which is pure water) is removed, leaving an intensely concentrated must of high sugar (the same minimum must weight as Beerenauslese) and acidity, but without the specific flavour of 'noble rot' normally associated with Beeren- and Trockenbeerenauslese.

Sekt, Germany's sparkling wine, is made with the excess of under-ripe grapes which are the inevitable product of Germany's northerly situation. Sekt may be fermented in bottle or in tank, may be made from grapes from any region and may even include imported wines. All the better Sekts are called either Deutscher Sekt, which means the wine must be made from 100% German-grown grapes, or Sekt bA, in which case it must be made from grapes from one of the 11 designated German wine-growing regions. The label here illustrates the highest category: Vintage Sekt from a single vineyard.

Southern & Eastern Europe and the Mediterranean

Italy

Colonizing Greeks called Italy Oenotria – the land of wine. The map reminds us that there is little of Italy that is not, at least marginally, wine country. Her annual production is now easily the biggest in the world.

The first edition of this Atlas described the Italian attitude to wine as amiably insouciant: chaotic enough, with its delights and disappointments, to drive a tidy-minded wine merchant to drink. The past twenty years have seen radical changes to every aspect of the making and selling of Italian wine. The insouciance is gone. The business has become deadly earnest, and highly aware of international tastes and trends. Yet the Italians still have ways that can take patience and goodwill to understand.

In terms of geography, Italy cannot fail to produce good wine in great variety. If hill slopes, sunshine and a temperate climate are the essentials, Italy has more than any country in Europe. Her peculiar physique, that of a long spine of mountains reaching south from the sheltering Alps almost to North Africa, means that there can hardly be a desirable combination of altitude with latitude and exposure that is absent. Many of her soils are volcanic; much is limestone or tufa; there is plenty of gravelly clay: Oenotria indeed.

To the consumer, however, Italy has a serious drawback: an impossible confusion of names. Because wine is omnipresent, so much a part of everyday life, made by so many proud and independent people, every conceivable sort of name is pressed into use to mark originality. Thus one bottle may carry on it not only the official (DOC) name, often the name of the grape and the name of the producer, but also the name of the property, of a part of the property, or of anything else that takes the producer's fancy – and fantasy it often is. Matters are made much worse by the habit of omitting the name of the region. Often the name of an obscure town is the only geographical reference on a label.

Italy, like Germany, desperately needs a labelling system – which is not necessarily the same thing as a new wine law – in which it is clear who made the wine, where it was made, and how it should be referred to.

During the past two decades the Italian government has done a monumental job of tidying up the multiplicity of Italian wines into defined identities. The Italian DOC (Denominazione di Origine Controllata) system is described opposite – see Wine Law. Over these years, though, a serious drawback in the DOC system became clear. What it effectively does is to fossilize the current practice of the majority of winemakers in each region, regardless of whether it leads to the best results or not. Indeed, it penalizes progressive winemakers who know that certain changes of practice (whether, for example, of grape varieties, their treatment, or the ageing of the wine) could greatly improve their products.

The result has been the proliferation of *vini da tavola* – that is unclassified and undemarcated wines of the lowest official standing – which frequently excel the DOC wines in both quality and price; a number are brilliant. *Vini da*

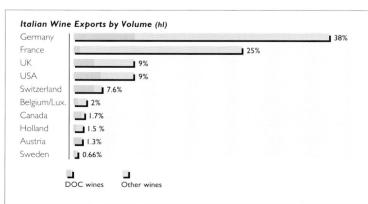

International boundary

Regione boundary

DOC areas

Land above 600 metres

173 Regional map page number

1:6,000,000

Km. 0 — 100 — 200 Km.
Miles 0 — 60 — 120 Miles

N

Italian Wine Exports by Volume (hl)

Germany	38%
France	25%
UK	9%
USA	9%
Switzerland	7.6%
Belgium/Lux.	2%
Canada	1.7%
Holland	1.5 %
Austria	1.3%
Sweden	0.66%

DOC wines   Other wines

Italy is the world's leading wine-producer, with 63.8 million hectolitres in 1992. Of the total production, over 20% (12.4 million hl) was exported, which reflects a 5.4% drop in quantity on the previous year, but a rise of 1.75% in terms of quality. The chart shows the volume of DOC (best-quality) wine and other wines exported to the top ten importers of Italian wine (excluding *spumante*). The average price per litre of DOC wine was 2,957 lire; other table wines fetched on average 992 lire.

ITALIAN WINE LAW

From 1963 to 1992 the demarcation and regulation of Italian wine names was embodied in one rigid concept, **DOC** (**Denominazione di Origine Controllata**) and its superior rank **DOCG** (the G is for **Garantita**). Some 250 wines and regions are thus denominated. The requirements are a body of producers who agree on the 'tradition' of their wine, its zone of production, grape varieties, methods, yields and characteristics. DOCs have brought some order out of chaos, but at the expense of progress; they fossilize the status quo rather than enhance or guarantee quality.

The result of this rigidity is that many producers, and by definition all innovators, decided that a DOC was a hindrance and worked outside the system. For them, however good their wine, the only legal category available was the lowest: *vino da tavola*. An absurd situation had arisen by the mid-80s where in certain regions, notably Tuscany, many of the best wines were *vini da tavola*, involving non-traditional varieties and methods.

Long overdue reform came in 1992 with the sudden passing of the 'Goria' Law (named after the Minister-in-a-hurry who pushed it through), probably the world's most progressive and complete concept for wine regulation and labelling. A concept it remains for the time being, though; parts of it will not become effective for several years.

Philosophically its main plank is that geographical origin should be the principal element in labelling. The most fundamental departure is to allow for flexibility and movement within the hierarchy by high- or low-performing wines or regions. At the bottom end this means that some 50 under-performing DOCs will cease to exist. At the top it means that specially fine wines will be granted DOC status after five years steady quality and DOCG status five years after that, subject to honouring their self-imposed standards. It will also give official recognition and status to top-quality sub-zones or even individual vineyards for the first time.

Law 164 is most graphically represented by a pyramid, whose base is the simple *vino da tavola*. No geographical or varietal claims can be made; only a brand name. Next is a new creation: **Indicazione Geografica Tipica** (**IGT**) which mirrors France's Vin de Pays. IGTs can use the geographical name and the varietal name – strictly in that order. The principle is that varietal identification must remain secondary to geographical. Above the IGT come the DOC and DOCG. In these bands the label can carry detail as specific as a single vineyard (*vigna*) name – but only by sacrificing quantity for quality. Overproduction by over 20% will demote a wine.

Thus the top rank will be a *vigna* wine from a DOCG. Once limited to a dozen areas, DOCG rank will become the right of any DOC which meets the five-year rule. More radically, an outstanding proprietorial wine 'which does honour to Italy' may be eligible for its own DOCG.

A distinct advantage of the pyramid system is that producers can decide at vintage time how high they are going to pitch their wine. Self-discipline can give them the right to the top appellation; high yields and low strength will automatically demote them.

Sound foundations have been laid: now comes the test for the administration.

tavola are the test-benches of all new ideas, imported grape varieties, techniques borrowed from around the world. By the 1980s the situation had become absurd. In 1992 a new law was passed, Law 164, to restructure the whole system of classification.

On the maps that follow the lead is given by the DOC system, because it is DOCs that have officially delimited zones. The principal *vini da tavola* are also marked. Over the course of the next decade the new system will come slowly into play – but it is not the map that will change, rather the relative standing of the wines on it.

The Italian section of this Atlas is again much extended in this edition in response to innovations and the dramatic raising of standards in many regions. The map on this page is intended as a reminder of the whereabouts of the regions (eg Tuscany or Campania) and as a key to the subsequent more detailed maps. All the current DOCs and DOCGs appear on the four pages that carve up the country into northwest, northeast, centre and south, except those in the complex centres of quality winegrowing which are given large-scale maps of their own. As many VDTs as have plottable locations and more than local reputations are also shown.

And the wine? Are all Italy's best wines still red? Most, but by no means all. Italy learned to make 'modern' white wine in the 1960s. In the 1980s she began to add back the character that was lost in the process. But national taste is still for ultra-dry whites with the fruit flavours stripped out. Italian white wine, you sometimes feel, would be water if it could. There is still only one region of truly fine white wines by international standards: the extreme northeast. Many other fine whites certainly exist, but they are exceptions.

Italy's red wines have meanwhile leapt ahead. They range from the silky and fragile to the purple and potent, in every style and aroma from redoubtable natives to the international Cabernet standard. Yet to be true to the spirit of Italy the qualities of all her wine must be seen in the context of the incredibly varied, sensuous Italian table. The true genius of Italy lies in spreading a feast. In the great Italian feast, wine plays the chief supporting role.

A north Italian grower returns to the primitive method of testing the ripeness of his grapes. A refractometer is more precise, but a mouthful can give a foretaste of the wine to come: its ripeness, acidity and aroma.

THE LANGUAGE OF THE LABEL

Tenuta Holding or estate
Vendemmia Vintage
Denominazione di Origine Controllata e Garantita Similar to Appellation Contrôlée (see *Wine Law*)
Riserva Wine aged for a statutory period (usually three years)
Classico From the central and best area of its region
Imbottigliato (or **Messo in bottiglia**) **ne l'origine** (or **del produttore all'origine**) Estate bottled
Imbottigliato nello stabilimento della ditta Bottled on the premises of the firm
Fiasco (pl. **flaschi**) Flask (eg Chianti)
Infiascato alla fattoria Bottled in *flaschi* at the winery
Vino da tavola Table wine (see *Wine Law*)
Bianco White
Rosso Red
Nero Very dark red
Chiaretto Very light red
Rosato Pink
Secco Dry
Amaro Bitter or very dry
Amabile or **Abboccato** Medium sweet
Dolce Very sweet
Spumante Sparkling
Frizzante Semi-sparkling
Gradi (or **Gradi alcool** or **Grado alcoolico**) followed by a number: percentage of alcohol by volume
Casa vinicola Wine firm
Cantina Cellar, winery or bar
Cantina sociale (or **cooperativa**) Winegrowers' cooperative
Consorzio Local growers' association with legal standing
Vin or **Vino Santo** Wine made from grapes dried indoors over winter
Passito Similar
Cotto Cooked (ie concentrated) wine, a speciality of a few regions
Recioto Wine made of half-dried grapes: strong and/or sweet
Stravecchio Very old, ripe, mellow
Vino liquoroso Fortified wine

Northwest Italy

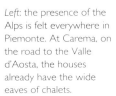

Left: the presence of the Alps is felt everywhere in Piemonte. At Carema, on the road to the Valle d'Aosta, the houses already have the wide eaves of chalets.

Above: Piemonte, Lombardy and Liguria on the coast offer the widest range of high-quality wines in Italy, from pungent Nebbiolos to crisp sparkling wines.

Northwest Italy means Piemonte to any wine-lover. In its bitter-sweet vermouths, its grapey *spumantes*, its pungent purple wines for dishes of game and cheese, it epitomizes the sensuality of the Italian table at its best. On the next three pages its heart is shown in detail.

But the Langhe and Monferrato hills around Alba and Asti are not the only great vineyards of the northwest. The noble grape that makes Barolo, the Nebbiolo, gives excellent, if different, results in several corners of the region – most notably between Novara and Vercelli (famous for rice), 50 miles (80 kilometres) north, where under the name of Spanna it rejoices in no fewer than six different DOCs – surely a case for rationalization.

The DOCG Gattinara (above all Monsecco) is considered the king of these, with Ghemme and Lessona as consorts and Bramaterra not far behind. All benefit from a sub-alpine climate, a southern exposure and fast-draining glacial soil. In practice all depends on the grower and the amount of the permitted Bonarda or Vespolina grapes added. The weight and intensity of Barolo is not quite there, but perfume is not lacking. With age Spanna can grow extremely gamey.

The very different Valtellina wines are mapped on page 177. North of Turin on the road up to the Valle d'Aosta and the Mont Blanc

tunnel to France there are two more Nebbiolos, of high reputation but low output, Carema and Donnaz. Carema is still in Piemonte (but nonetheless calls the Nebbiolo Picutener); Donnaz is over the provincial boundary in the Valle d'Aosta, Italy's smallest wine region. Alpine conditions make these Nebbiolos less potent and deep-coloured but scarcely less fine than Barolos. They are rarities that can fetch a high premium.

Aosta's other notable red rarity is the Enfer d'Arvier, made of a grape known as the Petit Rouge which tastes not unlike the Mondeuse of Savoie: dark, fresh, berryish and bracing; altogether an excellent alpine wine. The busy valley also has some recherché whites: the very light Blancs de la Salle and de Morgex, and some winter-weight Malvoisies.

Where Piemonte merges with Lombardy to the east conditions become less alpine and extreme. The Oltrepò Pavese is mapped on page 177. Just beyond it the valley of the Trebbia, as the river flows north to Piacenza to contribute to the Po, is a centre of determinedly traditional vines and wines that quietly express the history and individuality of their region. The taste for a light fizz in these Colli Piacentini whites and reds is so general that any without is called *morto*. A good wine is *vivace*.

And far across the Lombard plain, east of Milan and again within sight of snow-capped Alps, the country between Brescia and Bergamo has built itself the reputation for making Italy's best *méthode traditionelle* sparkling: Franciacorta (see pages 178–79).

South from Piemonte over the final curling tail of the Alps, known as the Ligurian Apennines, we are on the Mediterranean, with scarcely enough room between the mountains and the sea to grow grapes. Liguria's production is tiny, but highly individual and worth investigating. Of its grapes only Vermentino and Malvasia are widely grown elsewhere: the white Bosco, Pigato, Buzzetto and Albarola are as esoteric as they sound. Cinque Terre is the white-wine name you will hear, for the 'fish wine' of the steep coast near La Spezia. Its liquorous version is called Sciacchetrà. Other less-known coastal whites should be tasted on a visit to Genoa: you will not find them elsewhere.

Potentially the most memorable Ligurian wine, however, is the red Rossese, whether of Dolceacqua near the French border or of Albenga, nearer Genoa. Unlike anything made west along the coast in the Alpes Maritimes, Rossese can be truly fresh, fruity in the soft-fruit or berry sense of Bordeaux, inviting to smell and refreshing to drink. Nor does it need any ageing.

International boundary
Regione boundary
Cinque Terre   White wine
Ghemme   Red wine
COLLI TORTONESI   Red and white wine
CALUSO PASSITO   Dessert wine
Coronata   Selected Vino da Tavola

DOC boundaries are distinguished
by coloured lines

175   Area mapped at larger scale
on page shown

Land above 600 metres

1:1,485,000

Km. 0   20   40   60   80 Km.
Miles 0   10   20   30   40   50 Miles

SVIZZERA

N

SVIZZERA

Chiavenna

177

Sondrio   Valtellina   *Tirano*

Livigno

Lago di Como

Lecco   *Glusone*

LOMBARDIA   Marzemino

VALCALEPIO   *Lovere*
MOSCATO DI SCANZO   *Lago d'Iseo*

Domodossola

Verbania

Lago Maggiore

Como

Bergamo

Monza

Franciacorta   *Cabernet*

Cellatica

Brescia

Capriano del Colle

Alagna Valsesia

Varallo

Boca   *Arona*

Rosso de Bellagio
Ghemme
Sizzano

Busto Arsizio

Milano

Crema

Cremona

Courmayeur

VALLE D'AOSTA
Aosta   St Vincent

VALLE D'AOSTA

Donnas

Carema
Canavese
Ivrea

Biella
Lessona
Gattinara
Fara

Novara

Vercelli

Abbiategrasso

Vigévano

Pavia

Mortara

San Colombano al Lambro

Lodi

Codogno

Piacenza

COLLI PIACENTINI

Cuorgné

Erbaluce di Caluso

CALUSO PASSITO

FRANCE

PIEMONTE

Chivasso

Vermut di Torino

Chieri

Grignolino del Monferrato Casalese

Casale Monferrato

175

Torino

Susa

Sestriere

Pinerolo

Freisa di Chieri

Freisa d'Asti

Chardonnay

Asti

Barbera del Monferrato

177

Alessandria

Voghera

Casteggio
Oltrepò Pavese
Clastidio

Tortona

COLLI TORTONESI

Cremona

Racconigi

Roero

Cortese dell'Alto Monferrato

Chardonnay

Novi Ligure

Cortese di Gavi

EMILIA-ROMAGNA

Fidenza

Parma

COLLI DI PARMA

Saluzzo

Bra   Alba
PELAVERGA
Dolcetto d'Alba

176

Acqui Terme
Dolcetto d'Acqui

Chiappera

Dolcetto di Dogliani

Dolcetto di Ovada

Argentera

Dolcetto delle Langhe Monregalesi

Cuneo   *Mondovì*

LIGURIA

Coronata
Polcevera

Genova

Rapallo

Rossese di Albenga

Pontremoli

COLLI DI PARMA

Savona

Barbera di Linero

TOSCANA

RIVIERA LIGURE DI PONENTE

Cinque Terre

La Spezia

Candia dei Colli Apuani

Albenga

COLLI DI LUNI   Massa

Rossese di Dolceacqua

Imperia

San Remo

Roma

173

Piemonte

Piemontese food and wine are as inseparable as those of Burgundy. They are strong, rich, individual, mature, somehow autumnal. Truffles play an important part. One feels it must be more than coincidence that this is the Italian province nearest to France.

Piemonte means at the foot of the mountains – the Alps. The Alps almost encircle the region, so that from its heart, the Monferrato hills around Alba, they form a continuous dark – or in winter sparkling white – horizon. Piemonte has a climate of its own, with a very hot growing season followed by a misty autumn and a cold, often foggy, winter.

At vintage time in Barolo the hills are half hidden. Ramps of copper and gold vines, dotted with hazel and peach trees, lead down to the valley of the Tanaro, lost in the fog. It is a magical experience to visit Serralunga or La Morra and see the dark grapes coming in.

The two best red wines of Piemonte, Barolo and Barbaresco, take their names from villages. They are mapped in detail on the next page. The rest have the names of their grapes – Barbera, Dolcetto, Grignolino, Freisa. If to the grape they add a district name (eg Barbera d'Asti) it means they come from a limited and theoretically superior area. The map shows the zones of central Piemonte – including that of the famous Moscato d'Asti *spumante*, the quintessence of sweet Muscat grapes in its most celebratory form. Asti *spumante* is often scorned by wine-snobs for the very cheerful simplicity that is its *raison d'être*. It also has the considerable merit of containing less alcohol than any other accepted – indeed celebrated – wine.

The still, dry white Cortese di Gavi is grown south of Alessandria to the east. In recent years new techniques and high-powered marketing have been used to make Gavi one of Italy's most prestigious white wines; almost, one might say, the nation's Chablis. The demand for whites has also led to the promotion of an old local grape, the Arneis, from a mere Nebbiolo-stretcher to make soft, light but plump wines not unlike Pinot Blanc – especially in the Roeri hills just north of Alba. More market-minded growers have successfully added Chardonnay (as *vino da tavola*) to their portfolios.

The Nebbiolo has no rival as the finest red grape of northern Italy. It does not have to come from Barolo or Barbaresco to make mellow fragrant wine. At the level just below noble, Barbera is the most important regional grape, certainly the one for less ideal sites and soils.

Barbera is dark, tannic, often rather plummy and acidic – ideal wine with rich food. Modern winemakers are not hesitating to test its potential for oak-ageing, but a more modest role (and price) usually becomes it better. Its one possible rival is Dolcetto: soft, where Barbera often bites, but capable of a marvellous balance between fleshy, dusty-dense and dry with a touch of bitter. The best Dolcetto comes from Alba, Diano d'Alba, Dogliani and Ovada (for its most potent style). Grignolino is consistently a lightweight but can be a fine and piquant one; at its best (often from Asti) extremely clean, stimulating and happy. All these are wines to drink relatively young.

Other specialities of this prolific region, the spaghetti-junction of *denominaziones*, include another frothy sweet red wine, Brachetto d'Acqui, sweet pink or red Malvasia di Casorzo d'Asti, the interesting yellow *passito* (made from semi-sweet grapes) with the DOC Erbaluce di Caluso and the agreeable blend of Barbera and Grignolino sold as Rubino di Cantavenna. One of the favourites of Turin itself is Freisa, often from Asti, a fizzy and frequently sweet red wine not unlike a more tart and less fruity form of Lambrusco.

Traditions mean even more in this proud and wine-conscious region than in most of Italy. But winemakers are becoming as inventive here as anywhere – and as ready to plant Chardonnay or Cabernet. One even makes a delicious blend of Nebbiolo and Barbera. Nothing is sacred.

A clear winter day in foggy Barolo shows the meaning of Piemonte – the foot of the Alps. Snowy peaks rise on three sides, with Monte Viso to the west. The foreground is a characteristic *bricco*: an ideal vineyard ridge.

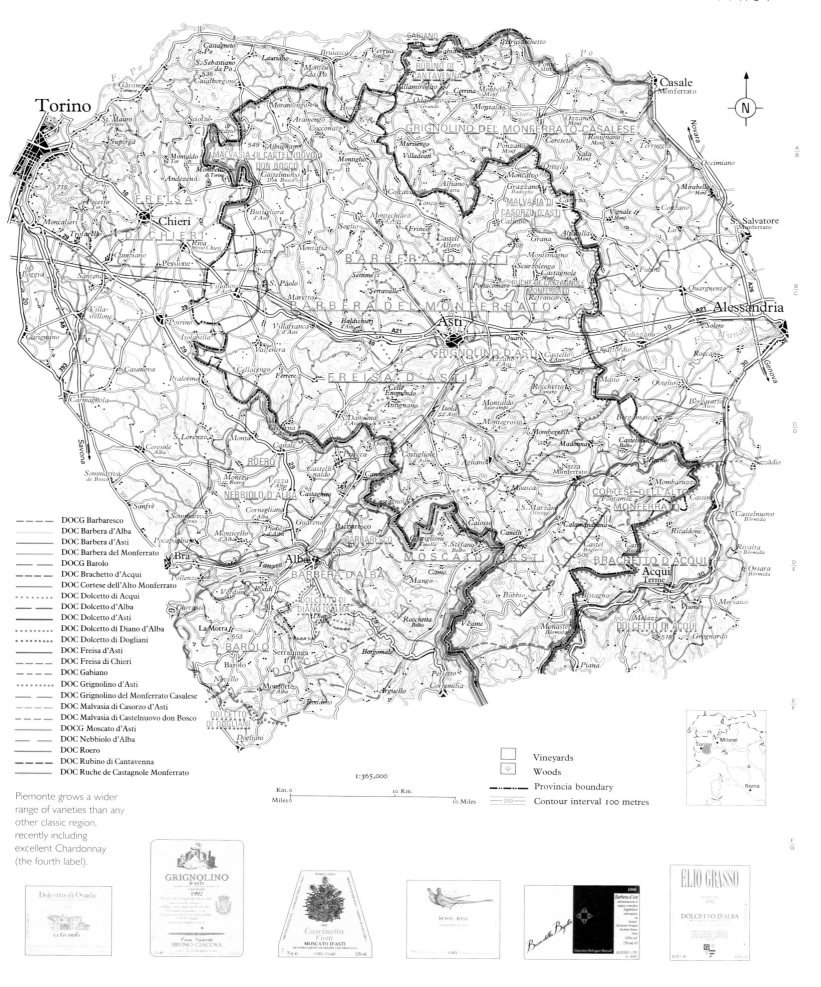

Torino

Chieri

Casale
Monferrato

S. Salvatore
Monferrato

Alessandria

Asti

Acqui
Terme

Bra

Alba

Map legend:

- – – – DOCG Barbaresco
- ——— DOC Barbera d'Alba
- ——— DOC Barbera d'Asti
- ——— DOC Barbera del Monferrato
- ——— DOCG Barolo
- ——— DOC Brachetto d'Acqui
- ——— DOC Cortese dell'Alto Monferrato
- ·········· DOC Dolcetto di Acqui
- ——— DOC Dolcetto d'Alba
- ——— DOC Dolcetto d'Asti
- ——— DOC Dolcetto di Diano d'Alba
- ·········· DOC Dolcetto di Dogliani
- ——— DOC Freisa d'Asti
- – – – DOC Freisa di Chieri
- ——— DOC Gabiano
- ·········· DOC Grignolino d'Asti
- – – – DOC Grignolino del Monferrato Casalese
- ——— DOC Malvasia di Casorzo d'Asti
- ——— DOC Malvasia di Castelnuovo don Bosco
- ——— DOCG Moscato d'Asti
- – · – DOC Nebbiolo d'Alba
- ——— DOC Roero
- – · – · DOC Rubino di Cantavenna
- ·········· DOC Ruche de Castagnole Monferrato

Piemonte grows a wider
range of varieties than any
other classic region,
recently including
excellent Chardonnay
(the fourth label).

☐ Vineyards

🌳 Woods

– · – · Provincia boundary

—200— Contour interval 100 metres

1:365,000

Km. 0 ———— 10 Km.
Miles 0 ———— 10 Miles

Barbaresco and Barolo

The Nebbiolo finds its most tremendous expression in the Langhe Hills, above the River Tanaro and its little tributaries, just north and west of Alba in the zones of Barbaresco and Barolo. All its finest wines are made on high sites with a southern tilt, on ridges that emerge from the October fogs (the Nebbiolo ripens very late). The soils are chalky clays, here with more iron, there with more magnesium or phosphorus: trace elements to which growers ascribe the some-times remarkably distinct styles of their wines.

Today the grower and his site (the terms *sorì* and *bricco* recur continually for distinguished ridges) hold the key to Barolo and Barbaresco. Tastings reveal consistent differences of quality, of aroma, of potency and of finesse that in the Côte d'Or would justify the term *cru*. And yet the emergence of these great wines from the limbo of legend into the critical limelight was only accomplished between 1980 and 1990.

It is the second time in 150 years that the region has been revolutionized. Up to the 1850s its Nebbiolos were vinified as sweet wines, their fermentation never satisfactorily concluded. A French oenologist, Louis Oudart, recruited by a reforming landowner in Barolo, demonstrated how the fermentation should be finished to make potent dry reds. His 19th-century techniques of late picking, long extraction and endless ageing in huge chestnut casks remained almost unaltered until the 1980s, when a newly critical public, putting 'fruit' firmly on the agenda, was respectful but unconvinced by wines that were vastly tannic, of overpowering strength, but often simply dried out by too long waiting for a maturity that never came.

Modern vinification had no problem finding the solutions: choosing the right (usually earlier) moment to pick, fermentation in steel at con-trolled temperatures, maceration for days rather than weeks or even months – and, more contro-versially, ageing in small new or newish barrels.

The results are still tannic wines that need to age, but in which the tannin is a crisp, mouth-cleaning frame for a stunning assembly of suggestive flavours. Great Barolos and Barbarescos can overlay smoky woodland notes on deep sweetness, the flavour of raspberries on leather and spice, leafy lightness on jam-like concen-tration. Older wines advance to animal or tarry flavours, sometimes suggesting wax or incense, sometimes mushrooms or truffles. What unites them is the racy cut of their tannins, freshening rather than overwhelming the palate.

A tour of the vineyards and their most accomplished interpreters might start from Barbaresco, whose profile has been raised sky-high by Angelo Gaja. Gaja has no inhibi-tions: his wines, whether classic Barbaresco, experimental Chardonnay or Sauvignon Blanc, or Barbera treated like first-growth claret, state their case, and cost a fortune.

Barbaresco is a big village on a ridge that wobbles west towards Alba, flanked all the way by vineyards of renown. Bricco Asili, Martinenga and Sorì Tildin are by-words for finest reds. A little lower to the east lies Néive, in whose castle M Oudart experimented with Nebbiolo. South on higher slopes lies the commune of Tréiso, also known for its high quality Dolcetto.

The Barolo zone starts two miles southwest, with the Dolcetto vineyards of Diano d'Alba lying between. Two little tributaries of the Tanaro split Barolo into three main though highly convoluted hill ranges that rise nearly 165 feet (50 metres) higher than Barbaresco. To the east lies the zone of Serralunga d'Alba with its enormous former royal estate of Fontanafredda. Gaja has recently bought vines at Serralunga to add Barolo to his portfolio.

Serralunga, with Monforte d'Alba to the south and Castiglione Falletto in the heart of the district, lies in the iron-rich zone where Barolos are beefiest. Bussia in Monforte, Ceretto's Bricco Rocche and Mascarello's Monprivato in Castiglione are prime examples.

The western hills of the zone in the communes of Barolo and La Morra tend to offer slightly less tense, more openly fragrant wines. The great vineyards here include Brunate, Rocche di la Morra and Monfalletto in La Morra and Barolo's most famous site, Cannubi, on slightly lower ground.

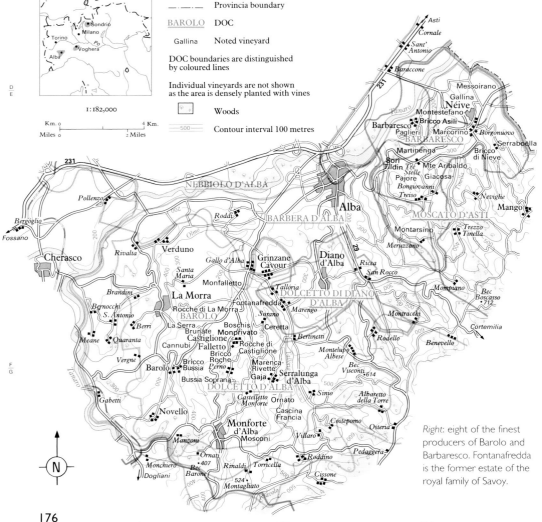

Right: eight of the finest producers of Barolo and Barbaresco. Fontanafredda is the former estate of the royal family of Savoy.

Lombardy: Valtellina and Oltrepò Pavese

Valtellina

Lombardy, land of contrasts. In this case between the plain of the River Po and the deep trench cut by Lombardy's northernmost river, the Adda, as it makes its way out of the Alps to join Lake Como.

The 30 miles (50 kilometres) where the Adda flows under the very walls of Switzerland give its north bank a long narrow southern slope, tilting its vines at the sun. Where the vines are the Nebbiolo of Piemonte, growing under the *nom de terre* of Chiavennasca, their wine has the DOC Valtellina Superiore. Four sub-zones have specific names: Sassella (considered the best of the group), Valgella, Grumello and Inferno. What they have in common is the early bite, the developing texture, the emerging autumnal fragrances of the Nebbiolo, here leaner and less sensuous than that found in Piemonte, but at best scarcely less fine.

Superiore is an essential qualification. The less-favoured sites produce plain Valtellina, which is welcome enough in Switzerland (St-Moritz is just over the hill), but contains little Nebbiolo. Half-dried grapes are used to make an alpine form of Recioto, known as Sfursat or Sforzato, with the concentration to age for many years.

Unlike Valtellina, which essentially produces just one red wine, the DOC Oltrepò Pavese covers no fewer than 14 kinds.

It is hard to offer a translation as musical as the name of this fulcrum of Lombardic viticulture (mapped below). Oltrepò Pavese means the part of the province of Pavia that lies beyond the River Po.

Far harder, though, is to convey in any orderly way the profusion of its wines, some with a DOC, some not, and much even sold without a geographical origin at all. Many of Italy's best Pinots Nero and Bianco for the making of sparkling wines come from here without mentioning the fact.

The best way to picture the region and its wines is as the dying ripples of the turbulence of hill and mountain in the northeast before the level ground of the Lombard plain. The DOC Oltrepò Pavese Rosso calls for two-thirds Barbera mollified with a variety of local grapes, of which Bonarda is the most prevalent. Bonarda balances sharply fruity Barbera with milder flavours and a touch of the bitterness

in the finish that Italians love. The Barbera unblended, though, is usually the better wine.

The best-known wine (and one of the best) to use the DOC is Frecciarossa, 'red arrow', from Castéggio. Buttafuoco and Sangue di Giuda are reds with bubbles more memorable for their names than for their flavours. Oltrepò white wines include 'Pinot', which can be either Bianco or Nero (made white) or Grigio or all of these. Pinot Grigio is most common without bubbles: a dense and potentially delicious wine that suggests its relationship to a German Ruländer.

Italian (in other words Welsch) Riesling is also a success in the Oltrepò Pavese; Moscatos are excellent and even Müller-Thurgau makes respectable wines.

In such conditions one can reasonably expect almost any grape to thrive. All that is lacking in this productive but scarcely celebrated area is a name to conjure with.

Oltrepò Pavese

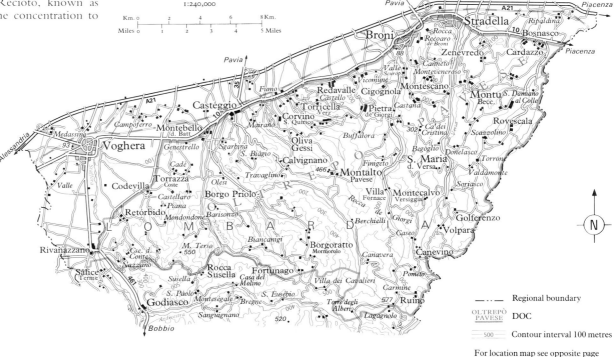

Northeast Italy

N orthest Italy owes less to tradition and more to modern ideas than the rest of the country. Whether it is the realism of the Venetians, the pressure of Austrian influence, the moderate climate, or all of these, more (bottled) wine is exported from the northeast than from anywhere else, more different grapes are grown and experimented with, and a more prosperous and professional air pervades the vineyards than in any but the most celebrated zones elsewhere.

Verona and its wines: Valpolicella, Soave, Bardolino and the southern Lake Garda wines, the Alto Adige with its Lago di Caldaro and Santa Maddalena are mapped and discussed in detail on pages 182–83. The other biggest concentrations of winegrowing are due north of Venice around Conegliano, on the Slovenian border in Friuli (mapped on pages 180–81) and in the Trentino, north of Lake Garda. The last red wines of Lombardy, the Valtellinas, are mapped on page 177.

Of the other Lombardy wines on this map, the Garda-side wines are very close in character to those of the Veronese Garda. There is little to choose between Chiaretto from the Riviera del Garda (of which the best part is south of Salo, particularly around Moniga del Garda) and Bardolino. Both are reds so light as to be rosé, or rosés so dark as to be red, with a gentle flavour, soft-textured and faintly sweet, made all the more appetizing by a hint of bitterness, like almonds, in the taste which is common to all the best reds in this part of Italy. They should be drunk very young.

Red Botticino (a Barbera blend) and Cellatica (a lighter one) are the very passable red wines of

The Roman arena at Verona, built in pink marble and holding some 25,000 spectators, is the largest in the world beside the Colosseum in Rome. 'Rhaeticus' was the Roman name for the famous wines from the surrounding hills praised by Virgil.

Brescia. The region's fame and fortune, though, come from Franciacorta; Italy's great sparkling success story, developed in the 1970s on the Berlucchi family estate in direct imitation of champagne, and since taken up by farm after farm in the region south of Lake Iseo. Chardonnay and Pinots Bianco and Nero are perfectly suited by a climate without extremes. The finest wines, both sparkling and still (and including *vini da tavola* modelled on both Bordeaux and burgundy) are from the Zanella family estate of Ca'del Bosco.

White Lugana, from the south end of Lake Garda, is a particularly appealing relation of Soave, offering a hint of lusciousness in a perfectly dry wine.

Only one name from the flat Po Valley is famous – the sparkling red Lambrusco from around Modena, above all from Sorbara. There is something decidedly appetizing about this vivid, grapey wine with its bizarre red foaming head. It cuts the richness of Bolognese food admirably. How its faint but unmistakable resemblance to Coca Cola founded a great American fortune (in one year Riunite, the cooperative of Réggio nell' Emília, shipped 11 million cases to the States) is one of the great success stories in the history of wine.

The character of the wine changes in the Veneto and eastwards. Already, on green volcanic

islands in the plain, the Colli Berici and Euganei near Vicenza and Pádova, the red grapes are the Cabernet and Merlot of Bordeaux, above all the Merlot, which plays an increasingly dominant role all the way from the valley of the Adige north of Lake Garda to Slovenia, and again in Italian Switzerland.

At their best both grapes succeed admirably here; some of the Merlots and Cabernets can seriously be compared with Bordeaux, having considerable character and staying power. Pinot Nero (Pinot Noir) also shows promise.

The white grapes are a mixture of the traditional – the Garganega of Soave, the Prosecco, the light, sharp Verdiso and the more solid Tocai (Pinot Gris) and Sylvaner, Riesling, Sauvignon Blanc and Pinot Bianco.

The DOCs of the region are a series of defined areas that give their names to whole groups of red and white wines. Those known simply as (for example) Colli Euganei Rosso are standard wines made of an approved mixture of grapes. The better wines use the varietal name with the DOC name – although there are also DOCs, like Gambellara between Soave and the Colli Berici, that are limited to a traditional grape, in this case the Garganega.

Breganze, north of Vicenza, is a case of a DOC brought to prominence (like Franciacorta) by one fanatical winemaker. Fausto Maculan outstripped the traditional whites of Tocai and Vespaiolo (although he makes them) by proving that this is a good Cabernet region – and by resurrecting the old Venetian taste for sweet wines from dried grapes with his white Torcolato. The productive north of the Veneto and its eastern neighbour, Friuli-Venezia Giulia, where most of the serious wines are white, is mapped on the next pages.

The country south of Bologna and Ravenna produces the rich white wine of which Italy is apparently proudest (judging by the fact that it was the first to be recommended for the rank of 'DOCG'): the Albana di Romagna.

Albana, in fact, like so many Italian wines, can be all things to all men. If it was the *amabile* style that was originally famous, today it is more often made dry (and often very dull, too). You can also buy it in a *spumante* version. To understand its reputation you must taste the work of the Fattoria Paradiso or one of this producer's few rivals: lovely, concentrated, faintly honeyed wine.

More reliable than Albana by far, if without claims to greatness, is Romagna's Sangiovese red: a big country boy whose company can easily grow on you.

Right: bubbles are an important element in many wines of the northeast, from Lambrusco in Emília to dry featherweight Prosecco in the Veneto and the splendid sparkling Ca' del Bosco.

SVIZZERA

ÖSTERREICH

N

TRENTINO-ALTO ADIGE

Meranese di Collina
Merano
Valle Isarco
Bressanone
Brunico

Livigno
Bórmio
Bolzano
Tiroler Leiten
Colli di Bolzano
Arabba
Cortina d'Ampezzo

Tolmezzo

FRIULI VENEZIA GIULIA

A23
Tarvisio

Valtellina
Tirano
Cles
ADIGE

San Martino di Castrozza

San Daniele del Friuli

COLLI ORIENTALI DEL FRIULI

Ramandolo

SLOVENJA

Edolo
Teroldego Rotaliano

VALDADIGE

Belluno
181
Udine
GRAVE DEL FRIULI
Schioppettino
Collio Goriziano

Clusone
Marzemino
VIN SANTO TRENTINO
Trento
Feltre
Vittório Veneto
Pordenone
56
Tunina
Gorízia
ISONZO

Lovere
Lago d'Iseo
Riva del Garda
Caseller
Marzemino
Rovereto
Prosecco di Conegliano Valdobbiadene
Conegliano
AQUILEIA
Monfalcone
CARSO

Franciacorta
Cabernet
BREGANZE
MONTELLO E COLLI ASOLANI
Bassano del Grappa
VINI DEL PIAVE
Portogruaro
LATISANA
Grado

Cellatica
Riviera del Garda Bresciano
184
Schio
Lison-Pramaggiore
Trieste

Botticino
Lessini Durello
182
Valpolicella Classico
Soave
Valpantena
Treviso
Verdiso

Bréscia
Bardolino Classico
Valpolicella Classico
Vicenza
Mestre

Capriano del Colle
Lugana
Verona
Gambellara
COLLI BERICI
COSTOZZA
Padova
Venézia

San Martino della Battaglia
Bardolino
Soave Classico
Bianco di Custoza

Mantova
COLLI MORENICI MANTOVANI DEL GARDA
COLLI EUGANEI
Moscato
Chióggia

Cremona
Legnago
VENETO
Friularo
Porto Tolle

Lambrusco Mantovano
Rovigo

Fidenza
Guastalla
Mirandola
Lambrusco Salamino di Santa Croce

Parma
Lambrusco Reggiano
Lancellotta
Sorbara
Lambrusco di Sorbara
Ferrara

Fogarina
Réggio nell' Emilia
Cento
Comácchio

COLLI DI PARMA
Modena
Montuni Del Reno
Ravenna

Lambrusco Grasparossa di Castelvetro
Bologna

Bianco di Scandiana
COLLI BOLOGNESI
Ímola
Albana di Romagna
Trebbiano di Romagna

EMILIA-ROMAGNA
Marano
Sangiovese di Romagna
Forlì
Cagnina di Romagna
Barbarossa
Pagadebit di Romagna
Cesena

TOSCANA
Candia dei Colli Apuani

Legend

— · — · International boundary

— · — Regione boundary

Lugana — White wine

Caseller — Red wine

COLLI BOLOGNESI — Red and white wine

VIN SANTO — Dessert wine

COSTOZZA — Selected Vino da Tavola

DOC boundaries are distinguished by coloured lines

181 — Area mapped at larger scale on page shown

— Land above 600 metres

1:1,485,000

Km. 0   20   40   60   80 Km.
Miles 0   10   20   30   40   50 Miles

179

Veneto and Friuli-Venezia Giulia

Italy's northeast corner is the country's one region where white wines regularly rise to high international standards and dominate production. They are not cheap. There is a strong demand from both Italy and its neighbours for these aromatic, naturally balanced and limpid wines.

Not that Friuli and Venezia Giulia were viticultural virgins, but the potential excellence of their wines has only become apparent since winemakers started using modern methods. In their planting, too, they are steadily adding the international favourites to the varieties traditionally grown. In their present state they offer a choice of wines as bewildering as any in the great Italian lexicon.

The map embraces most of the easternmost region of the north, Friuli-Venezia Giulia, and a small part of its neighbour the Veneto. The Veneto has two great wine centres, Verona (page 182) and Conegliano, 40 miles (65 kilometres) north of Venice. Northern Veneto runs into the Dolomites, and the region of Conegliano-Valdobbiádene already has a faintly alpine feeling. Its local speciality, the white Prosecco grape, is rather charmless as a still wine, but very good base material for (extremely dry) *spumante*.

Prosecco is thus the local fizz of Venice, and its *superiore* form, Cartizze from Valdobbiádene, one of Italy's best in the brisk, light-bodied manner. Nobody could accuse it of aping champagne, but it goes down well in the famous Bellinis in Harry's Bar.

Conegliano has another reason for fame in the wine world, as Italy's principal viticultural research station. Every sort of grape is tried out, and the local restaurants in the pretty old town can serve you anything from a local Merlot to a Gewürztraminer. On the evidence, Prosecco or the small-scale white Verdiso are what the area does best.

Still within the Veneto, the wide plain of the Piave, heavily planted with vines, is a useful source of both fresh dry white Verduzzo (an important grape of the northeast), of a minor Tocai (much more important in Friuli) and of Cabernet and Merlot of fair to substantial quality. Eastwards from Venice the great Bordeaux grapes make the running for red wine. Mass-produced they can taste very green; on such estates as Venegazzù and the Castello di Roncade, in the province of Treviso, they have been married into truly claret-like blends.

Cabernet (usually Cabernet Franc) pure or Merlot pure are the staples of the Piave DOC and five more to the east, made up of Pramaggiore, Latisana, Aquileia and Isonzo, and above all Grave del Friuli.

On the whole the Cabernet is heartiest to the west of the region, especially in Pramaggiore (where the Merlot can be a little dry and heartless for the grape that makes Pomerol). Going east, Cabernet remains the better of the two but the Merlot, although still light, gains definition and character. In the DOC Grave del Friuli and in Isonzo, Merlot is dominant. Neither grape

In the Colli Orientali del Friuli red wines of Cabernet, Refosco, Merlot, Schioppetino have equal billing with whites. The climate is relatively warm and dry between Udine and the Slovenian border, sheltered by the Alps to the east and north.

is as good in the coastal areas with their flat vineyards as in its more limited hillside plantations in the Colli Orientali del Friuli.

In the Piave an indigenous red grape, the Raboso, helps to define Venetian taste in red wine, which (as in white) is definitely for the austere and dry. The Raboso is sometimes blended with Merlot, also grown in the Piave.

The united DOCs of Lison and Pramaggiore, the latter for reds (Cabernet, Merlot, Refosco), the former for Tocai and other whites, make the transition from Veneto to Friuli-Venezia Giulia. Tocai di Lison (which has a Classico heartland

around the town of Lison) begins to promise the silky satisfaction this grape will give further east, in the Gorizian hills on the Slovenian border.

Grave del Friuli is much the biggest DOC of Friuli-Venezia Giulia, covering all the (literally) gravelly lowlands in the region's centre. Half its harvest is Merlot, with some Cabernet and also the often underrated Refosco, the lively red known as Mondeuse in the French Alps. Grave whites are chiefly the lean dry Verduzzo and the much more substantial Tocai, but a good quantity of Pinot Bianco (here often confused with Chardonnay) is also grown. Supplies of all these are plentiful, quality at least satisfactory and value assured. Certain producers' names stand out in the big and by no means homogeneous area: Duca Badoglio, Collavini and Plozner are among them – all in the province of Udine, towards the Colli Orientali del Friuli.

International boundary

Regione boundary

Provincia boundary

ISONZO   DOC

DOC boundaries are distinguished
by coloured lines

1:675,000

Km. 0   5   10   15   20 Km.

Miles 0   5   10 Miles

Wine quality mounts
steadily as you go east
from Venice. Piave makes
very acceptable reds
and whites; Collio (see
detailed map on page
183) very exciting ones.

Verona

The lovingly gardened hills of Verona, stretching from Soave, east of the city, westwards to Lake Garda, have such fertile volcanic soil that vegetation grows uncontrollably; the vine runs riot on every terrace and pergola, among villas and cypresses that are the image of Italian grace.

Their Soave is Italy's most famous white wine. The region is largely dominated by its *cantina sociale*, one of the biggest in Europe with 630 growers, and the firm of Bolla, which musters some 400. Considering the large-scale standardization involved, their wine is extremely good. It is relevant to wonder what the result would be if, say, all the wines of Pouilly-Fuissé were to be made together in one cellar.

Soave is a plain dry white wine made of the local Garganega and usually a good deal of Trebbiano. It is hard to characterize it in any more exciting way. And yet it has something – it may be a particularly soft texture – that singles it out and makes it always enjoyable. Its plainness also makes it very versatile.

The Soave region is centred on the eastern end of the Lessini Hills. This is the Classico zone, where such growers as Pieropan, Anselmi and Bertani concentrate on Garganega and a local (rather than the Tuscan or pan-Italian) form of Trebbiano to make wines – even single-vineyard wines – of an intensity and mouth-filling texture that bring the meaning of Soave (suave) into focus. Wines from the plain to the south (off the map) may be legally Soave, but cannot be expected to match this definition.

Above: the countryside of Valpolicella can be almost painfully pretty. Haymakers work under the vine pergolas in a scene that Virgil might have described. *Right*: estate wines of extraordinary quality have emerged recently in Valpolicella – even Soave. The labels on the right are from Collio where Mario Schiopetto is the pace-setter.

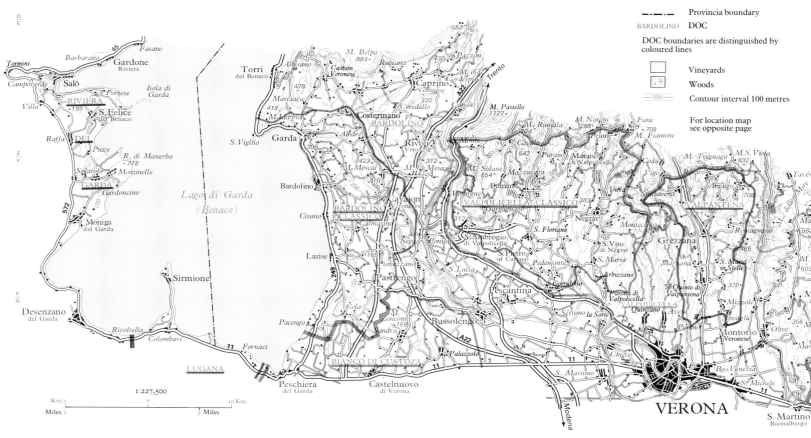

Collio

Soave cohabits with Valpolicella as a perfect couple. Plain Valpolicella should have a beautiful cherry colour, a gentle sweet smell, a soft light flavour and a trace of bitterness as you swallow. The mass-produced article is much despised, but there are many worse restaurant carafe wines.

Valpolicella Classico, from a clearly-defined massif of vineyards between San Ambrogio, Fumane and Negrar, has the same qualities in an intensified form. It still makes no great demands on the drinker, but satisfies at a deeper level with cherry- and almond-like flavours in a texture as suave as can be. The leading estates are extremely ambitious for Valpolicella Classico, seeing it, with justice, as one of Italy's most promotable products in every sense.

Its grandest form at present is as Recioto or Amarone, respectively the sweet (sometimes fizzy) and dry (also bitter) results of late-picking and loft-drying selected grapes – above all Corvina, the best of the region – to make highly concentrated and potent wines, the climax of every Veronese feast. Such wines are the direct descendants of the Greek wines shipped by the Venetians in the Middle Ages, adapted to the Venetian hinterland. Unfortunately today they are more admired than consumed – at least outside the region.

One answer lies in the old practice of *ripasso*, in which Valpolicella from the main crop is re-fermented on the pressed skins, preferably of Corvina, after an Amarone has finished fermentation. The first *ripasso* of modern times, Masi's Campofiorin, induced new respect for Valpolicella in the 1980s. Such estates as Allegrini, Guerrieri-Rizzardi, Quintarelli and Tedeschi, and such merchants as Bertani, are building up a constituency for Valpolicella Classico and its variants as one of Italy's surest things in wine.

Bardolino, from the lakeside of Garda, is surprisingly a paler, more insubstantial wine – almost a rosé (or *chiaretto*) – drinkable as soon as fermented. Chiaretto del Garda, from the further shore, is similar.

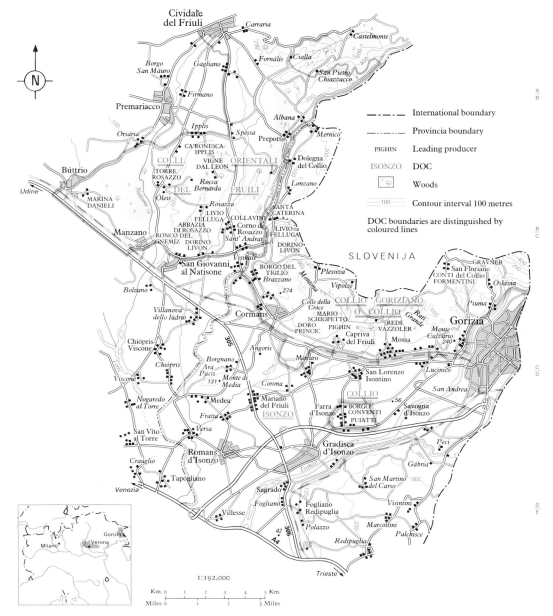

The Collio Goriziano and the Colli Orientali del Friuli in the far northeast form the natural boundary between Italy and Slovenia. Gorizia's hills have a mellow microclimate modified by the sea. Together they form the oldest-established and best vineyard of the region, often known simply as 'Collio'. A wine called straight Collio is a dry white of Tocai, Ribolla, Pinot and other grapes – which grow in confusing variety.

Whites include Italian Riesling, Sauvignon, Chardonnay, Traminer, Malvasia, Pinots Bianco and Grigio and the Tocai Friulano (whose distinguishing mark is said to be a smell of acacia blossom). Red varieties are Cabernet, Merlot and Pinot Nero.

Collio really rests its high reputation on the concentration and cleanness of its Tocai, supported by Pinot Bianco (sometimes Chardonnay) and Pinot Grigio. They combine high extract, and a texture that caresses the tongue, with vivid and lively flavour and fragrance. If they are not Europe's showiest wines, they still manage to convey a vitality, a feeling of class and a sense of satisfaction almost unique in Italian whites.

The hills inland do the same, if not in quite the same degree. The Colli Orientali del Friuli feel less of the Adriatic, more of the Alps: a marginally more extreme climate. All the Collio grapes are grown, with the addition of Rhine Riesling, Refosco and Cabernet Sauvignon (as opposed to Franc). The Refosco is a character no visitor to these beautiful hills should miss. Whether that or the smooth and vibrant Tocai goes better with Italy's best prosciutto (that of San Daniele, near Udine) is a good debate.

A great deal of local pride is tied up in Picolit, a strong white dessert wine which could be described as the Italian Jurançon: a wine more hay-like and flowery while less pungently honeyed than Sauternes.

Trentino

The valley of the Adige forms the dramatic corridor into the Alps that links Italy with Austria over the Brenner Pass. It is a rock-walled trench, widening in places to give views of distant peaks, but like the Rhône Valley an inevitably thronging north–south link with all the excesses of traffic and industry that go with it.

Its vineyards form a lovely contrast to the traffic at its heart. They pile up every available slope from river to rock-walls in a pattern of pergolas that from above gives the appearance of deeply leafy steps.

The catch-all DOC for the whole valley is Valdadige (in German, Etschtaler). But each part of the valley has its own specialities, indeed its own indigenous grapes. Growing conditions are fine for almost any white grape, and the usual candidates have been widely planted. Picked early they have every quality needed for good sparkling wine, the speciality of Trento.

But the native red grapes are too well-loved (as well as being too productive) to be deposed by a tide of imported varieties.

On the way north to Trento the snaking gorge is known as the Vallagarina, the home of Marzemino, a dark-hued light red whose fame comes almost entirely from the last act of *Don Giovanni*. The northern end of Trentino is the unique home of the full-blooded red Teroldego, from the grape of the same name grown on the cliff-hemmed, pergola-carpeted, gravelly valley floor known as the Campo Rotaliano, between Mezzolombardo and Mezzocorona. Teroldego Rotaliano is one of Italy's great characters, a dense purple wine of high extract and good ageing qualities, smooth and even soft in the mouth but marked, at least when young, with the penetrating bitterness that is the signal of the region. Wherever this (locally much appreciated) bitterness derives from, those who find it over-whelming can often eliminate it by decanting the wine early. After 24 hours in a decanter a four-year-old Teroldego has plenty of life and fruit, without so much of the Campari note.

The Schiava or Vernatsch, from the Tyrol, is another red grape with some of the same bitterness, made here in the Trentino into two DOCs, the light Casteller and the more sub-stantial Sorni (which also contains Teroldego and the Lagrein of Bolzano). The best Schiava, however, is a *vino da tavola rosato* sold under the name of Faedo.

The Cembra Valley and the eastern Adige slopes round San Michele are particularly successful for white grapes that are put to good use by the Istituto Agrario Provinciale (which also makes good Cabernet) and the firm of Pojer & Sandri, based at Faedo, the leaders of the sector. Pojer & Sandri scorn DOCs for their labels, but stay within the local idiom (which includes very good Müller-Thurgau).

The corresponding western arm of the valley near Trento, linking it with three small lakes, grows the same wide range of grapes (all these zones grow good base wine for *spumante*) but specializes in Vin Santo of high quality from yet another indigenous variety, the Nosiola.

DOC

Valdadige (Etschtaler)

Trentino

Sorni

Alto Adige (Südtiroler)

Teroldego Rotaliano

Caldaro (Kalterer)

Casteller

Provincia boundary

ZENI   Important cellar

Vineyards

Woods

400   Contour interval 200 metres

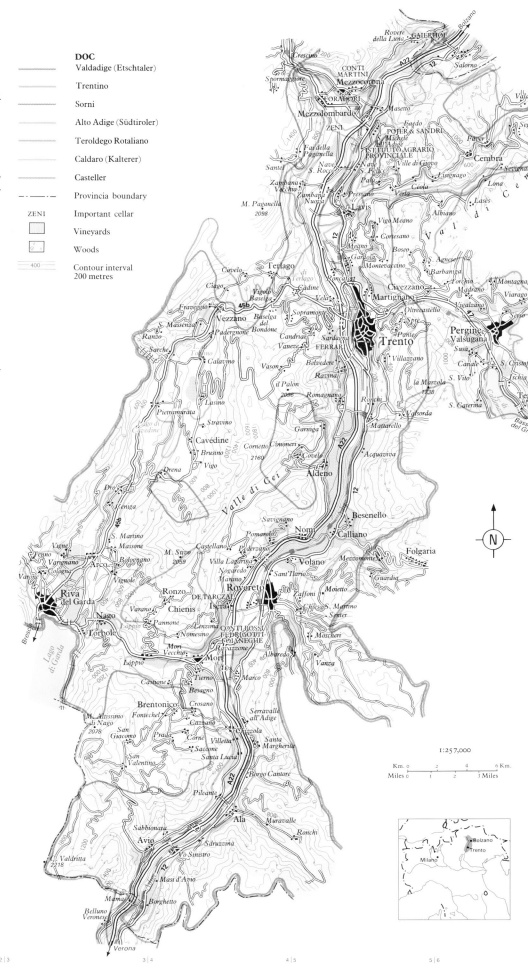

1:257,000

Km. 0   2   4   6 Km.

Miles 0   1   2   3 Miles

Alto Adige

The Alto Adige, alias the Südtirol, Italy's most northerly vineyard, is a vigorous and exciting region. Its Alpine peaks proclaim both a cultural and a viticultural melting pot. German is a more common language than Italian, yet French grape varieties are more widespread than Teutonic ones. Its vineyards have traditionally supplied red wines to northern neighbours, but despite the majority of production (65%) still being red, Alto Adige's modern reputation is based largely on a wide range of racy varietal whites.

Production is centred on the benchland of the Adige Valley. Vineyard altitudes varying from 650 to almost 3,300 feet (200–1,000 metres) allow for infinite permutations of microclimate and grape variety. Most wines are covered by the blanket DOC Alto Adige (Südtiroler) plus the name of the grape.

Higher vineyards, often steep and terraced as in the Isarco (Eisack) Valley northeast of Bolzano, are home to German varieties – Müller-Thurgau, Riesling, Sylvaner and even (so close is Austria) Grüner Veltliner, whose aromas benefit from wide fluctuations between day and night temperatures.

On slightly lower slopes Chardonnay, Pinot Bianco and Pinot Grigio are fruity and lively, while the village of Terlano, on the way north to Merano, is highly rated for Sauvignon. Despite its local origins, in Tramin, Gewürztraminer tends to be an underachiever in the Alto Adige.

The workhorse red grape is the Schiava (alias Vernatsch, also known in Germany as Trollinger). Its wines are light-coloured, soft and rather simple, with a bitter herbal twist. The best and most famous is Santa Maddalena. Lago di Caldaro, Colli di Bolzano and Meranese di Collina are all Schiava DOC, often made semi-sweet for the German market. The Lagrein, also a local grape, produces deeply fruity rosé – Lagrein-Kretzer – and darker -Dunkel, both with ageing potential.

Red varieties imported in the mid-18th century – Pinot Noir, Merlot and Cabernet – can be very good, especially from growers who have abandoned the traditional pergolas for low wires.

Most wine is made in cooperatives, but half a dozen specialists have international reputations. The house of Lageder, in Magré, is the regional leader, with a range of (mainly white) model wines, several single-vineyard selections and a barrel-fermented Chardonnay from the family's Löwengang estate.

DOC
- Meranese di Collina
- Santa Maddalena
- Caldaro (Kalterer)
- Teroldego Rotaliano
- Trentino
- Terlano
- Colli di Bolzano
- Sorni
- Provincia boundary

JOSEF BRIGL — Important cellar

Vineyards

Woods

—1000— Contour interval 200 metres

For location map see opposite page

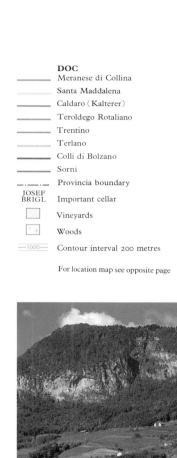

Above: the Adige has worn deep into the alpine foothills. Abrupt cliffs mark its course, sheltering sloping benches of fertile soil with a distinctly alpine air. These vineyards are at Cortaccio (Kurtasch), just south of Termeno (Tramin; the reputed source of the Traminer grape). *Below*: Alto Adige labels are usually bilingual; Trentino ones may be in Italian only. The Abtei Muri is a wine-producing monastery in the suburbs of Bolzano.

Central Italy

The best-loved Italian wines, best known to travellers, most drunk in restaurants from Soho to Sydney, are encompassed by the map opposite. Above all Chianti, whose zone with its Classico heart (see next page) occupies the better part of Tuscany.

Chianti and its blood-brothers (the blood being the juice of the red Sangiovese) are the dominant red wines of the northern part of the map. To the south they give way to the Cesanese of Latium and the Montepulciano of the Abruzzo. Going down the Adriatic coast the transition is in the Marche: Rosso Piceno is Sangiovese and Montepulciano mixed.

The white grapes that put their stamp on most central Italian wine are the Trebbiano of Tuscany and the Malvasia Bianco. Trebbiano is known as Procanico on the Tuscan coast and the island of Elba. The same grape is grown in the Midi as Ugni Blanc and in Cognac as St-Emilion, where its high acidity is welcome. In Italy even this attribute is commonly lacking. In the balance of central Italian white wines, whether Tuscan, Umbrian or Roman, Malvasia provides the body while Trebbiano gives the 'lift' – such as it is.

Neither, unfortunately, has any marked aromatic qualities. Hence there is a certain blandness and sameness only avoided by the best examples even of such famous names as Orvieto, Frascati, Est! Est!! Est!!! and the irresistibly named Bianco Vergine Valdichiana. Chianti has two DOCs for white wine: Bianco della Lega and Galestro (for a low-strength thirst-quencher). Both are the same dull mixture.

Where other white grapes contribute it is all to the good. Montecarlo from near Lucca, often called the best Tuscan (DOC) white, contains Sémillon, Sauvignon and Pinot Bianco.

Verdicchio, the standard fish wine of the Adriatic coast, relies on the contribution of the lively Verdicchio grape to the usual mix. Parrina from the Tuscan coast is seasoned with the more tasty Ansonica. Pitigliano can contain Grechetto, a minority grape with crispness and fragrance that also plays a large part in the very satisfying white of Torgiano near Perugia. Altogether more significantly, the DOC Pomino, devised by the Frescobaldi family of Chianti, abandons the Tuscan varieties but manages to make an original Florentine wine of Sauvignon, Pinot Bianco and Chardonnay.

Character is not all a matter of grapes. Orvieto and Frascati (pages 192 and 193) can (and should) be very distinct without noble varieties. When Michelangelo wrote of Vernaccia di San Gimignano that it 'kisses, licks, bites, thrusts and stings', he was not talking of an educated modern wine but of a white wine made like a red, stiff with extract and flavour. It is largely the dread of oxidation, of the wine going brown as it regularly used to, that robs it of identity.

Two famous red wines of the centre, Brunello and Vino Nobile, are discussed on pages 190–91. The Adriatic coast is thick with DOCs for reds of more or less lively, but generally sturdy, character. These include Sangiovese di Romagna and dei Colli Pesaresi, full-bodied Rosso Cònero from Ancona, and the lighter Rosso Piceno from a wider area (it is worth looking for the *superiore* version), Montepulciano

d'Abruzzo (which varies from fruity to flat) and its *rosato* version, Cerasuolo.

Further south the little-known region of Molise (just on this map) is rapidly gaining fame thanks to one great winegrower, Luigi Di Majo of Campomarino on the coast. His estate, the Masseria Di Majo Norante, started with a sturdy red, Ramitello (its DOC is Biferno; a blend of Montepulciano and Aglianico), then introduced the excellent Falanghina and other whites.

Over the border of Latium the Cesanese family is remarkable chiefly for its unpredictability; these wines can be still or sparkling, sweet or dry. Aleaticos, from wherever you may find them, are a more intriguing proposition: red dessert wines with a strong suggestion of Moscato.

These multifarious local wines apart, however, there are independent spirits at large who in the long run will influence them all. Dr Giorgio Lungarotti of Torgiano was the first to 'design' his wine from the ground up, then claim for it and be granted a DOC – a process which is now written into the Italian wine constitution. And this in a region that had no reputed red wines. (It now has several: look for Colli del Trasimeno and Colli Altotiberini.) Rubesco and other Lungarotti wines are mapped on page 192.

Other idiosyncratic planters were Tuscan noblemen who believed that whatever Sangiovese might be, Cabernet could make it better. Count Bonacossi of Carmignano, just west of Florence, was the first of these. He established the practice of flavouring his Chianti with Cabernet many years ago. Carmignano is now a separate (and excellent) DOC. But all this is beginning to seem like ancient history as the flood of newly coined wines grows. Today the pace is regularly set by these new 'super-Tuscans' – some super in quality, others only in price.

Below: a Tuscan press-house and its proprietor unconcerned about the approach of the 21st century. In the foreground are three of the curious little long barrels or *caratelli*, traditionally used for Vin Santo. Central Italy is moving faster than any region today into high technology, yet the homespun happily persists on little farms.

Left: pale Verdicchio is one of Italy's best-established 'fish' wines. Vernaccia an ancient Tuscan tradition. Montepulciano d'Abruzzo and Morellino are local reds with much to offer.

187

Chianti

Left: the Castello di Volpaia (behind, the town of Radda) has some of Chianti's highest vineyards – up to almost 2,000 ft (600 m). Besides Chianti Classico its red and white *vini da tavola*, from both Tuscan and French varieties, are among Tuscany's leaders.

The hills between Florence and Siena can come as near to the Roman poet's idea of gentlemanly country life as anywhere on earth. The blending of landscape and architecture and agriculture is ancient and profound. The villas, cypresses, vines, rocks and woods compose pictures that could be Roman, Renaissance, Risorgimento … there is no way of telling.

In this timeless scene vineyards, in the sense of ranks of disciplined vines, are the only new-comers. Traditionally vines and olive trees have clothed the dry, gritty and sandy slopes together. It is no surprise that the olives are losing, and files of vines now march up hill and down dale.

Chianti is more orderly than it seems. It was one of the first Italian wine areas to organize a *consorzio* of producers and discipline itself. The concept of Chianti Classico, the central and best area (mapped here), among six others with district names (Chianti Rufina, east of Florence, being the best of them), was established long before the present DOCG law. Recently, though, Chianti has gone through an identity crisis.

A formula was established more than a century ago by the illustrious Baron Ricasoli, sometime Prime Minister of Italy, at his castle of Brólio. His wine was made from four or five grape varieties, of which Sangiovese was the principal. A little Malvasia white was also admitted. Unfortunately the proportion of white grapes, easier for the farmers, grew – and Trebbiano crept in. When the DOC laws defined Chianti in 1963 they allowed up to 30% – far too much – of the white component. Pallid Chianti became the rule, and it became clear, to such as the ancient Antinori family of Florence, that either the rules must change, or it must make its best wine in its own way and give the wine a new name.

The Antinoris' excellent Tignanello is their rebel flag, made since 1978 with 10% of Cabernet in place of white grapes like Carmignano. To underline the point they rapidly added Solaia, with the proportions of Cabernet and Sangiovese reversed. There seems to be scarcely a castle or villa in Chianti that has not followed them with *vini da tavola* of their own construction, many of them excellent. No one, however, wants to throw out the true type of Chianti – and for good reasons.

The Chianti of tradition is (or was) livened up in an unusual way by the addition of a little unfermented must of dried grapes (a trick known as *il governo*) after it has fermented; the result is a faint prickle which helps to make it marvellously refreshing. The 1984 DOCG for Riserva Chianti, however, requires it to be aged for three years in oak before being bottled. It is distinguished by appearing in Bordeaux bottles instead of the *fiaschi* which mean Chianti to all the world. The bottle is appropriate for the nearest Italian equivalent to Bordeaux's chateaux wines – Chianti made and bottled on ancient private estates to higher and higher standards every year.

Both styles of Chianti, the current and the Riserva, can be outstandingly good in their respective ways. In a trattoria in Florence the house wine to drink with the pale, tender and tasty steaks can be as compulsively drinkable as Beaujolais, faintly sweet, just *frizzante*, grape-smelling, with a delicious slight edge. A bottle of ten-year-old Riserva, on the other hand, sums up the seductive warmth of Italian wine with a delicate and lingering astringency of its own.

At Siena a unique institution, the Enoteca or Wine Library of Italy, housed in an old Medici fortress, provides an opportunity to taste not only every possible Chianti but most other Italian wines of note.

The map shows, besides the chaotic hilliness of the Chianti countryside, and the scattering of vines and olives among woods, the cellars of most of the leading producers of Chianti Classico, who almost all use the black cock label.

The revival of Chianti Classico is one of the great success stories of the 1980s. It has prospered alongside such influential diversions as the Antinoris' Tignanello, the first 'super-Tuscan'; a blend of Sangiovese and Cabernet Sauvignon.

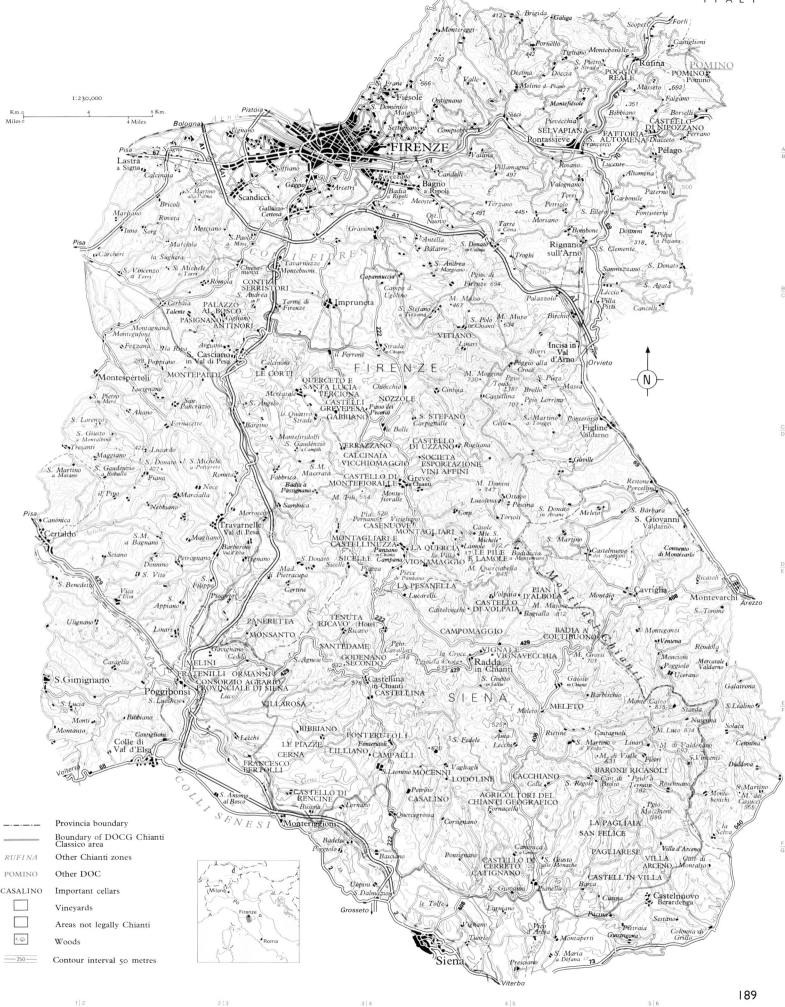

South Tuscany

The largest of the outlying areas of the huge (bigger than Bordeaux) Chianti region is the Colli Senesi, the Siena Hills. Forty miles (65 kilometres) south of Siena they roll in stately waves, woodland-topped, with here and there as a landmark a village, a rough stone castle or bare tufa cliff.

Until the 1970s little was heard of this part of the 'Putto' country. It was purely local knowledge that the climate here was more equable than farther north – the sea is only 30 miles (50 kilometres) away, via Grossetto – and that summers are regularly warmer and extremely dry. Monte Amiata, rising to 5,600 feet (1,700 metres) just to the south, collects the summer storms that come from that direction. Nor did many know that the Sienese form of Tuscany's red grape, the Sangiovese, is distinctly different and bigger, going here by the name of Sangioveto Grosso and, further east, at Montepulciano, as Prugnolo Gentile.

An enclave in the Colli Senesi around the little town of Montalcino went further in distinguishing its grape, calling it Brunello, and even further its wine, by making it of Brunello alone, without the blending customary in Chianti. At the same time as Ricasoli was devising an ideal formula for Chianti, Clemente Santi and his kin (now called Biondi-Santi) were established at their estate, Il Greppo, a model for what they labelled Brunello di Montalcino.

It is simple enough: the late-ripening Brunello is picked very late, in mid-October, from long-established vines with small crops. The strong dark wine is fermented long and slowly on its skins to extract the maximum colour and flavour. Then it is aged in big Tuscan barrels for at least four years. The result is the Italian equivalent of Spain's Vega Sicilia (coincidentally, a contemporary invention): a wine for heroes, or rather heroic millionaires, super-

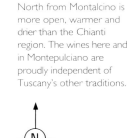

North from Montalcino is more open, warmer and drier than the Chianti region. The wines here and in Montepulciano are proudly independent of Tuscany's other traditions.

1:250,000

Km. 0   2   4   6   8   10 Km.
Miles 0   2   4   6 Miles

N

- - - - - - - - Regional boundary

- - · - - · - - Provincia boundary

BRUNELLO DI
MONTALCINO   DOC/DOCG

DOC/DOCG boundaries are distinguished
by coloured lines.

Bolgheri

charged with flavour, extract, tannin, acidity and impact.

The world at large did not meet Brunello (or Vega Sicilia) until the 1970s. Very ancient Biondi-Santi bottles were tasted and found exceptional. Other growers, though, thought not only that the price demanded was over the top, but that the same could be said of the wine. It was a 19th-century insurance policy to make over-strength wines and keep them in oak until they were rigid with tannin. Modern manners are better suited by equally potent wine bottled earlier, while fruity flavours are still dominant.

Among the subscribers to this theory was the man who has often been called Italy's greatest winemaker, and who is now in charge of the nation's wine laws, Ezio Rivella. Rivella was invited by Villa Banfi, the biggest importer of Italian wine into the USA, to prospect for a vast model wine estate in central Italy. Rivella settled for Montalcino, not only (or primarily) for its Brunello, but for its soil and climate, and the fact that as much as 7,000 acres (some 3,000 hectares) were available, at Sant'Angelo Scalo, in huge uncluttered blocks. The object was to make the rare Brunello available worldwide – and at the same time to experiment with almost every other noble grape in this favoured climate. So far Brunello has been the greatest success, encouraging dozens of other estates to compete on what has become a very fast track.

But Brunello is not alone. The neighbours to the east, across an intervening enclave of 'mere' Chianti, have ancient pretensions of their own embodied in their DOC, Vino Nobile di Montepulciano.

Montepulciano is a hill town of great charm surrounded with Chianti-style vineyards, a mixture of their own Sangiovese, the Prugnolo, with the other normal Chianti ingredients. Depending on the producer, the wine tends to resemble either a poor Chianti or a very good one. Logic suggests that it should be a halfway house between Chianti and Brunello. In practice the hallmark of true Vino Nobile is initial inkiness; an impenetrable youthful tannic hardness, giving ground only slowly to warmer and gentler flavours. (Two years in cask is the minimum legal age: three for a Riserva.)

To while away the waiting, the same producers will make a mild Chianti, and very mild Bianco Vergine in the Val di Chiana to the north. Bianco Vergine can be a lovely light and lissome wine, though with no great flavour. More challengingly, and led by the stylish house of Avignonesi, they are busy inventing 'super-Tuscans' of Merlot and Cabernet with conspicuous success, and not forgetting Chardonnay and Sauvignon Blanc.

Yet Montepulciano's greatest triumph, to this observer at least, is its Vinsanto – the forgotten luxury of many parts of Italy, Tuscany above all. It is orange coloured, smoky scented, extraordinarily sweet, intense and persistent, aged four years in tiny flat caratelli, traditionally (but no longer) under the roof tiles of a Renaissance palazzo.

The DOC Bolgheri began with a modest rosato. It has been overwhelmed by the de luxe *vini da tavola* that grew up alongside. Sassicaia lit the fuse that exploded the old appellation system.

It is debatable whether any winegrower since 'Chianti' Ricasoli has made such an impact on Italian wine as the founder of Sassicaia, the lonely little vineyard near the Tuscan coast that upset the whole DOC system. Sassicaia was totally non-traditional, unmistakably superb – and classed as a lowly *vino da tavola*. The system had to change.

When the Marchese Incisa della Rochetta chose a stony hectare of the big San Guido estate in the 1940s to plant Cabernet it was strictly a private affair. He hankered after the Médoc (his vines were from Château Lafite). The nearest vineyards were miles away. Bolgheri was neglected peach orchards and abandoned strawberry fields.

The estate lies 6 miles (10 kilometres) from the sea on the first slopes of the graphically named Colline Metallifere, a range rich in minerals that forms a shallow amphitheatre with a marvellous microclimate. Vines flower in May and grapes ripen early in September. When its early wines started to lose their tannin they revealed flavours not seen in Italy before. The Marchese planted more, nearer the sea on lower fields, building up to 60 acres (23 hectares) on his stoniest soils, and adding Cabernet Franc.

His nephews, Piero and Lodovico Antinori, tasted the wines. Piero talked to Professor Peynaud in Bordeaux. In 1968 Antinori started to bottle and market Sassicaia. By the mid-1970s it was world famous.

Castiglioncello, the original plantation, is on the east of the property at 1,000 feet (300 metres). The main coast road is the boundary to the west. An avenue of cypresses leads from it at right-angles to the ancient walled village of Bolgheri. Part belongs to the Incisas, part (by marriage) to the Antinoris' parents, who developed a minor DOC Bolgheri for rosato and bianco from standard Tuscan grapes at their Belvedere estate.

Then in the 1980s Lodovico Antinori began planting a selection of plots with varied soils on his property, Ornellaia, with Cabernet Sauvignon, Merlot and Sauvignon Blanc. Masseto, his highest plot, is clay, which suits the Merlot. Lower down are gravel, pebbles and sandy soils where he hopes Cabernet will develop finesse.

Meanwhile his brother Piero upgraded the rosato from his Scalabrone vineyard and in 1990 produced a Cabernet/Merlot blend called Guado al Tasso from the Al Tasso plot on higher ground.

The three estates are shown on the map; one mature, two young. Ornellaia has already proved its capacity to make another very fine Bordeaux-style red and its Sauvignon Blanc (labelled Poggio alle Gazze) shows promise. The limits of the isolated region have yet to be discovered. The DOC Bolgheri is in full evolution; under the new wine laws of 1992 this will be a test case. The *vino da tavola* that overtook the system has now been absorbed within it.

Umbria

Umbria is the one land-locked region of central Italy, slanted towards Tuscany and the west but with a distinct highland climate: cooler and with more regular rainfall than most of Tuscany. It is land-locked and backward in its traditions, too, apparently lacking the self-confidence of either the Tuscans (who have long imported its wine without acknowledgement) or the Romans, for centuries its overlords as one of the Papal States.

Its wine traditions are as ancient as any. Orvieto was an important Etruscan city. The magnificent cellars cut in the volcanic rock of its dramatic hilltop 3,000 years ago are unique examples of prehistoric technology, specifically designed for long cool fermentation, the object being sweet wine. Classic Orvieto is *amabile* – as sweet as possible, depending on the season and the amount of botrytis conjured by autumn mists in the vineyards.

Alas for Orvieto, the emerging modern market in the 1950s had little use for wine of unspecified sweetness. It was (and still is) easier to market dry wine. Dry Orvieto, though, was not different enough from any other pale bland product. Today, with such heavyweights as Antinori in play (though his Castello della Sala is far from being classic Orvieto), the future looks brighter. But meanwhile the limelight moved away to more interesting things being done near Perugia by one of the great pioneers in Italian wine history, the creator of Rubesco and the (1968) DOC Torgiano, Dr Giorgio Lungarotti.

Lungarotti set out in the 1950s with a clean slate to make a red Umbrian wine to rival those of Tuscany. Rubesco instantly outshone almost every Chianti of the time, and led him to experiment with other grape varieties. Cabernet and Chardonnay have both been outstandingly successful, the Cabernet blended in San Giorgio, the Chardonnay solo in Miralduolo.

Since Lungarotti's initiative several new DOCs have established the specific characters of the higher, cooler Colli Perugini, the lower, warmer hills around Lake Trasimeno, the Colli Martani, especially for Grechetto whites, and most promisingly, Montefalco, for the uninhibited reds of its apparently indigenous grape, the Sagrantino.

Above: the hill-town of Orvieto, founded by the Etruscans, dominates the vineyards that give its golden wine. *Below*: Umbria is asserting itself with variety and quality. The local hero is Dr Lungarotti of Perugia, founder of the DOC Torgiano.

-·-·-·- Regione boundary

-·--·-- Provincia boundary

ORVIETO DOC

DOC boundaries are distinguished by coloured lines

1:695,000

Km. 0   5   10   15   20   25 Km.
Miles 0   5   10   15 Miles

The Castelli Romani

The papal summer villa at Castel Gandolfo contains in its garden a long and lofty half-underground arcade: the very ambulatory in which the Emperor Domitian, whose summer house was on the same site, used to saunter in hot weather.

The villa commands views to the west over the Tyrrhenian Sea, and to the east over the round crater-lake of Albano. It perches, in fact, on the rim of an extinct volcano. That is what the Alban hills are. Reaching to 3,000 feet (900 metres) within 20 miles (30 kilometres) of Rome (and so near the sea) they provide today, as they did in ancient times, a wonderful retreat of green woodland and vineyard for summer weekends.

Villas of every prosperous period rejoice in them. And the Romans rejoice, flocking into Frascati or Marino, Grottaferrata or Monte Porzio Catone or Velletri to take their ease with a roast-pork sandwich and the thrilling local wine.

Frascati and its kin, found magical by Grand Tourists of the Augustan Age, must be the origin of the much-repeated truism that some wines 'don't travel'. It is made of the two central Italian white grapes, the Trebbiano and Malvasia, that are over-prone to oxidation – to turning brown and tasting flat. The traditional method of making it, skins and all like a red wine, gave oxidation every chance. (The object, often splendidly achieved, was to give it an almost fatty richness of texture, as well as the perfume of Malvasia skins.)

Deep cold cellars in the volcanic rock are enough to keep well-made Frascati fresh, even in barrel, until the summer visitors can drink it. Any other sort of handling, unfortunately, means changing its nature. It can be (and is) made by cold fermentation without skins today. The best producers make a good dense and aromatic wine. The interesting experiment is to compare a bottled Frascati with one straight from the barrel in an *osteria* on the hill or in a Roman tavern in Trastevere where the proprietor is a wine-lover.

Differences are commonly noted between the wines of Frascati and its neighbours in the Castelli Romani. Marino is the name most often mentioned as having a trifle more substance. Velletri also offers red wine. Colli Lanuvini is an adjacent DOC to the south for white wines which could be confused with some of the better products of the Castelli Romani.

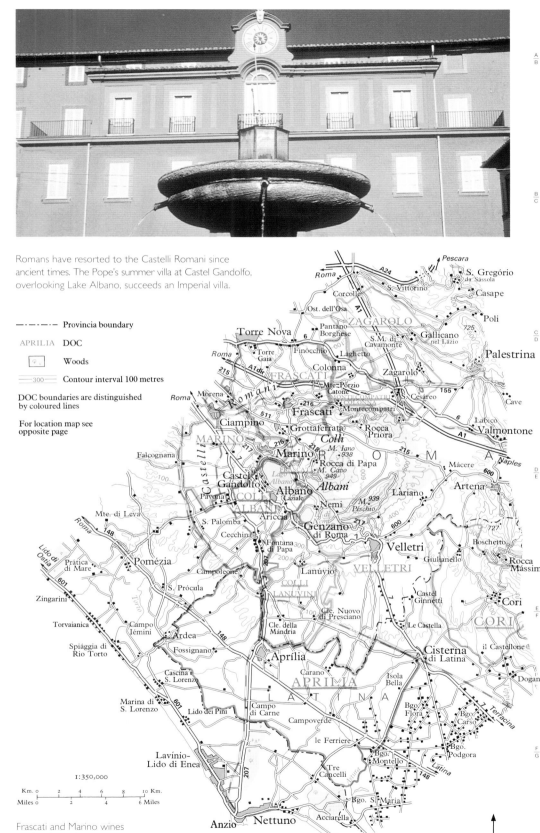

Romans have resorted to the Castelli Romani since ancient times. The Pope's summer villa at Castel Gandolfo, overlooking Lake Albano, succeeds an Imperial villa.

---·--- Provincia boundary

APRILIA DOC

Woods

——300—— Contour interval 100 metres

DOC boundaries are distinguished by coloured lines

For location map see opposite page

1:350,000

Km. 0   2   4   6   8   10 Km.
Miles 0   2   4   6 Miles

Frascati and Marino wines are hard to tell apart. Both should be rich-textured and grapey.

Southern Italy

There is always a faint air of unreality about any complete list of Italian wines. There are indeed that many names – but are there that many identities? A number of worthy local characters, especially in the south, go straight into the blending vat every year to emerge with much smarter labels.

But a good handful of southern wines have held their ground, and others are joining them to prove that southern does not necessarily mean sun-baked. Wines that used to sell on the power of association alone – the vine-hung terraces of Amalfi – have learned the simple facts of modern vinification and emerged as individuals.

For years the only familiar names were the ones tourists meet around Naples. Ischia was one of the first wines to claim a DOC, in 1966. It is easy enough for an island. Today its best producer, D'Ambra, has no need of a DOC to sell his well-made white Biancolella and Forastera. Capri has long been a sort of brand name; the island scarcely having room for vineyards. Lachryma Christi was famous but of very doubtful reputation until it became DOC Vesuvio in 1983.

Ravello wines, particularly those made by the Caruso family, are well balanced; fresher than most of the south (the altitude of Ravello and its sea mists are said to help). And I cannot resist writing the name of Gran Furore Divina Costiera, awful though the wine is.

The standard of the less publicized wines of inland Campania is set far higher. Taurasi is their majestic chief; deep-toned, tannic, fragrant – a wine to age in bottle. Its grape, the Aglianico (Ellenico, ie from Greece, like civilization itself down here), makes another good, rather lighter, red, Aglianico del Vulture, in vineyards on the hills of Basilicata up to 2,500 feet (760 metres). The name of Greco di Tufo, a white wine from Campania of remarkably original flavour, dry, brisk and fragrant, shares the credit between Greece and the tufa rock on which it grows.

In the same hilly province, Avellino, the acknowledged master winemaker of the region, Mastroberardino, makes an even more remarkable and unexpected white called Fiano, a wine

that combines lightness with firmness, lively length with deeply nutty flavour. Of Basilicata the only other well-known wine (not DOC) is Asprinio, which the Potenzans manage to make mercifully unpotent, pale and crisp.

Calabria has one strong red of reputation: Cirò (there is a white Cirò as well), but DOCs for several other districts, including Donnici, Savuto, Lamezia and Pollino. Calabria's most original wine is the sweetly perfumed Greco di Gerace from Bianco near the very tip of the toe.

Puglia's winegrowers have DOCs for a number of wines which have traditionally gone to market in bulk. Several are making their own reputations. The Primitivo from around Taranto is one; its full-bodied red is said to age very well. In California the theory goes that it may be the origin of the estimable Zinfandel.

Negroamaro is the cautionary name of the principal red grape here. It makes almost port-like roasted reds at Salento (as Salice Salentino), and under the DOCs Leverano, Copertino and Squinzano.

Both reds and whites in Puglia are being well made today, not over-strong, but neutral, without aroma, the whites particularly, which makes them an ideal base for vermouth. Locorotondo and Martina Franca are typical of this school of strong bland white. Quite exceptional is the almost-Californian produce of an estate near Foggia, Favonio, which grows Pinot Bianco, Chardonnay and Cabernet. Its one rival is the Torrebianco estate in the same area. These apart, the traditional rosés and new Pinots and Sauvignons of Castel del Monte are the most attractive product of the region at present. There are good dessert wines, of Moscato and Aleatico, on all hands.

More than any of the wines of Puglia, it is Sicilian wine that has made a name for itself in the past decade. Its Marsala, like a very distant cousin of sherry, has been famous since Nelson's day, when he fortified the Royal Navy with it. From deep doldrums as a mere cooking wine it has climbed back into respectability – even fashion. The best name is Samperi. The advent of Sicilian table wine, however, has been

spectacular. Vast government and EC grants have made the island Italy's biggest producer of inoffensive wines for blending, 75% of them white (and 80% made in cooperatives).

Brands rather than DOCs make the running. The one considerable table-wine DOC is Etna, for wines from the fertile volcanic soil of that threatening mountain. The Barone Vilagrande's red and white are typical examples: lively, well-balanced wines. Alcamo is the table-wine DOC for vineyards in the northwest and Cerasuolo for light reds from Vittoria on the south coast.

The best wines from other parts of Sicily are made on the Regaleali, Donnafugata and Rapitalà estates, all in the west. Most successful by far is Corvo from Casteldaccia, selling almost a million cases a year, apparently to every Italian restaurant on earth. Corvo's flagship is the fine dry red Duca Enrico.

The rest of Sicily's DOCs are reserved for her particular speciality: dessert wine. The Moscatos of Noto and the little island of Pantelleria, and the Malvasia of Lipari are outstanding examples of one of Italy's oldest vinous traditions. Carlo Hauner of Lipari has turned that tiny windswept island into a place of pilgrimage.

Most of Sardinia's DOCs, too, are for sweet wines. The distinction between a table wine and a dessert wine is even more blurred on Sardinia than in other parts of Italy; traditionally all her reds (Cannonau, Monica, Girò and Oliena are best known) were more or less sweet. Cannonau is the local form of Grenache; a chameleon of potentially high quality, sweet or dry. Her best whites were Vernaccia, which has a distinct affinity with sherry, and Nuragus, a dry wine without too much alcohol and (sometimes) with a firmness that makes it really appetizing.

One firm makes stylish, not over-modern reds and whites in vast new vineyards around Alghero in the northwest. Sella & Mosca wines are made and marketed by Piemontese and Milanese skills respectively. Their Torbato white, Tanca Farrà red and Anghelu Ruju dessert wines are models. Attractive and reliable wines like this could come from almost anywhere in Italy.

Above: Monte Vulture dominates northern Basilicata and the vineyards of Aglianico and Moscato of the brothers d'Angelo. The labels represent a variety of quality from the Italian south and its islands, unknown a decade ago.

Cesanese di Affile
Cesanese di
Olevano Romano

Avezzano
A25
Sulmóna

ABRUZZI

Termoli
A14

Ramitello

BIFERNO

SAN
SEVERO

Promontorio
del
Gargano

Manfredonia

Aleatico
di
Puglia

Cesanese
del Piglio

Frosinone

PENTRO
DI
ISERNIA

Isernia

Campobasso

MOLISE

A1

Sacco

Cassino

85

17

BIFERNO

Lucera

Cacc'e Mmitte
di Lucera

LAZIO

156

Latina

213

Terracina

7

Gaeta

Gaeta

Falerno
del Massico

A1

SOLOPACA

Tabarno

Torre Quarto

Orta
Nova

Torre
Giulia

Rosso di Cerignola

Barletta

MOSCATO DI TRANI

Troia

Benevento

Caserta

Conca

Greco di
Tufo

Cofone

Ariano Irpino

A16

Santo Stefano

Cerignola

Rosso
Canosa

Rosso Barletta

Molfetta

CASTEL DEL MONTE

Con-
verso

Bari

Taurasi

Aglianico
del
Vulture

Monopoli

16

Napoli

Per'e
Palummo

Gragnano

Avellino

Fiano d'Avellino

MALVASIA DEL VULTURE

MOSCATO DEL VULTURE

PUGLIA

GIOIA DEL
COLLE

Altamura

Gravina

100

Locorotondo

379

VESVIO

18

Lacrima
Christi

Salerno

A3

Eboli

CAMPANIA

Potenza

Aleatico di Puglia

Martina

Ostuni

Castellammare

RAVELLO

Amalfi

Tramonti

Sala
Consilina

Consilina

Aspríno

BASILICATA

Bradano

Matera

407

Brádano
Basento

Castelli
Acquaro

7

Brindisi

Brindisi

Squinzano

ISCHIA

Forastera
Biancolella

CAPRI

Costiera

Europe Divini

Vallo della
Lucania

598

Agri

106

Taranto

Lizzano

Copertino

Lecce

Manduria

MALARESE

FIVE ROSES

SALENTO

Cilento

Sapri

Lauria

Sinni

18

Castrovillari
Pollino

Primitivo di Manduria

Salice Salentino

Nardo

Gallipoli

Alezio

Matino

ROSA
DEL GOLFO

Golfo
di
Taranto

Lacrima di
Castrovillari

MOSCATO DI
SARACENO

Sibari

Crati

A3

Rossano

106

Páola

MOSCATO

Campana

Cosenza

Donnici

CIRO

MELISSA

107

CALABRIA

Savuto

18

Nicastro

Crotone

S. Anna di Isola

Capo Rizzuto

Lamezia

Catanzaro

106

280

Vibo
Valéntia

Monasterace
Marina

Is. Eólie o Lípari

Gittanova

Locri

Malvasia delle
Lípari

Faro

Palmi

Reggio di
Calabria

Pellaro

Bianco
Greco di
Bianco

106

Messina

Milazzo

Capo
Bianco

A20

SARDEGNA INSET:

Sta. Teresa
Gallura

Arzachena

Vermentino
di Gallura

MOSCATO

Tempio
Pausania

Olbia

125

Porto
Tórres

Sassari

MOSCATO DI
SORSO SENNORI

ANGHELU RUJU

Alghero

Ozieri

Bonnanaro

Monti

Budduso

Siniscola

Torbato
di Alghero

MALVASIA

Malvasia di Bosa

Bosa

Sígni

Macomer

Moscato di Sardegna

131D

Nuoro

MOSCATO

Oliena

Dorgali

Cannonau
di Sardegna

SARDEGNA

Vernaccia

Monica
di Sardegna

Vernaccia
di Oristano

Mandrolisai

ARBOREA

Arbatax

Oristano

Laconi

Lanusei

Monica di Cagliari
Moscato di Cagliari
Girò di Cagliari
Nasco di Cagliari
MALVASIA DI CAGLIARI

Uras

Kerri

Moscato di Sardegna

Campidano
di Terralba

NASCO

Sanluri

Guspini

131

Senorbi

MOSCATO

Nuragus di Cagliari

Iglesias

Carbónia

GIRÒ

Carignano
del Sulcis

MONICA

Cagliari

Sant' Antioco

SICILIA:

Trapani

Palermo

Lo
Zucco

Términi
Imerese

Cefalù

Corvo

A20

113

Mamertino

Capo
Bianco

A18

Str. di Messina

Alcamo

RAPITALA

REGALEALI

A19

Nicosia
Val di Lupo

ETNA

Taormina

Marsala

A29

121

Corleone

DONNAFUGATA

Paterno

Ciclopi

Catánia

VECCHIO SAMPERI

Castelvetrano

189

Enna

A19

Mazara
del Vallo

Menfi

SICILIA

Platani

Caltanissetta

Sciacca

115

640

Piazza
Armerina

417

Lentini

114

Agrigento

115

Caltagirone

Monali

Albanello

Siracusa

Gela

Cerasuolo di
Vittoria

CERASUOLO

Ragusa

Pachino

Eloro

MOSCATO
DI NOTO

Noto

Moscato di Siracusa

Modica

N

1:2,700,000

Km. 0   50   100 Km.

Miles 0   20   40   60 Miles

—·—·—   Regione boundary

Alcamo   White wine

Matino   Red wine

SOLOPACA   Red and white wine

MOSCATO   Dessert wine

MONICA   Selected Vino da Tavola

DOC boundaries are distinguished by
coloured lines

Land above 600 metres

195

Spain

Above: ventilation shafts above the cellars of the castle of Peñafiel in the DO Ribera del Duero. Powerful deep-coloured reds from this Denominación contrast with the finesse of the best Riojas.

THE LANGUAGE OF THE LABEL

Con crianza Aged (**sin crianza**, unaged)

Cepa Wine or grape variety

Viña, viñedo Vineyard

Cosecha Crop, or vintage

Vendimia Vintage

Denominación de Origen Similar to Appellation Contrôlée

Consejo Regulador Organization for the defence, control and promotion of a Denominación de Origen

Reserva Mature quality wine (of red, usually three years old)

Gran reserva Aged at least two years in barrel and three in bottle

Fino Good (particularly meaning the driest sherry)

Vino de mesa (or **de pasto**) Table wine

Vino corriente Ordinary wine, not usually bottled

Vino de cosecha propria wine made by the owner of the vineyard

Criado y embotellado por... Grown and bottled by. . .

Elaborado y añejado por... Made and aged by...

Embotellado or **Engarrafado de origen** Estate bottled

Blanco White

Tinto Red

Rosado Rosé

Clarete Light red or dark rosé

Seco Dry

Dulce Sweet

Espumoso Sparkling

4° Año (or **4 Años**) Bottled in its fourth year

Bodega Cellar, anywhere where wine is kept or made or even drunk

Spain and its wine are a pattern of riddles. It is the country with the most land under vines in the world, but only the third biggest wine producer. (Its average yield of 23 hectolitres per hectare is half what France allows for its finest wines.) Of all the countries in Europe Spain was the first to have laws defining quality, yet its entry into the quality wine market is no older than California's. A decade ago it had only half a dozen regions with any pretensions to quality: today it has twenty – and most of them are still so young in the business that an apt comparison is to New Zealand.

Where was Spain in the centuries when France, Germany, Hungary and parts of Italy were defining and refining their tastes and traditions? With the exception of the export-driven centres of Andalucia, Jerez and Malaga, it had slipped back almost to the Middle Ages. Rioja evolved out of trade with Bordeaux in the phylloxera years. But the proud traditions of Castile and the Duero had sunk into stupor, Catalonia was a downtrodden province, and the rest of the country either made double-strength wine for bulk export or swigged its own produce uncritically – often from goatskins.

The first signals of new self-awareness came in the late 1950s, from Rioja. The brilliantly aromatic, delicate and clean wines from this region were a challenge to all others. In 1970 the government put in place the machinery of Denominaciónes de Origen (DOs). In 1978

Spain's new constitution grouped the country's 50 provinces into 17 'autonomies', stimulating regional self-regard and rivalry. In 1986 Spain (and Portugal) joined the EEC and became eligible for technical and financial assistance on a vast scale, as well as having to match EC standards of definition and regulation of their wines.

The detailed results are still unclear in the frenzy of investment and upgrading, but the pattern is not difficult to see. Most of Spain is now technically equipped, at least in part, to make wines as good as its grapes will allow, and several of its varieties have inherent qualities as positive as any in the world. Like Italy, Spain sees the perils, as well as the benefits, of joining the international Cabernet club. Spain's contribution to the variety of the world's fine wines will expand all our horizons.

On the following pages the 'classic' areas are mapped in detail. The map opposite shows what a large part of the country is already demarcated either into full-fledged DOs (the nearest equivalent is Italy's DOCs) or the apprentice category of DE (Denominación Específica) where aspiring regions must wait for promotion. Already nearly half the nation's total vineyard area, which approaches 1.5 million

hectares of vines, is classed as DO, producing almost a third of Spain's wine (a third of which is exported). The top rank, equivalent to Italy's DOCG, is DOC (Denominación de Origen Calificada). The first was granted in 1991 – very properly to Rioja.

Spain is customarily divided into seven geographical macro-zones which are helpful in grasping the complexity of its multitude of physical variations and their consequent denominaciónes.

The smallest in terms of wine-production is the north-west, the 'green Spain' of Galicia, the Asturias and the Basque country, with the western part of León, El Bierzo. Traditions here are celtic and Christian with almost no Moorish influence. The sea, the hills, the wind and a good deal of rain (see the centre small map) are the chief physical factors. Wines are mainly white, light, dry, ideal for seafood, and range from the extremely tart Chacolí of San Sebastián to what is perhaps Spain's most exciting new kind of wine: aromatic and silky white Albariño from Rías Baixas. What was formerly (and can still be) no more than the Spanish version of Portugal's vinho verde has been dramatically upgraded. Old stories of Albariño really being Riesling abound. It does not need to be. This is an important original that challenges Spain's best white wines.

The Ebro is the river that flows southeast from the Cantabrian Cordillera on the north

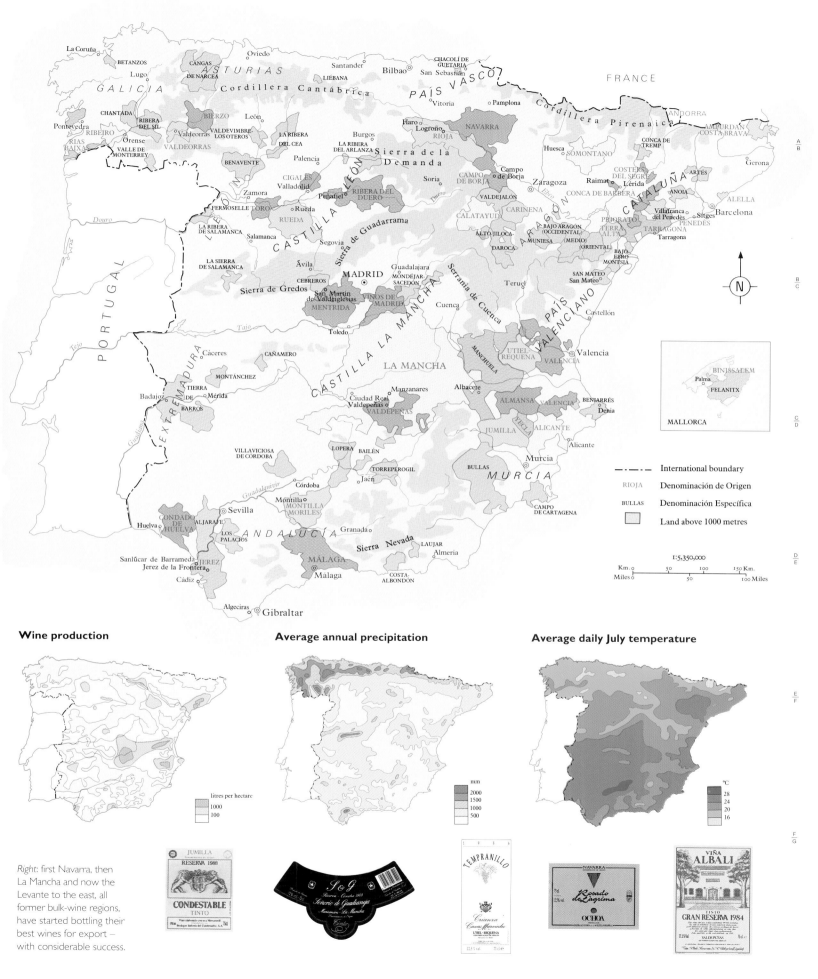

Wine production

Average annual precipitation

Average daily July temperature

litres per hectare
- 1000
- 100

mm
- 2000
- 1500
- 1000
- 500

°C
- 28
- 24
- 20
- 16

International boundary

RIOJA Denominación de Origen

BULLAS Denominación Específica

Land above 1000 metres

1:5,350,000

Km. 0 ... 50 ... 100 ... 150 Km.
Miles 0 ... 50 ... 100 Miles

Right: first Navarra, then La Mancha and now the Levante to the east, all former bulk-wine regions, have started bottling their best wines for export – with considerable success.

coast to the Mediterranean in Catalonia. The Upper Ebro embraces Rioja, Navarra and Aragón, with its one long-established red, Cariñena. Contact with France (Navarre and France were one kingdom) has its influence here, but only Rioja really showed it until recent years, when Navarra rosados made of Garnacha Tinta (French: Grenache) began to make their mark.

Things have moved fast here, too, especially on the technical front: top Navarra reds will soon challenge Rioja as more Tempranillo and Cabernet invade the Garnacha vineyards. Meanwhile the new-fledged DO of Somontano in Aragón with its almost sub-alpine climate, red earth and green grass, is already making fine whites of Viura (also Chardonnay) and clean fresh reds of good tight structure and acidity from Tempranillo, Cabernet and the local Moristel. The dominant producer is the cooperative of Barbastro.

The high, landlocked Duero Valley in Castile is mapped on page 206. The east coast of northern Spain is its very opposite: Catalan rather than Castilian, softly Mediterranean rather than harshly continental. Catalonia is mapped on page 204.

South down the east coast the vineyards inland from Valencia and Alicante have only modest traditions and no singularity of style – except strength. Valencia, Utiel-Requena, Almansa, Yecla, Jumilla and Alicante constitute the Levante; accustomed to providing potent bulk blending wine for an export market that is rapidly disappearing. Its salvation lies in diversification and as much lightening of style as it can manage in such a hot climate.

Most central of all to Spanish life is the Meseta, the high plateaux south of Madrid whose endless flat vineyards weary the eye. The extent of La Mancha, its chief DO, is clear from the map. The town of Valdepeñas traditionally gave its name to a large part of this production; strong (about 13%) but pale red made largely from the Airén, Spain's most-planted white grape. There are over a million acres (450,000 hectares) of Airén and only half a million of the next favourite, Garnacha. In La Mancha Airén is blended with an increasing proportion of Cencibel (alias Tempranillo). At best the result is fruity and almost delicate, despite its strength. Technology here is rushing straight from the antique (huge clay amphora-like *tinajas*) to stainless steel and oak, with very palatable results.

The southern quarter of Spain is dominated by sherry and brandy (pages 199–201) and the apéritif and dessert wines of Montilla and Málaga (page 207). Over 700 miles (1,150 kilometres) from the mainland the Canary Islands, once famous for sweet 'sack', are starting to revive a similar style There is one exception in the remote Tierra de Barros in Extremadura near the Portuguese frontier. The majority of its production goes into Brandy de Jerez, but Lar dos Barros suggests that some of the table wine potential of the not-distant Alentejo (see page 215) may be there.

Above: the green extreme of Spain is Galicia in the northwest, where the River Miño forms the border with Portugal. Light and fragrant Albariño whites from here have become high fashion.

Below: the wine is as brown as the landscape in Málaga in the southeast of Spain. Mules and donkeys are still used to carry the grapes (chiefly Pedro Ximénez and Moscatel) from steep patches of vineyard.

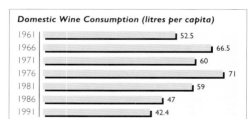

Domestic Wine Consumption (litres per capita)

Year	Litres
1961	52.5
1966	66.5
1971	60
1976	71
1981	59
1986	47
1991	42.4

Above: Wine consumption in Spain has been in decline since the mid-1970s, though the trend now appears to be stabilizing. Spain is now seventh in the world, behind France, Portugal, Italy, Luxembourg, Argentina and Switzerland.

Below: In 1991 Spain produced almost 31.2 million hectolitres of wine, of which almost a third (10 million hl) was DO quality wine. Exports accounted for almost 46% of the total (14.4 million hectolitres), of which 26.4% (3.8 million hectolitres) was DO quality wine. Germany is the biggest importer of DO Rioja, while the main importer of DO Cava is the USA, which took over a quarter of the total exported.

Spanish Production and Exports 1991 (millions of hectolitres)

	Exports	Production
DO Quality	3.8	10
Other wines	10.6	21.2

■ Exports　■ Production

Jerez de la Frontera

There are little bars in Jerez where the tapas, the morsels of food without which no Jerezano puts glass to mouth, constitute a banquet. From olives and cheese to prawns, to raw ham, to peppery little sausages, to lobster claws, to miniature steak streaked with amber onions, the path of temptation is broad and long.

Your copita, a glass no more imposing than an opening tulip, fills and empties with a paler wine, a cooler wine, a more druggingly delicious wine than you have ever tasted. It seems simultaneously dry as dust and just teasingly sweet, so that you have to sip again to trace the hint of grapes.

It comes in half-bottles, kept on ice. A half-bottle is reckoned a reasonable drink to spin out over an hour or two among the tapas. And in half-bottles it stays as fresh as it was when it left the bodega – for no bottle is left half full.

The most celebrated sights of Jerez are the bodegas of the shipping houses. Their towering whitewashed aisles, dim-roofed and crisscrossed with sunbeams, are irresistibly cathedral-like. In them, in ranks of butts sometimes five tiers high, the new wine is put to mature. It will not leave until it has gone through an elaborate blending process which is known as the solera system. Only the occasional wine of notable distinction is sold unblended as an 'almacenista'.

The first job when the new wine has got over its fermentation is to sort it into categories; better or worse, lighter or more full-bodied. Each wine is put into the *criadera* (nursery) appropriate to its character. Each character or category of wine has a traditional name.

From the *criaderas* the shipper tops up a number of soleras, consisting of perhaps 20, perhaps several hundred butts; each wine going into the solera nearest to its character. As new wine goes into butts at one end of the solera, mature wine

The sherry bodegas of Jerez de la Frontera

1	Williams & Humbert	5	Pedro Domecq
2	Garvey	6	Gonzalez Byass
3	Valdespino	7	John Harvey
4	Sandeman		

for blending is drawn from the other. The solera system is simply a progressive topping-up of older barrels from younger of the same style, so that wine is continuously being blended, and hence always emerges tasting the same.

The solera wines are the shipper's paintbox for blending the house brand, or for brands ordered by other wine merchants for sale under their own names. Most sherry when it is sold is a blend of several, sweetened and strengthened to the consumers' taste. The few 'straight solera' sherries which are sold tend to be unsweetened and therefore wines for the connoisseur.

The categories into which all young sherry is classified begin with fino. Finos are the best; delicate and distinctive wines which will need a minimum of blending and sweetening. They

will age excellently, but also have qualities that make them perfect young. Their strong individuality comes from an unusual form of yeast, flor, which forms on their surface. Tasted from the butt, when the *capataz* of the bodega thrusts a long-handled *venencia* through the flor into the pale wine to bring out a sample, they have a magical new-bread freshness and vitality; they are, beyond question, Spain's finest wine of all.

Amontillado – a softer, darker wine – comes next. The best amontillados are old finos, finos which did not quite have the right freshness to be drunk young, although the name is often used in commerce for middle-character blends of no real distinction. Great amontillado soleras (for only from the solera can you taste the real individuality of the wine) are dry and almost stingingly powerful in flavour, with a dark, fat, rich tang – but words fall short.

Oloroso is the third category. Wines which have great possibilities for ageing but are a little heavy at first go into this solera. They are the basis for the best sweet sherries – often known as milk or cream, which suggests a silky fatness.

Sweetening wines and colouring wines for blending are made separately from sun-dried grapes and kept in their own soleras. Lesser wines which go into cheaper blends are known as *rayas*, and a final rare character, something between fino and oloroso, as palo cortado.

In addition there are the manzanillas of Sanlúcar de Barrameda. Manzanilla finos are some of the most delicate and lovely of all, always with a faintly salty tang which is held to come from the sea. A manzanilla amontillado is rare, but can be exquisite, salty and brown as burnt butter.

No blend, medium-sweet or sweet as most blends are, can compare with these astonishing natural sherries. They are as much collectors' pieces as great domaine-bottled burgundies.

Excellent fino from Valdespino's Ynocente vineyard in Machamudo: unique in naming its origin.

The most famous fino of all does not mention fino on the label. Extremely dry, fresh and delicate.

Duff Gordon is owned by Bodegas Osborne. Their best-known wine is the amontillado, El Cid.

Marqués Real Tesoro is an expanding bodega famous for manzanilla, amontillado as well as Tio Mateo fino.

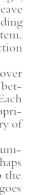

Barbadillo, Sanlúcar's largest bodega, has a range of excellent manzanillas, including old dark *pasada*.

Perez Megia is one of Sanlúcar's smaller bodegas, with pale Alegria and good Jalifa amontillado.

Sandeman's (now Seagram-owned) began in the port trade. Its fino Apitiv is good, old sweet sherries superb.

Dos Cortados signifies very dry oloroso with great distinction: a true connoisseur's sherry.

A magnificent old dry oloroso from Machamudo, one of the top wines from the house of Domecq.

'Croft Original' is a modern style of pale sweetened fino. The company's ports are better.

The most famous of creams from a British firm in Bristol, now the biggest sherry company.

Emilio Lustau is famous for highly distinctive top-quality sherries over a wide range.

The Sherry Country

Finesse – meaning fine-ness in its most literal sense, a combination of strength and delicacy – is not one of the qualities you normally find in scorched-earth wines. Where the sun fairly grills the ground, and the grapes ripen as warm as fruit in a pie, wine sometimes develops wonderful thews and sinews, power and depth. But finesse?

This is sherry's great distinction. It is a question of chalk; of the breed of the Palomino grape; of huge investment and long-inherited skill. Not every bottle of sherry, by a very long way, has this quality. But a real fino, the rarely shipped unstrengthened produce of the bare white chalk dunes of Macharnudo or Sanlúcar de Barrameda, is an expression of wine and wood as vivid and beautiful as any in the world.

One does not think of sherry normally in direct comparison with the world's other great white wines – but it is, strange to say, the cheapest of them, even bodega bottled and fully mature, ready to drink.

The sherry country, between the romantic-sounding cities of Cádiz and Seville, is almost a caricature of grandee Spain. Here are the bull ranches, the caballeros, the castles on the skyline, the patios, the guitars, the night-turned-into-day. Jerez de la Frontera, the town that gives its name to sherry, lives and breathes sherry as Beaune does burgundy and Epernay champagne.

The comparison between sherry and champagne can be carried a long way. Both are white wines with a distinction given them by chalk soil, both needing long traditional treatment to

Below: the Gonzalez Byass bodegas in Jerez reflect the Moorish past of Andalucia. *Right*: there is a strange dazzling white light reflected off the chalk soil in the sherry vineyards. Golden Palomino grapes almost cook in the heat and their high sugar content gives strong, stable wine. The miracle is that it is delicate, too.

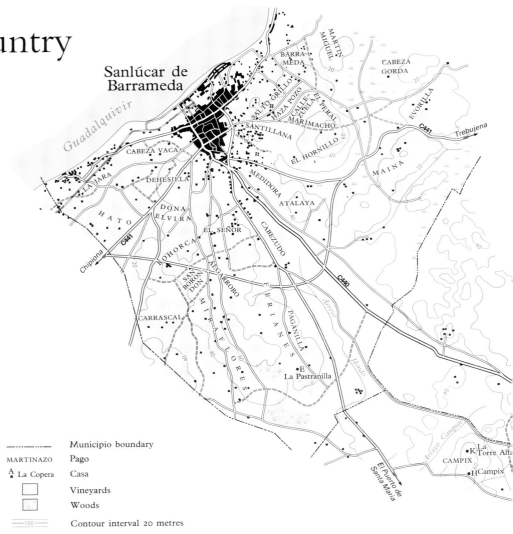

Sanlúcar de Barrameda

–·–·–·–	Municipio boundary
MARTINAZO	Pago
A La Copera	Casa
☐	Vineyards
☐	Woods
═100═	Contour interval 20 metres

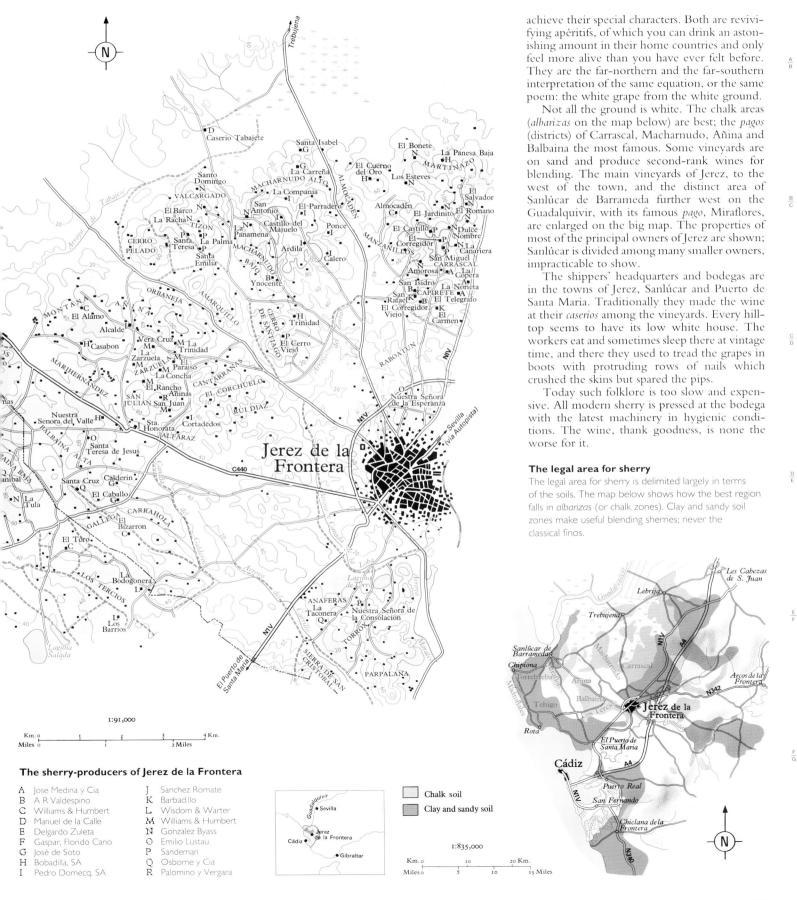

achieve their special characters. Both are revivifying apéritifs, of which you can drink an astonishing amount in their home countries and only feel more alive than you have ever felt before. They are the far-northern and the far-southern interpretation of the same equation, or the same poem: the white grape from the white ground.

Not all the ground is white. The chalk areas (*albarizas* on the map below) are best; the *pagos* (districts) of Carrascal, Macharnudo, Añina and Balbaina the most famous. Some vineyards are on sand and produce second-rank wines for blending. The main vineyards of Jerez, to the west of the town, and the distinct area of Sanlúcar de Barrameda further west on the Guadalquivir, with its famous *pago*, Miraflores, are enlarged on the big map. The properties of most of the principal owners of Jerez are shown; Sanlúcar is divided among many smaller owners, impracticable to show.

The shippers' headquarters and bodegas are in the towns of Jerez, Sanlúcar and Puerto de Santa Maria. Traditionally they made the wine at their *caserios* among the vineyards. Every hilltop seems to have its low white house. The workers eat and sometimes sleep there at vintage time, and there they used to tread the grapes in boots with protruding rows of nails which crushed the skins but spared the pips.

Today such folklore is too slow and expensive. All modern sherry is pressed at the bodega with the latest machinery in hygienic conditions. The wine, thank goodness, is none the worse for it.

The legal area for sherry

The legal area for sherry is delimited largely in terms of the soils. The map below shows how the best region falls in *albarizas* (or chalk zones). Clay and sandy soil zones make useful blending sherries; never the classical finos.

1:91,000

Km. 0   1   2   3   4 Km.
Miles 0   1   2 Miles

The sherry-producers of Jerez de la Frontera

A	Jose Medina y Cia	J	Sanchez Romate
B	A R Valdespino	K	Barbadillo
C	Williams & Humbert	L	Wisdom & Warter
D	Manuel de la Calle	M	Williams & Humbert
E	Delgardo Zuleta	N	Gonzalez Byass
F	Gaspar, Florido Cano	O	Emilio Lustau
G	José de Soto	P	Sandeman
H	Bobadilla, SA	Q	Osborne y Cia
I	Pedro Domecq, SA	R	Palomino y Vergara

Chalk soil
Clay and sandy soil

1:835,000

Km. 0   10   20 Km.
Miles 0   5   10   15 Miles

201

Rioja

Fonzaleche in the Rioja Alta has the bare highland feeling of much of the region outside the river valley, emphasized by the Sierra de Cantabria in the distance. Vineyard, crops and pasture alternate, the vines low bushes without posts and wires.

For many years Rioja had a virtual monopoly of the wine lists of good restaurants in Spain. They offered local wines in carafes. But if you wanted bottled wine, especially red wine, Rioja was the Bordeaux and burgundy of Spain. You were pointed towards Rioja.

It is partly a question of human geography, as well as physical. Rioja is not far from the French frontier; not far from Bordeaux. When phylloxera arrived in the 1870s many winegrowers took off for Spain. They found in Rioja rather different conditions but an opportunity to make good wine all the same. Then the phylloxera caught up with them, and they went home. But they left French methods and ideas.

Rioja is distinctly mountainous in atmosphere. It lies in the shelter of the Sierra de Cantabria to the north, but its best vineyards are still 1,500 feet (460 metres) above sea level. They get plenty of rain and long springs and autumns, rather than endless parching summers. The wine is correspondingly delicate by Spanish standards: well made and at the right age exceedingly fragrant and fine, yet with a faintly toasted sweet warmth, which seems to proclaim it Spanish.

The area is divided into three by terrain and altitude. The areas further up-river are cooler and wetter. Rioja Alta (the high Rioja) has the coolest climate and a mixture of clays, chalky and iron-rich, and silts that give its wine acidity, finesse and 'structure': it makes the longest-lived and potentially the best wines of the region. Rioja Alavesa has warmer, more alkaline slopes. Its Tempranillo is fragrant and pale, less sinewy, quicker to mature, but excellent in blends. Rioja Baja (the low Rioja) has a more Mediterranean climate with heavier soil, largely planted with Garnacha for the strongest but coarsest wine of

the three, the right booster for many blends but rarely becoming a Reserva in its own right. The three zones meet near the town of Logroño, one of the two main centres of the wine trade.

The chief wine centre is Haro. The dignified little town, old stone mansions in its centre, is dwarfed by its outskirts, which contain 13 large bodegas – almost a third of the total of Rioja. The surrounding countryside is beautiful in an upland way: tall poplars and eucalyptus trees line the roads; orchards cover slopes along with tilting fields of vines. In the rocky valley bottom the infant Rio Ebro is joined by the little Rio Oja, whose shortened name the region has adopted.

There are very few wine estates, large or small, in Rioja which grow, make and bottle all their own wine. In many matters of technique the Bordelais left their mark, but châteaux (with the possible exception of Castillo Ygay) are not among them. To qualify for a Rioja Certificate of Origin a bodega has to be large enough, and almost all bodegas buy in grapes from other growers or cooperatives to supplement those they grow themselves, and make a blend of wine of their own house style. Vineyard names appear frequently on Rioja bottles: Paceta, Pomal, Tondonia, Viña and Zaco are all well known. They are not regulated as individual sites are in, say, Burgundy, but the style of the wines bottled with their names is generally very consistent and high.

Red wine is far more important than white. It is made from a mixture of grapes, in which the Tempranillo, Spain's best red wine grape, is backed up with Garnacha for strength, Graciano for tannin and fragrance and/or Mazuelo (alias Cariñena or Carignan) for colour and acidity. Bordeaux- and burgundy-shaped bottles tend to

be used for, respectively, the lighter (formerly 'clarete') and fuller ('tinto') wines.

By and large these wines are still made rather as Bordeaux was 50 years ago, to be aged for several years in barrels (two or three for standard, but far more than Bordeaux, up to five or ten, for Gran Reservas), until their darkness and fruitiness has been tamed and replaced with the almost tawny colour and soft dry vanilla flavour that come from oak. In Spain, where most red wine was traditionally inky, they are much appreciated light and smooth, the effect of long ageing in wood. The greatest change in Rioja in recent years has been the move to bottle earlier; to reduce the dominance of the oaky aroma and allow the grapey flavours to blossom. It is a marked improvement: only exceptional wines could stand up to the traditional Reserva treatment. Yet a few, from such conservative bodegas as López de Heredia and Muga, still do, with glorious results.

White Riojas are made of the freshly acidic Viura (alias Macabeo) blended with Malvasia Riojana which adds a little body and aroma. Garnacha Blanca can be used, but adds little except alcohol. Even white Rioja wines were often given four or five years in barrel. When they had grown golden and rather thin, or flat with oxidation, they were reckoned at their prime, whereas earlier, sometimes marvellously stony and up to good Graves standards, they were considered too young. Today many bodegas go to the other extreme, fermenting the aromatic must of the Viura grapes very cold in steel tanks, and bottling it while it still tastes more of fruit than of wine. Others hold to a middle course, ageing whites briefly in wood. The minority toe the classic line; theirs is the most memorable wine.

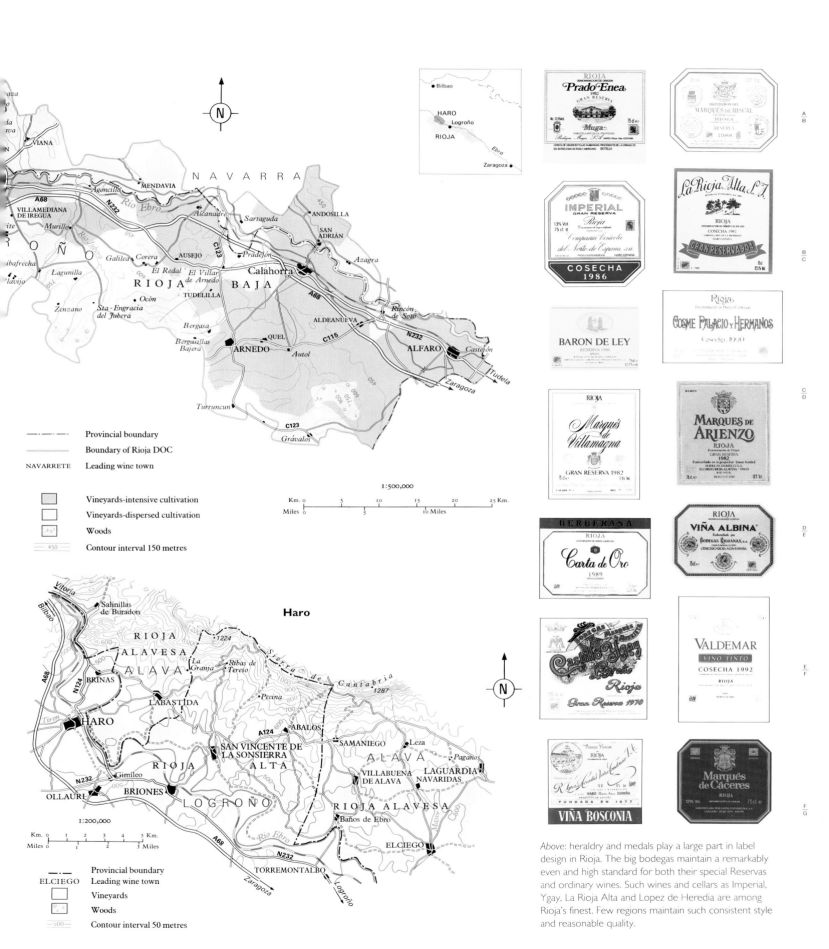

Map (top, 1:500,000):

NAVARRA

VIANA
MENDAVIA
Agoncillo
Río Ebro
Alcanadre
Sartaguda
ANDOSILLA
SAN ADRIÁN
A68
VILLAMEDIANA DE IREGUA
N232
Murillo
Galilea
Corera
Pradejón
AUSEJO
C123
Azagra
El Redal
El Villar de Arnedo
Calahorra
A68
RIOJA
BAJA
Lagunilla
Ocón
TUDELILLA
Rincón de Soto
Zenzano
Sta - Engracia del Jubera
ALDEANUEVA
Bergasa
QUEL
C115
ALFARO
Castejón
N232
Bergasillas Bajera
ARNEDO
Autol
Tudela
Zaragoza
Turruncun
C123
Grávalos

Inset map: Bilbao, HARO, Logroño, RIOJA, Ebro, Zaragoza

1:500,000
Km. 0 5 10 15 20 25 Km.
Miles 0 5 10 Miles

Legend (top map):

Provincial boundary
Boundary of Rioja DOC
NAVARRETE — Leading wine town

Vineyards-intensive cultivation
Vineyards-dispersed cultivation
Woods
Contour interval 150 metres

Map (bottom, 1:200,000):

Haro

Vitoria
Bilbao
Salinillas de Buradon
A68
RIOJA ALAVESA
ALAVA
La Granja
Ribas de Tereso
Sierra de Cantabria
BRINAS
N124
Pecina
LABASTIDA
Tirón
HARO
ABALOS
A124
SAMANIEGO
Leza
SAN VINCENTE DE LA SONSIERRA
ALAVA
Paganos
RIOJA ALTA
Gimileo
VILLABUENA DE ALAVA
LAGUARDIA
NAVARIDAS
N232
BRIONES
LOGROÑO
OLLAURI
RIOJA ALAVESA
Baños de Ebro
Río Ebro
A68
ELCIEGO
N232
TORREMONTALBO
Zaragoza
Logroño

1:200,000
Km. 0 1 2 3 4 5 Km.
Miles 0 1 2 3 Miles

Legend (bottom map):

Provincial boundary
ELCIEGO — Leading wine town
Vineyards
Woods
Contour interval 50 metres

Wine labels (right column):

Rioja — Prado Enea 1982 — Gran Reserva — Muga
MARQUÉS DE RISCAL — RIOJA — RESERVA 1988
IMPERIAL GRAN RESERVA — Rioja — Compañia Vinicola del Norte de España, s.a. — COSECHA 1986
La Rioja Alta, S.A. — RIOJA — COSECHA 1982 — GRAN RESERVA 904
BARON DE LEY — RESERVA 1986 — RIOJA
Rioja — COSME PALACIO Y HERMANOS — Cosecha 1990
Marqués de Villamagna — GRAN RESERVA 1982
MARQUES DE ARIENZO — RIOJA — GRAN RESERVA 1982 — BODEGAS DOMECQ S.A. ELCIEGO-RIOJA ALAVESA · SPAIN
BERBERANA — RIOJA — Carta de Oro 1989
RIOJA — VIÑA ALBINA — Embotellado por BODEGAS RIOJANAS, s.a.
CASTILLO YGAY Rioja — GRAN RESERVA 1970
VALDEMAR — VINO TINTO — COSECHA 1992 — RIOJA
R. Lopez de Heredia Viña Tondonia, S.A. — RIOJA — VIÑA BOSCONIA — FUNDADA EN 1877
Marqués de Cáceres — RIOJA

Above: heraldry and medals play a large part in label design in Rioja. The big bodegas maintain a remarkably even and high standard for both their special Reservas and ordinary wines. Such wines and cellars as Imperial, Ygay, La Rioja Alta and Lopez de Heredia are among Rioja's finest. Few regions maintain such consistent style and reasonable quality.

Catalonia

On a coast whose traditional production was nearly all heavy dark red wine for the world's blending vats, it is a surprise to find the world's biggest cellars for sparkling wine. But Catalonia is unlike the rest of Mediterranean Spain. Catalans have more vitality, are more demanding, destructive, creative. They also have, on rising ranges of inland hills in the shelter of the eastern Pyrenees, with the ocean at their feet, a superbly temperate and reliable climate.

In the past it was the hottest areas near the sea, with their super-potent wine, that were most in demand. Today it is the higher ground that has brought recognition to a new sort of well-balanced table wine, combining the qualities of ripe Mediterranean grapes with the sort of finesse that is found in the best Riojas.

There are eight Denominaciónes de Origen in Catalonia today, but by far the most important is not a regional name, but the DO Cava, whose heart, if not its only legal address, is the town of St Sadurní d'Anoia in the limestone hills of Penedès. It is the most-visited wine centre, they say, in Spain: the city of sparkling wine.

Cava, though, is not purely a geographical appellation. It is granted to certain towns in La Rioja, Navarra, Aragón and the Basque country as well as Penedès – but always and only for their *metodo tradicional* (ie what was formerly known as 'champagne method') sparkling wines.

Two vast concerns, Codorníu and Freixenet, control the industry. They use local white grape varieties, well adapted to produce acidic wines despite the hot weather, to make Cava fresh and well-balanced, if not very aromatic. Parellada,

Xarel-lo and Macabeo (alias, in Rioja, Viura) are the principal sorts. But Chardonnay is increasingly entering into blends, and some are being sparkled straight. Young, their creaming cava can be exquisitely fruity. Where too much stress is laid on ageing they have not yet been so successful; though technology here advances in leaps.

One name has dominated the table wines of the region for thirty years or more: Torres. The bodegas at Villafranca de Penedès, family-owned for 300 years, led the revolution of ideas and technology that put Catalonian wine alongside Rioja as Spain's best reputed and best distributed.

Bodegas Torres made the running by studying abroad, ignoring the rules, planting such non-traditional grapes as Cabernet and Pinot Noir, Chardonnay and Gewürztraminer, opening new vineyard areas at higher altitudes, using cold fermentation in stainless steel and ageing more in bottle and less in cask. The traditional red grapes of the Penedès are not greatly different from those of Rioja, with Garnacha and Tempranillo (known here as Ull de Llebre) preponderant. Torres' standard brands, Tres Torres and Gran Sangre de Toro, have a certain extra richness and ripeness which distinguishes them from Riojas Reservas. Oak still plays an important part. The Torres top red, Gran Coronas Mas la Plana, almost pure Cabernet, tastes more like a complex, fruity, somehow faintly decadent Bordeaux.

Torres, followed by several of its neighbours, has also reinterpreted the white wines of Penedès, adding the classic French and even German grapes. One neighbour, Jean León,

Above, left: the Raimat bodega near Lérida, an enterprise started in the 1930s, was reborn in the 1980s to make high-quality Cabernets and Chardonnays, now called DOC Costers del Segre.
Above: the high Penedès on the way up to Lérida. The hermitage of Pierola, with the Sierra de Montserrat in the background. The altitude here expands the range of growing conditions.

took the California view and planted nothing but Cabernet and Chardonnay.

The owners of Codorníu meanwhile had long intended to exploit the potential of inland Catalonia. In the 1930s, just before the Civil War, the Raventos family built an ambitious modern bodega at Raimat, on the high plateau near Lérida (see page 197) to make fine table wines. So far inland the climate is more continental, with minimal rainfall. After a 50-year delay, the Raimat estate started afresh to produce exceptional red and white wines, again using native and French varieties. The Cabernet in particular is excellent. In 1988 part of the Lerida region was given the DO Costers del Segre: Raimat, though, remains its only star.

The same family now owns the extravagant Masia Bach estate in Penedès, at St Esteve Sesrovires. Extrisimo Bach, formerly its best-known wine, was sweet and oak-aged, much in the style of the neighbouring Denominación of Alella, to the north of Barcelona.

Alella is a dwindling vineyard, interesting as its wines may have been. Further north the Costa Brava has its Denominación of Ampurdan (shown on page 197), centred around Perelada in the province of Gerona, producing sparkling wines (not up to Penedès standards) and (the bulk of production) rosado.

More important are the ancient vineyards of Tarragona and Priorato, to the south, and the more recently created DOs of Conca de Barberá, extending Penedès-style wine further up into cooler hills, and Terra Alta, a similar inland extension to the sprawling region of Tarragona.

Priorato is the true heart of Tarragona, a hot and rocky region of volcanic soil that produces red wines of formidable colour, strength and blackberryish flavour. Fermented dry, they have been more used for blending than drinking. Recent examples, though, have revealed uninhibited and luscious flavours that bring parts of Australia to mind. As sweet fortified wine, aged for many years to acquire dusty *rancio* flavours, Priorato Dulce can also be superb.

Superlatives excluded, much the same can be said of the rest of Tarragona. Its wines, exploited and appreciated by the Romans (whose architecture is still much in evidence) are either strong dry reds for blending or passable substitutes for port. A very few are much better. But more could be, and Spain's entry into the EC has encouraged the quality producers in all regions.

Below: the foundation of the Penedès wine industry is its sparkling cava. Codorníu's cellars are reputed the biggest of their kind on earth. Codorníu also owns Raimat (see opposite). The other pillars of Penedès are the noble red Gran Coronas of Bodegas Torres (recently renamed Mas la Plana), its stablemates, and a handful of their rivals.

-------	Provincial boundary
————	Boundary of DO
TARRAGONA	DO
PIERA	Leading wine town

1:615,000

Km. 0   10   20   30 Km.
Miles 0   5   10   15 Miles

Rueda and the Duero

For many years, before the late 1970s, Spain's most prestigious and expensive red wine appeared a complete maverick. Few had tasted Vega Sicilia, and fewer still knew where, in the vast dustbowl of central Spain, such a remarkable vineyard could be found.

The plain of Old Castile, stretching in tawny leagues north from Segovia and Avila to the old kingdom of León, is traversed by the adolescent Duero, the river that in Portugal becomes the Douro and the home of port. It is the shallow valleys of the Duero and its tributaries, around Valladolid, from Zamora upstream to Aranda de Duero, that have an ancient winemaking tradition – more, one would think, because they had a thirsty population (Valladolid, as the capital of 17th-century Spain, formulated strict wine laws) than because the fierce climate favoured the vine. The wines were very alcoholic: the reds black; the whites like primitive sherry. On the credit side there were chalky clay soils that retained the sparse rainfall and gave the wine at least a suggestion of the quality associated with chalk. And at 2,000 feet (610 metres) the nights are remarkably cool.

Vega Sicilia, the one perfectionist property at Valbuena de Duero, proved that very fine red could be made. The estate was planted in imitation of Bordeaux in the 1860s, at the same time as the first such steps were being taken in Rioja. But here the Bordeaux grapes were used, with only a minority of the native Garnacha and Tempranillo (known here as Tinto Fino or Tinto del País). Vega Sicilia's Unico, aged ten years in barrel, is a wine of astonishing, penetrating personality. For many people its younger brother, the five-year-old Valbuena from the same estate, is an easier wine to understand.

Rather than imitate the local hero by planting Cabernet, the region has now won its spurs

with the Tinto Fino almost single-handed. About 1970 the cooperative at Peñafiel, just to the east, its cellars under the Moorish castle, greatly refined its winemaking, using the Tinto Fino and ageing its Reservas, notably the extremely tasty Protos, in oak. Next to follow was Alejandro Fernández at Pesquera de Duero. Since the early 1980s Fernández has had a near-fanatical following for his 100% Tinto Fino, which here makes perhaps its grandest wine. Concentrated fruit and high alcohol sound merely aggressive, but Pesquera has a luscious quality which promises many years of staying power.

In 1982 the region was defined as a Denominación de Origen under the name Ribera del Duero, along with the neighbouring Ribera de Burgos around Aranda in the province of Burgos (whose wines, Torremilanos for example, tend to be paler and lighter than the hefty reds of Valladolid).

Meanwhile south of Valladolid something more like a revolution was taking place. The old wine centres of Rueda and Nava del Rey,

traditional producers of sherry-like whites, came under the prospecting eye of the famous Rioja bodega, Marqués de Riscal, looking for a new source for white wines of fashionable fruity freshness. It was not the landscape, flat and bare, but the local white grape, the Verdejo – also the ancient network of deep cellars which once supplied the court at Valladolid – that attracted Riscal's attention.

Carefully vinified, the Verdejo has good fruity acidity and the ability to age well in cask. In 1971, with the advice of Professor Emile Peynaud from Bordeaux, Riscal built a modern 'inox' bodega. In 1980 Rueda was made a denominación. At the same time the local Sanz family's Bodegas de Crianza de Castilla la Vieja went into partnership with the Marqués de Griñon, who had already attracted attention by growing Cabernet at, of all places, Toledo. Griñon, like Riscal (and also with Peynaud advice) makes a Rueda Superior (which must be at least 60% Verdejo), but sells it unaged. It is remarkably crisp and aromatic, certainly one of Spain's best white wines.

Right: Vega Sicilia is the Grange Hermitage of Spain: its eccentric red champion. Pesquera leads Ribera del Duero reds, while Marqués de Griñon is the freshest of Rueda whites.

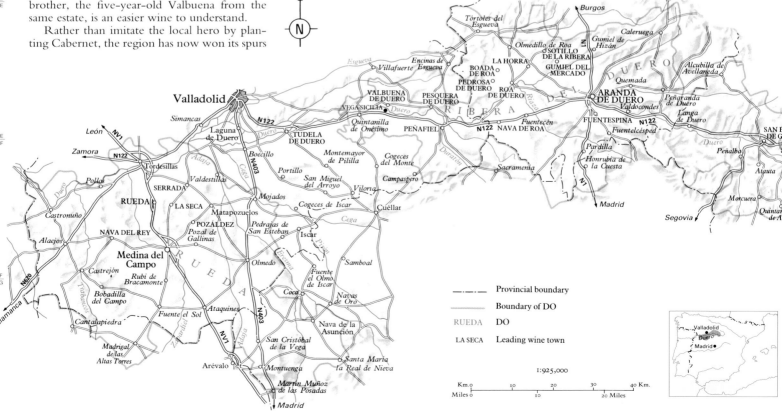

Montilla and Málaga

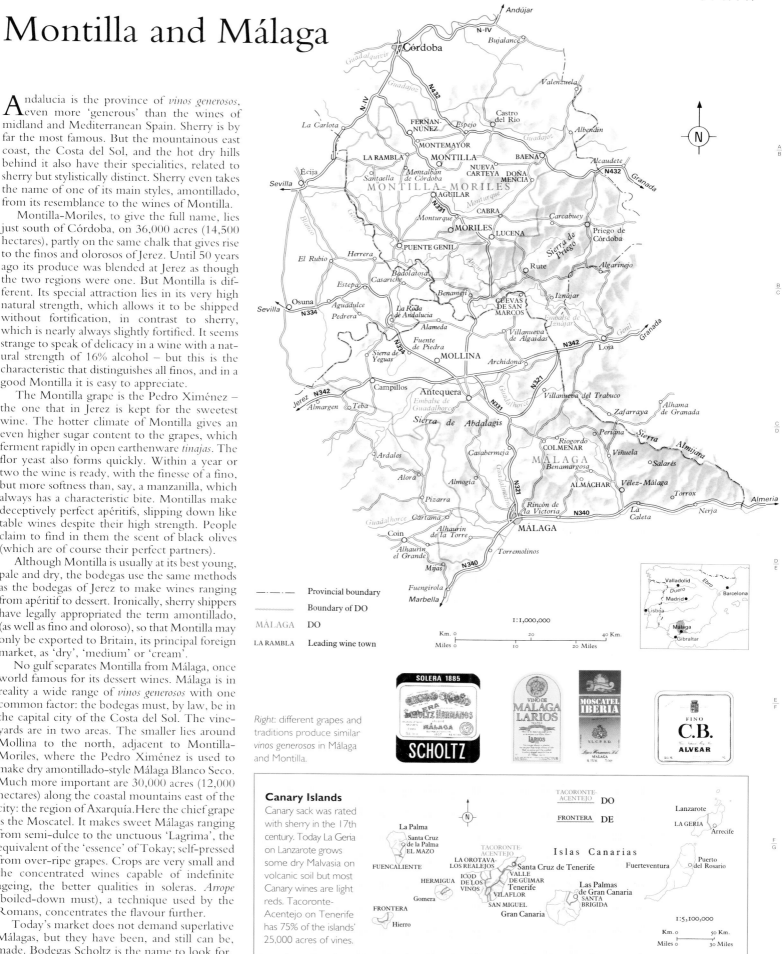

Andalucía is the province of *vinos generosos*, even more 'generous' than the wines of midland and Mediterranean Spain. Sherry is by far the most famous. But the mountainous east coast, the Costa del Sol, and the hot dry hills behind it also have their specialities, related to sherry but stylistically distinct. Sherry even takes the name of one of its main styles, amontillado, from its resemblance to the wines of Montilla.

Montilla-Moriles, to give the full name, lies just south of Córdoba, on 36,000 acres (14,500 hectares), partly on the same chalk that gives rise to the finos and olorosos of Jerez. Until 50 years ago its produce was blended at Jerez as though the two regions were one. But Montilla is different. Its special attraction lies in its very high natural strength, which allows it to be shipped without fortification, in contrast to sherry, which is nearly always slightly fortified. It seems strange to speak of delicacy in a wine with a natural strength of 16% alcohol – but this is the characteristic that distinguishes all finos, and in a good Montilla it is easy to appreciate.

The Montilla grape is the Pedro Ximénez – the one that in Jerez is kept for the sweetest wine. The hotter climate of Montilla gives an even higher sugar content to the grapes, which ferment rapidly in open earthenware *tinajas*. The flor yeast also forms quickly. Within a year or two the wine is ready, with the finesse of a fino, but more softness than, say, a manzanilla, which always has a characteristic bite. Montillas make deceptively perfect apéritifs, slipping down like table wines despite their high strength. People claim to find in them the scent of black olives (which are of course their perfect partners).

Although Montilla is usually at its best young, pale and dry, the bodegas use the same methods as the bodegas of Jerez to make wines ranging from apéritif to dessert. Ironically, sherry shippers have legally appropriated the term amontillado, (as well as fino and oloroso), so that Montilla may only be exported to Britain, its principal foreign market, as 'dry', 'medium' or 'cream'.

No gulf separates Montilla from Málaga, once world famous for its dessert wines. Málaga is in reality a wide range of *vinos generosos* with one common factor: the bodegas must, by law, be in the capital city of the Costa del Sol. The vineyards are in two areas. The smaller lies around Mollina to the north, adjacent to Montilla-Moriles, where the Pedro Ximénez is used to make dry amontillado-style Málaga Blanco Seco. Much more important are 30,000 acres (12,000 hectares) along the coastal mountains east of the city: the region of Axarquía. Here the chief grape is the Moscatel. It makes sweet Málagas ranging from semi-dulce to the unctuous 'Lagrima', the equivalent of the 'essence' of Tokay; self-pressed from over-ripe grapes. Crops are very small and the concentrated wines capable of indefinite ageing, the better qualities in soleras. *Arrope* (boiled-down must), a technique used by the Romans, concentrates the flavour further.

Today's market does not demand superlative Málagas, but they have been, and still can be, made. Bodegas Scholtz is the name to look for.

‑‑‑‑‑‑‑	Provincial boundary
	Boundary of DO
MÁLAGA	DO
LA RAMBLA	Leading wine town

1:1,000,000

Km. 0   20   40 Km.
Miles 0   10   20 Miles

Right: different grapes and traditions produce similar *vinos generosos* in Málaga and Montilla.

Canary Islands

Canary sack was rated with sherry in the 17th century. Today La Gería on Lanzarote grows some dry Malvasia on volcanic soil but most Canary wines are light reds. Tacoronte-Acentejo on Tenerife has 75% of the islands' 25,000 acres of vines.

1:5,100,000

Km. 0   50 Km.
Miles 0   30 Miles

Portugal

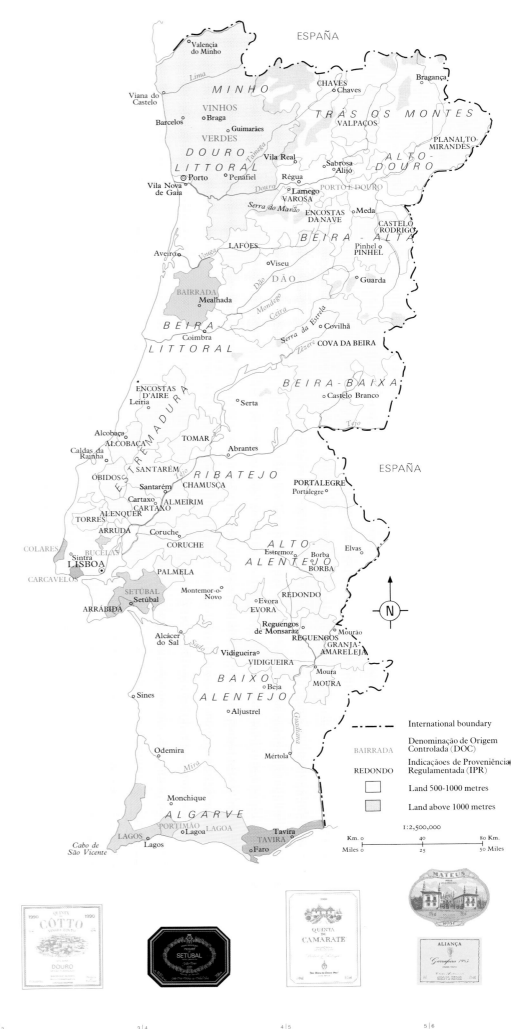

Portugal is the place for wine romantics. Even more than Italy it remains the country of ancient ritual, of groaning ox carts, of dappled sunlight through arbours of vines, of treading the purple must, of maidens bearing pitchers, of songs handed down for centuries.

The climate is ideal for wine grapes. The northern two-thirds of the country has ample rain, except in the high Douro beyond the mountains, and a long, bright rather than blazing, summer; Atlantic characteristics which make it rather like a more southerly Bordeaux.

Portugal's greatest wine is port. It is treated in detail on pages 212–14. Port was conceived as an export wine – as was, oddly enough, Portugal's other (though far more modern) best-seller, the sweet rosés led by Mateus and Lancers.

Thus undistracted by any further need to compromise with foreign tastes, the Portuguese have continued, right up into the last years of the 20th century, to grow their own grapes in their own ways and make wines to their own liking.

Not that Portuguese wine has been without laws and regulations. Long before her entry into the EC in 1986 certain districts were demarcated and every aspect of their wines controlled – not always to the benefit of their quality, or to the liking of merchants and their local clients, who routinely ignored what the law prescribed to blend the kinds of wines they preferred.

Among the original 'demarcated' wines the most famous and singular remains vinho verde, the 'green' wine of the northernmost province, the Minho (see page 211), which accounts for a quarter of Portugal's wine harvest. In contrast all other wines used to be classed as 'maduro' (aged).

Until the 1970s only the Dão region (page 211), three historic but scarcely significant Lisbon vineyards (opposite), and the unique Moscatel de Setúbal were demarcated. In 1979 Bairrada was added (page 210), and the Algarve – though for reasons more connected with tourism than taste.

The rest of Portugal's table wine was merged into an anonymity out of which skilful merchants produced their own favourite blends. Portugal's red grapes, processed in traditional fashion, give robust and invigorating, tannic and earthy wines, good value but not notably aromatic or complex. Ten years is rarely excessive ageing and sometimes not enough. The better wines would be aged as Reservas; the best as Garrafeira, which might be rendered as 'selected old wine'.

Today the trend is to become much more specific. Individual estate wines were formerly almost unknown; today there are dozens. The first, and still the best, was begun in the 1950s by the port house of Ferreira in, of all places, the high Douro. Its rare and sumptuous Barca Velha

Right: Portugal's best table wines used to be Garrafeira blends. Today each region from the Douro to the Alentejo is asserting its individuality, with increasingly interesting results.

Lisbon

soon became for Portugal what Vega Sicilia is for Spain. J M da Fonseca, across the Tagus from Lisbon, remains the largest and most important producer of Setúbal and makes admirable Periquita and Camarate reds, the latter with a proportion of Cabernet. In the early 1980s J P Vinhos released an estate Cabernet Sauvignon, Quinta de Bacalhoa, which tasted more like a modern Bordeaux than a traditional Portuguese red. Yet a full-scale invasion of Cabernet and Merlot has not followed: Portugal has excellent grapes of her own, and the will to use them.

With entry into the EC has come a rush of what Brussels calls VQPRDs, Paris VDQS areas and Lisbon IPRs (Indicacães de Proveniência Regulamentada). The map shows the resulting rash of new names. While some of the new-hatched regions have authentic character and important potential others are likely to be mere straws in the wind. Time will tell.

The previously neglected regions whose life may be changed by their new status start in the north with Trás os Montes; remote uplands most beautiful at their golden harvest time. Its IPRs, Chaves, Valpaços and Planalto-Mirandês, offer quantities of strong coop-made wines, but are also a major source of rosé long tapped by the Sogrape company for Mateus. Sogrape also uses the name Planalto for a dry white.

The mountainous Beiras, Alta and Baixa (Upper and Lower) are the border regions with Spain south of the Douro. (Beira-Littoral to the west contains Bairrada.) None of their six IPRs (see map) is a name to conjure with, although major merchants have drawn steadily on their vineyards in the past for their house blends.

The coastal region south of the Beira-Littoral is the Estremadura, informally known as Oeste, 'the west'. There are six IPRs here too; none of note. If Torres Vedras is a familiar name it is on account of Wellington's thin red line, not its thin red wine. Alenquer is perhaps the most promising IPR; its Quinta das Pancas especially. The mystery is that in the 18th century the mighty monastery of Alcobaça was the richest of all Cistercian houses, and the 'greatest temple of gluttony in Europe': strange that the Cistercians (who planted the Clos de Vougeot and the Steinberg) left the wines of Oeste unimproved.

The valley of the Tagus (Tejo) is the highly productive Ribatejo, of whose six IPRs Cartaxo and Almeirim are the most promising. The Ribatejo Garrafeiras of Carvalho, Ribeiro and Ferreira have been some of Lisbon's favourite drinking for a century; further back the name Charneco found on silver labels refers to this area.

Today all eyes are turned south of the Tagus, to the Alentejo, mapped on page 215.

In keeping with Portugal's reputation as a maritime nation she brings vines as near as they ever get to the sea. At Colares they grow on the sandy beach, immune to phylloxera. They hug the ground, their old limbs like driftwood, bearing small bunches of intensely blue grapes: the Ramisco. Its wine is black and tannic and needs as long to mature as claret of 100 years ago. It was traditionally esteemed Portugal's best red table wine, but now little is made, at least in the sandy soil where it is best, and less is exported.

Less still remains of Carcavelos, whose luscious amber wine became famous during the Peninsula war. Estoril has swamped all but one remaining vineyard, the Quinta dos Pesos at Caparede. There are more profitable investments today around Lisbon than vineyards.

Of Lisbon's local wines Bucelas (some labels still use the old spelling 'Bucellas') is probably in best shape – pleasant, white and dry, slightly oaky, but scarcely memorable. Much more important today are the vineyards of the Arrabida peninsula across the Tagus, where the house of Fonseca looks forward rather than back. Fonseca's Moscatel de Setúbal is one of the world's very best sweet Muscats. It is fortified, although much less than port, and the grape skins, which in Muscats contain much of the aromatic elements, are steeped in it to intensify the scent. Unlike Muscats from the south of France, Setúbal improves with age – even with great age. It can be exquisite young or old.

The village of Azenhas do Mar, north of Colares. Tucked into the cliff, fishermen's cottages shelter from the Atlantic's blasts.

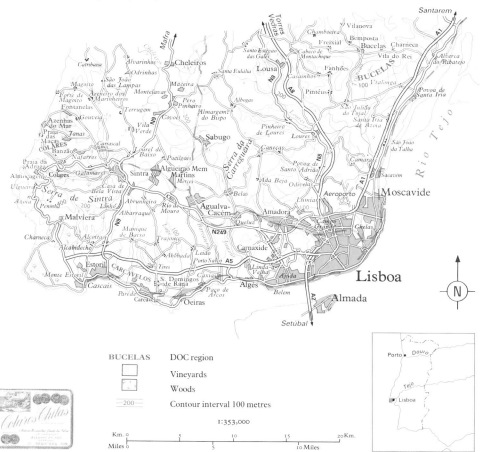

| BUCELAS | DOC region |
| Vineyards |
| Woods |
| 200 | Contour interval 100 metres |

1:353,000

Bairrada

The region of Bairrada was added in 1979 to the then short list of Portugal's *selos de origem*. It is a rural district lying astride the highway that links Lisbon and Oporto, filling most of the area between the granite hills of Dão and the Atlantic coast. Its low hills are of heavy lime-rich clay which gives body and typical Portuguese bite to its overwhelmingly (85%) red wine. A moderate climate, prone to sea mists, helps its balance and acidity.

Most of the credit for quality, though, must go to the local red grape, the Baga. On its own it is too tannic for non-Portuguese tastes, but wines blended with a high proportion of Baga have deep fruitiness, splendid colour and vigour, and in ageing will resist oxidation for years. An active research station and modern wineries have experimented with the ideal blend of grapes, and recent vintages from such merchant-makers as Caves Aliança, São João, Barracão and Messias are heartily to be recommended.

The region's white grape, Maria Gomes, is fairly neutral, but leavened and made aromatic by the obscure but excellent Bical. Most is now made sparkling, although old bottles of the still wine can have considerable quality.

The potential of the region for truly remarkable table wines has one eccentric and wonderful witness. Right on its southeast boundary, on the slopes of the hill of Buçaco, where Wellington first turned back Napoleon's Peninsular force in a famous battle, the Buçaco Palace Hotel makes and matures red and white wines in a wholly traditional way. The grapes are trodden in stone *lagars* and the wine aged for years in barrel in the Palace cellars. Both reds and whites on the hotel wine list go back for decades. The whites seem to be at their best at about 20 years and the reds, velvety but intense, at about 30.

Above: the magnificent Palace Hotel at Buçaco overlooks the Bairrada region from its wooded ridge to the east. Its cellars (*right*) age some of Portugal's very best and truly traditional wines. Both red and white are kept for years in barrel and in bottle for decades.

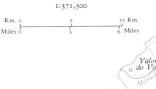

- ● Barrô   Leading wine town
- Boundary of DOC
- — 200 —   Contour interval 100 metres

1:371,500

THE LANGUAGE OF THE LABEL

Vinha Vineyard
Quinta Farm, estate
Colheita Vintage
Denominação de Origem Controlada (DOC)
Established demarcated area. Cf. Appellation Contrôlée
Indicação de Proveniência Regulamentada (IPR)
Demarcated legal area
Reserva Better quality wine
Garrafeira 'Private cellar' – ie best quality
Vinho verde 'Green' wine from the Minho (page 211)
Vinho de mesa Table wine
Vinho de consumo Everyday wine
Maduro Old or matured
Engarrafado na origem Estate-bottled
Branco White
Tinto Red
Rosado Rosé
Clarete Light red or dark rosé
Séco Dry
Doce, Adamado Sweet
Espmante Sparkling
Adega The premises of a wine company; cellar
Aguardente Brandy
Armazem Cellar

Top is the label of the Buçaco Palace Hotel. There are few producers in the region, but all are sound or better.

Minho and Dão

Portugal's most distinctive contribution to the world's table is the speciality of her northern counties: their vinho verde. The name green wine describes its fresh, slightly under-ripe style, not its colour, which is red (three-quarters of it) or almost water-white.

Partly as a result of land shortage in this most densely populated part of the country, vines in the Minho are grown up trees and on pergolas around the little fields. In late summer the sight of the grape-bearing garlands along every road gives almost pagan pleasure. High off the ground, the grapes stay cool and keep their fresh acidity.

The crop is picked early and fermented briefly – the object being wine with a low alcohol content and a decided tartness. Secondary fermentation is encouraged to convert excess malic acid to lactic. The red wines tend to be cloudy, but both they and the whites (which foreigners prefer) have a scintillating little bubble about them which is marvellously refreshing. It is all too easy to gulp them like beer on a hot day. To a romantic they are best from the barrel in the spirited little taverns of Monção and Barcelos and Penafiel. Export versions tend, with some exceptions, to be sweetened and carbonated; still good, but less magically fresh and bracing.

Far better wine is made from the white Alvarinho grape around Monção. Alvarinho (Spanish: Albariño, see page 196) will keep for several years in bottle, developing a freesia-like scent and losing its bubbles. Almost certainly it is Portugal's best white wine.

Basto and Amarante are considered the next best areas of the Minho, followed by the more productive Braga and Penafiel. Lima makes a slightly stronger and deeper-coloured red wine than the others. But officially it is all vinho verde, and wines from the different regions are often blended together.

The name of Dão has long been associated with solid reds, reliable but tannic and dull, the result of a ridiculous statute that sent all its grapes to heavy-handed cooperatives. Happily the European Community has disallowed this monopoly; the result is some far juicier and friendlier wines.

Dão is granite hill country, where bare rocks show through the sandy soil. Vineyards are only a subplot in the landscape, cropping up here and there in clearings in the sweet-scented pine forests. Its capital, Viseu, is one of Portugal's prettiest towns.

There are both red and white Dãos. While they are young the whites can be firm and fragrant. The red as it is usually sold – a blend from a big merchant perhaps four years old – is a clean, tannic but scarcely interesting wine. Good Reservas in the traditional style (such as Porta dos Cavaleiros) can take 15 years to blossom, and even then be fairly earthy.

A brighter future is promised by such enterprises as the huge new Quinta dos Carvalhais of the Sogrape company – the brand is Grão Vasco – by Fonseca's Quinta da Insua and the Conde de Santar's estate.

Fizzy and tart vinho verde comes in infinite variety. Good Dãos, the complete contrast, smooth and solid, are made by relatively few producers.

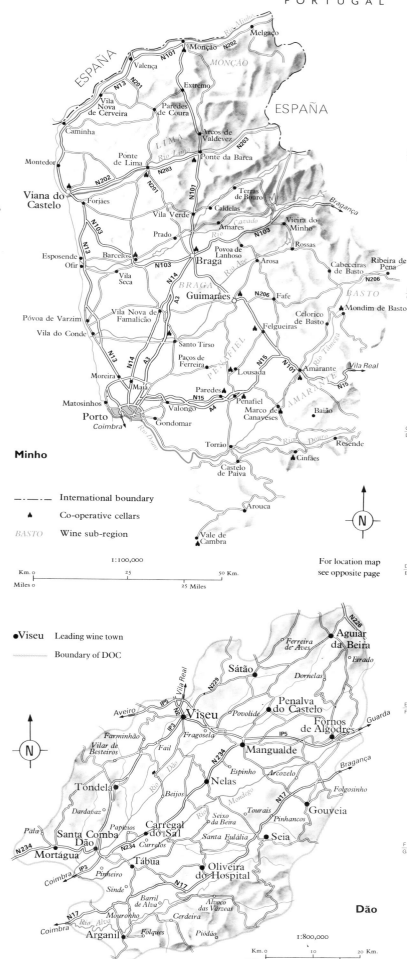

Minho

—·—·— International boundary

▲ Co-operative cellars

BASTO Wine sub-region

1:100,000

Km. 0   25   50 Km.

Miles 0   25 Miles

For location map see opposite page

● Viseu Leading wine town

Boundary of DOC

Dão

1:800,000

Km. 0   10   20 Km.

Miles 0   10 Miles

The Alto Douro

Of all the places where men have planted vineyards, the upper Douro is the most improbable. To begin with there was not even soil: only 60° slopes of slate and granite, flaking and unstable, baked in a 100° sun. It was a land of utter desolation.

The vine, however, is the one useful plant that is not quite deterred by these conditions. The Mediterranean-type climate suits it. What was needed was simply the engineering feat of putting soil on the Douro slopes and keeping it there. Which meant building walls along the mountainsides, thousands of them, like contour lines, to hold up patches of ground (one could hardly call it soil) where vines could be planted.

Once the ground was stabilized and rainwater no longer ran straight off, it began to form soil, and plants began to add organic matter. Now olives, oranges, cork oaks and pines flourish. But before this could happen men had to blast and chip away at the slate, piling chunks of it into towering terrace walls.

Steps are the nightmare of workers in these vineyards. Every grape must be carried off the hill on the back of a man. New vineyards today are contoured with dynamite and bulldozers as far as possible to eliminate steps and walls.

The Douro reaches Portugal from Spain in a wilderness which is still inaccessible except by mule or canoe. It has carved a titanic canyon through the layered rock uplands. This is the port country. The 4,600-feet (1,400-metre) Serra do Marão to the west prevents the Atlantic rainclouds of summer from refreshing it. Often there is no summer rain at all.

Many of the original terraces dating from the 17th century survive in the mountains above Regua, in the original port-wine zone, given its first official limits (the first such limits ever given to any wine) in 1756. Today this area remains the biggest producer, but the search for quality has led further and further upriver. The modern zone is 20 times the size it was in the 18th century, and all the best part is comparatively new. Below the tributary Corgo the wine is reckoned definitely inferior. The best vineyards of all today are those around and above Pinhão, including the tributary valleys of

The vineyards of the upper Douro are some of the most spectacular on earth. The view here, from the Quinta do Bom Retiro, looks down the valley of the tributary Rio Torto towards Piñhao, the little capital of the remote region. These are modern, rebuilt vineyards with their old terracing removed for easier labour.

	District boundary
	Parish boundary
QTA. DA FOZ	Quinta
	Vineyards
	Woods
500	Contour interval 100 metres

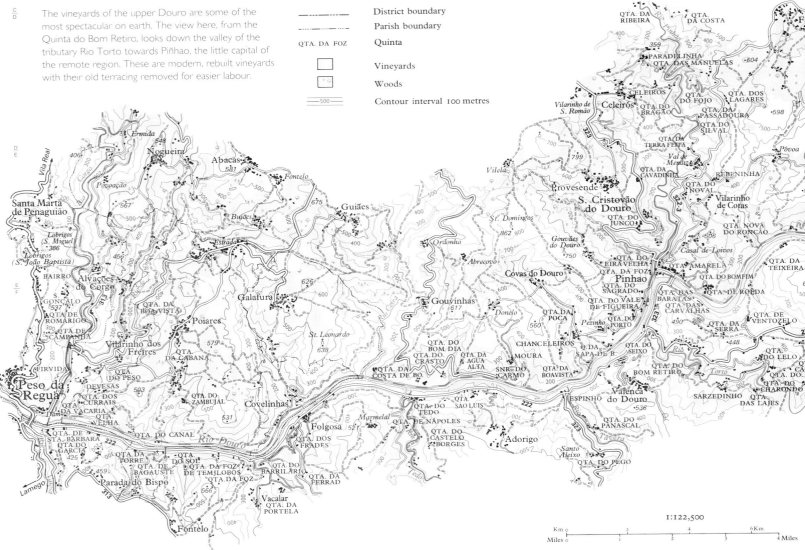

1:122,500

the Távora, Torto, Pinhão and Tua rivers.

Vintage time anywhere is the climax of the year, but on the Douro, perhaps because of the hardship of life, it is almost Dionysiac. There is an antique frenzy about the ritual, the songs, the music of drum and pipe, the long nights of treading by the light of hurricane lamps while the women and girls dance together.

The famous shipping firms have their own quintas up in the hills, where they go to supervise the vintage. They are rambling white houses, vine-arboured, tile-floored and cool in a world of dust and glare. Most of the famous quintas are shown on the map on these pages. Quinta names, however, rarely appear as wine names. Only half a dozen of the whole valley, of which the most famous is Quinta do Noval above Pinhão, sell their wine unblended. The names of Taylor's Vargellas, Croft's Roeda and Graham's Malvedos are used for vintage wines in years not quite fine enough to be generally 'declared'. For the essence of port is blending, and the main source of grapes and wine is not big estates but a multitude of small farmers.

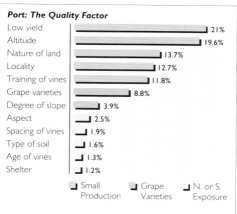

Port: The Quality Factor

Low yield	21%
Altitude	19.6%
Nature of land	13.7%
Locality	12.7%
Training of vines	11.8%
Grape varieties	8.8%
Degree of slope	3.9%
Aspect	2.5%
Spacing of vines	1.9%
Type of soil	1.6%
Age of vines	1.3%
Shelter	1.2%

☐ Small Production   ☐ Grape Varieties   ☐ N. or S. Exposure

Above: The port vineyards are graded into six classes. The quantity of wine they can sell as port is regulated by their standing. The factors by which they are judged are the same as in Burgundy, say, or Germany, but the emphasis is different. The diagram shows how for port small production – as little as 600 litres per 1,000 vines – and the altitude of the vineyard – it should be below 1,500 feet (300 metres) are considered of primary importance in the marking.

Above: the old way of bringing new port wine down the Douro on square-sailed boats ended in the 1960s when the river was dammed and its perilous rapids silenced. The antique *barcos rubelos*, said to derive from ancient Phoenician vessels, still bring colour to the scene, here by the Quinta da Foz at Pinhão.

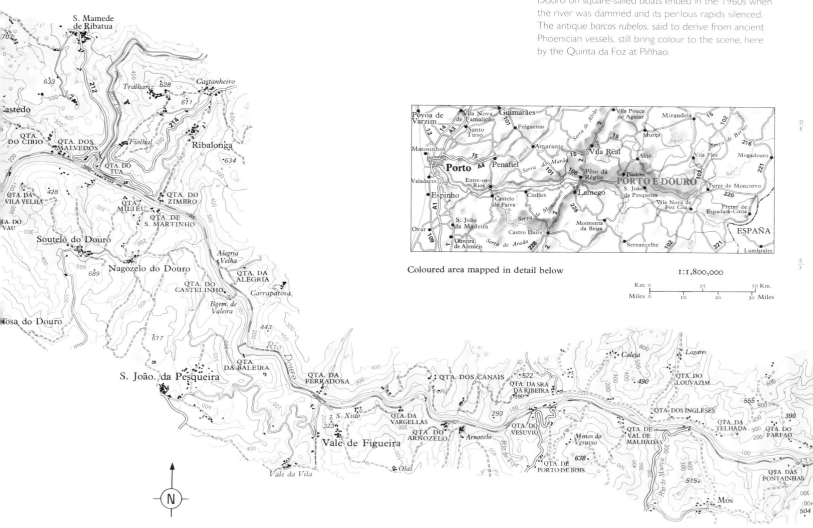

Coloured area mapped in detail below

1:1,800,000

The Port Lodges

Port is made by running off partially fermented red wine, while it still contains at least half its grape sugar, into a barrel a quarter full of brandy. The brandy stops the fermentation so that the resulting mixture is both strong and sweet.

The wine also needs the pigmentation of the grape skins to colour it, and their tannin to preserve it. In normal wines these are extracted during the course of fermentation. But since with port the fermentation is unnaturally short, pigmentation and tannin have to be procured some other way – which traditionally in the Douro means by treading.

Treading is a means of macerating the grape skins in their juice so as to extract all their essences. The naked foot is the perfect tool for this, being warm and doing no damage to the pips, which would make the juice bitter if they were crushed. Rhythmically stamping thigh-deep in the mixture of juice and skins in a broad stone trough (a *lagar*) is the traditional treatment for giving port its colour, its grapiness, and its ability to last and improve for many years.

For most port a mechanical substitute for treading has now been introduced. It consists of a closed fermenting vat in which the carbon dioxide pressure makes the juice circulate up a pipe from the bottom to the top, where it pours over the 'cap' of floating skins. In several days this continuous churning has the same effect as the more expensive man-hours in the *lagar*. But there are still shippers who feel that treading is best, and still many quintas where it goes on, particularly in the best area, above the Corgo (the area mapped on the following pages).

Port that is kept up the Douro is rare. Virtually all port is taken down the river soon after it is made, to complete its processing in the port suburb of Oporto, Vila Nova de Gaia.

The journey downriver used to be made in high-prowed sailing boats like Viking long ships, which had to be controlled through the rapids by eight men working long sweeps in the bows. Now the port is taken by truck.

The shippers' warehouses in Vila Nova de Gaia are known as lodges. They have much in common with the sherry bodegas. In the lodges the port is kept in pipes, 522-litre barrels, for anything from two to 50 years.

Perhaps three years out of ten conditions are near perfect for port-making. The best wine of these years needs no blending; nothing can be done to improve it except wait. It is bottled at two years like claret, labelled simply with its shipper's name and the date. This is vintage port, and there is never enough of it. Eventually, perhaps after 20 years, it will have a fatness and fragrance, richness and delicacy, which is incomparable.

A great vintage port is incontestably among the world's very best wines. Most other port, from near-vintage standard to merely moderate, goes through a blending process, to emerge as a branded wine of a given character. This wine, aged in wood, matures in a different way, more rapidly, and loses some of its sugar in the process. A very old wood port is comparatively pale

The port lodges of Vila Nova de Gaia

1 Fonseca
2 Graham
3 Diez Hermanos
4 Ferreira
5 Companhia Velha
6 Gran Cruz
7 Niepoort
8 Martinez Gassiot
9 Cockburn
10 Barros
11 Instituto do Vinho e da Vinha
12 Dow
13 Burmester
14 Mackenzie
15 Ramos Pinto
16 Sandeman
17 Smith Woodhouse
18 Rozés
19 Kopke
20 Wiese & Krohn
21 Companhia do Comércio de Vinho do Porto (CCVP)
22 Rainha Santa
23 Croft
24 Taylor
25 Offley Forrester
26 Warre
27 Noval
28 Borges
29 Calem
30 Churchill
31 Osborne
32 Delaforce

Above: Vila Nova de Gaia is composed almost entirely of shippers' warehouses, or lodges, where port is matured.

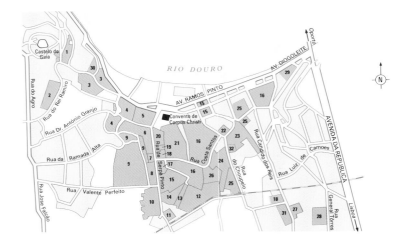

THE LANGUAGE OF THE LABEL

Vintage The wine of a single exceptional year bottled early for laying down

Late-bottled vintage Similar wine bottled when mature, lighter than vintage

Crusted Good but not vintage port bottled early for laying down

Vintage character A superior ruby, aged 4–5 years in wood

Tawny Port kept many years in wood until it fades to a tawny colour; smooth and lighter than any of the foregoing. Also pale young port (at a much lower price)

Ruby Port aged 2–3 years in wood; darker and fruitier

White port From white grapes; often much drier than red and sold as an apéritif

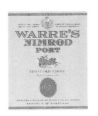

Left: traditionally, vintage port bottles had no labels, only a stencilled name in white paint. More durable than paper, stencilling is still used by the shipper Niepoort (see the plan of Vila Nova de Gaia above, left). Many of the best names in the port trade are British; a reminder that it was the British taste for sweet wine that built up the industry in the 18th century. Today France is the biggest customer.

Alentejo

Fishing boats evoke the old harbour life on the river between Oporto and Vila Nova de Gaia. Eiffel's great iron bridge spans the Douro with, on the left, the dominating bishop's palace and cathedral.

In comparison with the tapestry of vines that seems to smother northern Portugal, the Alentejo, the southern third of the country, is almost vineless. Its wide sun-browned spaces are dotted with silver olives and dark cork oaks (it is the world's most important source of cork), browsed bare by sheep, but only occasionally green with low vines. Farms are rare. Ranch-like estates, unknown in the densely peopled north, were the cause of violent trouble here in the revolutionary 1970s. Landowners were dispossessed and crops and vines went to wrack and ruin.

It was a well-kept secret that wine from the Alentejo, primitive as it might be, had potential, not just for strength but for profound fruitiness. Some wines are still fermented the (very) ancient way in earthenware amphoras, which have a disconcerting tendency to burst at the height of fermentation. Yet even in Porto the shippers' Factory House sometimes bought a barrel from an Alentejo estate. Thirty years (in bottle) later the wine was fleshy, fragrant; almost fine. A 1979 red from the Mouchão estate of the long-resident (British) Reynolds family was splendid, though still very tannic, in

1993 – and this despite the 'troubles'.

The Alentejo has now been given no fewer than eight IPRs, six of them based on cooperatives. More significantly, some very sophisticated international investors have targeted the region. The range of permitted grapes is wide, but the great majority of the production, rather surprisingly, is white, largely from the Roupeiro grape, which stands up well to the heat (but still needs drinking young).

The best of many red varieties are the Periquita (made famous by Fonseca) and the Aragonez (alias, in Spain, the Tempranillo). Curiously, though, the most ambitious estates are prepared to dispense with the IPR label in order to grow Alicante Bouschet, a poor grape in France but seemingly valuable under Alentejo skies. So far the Cabernet has almost been kept at bay.

Fame came to the Alentejo in 1991 when the Domaines Rothschild bought the stately Quinta do Carmo at Estremoz in the Borba region. Its reds, 50% Alicante Bouschet, are already impressive. Another half-dozen quality-oriented quintas are mapped. Among the large cooperatives Borba is the best equipped.

('Tawny' is the term) and dry, but particularly smooth. The best tawnies, at 20 years or so, cost as much as vintage ports; many people prefer their mellowness and moderated sweetness to the full, fat and flowery flavour which vintage port can keep for decades.

Run-of-the-mill 'wood' ports are not kept for nearly so long, nor would such age find any great qualities in them to reveal. They taste best while they are still fruity with youth, and often fiery, too, with perhaps five years as the average age of a blend. France is the great market for these wines. They used to be the staple winter drink in British pubs, where they were kept in a barrel in the bar.

Vintage port has disadvantages. It needs keeping for a very long time. And it needs handling with great care. As the making of the wine does not reach its end until after bottling, the sediment forms a 'crust' on the side of the bottle: a thin, delicate, dirty-looking veil. If the bottle is moved, other than very gingerly, the crust will break and mix with the wine, so that it has to be filtered out again. In any case the wine must be decanted from its bottle before it is served. Which is enough to discourage many people from buying it.

As a compromise between vintage and wood port, shippers now also offer Late-bottled Vintage wines – port from good years (although not always the very best) kept unblended but in barrel instead of being bottled at two years. After eight years or so it has rid itself of its crust and matured as far as it would in twice as long in bottle. In many ways it is the modern man's vintage port, being speeded up and cleaned in this way. Yet there are those who argue that vintage port is not a modern man's drink, and that if you are going to indulge in an old-fashioned pastime you might as well do it properly.

The Alentejo has no history of quality wine production but high aspirations and influential investors.

International boundary
District boundary
ÉVORA   IPR
■ FINAGRA   Leading producer
—200—   Contour interval 200 metres

1:1,000,000

Km. 0   10   20   30   40 Km.
Miles 0   10   20 Miles

Madeira

Above: the breakneck slopes of Madeira are terraced for vineyards from near sea level up to heights of almost 3,250 ft (990 m). Irrigation channels from the mountain peaks keep the fields green and fertile.

The cluster of volcanic islands 400 miles (640 kilometres) off the coast of Morocco, which the ancients knew as the Enchanted Isles, are known to us as Madeira, Porto Santo and the Desertas. Madeira is the largest island of the little archipelago and one of the prettiest in the world, as steep as an iceberg and as green as a glade.

The story goes that when the Portuguese landed on the island (in 1420, at Machico in the east) they set fire to the dense woods that gave the island its name. The fire burned for years, leaving the already fertile soil enriched with the ashes of an entire forest.

Certainly it is fertile today. From the water's edge to over halfway up the 6,000-foot (1,800-metre) peak it is steadily terraced to make room for patches of vine, sugarcane, banana and little flower gardens. As in northern Portugal the vines are grown above head height in arbours, making room for yet more cultivation beneath. Hundreds of miles of little irrigation canals distribute water from the peaks to the crops.

Wine has been the principal product of the islands for 400 years. Madeira, though, was not the first of the islands the Portuguese planted. From the outset the settlers saw them as an extension of the sweet-wine vineyards of the Mediterranean. The Ottoman Empire was then enveloping the sources of Malmsey: Crete and the Aegean Islands. Porto Santo, low, sandy and with a North African climate, looked much more promising than tall green rainy Madeira.

The settlers planted the Malmsey grape, the Malvasia, concentrated its sugar in the sun (in Cyprus Commandaria is still made this way), and found a ready market for their sweet wines – even at the court of François I of France.

The planting of Madeira itself – with both vines and sugarcane – came later. Settlement of the American colonies meant increased traffic and trade and the bigger island, with its port of Funchal, became the victualling place for west-bound ships. Conditions here are very different from those on Porto Santo; rain is rarely far off; Malvasia, Verdelho and the other vines they introduced often struggled to ripen. The marriage of sugar with acid and astringent wines was an obvious expedient.

The sweet-and-sour result was more than adequate as ballast on sailing ships, and an effective anti-scurvy protection into the bargain. It was travelling as ballast that made madeira. 'A bucket or two' of brandy (or cane spirit) fortified it for its long sea voyages. One crossing of the equator would finish off any normal wine, but it was found to mellow madeira wonderfully – and a double equator crossing even more so. In the 18th century it became the favourite wine of the American colonies. Savannah, Georgia, was famous for its madeira merchants and connoisseurs. Bottles of 18th-century madeira, labelled with the names of the ship that brought them, are still kept, not in cellars but in sunlit rooms – and the wine survives.

Instead of long sea voyages, madeira today is subjected to ordeal by fire. A similar effect to the

Madeira today must be strictly 'varietal' to carry its traditional (from sweetest to driest) names of Malmsey, Bual, Verdelho and Sercial. Henriques & Henriques is the largest independent shipper today; the other famous names are grouped in the Madeira Wine Association.

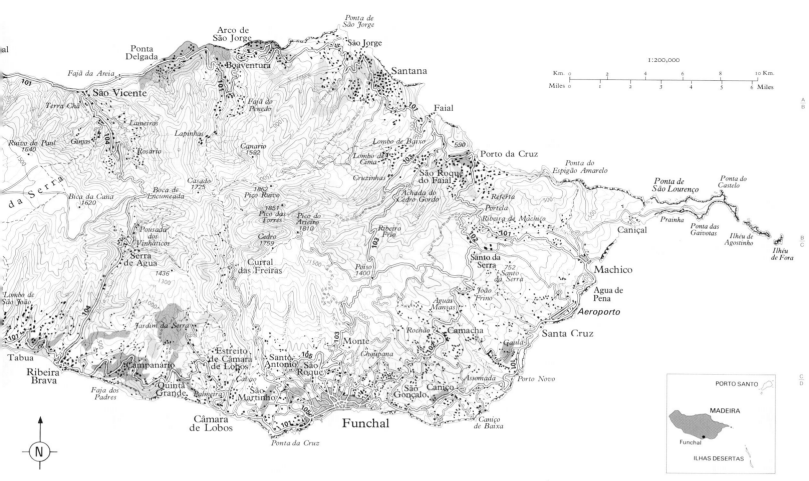

PORTO SANTO

MADEIRA

Funchal

ILHAS DESERTAS

tropical heat is produced by warming the wine over a long period to 120°F (45°C). It stays in hot stores (*estufas*) for three or four months. (More moderate temperatures for longer periods are better; best is no artificial heat at all, but many years in a sun-baked loft.) When it comes out it has the faintly caramel tang by which all madeiras can be recognized. Too much of a burnt sugar taste means that the *estufa* was too hot.

Today Madeira shippers blend their wine into consistent brands. The old practice was a solera system like that used for sherry, now disallowed by the EC for wines older than ten years. Some older bottled solera wines are very fine, if you can find them, but the very highest quality of madeira, as of port, has traditionally been the reserve wine of a single vintage – and in the case of madeira, of a single grape variety.

The double disaster of oidium in the 1850s and phylloxera in the 1870s, then the Russian Revolution and American Prohibition, almost put an end to madeira, caused the closure or amalgamation of many merchant firms, and for a long while interrupted the flow of quality wine. The vineyards were largely turned over to American hybrids (Black Spanish, the chief one, is known in Madeira as Jacquet), while the classic varieties became rarities. The most planted *vinifera* vine was the Tinta Mole, at best a fair substitute for the vines that made the island's reputation.

Bottles of the pre-phylloxera years still survive, none the worse for being over 100 years old. Vintage madeira, like Tokay, is a wine that

age seems unable to exhaust or diminish. The older it is the better it is. Centenarian wines can combine intensity with freshness, depth with pungency like no other product of the grape.

The practice until Portugal joined the EC was to cite the classic vine varieties of Madeira on labels whether the wine was really made from them or (more likely) not. There are four, corresponding approximately to degrees of sweetness, although the actual sweetness is controlled not by the grape but by the addition of *vinho surdo* or 'deaf wine': grape juice prevented from fermenting at all by adding brandy. Less 'classic' madeiras are also made port-style by stopping the fermentation with spirit.

The sweetest of the four, and often the best, is Malmsey or Malvasia: dark brown wine, very fragrant and rich, soft textured and almost fatty, but with the tang of sharpness that all madeiras have – the perfect wine to end a rich dinner on an uplifting note.

Bual madeira is lighter and slightly less sweet than Malmsey – but still definitely a dessert wine. A smoky note steals in to modify its richness. Alas the Bual is a rare vine today.

Verdelho (the most planted white grape on the island) is made less sweet and softer than Bual. The faint honey and distinct smoke of its flavour make it good before or after meals.

Sercial, the driest wine of Madeira, is grown in the highest vineyards and harvested late. Sercial wine is light, fragrant, distinctly sharp – unpleasantly astringent young, in fact – but

marvellously appetizing old. It is more substantial than a fino sherry, but still a perfect apéritif.

Under new regulations the four varietal names are permitted only if the wine is made from 85% of the variety in question (even the *vinho surdo* is included). All other wines must simply be labelled as rich, sweet, medium or dry, corresponding roughly to the four varieties.

Laws relating to vintage madeira have also been updated. To be labelled Vintage, the wine must be from a single year, of a single variety, aged in cask for at least 20 years. In practice the very finest wines may spend a century in the barrel, or decanted into glass demijohns, before being bottled. In bottle they develop at a snail's pace.

After Prohibition spelled the collapse of trade with the USA in the 1920s the island's main market was France, which bought only cheap wines for *sauce madère*. The majority of shippers had to pool their resources to survive. Twenty-seven companies formed the Madeira Wine Association, which now (as the Madeira Wine Company) sells its best wines under the historic names of Blandy and Cossart. Leacock and Miles are labels used for cheaper blends. Henriques & Henriques (the largest independent), Barbeito (now Japanese controlled) and H M Borges are the remaining shippers of bottled wines.

The EC, however, has stirred the industry with its new rules. More activity in the 1990s, including investment by the redoubtable Symington family from the world of port, promises a much brighter future.

Switzerland

Switzerland is an intensely wine-conscious, insatiably wine-importing country. As a producer she is small but impeccable, with a mere 35,000 acres (14,000 hectares), divided into countless tiny properties. The Swiss are loyal to their own local wines, without pretending that better things do not happen in France. They are among the world's biggest importers of burgundy; Beaujolais is almost their national drink. As for exporting, it hardly happens at all.

The Swiss are efficient, if sometimes unromantic, winemakers. By scrupulous care of their vines, making use of fertilizers and irrigation, they achieve yields twice as high as those in French appellation areas. They take chaptalization for granted: there are no German-style indications of natural unsugared wine. By managing to produce such big quantities, assisted by sugar when necessary, they make growing grapes pay in difficult terrain with a high standard of living.

At the same time the long near-monopoly of white wine in Switzerland has been broken. Red wine is in fashion, a development of the last 30 years – and now accounts for nearly a quarter of the total. There has been an enormous increase in the planting of Pinot Noir and Gamay in the most important areas: Vaud, Valais and Geneva. Italian Switzerland, the Ticino, has concentrated on the Merlot, introduced from Bordeaux in 1907. The red-wine fashion has also saved the formerly dwindling vineyards of German Switzerland, which have long specialized in the Blauburgunder (Pinot Noir).

Almost every canton in Switzerland makes a little wine. Two areas apart from the Rhône Valley and Lake Geneva have fair-sized industries: the Ticino and Neuchâtel.

The Ticino has not long been an exporter of wine and with only 2,000 acres (800 hectares) has little to spare. The local tradition is a peasant one. It was devastated by phylloxera and oidium, and 50 or 60 years ago hardship was still sending emigrants to America. (The famous Italian Swiss Colony vineyards near Santa Rosa in California are one result.) America sent vines in return: non-*vinifera* vines and hybrids are still grown in odd corners of the Ticino. The typical local red wine, called Nostrano, is hard to find these days. But the Merlot grows lustily, as it does in northeast Italy, making wine which is aromatic, soft-textured and can be delicious. Better Ticino Merlots, attaining 12% alcohol (normally about one-third of the total) use the name 'Viti' to distinguish themselves from the rest.

Neuchâtel is equally known for its red and its white wine – although the white is three-quarters of the crop. Without doubt the simplicity of the whole area (it is just 1,500 acres, 600 hectares) calling its wine by the famous name of its capital has been a help. The north shore of the lake is temperate, except for cold winds from the Jura which often hamper flowering and reduce the crop. The Pinot Noir grows well on limestone here (there is no Gamay), giving a pale

light wine but with character and definition, most delicious rosé, sold as *oeil de perdrix*. The village of Cortaillod, south of Neuchâtel, is said to make the best.

White Neuchâtel is made from the Chasselas, like Fendant wine from Valais. It is lighter than Fendant and encouraged to fizz faintly by being bottled *sur lie* – without being separated from its yeasty sediment. In some cases the process is carried further to making fully sparkling wines. There is also a litle Müller-Thurgau and even Chardonnay.

Lake Bienne (the Bielersee) just to the north-

east of Neuchâtel has similar wines which fetch high prices, under the alternative names of 'Schafiser' or 'Twanner', in the cantonal capital of Bern. Dearest of all is Inselwein, from the tiny Peter Island.

The wines of other cantons do not travel much. The Bundner Herrschaft, a little district on the borders of Austria and Liechtenstein, has the distinction of being the first wine region of the infant Rhine. It grows Blauburgunder (or 'Clevner') almost exclusively; the best are dear and can be excellent, benefiting from the warm autumn wind, the foehn. The Herrschaft

Swiss wines are known by regional names relating to grape varieties and qualities as well as to geographical origin. The following may be seen on labels:

Amigne: a local Valais white grape giving full golden dessert wine.
Arvine or Petite Arvine: Valais grape for full-bodied, tasty, often tart wine.
Blauburgunder: Pinot Noir from a German-speaking canton.
Chasselas: the main grape variety in Switzerland. It is not usually identified on the label.
Clevner: another name for Blauburgunder.
Dôle: red Valais wine of Pinot Noir and Gamay, of tested quality.
Ermitage: white Marsanne vines from the French Rhône grown in the Valais: rich, concentrated, heavy wine, usually dry.
Fendant: white Valais wine of Chasselas; Switzerland's most famous.
Gamay: the Beaujolais grape, largely grown around Geneva, in La Côte and the Valais.
Goron: red Valais wine; Dôle that failed the test.
Humagne: rare red or white Valais varieties: unrelated but both strong characters.

Johannisberg: Sylvaner from the Valais.
Malvoisie: heavy white Pinot Gris from the Valais; often made sweet from dried ('*flétri*') grapes.
Merlot: red Bordeaux grape grown for the best Ticino wine.
Nostrano: ordinary Ticino wine from a variety of French and Italian grapes.
Oeil de Perdrix: term used for light rosé from Pinot Noir, particularly in Neuchâtel.
Perlan: white Geneva (or Mandement) wine from Chasselas.
Rèze: rare grape traditionally used for 'glacier' wine.
Riesling-Sylvaner: Müller-Thurgau wine, common in eastern Switzerland.
Salvagnin: red Vaud wine of tested quality; the equivalent of Dôle from the Valais.
Schafiser or **Twanner**: the light but expensive wine of Lake Bienne in the canton of Bern, red or white.
Viti: red Merlot wine of a certain standard from Ticino.

Any Swiss wine which is not completely dry must by law carry the words '*légèrement doux*' or '*avec sucre residuel*'.

also grows the otherwise-unknown Completer, which is picked in November to give a sort of Beerenauslese – although the early-ripening Müller-Thurgau is the commonest white grape in the German-speaking cantons.

Zürich, Schaffhausen, St Gallen, Basel and even Luzern maintain diminutive wine industries based predominantly on the Blauburgunder grape. All agree that their wine is expensive, and most that it has charm and delicacy. Certainly the evidence disappears promptly enough: none is available for export – even as far as Geneva.

Left: houses compete for space with the terraces of vines on the steep north shore of Lake Geneva. Reflected sun from the lake helps to ripen the golden Chasselas to make delicate but sometimes excellently lively wine.
Right: German- and Italian-speaking Switzerland relies for its red wines respectively on the Burgundian Pinot Noir and the Merlot of Bordeaux. The best Ticino Merlot carries the legend 'Viti'. Pinot Noir and Gamay are meanwhile increasingly being planted around Geneva.

- - - - - International boundary

Gamay Chief wine or grape names

[ ] Principally white wines

[ ] Red wines

[ ] White and red wines

VAUD Wine region

LAVAUX Wine sub-region

[ ] Land above 2000 metres

[220] Area mapped at larger scale on page shown

1:1,675,000

Valais and Vaud

The steep sides of the Valais, the valley which the young River Rhône has carved through the Alps, are followed by gentler slopes in the Vaud, where it broadens into Lake Geneva (Lac Léman). An almost continuous band of vines hugs the river's sunny north bank all the way.

In the higher valley peculiarly alpine conditions, brilliant sun and summer drought, and by the lake the mildness brought about by a great body of water both favour the vine in different ways. The Valais and the Vaud are Switzerland's biggest and best vineyards. The production of Geneva included, the Rhône Valley gives more than three-quarters of the national total.

Almost three-quarters of this is white wine. The proportion used to be even higher, but growers have been planting the Pinot Noir on a large scale and the Gamay of Beaujolais on an even larger one still.

The great grape of both the Valais and the Vaud is the Chasselas. In the Valais it is called Fendant. It is not reckoned a fine-wine grape in France, but in Switzerland its very neutrality can combine with different *terroirs* to produce strikingly distinct wines.

In the Valais the centre of Fendant-growing is Sion and the villages just to the west, Conthey, Vétroz and Ardon. There is little rain (Sierre is the driest place in Switzerland) and endless sun. If the vines escape spring frosts they make a powerful wine with as much as 13% alcohol. Irrigation, traditionally done by wooden channels called *bisses* coming break-neck down the mountainside, is essential.

The average grower's holding is a mere half-acre: 20,000 share the 12,000-acre (4,800-hectare) total – so nearly all are part-timers. Some 60% of the wine is made by one concern: the Union des Négociants en Vin du Valais; 30% by the Provins cooperative – leaving only 10% to be made by individuals.

Of these the 50-acre (20-hectare) Domaine du Mont d'Or has the best site of all: a steep south slope protected at the foot by an outlying hill. The Sylvaner ('Johannisberg') excels itself here, shrivelling on the vine to make splendid rich wines. Fendant puts on flesh and stiffens its sinews. These are the mainstay white grapes, but the Valais has a unique repertoire of alpine specialities that are all worth exploring – if you can find them. Notes on their wines appear on page 218.

Valais reds of blended Pinot Noir (minimum 51%) and Gamay must reach a statutory sugar level to qualify for the name of Dôle. The best come from the calcareous slopes round Sierre. Disqualified Dôle is sold as Goron. In the Vaud (where 20% of the wine is now red) Dôle-type wine is called Salvagnin. Pinot Noir and Gamay are also made separately here.

Chablais, the district between Valais and Vaud, between Martigny and Montreux, although in the canton of Vaud, is transitional in character. Aigle and Yvorne and Bex are its best-known villages. Their white wine (they also make sought-after reds) is strong, but drier and less full than Fendant. Villeneuve, at the

very start of the lake near Montreux, makes particularly lovely wine.

The central part of the Vaud, between Montreux and Lausanne, is confusingly called Lavaux. Switzerland's most appealing Chasselas wines, dry and gentle, some more fruity, some with a more distinct *goût de terroir*, are grown on the terraces of Lutry, Villette, Epesses, St-Saphorin and Chardonne. They are usually sold with the village name. Dézaley, widely considered the best wine of the Vaud, and Calamin are the exceptions. They are lively, harmonious and long and have their own appellations as crus.

After Lausanne, La Côte has lighter (or more delicate) and perhaps less distinguished wines; 40% of the Vaud total. The best can be irresistibly fresh; faintly bubbly. Féchy and Mont-sur-Rolle are the best-known villages. Nyon, the commercial centre, sees more and more light Gamay reds.

The same is true of the Geneva vineyards, where Chasselas (now 50% of the crop; Gamay is 35%) is known as Perlan. The big Geneva coop, Vin-Union, draws on three areas. The largest is Mandement (Satigny is the country's biggest wine commune) which has the ripest and tastiest Perlan. The vineyards between the Arve and the Rhône are milder, and those between the Arve and the lake pretty dry and pallid: a far cry from the potent Fendant of Sion.

Map legend

_._._	International boundary
_..._	Canton boundary
VINZEL	Leading wine commune
▦	Vineyards
▦	Woods
═1000═	Contour interval 200 metres

1:450,000

Km. 0   5   10 Km.
Miles 0   3   6 Miles

The vineyards of Lavaux tilt breakneck down to Lac Léman. Dézaley (*above*) is the most famous village for lively, limpid, gentle whites.

Below: Vétroz, near Sion in the Valais, has some of Switzerland's driest and warmest slopes. Valais wines are the headiest and most potent of the Alps.

Swiss labels are so original and exuberant that one is tempted to think they vary more than the wine. Some of the main Valais and Vaud producers are represented here.

221

Austria

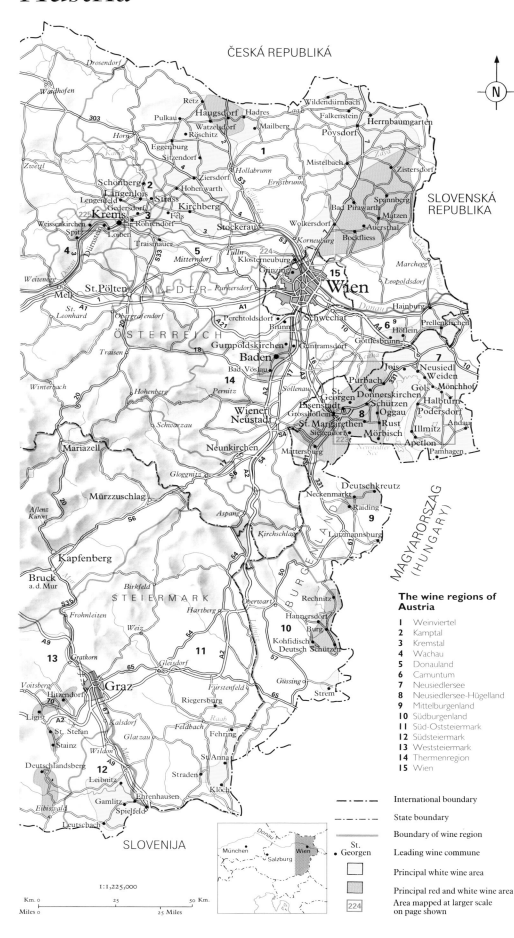

CESKÁ REPUBLIKÁ

SLOVENSKÁ REPUBLIKA

ÖSTERREICH

NIEDER-

STEIERMARK

BURGENLAND

MAGYARORSZÁG (HUNGARY)

SLOVENIJA

The wine regions of Austria

1 Weinviertel
2 Kamptal
3 Kremstal
4 Wachau
5 Donauland
6 Carnuntum
7 Neusiedlersee
8 Neusiedlersee-Hügelland
9 Mittelburgenland
10 Südburgenland
11 Süd-Oststeiermark
12 Südsteiermark
13 Weststeiermark
14 Thermenregion
15 Wien

—·—·— International boundary

— — — State boundary

——— Boundary of wine region

St. • Georgen   Leading wine commune

☐ Principal white wine area

▨ Principal red and white wine area

224 Area mapped at larger scale on page shown

1:1,225,000

Km. 0   25   50 Km.
Miles 0   25 Miles

Above: Gumpoldskirchen is the name of the hill-slope south of Vienna. Its wines were traditionally late picked, rich and sweet. Today dry wines are in vogue, and even Chardonnay is appearing.
Right: Growers have no inhibitions about varieties. Morillon is an alias for Chardonnay

Austria comes 8th in the world league table of wine consumption, 16th for wine production, but for uninhibited enthusiasm and experimentation her producers today rate somewhere between Australia and New Zealand.

No country in Europe has changed its attitude and upgraded its standards so much in the past decade. And it all began with a storm in a wine-glass, a minor scandal in 1985 in which a few idle and dishonest (not to say criminal) growers and merchants were caught adding diethylene glycol to their thin wines to give them more body. No one was poisoned, but the 'Austrian Wine Scandal' made such international headlines that (for example) the president of one of Japan's biggest companies was forced to resign.

The Austrian government had no alternative but to change its entire wine-control system, and the Austrian wine industry to about-face into frantic activity.

Not that it was inactive before. Austrian merchants were adept at blending cheap wines from East Europe or Italy and labelling them Austrian, careless of the cut-price image it gave their country. Wine-laws on the German model were enacted in 1972 with considerable effect: exports both improved and increased. But the country's fame still centred round her inimitable easy-drinking tavern wines; almost impossible to

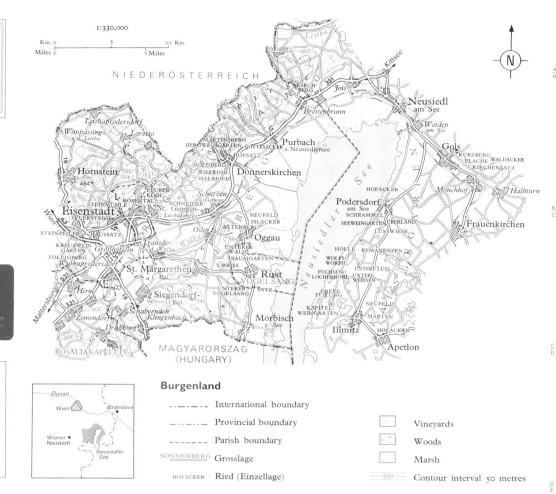

Burgenland

–·–·–·– International boundary	▢ Vineyards
–·····– Provincial boundary	▨ Woods
–––––– Parish boundary	▢ Marsh
SONNENBERG Grosslage	
HOFÄCKER Ried (Einzellage)	══250══ Contour interval 50 metres

bottle and export with their character intact. It took the shock of 1985 to make growers extend themselves and start bottling and selling their best wines competitively. Even they have been astonished at the range and quality of what their country can produce.

Modern Austria is a mere fraction of what the name meant before the First World War. But its kernel, Lower Austria, where the Alps descend to the great Pannonian plain that reaches across Hungary, is a region full of variety. It embraces granite, slate, chalk, tufa, clay and fertile loess, parched fields and perpetually green ones, craggy precipices along the Danube and the tranquil shallow mere of the Neusiedlersee.

All Austria's best wines used to be white – and most still are. Her central position among Europe's northern and eastern vineyards shows in the character of the wine she makes. There is something of the freshness of the Rhine in it but more of the fieriness and high flavour of the Danube.

Only eastern Austria makes wine. The vineyards are concentrated all around Vienna except to the southwest. The principal regions are the Wachau, Kamptal and Kremstal (former Kamptal-Donauland), Vienna, Thermenregion (mapped in detail overleaf), Carnuntum and Donauland (former Donauland-Carnuntum) straddling the capital, Burgenland around the

Neusiedler See southeast of Vienna, and the Weinviertel (formerly Falkenstein and Retz) north of the capital.

Styria (Steiermark) in the south, bordering on Slovenia, has only 5% of Austria's vineyards but a soaring reputation for intense-flavoured whites of Welschriesling, Sauvignon and Morillon (ie Chardonnay), and at Kloch, on volcanic soil, Traminer. The pale but piercing rosé Schilcher is the speciality of Western Styria.

Burgenland (mapped above) lies on the Hungarian border – indeed the Hungarian redwine district of Sopron is carved out of it. Like much of Hungary, its historic speciality is sweet wines. The country is flat and sandy around the lake (an extraordinary pool, more than 18 miles (30 kilometres) long and only a metre deep) and mists envelop it through its long warm autumns, making the noble rot a regular occurrence.

The most historically famous wine of Burgenland comes from Rust. Ruster Ausbruch was regularly compared with Tokay. Ausbruch means the same as the Hungarian Aszú; a wine made of shrivelled grapes caused to ferment by mixing them with normal ones – except that in Tokay the former are added to the latter; in Rust vice versa. In sweetness Aszú is ranked between Beeren- and Trockenbeerenauslese.

Burgenland today is divided into four areas: South, Middle and, east and west of the lake,

Neusiedlersee and Hügelland, whose centres are Rust, Eisenstadt and Mörbisch. Its grapes include Welschriesling, Müller-Thurgau, Muskat-Ottonel, Weissburgunder, Ruländer, Traminer and Hungary's Furmint for its sweet wines, but growers are becoming increasingly interested in what their relatively warm climate can achieve with red, both traditional Blauburgunder, Blaufränkisch and Zweigelt and new-fangled Cabernet, and even Sangiovese and Nebbiolo.

In contrast to those of Burgenland, the wines of the Weinviertel (meaning 'wine quarter') are in the main light and dry. The great grape here is Austria's favourite, the Grüner Veltliner, at its most typical in the aromatic wines of Falkenstein. But in Retz and Mailberg to the west the emphasis is on reds.

Veltliner wine when it is well made and drunk young is marvellously fresh and fruity, with plenty of acidity and an almost spicy flavour. To compare it with Rhine Riesling is like comparing a wild flower with a finely bred garden variety.

There are times, when Grüner Veltliner wine is drawn straight from the barrel into a tumbler, frothing and gleaming a piercing greeny gold, when it seems like the quintessence of all that a wine should be. Drink it then, with a sandwich on the terrace. It will never taste like that under any other conditions.

Vienna

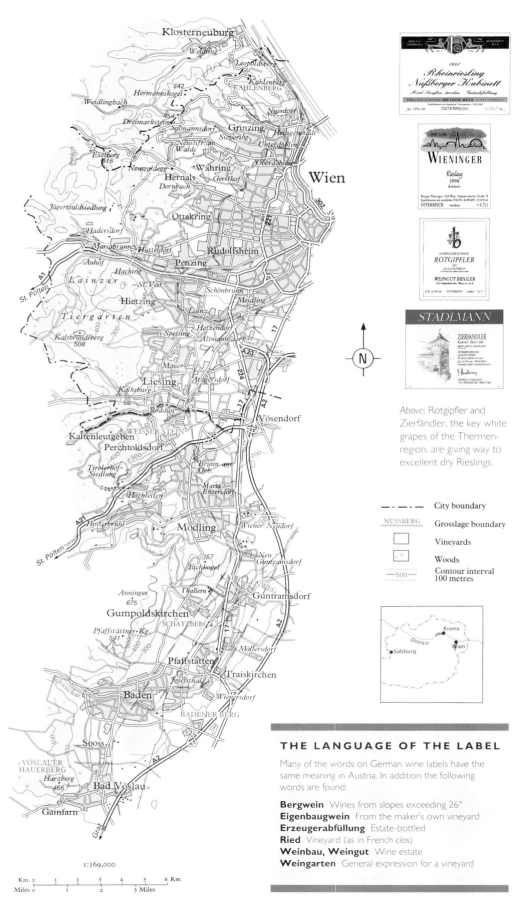

Above: Rotgipfler and Zierfändler, the key white grapes of the Thermen-region, are giving way to excellent dry Rieslings.

- – – · – — City boundary
- NUSSBERG — Grosslage boundary
- ☐ — Vineyards
- ☐ — Woods
- —500— — Contour interval 100 metres

No capital city is so intimate with wine as Vienna. Vineyards hold their ground within the heart of the residential districts and surge up the side of the surrounding hills into the Vienna woods. North, east and south, where the line of hills circles and protects the city, there are vines. To the south they continue along the Südbahn (now called the Thermenregion, for its hot springs) flanking the last crinkle of the alpine foothills facing the Hungarian plain.

Most of their wine is drunk as *Heurige*, in *Heurigen* – for this untranslatable word means both the new wine and the tavern where it is drunk. Every vintner seems to be tavernkeeper too, and chalks up on a board the wines and their (modest) prices, by jug or litre bottle, labelless, to be drunk on the spot or carried away. Good *Heurige* is sensational; spirited, sprightly stuff which goes straight to your head. Most of it is Grüner Veltliner. Some is Müller-Thurgau, Weissburgunder, Riesling; some is Traminer. The best of the new wines are not too dry.

Viennese connoisseurs know every grower in Neustift, Grinzing, Sievering, Nussdorf and Kahlenberg, the wine villages of Vienna. The atmosphere in their leafy taverns varies from idyllic to hilarious. In most of them Beethoven wrote at least a concerto. The region is dominated by the splendid monastic cellars and wine school at Klosterneuburg.

Thermenregion wines were formerly summed up by the rich produce of Gumpoldskirchen; fine late-gathered wines made from the lively Zierfändler, the heavier Rotgipfler or the local hero Neuberger. The trend today is more for dry Rieslings, Neuburgers, even Chardonnay, of which Traiskirchen has fine examples.

The spas of Baden and Bad Vöslau are better known for their reds: Portugiesers, Zweigelts and St Laurents made dark, dry and appetizing, though hardly inspiring. They are daily growing more ambitious, with Blauburgunder, and even Cabernet, and new French oak in their cellars.

THE LANGUAGE OF THE LABEL

Many of the words on German wine labels have the same meaning in Austria. In addition the following words are found:

Bergwein Wines from slopes exceeding 26°
Eigenbaugwein From the maker's own vineyard
Erzeugerabfüllung Estate-bottled
Ried Vineyard (as in French *clos*)
Weinbau, Weingut Wine estate
Weingarten General expression for a vineyard

1:169,000

Km. 0   1   2   3   4   5   6 Km.
Miles 0   1   2   3 Miles

Wachau

The village of Dürnstein with its castle and excellent hotel, is the spiritual heart of the Wachau. Richard Coeur de Lion was imprisoned here.

1:62,500

Km. 0   1   2 Km.
Miles 0   1 Mile

Above: in the Wachau the cooperative is the biggest bottler, but individual growers and vineyards are becoming better known.

FRAUENWEINGARTEN Grosslage boundary

RITZLING   Ried boundary

       Ried vineyard

       Other vineyard

       Woods

—500—   Contour interval 100 metres

Forty miles (65 kilometres) west of Vienna the broad grey Danube broaches a range of 1,600-foot (490-metre) hills. For a short stretch the craggy north bank of the river, as steep as some of the Mosel slopes, is patchworked with vines on ledges and outcrops, along narrow paths leading up from the river to the crowning woods.

There are patches of deep soil and others where a mere scratching finds rock, patches with day-long sunlight and others that always seem to be in shade. There is no grand sweep of vines here; no big estates and no unique vine variety. But this is the Wachau; Austria's Rheingau and Mosel rolled together.

Grüner Veltliner is the traditional Wachau grape and makes its most vivid, persuasive, agreeable wines here – at their best high-spirited and fiery, almost peppery performances. But growers have more recently been dedicating their best and steepest *rieds* to Riesling, and their clientele is enraptured. Top Wachau Rieslings from such growers as Hirtzberger at Spitz (just off the map to the west), Jamek at Joching, Prager at Weissenkirchen, F X Pichler at Oberloiben, Alzinger at Unterloiben, and the famous Freie Weingärtner cooperative at Dürnstein can have the steely cut of the Saar in a mouth-filling structure which is closer to Alsace.

The Wachau growers have their own system of designating wines which would all fall into the Prädikat and Trocken categories; local taste codified, in fact. Steinfeder is a light Kabinett, Federspiel is a more vibrant version, while Smaragd, still dry, is at least Spätlese – which means more like a German dry Auslese.

Dürnstein is the natural capital of the Wachau and the scenic climax of the valley. A very good hotel by the river is named after Richard the Lionheart, who was imprisoned here. The baroque steeple, the ruined castle and the tilting vineyards of Dürnstein are irresistibly pretty and suggestive.

Krems marks the end of the Wachau and the start of Kremstal, which falls naturally into four disparate sectors. The Krems Valley is the first, and takes Krems itself and Stein next door (with its famous *ried* Steiner Hund) technically out of the Wachau. The Krems Valley runs north up to Langenlois in the valley of the Kamp, on strange soft loess, half soil, half rock, source of some famous Veltliners but also of full-bodied reds. Brundlmayer is the great name here.

To the east of Krems lies Rohrendorf, on lower hills of sandier soil, famous as the base of the long-established firm of Lenz Moser, viti-cultural pioneers and still producers of fine wines both here, at Mailberg in the Weinviertel and at Siegendorf near the Neusiedlersee.

Finally the Kremstal area leaps the Danube to include the territory of the massive Bene-dictine house of Gottweig and the villages adjoining. The chief of these is Furth, where the names of Malat-Brundlmayer and Maier conjure up a remarkable range of both red and white wines.

Hungary

Hardly any country has a national character so pronounced in its traditional wine – and food – as Hungary. Historically, the wine culture of Hungary is third in seniority, in tradition and refinement, to those of France and Germany. While most Italian and Iberian wine was still primitive, each wine region of Hungary had developed specific tastes, embodied in her singular grape varieties, to a very high standard.

For this reason no country has more to lose by accommodating the taste of foreign buyers who look on it as another cheap source of same-again wines. From the 1960s on Hungary began to lose confidence in her traditions, her wines became less special – made to a price rather than a standard. The 1970s and 1980s saw planting of international grape varieties on a large scale – a trend that is likely to accelerate in the 1990s as formerly state-held land is privatized.

The characteristic Hungarian wine is white – or rather warmly gold. Those who look for fresh-fruitiness above all in white wine should look elsewhere. It smells more of a pâtisserie than a greengrocer, if one can so distinguish between ripe, yeasty smells and the acidic ones of fresh fruit. It tastes, if it is a good one, distinctly sweet, but full of fire and even a shade fierce. It is not dessert wine; far from it. It is wine for meals cooked with more spice

and pepper and fat than a light wine could stand.

Like Germany, Hungary treasures her sweet wines most. Tokay (see the next pages) is her pride and joy. But most of the country makes wine. The variety is rich in both traditional and international types.

On the map, the chief wine types are listed where they grow. They bear the district names followed by their grape names – the standard Hungarian system. Hungary's great grape varieties begin with the strong acidic Furmint and the softer perfumed Hárslevelü – the grapes of Tokaj, but not only Tokaj. They continue with the now rare Kéknyelü ('Blue-stalk') of Lake Balaton, capable of wonderful richness and attack, the Szürkebarát, alias Pinot Gris, also lushest on Lake Balaton. Quite different are the aromatic, lively Leányka (the Feteasca Alba of Romania), the fresh, even tart Ezerjó, the Olaszrizling, tastier in Hungary than in most places, the Mézesfeher ('white honey'), rich and mouthfillling - and usually sweet; the tart and fragrant Juhfark … and all these before the Tramini, Sauvignon, Chardonnay and Pinot Blanc are counted.

Red varieties are few in Hungary. The Kadarka (called Gamza in Bulgaria) is the most important; a good worker rather than a star. Kékfrankos is Blaufränkisch, a lightweight here

as elsewhere. Pinot Noir (Nagyburgundi) makes very solid wines in the south; Merlot (oddly called Médoc Noir) contributes to Bull's Blood at Eger. Cabernet is a more recent introduction.

More than half Hungary's vineyards are on the Great Plain, the Alföld, between the Danube (Duna) and the Tisza in the southern centre of the country, on sandy soil which is little use for anything but vines. The vine, indeed, has been used for reclaiming sand dunes which used to shift in storms. Great Plain wine, the red mainly Kadarka, the white Olaszrizling or Ezerjó, is the daily wine of Hungarian cities.

The other half is scattered among the hills that cross the country from southwest to northeast, culminating in the Tokajhegyalja – the Tokaji hills. In the south the districts of Szekszárd, Villány and Mecsek grow both red and white wines, but here the red are coming to the fore. Kadarka is the historic grape; Nagyburgundi well-entrenched and Cabernet the rising star, making fruity, lightish wine of good quality. Cabernet from Hajós can be very fine.

Lake Balaton, besides being the biggest lake in Europe, has a special significance for Hungarians. In a country with no coasts and few landmarks, it is the sea and the chief beauty spot. Its shores are thick with summer villas and holiday resorts, fragrant with admirable

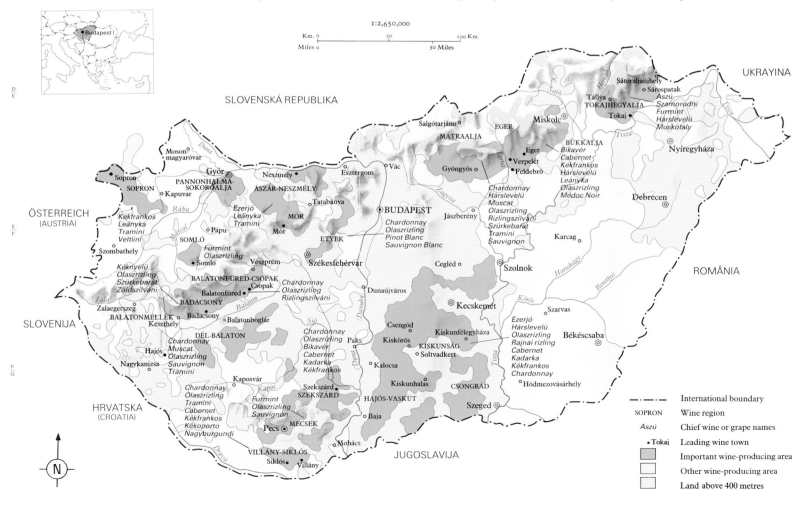

THE LANGUAGE OF THE LABEL

The language of the Hungarian label is like the industry itself, in rapid evolution since the dismemberment of the state system began in 1991. Normally there are few descriptive words or phrases.

The place-name, ending in 'i' (which is equivalent to the German 'er'), is usually followed by the grape variety.

Aszú The equivalent of the German Beerenauslese – over-ripe grapes collected for the sweetening of Tokay

Aszú Essencia The highest quality of Tokay commercially available: superb amber wine of Yquem-like quality

Szamorodni Literally 'as it comes', ie Tokay not specially treated with *Aszú*, and therefore more or less dry. Also sometimes used for wines other than Tokay

Különleges minöségü bor Finest quality wine

Minöségi bor Best-quality wine

Tájbor Country wine

Asztali bor Table wine

Palackozott Bottled

Fehér White

Vörös Red

Száraz Dry

Édes: Sweet

Pezsgö Sparkling

cooking. It has good weather and a happy social life. The north shore of Lake Balaton has all the advantages of good exposure and shelter, as well as the air-conditioning effect of a big body of water. It is inevitably a vineyard.

Its special qualities come from the climate, and from the combination of a sandy soil and extinct volcano stumps (Mount Badacsony is the most famous), dotted around among otherwise flat land. The steep slopes of basalt-rich sand drain well and absorb and hold the heat.

Olaszrizling is the common white grape. Its wine is very good when it is only a year old; dry but fresh and clean and not too strong. The real specialities, however, are the grapes that make powerful, honey-scented wine: Furmint, Szürkebarát and Kéknyelü. Even at a year old, tasted from the barrel, a Szürkebarát can still be as white as milk and prickly and fierce with fermentation. In two or three years these wines – of which the Kéknyelü is reckoned the 'stiffest' and best – have remarkable presence. They are aromatic and fiery; not exactly dessert wines but very much the wines for the sort of spiced and pungent food the Hungarians love.

Csopak, Balatonfüred and Badacsony are the main centres. Normally the standard quality will carry the simple name Balatoni, with the grape-name. The name Badacsonyi on a label implies a stronger, sweeter, and to the Hungarian way of thinking altogether better wine.

The singular flavour of Balaton is not limited to its native vines. More and more foreign grapes have been planted, and each picks up something of the dense and spicy style – here Sauvignon and Chardonnay become honorary Hungarians. South of the lake, Balatonboglár is a recently developed region of sand and fertile loess more or less dedicated to introduced varieties, from Chardonnay to Merlot.

The small, isolated hill districts of Somló to the west, growing Furmint and Olaszrizling, and Mór to the north, growing Ezerjó, also have very distinct characters: Somló for gentler, Mór for drier, more highly flavoured wine. Both are among what Hungary calls its historical wine regions. Sopron, almost on the Austrian border, is a red-wine outpost, growing Kékfrankos, a lively wine but hardly a great one. Moving east Ászár-Neszmély uses traditional grapes for dry whites while Etyek, west of Budapest, is a flourishing source of largely untraditional whites.

Along the south of the Mátra range to Eger is Hungary's second-biggest vineyard, formed of the old districts of Gyöngyös-Visonta and Debrö. The sweet white Hárslevelü of Debrö (ie the villages of Aldebrö, Feldebrö and Verpelét) is its great historic wine. Traditional Olaszrizling and Kadarka are being supplanted by the international favourites. Gyöngyös Chardonnay and Sauvignon are prime export wines.

Best known of all Hungary's table wines is Eger's Bikavér, or Bull's Blood. Eger is one of Hungary's most important wine centres, with huge cellars, magnificent caverns cut in the soft dark tufa of the hills. Hundreds of time-blackened oak casks, 10 feet across and bound with bright red iron hoops, line their galleries.

Unfortunately, the recent production of Bull's Blood has been less than remarkable; Kékfrankos has been substituted for Kadarka and the blood has been thinned. The best wine of Eger today is its Leányka – a Hungarian white that should satisfy anyone.

Above left: Lake Balaton is Europe's biggest lake, its shores the summer resort of half Hungary and the source of many of its most splendid white wines. Volcanic stumps along the north shore provide warm fertile soil. *Below:* Hungary's traditional grapes are in retreat before international sorts. But they still make its most rewarding wines.

Tokay

The word legend is more often used about Tokay than any other wine. (Tokay is the English spelling: the original is Tokaji; the place Tokaj.) There are good recent reasons for this. When Hungary became communist in 1949 the ultimate quality of what all agreed was the greatest wine of Eastern Europe was compromised. The famous vineyards and great estates of Tokaj lost their identity. They were confiscated; their wines were homogenized in the vast collective cellars that took control.

What was exported was indeed Tokay, and sometimes excellent. But individuality was lost, and with it the heights of quality. It was as if all the châteaux of the Médoc sent their wines to be finished and bottled in one cellar – which then pasteurized them. After 50 years memories even of Lafite and Latour would become dim.

Tokay, though, has been legendary for 400 years. Only champagne has spawned as many anecdotes. History relates how the sumptuous Tokay *aszú* was first produced – methodically, rather than by chance – by the chaplain of the Rákóczi family in their vineyard called Oremus at Sárospatak (his name was Szepsi; the year 1650). How the Polish knights who raised the Turkish siege of Vienna in 1683 took home a passion for Tokay. How in 1703 the great patriot Prince Rákóczi of Transylvania, used it to woo the support of Louis XIV against his Hapsburg overlords. How Peter and Catherine the Great kept a permanent detachment of

Above: shrivelled Aszú grapes are the essence of Tokay. This was the first region, long before Sauternes, to use 'noble rot' to make luscious wines.
Below: intensely sweet Tokay is virtually immortal. Antique bottles are stored standing in damp cellars, grey cellar mould masking their glowing amber. Their corks are changed every 25 years.

Cossacks in Tokaj to escort their supplies – and how its miraculous restorative properties led potentates to keep Tokay at their bedsides.

Tokay was the first wine knowingly to be made from botrytised or 'nobly rotten' grapes; over a century before Rhine wine, and perhaps two centuries before Sauternes. The conditions that cause the rot, the shrivelling of the grapes and the intense concentration of their sugar and flavour are endemic to the Tokaji hill range, Tokajhegyalja, southernmost bastion of the Tatra, the western extension of the Carpathians.

The range is volcanic, rising in typically sudden cones from the north edge of the Great Plain. Two rivers, the Bodrog and the Hernád, tributaries of the Tisza, converge at the southern tip of the range, where Mount Kopashegy, Bald Mountain, rises 1,700 feet (528 metres) above the villages of Tokaj and Tarcal. From the plain come warm summer winds, from the mountains shelter and from the rivers rising autumn mists.

Of the three grape varieties in Tokaj today, some 70% of the vines are the late-ripening, sharp-tasting, thin-skinned Furmint, highly susceptible to botrytis infection. Another 25% is Harslevelu ('lime-leaf'), less susceptible but rich in sugar and aromas. The rest is Muscat Blanc à Petits Grains – either used as a seasoning grape, as Muscadelle is in Sauternes, or as a rich speciality on its own.

The map shows the principal villages of the region, whose slopes form a wide V, thus facing southeast, south or southwest. The vineyards were first classified in 1700 by Prince Rákóczi. By 1804 they were divided into first, second, third and unclassed growths, besides three Great Growths, one in Tokaj itself and two in Tarcal, which had an Yquem-like standing *hors concours* (literally, because their wine did not enter commerce: it was Imperial property and went straight to crowned heads and their favourites).

One of these, Csarfas, is now run as the national research station. The other two were both called Mézesmály ('honeycomb'). The one in Tokaj has been subsumed into other first-growths. Mézesmály in Tarcal is a mere 50 acres (20 hectares) on the lower western skirts of the hill. The soil in Tarcal, parts of Tokaj and neighbouring Mád is loess; fertile, open and warm: so fast-draining that even after rain it does not stick. Drought can be a problem here. The bulk of Tokajhegyalja soils are more or less stony clays, much harder to cultivate but retaining moisture well. Vines on loess ripen faster and give the richest, most aromatic wines; those on clay tend to higher acidity and possibly greater longevity.

Tokay is made by a unique two-stage process. In a good vineyard and vintage, shrivelled *aszú* grapes are picked separately and taken to the cellars as a more or less dry mass. The rest of the crop is meanwhile crushed and pressed to make the 'base' wine. *Aszú* is then added to the base wine (or vice versa) in proportions traditionally measured by the number of 20-litre *puttonyos* of *aszú* per barrel, from two to six. Tokay barrels (*gönci*) hold only 140 litres, so seven *puttonyos* would be pure *aszú*. The *aszú* is steeped in the

wine for up to a week to extract its sugar and flavour. The wine is then drawn off to ferment again in its *gönci* in very cold damp cellars – a process that can take months – even years.

Three *puttonyos* make it the rough equivalent of a German Auslese, four or five put it into the Beerenauslese class of sweetness and concentration. The conventional minimum age in barrel for these *aszú* wines is the number of *puttonyos* plus two: a five-'putt' wine cannot be bottled, therefore, for seven years. Whether this is the ideal age is a matter for debate. If no *aszu* has been added the wine is 'Szamorodni' (literally 'as it comes') – developing a style rather like a light sherry and either 'Szaraz' (dry) or 'Edes' (fairly sweet). To many Hungarian connoisseurs four-'putt' *aszu* has the most balance and finesse.

Two more peculiarities of circumstance give Tokay its unique character. The casks are rarely topped up, but left with space for oxygen. And the pitch-black, small-bore tunnels are thickly veiled in cellar-mould, *Cladosporium cellare*. A rich store of yeasts and bacteria therefore attacks and feeds on the wine, just as flor does on fino sherry, very slowly oxidizing it and weaving a complex web of flavours.

In exceptional years (1993 was one) the best vineyards produce the equivalent of a Trockenbeerenauslese; must so sweet that, even diluted with base wine, and even with Tokay's potent native yeasts, it takes years to ferment and remains intensely sweet. Ten years is the minimum

Above: the variety of modern Tokay labels is the signal that the State monopoly has ended. The region is returning to its former system of château-like estates, with spectacular implications for quality.

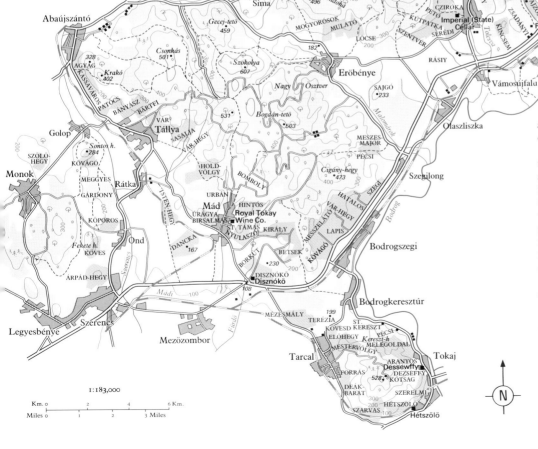

age for this 'Aszú Essencia'. At 30 only the cream of old Sauternes can be compared with it.

The most luxurious Tokay of all is made only from the juice that *aszú* berries naturally exude as they are waiting to be crushed. This Essencia is up to 60% sugar and will hardly ferment at all. Of all the essences of the grape it is the most velvety, oily, peach-like and penetrating. Its fragrance lingers in the mouth like incense. No age is too great for it (or for any *aszú* wine). What it is like at 200 years (some of the great Polish cellars kept it that long) only the Tsars can tell.

What does the future hold? Since 1990 the state has been privatizing its land and cellars, restoring them to their rightful owners or selling them to newcomers. Six joint ventures were begun by 1993, three of them by French insurance companies. Millions of capital has been poured in to upgrading vineyards, renewing equipment and researching the finest qualities of the land. Estate-bottled Tokays are again on the market and the names of the first-growths will again become familiar. It is an exciting prospect.

The Czech and Slovak Republics

Lying along the northern border of such incorrigibly vinous countries as Austria and Hungary it would be strange if the Czech and Slovak republics did not make good wine too. How good has only been revealed since 1989, when tourists flooding into free Prague found the white wines in the cafés, especially those labelled Moravenka (Moravian), as delicious as their equivalents in Vienna.

Slovakia has much the biggest wine region of the formerly united country, with about two-thirds of its acreage and production. Moravia, now the eastern half of the Czech republic, makes most of the rest, while Bohemia has only 1,000 acres (400 hectares), mainly along the right bank of the Elbe north of Prague, making light Germanic style wines, most notably at Mělník and Roudnice nad Labem.

Most of the Czech vineyards are indeed close neighbours to Austria's Weinviertel. Those of Moravia are concentrated between its capital, Brno, and the Austrian border, from Znojmo spreading east across the peaceful Pálava Hills for some 70 miles (110 kilometres). In this region the most successful wines are Sauvignons (which have real zest without exaggerated aromas) from Znojmo's two well-equipped cellars at Satov and Novy Saldorf, also from Valtice, Pavlov and Velké Pavlovice, Ruländers from Pavlov, Mikulov and Znojmo, Rieslings from Valtice, Mikulov, Bzenec and Novy Saldorf, some Traminers and Müller-Thurgaus, and the local and very tasty variety Palava from Pavlov and Satov. Reds are not so interesting. St Laurent is the most satisfactory grape at present; from Velké Pavlovice, Valtice and Bzenec.

Slovakia's vineyards cluster round Bratislava and scatter east along the Hungarian border,

enjoying a marginally warmer climate and adding Ezerjó and Leányka to their repertoire. Raca, just north of Bratislava, is known for hearty red Frankovka, St Laurent and also Pinot Noir. Pezinok makes good Veltliners, Rieslings … a wide range including a popular Silvaner blend. Modra has the best name for Riesling and Ruländer; Nitra perhaps ranks slighter lower for the same wines. Further south Sered has produced Hubert sparkling wine since early in the 19th century, while the Ruban cellars near Nové Zámky are respected for their spicy Ruländers, Veltliners and Traminers and ripe red Limberger.

Slovakia has also inherited in its extreme east two villages of the Tokaji region from Hungary. The Tokay and yellow muscat, as well as Traminer, from Nové Mesto, are nothing to be ashamed of.

Above: Prague, famous for palaces, has handsome wine estates (here, Troja) nearby. *Below*: the best Czech and Slovak wines are from southern Moravia, specializing in fragrant whites (Palava is a local grape) and Slovakia, with good red Frankovka and a tiny corner of the Tokay region.

DEUTSCHLAND

1:3,650,000

Km. 0   50   100 Km.
Miles 0   50 Miles

Liberec

Velké Žernoseky
Most Žalhostice Litoměřice
Loumy Roudnice Mělník
Chlumčany nad Labem
Karlovy Vary
B O H E M I A
PRAHA (PRAGUE)
Karlštejn
Plzeň Starý Plzenec
Č E S K Á   R E P U B L I K A
Tábor
Jihlava
Hradec Králové
Ostrava

POLSKA

M O R A V I A
Brno
BZENEC/STRÁŽNICE
ZNOJMO/MIKULOV HUSTOPEČE/HODONÍN Polešovice
Hustopeče Velké Bzenec
Znojmo Pavlovice Strážnice
Novy Šaldorf Pavlov Hodonín
Šatov Mikulov Skalica
Valtice Břeclav

Žilina
SLOVENSKÁ Poprad Prešov **REPUBLIKA**
Tatry
Nízke Tatry
SLOVAKIA
Trenčín Prievidza Banská Bystrica
Košice
Moldava nad Bodvou VYCHODOSLOVENSKÁ
Čerhov
Rimavská Sobota TOKÁJSKÁ
Slovenské Nove Mesto
Streda nad Bodrogom Chlmec
Sečovce
Královský

HLOHOVEC/TRNAVA
ÖSTERREICH (AUSTRIA)
SKALICE/ZAHORSKÁ
Smolenice Topolčany
MALOKARPATSKÁ Častá Hlohovec Zlaté Moravce
Modra Trnava Nitra
Pezinok Sered **NITRA**
Raca Senec Vráble Levice
BRATISLAVA Šahy
MODRY KAMEN
Velký Krtíš
Krupina

MAGYARORSZAG (HUNGARY)

Dunajská Streda Nové Zamky Hurbanovo
PODUNAJSKÁ
Komárno Štúrovo

Praha
Bratislava
Ljubljana

N

— · — · — International boundary
NITRA   Wine region
• Mělník   Wine town/village
   Vineyard
   Land above 1000 metres

Slovenia

The new-minted (1991) nation of Slovenia just touches the Adriatic in Istria, then runs north up the Italian border to the Carnatic Alps and east through the dwindling Julian Alps to border on Hungary. Both ends of the country, west and east, are long-established wine regions.

Predictably the west favours the Italian style of dry whites (Collio, mapped on page 183, reaches across from Friuli into Slovenia) and husky reds; notably Teran from Refosco grapes on the harsh Istrian Hills. Similarly in the east the taste is for flavours as rich as possible from late-picked grapes, Magyar-style. Between the two the Sava Valley, the country's third region, is more alpine and makes lighter wine, much of it Cvicek rosé from Blaufränkisch, known here as Modra Frankinja.

The map shows the country's biggest and most historic wine region, Podravje, the valley of the Drava and the jumbled hills between the Drava and the Mura, flowing parallel to the north.

This is overwhelmingly a white-wine region. Laski (Welsch) Riesling is its basic grape, and grows here as well as anywhere but the range of alternatives is bewildering. Pinots Blanc and Gris, Chardonnay, Sauvignon (called here, with a flash of inspiration, Muscat-Silvaner), real Riesling, Traminer, 'yellow' muscat, Rizvanec (Müller-Thurgau) and Kerner are joined by the native Rebula (Ribolla in Friuli), Sipon or Furmint, and Ranina, known in Austria as Bouvier and the speciality of Radgona, where its wine is sold as Tiger's Milk – a mild enough tiger.

As if selection amid this plethora was asking too much, local blends sometimes appear to be random mixings. Halozan, for example, a speciality of the central winery at Ptuj, is a blend of Rhine Riesling, Muscat, Pinot Blanc, Sauvignon and Traminer.

Whatever the thoughts behind the choice of variety, vintage time conditions throughout the region, strongly influenced by the radiator of the Pannonian plain, favour late-harvest wines of full body and measured sweetness.

The region is divided into six districts, based on Maribor, the Haloze Hills, Ptuj, Gornja-Radgona, Ljutomer-Ormoz (whose Jeruzalem vineyard has been so named since the time of the Crusades) and, north-east of the River Mura, Lendava.

With winemaking centralized in their huge cellars detailed district characteristics have tended to be lost (and much wine neutralized in budget blends for export). But Slovenia sees its role clearly as a quality producer. Its 50,000 acres (20,000 hectares) can only supply half the needs of its two million people. Everyday wine has to be imported, while enterprising individual growers build reputations which will soon be more than local.

Right: the Sava region and the rolling hills of the Bizeljsko district in southern central Slovenia are a potentially important source of light, dry reds and ripe whites, local and international varieties, including some of the country's best Laski Riesling. The castle in the background is Bizeljski Grad.

For location map see opposite page

International boundary
Boundary of demarcated region
HALOZE Boundary of Okoliš (Appellation)
■ VINAG Wine cellar
First-class vineyard
Second-class vineyard
Other vineyard
—600— Contour interval 150 metres

Above: Kraski Teran is a red from Istria. Radgona and Jeruzalem are historic wine centres of the Drava Valley.

The Former Yugoslavia

The Bosnian war of the 1990s makes any account of the wine regions of the countries involved both provisional and academic. Slovenia miraculously slipped its leash in 1991. Its Drava vineyards, the most famous of the former federation, are mapped on page 231.

This map shows the main production regions before Yugoslavia disintegrated in 1991, with the names of their most widely grown wines. The Balkans are rich in ancient grape varieties that persist, despite the inevitable invasion of French sorts, on the strength of their character and perfect adaption to local conditions. Some 300 varieties are said to grow between the Pannonian plain to the north and Greece to the south.

Mountainous Bosnia-Hercegovina is the exception. Both its terrain and its Muslim inheritance make commercial winegrowing an unlikely occupation, except on the Dalmatian coast and inland to Mostar. Mostar's Zilavka is a white grape of memorable character: its wine full-flavoured and dry with a unique apricot smell. The local red, Blatina, pales beside it.

North of the River Sava, between Zagreb and Belgrade, is largely white-wine country. Its commonest grape, the Welschriesling (known in Slovenia as Laski Riesling), bears the name of Grasevina. Slavonia, with its mountains, provides its best growing conditions, especially round Kutjevo, source of much of the low-price (and sadly nondescript) 'Yugoslav Riesling' of British supermarkets.

Most of northern Serbia, Vojvodina, shares the characteristics of the Pannonian plain with Hungary to the north and Romania's Banat to the east. Its grapes are the same, too: largely Ezerjó and Kadarka. Its best white wines, though, are the Sauvignons, Traminacs and Grasevinas from the Fruska Gora Hills, a range 40 miles (60 kilometres) long, 1,500 feet (450 metres) high at best, that relieves the flatness of Vojvodina along the Danube north of Belgrade.

South of Belgrade the town of Smederevo gives its name to the white Smederevka, a scarcely memorable grape that rapidly gives way to more invigorating red wines in southern Serbia: above all to Prokupac. Until recent plantings of Cabernet, Gamay, even Pinot Noir from Serbia southwards, the near universal red grape here was Prokupac. Between Smederevo and Svetozarevo, in Zupa and Kruzevac and south into Macedonia it forms about 80% of the production. It makes good rosé, Ruzica, firm, with plenty of flavour, and a red wine varying from dark and bitter to pleasantly fruity and drinkable. Often it is blended with the milder Plovdina and given local names (eg in Zupa, Zupsko Crno).

Kosovo is different. It has discovered a readier market for Cabernet (which it makes well) and a sweetish Pinot Noir blend designed for the German market under the name of Amselfelder. Of the indigenous reds in the south the best is the Vranac of Montenegro and Macedonia, heady but with structure and even, with three or four years' ageing, class.

Northern Croatia and Serbia are essentially mass-production cooperative country. The long coastal strip of Dalmatia is a complete contrast – a region full of original, if elusive, rewards. From Rijeka south the great red grape is the Plavac Mali. If it is true that the original home of the Cabernet was in Albania, it is possible to imagine that this small dark berry, giving tannic, strong and chewy wine, is a long-lost relation.

Among its most potent manifestations are dense and sweetish Dingac and Postup from the Peljesac Peninsula, north of Dubrovnik. It turns up in formidable home-made Prosek, from little rocky patches under fig trees – at best a fair substitute for port. Pale versions are called Plavina or Opol. But Plavac is worth tasting anywhere.

Several more or less white wines of strong personality are made on the islands, often pressed by an antique press and hoarded as a treasure which is none of the government's business. The dry white (sometimes brown) Grk of Korcula, the pale and even perfumed Bogdanusa of Hvar and the similar Vugava of Vis, Marastina, delicate (as at Smokvica on Hvar) or potent in white Prosek, and Posip – reputedly the same grape as Furmint – are all characters as different from a modern Sauvignon Blanc as you could hope to find.

With Dalmatian food – tiny oysters, raw ham, grilled fish, smoky and oniony kebabs and mounds of sweet grapes – the fire and flavour of such local wines could seem ambrosial.

Above: the Dalmatian coast of the Adriatic is limestone country called karst. The Peljesac peninsula is known for powerful sweet Prosek from the native red grape, Plavac Mali. *Right*: the 300-odd traditional grape varieties are still holding their own against the international ones.

ÖSTERREICH
(AUSTRIA)

Julijske Alpe

ITALIA

PRIMORSKA
SLOVENIJA
*Merlot
Rebula*
Vipava

S L O V E N I J A

LJUBLJANA

Brda

POSAVJE

*Teran
Refoško
Cabernet
Borgonja*
*Poreč
Muškat
Merlot
Malvazija
Pinot Bijeli*

ISTRA

*Vinodolsko
Trbjan*

Cres

Rijeka

Karlovac

Cviček

231

Gorna
Radgona
Maribor PODRAVJE
Ptuj Ljutomer
Ormož
Haloze

Kapela

Sauvignon
Laski Rizling
Renski Rizling
Traminec
Beli Pinot
Rumeni Muškat
Šipon
Radgonska Ranina (Tigrovo Mleko)
Kerner

Varaždino

*Graševina
Traminac*

Graševina

MAGYARORSZAG
(HUNGARY)

ZAGREB

Mladina

*Rizling Rajnski
Portugizac*

KONTINENTALNA
HRVATSKA

H R V A T S K A
(C R O A T I A)

*Graševina
Burgundac Bijeli*

Kutjevo

*Graševina
Plemenka Ružica*

Osijek

Drava

Slavonski Brod

Vukovar

Graševina

*Bijeli Klikun
Semilon
Sauvignon
Ružica*

SREMSKI KARLOVCI
FRUŠKA GORA

Novi Sad

Kadarka
Ezerjó
Italijanski Rizling
Kevedinka
Frankovka

SLIBOTIČKO-
HORGOŠKA
PEŠČARA
Subotica

Sombor

VOJVODINA

Novi Bečej

Italijanski Rizling
Muskat-Ottonel
Cokanski Merlot
Samorodno
Banatski Rizling

BANAT

ROMANIA

*Traminac
Italijanski Rizling
Semillon/Sauvignon
Plemenka
Bermet
Biser*

*Italijanski Rizling
Smederevka*

BEOGRAD
(BELGRADE)

Bosna

Banja Luka

B O S N A I

H E R C E G O V I N A

Bijeljina

Tuzla

POCERINA

Smederevo

*Prokupac
Oplenačka Ružica*

*Smederevka
Prokupac/Ružica*

ŠUMADIJSKO-
VELIKOMORAVSKI

Zadar

*Trboljan
Plavina
Opol
Marastina*

Šibenik

PRIMORSKA HRVATSKA

Plavac Mali

Split

*Plavac Mali
Prošek
Opol
Bogdanuša*

Plavac Mali

Hvar

*Vis
Vugava*

Korčula

*Plavina
Grk
Maraština
Pošip*

Mljet

*Jadransko Morje
(Adriatic Sea)*

Dubrovnik

*Kujunduša
Rudežuša*

HERCEGOVINA

Mostar

*Žilavka
Blatina*

*Plavac Mali
Dingač
Postup*

Pelješac

SARAJEVO

Konjic

Pljevlja

S R B I J A
(S E R B I A)

Čačak

*Zupsko Crno
Zupska Ružica
Vinjak*

Ž U P A

ZAHODNOMORAVSKI

Prokupac/Plovdina

Svetozarevo

TIMOČKI

*Prokupac
Začinka
Bagrina
Dubravka*

Kruševac

Aleksinac

Niš

Leskovac

NIŠAVSKO-JUZNOMORAVSKI

*Plemenka
Grom*

Vlasotinci

BÂLGARIJA

C R N A G O R A
(MONTENEGRO)

Nikšić

Kotor

*Vranac
Plavka*

Titograd

CRNA GORA

KOSOVO

Peć

*Burgundac
Cabernet Franc
Gamay
Italijanski Rizling*

Djakovica

KOSOVO

Prizren

Priština

Vranje

SHQIPËRI
(ALBANIA)

SKOPJE

PČINSKO-
OSOGOVSKI

M A K E D O N I J A
(M A C E D O N I A)

Titov Veles

POVARDARSKI

*Prokupac
Ružica
Rizling
Kratosija
Samotok
Belan
Teran
Muškat-Hamburg
Kavadarka
Krater
Smederevka
Zilavka
Vranac*

*Prokupac
Plovdina
Ružica*

PELAGONIJSKO-
POLOŠKI

Prilep

Kavadarci

Ohrid

Bitola

ELLINIKI
(GREECE)

THE LANGUAGE OF THE LABEL

Visokokvalitetno High quality
Cuveno vino Special or selected wine
Stolno vino Table wine
Punjeno u... Bottled at...
Proizvedeno u vinariji... Produced at...
**Proizvedeno u vlastitoj vinariji poljoprivredne
zadruge...** Made in the cooperative winery of the
place named
Prirodno Natural
Bijelo White
Crno Red
Ruzica Rosé
Biser (literally, pearl) Sparkling
Suho Dry
Polsuho Medium dry
Slatko Sweet
Desertno vino Dessert wine

– · – · – International boundary

– – – – – Republic boundary

BANAT Wine region

Semillon Chief wine or grape names

☐ Principally white wines

▨ White and red wines

▨ Principally red wines

☐ Land above 1000 metres

231 Area mapped at larger scale
on page shown

1:3,400,000

Km. 0   50   100 Km.

Miles 0   50 Miles

1|2   2|3   3|4   4|5   5|6

Bulgaria

Of all the wine countries of Eastern Europe Bulgaria has been the most single-minded in directing its wine industry towards exports and designing it to earn hard currency. Massive plantings on rich land in the 1950s were intended to pump out a river of everyday wine for the USSR (and later for the West) from quality grape varieties. The plan succeeded beyond anyone's dreams.

By 1966 Bulgaria had become the sixth-largest wine exporter in the world. In 1978 it made a serious impression on the British market. Britain remains its most important customer, even having helped to frame its new EC-style wine laws. Today Bulgaria is apparently the world's second largest exporter of bottled wine, after France, exporting 90% of its entire crop.

Compared with Romania Bulgaria has little in the way of a continuous winemaking tradition or 'classic' wines. In ancient times, under Greek influence, wine was endemic, but modern Bulgaria's architecture, folk costumes and food all bear the marks of the Turkish domination, with its Islamic prohibition, which ended a bare century ago.

The wines that succeed beyond all expectation in Bulgaria are Cabernet, Chardonnay and Merlot. The Cabernet and Merlot have fruit, vigour, balance – the robust qualities of red Bordeaux in a good vintage, if not its finesse. Bulgaria, if its figures are to be believed, has four times as much Cabernet vineyard as California.

But the national varieties are not neglected, nor without character. Of reds there is Gamza (or Gumza) – the lively Kadarka of Hungary; Pamid, which gives pale gulping wine; Mavrud, which gives the opposite – the country's national pride; and Melnik, from that town in Harsovo in the far southwest. Melnik could be called the Syrah of Bulgaria; strong, dark and very flavoury, ageing almost indefinitely.

Among whites, the dominant local varieties are Rkatziteli and Dimiat (Serbia's Smederevka). Red Misket (not a muscat, despite of its name) and Muscat Ottonel are popular, but success with Chardonnay, Riesling, Gewürztraminer and Aligoté is elbowing most of the traditional varieties (except Misket and Muscat) aside.

In 1978 the Bulgarian government initiated a useful and thorough system of geographical appellations, now quite as strict, on paper, as French appellations contrôlées. The main quality categories are plain 'Quality', the lowest export standard, then DGO or 'Country Wines', in which two varieties are blended to produce an original taste. Controliran is the equivalent of a full appellation, limited mainly to single varieties from a select two dozen regions.

In addition Reserve wines must be matured for up to three or four years in oak vats, often of American oak. Special Reserve is a category intended for limited lots, which may or may not be Controliran but are often the country's best.

The new laws redivided the country from nine former regions into five, corresponding to natural physical zones. The northern region along the Danube grows largely red wines, its cooler climate giving particular quality to both the Cabernet and Gamza and a little Pinot Noir, Gamay and Muscat. The most famous estate here is Lovico Suhindol, Bulgaria's first cooperative in 1909 and the first winery to be privatized in 1992 after the Revolution. Suhindol is Controliran for Gamza, but better-known for its ripe dark Cabernet. In the same region Svischtov is Controliran for Cabernet, while Pavlikeni is well-known both for Gamza and Cabernet and a Country Wine blend of Gamza and Merlot. The Yantra Valley is Controliran for Cabernet, Pleven is the home of Pamid, while Russe on the Danube specializes in white wines.

Russe borders on the Eastern Region, whose temperate Black Seaside climate seems to favour white grapes. Bulgaria's best-known Chardonnays come from Khan Khrum and Novi Pazar, Shumen and Varna, oaked or unoaked. They do not reach the quality of the country's better reds, but nobody can complain about their price.

The Stara Planina, the Balkan Mountains, divide the centre of Bulgaria into north and south. Karlovo, in the heart of the mountains, is white-wine country, with both Misket and Muscat – and also vast plantations of damask roses for their essential oils, or attar.

The warmer southern region, Haskovo, is the country of more full-bodied Cabernets and Merlots. Oriachovitza is Controliran for a Cabernet-Merlot blend that can be excellent, Stambolo and Sakar for Merlot, Sliven (with the country's biggest winery) for Cabernet and a Country Wine blend of Merlot and Pinot Noir. The speciality and price of Asenovgrad and Bulgaria's second city, Plovdiv, is its dense, purplish and potentially memorable Mavrud.

Over the Rhodope Mountains in the far southwest, close to the borders of Greece and Serbia, the capital of the Harsovo region, the town of Melnik is synonymous with Bulgaria's most original wine.

Left: what Bulgaria lacks in tradition and picturesque old cellars and estates she makes up in large-scale modern wine-factories. At this winery near Sliven the more exportable Chardonnay, has recently joined the native white Misket and Rkatziteli. *Right*: most Bulgarian export labels are in English or German. Ethnic labels in Gothic script are rarely seen abroad. The term to look for is Controliran, signifying a strict appellation of origin.

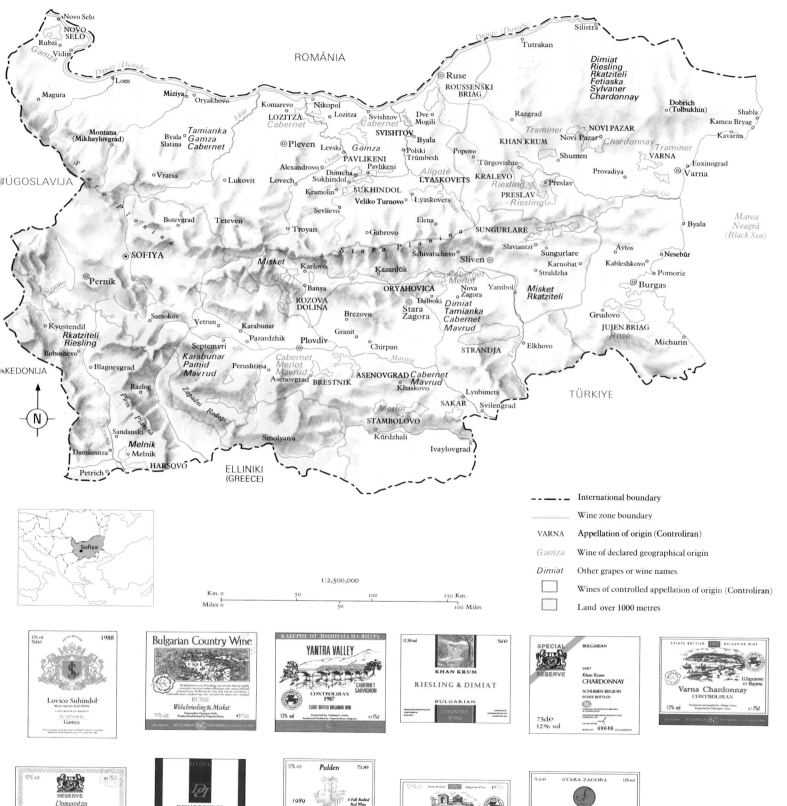

A
B

ROMÂNIA

Novo Selo
Rubzi
NOVO SELO
Vidin
Gamza
Lom
Magura
Miziya
Oryakhovo
Montana (Mikhaylovgrad)
Byala Slatina
Tamianka Gamza Cabernet
Vratsa
Lukovit

JUGOSLAVIJA

Stara Planina

Komarevo
Nikopol
LOZITZA
Cabernet
Lozitza
Svishtov
SVISHTOV
Byala
Dve Mogili
ROUSSENSKI BRIAG
Ruse

Silistra
Tutrakan
Dunav (Danube)

Dimiat Riesling Rkatziteli Fetiaska Sylvaner Chardonnay
Razgrad
Dobrich (Tolbukhin)
Shabla
Kamen Bryag
Kavarna

Pleven
Levski
Gamza
PAVLIKENI
Pavlikeni
Alexandrovo
Sukhindol
Dimtcha
Kramolin
SUKHINDOL
Veliko Turnovo
Sevlievo
Polski Trumbesh
Aligoté
LYASKOVETS
Lyaskovets

Popovo
Türgovishte
KHAN KRUM
Provadiya
KRALEVO
Preslav
PRESLAV
Riesling

Traminer
NOVI PAZAR
Novi Pazar
Shumen
Chardonnay
VARNA
Traminer
Euxinograd
Varna

B
C

Botevgrad
Teteven
Troyan
Gabrovo
Elena

Stara Planina

SOFIYA
Pernik

Misket
Karlovo
Banya
ROZOVA DOLINA
Kazanluk
ORYAHOVICA
Brezovo
Granit
Stara Zagora
Dalboki
Dimiat Tamianka Cabernet Mavrud

SUNGURLARE
Schivatschevo
Sliven
Slaviantzi
Sungurlare
Karnobat
Straldzha
Nova Zagora
Yambol
Misket Rkatziteli

Marea Neagrǎ (Black Sea)
Byala
Aytos
Kableshkovo
Nesebŭr
Pomorie
Burgas

C
D

Kyustendil
Rkatziteli Riesling
Boboshevo
Samokov
Vetrun
Karabunar
Pazardzhik
Plovdiv
Chirpan

Septemvri
Karabunar Pamid Mavrud
Perushtitsa
Asenovgrad
BRESTNIK
Cabernet Merlot Mavrud
ASENOVGRAD
Cabernet Mavrud
Khaskovo

STRANDJA
Elkhovo
Grudovo
JUJEN BRIAG
Rosé
Michurin

KEDONIJA

Razlog
Blagoevgrad
Zapadni Rodopi
Lyubimets
SAKAR
Svilengrad

Merlot
STAMBOLOVO
Kürdzhali
Smolyan

TÜRKIYE

D
E

N

Sandanski
Damianitza
Melnik
Melnik
HARSOVO
Petrich

ELLINIKI (GREECE)

Ivaylovgrad

Sofiya

1:2,500,000

Km. 0 ___ 50 ___ 100 ___ 150 Km.
Miles 0 ___ 50 ___ 100 Miles

— · — · —   International boundary

————   Wine zone boundary

VARNA   Appellation of origin (Controliran)

Gamza   Wine of declared geographical origin

Dimiat   Other grapes or wine names

☐   Wines of controlled appellation of origin (Controliran)

☐   Land over 1000 metres

E
F

F
G

1988
12% vol 75cl e
Lovico Suhindol
BULGARIAN RED WINE
SUHINDOL
Gamza

Bulgarian Country Wine
RUSSE
Welschriesling & Misket

КАБЕРНЕ ОТ ДОЛИНАТА НА ЯНТРА
YANTRA VALLEY
CABERNET SAUVIGNON
CONTROLIRAN 1987
ESTATE BOTTLED BULGARIAN WINE

11.5% vol 75cl e
KHAN KRUM
RIESLING & DIMIAT
BULGARIAN

SPECIAL RESERVE
BULGARIAN
1987
Khan Krum
CHARDONNAY
SHUMEN REGION
ESTATE BOTTLED
75cl e
12% vol
49646

ESTATE BOTTLED BULGARIAN WINE
Шардоне от Варна
Varna Chardonnay
CONTROLIRAN
12% vol 75cl e

RESERVE
12% vol e75cl
Damianitza
MELNIK
Melnik Region
1987

RESERVE
DOMAINE BOYAR'S
Stambolovo
MERLOT
HASKOVO REGION
VINTAGE 1988

12% vol 75cl e
Pulden
1989
A Full Bodied Red Wine
BULGARIAN
Cabernet Sauvignon & Mavrud
PLOVDIV REGION

Estate Bottled 1987 Bulgarian Wine
Assenovgrad Mavrud
CONTROLIRAN
МАВРУД ОТ АСЕНОВГРАД

75 cl e
STARA ZAGORA
12% vol
Controliran Region
ORIACHOVITZA
CABERNET SAUVIGNON & MERLOT
Bulgarian Red Wine
1987

Romania

Romania should have potential for fine wine as great as any of the old East European wine countries. It is not only a matter of situation – although Romania lies on the same latitudes as France – but of temperament. Romania is a Latin country in a Slav sandwich. It seems to have a natural affinity for the culture of France – and France a weakness for Romania. Its wine literature shares the sort of hard-headed lyricism of much of French gastronomic writing.

There is a great difference between the Atlantic influence which makes France moist and mild, and the continental influence which dominates Romania and its hot dry summers. But there are local moderating effects: the Black Sea and the height of the Carpathian Mountains.

In this part of the world political history is inescapable. Romania today is far larger than it was a century ago. Before 1918 Transylvania and Banat were part of Hungary; Dobrogea of Bulgaria. On the other hand the ancient region of Bessarabia, now the new-coined republic of Moldova, was the northern half of Romanian Moldavia.

The Carpathians curl like a snail in the middle of Romania. They occupy almost half the country, rising from the surrounding plain to about 8,000 feet (2,400 metres) at their peaks, and enclosing the Transylvanian plateau, which is still about 1,000 feet (300 metres) above sea-level. Across Wallachia, the south of the country, the Danube (Dunărea) flows through a sandy plain, turning north towards its delta and isolating the maritime province of Dobrogea. Moldavia and Wallachia, east and south of the Carpathians, are Romania's biggest vineyards.

In Romania, as in the old USSR, a great planting programme in the 1960s turned huge tracts of arable land into vineyard, making her at present with 600,000 acres (247,000 hectares) the sixth largest winegrower in Europe, with the eighth largest production. Most of the new vines, unlike those in Bulgaria in the same planting fury, were of the local varieties.

Three-quarters of consumption in Romania is of white wine: Feteasca Alba (famous in Hungary as Leányka) and Welschriesling are most widely planted, but four other white varieties of character are locally important: Feteasca Regala (perhaps a Furmint cross), Frîncusa, Grasa and Tamaioasa; the last two excellent for fragrant sweet wines. Two Romanian red varieties are also vital: Babeasca for big production and light wines, and Feteasca Neagra for dark, substantial *vins de garde*. In addition Cabernet, Merlot and Pinot Noir have long been acclimatized here, and Chardonnay, Aligoté, Pinot Gris, Gewürztraminer, Sauvignon and Muscat Ottonel are all extremely successful.

Like Hungary, Romania has one wine whose name was once famous all over Europe. But while Tokay struggled on through socialism to re-emerge in splendour, Cotnari, which used to appear in Paris restaurants as 'Perle de la Moldavi', faded from sight. It is now being resurrected. Cotnari is a natural white dessert wine, like Tokay but without oxidation: pale, delicate and aromatic; the result of botrytis attacking the indigenous Grasa and Frîncusa, perfumed with Tamaioasa and Feteasca. Barrel-ageing is brief: complexity develops in the bottle. Cotnari comes from the part of Moldavia that was left to the Romanians after first the Tsars, then the Soviets had annexed its northern half – annexation that led to intense planting further south.

The country today is divided into eight wine regions, of which Moldavia, east of the Carpathians, is much the biggest, with over a third of all Romania's vineyards. Wallachia, consisting of the Muntenian and Oltenian Hills, the southern ramparts of Transylvania, comes next with more than a quarter.

Northern Moldavia is white-wine country, with Cotnari as its pearl. The great concentration of production, though, is in the central Moldavian Hills: Vrancea, with Focsani as its capital and 100,000 acres (40,500 hectares) under vine. Cotesti, Nicoresti, Panciu (known for sparkling wine) and Odobesti (a brandy centre) are the lilting names of its wine towns. The terrain varies but much of it is sand, here as in the great plain of Hungary. The vines have to be planted in pockets dug deep enough for their roots to reach the subsoil, sometimes as much as 10 feet (3 metres) below the surface. It seems a desperate expedient, especially as it takes the vine some time to grow up to ground level and come into bearing. But good light wines are being made where nothing would grow before.

The red Babeasca of Nicoresti is a good example of the character of the country; it is pleasantly acidic with a clove-like taste, fresh, original and enjoyable.

Following the curve of the Carpathians Moldavia gives way to Muntenia, better known by the name of its most famous vineyards at Dealul Mare. These hills, well-watered, south-sloping and with the highest average temperatures in Romania, are largely dedicated to Cabernet, Merlot and Pinot Noir – as well as full-bodied Feteasca Neagra. In Soviet days red wines from here were generally made sweet for the demands of the Russian market. Happily, exports to the West have corrected this fault; many Cabernets and Pinot Noirs are now very well made; clean, distinct and not at all over-weight. One white speciality stands out: unctuous and aromatic dessert Tamaioasa (the name means 'frankincense') from Pietroasa.

Romania's short Black Sea coast gives Dobrogea, across the Danube to the east, the country's sunniest climate and lowest rainfall. Murfatlar has a reputation for soft red wines and luscious white ones, even sweet Chardonnays, from exceptionally ripe grapes grown on lime-

Cabernets, Merlots and Pinots of Dealul Mare grow among the bizarre contrast of churches and oil derricks. Wine is one of the first industries to recover from years of tyranny.

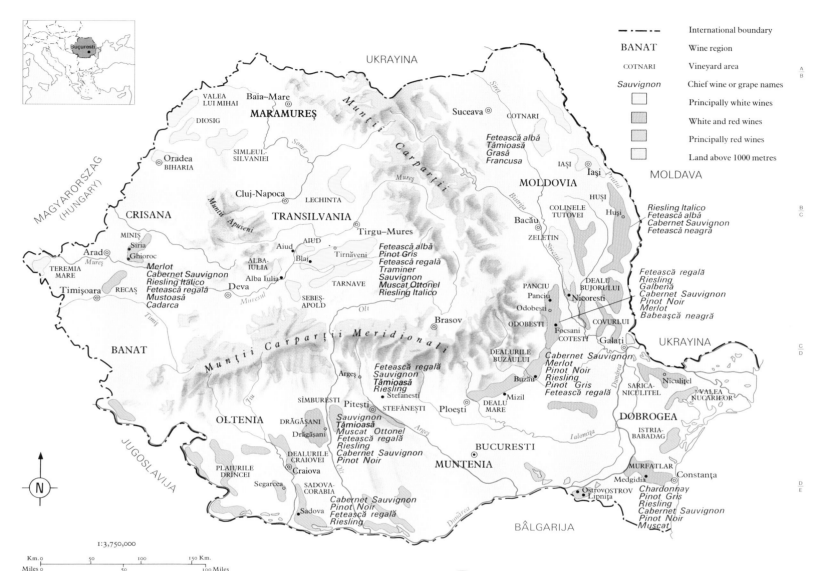

UKRAYINA

BANAT — Wine region (legend)
COTNARI — Vineyard area
Sauvignon — Chief wine or grape names
☐ Principally white wines
☐ White and red wines
☐ Principally red wines
☐ Land above 1000 metres
–·–·–·– International boundary

Bucuresti

MAGYARORSZÁG (HUNGARY)

VALEA LUI MIHAI
Baia–Mare
DIOSIG
MARAMUREȘ
Suceava
COTNARI

Oradea
BIHARIA
SIMLEUL-SILVANIEI

Fetească albă
Tămioasă
Grasă
Francusa

IAȘI
Iași
MOLDAVA

Cluj-Napoca
LECHINTA
Muntii Apuseni
TRANSILVANIA
MOLDOVIA
HUȘI
Bacău
COLINELE TUTOVEI
Huși

CRISANA
MINIȘ
Siria
Ghioroc
Tirgu–Mures
ZELETIN

Arad
BIHARIA
TEREMIA MARE

Merlot
Cabernet Sauvignon
Riesling Italico
Fetească regală
Mustoasă
Cadarca

AIUD
ALBA-IULIA
Aiud
Blaj
Tirnăveni

Fetească albă
Pinot Gris
Fetească regală
Traminer
Sauvignon
Muscat Ottonel
Riesling Italico

TARNAVE

Riesling Italico
Fetească albă
Cabernet Sauvignon
Fetească neagră

Timișoara
RECAȘ
Deva
SEBEȘ-APOLD
Muresul

BANAT

Brasov

Oltul

Munții Carpații Meridionali

PANCIU
Panciu
DEALU BUJORULUI
Nicoresti
Odobesti
ODOBESTI
Focsani
COTESTI
COVURLUI
Galati

Fetească regală
Riesling
Galbenă
Cabernet Sauvignon
Pinot Noir
Merlot
Babească neagră

DEALURILE BUZĂULUI
Buzău
Mizil
DEALU MARE

Cabernet Sauvignon
Merlot
Pinot Noir
Riesling
Pinot Gris
Fetească regală

UKRAYINA

SARICA-NICULITEL
Niculițel
VALEA NUCARILOR

DOBROGEA

Argeș
Ștefănesti
STEFĂNESTI
Ploești

Fetească regală
Sauvignon
Tămioasă
Riesling

ISTRIA-BABADAG

OLTENIA
SÎMBURESTI
Pitesti
DRĂGĂȘANI
Drăgășani

Sauvignon
Tămioasă
Muscat Ottonel
Fetească regală
Riesling
Cabernet Sauvignon
Pinot Noir

BUCURESTI
MUNTENIA

MURFATLAR
Medgidia
Constanța

DEALURILE CRAIOVEI
PLAIURILE DRÎNCEI
Craiova
Segarcea
SADOVA-CORABIA
Sadova

Cabernet Sauvignon
Pinot Noir
Merlot
Fetească regală
Riesling

OstrovOSTROV
Lipnița

Chardonnay
Pinot Gris
Riesling
Cabernet Sauvignon
Pinot Noir
Muscat

JUGOSLAVIJA

BÂLGARIJA

N

1:3,750,000
Km. 0   50   100   150 Km.
Miles 0   50   100 Miles

---

stone soils, tempered by on-shore breezes.

The outcrops of Carpathian foothills scattered through Muntenia and Oltenia each have their own specialities. Pitesti is known for aromatic whites (especially from Stefanesti); Dragasani for Cabernet, Merlot and Pinot Gris, especially from Simburesti. South of here on the Danube plain Segarcea has an established name for Cabernet, and a growing one for Pinot Noir.

In the western corner of Romania the Hungarian influence is plainly felt; many of the red wines of Banat are made from the Kadarka (here spelt Cadarca) of the Hungarian plain. The best come from Minis. The principal white grape is the Welschriesling.

Transylvania, meanwhile, remains like an island in the centre of the country: a plateau 1,500 feet (460 metres) and more above sea-level, cool and relatively rainy, favouring much fresher and crisper white wines than the rest of Romania. Tarnave makes the best dry Feteasca; Alba Julia its most aromatic Muscat Ottonel and Gewürztraminer.

Cotnari is Romania's most distinguished white wine; a strong, dryish, natural dessert wine based on the Grasa grape, which is subject, like the Sémillon (see page 25) to 'noble rot'. Most Romanian labels name the grape variety first and foremost; the whites (Riesling, Feteasca, Furmint, etc) are best. French is commonly used as the label language.

237

Greece

The modern history of Greece has not been kind to its people, nor conducive to international standards of winemaking. Greek wine today presents a strange mixture of domestic secrets and jealousy and Brussels-led regulations. To anyone who is tired of safe international wines, though, it offers vivid and original flavours that make it a vital area of exploration.

Since Greece joined the European Community the process of designating wines according to Community law has brought neglected local specialities into focus. Some are memorable; all are worth trying, even if branded wines from the major négociants still seem to dominate the market. Demestika from Achaia-Clauss at Patras, Lac des Roches and other brands from Boutari at Thessaloníki, Kouros from Kourtakis in Attica … these are the wines you are most likely to find in tourist hotels and restaurants.

Ancient and modern Greece are divided by a gulf with few bridges. The taste for resinated wine, or retsina, is one; perhaps the only characteristic habit of Greece that goes straight back 3,000 years and beyond, to the time when gods walked on earth.

Traces of pine resin have been found in wine amphorae from earliest times – and not only in Greece. It is usually assumed that it was used to preserve the wine. But resinated wine does not age well. There is reason enough in the fresh, sappy, turpentine-like flavour which resin gives if added during fermentation. The result is one of the most individual and appetizing of all drinks, and can also be ideally palate-cleansing with oil-rich rustic food.

Attica, the region of Athens, and the big island of Euboea is the home of retsina – though not uniquely. It can be made anywhere: Lemnos, for example, makes a muscat version. Most of it is white, from the Savatiano grape, but some rosé or *kokkineli* is also made.

The Peloponnese produces one-quarter of Greece's wine from rather more than a half of her vineyards. The conundrum is solved by currants – named 'from Corinth' and still a major industry along the south coast of the Gulf. Although 60% of Greek wine is white, this is red-wine country. Nemea, near Mycenae, uses its apparently unique and presumably ancient Agiorgitiko grape to make spicy, structured wine. The Nemean cooperative, the principal source, calls its best wine Kava Nemea. Grand Palais is another good brand.

Mavrodaphne from Patras is the other celebrated red: a sweet dark wine between an Italian Recioto and a sort of port, concentrated (also slightly fortified, to 15°) and intended for long ageing and solemn tasting – though hard to resist young. Whites in the Peloponnese are rather less interesting. Mantinia is the fresh white of Arcadia (promising address); Patras an appellation for dry white Rhoditis, which is in plentiful supply, and dessert muscats, which are harder to find.

Mountainous central Greece is the least endowed region for designated wines. In Epirus the often fizzy white Zitsa, from near the

Vineyards of the Côtes de Meliton, the oddly named appellation of the Domaine Carras in Sithonia, the central peninsula of Halkidiki. Here both native and French varieties are grown. In the background is the Aegean resort village of Neos Marmaras.

Ottoman city of Ioannina, was enjoyed by both Byron and his theatrical acquaintance Ali Pasha. Epirus has Greece's highest vines at Metsovo, at nearly 4,000 feet (1,200 metres); even some Cabernet sold as Katoyi (not an appellation) at correspondingly high prices. In Thessaly to the east, facing the Aegean, Ankialos is the white for calamari and Rapsani (on Mount Ossa) the red to drink young and – hopefully – rasping.

Physically Macedonia relates more to the Balkan landmass then the Mediterranean limbs of Greece. This is red-wine country, dominated by one variety, the Xynomavro, whose name denotes sourness but whose wines are some of

THE LANGUAGE OF THE LABEL

Παλαιόν (Palaion) Old wine
Ἐνδίκως διατηρημένον (Endikos diatirimenon) Mature quality wine
Ἐπιτραπέζιο κρασί (Epitrapezio) Table wine
Οἰνοπαραγωγᾶς (Oinoparagogas) Wine-producer
Οἰνοποιεῖον (Oinopoieion) Wine factory
Παραγωγὴ καὶ Ἐμφιάλωσις (Paragogi ke emfialosis) Produced and bottled
Οἶνος Λευκός (Oinos lefkos) White wine
Οἶνος Ἐρυθρός or **Μαυρος** (Oinos erythos) or (Mavros) Red wine
Ροζέ (Rosé) or **Κοκκινέλι** (Kokkineli) Rosé
Ρετσίνα (Retsina) Retsina
Ξηρός (Xiros) Dry
Ἀφρώδες κρασί (Afrothes) Sparkling wine

the tastiest in Greece. Naoussa is the best and most important, with 2,000 acres (800 hectares) and the firms of Boutari and Tsantalis, as well as a modern cooperative, are making good examples: dark, heady, full of flavour and astringent in the finish.

Goumenissa, from a much smaller area to the north, is similar but milder; Amindeo, from 1,100 acres (445 hectares) of vines planted at 2,100 feet (650 metres) is lighter, red or rosé and often pétillant.

Naoussa also appears in blends: Cava Boutaris, one of the firm's best wines, blends Naoussa with Nemea, the north with the south. Cava Tstantalis is Naoussa with an addition of Cabernet.

The entry of Greek wine into the modern world was heralded in the 1960s by the arrival of John Carras in Macedonia's very different sea-girt extension, Halkidiki. Carras planted over 1,000 acres (400 hectares) of the central peninsula, Sithonia, with Greek and French varieties – besides developing yachting and tourist facilities.

In 1981 the Carras estate was granted an appellation which reflects its internationalist tendencies: Côtes de Meliton. Cabernet is the principal red grape blended with the Limnio (imported by Carras from the island of Limnos). Meliton whites are from mostly Greek grapes – although Carras also makes non-appellation wines including Sauvignon Blanc. Château Carras is the first label, Domaine Carras the second. Both are well-made, if not precisely vernacular. Surprisingly, the Tsantalis Agiorgitiko wines from the monks of Mount Athos are not without foreign blood either.

Of the Greek islands, Crete is much the biggest wine producer, famous in Venetian times for its sweet Malmseys. They seem, alas, to be extinct. Arhanes, Peza and Dafnes cluster in the mountainous centre of the island: big reds, either dry or sweetish, more suited, perhaps, for Minoan than modern man. (There is also dry white Peza.) Sitia to the east also makes strong but aromatic reds that can be dry or sweet.

Cephalonia and its Ionian neighbours come next in importance, especially for fresh white Rombola (or Robola) and Verdea of Zakinthos.

In the Aegean, several islands make sweet wines of Malvasia, and some of Muscat. Samos is the best and most famous of these and perhaps the only exporter, with utterly clean and tempting wines, although it is rare to find aged examples of Nectar (it can scarcely be too old), its true essence, off the island.

Santorini is the most original and compelling. Its potent and intense wines, white and (very) dry, grow in little nests crouching on the windswept heights of this not-very-extinct volcano. The sweet Visanto of Santorini was once a great industry: the mass-wine of the Russian church.

Rhodes has an ideal climate, and recently has started making wines worthy of it: red Chevalier de Rhodes, white Ilios, some sweet muscat and a sparkling wine which is very refreshing in this Elysian context.

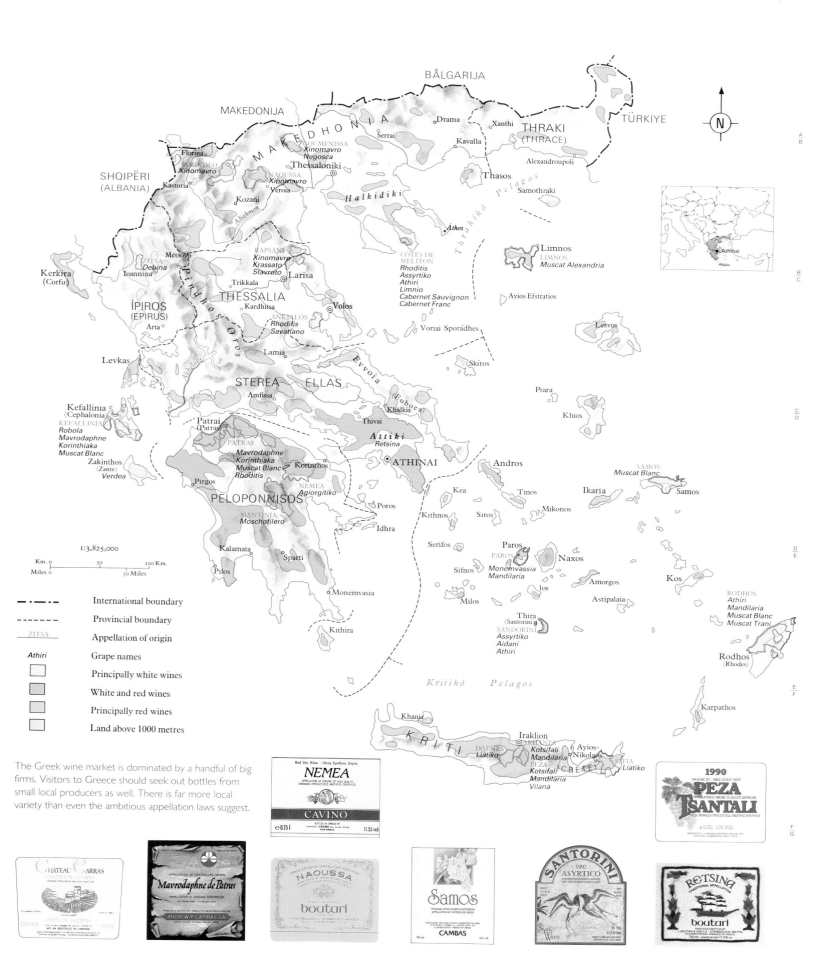

The Greek wine market is dominated by a handful of big firms. Visitors to Greece should seek out bottles from small local producers as well. There is far more local variety than even the ambitious appellation laws suggest.

Russia, Crimea

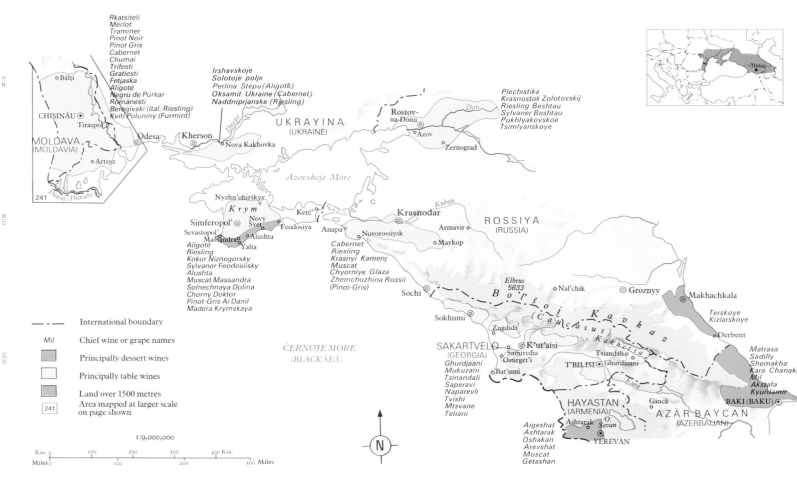

Rkatsiteli
Merlot
Traminer
Pinot Noir
Pinot Gris
Cabernet
Chumai
Trifesti
Gratiesti
Fetjaska
Aligoté
Negru de Purkar
Romanesti
Beregivski (Ital. Riesling)
Kviti Poloniny (Furmint)

Irshavskoje
Solotoje polje
Perlina Stepu (Aligotē)
Oksamit Ukraine (Cabernet)
Naddniprjanske (Riesling)

Plechistika
Krasnostok Zolotovskij
Riesling Beshtau
Sylvaner Beshtau
Pukhlyakovskoe
Tsimlyanskoye

Aligoté
Riesling
Kokur Niznegorsky
Sylvaner Feodosiisky
Alushta
Muscat Massandra
Solnechnaya Dolina
Chorny Doktor
Pinot-Gris Ai Danil
Madera Krymskaya

Cabernet
Riesling
Krasnyi Kamenj
Muscat
Chyorniye Glaza
Zhemchuzhina Rossii
(Pinot-Gris)

Ghurdjaani
Mukuzani
Tsinandali
Saperavi
Naparevli
Tvishi
Mtsvane
Teliani

Aigeshat
Ashtarak
Oshakan
Arevshat
Muscat
Getashan

Terskoye
Kizlarskoye

Matrasa
Sadilly
Shemakha
Kara Chanak
Mil
Akstafa
Kyurdamir

— - — International boundary

Mil Chief wine or grape names

Principally dessert wines

Principally table wines

Land over 1500 metres

241 Area mapped at larger scale on page shown

1:9,000,000

The Soviet Union officially decided in favour of wine – theoretically at the expense of vodka – in the fifties. In 1950 she had nearly a million acres (400,000 hectares) of vineyards. By 1985 she had almost 3.5 million (1.4 million) which made her second only to Spain in the world league table of area under vine, and third in production, behind Italy and France. This is certainly the biggest and fastest extension of the world's winegrowing capacity ever seen. Yet even this was not enough: the Union was an insatiable wine importer, buying in some 7 million hectolitres a year.

Quality, of course, was not the object. To handle these vast quantities a network of primary and secondary wine factories was set up. Primary plants crushed and fermented, then sent wine by tankers to secondary plants in consumer areas – mainly Moscow, Kiev, Leningrad and Vladivostok – where it was finished and bottled at high temperatures that often cooked and effectively ruined it.

The second Russian Revolution of 1989 has not changed the system overnight, but it has opened the door to those enterprises with quality to offer to bypass Moscow. There are numerous chronic difficulties; no bottling equipment or even bottles, for example, in many producing wineries. But the spotlight is now back on the regions which gave Russia her best wines in the past.

The south coast of the Crimea was the Riviera of Tsarist Russia and its chief source of dessert wines. Magnificent muscats, 'ports', 'sherries' and 'madeiras' from the Massandra cellars were sold by Sotheby's in 1990. Russia's best 'champagne' comes from the same coastal strip of vineyards.

Moldova (see opposite) is the most advanced and most promising. This map locates the others – of which the Crimea and Georgia are historically the most important.

The Crimea became part of the Russian Empire under Catherine the Great at the end of the 18th century. The Mediterranean climate of its south coast soon made it the natural resort area for the more adventurous aristocracy. It was developed by the famously rich and cultured anglophile Count Mikhail Woronzov in the 1820s. Woronzov built a winery, and later his palace, at Alupka, southwest of Yalta, and founded a wine institute (wine being his passion) at Magarach nearby.

In a precise parallel with what was going on in Australia at the same time (and California a generation later) Woronzov began by imitating as closely as possible the great wines of France. His success was as limited as someone trying to make burgundy in Barossa. The south coast was too hot. Only 6 miles (10 kilometres) inland, on the other hand, it was too cold. Winter temperatures go down to −10°F (−20°C) and *vinifera* vines have to be entirely buried to survive at all. Notwithstanding there are vast inland plantings by the soviets, mainly of Rkatsiteli, but also of winter-hardy hybrids bred at Magarach.

A generation after Woronzov, Prince Lev Galitzine was more scientific. After the Crimean war of 1854–56 the Tsar built a summer palace,

Moldova

Livadia, between Alupka and Yalta. Galitzine had remarkable success making Russia's second favourite drink, 'champagne', 30 miles (50 kilometres) east along the south coast at his estate Novy Svet ('New World') – a tradition that continues. But the destiny of the Crimea was clearly dessert wines. In 1890 the Tsar built 'the world's finest winery' at Massandra, near Livadia, with Galitzine in charge, to develop the potential of the south coast, a narrow 50-mile (80-kilometre) belt between mountains and sea, for sweet wines of all sorts.

The names of Massandra, Livadia, Alupka and Novy Svet, as well as those of Alushta, Ai-Danil and Ayu-Dag, re-emerged in the West in 1990 at a unique sale held in London by Sotheby's, when wines from the official collection at Massandra, started by Galitzine and dating back to 1880, were auctioned.

The majority were called 'Port' (red or white), 'Madeira', 'Sherry', 'Tokay', 'Cahors', or even 'Yquem', with the exception of the muscats, white, rosé or black. Most of the wines were extremely fine, a large number superb, and the white Massandra Muscat de la Pierre Rouge and the Rose Muscat of Livadia perhaps best of all.

Georgia is a very different case. Far from being a recent colony of the vine, it may be the oldest wine region of all. Its native grape varieties number over 500, and the micro-climates of its many valleys, from its warm and humid Black Sea coast into the almost arid interior of Kakhetia offer different *terroirs* for them all. Georgian peasants still use pre-classical methods, fermenting their wine in *kwevris*, or amphoras, buried up to their necks, with highly aromatic and marvellously varied, if primitive, results.

Nonetheless Pushkin drank Kakhetian in St Petersburg and compared it to 'the finest burgundy'. Despite their epic wars with Caucasian Muslim tribes Russo-Georgian aristocrats established châteaux, of which Tsinandali was and is the most famous, and made highly appreciated wines.

Georgians are notorious for their relish and capacity for wine. But their crippled country is in no state to improve the quality of the wine it currently makes. Today the red Saperavi gives the best available wines (also sold as Mukuzani and Napareuli). Less interesting are the white Tsinandali and Ghurdjaani. Visitors will find Georgia's incredibly cheap and popular 'Champanski', made by the 'continuous flow' method, one of Russia's more benign technological innovations, more tempting.

The Don basin round Rostov specializes in sparkling wine. The red, sweet and sparkling Tsimlyanskoye is best-known. Anapa, south of Krasnodar, has a reputation for Riesling. Chyorniye Glaza ('Black Eyes') is the 'port' of Russia.

Armenia, Azerbaijan and the Caspian Sea coast up to Machackala are dessert-wine country. All the types listed are sweet and strong, red, brown or white, some cooked like madeira. The Matrasa and Sadilly of Baku, red and white table wines, are the notable exceptions.

If the Kremlin cellars of the Tsars took their dessert wines from the Crimea, they turned for their finest table wines to what was then Moldavia (and anciently Bessarabia). Moldova's history has been a tug-of-war between Russia and Romania. Happily for its (largely Romanian) people neither side prevailed. Moldova won the prize of independence in 1991.

During the commissar years the country's natural affinity for the vine was paid the backhanded compliment of a colossal, indiscriminate planting programme, reaching almost 600,000 acres (235,000 hectares) and furnishing one-fifth of the wine of the Soviet Union when that empire was the world's third biggest producer. A combination of very severe winters in the 1980s with Gorbachev's anti-alcohol campaign removed 140,000 acres. But for a country with a population of 4.3 million 450,000 acres (180,000 hectares) – half as much again as Bordeaux – is still a lot of vines.

The elements that combine to grow first-class grapes in Moldova are the latitude of Burgundy, fertile soils, the valley slopes of many rivers and a climate tempered by the Black Sea (although Moldova has no coast; the coastal strip is Ukrainian). Winter is occasionally cold enough to kill unprotected vines, but long-established vineyards in the best sites have an almost model climate, wet in winter and dry in summer.

Like the Napa Valley, which it resembles both in shape and its relationship to the sea (or bay) – though not in size – Moldova is warmer in the north, but also cloudier and damper with colder winters. The south centre, north, east and west of the capital, Chisinau, is the most favoured area. It was chosen by the Romanovs, who invited French vignerons to plant their 1,500-acre (600-hectare) château at Romanesti. They introduced Cabernet, Merlot and Malbec for red wines and Russia's favourite grapes for white: Rkatsiteli and Aligoté. The Romanovs also founded Russia's first wine school at nearby Stauceni (now the top source of Aligoté).

In its role as supplier to Russian society, 19th-century Moldova developed sophisticated (and enormous) cellars not only for table wines, but for 'sherry' (at Ialeveni, south of Chisinau), sparkling wine (at Cricova) and brandy (at Balti in the north). Its most famous vineyard today, though, is at Purcari in the southeast, where Cabernet and Saperavi, the splendid red grape from Georgia, dark, plummy, acidic and long-ageing, make a formidable claret-like blend. When the 1963 vintage of Negru de Purcar was released in the West in 1992 it caused a sensation. At least three joint-venture companies were under way by 1993, one involving Penfold's of Australia, another a Dutch and French team.

A dozen specific small vineyards have already been selected for a rudimentary appellation status to show the best of what Moldova can produce. Politics permitting, it will become one of Europe's most exciting 'new' wine regions.

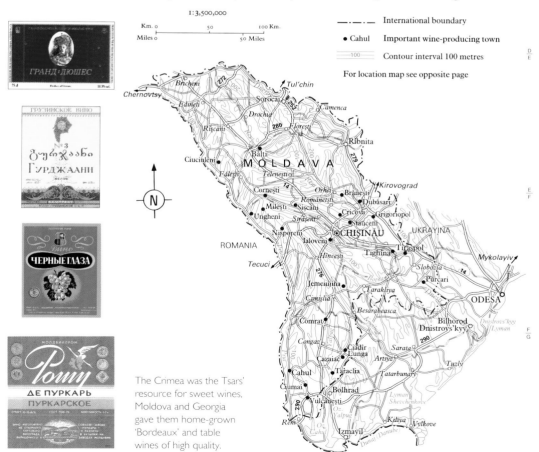

1:3,500,000

Km. 0   50   100 Km.
Miles 0   50 Miles

— · — · —   International boundary
● Cahul   Important wine-producing town
—100—   Contour interval 100 metres
For location map see opposite page

The Crimea was the Tsars' resource for sweet wines, Moldova and Georgia gave them home-grown 'Bordeaux' and table wines of high quality.

The Eastern Mediterranean

Grape vines flourish alongside fig trees in the Bekaa Valley, east of Mount Lebanon. Defiant in the face of two decades of civil war, Château Musar is a wild card among the world's great red wines.

Israel has good, sometimes excellent, red and white wines on offer. Château Musar (*top right*) is the Lebanon's First-Growth. Turkey's growing range of soft reds and fresh whites has not forsaken the indigenous varieties.

It is a sobering thought that some spot on this map may be the very place where man first tasted wine. Whether it was in Turkey or Armenia that the first wine was made, there is no doubt that the Middle East is its home country. Noah, Naboth, Babylon and Baalbek are all evidence that the eastern Mediterranean was the France and Italy of the ancient world – until the eighth century, the advent of Islam.

The Prophet forbade his followers to use wine. How effectively has often been discussed. Caliphs and Sultans were by no means all abstainers. Christians and Jews made the wine – no matter who drank it. But not until the end of the 19th century did wine begin to return to its homeland in earnest. As phylloxera destroyed Europe's vineyards, Asia stepped into the breach. In 1857 the Jesuits founded the cellars of Ksara, still the biggest in the region. In the 1880s a Rothschild started winegrowing once more in Israel. The Ottoman Empire exported nearly 70 million litres in one year in the 1890s (mainly from Thrace and the Aegean). In 1903 Nestor Gianaclis planted the first vines of a new Egyptian wine industry, near Alexandria, whose wine was famous in Roman times.

Gastronomic (as well as sympathetic) interest has long centred around the Lebanon, where one remarkable man, Serge Hochar of Château Musar, continued to make outstanding wine through twenty years of civil war. Musar's vines are on the east slope of Mount Barouk, over-looking the war-ravaged Bekaa Valley. At 3,000 feet (900 metres) Cabernet and Cinsault, the main grapes in the 325-acre (130-hectare) vine-yards, produce extraordinarily aromatic wines, like rich and exotic Bordeaux, long-aged before sale and ageable for decades after. Musar now has a rival, though one with a different style and philosophy. Château Kefraya is made for drink-ing young. The evidence that Château Musar represents of the potential of the Levant for truly fine wine has fascinating implications. It was after all from Canaan (now Lebanon) that the Pharaohs imported their favourite wines.

Turkey is the biggest producer and exporter of the Levant. She has the fifth largest vineyard acreage in the world, but only 3% of her grapes are made into wine. The rest are eaten, fresh or dried. The wine industry is held back by lack of a domestic market, for 99% of the population remains Muslim. Kemal Ataturk, founder of the secular republic, built state wineries in the 1920s in the hope of persuading his people of the virtues of wine. He ensured the survival of indigenous Anatolian grape varieties. But Turks are apparently hard to persuade.

The country is divided into nine ecological zones. Zones II and III, the Aegean coast and Thrace/Marmara, are by far the biggest wine producers, making three-fifths of the total. The state monopoly has 21 wineries and accounts for most exports (mainly in bulk). High-strength blending wine is most in demand, although the names of Trakya and Buzbag, its lighter and darker red wines (from Thrace and southeast Anatolia respectively) are familiar. Buzbag is a noted bargain, a wine of powerful yet pleasing character from one of the nearest vineyards to Noah's. There is also a white (Semillon) Trakya.

Of the private firms, Doluca and Kavaklidere are the leaders. Doluca operates in Thrace (its Villa Doluca and Villa Neva, from Thrace and eastern Anatolia, are reliable); Kavaklidere near Ankara, concentrating on Anatolia's own vari-eties: Narince, Emir and Sultanine whites (including a very fresh Primeur) and Bogazkere, Kalecik Karasi and Öküzgözü reds.

The considerable wineries at Rishon-le-Zion and Zichron-Yaacov were a gift to Israel from Baron Edmond de Rothschild. They make over three-quarters of Israel's wine, mostly from vineyards in the Carmel Valley. Until the 1980s Israeli wines were of Kosher interest only. But planting on the Golan Heights, from the Sea of Galilee up to 4,000 feet (1,200 metres) towards Mount Hermon, began in 1976, Californian technology was shipped in, and in 1987 a Sauv-ignon Blanc emerged to amaze the world. Since then the top Galilee red and white varietals, under the Yarden label, and Gamla and Golan second and third labels, have been consistently good and sometimes excellent. The Rothschild Reserves have been working hard to keep up.

The Gianaclis vineyards still operate in Egypt, northwest of the Nile Delta at Abú Hummus. Four times more white grapes than red are grown, but three-quarters of the white wine is distilled. Among the best-known whites are Cru des Ptolemées and Reine Cléopatre. The Queen would not have been amused.

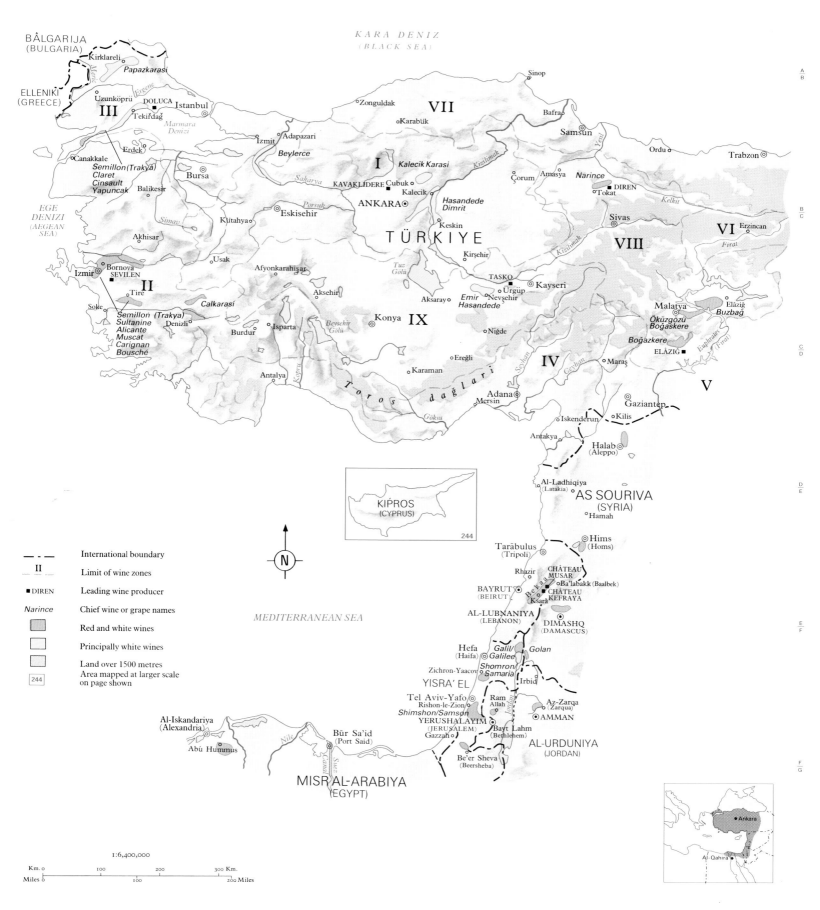

BÂLGARIJA
(BULGARIA)

ELLENIKÍ
(GREECE)

KARA DENIZ
(BLACK SEA)

Kırklareli
Papazkarası

Uzunköprü
DOLUCA
İstanbul

III

Tekirdağ

Sinop

Zonguldak

VII

Karabük

Bafra

Samsun

İzmit
Adapazarı

Beylerce

Ordu

Trabzon

Marmara
Denizi

Erdek

Çanakkale
Semillon(Trakya)
Claret
Cinsault
Yapuncak

Bursa

Balıkesir

I

Sakarya

KAVAKLIDERE Çubuk

ANKARA⊙

Kalecik Karası

Kalecik

Kızılırmak

Çorum

Amasya

Narince

DİREN
Tokat

Kelkit

Sivas

VI
Erzincan

EGE
DENİZİ
(AEGEAN
SEA)

Akhisar

Kütahya

Eskişehir

Porsuk

Hasandede
Dimrit

Kızılırmak

VIII

Fırat

TÜRKİYE

Kırşehir

İzmir
Bornova
SEVİLEN

Tire

II

Simav

Uşak

Afyonkarahisar

Tuz
Gölü

Aksaray

TAŞKO
Ürgüp
Nevşehir

Kayseri

Emir
Hasandede

Malatya

Öküzgözü
Boğaskere

Elazığ
Buzbağ

Söke

Semillon (Trakya)
Sultanine
Alicante
Muscat
Carignan
Bousché

Denizli

Çalkarası

Burdur
Isparta

Beyşehir
Gölü

Konya

IX

Niğde

Boğazkere

ELAZIĞ

Euphrates/Fırat

Ereğli

Antalya

Köprü

Toros   dağları

Karaman

Seyhan

Ceyhan

IV

Maraş

V

Göksu

Adana
Mersin

Gaziantep

İskenderun

Kilis

Antakya

Halab
(Aleppo)

Al-Ladhiqiya
(Latakia)

AS SOURIYA
(SYRIA)

Hamah

KIPROS
(CYPRUS)

244

Hims
(Homs)

Tarābulus
(Tripoli)

Rhazir

CHÂTEAU
MUSAR

Ba'labakk (Baalbek)

BAYRUT
(BEIRUT)

Beka'a

Ksara

CHÂTEAU
KEFRAYA

AL-LUBNANIYA
(LEBANON)

DIMASHQ
(DAMASCUS)

MEDITERRANEAN SEA

Hefa
(Haifa)

Galil/
Galilee

Golan

Zichron-Yaacov

Shomron/
Samaria

Irbid

YISRA'EL

Tel Aviv-Yafo
Rishon-le-Zion

Shimshon/Samson

Ram
Allah

Jordan

Az-Zarqa
(Zarqua)

⊙ AMMAN

YERUSHALAYIM
(JERUSALEM)⊙

Bayt Lahm
(Bethlehem)

AL-URDUNIYA
(JORDAN)

Gazzah

Al-Iskandariya
(Alexandria)

Abū Hummus

Nile

Būr Sa'id
(Port Said)

Suez Canal

Be'er Sheva
(Beersheba)

MISR AL-ARABIYA
(EGYPT)

International boundary

II   Limit of wine zones

■ DİREN   Leading wine producer

Narince   Chief wine or grape names

Red and white wines

Principally white wines

Land over 1500 metres

244   Area mapped at larger scale
      on page shown

N

1:6,400,000

Km. 0   100   200   300 Km.

Miles 0   100   200 Miles

Ankara

Al-Qahira

Cyprus

Cyprus not only has one of the oldest wine-growing traditions in the world, it is the most developed and successful of the wine countries of the eastern Mediterranean; the first (during its period of British rule, starting in 1878) to restore wine to the prime place in the economy it had before the Muslim invasion.

In the last 30 years methodical innovations opened a huge export market. The fall of the USSR was a serious blow: the Soviets bought vast quantities of dry red and Commandaria. Cyprus sherry made the running for many years, but with declining demand the island's potential for good-quality table wines is slowly emerging.

The Troodos Mountains, attracting rain, make viticulture possible on what would otherwise be too dry an island. The vineyards lie where the rains fall, in idyllic green valleys up to nearly 3,000 feet (900 metres) into the hills. The whole south-facing Troodos is possible wine country. Limassol, the port on the south coast, is the entrepôt and headquarters of the four big wine firms, ETKO (the oldest winery on the island, dating from 1844), KEO, Laona and Loel, and the cooperative SODAP.

The most individual of Cyprus wines is the liquorous Commandaria, made of dried grapes, both red and white, in fourteen villages, of which Kalokhorio, Zoopiyi and Yerasa are best known, the lower slopes of the Troodos. Commandaria has been made at least since the crusading Knights Templar established themselves in their Grande Commanderie on the island at the end of the 12th century. Its intense sweetness (it can have four times as much sugar as port) harks back far further than records go; there are references in Greek literature to such wines, which were invariably drunk diluted with water (sometimes seawater). The sweetness is achieved by drying the grapes to raisins on sheets spread on the ground among the vines.

Commandaria is now made both as a straight commercial dessert wine of moderate age, popular for the Sacrament in churches, cheap and pleasant but without interest, and in very small quantities as the quite alarmingly concentrated wine of legend. The taste and texture of an old true Commandaria are more than treacly; the best have a remarkable haunting fresh grapiness.

The range of grapes grown on Cyprus is much less eclectic than in most developing wine countries. The island has never had phylloxera, and rather than risk it by importing new stock, growers until recently kept to the island's traditional grapes: the black Mavron (still 70% of the vineyard), the white Xynisteri, Ophthalmo and the Muscat of Alexandria.

The last decade, though, has seen an increase in vineyard acreage (to 60,000 acres; 24,000 hectares), and the introduction of new varieties. The Palomino of Jerez is used both for sherry and a very pleasant soft dry white wine. Grenache is used for lighter reds than the heavyweight Mavron normally produces (Domaine d'Ahera is one), and experiments with Shiraz, Cabernet and Chardonnay have encouraged further planting.

Earlier picking has raised standards generally. We can expect to see new, more aromatic wines from this lovely island. For the moment, diners at the best Greek restaurants (all of which seem to be run by Cypriots) are very content with such plain but appealing reds as Othello and Semeli, Negro or Afames. They are best at three or four years old. The first choice for a refreshing white wine in the Cyprus sun is the lightly fizzy Bellapais, made by KEO and named after the abbey of Bellapais near Kyrenia.

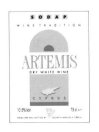

Above: Commandaria is sadly underrated: a true original. Cyprus table wines and sherry are reliable.

Chief wine village · Arsos

Leading vineyard area

Other vineyard area

Land above 1000 metres

1 : 1,065,000

North Africa

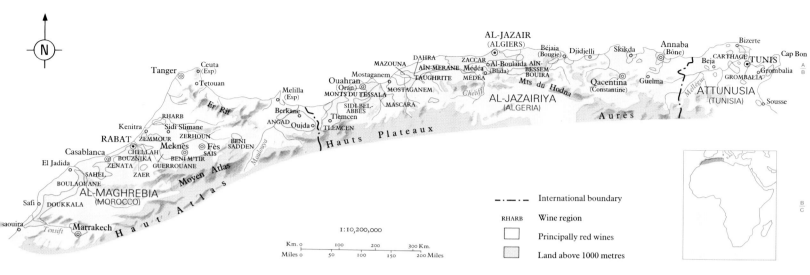

Map legend:
- —·—·— International boundary
- RHARB — Wine region
- □ Principally red wines
- ▨ Land above 1000 metres

1:10,200,000

Km. 0 — 100 — 200 — 300 Km.
Miles 0 — 50 — 100 — 150 — 200 Miles

North Africa's profile as a wine producer has sunk ever lower since its palmy days of 40 years ago, when Algeria, Morocco and Tunisia between them accounted for no less than two-thirds of the entire international wine trade. Algeria alone had one million acres (over 400,000 hectares).

Almost all this vast quantity went to Europe (mainly to France) as blending wine, appreciated for its strength, colour and concentration. Algeria was by far the biggest source. When it became independent from France in 1962 the decline was immediate: there was practically no domestic business. Algeria has continued to either pull up or neglect her vineyards. Between 1966 and 1991 her crop has shrunk from 16 million hectolitres to less than one million. Eighty percent of her vines are more than 40 years old and presumably will not be replaced.

This is not to say that all Algerian wine is, or need be, of poor quality. Light soils and hot sunshine make them strong, but certain wines of the hills were given VDQS status in French colonial days. Moreover, it is the best hill vineyards that have been maintained, while the plains now grow cereals.

There are seven designated quality regions, all in the western provinces of Oran and Alger. The Coteaux de Tlemcen, nearest to Morocco, produces very adequate red, rosé and white; powerful and dry but not coarse. Wine from the Monts du Tessala seems not so good, but the Coteaux de Mascara has an old reputation and makes both rich reds and respectable smooth and fruity white.

Taughrite, Aïn-Merane and Mazouna, the modern names of the Dahra crus formerly called

Robert, Rabelais and Renault, make strong, clean reds and attractive lighter rosé. The Coteaux du Zaccar, further from the sea, seems to produce less fruity flavours. To the east again the Médéa Hills, with vineyards up to 4,000 feet (1,200 metres), and Aïn-Bessem Bouira make some of Algeria's best wines. All in all it is the rosés that are most appealing. The top prestige wine, Cuvée du Président, is not necessarily as good as the best of the local offerings.

Commonsense would suggest that Morocco, benefiting from the influence of the Atlantic, should have North Africa's best vineyards. Although they too have shrunk to about half their acreage in 1970, they have never been huge, and have aimed at quality rather than quantity. The Moroccan Appellation d'Origine Garantie is enforced by the central organization, SODEVI, that organizes all wine production.

The region of Meknès-Fès, at more than 1,500 feet (450 metres) in the middle Atlas foothills, is the most important, making the impressive red exported as Tarik and Chantebled (respectively heavier and lighter, but both smooth and well made). Since 1993 the Domaine de Sahari near Meknès, with 3,000 acres (1,200 hectares), has added Cabernet and Merlot to its range of Rouge de Guerrouane (a blend of Cinsault, Carignan, Grenache and Alicante Bouschet with a little Syrah) and a Gris made of Cinsaut. Around Rabat on the coastal plain, satisfying soft reds are sold under district names: Rharb, Chellah, Zemmour and Zaer. South of Casablanca vin gris is the speciality, white made of red grapes which should be served ice-cold. The Gris de Boulaouane is the one wine you will find east of the Atlantic

still made of the Criolla grape, alias the Mission of California (and País of Chile). It becomes a familiar friend to visitors in a land that lacks white grapes.

Tunisia, like Morocco, is trying to improve quality to generate exports. Muscat wines have always been her speciality – and probably were in Carthaginian times. Today she makes muscats both sweet and dry (the dry on Cap Bon), but some of her red and rosé wines may appeal more to conventional taste.

The union of cooperatives is the biggest producer. Its standard lines are red Coteaux de Carthage from the hills around Tunis, Château Mornag rosé from hills further east, dry Muscat de Kelibia from Cap Bon, and Magon, a richer red than the Coteaux de Carthage, from Tébourba in the Medjerdah Valley to the west.

The state winery makes Château Thibar, a red from the northwest of Tunisia, and Sidi Selem, another red from Mornag. Two independent producers, Lamblot and Château Feriani, make their notable reds north of Tunis, in the Coteaux d'Utique. Two others, Lavau and Tardi, are in the Tébourba region and the hills to the north.

Tunisia has plenty of sound red wine, good sweet mucats, attractive rosés (some of them, admittedly, muscat-scented). So far there is a shortage of good white wine. Algeria, in this regard, still leads both her seemingly more ambitious neighbours.

Below: the dwindling Algerian vineyards maintain their former French VDQS names. But Morocco and Tunisia have overtaken Algeria in quality. Pale *vin gris* is a Moroccan staple, especially south of Casablanca.

Asia

The human geography of wine poses some questions that must intrigue anyone who believes in wine as a blessing to mankind. The most imponderable concerns the East.

The Arab world renounced wine in the 8th century – at least in theory: certain Caliphs, and certainly Seljuk and Ottoman Sultans, saw no sense in postponing the pleasure until the after-life. The Persians were the most reluctant to abandon it, as the Rubaiyat of Omar Khayyám so clearly explains. Shiraz in the Zagros Mountains in southern Persia was a great centre of export-quality wine (mainly to India) until the 19th century. Indeed it is recorded that in 1677 Shiraz was exporting its wine in bottles, something hardly ever done in Europe at that time.

In the 16th century Afghan vineyards supplied the Indian Mogul court. Today Poona in the Maharashtra Hills above Bombay produces sparkling wines (Omar Khayyám and Pompadour) of a quality well worth exporting to Europe. As far south as Bangalore Cabernet Sauvignon is growing in the Dodballapur Hills. Grover Vineyards is planning to produce 100,000 cases a year. There also remain scattered traces of the Hounza vineyards, high in the Hindu Kush, that lined the more fertile parts of the Silk Road – the route the wine-vine travelled to China.

The vine was known to 2nd-century gardeners in China – who called one variety 'vegetable dragon pearls'. They knew how to make wine with it, and did so. Why did it not become part of their way of life, as it has in every Western country where it will grow successfully?

The late Edward Hyams, who made a study

Below: Asiatic ambivalence about wine has a long history. It was openly enjoyed by the 16th-century rulers of Mogul India, Muslims though they were. India is still ambivalent today, with excellent sparkling wine from near Bombay (*right*) being labelled 'for export only'. China (*far right*) has no such inhibitions. Huadong is the quality leader.

1:5,128,000

of the references to wine in oriental literature, concluded that it simply does not suit the Asiatic temperament. It clearly brings out the best in Western man, but, for the Chinese, wine from grapes, with its complexity of flavours and its soothing, inspiring effect, has never 'taken'. Perhaps today there is an even simpler reason. The Chinese eat strongly seasoned food hurriedly. They need something simply liquid to wash it down, plus a strong drink, a rice spirit, to toast each course with. To the Chinese, any alcohol should have fire in it.

This being said, there have been substantial vineyards in northern China during this century at least. The district of Tsingtao (Qindao) in

Shantung (Shandong) Province was under strong missionary influence early this century; vineyards were planted and cellars constructed. Germans built the first winery in Tsingtao. When they left, their barrels continued to be used – eventually with disastrous effects on the wine. The taste of oxidation became familiar in the sherried condition of what little Tsingtao wine was seen in the West.

Recently, in China's new mood of openness, several moves have been made to install a modern wine industry. It seems that soils are suitable. Climate is more problematical. Inland it suffers typical continental extremes, while the coast is subject to monsoons. Nothing wonderful has

Japan

happened yet, but on the map you may be looking at an important wine region of the future.

The Shandong Peninsula (shown here) is the only region with any recent wine history. Yantai (formerly Cheefoo: the name on labels is now Changyu) and Tsingtao had the first 20th-century wineries. There are said to be some 35,000 acres (14,000 hectares) of vines in the province today (mainly of table grapes) producing about one million cases in five main wineries – the two mentioned plus Wei Fang, He Ze and Ji Nan. Little village operations add to the total. The old grape varieties seem to have been largely Russian and German.

The Rémy Martin Company was probably the first to collaborate with the Chinese in making a white wine of local Dragon Eye grapes, flavoured with Muscat (brought from Bulgaria in 1958). They called it Dynasty. Its success in Chinese restaurants has encouraged them to plant classic varieties in Tianjin municipality, southeast of Peking (north of Shandong).

A second joint venture produced Great Wall, also in Tianjin. A third, involving the French Pernod-Ricard company, took the vine 75 miles (120 kilometres) northwest of Peking, to the rainshadow of the Yan Mountains near the Great Wall (the winery is in western Peking). The local Dragon Eye is being augmented with Chardonnay, Cabernet . . . all the usual suspects, plus Muscat, much appreciated in China, and quality is promising. The main problem is winter cold, which makes it necessary to dig trenches and bury the vines each season.

On the face of it the Shandong Peninsula looks the most likely place to grow European grapes. It is the only part of China with a maritime climate, and offers well-drained south-facing slopes near the sea. The initiative here was taken by an Englishman in Hong Kong, Michael Parry; a joint venture with the Tsingtao winery (the name is familiar from China's best-known beer). A promising start was interrupted by fallout from the Tiananmen Square massacre in 1989. Parry died. But his assistant introduced Hiram Walker to the business, which has taken wine-quality in China to a new level by exploiting slopes on the south side of the Peninsula. So far Riesling and Chardonnay have both reached fair international levels of quality. The brand name is Huadong.

Thus much is perhaps not surprising, simply the thin end of a hopeful wedge. What is truly strange to learn is that the greatest concentration of vineyards in China is as far from Western influence – and from the sea – as it is possible to get: in the extreme northwest, north of Tibet and close to Kazakhstan, in the Turpan Depression in the autonomous province of Xinjan Urgur. In the very heart of Asia, it lies on almost the perfect latitude for the vine: that of the south of France and north of Italy. There are 28,000 acres (11,000 hectolitres) of vines. Unfortunately, however, no wine. In the heart of the huge Asian landmass, summer is so fiercely and continuously hot that the grapes turn to raisins on the vine.

Nature, in constructing Japan, seems to have had almost every form of pleasure and enterprise in view except wine.

Although the latitude of Honshu, the main island of the Japanese archipelago, coincides with that of the Mediterranean, its climate does not. Like the eastern United States (lying in the same latitudes), it suffers from having a vast continent to the west. Caught between Asia and the Pacific, the greatest land and sea masses in the world, its predictably extreme climate is peculiar to itself. Winds from Siberia freeze its winters; monsoons from the Pacific and the Sea of Japan drench its springs and summers. At the precise moments when the vine needs sunshine, for flowering in early summer, and for ripening towards harvest, the rainy seasons, *baiyu* and *shurin*, come pat upon their cue. And between the two come the summer typhoons.

The land the typhoons lash is hard-boned and mountainous, almost two-thirds of it so steep that only the forests prevent the acid soil from being washed into the short, turbulent rivers. The plains have alluvial 'paddy' soils, washed from the hills, poor-draining and good for rice, not vines. The little gently sloping arable land there is is consequently extremely valuable and demands a high return.

It is not surprising, perhaps, if Japan has hesitated about wine; hesitated, that is, for about 1,200 years. History is exact. Wine was grown in the 8th century AD at the court of Nara.

Buddhist missionaries spread the grape vine around the country – although not necessarily with wine in mind. In 1186, near Mount Fuji, a seedling vine with thick-skinned grapes (*Vitis vinifera orientalis* 'Caspica') was selected and named Koshu: it remains the variety best suited to Japanese conditions, making decent white wine. Another is Zenkoji, the grape known in China as Dragon Eye.

In the 15th century Portuguese traders, and in the 16th St Francis Xavier, preaching to the Yamaguchi court, introduced red 'tinta wine'. In 1569 a great warlord, Oda Nobunaga, held a famous wine-tasting party for his samurai generals. By the 17th century the characteristic form of Japanese vineyard had been invented: a way of training the vine that counteracts, as far as possible, the tendency to rot brought on by summer rain. The 'tanazukuri' system trains a vine vertically, about as high as a man's reach, then fans out its branches horizontally on wire supports for 30 feet (10 metres) or more in all directions. A traditional Japanese vineyard is one vast pergola, with the advantages of taking up the minimum of valuable land, and allowing the maximum circulation of air around the hanging grapes.

Below: old-style Japanese vineyards are a strange sight: overhead vines trained on wires to cover large areas. The aim is air-circulation to avoid rot in a warm humid climate. Straw jackets guard against winter cold. But quality suffers and new vineyards are conventionally trellised and pruned.

Above: Mann's (owned by Kikkoman), Suntory and Mercian (Sunraku Ocean) are the real driving forces in Japan's new quality wine industry. Iwanohara is a subsidiary of Suntory.

Japanese grape-producing regions

1 : 1,333,000

------- Prefecture boundary

■ SUNTORY Winery

Jyonohira Vineyard name

▨ Vineyard

▨ Land 1000-2000 metres

☐ Land above 2000 metres

The disadvantages of this system of vine-growing is that the spreading plant, its roots constantly watered, even in shallow soil, produces a huge crop of watery grapes. Sugar levels are so low that the law allows unlimited addition of sugar up to an amazing 260 grams per litre. 'Extract' is also low: the wine tastes at best mild, at worst downright watery.

A wine industry, in the modern sense, has nonetheless existed for 100 years. Japan's first outward-looking government, in the 1870s, sent researchers to Europe to study methods and to bring back vines.

It soon became clear that American vines did better than French or German. Nor were the Japanese averse to the 'foxy' flavour of eastern American grapes. The Delaware became the most planted variety, with the Muscat of Alexandria the only popular *vinifera* vine.

The industry, from the start, was based in the hills around the Kofu Basin, in Yamanashi Prefecture, within view of Mount Fuji and convenient for the capital. The original winery built by the Mercian company can still be seen, a historic landmark with its water-powered crusher and vats made from bamboo.

Up to the 1960s many small firms in Kofu made wine as sweet as possible for an unsophisticated market. Since 1970 three big companies, able to distribute nationally, have taken over. Only one, Suntory, is a major grape grower, with 370 acres (150 hectares). Mercian and Mann's buy mostly from farmers. All three now have at least small supplies of the best European grapes. To protect them from untimely rain a polymer sheet is permanently installed in the 'lyre' trellis. In general their Cabernets and Chardonnays are correct, if a trifle faint. Until 1985 the one outstanding wine was made from 'nobly rotten' Riesling and Sémillon by Suntory: a truly memorable (and incredibly expensive) imitation of Sauternes. Suntory's Chateau Lion Cabernet can also be remarkably good.

All three firms have now gone further, experimenting with Chardonnay, Cabernet and Merlot with remarkable success. Château Lumière is another producer with Chardonnay and Cabernet. The map shows the 1993 distribution of premium vineyards and wineries.

All Suntory's vines are in Yamanashi. Mann's grows Cabernet in Yamanashi; mainly white grapes and Merlot in Nagano to the west, and Chardonnay in Fukushima to the east. (Rainfall diminishes as you go east, while Yamanashi has the highest average temperatures and earliest budbreak, flowering and vintage.)

Mercian favours Nagano for Merlot and Chardonnay. Its Kikyogahara Merlot of 1985 led the way in colour and concentration and had all the characteristics of a very good French example. Mercian believes the higher temperatures of Yamanashi are better for Cabernet Sauvignon. No one who has tasted the Jyonohira Cabernet of recent vintages would argue.

248

The New World

North America

'The goodliest soil under the cloak of heaven' was how one of Raleigh's men described the new-found Carolinas. One of the most impressive sights was their grapevines, whose fruit festooned the forests. The grapes were sweet, if strange to taste. It was natural to assume that wine would be one of the good things of the New World.

Yet 300 years of American history are a saga of the shattered hopes of would-be wine-growers. First, of those who used the wild grapes they found. 'They be fatte, and the juyce thicke. Neither doth the taste so well please when they are made into wine', wrote Captain John Smith in 1606. Then, of those who imported European vines and planted them in the new colonies. They died.

The colonists did not give up. Having no notion what was killing their vines, they assumed it was their fault and tried different sorts and different methods. As late as the Revolution, Washington tried, and Jefferson, a great amateur of wine who toured France for the purpose, had a determined attempt. Nothing came of it. The American soil was full of the European vine's deadliest enemy, phylloxera. Aided by bitter winters and hot humid summers such as Europe never sees, which brought with them fungus diseases, America foiled everyone who tried to make European wine.

If American wines of American grapes were bad, some were worse than others. The ancestry of grapes is almost impossible to trace, but either a chance sport of an American vine, or else a natural hybrid between an American and a European vine, gave its grower hope of better things. More improvements came to diligent gardeners who planted pips and tried out the results. Some of these hybrids became famous. The Catawba was born thus, and in 1843 the Concord – one of the healthiest, most prolific, best-looking and tastiest grapes ever introduced.

The peculiarity of American grapes the colonists disliked only emerges fully when they are made into wine. The wine has a flavour known as 'foxy' – a distinct and easily recognized scented taste, which precludes any subtlety or complexity. There are many American species. Foxiness is most pronounced in *Vitis labrusca*. Unfortunately *V. labrusca* must have had its genes in Catawba and been one, if not both, of the parents of the Concord. And it continued to be used by hybridizers who produced such other famous American grapes as the Delaware.

Since these were the best grapes Americans could grow, Americans grew them. Vineyards were started in New York, New Jersey, Virginia and, above all, Ohio. It was at Cincinnati, Ohio, that the first commercially successful American wine was born – Nicholas Longworth's famous Sparkling Catawba. Longworth hit on the fact that foxiness is least objectionable in sparkling wine. By 1850 he had 1,200 acres (485 hectares) of Catawba vineyards and was making a fortune.

It was short lived. Vine disease, the Civil War and finally Longworth's death in 1863 ended Cincinnati's challenge to Reims. But the point

The Franciscan missionary Father Junípero Serra is said to have planted the first vines in California in 1769.

Thomas Jefferson, wine connoisseur and would-be winegrower, promoted wine as the best means of combating intemperance.

------- State boundary
• Austin State capital
⬤ Pre-Prohibition vineyard area
· Vineyard
· Winery

was made. Longworth's champagne makers soon found new employers: the new Pleasant Valley Wine Co. of Hammondsport on New York's Finger Lakes. This time American wine had found a permanent home. From the Finger Lakes the eastern wine industry has spread to such promising new pastures as Long Island (described on page 274). Here we must trace the progress of America's other winemaking tradition, which came in under Spanish colours by the back door, while the Anglo-Saxons were struggling with the native vines at the front.

The earliest Spanish settlers in Mexico had established the vine there in the 16th century with tolerable success. Their primitive vine, known as the Mission (presumably a seedling, since it is unknown in Europe) flourished in Baja California. But not for 200 years did the Franciscan fathers move north up the coast of California. In 1769 the Franciscan Junípero Serra, founding the San Diego Mission, is said to have planted California's first vineyard.

There were none of the problems of the East Coast here. *Vitis vinifera* had found its Promised Land. The vine moved up the coast with the chain of missions, arriving at the northernmost, Sonoma, by 1805. There, although the missions declined, viticulture flourished. Jean-Louis Vignes brought better grapes than the Mission from Europe to Los Angeles. Came the Gold Rush and massive immigration. By the 1850s the redoubtable figure of Agoston Haraszthy had taken over, organizing, after a fashion, the new wine industry, and personally bringing 100,000 cuttings of innumerable varieties from Europe.

Thus by the mid-19th century America had two wine industries, poles apart. She still has – but the gap is narrowing; the east is struggling to emulate the west. Both limped through the disaster of Prohibition making sacramental wine (even sparkling sacramental wine) and selling grape juice with the warning 'Caution – do not add yeast or the contents will ferment'. They took over a decade to find their feet again after Repeal, and Americans took more than a generation to take up regular wine drinking. It still remains a minority taste. But today the scene is

1:21,750,000

m. 0   200   400   600   800 Km.

les 0   200   400 Miles

The Hungarian Agoston Haraszthy galvanized the California wine industry by introducing scores of new vine varieties in the 1840s.

Frank Schoonmaker, writer and wine merchant, influenced California to make quality wine after Prohibition by promoting 'varietal' labelling.

Philip Wagner, writer and winemaker, introduced hybrid grapes to the eastern States; a historic move in American wine history.

Eugene Hilgard, at the Agricultural Experiment Station, started in 1880 to lay the foundations of scientific viticulture in California.

James D Zellerbach pioneered the use of French oak for ageing California wine. His Chardonnay of the '50s were a turning point.

Dr Konstantin Frank proved that good wine can be made from European grapes in the Finger Lakes district of New York.

full of activity and experiment, with vineyards being planted (in many cases replanted) not only in California and New York but in most of the other states of the Union as well.

The South has a small wine industry of its own based on the native grape of its hot, damp woods: *Vitis rotundifolia*, the Scuppernong. The Scuppernong holds its big cherry-like grapes in clusters, not pressed together in bunches, and thus avoids the inevitable bunch-rot of normal grapes in the climate of Georgia and the Carolinas. Scuppernong wine is very sweet and uncompromisingly strange to *vinifera*-trained tongues.

Most of the other states with infant industries started by planting either the well-proven American vines (of which Concord is by far the most popular, dreadful though its wine is) or else the new French-American hybrids which were bred in France in the hope of solving the phylloxera problem, but are more appreciated in America as possible solutions to the riddle of the fox. The hybrids were first introduced by Philip Wagner of Boordy Vineyards in Mary-

land – perhaps a contribution as significant as that of Jean-Louis Vignes.

On the other hand, most are now planting, gingerly at first, at least some of the classic *vinifera* varieties that give them their one chance of entering the mainstream of wine.

The young vineyards of the mid-Atlantic States and the older ones of New York, Ohio and Michigan are mapped on pages 274–75. The most recent recruit to their number, recent at least for the making of quality wine, is the Canadian province of Ontario, which benefits, like Ohio and Michigan, from the almost maritime influence of the Great Lakes.

Meanwhile on the West Coast the states of Washington, Oregon and Idaho have demonstrated their ability to make wine at least as good as California's. Their enthusiasm has spilled over the Canadian border, too, into an infant wine industry in British Columbia. The wine country of the Northwest is mapped on pages 270–73. More surprising is the current activity in southern and western states which appeared complete strangers to the vine. West Texas is doing things

on the biggest scale, with considerable plantings near Lubbock, but New Mexico and Arizona also have promising vineyards (see pages 268–69). The secret here is a high enough altitude to provide cool growing conditions. Rainfall is too scant to be reliable; irrigation is essential.

In the Midwest, Missouri has a long history of growing American grapes, and more recently hybrids. Augusta made this point when in 1980 it became America's first designated viticultural area or AVA. Few people realize, though, that Swiss immigrants in Arkansas planted *vinifera* grapes there more than 100 years ago, and are still working on it.

The question raised by all this enthusiasm is really an economic one. Given that it may be possible to make wines of adequate or better quality in almost all of the 50 states (Hawaii is included; alas, Alaska not), will it be worthwhile? California currently produces nearly 90% of American wine in near-ideal conditions. How long will it take for more than a local market to develop in the offerings of aspiring new vineyards, however good?

California

Thirty years ago, in the mid-1960s, the ground rules of California wine were simple. A handful of traditional wineries, all grouped around San Francisco Bay but most of them in the Napa Valley, were making a few wines of remarkable quality. Vast, technologically advanced wineries elsewhere in the state, using grapes drawn from both the Bay Area and the Central Valley, were making sound and extremely good value everyday wines. Life was quiet in the vineyards: America did not appreciate her luck. You could buy a beautiful mature Beaulieu or Martini, Krug or Inglenook Cabernet for the price of a steak – but few people did.

The perceptive at the same time were aware of developments that were to start a revolution. It began with small-scale, almost 'hobby' wineries: Stony Hill in the Napa Valley making Chardonnay in a new style, firm yet delicate; Hanzell, over the hills in Sonoma, importing French oak barrels to bring burgundian flavours to Chardonnay and Pinot Noir; Heitz, in St Helena, buying wines and grapes, elaborating them with a bold touch and demanding a price that rocked people on their heels; the little Château Souverain, near Geyserville, making such fine-tuned Riesling, Zinfandel and Cabernet that classic European wines sprang to mind.

In 1966 Robert Mondavi left his old family firm of Charles Krug to build his own winery at Rutherford. The rest had been jostling at the gate. This was the gun. With Mondavi, wine became news; everything was in the open; not to know was to be behind the times. A trickle of new wineries grew rapidly to a spate. There were 25 Napa wineries in 1960; by 1972 the number was 44. Between 1972 and 1982 both the number of wineries and the vineyard acreage multiplied again by three; from 1982 to 1992 the number of wineries doubled again. The figures for the whole of California show an increase in the same decade of 50% in wine-grape acreage, and 30% in the number of wineries, to 820.

Change has been almost as prodigious as growth. The accepted wisdom of California's wine geography has had a series of surprises. A glance at the map shows a broad and simple division into inland vineyards, running the length of the Central Valley behind the Coast Ranges, and more or less coastal grape-growing regions. An early study by the influential Department of Viticulture and Enology of the University of California divided the state into a series of zones, using the method known as heat summation (see the map opposite). In 1944 five zones were plotted, the coolest nearest to northern Europe in climate (or rather in growing-season temperature), the hottest comparable to North Africa.

The constant contention of the Department has been that the way ahead lies in planting the right grape variety in the right place – place, that is, defined by climate. After a generation of following the Department's recommendations, growers have found that nothing is as simple as it seems. In France, growers are fond of saying that their soil changes with every step. In California, anyone can see that it is the climate

Nothing has changed the status and self-esteem of wine-growers in California as much as discovering what the aromas and flavours of French oak barrels have to offer.

that ducks and swerves. California's attitude to France's attitude to soil was sceptical – even sniffy. California's coastal soils are pretty consistent, ran the argument. Where they vary it is mainly in depth and porosity, and hence in the speed of drainage they provide. But by the time the exposure, elevation, heat summation, sun hours, frost risk and ten other factors have been counted, soil has generally been discounted. It seemed safer to stick to the obvious facts: above all, that the more mountains there are between you and the sea, the less chance there is of the sea air reaching you to moderate the climate.

So cold is the inshore water of the Pacific, from Mendocino in the north down to Santa Maria (or Point Concepción) that it causes a perpetual fog-bank all summer just off the coast. Each day that the summer temperatures reach 90°F (32°C) inland, the rising hot air draws the fog inland to fill its space. The Golden Gate is its most famous pathway, but everywhere up and down the coast that the ridge of hills dips below about 2,000 feet (610 metres) the fog, or at any rate cold Pacific air, spills over and cools the land. Certain valleys that are end-on to the ocean act as funnels to allow sea air to invade 100 miles

(160 kilometres) inland. San Francisco Bay even has an effect on the climate in the Sierra Foothills, nearly 200 miles (320 kilometres) to the east.

The first editions of this Atlas mapped the coastal regions immediately north and south of San Francisco Bay, from Sonoma's Russian River down to the Salinas Valley in Monterey County (and also the Central Valley). The last edition added the new-minted Central Coast area, the newsworthy extreme north in Mendocino County, and a then-promising chunk of southern California: Temecula. This edition records the rapidly-evolving official concept of Approved Viticultural Areas, instituted in 1980 as a form of appellation to help guide and to some slight extent protect the consumer. Compared with a French appellation contrôlée the AVA is a toothless instrument, concerned only with geography, not with quality. Its one demand is that 75% of grapes used must come from the area named on the label and be of the variety (if any) specified.

Some of the viticultural areas are so small that they affect only one winery. Others are as large as several counties. Like Italian DOCs, they are requested by parties in the district in question and granted, modified or rejected by – strange to say – the Bureau of Alcohol, Tobacco and Firearms. How far an AVA relates to a real geographical identity is thus largely a matter of chance.

There are excellent winemakers who still ignore AVAs, preferring to use good grapes from wherever they can get them. Others are already totally specific about one vineyard and will presumably develop along these lines. Well over 300 individual vineyard names are now in use on California labels – powerful confirmation that California is moving on from the stage where it was only the grape variety and the brand name that counted. The region and specific district have definitively entered the picture.

In several cases grapes and districts are pairing off with their most suitable partners, as in all the longest-established wine regions. Napa Cabernet, Dry Creek Valley Zinfandel, Carneros Pinot Noir and Chardonnay are some evidence to date.

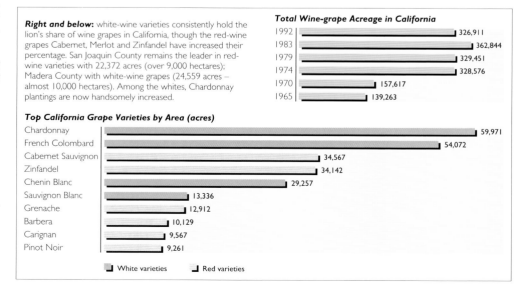

Right and below: white-wine varieties consistently hold the lion's share of wine grapes in California, though the red-wine grapes Cabernet, Merlot and Zinfandel have increased their percentage. San Joaquin County remains the leader in red-wine varieties with 22,372 acres (over 9,000 hectares); Madera County with white-wine grapes (24,559 acres – almost 10,000 hectares). Among the whites, Chardonnay plantings are now handsomely increased.

Total Wine-grape Acreage in California

Year	Acreage
1992	326,911
1983	362,844
1979	329,451
1974	328,576
1970	157,617
1965	139,263

Top California Grape Varieties by Area (acres)

Variety	Acres
Chardonnay	59,971
French Colombard	54,072
Cabernet Sauvignon	34,567
Zinfandel	34,142
Chenin Blanc	29,257
Sauvignon Blanc	13,336
Grenache	12,912
Barbera	10,129
Carignan	9,567
Pinot Noir	9,261

White varieties   Red varieties

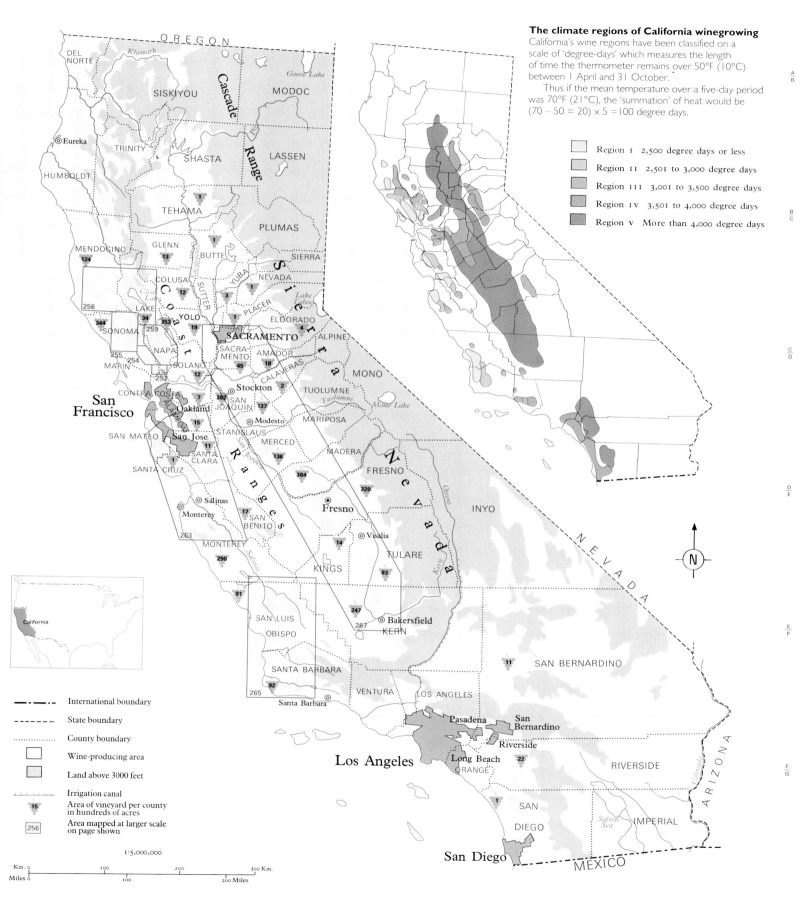

The climate regions of California winegrowing
California's wine regions have been classified on a scale of 'degree-days' which measures the length of time the thermometer remains over 50°F (10°C) between 1 April and 31 October.

Thus if the mean temperature over a five-day period was 70°F (21°C), the 'summation' of heat would be (70 − 50 = 20) × 5 =100 degree days.

Region I   2,500 degree days or less
Region II   2,501 to 3,000 degree days
Region III 3,001 to 3,500 degree days
Region IV   3,501 to 4,000 degree days
Region V   More than 4,000 degree days

OREGON
DEL NORTE
SISKIYOU
Klamath
Goose Lake
MODOC
Eureka
TRINITY
Cascade Range
SHASTA
LASSEN
HUMBOLDT
MENDOCINO
124
TEHAMA
1
PLUMAS
GLENN
1
13
BUTTE
SIERRA
256
COLUSA
Clear Lake
YUBA
NEVADA
Lake Tahoe
12
SUTTER
3
1
LAKE
34
PLACER
1
344
353
19
ELDORADO
SONOMA
259
YOLO
4
SACRAMENTO
ALPINE
255
NAPA
254
SACRA-MENTO
AMADOR
MARIN
SOLANO
45
18
257
12
CALAVERAS
MONO
San Francisco
CONTRA COSTA
Stockton
2
TUOLUMNE
7
382
Mono Lake
Oakland
ALAMEDA
San JOAQUIN
137
Tuolumne
15
Modesto
MARIPOSA
SAN MATEO
STANISLAUS
San Jose
11
MERCED
SANTA CLARA
San Joaquin
MADERA
1
136
SANTA CRUZ
384
FRESNO
Salinas
320
Monterey
17
INYO
SAN BENITO
Fresno
263
Salinas
Visalia
14
MONTEREY
TULARE
290
KINGS
93
91
SAN LUIS OBISPO
247
267
Bakersfield
KERN
SANTA BARBARA
92
265
VENTURA
11
SAN BERNARDINO
Santa Barbara
LOS ANGELES
NEVADA
N
Pasadena
San Bernardino
Riverside
Los Angeles
Long Beach
22
RIVERSIDE
ORANGE
ARIZONA
1
SAN DIEGO
Salton Sea
IMPERIAL
San Diego
Colorado
MEXICO

California

International boundary
State boundary
County boundary
Wine-producing area
Land above 3000 feet
Irrigation canal
15   Area of vineyard per county in hundreds of acres
256   Area mapped at larger scale on page shown

1:5,000,000

Km. 0   100   200   300 Km.
Miles 0   100   200 Miles

Sonoma Valley

The California wine pilgrim should go first to Sonoma. The town has all the atmosphere of a little wine capital – in fact of the capital of a very little republic: the momentary Bear Flag republic of California. Sonoma's tree-shaded square, with its old mission buildings and barracks, its stone-built City Hall and ornate Sebastiani Theatre, is faintly Ruritanian in style, and thickly layered with history.

The hills overlooking the town were the site of Agoston Haraszthy's splendid estate of the 1850s and 1860s. Part of his Buena Vista cellars still stands in the side-valley to the east, although the winery has migrated to Carneros. Another famous 19th-century winery, Gundlach-Bundschu, has been revived more recently on the same southern slopes. On the road to Santa Rosa, in Jack London's 'Valley of the Moon', Grand Cru is a revival of a centenarian heyday. This was where winemaking started in northern California. Today it represents only a small proportion even of Sonoma County's output – most of the vineyards have moved north to the Russian River and adjacent valleys.

The Sonoma Valley AVA runs from Carneros (see page 257) in the south up to (and just over) the watershed dividing the Sonoma and Russian River basins. Like the Napa Valley, but in a smaller compass, the Sonoma Valley shades from cool at Carneros to warmer at its northern end, sheltered from the north all the way by the Mayacamas Mountains. It would be a brave taster who would claim to identify a Sonoma Valley character; too much depends on three variables: site, grape and winery.

Yet there has been continual renewal of interest in what history has proved an excellent vineyard. In the 1940s Buena Vista was the first defunct winery to be revived. In the 1950s James D Zellerbach built the tiny Hanzell, high on the hill above Sonoma, and installed the historic barrels that taught Chardonnay to taste like burgundy. In the 1970s Kenwood, from humble beginnings, and Chateau St Jean, from grander ones, began to be short-listed among California's best and most original wineries.

Kenwood's name is largely for Cabernet and Zinfandel with the Sonoma Valley appellation. Chateau St Jean makes only whites, of good to excellent quality, and was one of the first to cite the precise vineyard for its best Chardonnays and truly remarkable late-harvest Rieslings ('Robert Young', in the Alexander Valley, and 'McCrea', above Kenwood in this valley, for Chardonnay).

Kistler, Landmark, Gundlach-Bundschu and perhaps above all the exceptional Sonoma-Cutrer 'Les Pierres' vineyard (just west of Sonoma city) are all evidence that this AVA can grow perfect Chardonnay. Les Pierres is one of America's best-structured Chardonnays – ageing five years easily. Evidence of excellent Cabernet first came from Martini's famous Monte Rosso vineyard in the eastern hills, and more recently from the outstanding Laurel Glen Cabernets from Sonoma Mountain, which forms a significant sub-appellation in the west. Benziger-Glen Ellen also makes fine Sauvignon Blanc in the same area.

Sonoma labels illustrate the variety of appellations available under the new system: Sonoma County, Sonoma Valley, Russian River, Alexander or Green Valley. Several name a particular vineyard or 'ranch'.

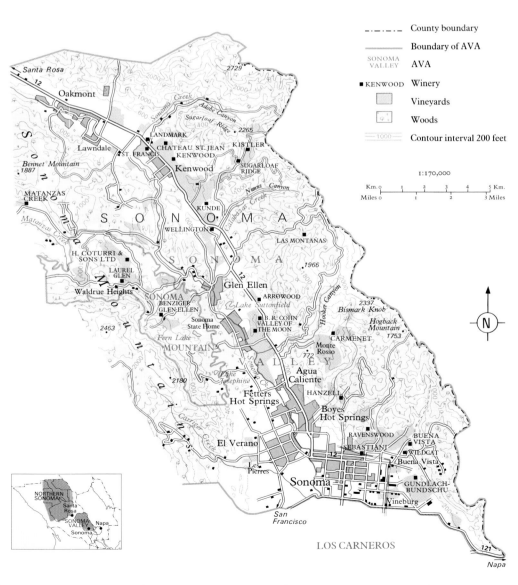

254

North Sonoma

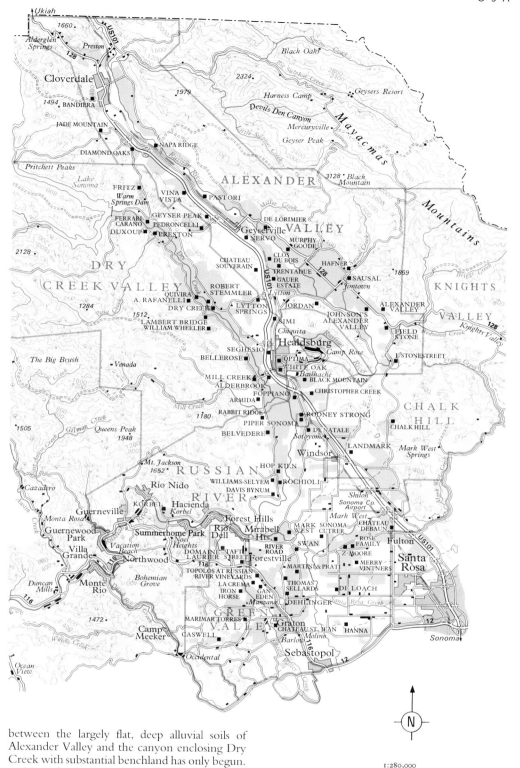

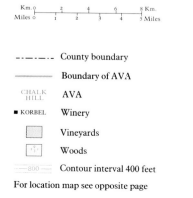

The new system of viticultural areas imposed a pattern on the sprawl of vineyards over Sonoma County – at present the most complete and potentially helpful of any such demarcation.

Sonoma County runs north up the coast from the head of San Francisco Bay, between the Napa Valley and the sea, its northern half drained by the Russian River (named after a Russian trading post) and its tributary creeks. Most of the county's vineyards now lie in this region, mapped here, between Santa Rosa, 20 miles (32 kilometres) north of Sonoma city, and Cloverdale, 35 miles (56 kilometres) beyond. The map opposite shows the original core of vines around the old county capital. A separate appellation, Carneros, links the county's southern end with Napa (see page 258).

Traditionally northern Sonoma has been the source of good-quality 'bulk' wine, bought or made by the big firms of the Central Valley for blending. It is still a major source of Gallo's standard wines, not to mention its up-market varietals. Wineries have flourished here (barring Prohibition) for a century, but in the main anonymously. The most famous exceptions were the Italian Swiss Colony, founded in 1881 at Asti, and Korbel, long the source of California's best-known sparkling wine, near Guerneville.

It is 20 years since the sense of purposeful excitement spilled north from the Napa Valley and flooded the Russian River basin. Alexander Valley, whose first quality vines are a mere 25 years old, was the first appellation to command respect. In 1970 the veteran Simi Winery at Healdsburg woke to new life. A new Château Souverain was built in the expense-no-object style. The Pedroncellis found recognition for years of quiet work; wineries began to spring up.

Piper-Heidsieck of Champagne was among the prospectors, joining with Sonoma Vineyards to outdo Korbel at what had been the region's best speciality. They were joined by Iron Horse Vineyards in the cool Green Valley. Chateau St Jean turned to the Russian River for fruity-acid, not over-golden wines to make sparkle.

The coolest parts of Sonoma (as of every other part of the state) have the most direct access to Pacific air: Carneros by the Bay in the south, and the Russian River Valley, particularly at its seaward end where the river penetrates the 1,500-foot (460-metre) coastal hills. Within the Russian River AVA two sub-AVAs are distinguished. Green Valley, first instigated by Iron Horse Vineyards, specializes in lively Chardonnay and Pinot Noir, perfect for sparkling wine. Chalk Hill, though a shade warmer, is also white wine country, led by Rodney Strong's Chardonnays.

Progressively warmer conditions are found in Dry Creek Valley, then the broader and much more open Alexander Valley. Densely-planted, they both grow warmer to the north, away from the air-flow of the Russian River at Healdsburg. Knight's Valley, almost an extension of the head of the Napa Valley, is warmer than Dry Creek but cooler (because higher) than Alexander Valley.

These, so far, appear to be the temperature readings as regards grape quality. Soil is another matter. Methodical exploration of the differences between the largely flat, deep alluvial soils of Alexander Valley and the canyon enclosing Dry Creek with substantial benchland has only begun.

New plantings are tending to follow the logic of temperature. Pinot Noir and Chardonnay, best with cooler conditions, are gravitating into the Russian River Valley and the cooler parts of Chalk Hill and Dry Creek. Tiny Williams & Selyem has shown how fine Russian River Pinot Noir can be, but Gewürztraminer, Sauvignon Blanc and Riesling also enjoy the relatively cool climate. Cabernet and Zinfandel are dominant in the warmer parts of Dry Creek (Zinfandels made by Ridge of grapes from here are famous).

Alexander Valley seems to confer a gentle nature on almost any grape, as epitomized by the suave productions of Jordan, the stately winery that first brought it into fashion in the 1970s.

1:280,000

Km. 0   2   4   6   8 Km.
Miles 0   1   2   3   4   5 Miles

—·—·—·— County boundary
———————— Boundary of AVA
CHALK HILL AVA
■ KORBEL Winery
▢ Vineyards
▢ Woods
—800— Contour interval 400 feet

For location map see opposite page

Mendocino and Lake County

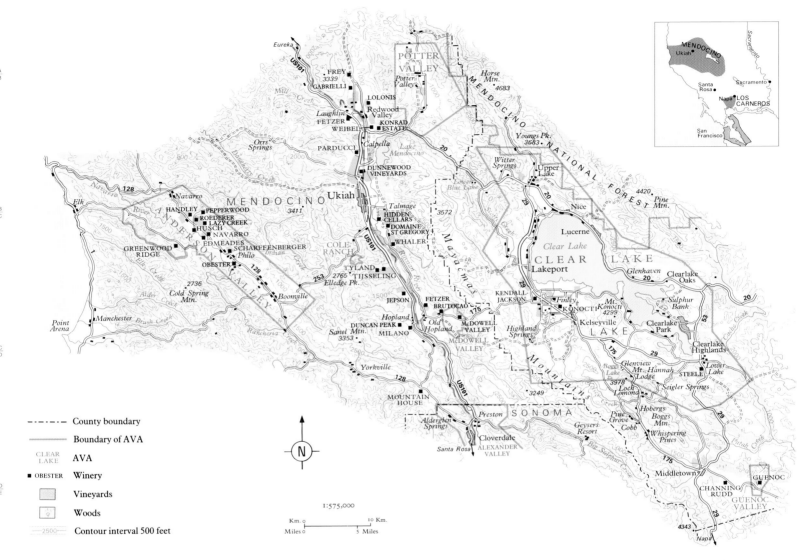

County boundary

Boundary of AVA

CLEAR
LAKE   AVA

■ OBESTER   Winery

Vineyards

Woods

2500   Contour interval 500 feet

1:575,000

Km. 0   10 Km.

Miles 0   5 Miles

Mendocino County is the northernmost outpost of the vine in California. The instinct that tells you that it must be a cool-climate region is wrong. North of Cloverdale and the Sonoma county line the coastal hills rear up as more sudden and accentuated features, in redwood country that stretches on up the coast it seems endlessly, misty and resin-scented. But because the hills are higher, the valleys behind them are drier and warmer.

Most of the established vineyards of Mendocino are well tucked in behind a 2,000–3,000-foot (600–900-metre) range. The sea breezes do not reach Ukiah and the Redwood and Potter valleys – the latter one of the five AVAs of the county. They are warm enough to be rated Region III, or even IV in places, on the heat-summation scale. Their typical wines (from some deep alluvial soils) are full-bodied, often rather soft reds of Cabernet, Pinot Noir, Zinfandel or Petite Syrah.

The oldest winery in this region is Parducci (founded in 1931, a date that proclaims a visionary: Prohibition was still in force). Fetzer was an important addition of the late 1960s; so

important that today its 1,600 acres (648 hectares) of vines supply only one fifth of its needs. With over 2.5 million cases (half under the Bel Arbors label) it leads this northern region with wines of famously reliable value – most of them white. Weibel, next in size, is a refugee from the urban sprawl of the East Bay that hides the greater part of its production (60% sparkling) behind buyers' own labels. A dozen smaller wineries are too variable for any real consensus about their products, but the unexpected star of the area is a brandy distillery, Germain-Robin, reputed California's best.

At the same time Mendocino has built quite a different reputation for the one area where the coastal hills part and fogs find a limited access inland. The little Navarro River tumbles down the Anderson Valley through the redwoods. Anderson Valley has a super-cool, sometimes too-cool, ripening season, at least in its lower reaches below Philo. Higher, on the ridges above the fog, Zinfandel ripens splendidly – a fact that a few reclusive Italian families discovered long ago.

Edmeades (now part of Kendall-Jackson), Navarro and Husch are three of the more recent

pioneer wineries that first made highly aromatic white wines in the Anderson Valley from grapes that would ripen in Germany. Riesling and Gewürztraminer are perfectly in tune. By 1982 Champagne Roederer was installed here, alongside Scharffenberger (sparkling) Cellars, which has since been bought by the Champagne house of Pommery.

The meeting place of the two extremes of Mendocino climate is McDowell Valley, a tiny appellation established by the highly competent owners of McDowell Valley Vineyards, on the winding Route 175 from Hopland to the out-of-the-way resort of Clear Lake.

Lake County is a warm region, too, comparable to the head of the Napa Valley, not far to the south. Its tranquillity once attracted the troubled beauty Lillie Langtry to settle here. She imported a Bordeaux vigneron and started an ambitious winery at Guenoc – unfortunately just before Prohibition. But Guenoc has revived and the new venture promises well. Clear Lake is more famous as a resort than as an AVA. It is dominated by Kendall-Jackson and a grower group: Konocti Cellars.

Carneros

Above: vineyards are rolling over the former sheep-walks of Carneros, cooled by Bay breezes. Chardonnay and Pinot Noir ripen here with fine acidity that gives table wines 'elegance' and sparkling ones liveliness. Half of Carneros is in Napa County, half in Sonoma.

Left: Parducci and Fetzer are pioneer Mendocino names; Roederer an invasion from Champagne. On the right are Carneros leaders' labels: Domaine Carneros is the Champagne (Taittinger) invader here.

Los Carneros (commonly known as Carneros), literally 'the rams', is a district relatively new to the vine, but increasingly looked-to for the highest quality of grapes that require cool ripening conditions. It lies to the south of Napa city on the north shore of San Pablo Bay, the northern arm of San Francisco Bay: low rolling hills of variably clayey and coarse, rocky soil, where the wind rattles the vine-leaves more often than not. Old farm buildings proclaim it until recently grazing land. But grapes grown and sold to various wineries in the 1970s by one of its farmers, Rene di Rosa, made the reputation of his property, Winery Lake, and attracted others to buy and plant the sheep-walks. Winery Lake was bought by Seagram and its grapes are used by Sterling.

First of the newcomers to make a name were Carneros Creek, which started to produce outstanding Pinot Noir here in the 1970s, and Acacia, which since 1979 has made both Pinot Noir and Chardonnay of steady quality. Acacia was a leader in the practice of creating individual vineyard wines that were, and are, consistently different. Saintsbury, nearby, takes a different line, effectively reserving the winery label for its (excellent) best selection.

The famous old name of Buena Vista, owned by the German Racke family, has moved down here from its original site in Sonoma. The evidence of its Carneros-grown Cabernet suggests that the region gives quite pointed acidity to this variety. Carneros-grown grapes (especially Chardonnay) are used, though, by many wineries outside the region, either alone or in blends, to leaven wines grown in warmer areas. Cuvaison is an example of a winery far up the Napa Valley whose style is derived from Carneros grapes.

Present evidence points to the true destiny of the district being sparkling wine. Three recent installations: Gloria Ferrer and Codorníu from Spain, and Domaine Carneros with Champagne (Taittinger) parentage, are extremely convincing.

Politically, Carneros straddles the Napa/Sonoma county line. As a viticultural area, therefore, it has three appellations: Carneros, Napa Valley and Sonoma Valley.

- - - - - - County boundary
─────── Boundary of AVA
NAPA VALLEY   AVA
■ ACACIA   Winery
    Vineyards
    Woods

Contour intervals:
below 100 ft every 20 ft
above 100 ft every 100 ft

1:200,000

For location map see opposite page

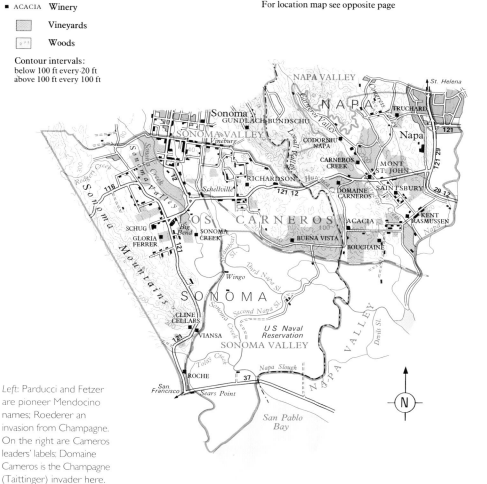

Napa Valley

The Napa Valley is the symbol as well as the centre of the top-quality wine industry in California. It has never had a monopoly. But in its wines, its winemakers and the idyllic atmosphere which fills it from the green hills on one side to the golden ones on the other, it captures the imagination and stays in the memory.

The valley runs in a shallow arc northwest from Napa city, most of its vineyards lying on its nearly flat floor, which is broken here and there by wooded knolls rising 200–300 feet (60–90 metres). The vineyards creep up the benchland on either side of the valley until (along the east side) the soil becomes too thin and rocky grassland takes over, dotted with dark oaks, or (on the west) the slope becomes too steep and forest of maple, madrone, laurel and redwood covers the ground, giving way here and there to bowls or ramps or amphitheatres of vineyard, even high up in the mountains.

The typical Napa Valley winery, large or small, is set beside a valley road in the vines. Others, such as Schramsberg, Mayacamas, Chappellet or the Newton Vineyard, lie in elevated enclaves of their own, remote from the bustle of the valley floor.

The valley falls into three climate zones. Its southern end, the separate district of Carneros (see page 257) and the valley proper from Napa north to Oakville, is Region I, the coolest. From Oakville to the northern end of St Helena is Region II. The head of the valley, around Calistoga, remotest from the influence of the Bay, is Region III.

For all this Napa Valley is one AVA, and is anxious to retain the identity that gives its grapes a premium over almost all others in California. The area, in other words, is political rather than physical. It covers not only the valley, nor simply its more complex drainage area, but almost the entire county: bayside, mountainside, valley floor and high plateau. It is not reasonable to argue that there can be one 'Napa style', however resounding the Cabernets and succulent the Chardonnays that keep its reputation at the top. Hence a continuing process of hammering out sub-AVAs which began a generation ago, informally and not uncontroversially, with the suggestion that low benchland (in other words the very foot of the hill-slopes) from Rutherford south into Oakville on the west side had a long track record for characteristically forceful and long-ageing Cabernets and might be dubbed 'The Rutherford Bench'.

The famous Inglenooks of John Daniel in the 1940s and 1950s, the Georges de Latour Private Reserve of Beaulieu Vineyards in the 1940s, 50s and 60s, Heitz' Martha's Vineyard from 1966 on

and more recently his Bella Oaks, Cesare Mondavi Selection Cabernet from Charles Krug, Cabernet Bosché from Freemark Abbey, Robert Mondavi Reserve Cabernet from the late 1960s and, since 1979, the Mondavi/Rothschild Opus One – all these famous wines were made of grapes grown in this stretch of dirt. Different as their styles of winemaking may have been, they have set a certain standard and evoked in those who have known them the pleasure of recognition. 'Rutherford dust' is one term sometimes used to try to pinpoint a characteristic taste they often share.

Why this mid-point in the valley should be so ideal is a matter for debate. Good drainage is certainly a factor. Another may be underground springs. Yet another may be the generally north-eastern exposure of the gentle slopes, which therefore catch the earliest morning sun in summer. Their soils warm up rapidly, then lose the hottest rays in the afternoon – like, incidentally, those of the Côte d'Or. As the shadow of the western hills falls over their vines, with soil and air both very warm, they enjoy a

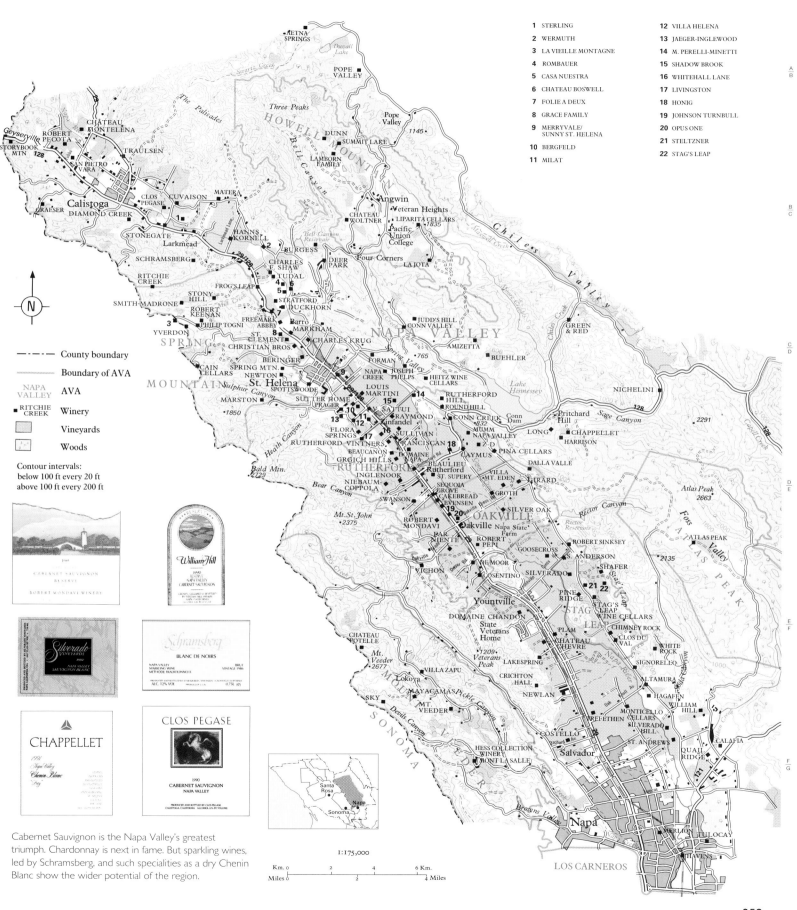

1	STERLING	12	VILLA HELENA
2	WERMUTH	13	JAEGER-INGLEWOOD
3	LA VIEILLE MONTAGNE	14	M. PERELLI-MINETTI
4	ROMBAUER	15	SHADOW BROOK
5	CASA NUESTRA	16	WHITEHALL LANE
6	CHATEAU BOSWELL	17	LIVINGSTON
7	FOLIE A DEUX	18	HONIG
8	GRACE FAMILY	19	JOHNSON TURNBULL
9	MERRYVALE/ SUNNY ST. HELENA	20	OPUS ONE
10	BERGFELD	21	STELTZNER
11	MILAT	22	STAG'S LEAP

County boundary

Boundary of AVA

NAPA VALLEY — AVA

RITCHIE CREEK — Winery

Vineyards

Woods

Contour intervals:
below 100 ft every 20 ft
above 100 ft every 200 ft

CHAPPELLET
1990
Napa Valley
Chenin Blanc
"Dry"

CLOS PEGASE
1990
CABERNET SAUVIGNON
NAPA VALLEY
PRODUCED AND BOTTLED BY CLOS PEGASE
CALISTOGA, CALIFORNIA ALCOHOL 12% BY VOLUME

William Hill
1990
RESERVE
NAPA VALLEY
CABERNET SAUVIGNON
GROWN, CELLARED & BOTTLED BY
WILLIAM HILL WINERY
NAPA, CALIFORNIA

Silverado
VINEYARDS
1992
NAPA VALLEY
SAUVIGNON BLANC
PRODUCED AND BOTTLED BY SILVERADO VINEYARDS
NAPA, CALIFORNIA · ALC. 13.5% BY VOL.

Schramsberg
BLANC DE NOIRS
NAPA VALLEY
SPARKLING WINE
METHODE TRADITIONNELLE
VINTAGE 1986
PRODUCED AND BOTTLED BY J. SCHRAMBERG VINEYARDS · CALISTOGA CALIFORNIA
ALC. 12% VOL   (.75L ℮)

Cabernet Sauvignon is the Napa Valley's greatest triumph. Chardonnay is next in fame. But sparkling wines, led by Schramsberg, and such specialities as a dry Chenin Blanc show the wider potential of the region.

1:175,000

Km. 0   2   4   6 Km.
Miles 0   2   4 Miles

259

long, slow period of cooling. Grapes on an eastern slope ripen more slowly and later. Other things being equal, all these are factors that enhance flavour and aromas in the fruit.

On the other hand, say growers in Oakville, just to the south, these factors affect 'the Oakville bench' too. None of which pleases growers based in these townships but off the 'bench' (if there is one). Hence the decision to make Rutherford and Oakville – the whole communities – AVAs, and drop (if not forget) their benches.

Just south of Oakville, on Route 29 at Yountville, the valley floor is considerably narrowed by two major outcropping eminences which interrupt the flow of cool air northwards from the Bay. Tucked behind one of these hills, on the eastern side, is another area with a claim to distinctiveness and now an AVA: Stag's Leap (named for the cliff edge above it). Stag's Leap Wine Cellars and neighbouring Clos du Val led the way here with Cabernets in a more supple, delicate style than those of Rutherford and Oakville. What they discovered is confirmed by, among others, Silverado and Shafer Vineyards.

These are the AVAs of the valley itself (so far). The mountain districts around have been easier to designate, as (clockwise from Carneros) the sub-AVAs of Mount Veeder and Spring Mountain in the Mayacamas Range, Howell Mountain to the north and the fledgling Atlas Peak to the east. High in the western hills it is Riesling, followed by Chardonnay, that have made the best wine for longest; on Howell Mountain it is Zinfandel, Cabernet and now Merlot. Atlas Peak, under Antinori influence, has opened its batting with Sangiovese.

There are two much-frequented routes for visiting the Napa Valley: the commercial artery, Highway 29, up the west side, or the more romantic Silverado Trail up the east. Infrequent and at times baffling cross-valley roads link them.

The first considerable winery going north on Highway 20 is on the first of the crossroads, Oak Knoll Avenue. Trefethen Vineyards is remarkable not only for its huge spread of immaculate vineyard and noble old wooden barn, but also for the well-judged elegance (the only word) of its wines. This is the cooler end of the valley, as the

nerve and balance of Chardonnay, Riesling and even Cabernet grown here bear witness.

Follow Oak Knoll Avenue and turn north on the Silverado Trail to find the Stag's Leap AVA, where the trail runs under the brown crags where the stag presumably leapt.

The next essential visit on Route 29 is a few miles on: Domaine Chandon, its sparkling-wine cellars and its admirable restaurant. Next, beyond Oakville, on the 'benchland' and surrounded by the valley's most prestigious vines, is Robert Mondavi's adobe mission-style winery, arguably the most influential in America. Opposite across Route 29 lies the extravaganza of Opus One.

These places of pilgrimage are beginning to challenge Disneyland in popularity. From here on up the valley the famous names clock up with increasing frequency: Inglenook, Beaulieu, Louis Martini – with a dense concentration around St Helena. Just north of the little town (which retains, despite the crowds, a potent charm) the Beringer Winery has extensive caves and excellent wines to show behind its 'Rhine House', a building almost ghoulishly faithful to Germanic tradition. Charles Krug is another of the great old names of the valley surviving from the 19th century. Freemark Abbey, by the road, founded in 1895 and refounded in 1967, has very high standards – but the same can be said for another dozen smaller wineries in this top section of the valley, from Smith-Madrone on Spring Mountain to the west and the Schramsberg that Robert Louis Stevenson loved to the spectacular (though secluded) Phelps and Chappellet wineries to the east.

The country here where the valley narrows becomes more and more beautiful. Oaks and pines, streams, darting birds, fruit trees, sunlit meadows stretch to the pretty little spa of Calistoga and beyond up into Knight's Valley over the Sonoma county line.

Before Calistoga is one mandatory tourist stop, the astonishing vision of an apparent Greek monastery perching on a steep mid-valley knoll: Sterling, the flagship winery of Seagram. Ascent is by canary-coloured cable car. Just beyond is another: Clos Pegase, a winery that would not look out of place at Luxor on the Nile.

Napa: the Quality Factor

It used to be said that 'every year is a vintage year' in California. In the Central Valley it is true that grapes ripen regularly and the wine of one year is much like that of the next. But the coastal counties' vineyards have a more wayward climate, more varying microclimates and more differing soil structures than broad generalizations can convey. As the wine industry matures it is learning to take advantage of local conditions to produce consistently distinctive wines by planting the right grape in precisely the right place.

In Europe such experiments have taken centuries. California is moving faster. Individual sites have established reputations for growing particular grapes outstandingly well. Martha's Vineyard Cabernet was first to make the point, but today such investigations are commonplace; witness the discussion of Napa AVAs on page 258.

The maps opposite were drawn as a first step in plotting the fundamental quality factors for one small area, the northern Napa Valley, by James Lider (for many years official agricultural adviser in the area) in collaboration with his brother Lloyd Lider of the University of California.

Three easily measurable variables affect the Napa grower's decision as to what vines to plant where. Soil is the first. The area's two principal soil types are 'upland soil', gravelly loam, quick-draining and warm, on the lower slopes of the surrounding hills, and the heavier clay of the valley floor. The former, as a general rule, gives finer quality and will usually be reserved for Cabernet and Chardonnay. Merlot, Sauvignon Blanc and Semillon are more tolerant of the latter.

The second factor is the average temperature, measured in California on the scale described on page 253. Even within this small area, 17 miles by 5 (27 by 8 kilometres), three different temperature zones are discernible. The bottom map shows innumerable local pockets of warmer or cooler conditions that in due course may create wines of particular character.

The third factor is the risk of destructive late spring frosts, worst on the valley floor where the cold air drains to. Vines coming into leaf early are most at risk. Those affected are likely to replace damaged flowers with a second flush, whose grapes will ripen later than those remaining. Uneven ripeness makes high-quality wine unlikely.

In simple terms, therefore, the vineyards with the highest quality potential are those with upland soil and low frost risk (which usually go together), planted with the grapes indicated for that temperature zone. In practice, many more complex factors come into play, perhaps the next most essential being the timing and speed of ripening.

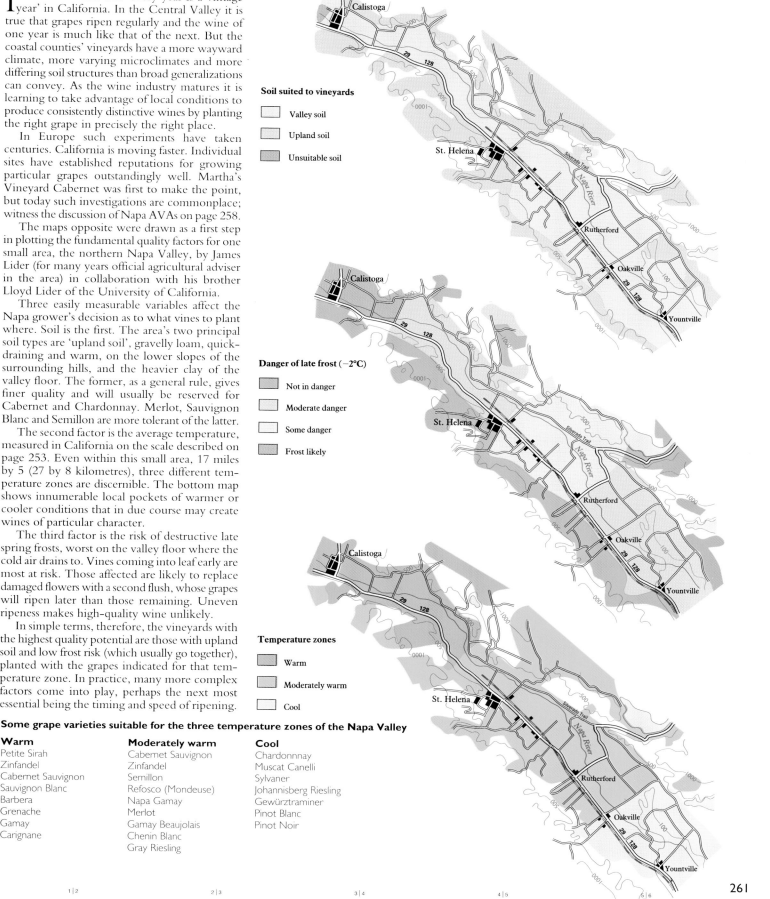

Soil suited to vineyards

- Valley soil
- Upland soil
- Unsuitable soil

Danger of late frost (−2°C)

- Not in danger
- Moderate danger
- Some danger
- Frost likely

Temperature zones

- Warm
- Moderately warm
- Cool

Some grape varieties suitable for the three temperature zones of the Napa Valley

Warm	Moderately warm	Cool
Petite Sirah	Cabernet Sauvignon	Chardonnnay
Zinfandel	Zinfandel	Muscat Canelli
Cabernet Sauvignon	Semillon	Sylvaner
Sauvignon Blanc	Refosco (Mondeuse)	Johannisberg Riesling
Barbera	Napa Gamay	Gewürztraminer
Grenache	Merlot	Pinot Blanc
Gamay	Gamay Beaujolais	Pinot Noir
Carignane	Chenin Blanc	
	Gray Riesling	

South of the Bay

The area just south and east of San Francisco Bay is wine country as old as the Napa Valley. Its wineries are far fewer, but several of them are among California's most famous names. The dry gravelly soil of the Livermore Valley has long been famous for white wine, especially Sauvignon, with perhaps the most individual style in the state.

Paul Masson and Almaden in Saratoga and Los Gatos (both companies are now, alas, virtually defunct) were the pioneers and for many years leaders of the industry. In the 1960s the exploding conurbation of the Bay Area drove them to look for new vineyards. Encouraged by climate studies from the University of California, they moved south.

Almaden was the first company to make a move on a big scale, planting Cabernet and Chardonnay at an elevation of 1,000 feet (300 metres) at Paicines in San Benito County. Further south still, said the University. Paul Masson, Mirassou from San Jose and Wente Bros from Livermore all planted in what promised to be a wonderfully cool-climate zone: the Salinas Valley. With its mouth open to the ocean just north of Monterey it forms a highly efficient funnel for a regular afternoon visitation of cold sea air.

The valley has a history of growing excellent salads and vegetables. It was enthusiastically turned over to vines in a planting spree that covered more than 30,000 acres (12,000 hectares), largely between Gonzales and King City. Unfortunately, the funnel proved all too efficient. On a hot day inland, clammy coastal air comes rushing up the valley with such force that it actually tears off vine shoots. Some remarkable wines were made. A Zinfandel, for example, that did not ripen until December. 'Green' flavours in Salinas wines were fancifully attributed to the lettuces that had been grown there before.

In reality, the search for coolness had gone too far. Some of the huge planting of the early 1970s has now been removed; the rest, still a vast area, is mechanically farmed to provide cool-climate jug material for such Central Valley giants as Delicato.

On the present evidence Arroyo Seco (an AVA since 1983) is as close to the sea as is possible for quality wine to be made in the valley – Wente and Mirassou both use grapes from this area. Jekel has produced almost over-ripe Chardonnays and Cabernets and rich Rieslings. But now the concentration is on planting south of King City, on down towards the county line of San Luis Obispo, or alternatively up on the valley's western slopes in the 1992 AVA, Santa Lucia Highlands.

Wineries did not proliferate among the new vineyards. There are more in the Santa Cruz Mountains which, in comparison, have scarcely any vineyards at all. The Hecker Pass has a cluster of long-established family affairs, but it is isolated wineries in the hills above Santa Cruz that have nationwide reputations for their diminutive output.

Martin Ray was the first winemaker to bring renown to this beautiful forested mountain area, in the 1950s. His eccentric, expensive wines caused arguments and amusement in just the opposite proportion to those of his spiritual successor, Randall Grahm of Bonny Doon. Grahm is a wag, but also an inspired improviser, issuing highly original blends with such leg-pulling names as Le Cigare Volant and Le Sophiste. His inspiration is the Rhône – he calls himself a 'Rhône Ranger' – and increasingly Italy; traditions never taken so seriously in California before, now unmistakably beacons for the future.

The established leader in the region is Ridge Vineyards, high on a ridge overlooking the ocean one way and the Bay the other, with Cabernet from the highest patch, Montebello, often as fine and long-lived a red wine as any in California. (Ridge also makes a splendid Napa Cabernet under the name York Creek, as well as celebrated Zinfandels from Northern Sonoma).

In almost the same quality league, but with completely different wines, is the isolated Chalone Vineyard, remote on a sun-scorched 2,000-foot (600-metre) limestone hilltop on the road from Soledad to nowhere – except the Pinnacles National Monument. Chalone (which has its own AVA) makes Chardonnay and Pinot Noir with the conviction that Burgundy's Corton has somehow migrated west. It is a thought that must have occurred to the equally go-it-alone Josh Jensen, who founded Calera to grow Pinot Noir just 20 miles (32 kilometres) north in the same range (Mount Harlan AVA). The soil is right; the sun just too hot.

Below left: looking west from Smith & Hook's vines above Soledad to the Pinnacles National Monument. Cabernet from here is intensely 'herbaceous'. *Below*: the barrel room at Ridge Vineyards above Santa Clara. Ridge Cabernet and (from N. Sonoma) Zinfandel are among California's finest.

Wineries south of the Bay
are a mixture of such
old-timers as Wente and
Mirassou, classics such as
Ridge and Chalone, and
stylish pioneers,
represented here by
Calera and 'Le Cigare
Volant' of Bonny Doon.

County boundary

Boundary of AVA

CHALONE AVA

JEKEL Winery

Vineyards

Woods

1000 Contour interval 1000 feet

1:710,000

Km. 0 .... 15 .... 30 Km.

Miles 0 .... 15 Miles

The South Central Coast

The pattern is familiar by now: a river-worn gap in the Coast Ranges, access to a fertile valley for the cold foggy sea air, and grapes taking over from cattle, or apples, or whatever farmers raised before the vine began its colonizing progress down the coast.

The logic that filled the Salinas Valley in Monterey County with grapevines in the early 1970s scarcely paused to take stock, but applied the same principle to the next two counties southwards: San Luis Obispo and Santa Barbara. By 1980, both had enough vines in enough locations for serious investigations into their relative qualities to begin.

Already they have been divided into six AVAs. There may well be more to come. But the variety of coastal conditions is adequately evidenced by these six.

To the north, the appellation Paso Robles covers a wide stretch of country, varying from wooded hill terrain west of Highway 101 to rolling grassland east of the road. The fame of Paso Robles, such as it is, comes largely from potent Zinfandels, with Templeton as their favoured centre. It rates as Region II or warmer, with no direct access for cooling ocean breezes. Its best vineyards, for this reason, are probably those that are cooled by their altitude.

The pioneer new-generation winery of the district was HMR, started in 1964 as Hoffmann Mountain Ranch, which used Pinot Noir, Riesling and Chardonnay grown locally. Zinfandel would probably have been a better choice. The latest to choose the same corner, near Adelaida, is the Perrin family of Beaucastel

Estate from Châteauneuf-du-Pape, with Rhône grapes in mind. Martin Brothers is one of the few wineries to take Italian vines seriously, the Nebbiolo in particular, while Meridian (formerly Estrella River) stands out for its hilltop site, a vantage point dominating the increasingly viticultural landscape to the southeast. Cabernet seems to be its destiny.

Edna Valley, over the Cuesta Pass to the south, could hardly be more distinct. If sea air hardly touches Paso Robles, it swirls in from Morro Bay and cools the valley above San Luis Obispo to a Region I climate. Chardonnay appears so far to be the prime grape for the area, Edna Valley Vineyards (related to the celebrated Chalone) its prime local user, although wineries elsewhere buy grapes. The Champagne firm of Deutz has built a sparkling-wine cellar at Arroyo Grande. Corbett Canyon winery has the resources to do great things.

South again across the county line in Santa Barbara, Santa Maria Valley provides conditions that are, if anything, cooler still. Its river runs out to sea in flat land that offers no opposition at all to the Pacific air. Some of its vineyard land is so low-lying that sea fog moves in at midday and the fruit can be under-ripe and over-acid. Almost all the land is owned by farmers rather than wineries, making vineyard names unusually prominent; they crop up on different wineries' labels. Bien Nacido, Cambria and Byron proceed in that order up the valley, growing slightly warmer as they go. Rancho Sisquoc is the most sheltered, except for the positively secluded Foxen in its canyon. The best grapes, Chardonnay

Above: fog clears as the sun rises over young vineyards in Paso Robles. High day-time temperatures ripen potent Zinfandels here. Local growers are now looking seriously at grapes from the Rhône Valley and northern Italy.

in the main, are grown on the south slope high enough – 600 feet plus (180 metres) – above the valley floor to be on the fringe of the fog belt. Their fruity intensity and high acidity sometimes brings New Zealand to mind.

Much the most exciting winery in the area, with an air of frenetic experimentation matched only by Bonny Doon in Santa Cruz, is Au Bon Climat and its partner in the same unprepossessing premises, Qupé.

Conditions are warmer and more stable over the Solomon Hills to the south. The Santa Ynez Valley AVA is no obvious physical feature, but a sprawl of vineyards in rolling oak-dotted hills around and to the north of Solvang, a town as peculiarly Danish as its name. The grapes that seem best suited to the area are Sauvignon Blanc, the Cabernets and Merlot.

Firestone is the biggest winery, and (with its stable-mate, J Carey) a landmark for reliability and value. Zaca Mesa comes next in size. Babcock, Brander and Gainey are all highly regarded. The true excitement of Santa Ynez, though, lies westward towards Lompoc and the ocean, where the Sanford & Benedict vineyard occupies a sheltered north-facing niche that perfectly suits Pinot Noir and Chardonnay. The Sanford winery uses some of its grapes and sells others. In the right hands this is California's best Pinot Noir so far.

San Francisco

MONTEREY

San Miguel
MISSION VIEW
ABBEY D'OR
CASTORO
CAPARONE
Estrella
Cholame
46
JUSTIN
TWIN HILLS
MARTIN BROS.
J. LOHR
46
MERIDIAN
Adelaida
HMR
EBERLE
ARCIERO
Whitley Gardens
Shandon
ADELAIDA CELLARS
BARON
Paso Robles
PEACHY CANYON
PASO ROBLES
Cypress Mtn. 2933
HOPE FARMS
46
PESENTI
Templeton
YORK MTN
46
MASTANTUONO
WILD HORSE
Creston
YORK MTN
CASTORO CELLARS
41
Atascadero
CRESTON MANOR
Cayucos
Cerro Alto 2624
SAN LUIS
Black Mtn. 3622
LOS PADRES NATIONAL FOREST
Morro Beach
41
58
58
Estero Bay
Morro Bay
Cuesta Pass
Santa Margarita
Santa Margarita Lake
Baywood Park
OBISPO
Pozo
Los Osos
San Luis Obispo
SANTA LUCIA
Point Buchon
CLAIBORNE & CHURCHILL
EDNA VALLEY
Irish Hills
1819
Bald Mtn. 2834
WILDERNESS
Edna
EDNA VALLEY
Avila Beach
CHAMISAL
SAUCELITO CANYON
Port San Luis
CORBETT CANYON
VALLEY VINEYARDS
ARROYO GRANDE
Shell Beach
Huasna
Pismo Beach
Grover City
Arroyo Grande
Oceano
MAISON DEUTZ
Nipomo
1902
Twitchell Reservoir
166
Los Coches Mtn. 3016
Bakersfield
Guadalupe
166
SANTA MARIA VALLEY
Point Sal
Betteravia
AU BON CLIMAT
QUPÉ
Tepusquet 3253
LOS PADRES
Santa Maria
Orcutt
Garey
CAMBRIA
Casmalia
Sisquoc
BYRON
RANCHO SISQUOC
135
Solomon Hills
FOXEN VINEYARD
Purisima Point
San Antonio Creek
135
NATIONAL FOREST
ZACA MESA
Vandenburg Air Force Base
Los Alamos
FESS PARKER
Purisima Hills
SANTA
SANTA YNEZ VALLEY
Surf
Vandenburg Village
1984
FIRESTONE
AUSTIN CELLARS
Los Olivos
BRANDER
Babcock
246
HOUTZ
CAREY
Honda
Buellton
BUTTONWOOD FARM
Santa Ynez
Lompoc
246
MOSBY
THE GAINEY VINEYARD
Point Arguello
Tranquillon Mtn.
Arlight 2159
SANFORD
246
Solvang
SANTA YNEZ VALLEY
Lake Cachuma
Santa Barbara
BARBARA
Santa Ynez
154
Santa Ynez Mountains
Santa Ynez Peak 4298
Jalama
1759
Las Cruces
LOS PADRES NATIONAL FOREST 2548
Santa Barbara
Concepcion
Drake
Gaviota
US101
Point Concepcion
Tajiguas
Capitan

Sacramento
San Francisco
Los Angeles

1:725,000

Km. 0   10   20 Km.
Miles 0   5   10 Miles

─ ∙ ─ ∙ ─ County boundary
────── Boundary of AVA
YORK MTN AVA
■ HOUTZ Winery
▨ Vineyards
▨ Woods
─ 2500 ─ Contour interval 500 feet

N

A
B
C
D
E
F
G

Left: the top and bottom labels come from the same uninhibited Santa Maria winery. The 1980s saw this part of the coast, pioneered by Firestone, regularly making headlines.

The Central Valley

The San Joaquin Valley, alias the Central Valley, produces four bottles out of five of California wine. Put another way, if all America's wine filled one bottle, all but one-and-a-bit glasses of it would come from this giant vineyard.

Conditions are totally different here from those among the coastal hills. The soil is rich, fertile and flat for 400 miles (645 kilometres) north–south and up to 100 miles (150 kilometres) across. Vines take their place with orchards, and, among the vines, table and raisin grapes with wine grapes. The total vineyard acreage is approximately twice that of Bordeaux – but of this only one-third is planted to wine grapes. White wine grapes are dominated by Colombard, with one-third of the total wine grape acreage, followed by Chenin Blanc at 12%. Among reds Zinfandel has 10%, with Grenache, Barbera and Carignane at about half this level each. The biggest acreage of all, though, is of the raisin grape Thompson Seedless, which accounts for nearly one-third of the entire 550,000 acres (223,000 hectares). Thompson Seedless can also be fermented.

The climate is reliably, steadily, often stupefyingly, hot. For most of the length of the valley the Coast Ranges seal it off from any Pacific influence. On the University of California scale most of it is Region V. The natural produce of such a climate is grapes with high sugar content and virtually no acidity. In practice, high cropping levels (9 tons an acre (4 tons a hectare) is common) caused by generous fertilizing and irrigation tend to make watery wine – the equivalent of France's notorious 11° Midi *ordinaire*. Strong sweet dessert wines were the best the valley could do, until technology came to its rescue.

Thirty years ago America drank 70% high-strength wine, 30% light table wine. Today the proportions are reversed. The valley adapted to the new demand with creditable speed and success – indeed helped to shape the pattern of American winedrinking by designing new kinds of light wine, making them reliably and selling them reasonably.

The University of California provided the means, in the form of new grape varieties, new ways of growing them and new winemaking techniques – not to mention new winemakers. Some of its new varieties, such as Ruby Cabernet and Rubired, are now established as California standards. New varieties apart, the elimination of unsuitable old ones has been an important part of the improvements.

New ways of growing them have consisted mainly of high trellising with various devices to give the maximum curtain of leaves over the grapes, of mist sprays to cool the vines, and of mechanical harvesting – now standard practice in these industrialized vineyards.

In the cellar the great developments have been in using stainless steel and other neutral tanks, protecting the must and wine from oxygen, employing various forms of presses, pumps and filters – but above all in temperature control. Refrigeration, more than any single factor, made good light wine possible in the Central Valley.

The lead in these developments was taken by the brothers Ernest and (the now late) Julio Gallo. The lead has been held firmly and this family-owned business at Modesto is today the biggest single wine operation on earth. Its statistics are startling: 9,000 acres of vines, an output of almost 100 million cases; the biggest glass factory west of the Mississippi at the start of the bottling line.

The figures would be impressive if it were beer being dispensed, or even soda water. What makes them awe-inspiring is that the product is wine: on the whole very good wine. Gallo has been the major influence on America's taste for wine – it could hardly be otherwise, as it makes every third or fourth bottle (the figures are not available). The winery takes the responsibility seriously, providing as it were a beginners' course from apple and other 'pop wines' by easy degrees of sweetness and fruitiness to some of the best standard 'burgundy' and 'chablis' in the business and beyond to fully dry, well-matured varietals. In 1990 it launched its 'super-premium' Cabernet and Chardonnay.

Gallo, as other good valley producers, does not limit itself to valley grapes. It is one of the biggest growers and buyers in the North Coast counties, including the Napa Valley and North Sonoma.

E & J Gallo has several big colleagues in the San Joaquin Valley – big enough for its wineries to remind you more of oil refineries than of any agricultural operation.

Guild, based at Lodi, is a growers' cooperative whose Italian-style (in other words sweet) Cribari brand wines are immensely popular. Guild is now owned by Canandaigua of New York, as are Cresta Blanca and the hugely successful Cook's Champagne Cellars.

The Wine Group is a conglomerate whose brands include Colony, Italian Swiss Colony, Petri and Lejon. Franzia Winery identifies all its wines as 'made and bottled in Ripon'. Heublein at Madera unites a clutch of once-respected names, now sadly debased to jug-wine level, Almaden and Inglenook Navalle among them.

Smaller but still huge concerns (with higher standards) include Delicato at Manteca, Bronco at Ceres and, most revolutionary, the Woodbridge Cellars of Robert Mondavi. The Mondavis' ambitions are not limited to top-quality Napa wines. Everyday Woodbridge wines reach much deeper into the nation.

One section of the valley can be said to have a different character and style from the rest: the northern end, where the San Joaquin River curls west and flows sluggishly into San Francisco Bay. The influence of the distant Bay is still felt here in much cooler nights than further south. Lodi, the heart of these vineyards, correspondingly has its own reputation for better table wines than the average. Most Lodi wine is used for blends, but this is where Mondavi has its Woodbridge cellars. Further northwest, in the

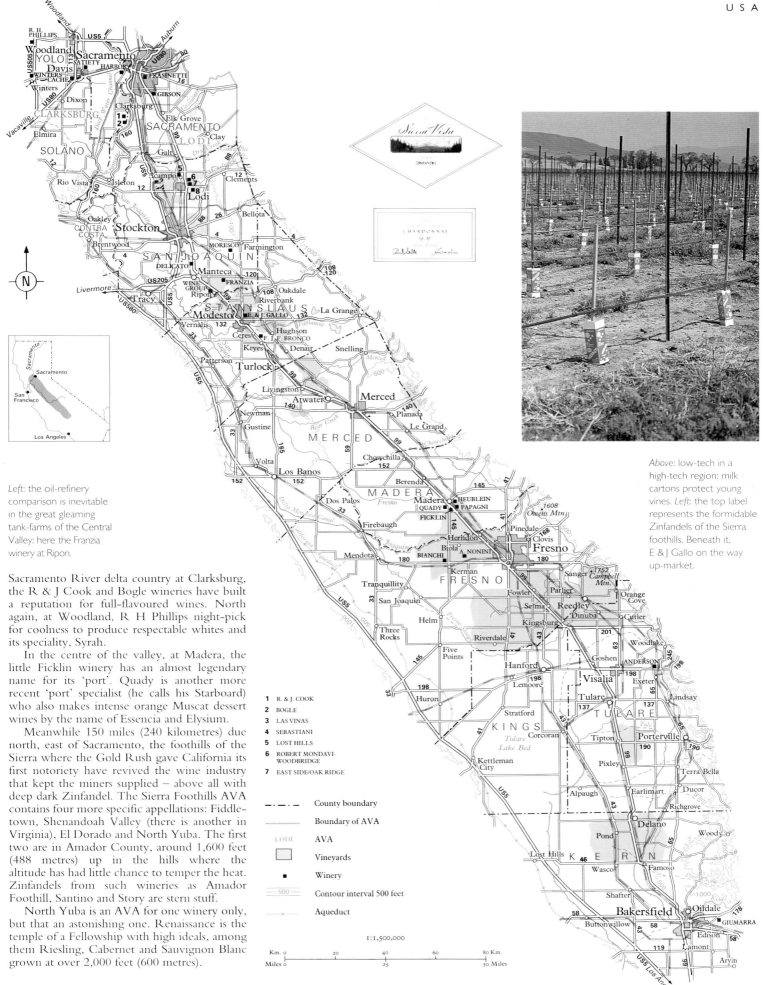

Left: the oil-refinery comparison is inevitable in the great gleaming tank-farms of the Central Valley: here the Franzia winery at Ripon.

Above: low-tech in a high-tech region: milk cartons protect young vines. *Left*: the top label represents the formidable Zinfandels of the Sierra foothills. Beneath it, E & J Gallo on the way up-market.

Sacramento River delta country at Clarksburg, the R & J Cook and Bogle wineries have built a reputation for full-flavoured wines. North again, at Woodland, R H Phillips night-pick for coolness to produce respectable whites and its speciality, Syrah.

In the centre of the valley, at Madera, the little Ficklin winery has an almost legendary name for its 'port'. Quady is another more recent 'port' specialist (he calls his Starboard) who also makes intense orange Muscat dessert wines by the name of Essencia and Elysium.

Meanwhile 150 miles (240 kilometres) due north, east of Sacramento, the foothills of the Sierra where the Gold Rush gave California its first notoriety have revived the wine industry that kept the miners supplied – above all with deep dark Zinfandel. The Sierra Foothills AVA contains four more specific appellations: Fiddletown, Shenandoah Valley (there is another in Virginia), El Dorado and North Yuba. The first two are in Amador County, around 1,600 feet (488 metres) up in the hills where the altitude has had little chance to temper the heat. Zinfandels from such wineries as Amador Foothill, Santino and Story are stern stuff.

North Yuba is an AVA for one winery only, but that an astonishing one. Renaissance is the temple of a Fellowship with high ideals, among them Riesling, Cabernet and Sauvignon Blanc grown at over 2,000 feet (600 metres).

1   R. & J. COOK
2   BOGLE
3   LAS VINAS
4   SEBASTIANI
5   LOST HILLS
6   ROBERT MONDAVI-WOODBRIDGE
7   EAST SIDE/OAK RIDGE

–··–··–   County boundary

————   Boundary of AVA

LODI   AVA

☐   Vineyards

■   Winery

500   Contour interval 500 feet

Aqueduct

1:1,500,000

Km. 0   20   40   60   80 Km.
Miles 0   25   50 Miles

267

The Southwest States and Mexico

California's first Mission vines were planted between what is now downtown Los Angeles and the city of Pasadena to its north. The Mission San Gabriel still stands, but subdivision and smog have long since driven vineyards out of their original California home. Los Angeles' vines migrated west into what was then the desert area of Cucamonga. Early in the 20th century Cucamonga was a vast and prosperous vineyard, producing 'common table wines and fine dessert wines'. The road maps still credit it with the 'Oldest winery in California'.

Long before even the Mission grape reached California, however, it was being fermented for the needs of Spanish missionaries in Arizona, New Mexico, and near El Paso in Texas.

Texas has a special place in the history of the vine, if not of wine. It is the botanical heart of America as 'Vinland' – indeed the region with more native grape species than any other on earth. Of 36 species of the genus *Vitis* scattered around the world no fewer than 15 are Texan natives – a fact that was turned to important use during the phylloxera epidemic. Thomas V. Munson of Denison, Texas, made hundreds of hybrids between *Vitis vinifera* and native grapes in the search for immune rootstock. Working with Professor Viala of the University of Montpellier he introduced many of the resistant roots that saved not only France's, but Europe's wine industry.

That of Texas itself was killed by Prohibition. In 1920 the state had a score of wineries. Revival after Repeal was slow and painful: half of the state's 254 counties are still 'dry' today. But a Farm Winery law in 1977 gave encouragement to pioneers: the first of them, high on the 'staked plains' at nearly 4,000 feet (1,200 metres) near Lubbock, Llano Estacado and Pheasant Ridge. They chose well. Despite the infinite exposure and dismal flatness of the region its soil is deep, calcareous and fertile, its sunshine brilliant, its nights cool (and its winters very cold). The air is dry, rain falls in early summer and violent weather is relatively rare. Having started with a trial mixture of *vinifera* and hybrid vines both wineries now produce Chardonnays, Sauvignons, Chenins, Cabernets and Merlots comparable to good examples from northern California.

Texas' biggest wine enterprise by far is 200 miles (320 kilometres) south at Fort Stockton, where the land-rich University of Texas formed a joint venture in 1984 to plant over 1,000 acres (400 hectares) with Domaines Cordier of Bordeaux. The label of their adequate varietal range is Ste Geneviève.

More promising for quality is the vaguely defined region known as the Hill Country, south of Lubbock and west of Austin, which has staked out three AVAs: Texas Hill Country, Fredericksburg and Bell Mountain (the last for a single estate winery of the same name specializing in Cabernet). The first two comprise over 500 acres (200 hectares) and some ten wineries each. This is popular vacation country (vital to cellar-door sales) which prides itself in its

Above: without the Rockies to keep the temperature down vineyards would not exist in New Mexico. La Chiripada winery, near Dixon, is producing medal-winning wines, among them a Special Reserve Riesling and a blend of Vidal/Villard Blanc.

Above: riddling sparkling wine at Domaine Mont-Jallon in New Mexico. Several French concerns have seized the opportunity to make sparkling as well as still wines in Texas and New Mexico. Both states now produce a good range, the best beating California at wine shows.

cuisine. Since beer is the logical drink with typical Tex-Mex food the menu is an important consideration.

It is the Rockies that allow New Mexico to even think of growing wine: elevation cools the climate down to the point where, in the north of the state, only hydrid vines will survive. The Rio Grande Valley provides almost the only agricultural land, falling from over 7,000 feet (2,000 metres) at Santa Fe to 4,500 (1,300) at Truth or Consequences. Its three AVAs, from north to south, are Middle Rio Grande (which has the state's biggest and perhaps best winery, Anderson Valley), Mimbres Valley and Mesilla Valley, almost on the Mexican border.

Insofar as New Mexico is making a reputation for wine it is, surprisingly, for bubbly, led by the Gruet winery and followed by Domaine Mont-Jallon and Domaine Cheurlin.

Southeast Arizona, with its one AVA, Sonoita, shares much of the character of southern New Mexico. The Callaghan and Santa Cruz wineries seem to see their main chance with Merlot and Sauvignon Blanc.

To the north Colorado now has nine wineries, sheltered in the Grand Valley of the Colorado River near Grand Junction at an elevation of 4,000 feet (1,200 metres). Its best wines, of Chardonnay, Merlot, Riesling and even Viognier and Shiraz (Colorado is a trendy state) are said to have an aromatic intensity comparable to wines from the Columbia Valley.

Meanwhile in southern California the vine has moved south and closer to the ocean. Rancho California (now known as Temecula) rises in bumps and hillocks to elevations of up to 1,500 feet (450 metres), a mere 20-odd miles from the ocean and linked to it by a vital (if scarcely spectacular) corridor for cool air known as Rainbow Gap. The Gap cools this essentially sub-tropical area down to Region III: no hotter

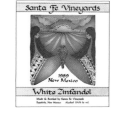

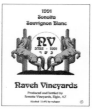

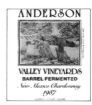

than the upper Napa Valley. The pioneer planter of the region, in the early 1970s, was Ely Callaway. From the start he made high quality his goal, content with small crops to obtain it.

Unexpectedly, it has been white grapes rather than red that have benefited most from the long growing season and relatively cool late summer of the region. After ten years of experience Callaway became an all-white winery, with fog in fall even provoking noble rot and allowing the making of luscious 'botrytized' wines. A number of small estate wineries have followed similar patterns, though without abandoning the red varieties. But the quality of the white grapes of Temecula is such that an avocado-grower from Fallbrook, over the county line in San Diego county, decided to risk his name on sparkling wine (the name is Culbertson) made of Temecula-grown Pinot Blanc, Chardonnay and Chenin Blanc. Now he buys most of his fruit in Santa Barbara – but then he needs much more of it.

Left, below: Colorado's Grand Valley makes good wine from classic grapes. Arizona's wines (including kosher) are similar in style to those of New Mexico. Texas winemaking has flourished since the 1977 law. In Mexico Cetto (last label) is among the leaders.

Hernando Cortés founded the Mexican wine industry in 1524. For 450 years it almost marked time. In the past fifteen years it has moved further than in its entire history.

Change started with the planting of noble grape varieties to replace the ignoble Mission. At first in the Guadalupe Valley near Ensenada in Baja California, then later in Queretaro Province, just north of Mexico City – but at an altitude of 6,700 feet (2,040 metres). The pioneers were Bodegas Santo Tomas at Ensenada, Bodegas Pinson with its Don Eugenio brand, and L A Cetto, who now owns some 3,000 acres (1,200 hectares) in Baja California, two-thirds of them in the Guadalupe Valley. Cetto makes remarkably successful wines from the Nebbiolo of his native Piemonte as well as Cabernet and very palatable Petite Syrah. White wines are fair, but scarcely interesting.

But it was Pedro Domecq from Spain, investing with remarkable confidence, that really set Mexican wine on a new course. About half of the 6,500 acres (2,600 hectares) in the Guadalupe Valley are Domecq's, producing both its very satisfactory standard Los Reyes and its premium Cabernet blend, Château Domecq.

Down south near Mexico City in the mountains of Querétaro, Cavas de San Juan at San Juan del Río were the pioneers, with respectable Cabernet and Pinot Noir. Domecq has joined them in Querétaro, while Pinson has planted further north at Zacatecas.

The newest Mexican winery was founded in 1988, back in the Guadalupe Valley. Monte Xanic is a 150-acre (60-hectare) estate of a kind that Mexico has not seen before, intent on setting a new standard of quality.

The irony is that Mexican taste lags far behind the potential of Mexico's modern vineyards and wineries. Most bodegas lean heavily for their profits on low-quality sweet wines, and above all on brandy, to mix with the national drink, Coca Cola.

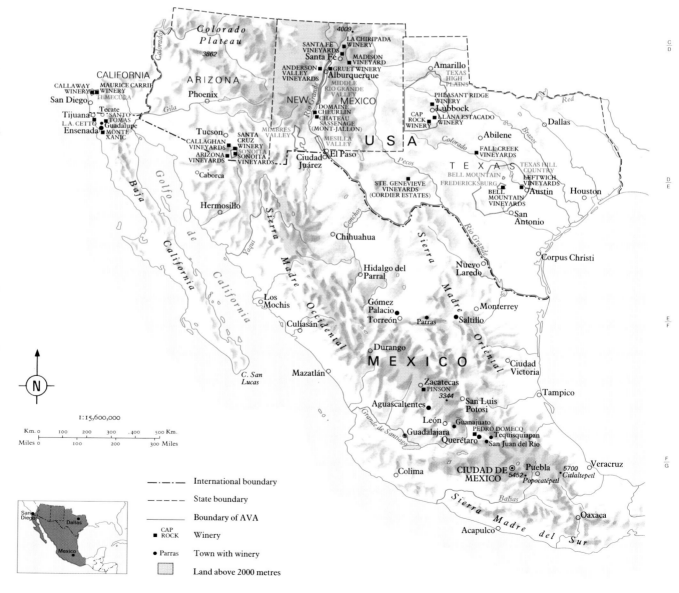

1:15,600,000

Km. 0   100   200   300   400   500 Km.

Miles 0   100   200   300 Miles

--- · --- International boundary

- - - - State boundary

——— Boundary of AVA

■ CAP ROCK   Winery

● Parras   Town with winery

▦ Land above 2000 metres

The Pacific Northwest

Mendocino County is as far north as California's vineyards go. It is not just the redwood forests that stop them, but also the configuration of the coastal hills. No longer a persistent ridge, admitting fog through occasional chinks, they rise and fall in disorder, beset by the perpetual drizzle the redwoods love. Not until the Oregon border does the Coast Range line up again as a sheltering sea wall. But here the ocean is different, too, with the warm North Pacific current bringing rain instead of fog and modifying what might otherwise be more severe temperatures. Portland, Oregon is, after all, further north than Portland, Maine.

Conditions, in a word, become much more European. The valleys of Oregon suffer the same sort of irregular and perplexing weather as Bordeaux or Burgundy. It seems odd that there is no history of winegrowing here. But it is barely 30 years since the pioneers began – both here and in the equally promising, but utterly different, eastern Washington.

Now the Northwest has two thriving wine industries. Western Oregon rapidly found that its gentle climate could produce a style of wine that California, at that juncture, was lacking: wines of moderate alcohol, good acidity and balance, flavoury but not over-emphatic. Pinot Noir, at that time California's despair, showed the fresh juiciness of some of the lighter burgundies. Chardonnay made delicate wines and Riesling racy ones. There was a catch, though: rain, especially at vintage time.

Eastern Washington (and eastern Oregon) is another world. Rain at any time is unlikely. The vineyards are two mountain ranges inland: the towering Cascades, which fend off all but a bare 10 inches (250mm) of rain a year. In this semidesert, irrigation is essential. But the Columbia River provides endless water, and the clear skies give long hot days contrasting sharply with low temperatures at night.

Grapes in this northern continental climate taste quite different from either the low-key subtlety of western Oregon's or the frank fruitiness of California's. They ripen reliably but slowly, night-time temperatures keeping their acidity remarkably high for all their ripeness, with consequent intensity and length of flavour.

Just as distinct as their grapes are the scale and styles of the two industries. Though both grew prodigiously (especially in reputation) through the 1980s, reaching a total of over 20,000 acres (8,100 hectares) by 1992, Oregon still only had (in round figures) half of Washington's 12,000 acres (4,860 hectares). (The total grape acreage is double this, but half is in Concord and similar non-*vinifera* grapes for juice and jam production.) To put the entire Northwestern wine industry in perspective, it still boasts only about two-thirds the *vinifera* acreage of the Napa Valley.

The two states now have the same number of wineries – about 90 each – but Washington's are on average bigger and more lavishly equipped. Washington's eight largest wineries make 95% of the state output, while Oregon's top seven only manage a third of the total.

Above: young Pinot Noir vines in the Willamette Valley at Dundee, Oregon. Untimely rain is the constant threat in this region of rich greens. But even Burgundians admit the risk can be worth running.

The roots of this difference lie in the terrain. The great concentration of Oregon's winegrowing is in the settled valleys west and south of Portland that have raised cattle, fruit and a wide range of crops for a century. Vineyards have been slipped piecemeal into this busy, well-worked landscape. There is no monoculture here; you could drive through the Willamette Valley without seeing a vine. When the grapevine came to Washington, by contrast, it moved straight out onto the steppe-like wastes beyond the mountains where monoculture under irrigation is the only form of agriculture.

Oregon strictly regulates, with tighter laws than any other state, three separate AVAs, plus two which it shares with Washington and which are much more Washingtonian in character. The Willamette Valley (see page 273) is by far the most developed. South of it the Umpqua Valley, although it has only 500 acres (200 hectares) and ten wineries, benefits from more shelter, warmer summers and drier autumns. Its reputation starts with Riesling, from such wineries as Hillcrest and Callahan Ridge, but by no means finishes there. South again, near the California border, the Rogue Valley has promising prognostications, being warmer and much drier than its northern neighbours. The wineries that lead this appellation – Bridgeview, Valley View, Siskiyou and Foris – have set their sights on Cabernet and Merlot but create excitement with Gewürztraminer and other white grapes as well.

Finally, the shared AVAs are a small part of the Columbia Valley and an even smaller piece of Walla Walla. The Walla Walla region has a less extreme, more humid climate than Yakima and shows promise of excellent Chardonnay, Cabernet and Merlot. Its development, begun in about 1980 by Leonetti, spills over into Oregon with the Seven Hills Vineyard. Canoe Ridge Vineyard is the beacon for the future, being jointly operated by the Woodward Canyon winery and California's Chalone.

As their reputations stand after some 20 years of coherent experiment the core wine of Oregon is Pinot Noir, that of Washington Merlot, closely followed by Cabernet, Semillon, Riesling, Sauvignon and Chardonnay in that order. Yet there are still doubters about Pinot Noir in Oregon, critics who, after too many unsatisfactory bottles, believe the whites, whether Riesling or Gewürztraminer, Chardonnay or Pinot Gris (a growing favourite) are more promising in the whole context of American winegrowing.

Perhaps the most surprising high-quality vineyard in the USA today is far off this map to the east in the Snake River Valley of Idaho. The Symms family pioneered the region, on the latitude of Oregon's Umpqua Valley but 400 miles (640 kilometres) from the Pacific. Like eastern Washington's, the climate is continental, more extreme from being further south, but also considerably higher, at 2,700 feet (820 metres). The Yakima Valley is at about 900 feet (274 metres).

The Symms' Ste Chapelle Winery is now the fourth largest in the Northwest. At the outset it used mainly Washington-grown grapes. But as the quality of grapes from the Symms' own fruit ranch near Caldwell became clear Idaho moved into its own as a producer of splendid Chardonnay and (often late-harvest) Riesling and Chenin Blanc. The Chardonnay combines intensity with silky richness that challenges the best in California. With such success, they were not alone for long: Idaho now has ten wineries.

British Columbia arrived on the scene, somewhat tentatively, a shade earlier. The centre of the small wine industry is the Okanagan Valley, 200 miles (320 kilometres) east of Vancouver, where a long narrow lake runs north–south. Hybrids have been grown here for 45 years, but only in the last 15 have trials with *vinifera* been encouraging. Gewürztraminer, Riesling (not the inferior 'Okanagan Riesling') and Chardonnay have all made highly promising beginnings.

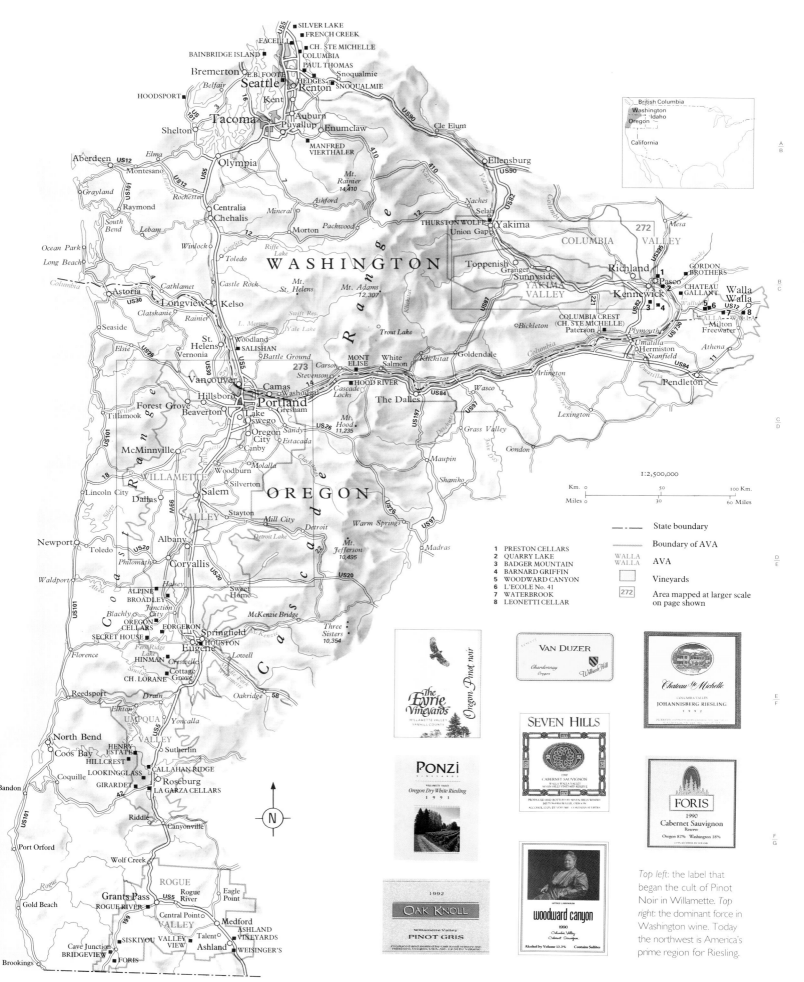

Top left: the label that began the cult of Pinot Noir in Willamette. *Top right*: the dominant force in Washington wine. Today the northwest is America's prime region for Riesling.

Yakima

The Yakima Valley just pre-dates the Willamette as a select site for the vine. Although the first winery in this remote spot, Hinzerling, was not built until 1974, grapes from here were already celebrated in Seattle. Academics at the University of Washington made their first wines from Yakima grapes in the early 1960s – and were delighted. In 1966, as Associated Vintners, they made a Riesling and a Gewürztraminer that turned heads.

The next year the American Wine Growers Corporation, an industrial producer of mainly non-*vinifera* bulk wines, turned its thoughts to something far more ambitious. André Tchelistcheff, the senior winemaker of the Napa Valley, visited Seattle, tasted the professors' Gewürztraminer and pronounced it the best yet made in America. American Wine Growers hired him as consultant, and under his direction, in 1967, made its first Cabernet, Semillon and Grenache rosé.

What big-time fruit-growers had started as a low-cost farming area, a valley of scrub carved by the Yakima River on its way east to join the Columbia at Kennewick, had proved to have a climate close to perfect for ripening fine wine grapes, on a latitude between those of Bordeaux and Burgundy. The Yakima has worn its valley 1,500 feet (457 metres) deep between sheltering ridges: the Rattlesnake Mountains and Horse Heaven Hills. Where irrigation water is available (priority goes to the older plantations) the rainless summer and autumn minimize disease problems while the hot days and cold nights of the desert induce singularly well-defined flavours in some (not all) varieties.

So far the biggest red successes have been Merlot (from, for example, Columbia Winery, The Hogue Cellars and Chateau Ste Michelle), with Cabernet close behind (the same wineries, plus Staton Hills and Covey Run). White wines

Washington first made its reputation with Semillons, Gewürztraminer and Merlot. But the demand for Chardonnay and Cabernet is inexorable. In the Chateau Ste Michelle cellars Chardonnay is fermented in barrel. Unexpectedly, fermenting in barrel can be gentler to the wine than simple barrel-ageing.

are led in quantity by Chardonnay, but in quality by Riesling and Semillon, then Sauvignon.

The Yakima wine landscape is bizarre. The early vineyards were (and are) vast discs of green, as much as half a mile in diameter, clustered like pieces on a checkerboard in a tawny waste of undulating scrub. The hub of each disc is a mighty hydrant, pumping water from the Columbia along a quarter-mile irrigation boom rotating on tracks among the vines. Today the vineyards are no longer forced to be round. Drip irrigation allows them to be any shape. But they still stand out startlingly green against brown.

The leader of the Washington winemaking community today is Chateau Ste Michelle, the firm that Tchelistcheff guided. It is still based near Seattle, away from the vineyards, but owns a quarter of the 12,000 odd acres (4,858 hectares) of *vinifera* grapes in the state, both in the Columbia and in the Yakima valleys. It makes as consistent a range of wines as any in America, including excellent Cabernet and Merlot, very tasty Riesling and Chardonnay, extremely clean and dry Pinot Noir sparkling wine and notable Semillon. Semillon is also a staple of Columbia Winery, the Washington pioneer in the 1960s (then Associated Vintners). It is a wine to keep three or four years for its full quality to emerge. The Hogue Cellars, the most substantial estate-winery actually situated in the Yakima Valley, is also a marker for Semillon.

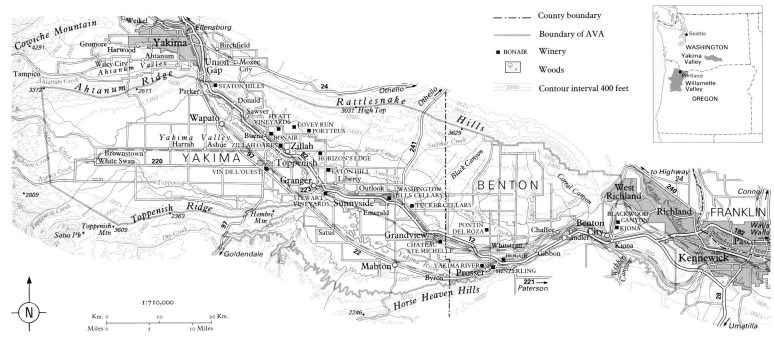

Willamette

The discovery (or invention) of the Willamette Valley as a winegrowing region was made in the late 1960s at Dundee, in the red hills of Yamhill County, by David Lett with his Eyrie Vineyards, and through the founding shortly after of the Knudsen Erath winery nearby.

Had Lett planted Chardonnay and Cabernet, fame would have been slow to follow. But he hit on Pinot Noir. Since 1970 Oregon and Pinot Noir have been linked for better or worse. The grey skies of this lush pastoral country can do what California has up to now found next to impossible: conjure up the illusion of drinking fine red burgundy. Over a third of the state's wine vineyards are planted in Pinot Noir, a quarter in Chardonnay, with Riesling at 15%, dwindling. Next come Pinot Gris (its only considerable plantation in America) and Gewürztraminer.

Almost as though this was the way Pinot Noir liked to be grown, the Willamette Valley stayed small-scale. The area attracted a different type of would-be winemaker from the high-rollers who head for Napa or Sonoma. Small means and big ideas produced a range of unpredictable wines, from the fascinating to the seriously flawed. If 25 acres (10 hectares) is an average holding on the Côte d'Or it will do nicely in Dundee too – or did, until investors from outside began to take it seriously. Most of the early wines, Lett's apart, were fragrant but ethereal. But by the mid-1980s the few substantial ones were becoming impressive in maturity. (Still in 1993 a 1978 Knudsen Erath Pinot Noir was at its peak, while a 1980 Eyrie was still dark and intense, asking for time.)

Whether or not this was what convinced them, very high-profile foreigners moved in – from California, among others, Stag's Leap and William Hill, from Australia Brian Croser, and most importantly, from Burgundy itself, Robert Drouhin (as well as Laurent-Perrier from Champagne). How satisfied they are with what they bought is still unclear. The Willamette Valley remains a place of uncertainties, its vintage pattern as wilful as any in France.

Broadly, the Willamette summer is coolest in the north in Washington County. But most vineyards here are well-sited on slopes to avoid late spring frost. The district favours aromatic whites. Montinore is much the biggest winery with nearly 500 acres (200 hectares), Tualatin (celebrated for Gewürztraminer) the oldest. Ponzi and Oak Knoll date back to 1970, Shafer to 1980.

Yamhill County has slightly more warmth but more frost problems: south slopes as steep as possible and well above frost pockets are best. Further south in Polk and Benton counties the pattern is less settled, vineyards more scattered, but conditions generally warmer again.

The towns of McMinnville, Yamhill and Newberg enclose the nucleus of this region, the red hills of Dundee. Iron gives the volcanic soil its colour; what is more important is the long cool growing season, a shade cooler than the Côte d'Or, measured in degree-days. Long hanging on the vine is what gives Pinot Noir (Riesling, too) its full range of flavours.

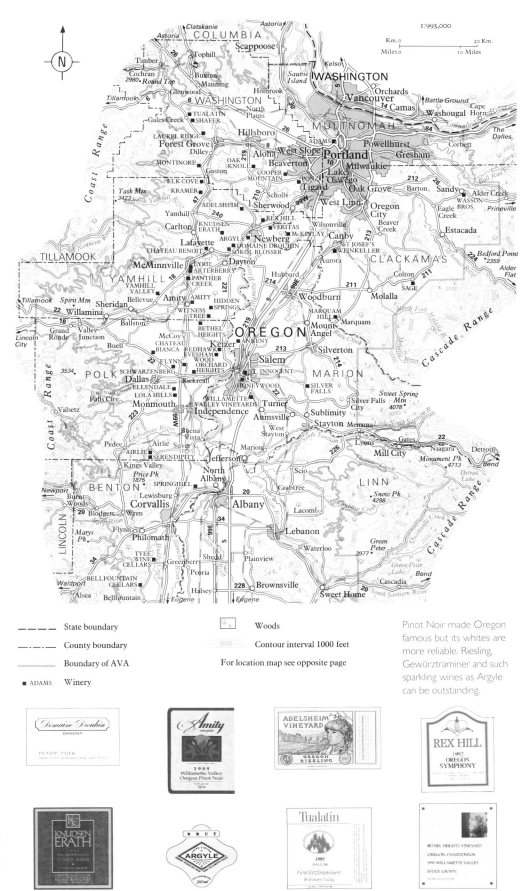

1:993,000

	State boundary
	County boundary
	Boundary of AVA
■ ADAMS	Winery

Woods

Contour interval 1000 feet

For location map see opposite page

Pinot Noir made Oregon famous but its whites are more reliable. Riesling, Gewürztraminer and such sparkling wines as Argyle can be outstanding.

New York, the Eastern States and Ontario

The centre of gravity of wine in the Eastern States has shifted decisively – critically, if not yet commercially. The industry has long been established in upper New York State, around the deep glacial trenches known as the Finger Lakes, just south of the great inland sea of Lake Ontario. Today the shift is due east and south, towards the coast and the mid-Atlantic states.

The Lakes moderate the climate, but it is tough and continental: there is a short growing season and a long, bitterly cold winter. Wine-growing started here in the 1850s and 1860s, while native American vines were the only ones that could be grown in the east (see pages 250–51). The 'foxy' taste of their wine is a long-established part of American tradition. Native vines are still the easiest to grow and still account for 26,000 (10,526) out of New York's 33,000 acres (13,360 hectares).

But the successful introduction, first of French-American hybrids, then of *vinifera* vines into the east is steadily marginalizing the native industry. Their market share understates their importance today. To all appearances they represent the future: Chardonnays and Rieslings are becoming routine in New York. Neighbouring states have no intention of missing the fun.

The central figure in the move to European grapes was Dr Konstantin Frank, a Russian-born German. His company, pointedly called Vinifera Wines, had the first successes with Riesling and Chardonnay in the Finger Lakes. His Riesling Trockenbeerenauslese, of 1961, caused a sensation. Frank's contention, now well proven, is that *vinifera* vines grafted on the right rootstocks and protected in winter are as hardy as American or hybrid ones. They also ripen just as well.

A considerable body of opinion still regards these vines as a risky proposition – not least because California can make *vinifera* wine so cheaply and well that a different product seems to make commercial sense. (And wineries are not above buying bulk California wine to blend and label 'New York'). But these are the thoughts of the old monolithic industry, of a few big wineries with famous old brands.

In 1976 a new farm winery law opened the way for small-scale, flexible operations. For them Frank had written the gospel. While the Finger Lakes remained the hub of the industry, with most vineyards, the apostles fanned out down the Hudson River (for long the scene of winegrowing experiments), headed for Lake Erie, and most importantly set up shop on Long Island, air-conditioned by the Atlantic.

The pioneers of Long Island were Alex and Louisa Hargrave. In 1973 they set their first vines in the silty-sandy potato fields of the North Fork, out at the eastern end of the island, almost surrounded by sea. The ocean influence slows the seasons: delays bud-break and maintains the mild weather for so long that total degree-days here equal those of the Napa Valley.

Long Island now has 1,300 acres (526 hectares) of vines, all *vinifera* (47% Chardonnay), 16 wineries and makes 90% of all New York state's premium wine. How could it fail, with

Above: although American vines and hybrids still dominate the north and east, the range and quality of classic varieties grows yearly, from Ontario to Virginia. *Below*: New York's Finger Lakes have been the centre of the industry for a century. Their strongest challenger today is Long Island.

New York City on its doorstep? The island has two AVAs: the original North Fork and the cooler (and smaller) Hamptons, or South Fork. Bedell, Bidwell, Gristina, Lenz, Palmer and Pindar are all North Fork wineries with a keen following in New York restaurants. Bridgehampton Le Rêve and Sag Pond represent the Hamptons; Banfi stands alone at Old Brookville.

The Hudson River region, with 1,000 acres (405 hectares) and more wineries than Long Island, is chasing hard. Its best-known concerns are Benmarl (mainly hybrids), Clinton (for sparkling), Rivendell and Millbrook, whose all-*vinifera* wines are the most impressive.

New York State has six AVAs in all. The biggest is Erie-Chautauqua with 20,000 acres (8,097 hectares) (partly in Ohio). Woodbury Vineyards with good Chardonnay, Riesling and sparkling wines is the shining star here in an ocean of Concord and Catawba juice-grapes. The Finger Lakes (Cayuga Lake is a separate small AVA) remains the most important in volume with 85% of the State's output and 48 wineries. By far the biggest concern is the Canandaigua Wine Co, the third largest in the US wine industry, owning Guild in California as well as Widmers, Manischewitz (including kosher) and many other brands. The best are Vinifera Wine Cellars (now owned by Frank *fils*) and its sparkling-wine offshoot, Chateau Frank, the Hermann J Wiemer Vineyard at Dundee on Lake Seneca and Wagner Vineyards (which still hedges its bets with non-*vinifera* vines, too).

But the 'fury of planting' in the east is not limited to New York. Ohio has a long history of winemaking in the Chautauqua area. Even here hybrids are ousting American grapes, and experiments with European vines are encouraging. The low-lying islands along the south lakeshore near Sandusky offer the best potential.

Michigan has a surprising number of wineries (Lake Michigan rarely freezes). Several, from Tabor Hill near the Indiana border, to Chateau Grand Travers on a lake-girt peninsula 200 miles (320 kilometres) further north, have succeeded in growing very creditable Chardonnay and Riesling, and even Merlot and Gamay.

Canada reaches its southernmost point at Pelee Island in Lake Erie. Southern Ontario, particularly where the Niagara Peninsula is air-conditioned by lakes both north and south, is Canada's natural vineyard – on the same latitude as northern Oregon. Until the 1970s those who knew Canadian wine found it hard to take seriously its sickly sherries. They still exist, but are almost forgotten in the revelation that Ontario can make fine Riesling, Chardonnay, Gewürztraminer and Auxerrois, and adequate Gamay, Pinot Noir and Cabernet. The biggest company, Brights, first experimented with Chardonnay in the 1950s with no real success. Chateau Gai tried bubbles in the 1960s. But it was not until the late 1970s that the new Inniskillin Estate by the Niagara River and nearby Chateau des Charmes dedicated themselves to *vinifera* varieties and encouraged their neighbours to do likewise.

The two dozen Ontario wineries are ex-

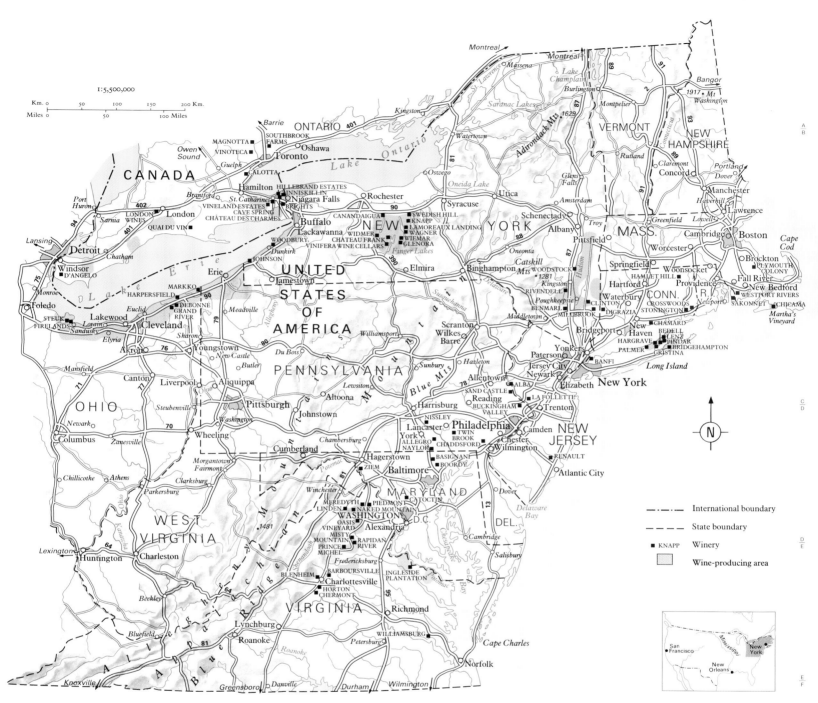

ceptionally well integrated. They have formed a Vintner's Quality Alliance to test and label wines that meet strict criteria of grape variety, ripeness and origin. But their real break has been the discovery that Ice-wine comes naturally to them. In 1991 Inniskillin's Vidal Ice-wine won a Grand Prix d'Honneur at Vinexpo in Bordeaux. Now almost every winery makes Ice-wine – the best of astonishing luscious freshness.

In the north, winter cold and the short growing season are the problems. Now that the mid-Atlantic states from New Jersey to Virginia have joined in earnest planting they face the diseases and summer humidity that frustrated Thomas Jefferson and so many would-be winegrowers in the past. Pennsylvania has two wine regions at opposite ends of the state: in the northwest as part of the Lake Erie complex; in the south, the

Lancaster and Cumberland valleys (both AVAs) near the Maryland borders. Modern winegrowing was launched in the Lancaster Valley at Conestoga. The region's winemakers, Allegro, Chaddsford, Naylor and Twin Brook, remain divided between *vinifera* and hybrid vines.

Maryland and Delaware are not big players. Catoctin Valley AVA is the principal area for Chardonnay and Cabernet. Basignani Winery and Boordy, famous for Philip Wagner's introduction of French-American hybrids, are split between these and *vinifera* vines. The Catoctin winery further south is more inclined to *vinifera*.

The state that, after New York's Long Island, offers the most excitement today is unquestionably Virginia. It has more vines than Long Island, but the same acreage of *vinifera* varieties and three times as many wineries. Its citizens see it as

true wine country. State laws back them, and recent results have been extremely impressive.

Five AVAs are in place, but the great concentration of planting is on the east slope of the Blue Ridge Mountains near Charlottesville, where the seasons are relatively reliable, the soil permeable and summer humidity not an insuperable problem. The heart of the region is the AVA called Monticello, after Jefferson's mansion. Prince Michel and its affiliate Rapidan River are the biggest concerns, the former for Cabernet (especially Le Ducq), the latter for Riesling. Montdomaine and Piedmont are other leaders, while Barboursville, owned by the Italian Zonin family, makes the usual *vinifera* wines very well and has produced a luxurious Malvaxia Reserve that makes one eager to see what else may be in store.

Australia

The Australian wine industry revolves round powerful personalities. Brian Croser's has been the name to conjure with since he brought Petaluma in S Australia to fame.

Of all the wine countries of the New World Australia took to the grape most readily and has developed her industry most consistently and to the best effect. Today she produces (albeit as a tiny proportion of her total harvest) red and white table wines, and certain dessert wines, comparable to the best in the world.

If Australia played wine test matches, it would have to be with California. Each would win the 'home' games, for the judges of each

Most of Australia is too hot and dry for vines to thrive. The evapo-transpiration index is a measure of the balance between heat and moisture; where evaporation exceeds precipitation the result is aridity.

have palates tuned to their national products. Some extreme exceptions apart, Australia's wines, whether red or white, tend to a fruity softness which may be direct but is also delicate and rather rapidly drinkable. In comparison California has tended to mask the grape flavours with higher levels of alcohol, and of oak in white wines, tannin in reds.

While Chardonnay reigns in both countries among whites, California's second grape is the Sauvignon Blanc; Australia still prefers Riesling. Australian 'Rhine' Riesling is very different from the German, a little closer to Alsace, but in reality one of the world's great originals, worthy of lengthy ageing and potentially very fine. In addition, Australia long ago developed the Semillon, a second-line grape almost everywhere else, into a noble solo variety.

For red wines, the Shiraz or Syrah (also called Hermitage from its home on the Rhône) long held pride of place. Old Australian Hermitage was usually heavy, often soft with an appetizing salty flavour, but also often tangy with what may have been unrestrained tannins, but could taste just like iron. In careful and creative hands it can be barrel-aged and judiciously blended to make superb red wine – even better than its makers used to realize. Penfolds' Grange Hermitage is the one first-growth of the southern hemisphere.

Excellent and original as Shiraz can be, in the marketplace it seemed for a while as though it might be swamped by the universal appeal of

The map plots the evaporation contour of 1500 mm, the reasonable minimum for vines. Onshore winds account for its curve round the coasts of South Australia, Victoria and New South Wales.

Cabernet Sauvignon. Cabernet pure, or blended with Shiraz, Merlot or sometimes Malbec, hogs most of the limelight in Australia today, although Shiraz from old vines still commands admiration, affection – and high prices.

New cooler vineyards have been opened up that suit Cabernet and Merlot to perfection. The latest development is that the notoriously hard-to-please Pinot Noir too has found a natural home in the coolest regions. Southernmost Victoria, around Melbourne, and northern Tasmania are both producing utterly satisfying, firm, fragrant, juicy Pinot Noirs.

Winegrowing got off to a flying start in Australia, even in Anglo-Saxon hands. The First Fleet of 1788, bringing the first permanent settlers, carried vines among its cargo; the first Governor made wine; and the initial number of the *Sydney Gazette*, published in 1803, carried an article (translated from the French) called 'Method of Preparing a Piece of Land for the Purpose of Forming a Vineyard'.

Almost all of the early Australian colonies (unlike the American) have the Mediterranean-type climate in which the vine luxuriates. Melbourne is near the 38th parallel of latitude, the same as Córdoba in Spain (and Sicily and San Francisco). Sydney is near the 34th, the same as Rabat, the capital of Morocco. Strong wines full of sugar but lacking acidity are what you would expect - and what Australia, for more than a century, was happy to produce. Certain areas were quickly identified as having soils and microclimates with special qualities. What is strange (as Max Lake, Hunter Valley wine-

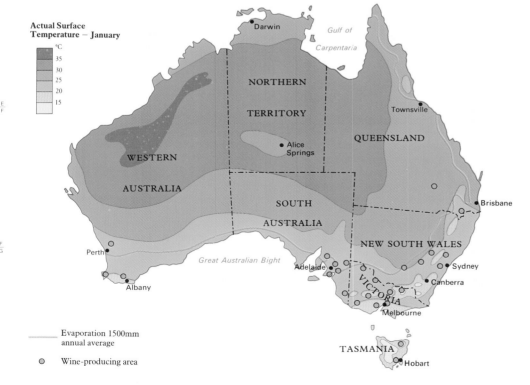

Actual Surface Temperature – January

°C
35
30
25
20
15

—— Evaporation 1500mm annual average

○ Wine-producing area

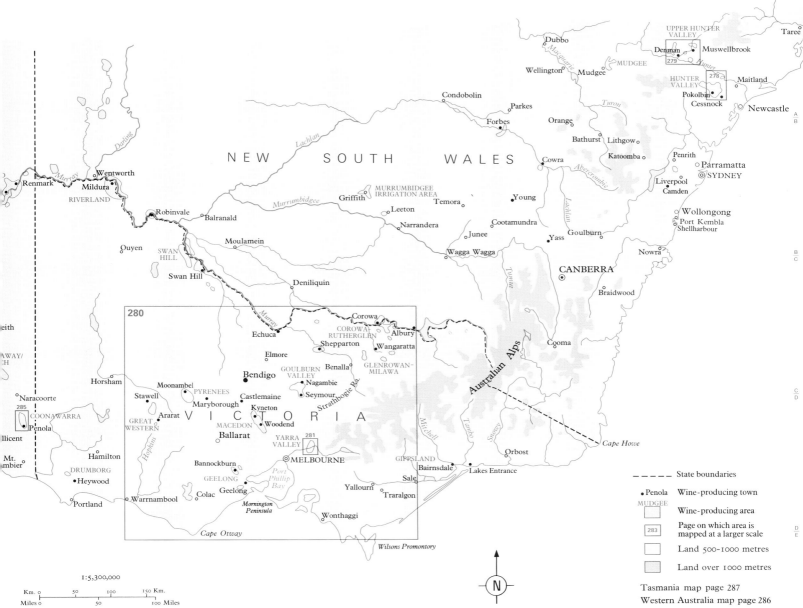

1:5,300,000

Km. 0   50   100   150 Km.
Miles 0   50   100 Miles

N

----- State boundaries

• Penola   Wine-producing town

MUDGEE   Wine-producing area

283   Page on which area is mapped at a larger scale

Land 500-1000 metres

Land over 1000 metres

Tasmania map page 287
Western Australia map page 286

grower and author, points out) is how adept the settlers were at choosing their sites. They sniffed out patches of potentially good vineyard miles from anywhere. To a great extent, it is still those early sites that produce the best wine today.

And as to 'style' (Australia's favourite wine word), everything began to change around about 1960. Controlled fermentation (first under pressure, then by refrigeration) revolutionized the making of white wines. The effect on consumption was revolutionary. For wine to be a refreshing drink was quite new. Dessert wines dwindled; red was rapidly overtaken by white. Even beer suffered.

Australia, in one generation, became a true wine-drinking nation, with a consumption per capita almost twice that of Britain and nearly three times that of the United States. Nearly 70% of this is so-called 'cask' wine: everyday quality in a plastic bag inside a box.

To convince the world market, though, such industrialized production had to be fine-tuned. Now the 'Riverland', the irrigated area along the Murray River, with its effortless mass-production of increasingly fresh, varietally distinct and even some very good wines, has become one of the major centres of power in the whole industry. Few paid much attention to the vast coops of Renmano and Berri until in 1992 a merger with Hardys suddenly made the new public company of BRL Hardy, the second largest in Australian wine. And not far down the road near Mildura is the new headquarters of Lindemans: Karadoc, which is the biggest single winery in the whole country. It can crush 10% of the entire Australian crop.

Wines at the top end of the market, meanwhile, have been refined by technological wizardry and constant open competition at shows. Australia's wine judges deserve much of the credit for her standards today. The wine can be no better than they are. In a country that still has no formal system of appellations, where labels can say as much or as little as they like with no central direction, the direct influence of experienced tasters is the crux of the whole business.

Australian Wine Production

South Australia	48%
New South Wales	31.6%
Victoria	19.5%
Others	0.9%

Above: Australia lies 14th in the world production league, with over 400 million litres in 1992 (1.8% of the world's total). The industry is concentrating on quality wines.
Below: Great Britain is Australia's largest export market, and the fastest growing one. In 1993 60% of all wine exports were of quality bottled wine, valued at Aus$ 299 million.

Australian Wine Exports

Great Britain	37.5%
New Zealand	14.23%
Sweden	14.16%
USA	9.95%
Canada	6.3%
Japan	2.2%
Ireland	1.75%
Czechoslovakia	1.6%
France	1.5%
Finland	1.16%

277

New South Wales

New South Wales, the cradle of Australian winegrowing, has long since been overtaken by South Australia as the nucleus of the industry. But there remains one district 100 miles (160 kilometres) north of Sydney as famous as any in the country: the Hunter Valley around Branxton and the mining town of Cessnock.

Surprisingly, being so far north, the Hunter area was one of the first in Australia to concentrate entirely on table wines. Its production is small. Vines were planted here (at Dalwood, near the river just east of Branxton) as early as 1828, but the soil that gave the Hunter Valley its reputation is found to the south in the foothills of the Broken Back Range. Around the east side of the hills there is a strip of weathered basalt, the sign of ancient volcanic activity.

The Hunter Valley is the most northerly of Australia's first-class vineyards – almost subtropical, in fact; the summer is very hot and the autumn often vexingly wet. To counter the extreme heat and northern sunshine, on the other hand, the summer skies are often cloud-covered and the direct sun is diffused. The ripening process is thus lengthened and delayed, giving grape aromas time to develop.

Hermitage (or Shiraz) is the classic red grape, and Semillon the traditional white. Rather soft and earthy but long and spicy, Hunter Hermitage lasts well and grows complex with time. Pinot Noir is surprisingly successful, too. Many think a blend of Pinot Noir and Hermitage has given some of the Hunter Valley's best wines. Cabernet is far less important here than in other areas.

Old-style white Hunter wines were broad and golden, soft and deceptively light in flavour when young. Such mild wines are normally a bad risk for ageing – but not the 'honey Hunters', as their friends call them. Age only intensifies and deepens their flavours and rounds out their texture. Today they are crisper and more aromatic when young, but the true virtue of 'Hunter Riesling', as the Semillon is wryly called, still lies at the end of a four- or five-year wait – at least.

The vogue grape, as almost everywhere in Australia, is the Chardonnay. In the 1970s Murray Tyrrell did what Max Lake had done with Cabernet: put down a marker no wine-maker could ignore, his Vat 47. Chardonnay now makes wines of surprising delicacy under Hunter skies, with each vintage and almost every winery adding to the accumulating experience of how long it can be kept with advantage in barrel, how long in bottle.

Two big wine companies once dominated the Hunter Valley. Lindemans (now all over Australia, and owned by Penfolds) has a powerful presence with the white wines that built its reputation (under such names as 'Chablis', now happily fading away). McWilliam's is atypical in being the only big-scale and long-established winery to (almost) confine its operations to one state, New South Wales. Most of its production is in the Murrumbidgee Irrigation Area further

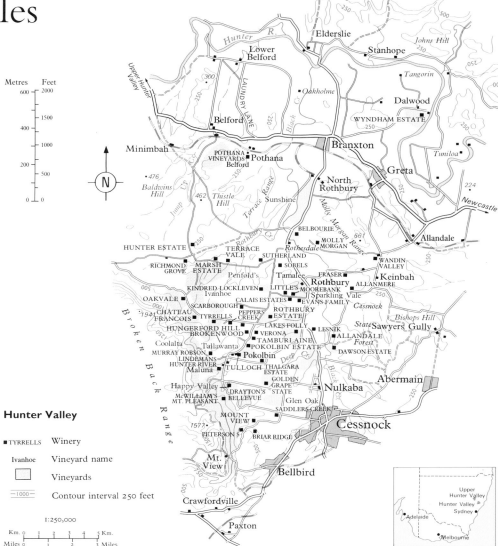

Hunter Valley

■ TYRRELLS   Winery

Ivanhoe   Vineyard name

[ ]   Vineyards

—1000—   Contour interval 250 feet

1:250,000

Km. 0 1 2 3 4 5 Km.
Miles 0   1   2   3 Miles

south (whose wines are much tastier than you would expect). It is a partner in Brand's Laira in Coonawarra. But McWilliam's banner is at Mount Pleasant near Pokolbin, using grapes from neighbouring Rosehill and Lovedale.

Long-established names also include Tulloch, Draytons Bellevue and above all the Tyrrell family who, after 120 years of a quiet life, became ringleaders of the rejuvenated region. New blood began with Max Lake, rapidly followed by the syndicate, led by Len Evans, that built the spectacular Rothbury Estate. If any one winery stands for Hunter Valley tradition it is Rothbury – above all for its Semillons, even if today its Chardonnays from Hunter and Cowra grapes (see below) are the best-sellers.

Hungerford Hill, a company split between the Hunter Valley and Coonawarra in South Australia, followed shortly after, often blending the products of the two regions. A third large-scale newcomer was Saxonvale; much smaller were the perfectionist Brokenwood and Petersons. At the same time Penfolds sold the then called 'Dalwood' to Brian McGuigan, who developed it over 20 years into the flourishing Wyndham Estate (which was bought by Orlando in 1990). Changes of ownership or control make the tracking of wineries a feat of mental gymnastics, but what was essential about

the Hunter Valley wines remains so: breadth and softness of style.

The Penfolds move from Dalwood was prophetic, if not perfectly timed. The group shifted further northwest onto higher ground in the upper Hunter Valley, to Denman, near Muswellbrook – then sold the property to the Rosemount Estate.

Rainfall is much lower here and irrigation, unknown in the Hunter Valley proper, essential. Nonetheless Rosemount has developed a style of super-rich Chardonnay which is extremely easy to understand at all levels up to its show-stopping single-vineyard 'Roxburgh'. Mountarrow (formerly Arrowfield) was not far behind initially, but the Upper Hunter has not spawned new wineries in the way that Rosemount's success would suggest. Rosemount indeed is now a national company, with other vineyards in Coonawarra and McLaren Vale.

Further west still, about 1,500 feet (450 metres) up on the western slopes of the Great Dividing Range, the little district of Mudgee (see page 277) has also made its mark since the 1970s. Its origins are almost as old as those of the Hunter Valley, but Mudgee dwelt in obscurity until the hunt began for cooler districts to make wines of more pronounced grape flavours. Intense Chardonnay and Cabernet are its real

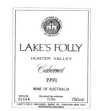

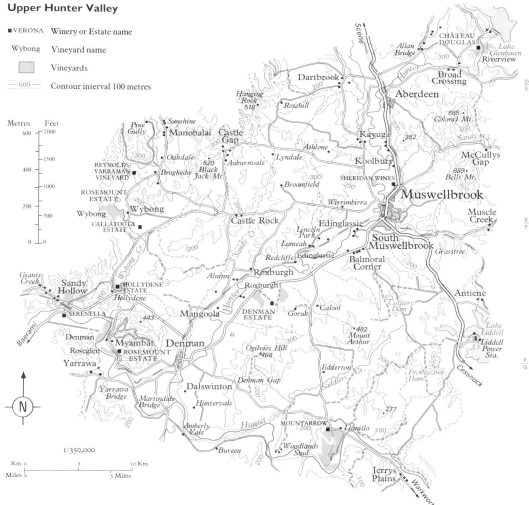

Above: the Rosemount estate's flagship vineyard at Roxburgh has been developed into an outstanding producer. Chardonnay from here is almost caricature Australian: sweet, toasty, creamy, overwhelming. Such 'show' wines – wonderful to taste, hard work to drink – have proved to be smash hits on the international scene.

Left: Tyrrell's introduced Chardonnay to the Hunter; Lake's, Cabernet. Rothbury's Semillon is a continuing classic, while the Rosemount estate dominates the Upper Hunter.

successes. Montrose is the biggest cellar in the district, Huntington the best, Craigmoor the oldest and Botobolar admirably organic.

No map is needed for the Murrumbidgee Irrigation Area 300 miles (480 kilometres) south-west near Griffith, where canalized water from the Murrumbidgee River turns bush into orchard and vineyard. After a long career making poor-quality wines, most of them fortified, Murrumbidgee was reborn in the era of re-frigeration. McWilliam's was the pioneer in producing light wines of startling freshness and quality on irrigated land at Hanwood.

Of the other scattered vineyards in New South Wales some belong to the past, some to the future. Camden, just outside Sydney on the Nepean River, was the site of famous early experiments. Cowra, 50 miles (80 kilometres) west and at 1,800 feet (550 metres), is an exciting new development, whose particularly lush and fulsome Chardonnays were originally made into Petaluma wines in the 1970s. Rothbury bought vineyards here in 1981 and others have followed. There are now over 1,000 acres (400 hectares) and planting is steady.

The Hilltops, a little to the south, near Young, and higher than Cowra, has half a dozen small wineries. Even the nation's capital, Canberra, has several enterprising small vineyards.

Upper Hunter Valley

- ■ VERONA Winery or Estate name
- Wybong Vineyard name
- ▨ Vineyards
- — 500 — Contour interval 100 metres

1:350,000

279

Victoria

At the end of the 19th century Victoria had as many vineyards as New South Wales and South Australia together. But phylloxera, which never reached South Australia, was fatally destructive. Between 1875 and 1900 it swept the state from Geelong to Rutherglen. Victoria's vineyards were reduced to a scattered rearguard.

The most important survivor was the north-east region, astride the Murray River and the border with New South Wales at Rutherglen and Corowa. Along with Wangaratta and Milawa further south they continued to specialize in forti-fied dessert wines, including Australia's finest: 'liqueur' muscat and 'Tokay' of astonishing silky richness. Both are in fact muscats: the first Muscat de Frontignan; the second Muscadelle (no relation to Hungarian Tokay). Morris has perhaps made the most velvety of all, but Baileys, Brown Brothers, Campbells, Chambers

Rosewood and Stanton & Killeen are all names to set the knowledgeable salivating.

The traditional table wines of warm-climate northeast Victoria can be summed up by Baileys' Bundarra Shiraz, once described by a French visitor as 'a three-course meal and a good cigar'.

Brown Brothers of Milawa have taken the opposite tack, looking outside the district for high-altitude sites – as high as 2,500 feet (760 metres) at Whitlands, above the King River Valley – to provide cool growing conditions. The all-family team has been prodigiously successful in widening its range with delicate dry whites (Semillon, Chardonnay, Riesling, even pale dry muscat) that were previously unheard of in inland Victoria. More surprising, Chardonnay now succeeds in the dessert wine country: St Leonards and Morris both make richly ripe specimens; HJT Vineyards produces

a remarkable model of balance at Glenrowan.

Of the other old Victorian vineyards that survive, much the largest are westwards along the Murray River, irrigated areas formerly used only for dessert wines and brandy. Here in the 'Riverland' (see map on page 277) the bound-ary between Victoria and South Australia is of no practical or stylistic significance. Renmark (in South Australia) and Mildura are the princi-pal centres. At Mildura the firm of Mildara [sic] for long made some of Australia's best 'sherries'. But as the industry turned away from dessert towards table wines, so did the Riverland, with astonishing success. Chardonnay and Cabernet of worthy quality at new low prices began a boom in the region. Mildara was the first to become a big player in the fine wine business, buying an important Coonawarra estate, merging with Wolf Blass, then buying a clutch of quality

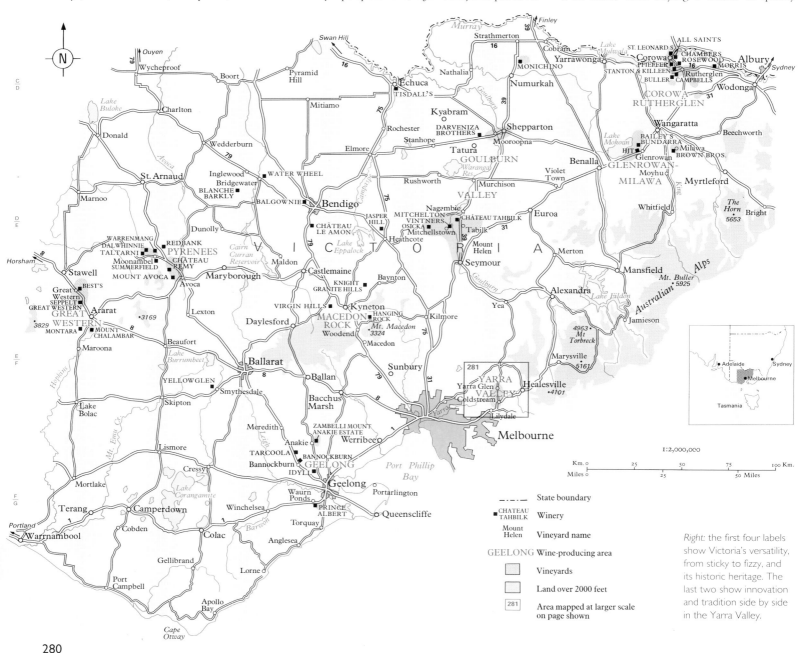

State boundary

CHATEAU TAHBILK ■ Winery

Mount Helen Vineyard name

GEELONG Wine-producing area

Vineyards

Land over 2000 feet

281 Area mapped at larger scale on page shown

Right: the first four labels show Victoria's versatility, from sticky to fizzy, and its historic heritage. The last two show innovation and tradition side by side in the Yarra Valley.

wineries in South Australia and Victoria.

Great Western, the district made famous by Seppelt's 'champagne', never gave up either. It lies 140 miles (225 kilometres) northwest of Melbourne, 1,100 feet (335 metres) up at the westernmost end of the Great Dividing Range, on lime-rich soil. Seppelt and Best's, a miniature by comparison, have a long record of producing good still and sparkling wines here (the grapes for bubbles come partly from Padthaway, partly from irrigated vineyards along the Murray).

One other district that never disappeared, although it dwindled to one estate, was on the Goulburn River 80 miles (130 kilometres) north of Melbourne. Chateau Tahbilk at Tabilk [sic], with estate, garden, stables and winery, remains like a film-set of Victorian Victoria. Tahbilk Cabernet is built like Latour – with no end in sight. Tahbilk Riesling can take age too – and so can the Marsanne brought here from the Rhône Valley. Since 1969 Tahbilk has had a worthy though very different neighbour, the ambitious Mitchelton winery at Nagambie, which uses grapes from both Goulburn and Coonawarra.

Pyrenees is the (ironic?) name of the rolling landscape east of Great Western between Avoca and Moonambel. This region is not notably cool (except sometimes at night) and its showpiece wines are big Cabernets from such as Taltarni and Dalwhinnie. The surprise is that Chateau Remy and Taltarni also make sparkling wines.

Bendigo, east again, is if anything warmer still: its wines are epitomized (and were launched) by Balgownie's sumptuous reds. Yet Balgownie has gone on to make splendid Chardonnay and even Pinot Noir. At Ballarat Yellowglen makes sparkling wines almost as though the climate was a factor you can ignore.

Yet the most exciting developments in Victoria over the past 20 years have resulted from the search for good vineyard land in cooler regions. The move has been either south towards the sea, or up into hilly areas. The Tisdall winery at Echuca was a pioneer in using grapes from Mount Helen in the Strathbogie Ranges to make vivid Chardonnay, and Riesling too. The Macedon Ranges between Kyneton and Sunbury north of Melbourne can be almost too cold. Virgin Hills near Kyneton has found an upland spot which stamps its Cabernet blend with cool concentration.

Meanwhile down by the sea at Geelong the Bannockburn and Idyll companies and on the Mornington Peninsula, south of Melbourne, the Dromana Estate, Stoniers Merricks and Hickinbotham are leading their respective regions – all now well past the experimental stage and demonstrating wonderfully vivid flavours that promise a brilliant future.

Yarra Valley

■ MONBULK Winery

▢ Vineyards

── 500 ── Contour interval 100 metres

For location map see opposite page

1:250,000

The eastern suburbs of Melbourne have spread up the valley of the Yarra River as far as Lilydale. Wine-lovers hope they will stop there. For the evidence of both historical records and recent wines suggests that this may be Victoria's, even Australia's, most promising area of all for grapes that require a cool climate.

From the 1840s to the 1920s the (primarily Swiss) growers of the Yarra Valley made Australia's finest light table wines. Then the industry died for 40 years. Yeringberg Winery remains intact (and functions again) to show us exactly how it was – and ancient bottles fill in the story. Many Australian wines are made as perfectly as science will allow from faultless fruit. The best Yarra Valley wines seem to have that rare quality known as 'breed': natural finesse.

Neither the climate nor the soil appears to be consistent enough to justify such a claim. The valley is complex in topography, with both steep and shallow slopes at altitudes from 160–1,300 feet (50–400 metres) and facing all points of the compass. Soils range from grey sandy or clay loam to vivid red volcanic earth so fertile that the great silver mountain ash trees along the creeks tower above the blue-leaved wattle.

The rebirth of the valley dates from the 1960s, when the once-powerful St Huberts reopened its doors, rapidly followed by the customary clutch of doctors fanatical about wine. Three of them, Drs Carrodus at Yarra Yering, Middleton at Mount Mary and McMahon at Seville Estate all set (and maintain) impeccable standards on a tiny scale. Those who followed included Dr Lance at Diamond Valley and the wine-author James Halliday at Coldstream Hills, both fired with the desire to grow Australia's first great Pinot Noir.

If one grape ever dominates in this region producing harmonious Chardonnay and clean-cut Cabernet, it may well be Pinot Noir. Its red wines come remarkably close to the Côte d'Or in clean, stone-fruity yet luscious flavours. It is also the foundation for Australia's best-yet sparkling wine. In 1988 Moët & Chandon opened Domaine Chandon in the valley. With the release of the first cuvées in 1989 the Yarra lost any chance of remaining a precious secret.

South Australia 1

Adelaide, the capital of South Australia, and hence of Australian winegrowing, is fittingly hemmed about with vineyards. A few still exist in the suburbs of the city. They stretch south through the Southern Vales and across the Mount Lofty Ranges to Langhorne Creek, 80 miles (130 kilometres) north up into the hills from Watervale to Clare, but most of all north-east to fill the Barossa Valley, only 35 miles (55 kilometres) from the city, a settlement that was originally largely German, and is not short of German characteristics to this day.

Barossa, with 17,500 acres (7,100 hectares), is Australia's biggest quality-wine district. It follows the Para River for about 20 miles (nearly 30 kilometres), and spreads eastwards into the next valley, from the 750 feet (230 metres) of Lyndoch to 1,800 feet (550 metres) in the east Barossa Ranges, where vineyards are scattered among rocky hills.

Almost every major Australian wine concern has a presence in Barossa, from Gramp's, whose founder planted the first vines (in 1847, at Jacob's Creek), to Lindemans from New South Wales, which today owns Leo Buring, the greatest Barossa Riesling specialist. Penfolds owns at least 1,000 acres (400 hectares), including the Kalimna Estate (source of at least some of the celebrated Grange Hermitage) and the Kaiser Stuhl Cooperative, in addition to huge blending cellars at Nuriootpa. Seppelt's began in the 1850s at Seppeltsfield, Smith's at about the same time at Yalumba, over the hill at Angaston.

The Barossa industry was founded on some of Australia's best dessert wines. The stocks of mature, sometimes ancient, 'ports' and 'sherries' at such wineries as Seppeltsfield and Yalumba are extremely impressive. When modern times called for table wines, it was the Rhine Riesling, strangely enough, that Barossa did best. Growers found that the higher they went into the hills to the east the finer and more crisply fruity the wine became. Gramp's planted a patch of schistous hilltop that a sheep would scarcely pause on, called it 'Steingarten', and gave Australian Riesling a new dimension.

Most Riesling is now grown up in the eastern ranges at Eden Valley, Pewsey Vale and Springton, while the main valley to the west grows Shiraz, Grenache and Cabernet, both for table wines and 'port'. There are exceptions. Henschke grows some of Australia's very best Shiraz at Keyneton, well up in the hills, and Mountadam has very fine Cabernet; even Pinot Noir.

Many Barossa reds in the past were rather dull and dry wines. Today's winemakers have learned what earlier picking, blending with grapes from other areas, and perhaps above all ageing in small casks can do. The region that produces Grange Hermitage must have potential for other great wines. Unfortunately the gold medals have tended to follow such loud, over-oaked wines as those made by Wolf Blass rather than the deeper, quieter productions of St Hallett or Peter Lehmann.

Barossa Valley

For location see map on page 277

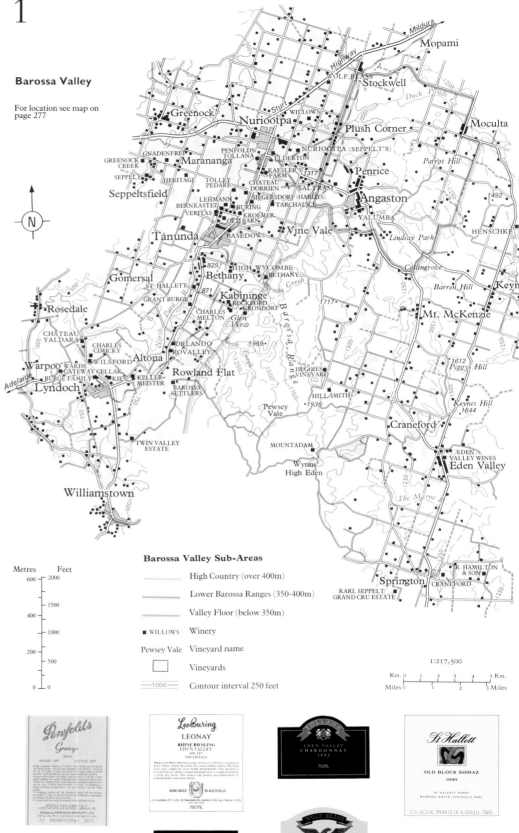

Barossa Valley Sub-Areas

	High Country (over 400m)
	Lower Barossa Ranges (350–400m)
	Valley Floor (below 350m)
■ WILLOWS	Winery
Pewsey Vale	Vineyard name
▢	Vineyards
1000	Contour interval 250 feet

1:217,500

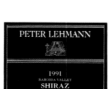

The district of Clare is a mere quarter of the size of Barossa, but with a history almost as long and a singular quality of wine that attracts some of Australia's most skilful makers and blenders. Its oldest brand name, Quelltaler, a soft dry white wine classified as 'hock', was for many years one of the best-known Australian wines abroad. (The firm, renamed Eaglehawk, now belongs to Mildara–Wolf Blass.)

Limestone soil and a warmer (or at least more extreme) climate than Barossa make the Clare style sturdy yet 'structured'. The red wines are no more juicy or delicate than those of Barossa, but they can seem to have more definition; more 'backbone'. Leasingham, Mitchell, Tim Knappstein, Jim Barry and Wendouree reds are the best examples.

Riesling from Clare is used by, among others, Petaluma, Mitchell, Tim Knappstein, Leasingham and, of course, Eaglehawk, to make wines which have both dash and delicacy: admirable examples of Australia's most distinct white 'style'.

Clare Valley

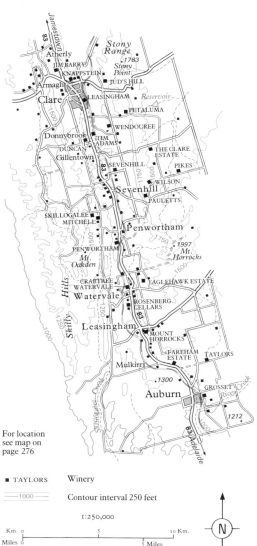

For location
see map on
page 276

■ TAYLORS Winery

═══ 1000 Contour interval 250 feet

1:250,000

Km. 0 ——— 5 ——— 10 Km.
Miles 0 ——— 5 Miles

N

Above: Henschke's old Hill of Grace vineyard, high in the Eden Valley, grows some of Australia's most perfect Shiraz.
Below right: the Clare Valley source of Petaluma's Rhine Riesling (the pedigree of this noble grape is often stressed in Australia).
Below left: the great names of Barossa, beginning with the majestic Grange Hermitage from Penfolds. Riesling and Shiraz are the classics of the region. Clare, despite its warm climate, is adept at producing balanced, dry, long-ageing Riesling.

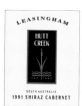

South Australia 2

Hardy's and Chateau Reynella represent the early history of Southern Vales, Petaluma the recent surge of the Mount Lofty ranges.

■ AMERY   Winery

☐   Vineyards

—1000—   Contour interval 250 feet

1:250,000

Km. 0   5   10 Km.

Miles 0   5 Miles

Metres   Feet

The Southern Vales district starts almost in the southern outskirts of Adelaide. It is the oldest vineyard in South Australia: the John Reynell who gave his name to Chateau Reynella planted his vines in 1838.

For much of the intervening one and a half centuries Reynella claret and 'port' have been respected names, and the original underground cellar Reynell built is one of the historic spots of Australian wine. Today it is the headquarters of the almost equally ancient firm of Thomas Hardy & Sons (now part of BRL Hardy, one of the big four of Australian wine). Young Tom Hardy went to work for John Reynell in 1850 before buying the Tintara property down the road. Talking to one of the Hardy family can make it seem like yesterday.

Natural conditions for the vine could hardly be better than in this coastal zone, a narrow band between the Mount Lofty Ranges and the temperate sea. There is usually adequate rainfall, a warm but not torrid summer, good air drainage to prevent frosts but a reasonably cool vintage season. Some of the earliest vineyards were actually in Adelaide and the foothills of Mount Lofty to the east. Much the most famous is Penfolds' 'Grange', from which at least a small part of the fabulous Hermitage still comes (nearly all of the original hill site has been sold as building land). The Piccadilly Valley on Mount Lofty was staked out in the 1970s by Brian Croser of the Petaluma and Bridge-water Mill wineries as a very cool microclimate for Chardonnay and Pinot Noir. (Petaluma's glorious Cabernets come from Coonawarra; its Riesling from Clare.)

Vineyards near the city were soon followed by others south across the Onkaparinga River in McLaren Vale, famous for sonorous 'port' and macho Shiraz but also capable of lively Chardonnay, Riesling and even Sauvignon Blanc. But it is increasingly in the cooler foothills of the encircling range that wine-makers are looking today, moving north to link up with the eastern hills of Barossa in what is effectively a continuous, if spasmodic, region.

The battle of the takeovers has made many changes among the respected old names in the Southern Vales. Seaview Cabernet is now a Penfold label; D'Arenberg marches on with husky red wines. The wines that best show the quality of the area come from Thomas Hardy, Geoff Merrill, Wirra Wirra and Woodstock.

Meanwhile, a few miles to the east, one of Australia's smallest but most historic little wine regions continues to produce its own salty idio-syncratic wines. Langhorne Creek (see page 277) is a bed of deep alluvium irrigated by (deliberate) flooding from the Bremer River. Bleasdale is the name of the vineyard planted by Frank Potts in the 1860s. Potts cut down the titanic red gums which thrived on the deep soil, sawing and working them with his own hands into (among other things) his winepress, yachts and a piano.

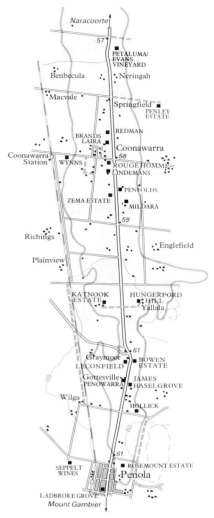

As far back as the 1860s early settlers became aware of a very odd patch of ground 250 miles (400 kilometres) south of the Adelaide region and its essentially Mediterranean climate. Just north and east of the village of Penola a long, narrow rectangle, only nine miles by less than one (15 by 1.5 kilometres), of completely level soil was distinctively red in colour and crumbly to touch. A mere 18 inches (45 centimetres) down, the red soil changed to pure limestone, and only five feet (1.5 metres) down to a constant table of pure water.

No land could be better designed for fruit growing. The entrepreneur John Riddoch started the Penola Fruit Colony and by 1900 the area, under the name of Coonawarra, was producing large quantities of a quite unfamiliar kind of wine, largely Shiraz, low in alcohol but brisk and fruity: in fact, not at all unlike Bordeaux.

Coonawarra's soil was not the only reason. The area is considerably further south, hence cooler, than any other South Australian vineyard, and only 50 miles (80 kilometres) from an exposed coast, washed by the Antarctic current and fanned by westerlies all summer. Frost is a problem in spring and rain at vintage time – enough to make a French grower quite nostalgic.

This great resource, an Australian vineyard producing wines with a quite different structure from most, was for a long time appreciated by very few. Only with the wine boom in the 1960s was its potential fully realized and the big names of the wine industry began to move in.

A substantial part of the strictly limited vineyard area belongs to growers who sell their grapes – to such as Petaluma at Adelaide, for example, which buys from the Evans Vineyard, but may blend the wine with something a little more powerful from Clare. Wynns is by far the biggest winemaking landowner, with 1,700 acres (690 hectares). Mildara has 600 acres (240 hectares), Lindemans 500 acres (200 hectares), and Hungerford Hill (from the Hunter Valley)

It seems a miracle that anyone noticed the patch of red soil miles from anywhere which has become Australia's most famous Cabernet Sauvignon region. Coonawarra wines have a crisp distinction and intensity of flavour.

350 acres (140 hectares). Penfolds recently purchased the big Katnook Estate with 500 acres (200 hectares). Others, such as Bowen's, Brand's Laira, Hollicks, Rouge Homme and Leconfield, are far smaller – more on the scale of a little St-Emilion château.

Shiraz was the original Coonawarra speciality. In the late 1960s Mildara demonstrated that conditions were just as near to ideal for Cabernet, and added Riesling with some success. Now, with Chardonnay in high demand, Riesling is giving way to the vogue grape, while Sauvignon Blanc, Pinot Noir and Merlot all grow happily to good effect. Nonetheless the Bordeaux red varieties are consolidating their dominance.

Coonawarra, strictly limited by the extent of its eccentric soil, has not been able to satisfy the demand for its type of cool-climate wines. Diligent research in country further north and nearer the sea produced an alternative at Padthaway (see page 277) with not dissimilar soil (but needing irrigation). Since the late 1970s several companies, led by Seppelt, Lindemans and Hardys, have been so happy with this source of grapes that it can almost claim the place of honour for white wines that Coonawarra does for red. Lindemans' Estate and Hardy's Eileen Hardy Chardonnays are supreme examples.

Coonawarra

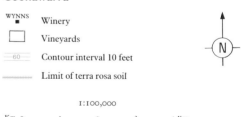

WYNNS ■	Winery
▢	Vineyards
══ 60 ══	Contour interval 10 feet
∼∼∼	Limit of terra rosa soil

1:100,000

Km. 0 ... 1 ... 2 ... 3 ... 4 Km.
Miles 0 ... 1 ... 2 Miles

There is only space for a handful of Coonawarra estates. Happily the last 25 years have seen the rise of Padthaway, 50 miles (80 km) north, which has as great a natural talent for white grapes as Coonawarra has for reds.

285

Western Australia

The first colonists of Western Australia were almost as quick to start winemaking as those of New South Wales. The Swan River Valley, just upstream from the state capital, Perth, saw its first vintage in 1834. From the searing heat of the summer, with dry winds from the interior keeping temperatures close to 100°F (38°C) for weeks, the early vintners realized that their forte was going to be dessert wines.

This is still what Swan Valley grapes do most memorably, yet strangely it was an experimental lot of dry white wine, made of Chenin Blanc in 1937, that put Western Australia on the nation's wine map. Houghton's 'White Burgundy' became a staple even in the east of the continent, recognized as a consistent bargain. Originally it was a huge golden wine of intense flavour. It has been tamed today to be soft yet lively, dry yet faintly honeyed in character; a blend of Chenin Blanc, Muscadelle and (recently) Chardonnay that remains year after year Australia's best-selling white wine. The extraordinary bonus is that it improves with age.

It is hard to imagine primitive techniques producing a better white wine from so hot a region. Perhaps this is why it took Western Australia another 30 years to realize what potential lay in the cooler parts of this vast, almost-empty state.

Perth has blistering summers, but south down the coast the influence of the Antarctic current and onshore westerlies is felt in much more temperate conditions. The southwestern corner of the Australian continent shares these conditions with the south coast of Victoria and South Australia. When the move to cool-climate areas began in the late 1960s, Western Australia produced two candidates, marked by quite different characteristics.

The first was the Margaret River region, enclosed within the coastal bulge of Cape Mentelle 160 miles (260 kilometres) south of Perth. 'The Margaret' has Mediterranean-type conditions, with plenty of winter rain but dry warm summers tempered by onshore winds and wet winters that scarcely merit the description. Australia has few landscapes as green, or forests as splendid as the soaring karri and jarrah woods of this area.

The second was what is now known as the Lower Great Southern Region, first staked out at Mount Barker in the 1960s and progressively extended westward, both inland to Frankland and along the coast from the port of Albany. Average temperatures are much lower here, particularly in autumn, giving a long cool ripening season. Rainfall is lower, too, but tends to occur in summer.

The two regions produced their first wines in the early 1970s. Vasse Felix was the first Margaret River label, followed by Moss Wood

1 TALIJANCICH WINES
2 HOUGHTON WINES
3 SANDALFORD
4 OLIVE FARM

■ CONTI   Winery
‒‒‒‒ 200   Contour interval 200 metres
287   Area mapped at larger scale on page shown

Metres Feet
300   1000
      750
200
      500
100
      250
0   0

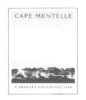

Above, left: Houghton and Sandalford are the two historic Perth-based wineries. The Margaret River came to the fore in the 1970s with the labels shown above. Mount Barker on the south coast is the latest excitement.

286

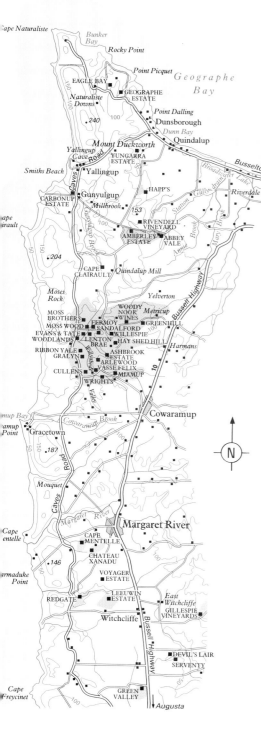

Tasmania

– and both were the enterprises of doctors. Critics immediately recognized a quite remarkable concentration of flavour in red wines (Cabernet, Shiraz, Pinot Noir, Merlot and a little Zinfandel) and whites (Chardonnay, Semillon, Sauvignon and Riesling). Sandalford, Houghton's neighbour and rival in the Swan Valley, rapidly moved in with a large plantation. Robert Mondavi of California became enthused and encouraged Denis Horgan to develop the enormously ambitious 220-acre (90-hectare) Leeuwin Estate. No winery in Australia ever started with loftier ideals (or prices). Its first triumph was Chardonnay: rich, intense, oaky, authoritative. Cabernet soon followed, equally intense, but well-aged before release. Delicious sappy Riesling is the third Leeuwin speciality. Now there are thirty wineries in the area, the most renowned internationally being Cape Mentelle for intense but measured Cabernet and Australia's best Zinfandel. (Even this, though, has been overtaken in reputation by the same owners' property in New Zealand, Cloudy Bay.)

The Margaret River region can be seen as the Coonawarra of the west; the best of its Cabernets being equally harmonious and distinctive. Great examples also come from Cape Clairault, Cullens, Moss Wood and Vasse Felix. The classic Margaret River white, though, is much harder to define. Semillon can be as aromatic as Sauvignon; the two are often blended (also with Chenin Blanc). Cape Mentelle, Cape Clairault and Evans & Tate could be taken as markers.

If Mount Barker grew less dramatically than the Margaret River at first, it holds no less promise. Grapes show their distinctive aromas equally forcefully here in the extreme south, but the red wines (Cabernet is dominant) have a tighter structure; less body and 'fat'. Whites, especially Riesling, are extremely aromatic and well balanced.

The Mount Barker pioneers were Forest Hill (a government research project) and Plantagenet. Plantagenet remained, along with the excellent Alkoomi at Frankland, the bellwether of the region until the late 1980s, when Goundrey Wines was recapitalized to become the largest and most ambitious company in the region. Houghton (which has also moved north of Perth, to a relatively cool coastal area called Moondah Brook) uses grapes from both the Lower Great Southern and the Margaret River. The two ventures have proved they can make some of Australia's best wines. Can they overcome the handicap of being so far from any important market?

The potential of Western Australia is by no means all explored yet. Just south of Perth a peculiar dusty grey soil formation known as Tuart Sands is adding yet another dimension: highly aromatic whites and relatively delicate reds. Capel Vale is the leader here, with vivid Chardonnay and Riesling. And experiments have begun just out of Perth to the east in the Darling Ranges.

The search for a cool climate in Australia logically leads to its southernmost, and sea-girt, state: Tasmania. As Andrew Pirie, its most successful pioneer, says, it is a land where the grass stays green all summer, as in northern Europe.

What little has been seen of Tasmanian wines so far has been highly encouraging. There is a mere fistful of players at present; the longest-established at Hobart on the South Coast. The evidence is that this is a very cool place to grow red grapes, particularly Cabernet, but that Riesling, Chardonnay and other whites, and sometimes Pinot Noir, can produce exceptionally lively and delicate aromas. South Australian dry Rhine Riesling has little or nothing to do with Germany; Tasmanian Riesling could be growing on the Moselle. And Australia's sparkling winemakers think they can almost taste champagne in the island's Pinot Noir-Chardonnay blend. The first all-Tasmanian sparkler, Clover Hill, appeared in 1993.

The Hobart estate is called Moorilla. The climate here tests Cabernet like a medium year in the Médoc: you can find finesse and stringiness in the same glass. Riesling is much more at home. Pipers Brook and Heemskerk (the latter now owned by Roederer) huddle together on a hill at the north tip of the island. The only condition that seems less than ideal in this vineyard carved out of Tasmania's rich and floriferous bush is the sea wind. Screens are necessary to preserve the vineleaves on the seaward slope. But ripening is as slow and sure as any vintner could hope for, and flavour correspondingly intense. Tasmania's future vintages are a certain pleasure in store.

HEEMSKERK　Winery

Land over 1000 metres

For location map see page 280

1:6,000,000

Km. 0   50   100   150 Km.

Miles 0   50   100 Miles

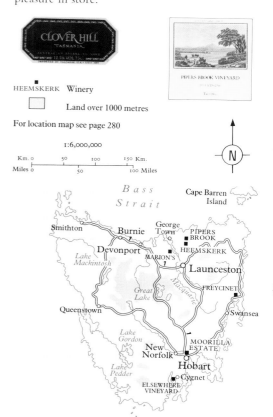

Margaret River

■ HAPP'S　Winery

Vineyards

—100—　Contour interval 50 metres

For location map see opposite page

1:350,000

Km. 0   5   10 Km.

Miles 0   5 Miles

New Zealand

There is no modern precedent for the revolution of manners and methods that has transformed New Zealand in the past 15 years from a footnote in the world's wine catalogue to a handsome chapter.

Before 1970 only interested locals knew that good red and white wines could be made, both near Auckland and along the east coast of North Island. The whole nation's cultural attitudes needed to change, though, before a serious wine industry could begin. When the time was ripe it took off far faster than anyone expected, to reach standards few can have dreamed of.

In 1960 the country had less than 1,000 acres of vines, mainly north of Auckland. By 1980 there were 14,000 acres (5,600 hectares), 2,000 of which were in the brand-new Marlborough region on South Island.

The 1980s saw stabilization and upgrading. In the initial boom poor varieties were planted in unsuitable places. Prices fell alarmingly. A government programme at the end of the decade grubbed out over a third of the acreage. But by 1993 the total was up to 15,000 acres (6,000 hectares), while prices, in a time of recession, were remarkably firm. In the same period the proportion of Chardonnay increased from 10% to 20% of the total vineyard, displacing Müller-Thurgau as the most planted vine.

Winegrowing New Zealand lies between the 35th and 45th parallels – in European terms, between Morocco and Bordeaux. The effects of latitude are countered, though, by the Pacific, by strong prevailing westerlies, by the effects of the mountains on their rain-clouds: factors that give the two islands a wide range of growing conditions – almost all cooler than the bare figures suggest. Enthused by the relative coolness (compared with Australia) most planters initially took Germany as their model. Far too much Müller-Thurgau was planted as a result.

Auckland's vineyards, mainly in the Huapai Valley, were established early in this century by settlers from Dalmatia working in the kauri-gum forests around the capital. They persisted despite a rainy subtropical climate; several of the families in what is now a surprisingly good red-wine area have Dalmatian names. As in Australia's Hunter Valley, cloud cover moderates what could be over-much sunshine and gives steady ripening conditions. Vintage-time rain and rot are problems. The most ingenious (and successful) answer has been to plant, as it were, out to sea – on an island that misses the mainland rain. Waiheke Island's Stony Ridge and Goldwater Cabernets are evidence of a microclimate miraculously right for Bordeaux grapes.

Of the wineries using Huapai grapes Kumeu River is the most successful. Matua Valley is another largely dedicated to local fruit. Most other Auckland wineries (eg Babich, Collards, Delegat's, Nobilo's, Selaks and Villa Maria) draw on other main vineyard regions for at least the majority of their white grapes. The biggest firms, Montana and Corban's, ferment in local sub-wineries in Gisborne, Hawke's Bay or Marlborough and finish their wines in Auckland. But

many transport white grapes long distances to their own crushers – a process not without risks.

A little wine had been made at Hawke's Bay, on the central east coast of North Island, for over a century. Climatic conditions are variable but at their best close to ideal, with Ruapehu and the other high central peaks catching the rain. An aerial view vividly shows the variety of deep glacial and alluvial soils and their distribution in a pattern flowing from mountain to sea. Silt and gravel have very different water-holding capacities; one vineyard can be at saturation point while another needs irrigation.

Some Cabernets made here in the 1960s for McWilliam's (of New South Wales) by the celebrated Tom McDonald indicated the long-term promise of the area. When serious planting began in the 1970s Hawke's Bay was logically the

Wine-producing area (in hectares)

- more than 1500
- 500-1500
- 50-500
- less than 50

NELSON — Main wine-producing area
Kumeu — Other wine-producing area
☐ Land over 1000 metres
289 Area mapped at larger scale on page shown

1:6,000,000

Below: celebrity came quickly to New Zealand with Sauvignon Blanc. As her range has expanded it is clear that Riesling, Chardonay, Cabernet, even Pinot Noir, will do well, too.

first region to expand, especially with Cabernet. Today it has been overtaken in acreage by Marlborough, but continues to produce New Zealand's most consistent red wines. Te Mata's Cabernet is generally considered the country's best, with Vidal and Villa Maria second. In 1990 Montana, the giant of the industry, revived the old McDonald winery (the label is now Church Road) with high ambitions for Cabernet.

Hawke's Bay Chardonnay and Sauvignon are almost equally celebrated. Most goes to Auckland (or to the Bay of Plenty, where Morton Estate makes heady use of Hawke's Bay grapes). Te Mata and Vidal, the chief local proponents, make excellent, if very different, use of them.

To the north of Hawke's Bay, Poverty Bay (the city of Gisborne gives the area its alternative name) provides a similar environment with less of a mountain backdrop. The principal differences are more cloud and rain, particularly in autumn, and much more fertile soil. Phylloxera is also a problem here. Gisborne is exclusively a white grape area, still massively planted with Müller-Thurgau but an extremely useful source of Chardonnay. One Gisborne wine stands out: Gewürztraminer, championed by Matawhero, one of only a handful of local wineries.

If there was a moment when it became clear that New Zealand was moving straight onto the fast track of New World wine regions it was a tasting in London in 1983 when Sauvignon Blanc from Marlborough made its first impact. The (Dalmatian-founded) Montana Wine Co led the way to South Island, cautiously at first, in the 1970s. In 1980 it made its first Sauvignon Blanc, and opened a Pandora's box of flavour no one could ignore. The cool bright sunny and windy climate of the northern tip of South Island induces exceptionally high sugar and acidity in grapes at the same time, and seems, in fact, to have been designed to intensify the scarcely subtle twang of Sauvignon. Marlborough Sauvignon is wine you either love or hate.

Such an exhilarating, easy-to-understand wine clearly had extraordinary potential, rapidly realized by, among others, David Hohnen of Cape Mentelle in Western Australia. In 1985 he launched Cloudy Bay, whose name, evocative label and smoky, almost chokingly pungent flavour have since become legendary. Other names to watch here are the well-established Hunter's and the very new Vavasour.

Marlborough's triumph became clear in 1990 when its planted acreage became New Zealand's highest. In 1993 it stood at 5,000 acres (2,000 hectares), substantially ahead of Hawke's Bay in second place and Gisborne in third.

The stony soils of Marlborough, helped by irrigation where necessary, seem capable of producing exceptional quality in Chardonnay and Riesling too. Few doubt that its red wines will eventually reach similar stature. Meanwhile the racy acidity of Marlborough grapes (it is routine to de-acidify table wines here and malolactic fermentation is crucial) makes them ideal material for sparkling wine. Deutz, Le Brun and Cloudy Bay's Pelorus are outstanding.

As New Zealand explores its *terroirs* the search for just-right combinations of micro-climate and soil continues. The little Nelson region west of Marlborough has higher rainfall and richer soil but does well with the same grapes – particularly Riesling (Seifried Estate is the leader), Chardonnay and Gewürztraminer.

Just across the straits on North Island, but only a little warmer and drier, the tiny Wairarapa region centred on Martinborough sees its destiny as neo-burgundian. Its eight wineries, led by Ata Rangi, Martinborough and Palliser Estate, have made some of New Zealand's most vividly varietal Pinot Noir so far. It has ranged from potently plummy to lean, dry

and earthy; but then so does burgundy. Here Chardonnay ripens well, keeping high acidity, while Riesling seems to have real potential.

Meanwhile, considerably further south of Marlborough, around Christchurch the rolling hills of Canterbury, famous for their sheep, are testing the limits of cool-climate grape-growing. Optimism is based on a dry sunny summer, while much further south still a singular summer microclimate gives the Central Otago region, between Lake Wanaka and Queenstown, a sporting chance. The old contention that New Zealand conditions are close to German is truer here than anywhere – but marginal vineyards can make wonderful wine.

Central Otago on South Island boasts the world's most southerly vineyards. Chard Farm, on the Kawarau River, is producing highly flavoured Chardonnay and Pinot Noir.

■ CLOUDY BAY   Winery

☐   Vineyards

—500—   Contour interval 100 metres

For location map see opposite page

1:250,000

Km. 0   5   10 Km.
Miles 0   5 Miles

Marlborough

South Africa

The scenery of Cape Province combines the luxuriant and the stark. Blue-shadowed crags rise from placid green pastures. Smooth rivulets of cultivation run between gaunt walls of rock. An almost perfect climate gives the vine everything it needs.

From these Elysian fields in the 18th and 19th centuries came one of the very greatest wines in the world – the legendary Constantia. Constantia was bought by European courts in preference to Yquem, Tokay, Madeira …

It takes certain political and social conditions, however, as well as the right climate, to develop a culture for fine wines. They existed briefly with the early Dutch governors: it was the second, Van der Stel, who planted the Constantia vineyard, as well as giving his name to Stellenbosch. But in the Cape politics, both under British rule and independence, have constantly hampered the wine industry, at first letting it run riot, then keeping it on far too tight a rein, so that only in the 1970s did a more promising scenario begin to emerge, and only in the late 1980s did it start to fructify.

The pattern of winegrowing in South Africa, unlike any other New World country, is overwhelmingly cooperative-based. Nearly 5,000 grape-farmers farm 250,000 acres (100,000 hectares) and most take their grapes to one of 70 coops. Over half the entire crop goes for either distillation or grape-juice concentrate (South Africa is the world's largest concentrate producer.) But the very size of some of the coops gives them the means to make very passable wine (especially white wine) at bargain prices, as northern European supermarkets are well aware.

At the other end of the spectrum are the country's 80-odd wine estates, defined as producers who grow all their own grapes, rather than buy them in. Their contribution in volume is relatively small; in quality and prestige vital.

The acute problems of wine farmers in the past left a powerful legacy in the form of a constitutional body to control prices and absorb surplus. This is the KWV, a sort of national cooperative with five wineries and, at Paarl,

some of the world's biggest and most modern wine-processing premises. Until 1992, though, the KWV also operated a quota system that smothered attempts to plant new vines in new places. The law-bending that resulted supplied the Cape with as many anecdotes as winemakers.

The most crippling problem of all was that good vines were desperately scarce. Until recently an absurd quarantine system made their import next to impossible. The most satisfactory white vine was Steen (still one-third of the whole vineyard today). Semillon was there, but Chardonnay and Sauvignon Blanc, Riesling, Cabernet, Merlot and Pinot Noir were practically unobtainable – and what vines there were were of poor clones or riddled with virus.

In 1972 the South African government, eager for international acceptance, introduced an elaborate system of control for 'Wines of Origin', which bears comparison with EC regulations. It designated 13 areas or origins, 12 of which are shown on the map opposite (the 13th, Benede-Orange – Lower Orange – is off the map, well north of Vredendal). At the same time it put firm limits on the use of the terms Estate and Superior, vintage dates and indications of grape variety. The idea was good, but no magic silk purse appeared. It is only since the late 1980s that enough healthy mature (or nearly) vines of first-rate varieties have been available to judge how good their wine can become.

The heart of the fine-wine region of South Africa, around the towns of Stellenbosch and Paarl, is mapped in detail on the following pages. Prevailing westerlies temper the climate of the Cape itself. The further south and west – and

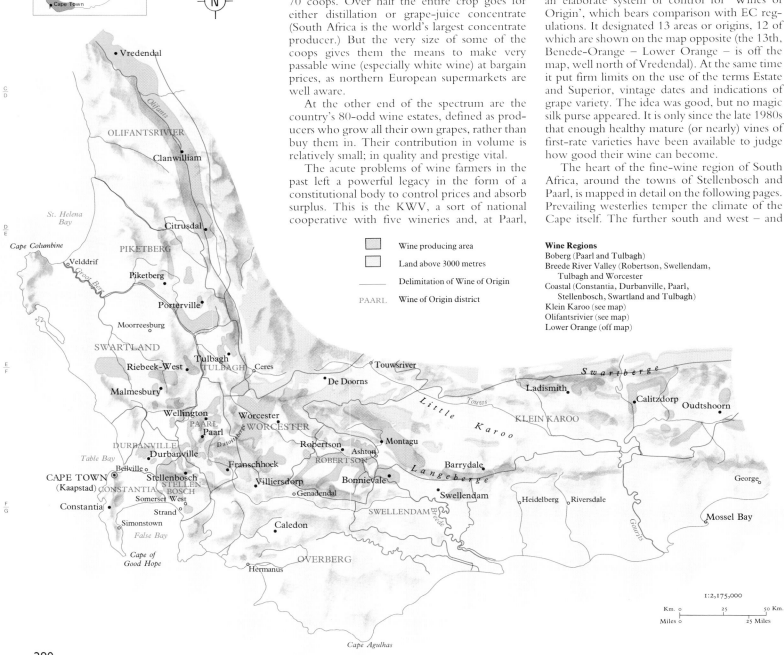

Wine producing area

Land above 3000 metres

Delimitation of Wine of Origin

PAARL. Wine of Origin district

Wine Regions
Boberg (Paarl and Tulbagh)
Breede River Valley (Robertson, Swellendam, Tulbagh and Worcester)
Coastal (Constantia, Durbanville, Paarl, Stellenbosch, Swartland and Tulbagh)
Klein Karoo (see map)
Olifantsrivier (see map)
Lower Orange (off map)

1:2,175,000

nearer the sea – the cooler and better supplied with rain. Until recently almost everything north and west of the Drakensteinberg, the mountains above Paarl and Franschhoek (see next pages) was considered dessert-wine or distilling-wine country. Certainly irrigation is essential. But several regions over the hills, Robertson in particular, are now talked about in much more respectful terms.

The principal red-wine grape in acreage is the Cinsaut, which often makes better wine in South Africa than in the south of France. In 1925 it was crossed here with the Pinot Noir to make the Pinotage; a true Cape speciality with a chameleon range of possibilities, from fresh *primeur* wines to deep fleshy ones. Pinot Noir is a fairly new arrival for which few held out hope, until a free-thinker took it as far south and as near the sea as you can get. Hamilton-Russell's Hermanus estate was almost as much a turning-point in the history of Cape wine as Constantia. Shiraz has gained a good footing, Merlot grows well, but the dominant quality red grape, inevitably, is Cabernet Sauvignon.

The white-wine harvest is completely dominated by the Steen, the local name for the Chenin Blanc of the Loire. South Africa's soils seem to suit it remarkably, and its naturally high acidity keeps its wine fresh and lively even after very hot summers. Its great virtue is its adaptability: the Steen makes everything from sweet or dry table wine to sparkling wine to 'sherry'. Semillon (or 'Green Grape'), so-called Cape Riesling (Crouchen Blanc) and Colombard have long been grown with some success, and Palomino for sherry, but other traditional white grapes have been of second-rate quality. For sweet wines, farmers inland grow red Muscadel and Muscat of Alexandria (which they call Hanepoot).

If one region outside the immediate Cape area stands out for the established quality of a clutch of estates, and good cooperative wine too, it is Robertson. The Breede River Valley is very warm and dry; its vineyards are almost all irrigated; in the big Worcester region they are mass-producers of no special repute (though the Nuy cooperative makes good wine). Worcester is where the KWV has its vast brandy headquarters.

But near Bonnievale a microclimate caused by cool ocean breezes coming inland to meet warm air gives misty days and dewy nights. In the 1970s the young Danie de Wet went to study in Germany, sniffed the potential in the air and started to experiment with dry white wines. He introduced cold fermentation to De Wetshof. Today the estate and several of its neighbours, Weltvrede and Van Loveren among them, are an important source of Chardonnay, Sauvignon Blanc, and even Riesling and Gewürztraminer.

Sea air from the Atlantic, on the other side of the Cape, also offers the cooperatives of Swartland and Piketberg, and right up north at Vredendal, the chance to make fresh-flavoured table wines.

Above: the soaring crags of the Drakensteinberg Mountains filter long beams of sunlight across the clustered wine farms of Paarl.
Below: good wines today come from as far east as Robertson and as far north as Olifantsrivier.

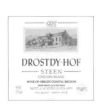

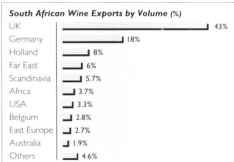

South African Wine Exports by Volume (%)

Region	%
UK	43%
Germany	18%
Holland	8%
Far East	6%
Scandinavia	5.7%
Africa	3.7%
USA	3.3%
Belgium	2.8%
East Europe	2.7%
Australia	1.9%
Others	4.6%

Above: South African wine exports increased by 14% in 1993 – to 18 million litres – half of which went to the UK. Exports still only account for 7.7% of total wine sales.
Below: Quality and top of the range wines now make up 51% of the production. 'Certified' wines comply with regulations concerning origin, varietal and vintage.

South African (Certified) Wine Production (litres)

Red Varieties

Natural wine	10, 714, 862
Fortified wine	8, 258

White Varieties

Natural wine	16, 041, 967
Fortified wine	914, 809

Non-Varietals

Natural wine	16, 151, 495
Fortified wine	919, 890

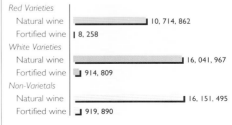

Paarl and Stellenbosch

Paarl and Stellenbosch are the hub of the Cape wine world. The majority of the Cape's wine estates, several of its best cooperatives, and its three biggest wine companies are all encompassed by this map.

Paarl has long been the centre of the sherry and fortified wine industry and headquarters of the KWV. Stellenbosch sums up the beauty of Cape Dutch architecture with the curling white gables of its buildings, both in town and scattered through the Arcadian countryside.

For most of this century it has been South African sherry and port-style wines that have paid the bills. Paarl sherry was and still is the world's best imitation of the Spanish original – to most people virtually indistinguishable. At their best its ruby and tawny versions of port have been equally remarkable.

But today's demand is for table wines, and it was largely around Stellenbosch, as soon as the vines became available, that growers first showed that good Chardonnay, Cabernet, Sauvignon Blanc and excellent vintages of their indigenous Pinotage were within their grasp.

The old Cape style of white, Steen-based, was always easy drinking. The reds were more of a problem, tending to be burly, coarse, tannic and dry. The grapes and technology to revolutionize standards arrived in a trickle until the late 1980s. Now they are present in force, and each vintage sees new successes.

The soils of Stellenbosch vary from light and sandy in the west (traditionally Steen country), to decomposed granite at the foot of the Simonsberg, Stellenbosch, Drakenstein and Franschhoek mountains in the east. North, further from the sea, the climate is warmer.

The best wines on the whole are coming from estates around Stellenbosch, which is open to southerly ocean breezes from False Bay, or high enough in the hills for altitude and cooling winds to be factors. (One of the aims, or at least results, of the estate system is that of marking wines clearly with their *terroir*.) The cooler areas include the detached and higher settlement of Franschhoek, originally farmed by Huguenots and still distinguished by its French place and family names. First-class estates in, or around the road up to, Franschhoek include La Motte, l'Ormarins and Thelema.

On the south side of Stellenbosch Meerlust, Rust-en-Vrede, Vriesenhof and Blaauwklippen are the top estates, best known for their red wines (the last especially for Zinfandel). North of Stellenbosch Rustenberg, Delheim, Kanonkop and Le Bonheur, clustering together along the west slope of the mountains, are also primarily red-wine estates. The excellent Simonsig and Villiera lie a little lower. Stellenbosch is also the base of the vast Bergkelder cellars which handle many top estates, as well as blending their own Fleur du Cap range to a high standard.

On the way to Paarl Backsberg, Fairview, Warwick and Glen Carlou are outstanding, while the showplace of the South African Winefarmers group, Nederburg, makes a vast range, including good Cabernets, but is most

Cape Dutch farms are the châteaux of South Africa: their architecture a constant wonder and delight. Schoongezicht (*above*) is the home farm of the famous Rustenberg Estate, its pastoral surrounds a National Preservation area. *Below, right:* the Cape's most historic wine, Constantia, has been reborn as Vin de Constance. Hamilton-Russell is even further south, at Walker Bay.

memorable for its late-harvest Rieslings and unique liquorous Steen, Edelkeur.

Two small regions of prime importance lie to the south, off the map and near the sea. One is the historic Constantia, recently revived with three estates: Groot Constantia, Klein Constantia and Buitenverwachting. The last two are currently making some of the country's best wines, notably Chardonnays. Since 1986 Klein Constantia has made Vin de Constance, a muscat re-creation of old Constantia. Its oil-smoky flavours with strong hints of orange resemble ancient bottles closely enough to be fascinating.

Perhaps the most significant move of all was south past Somerset West, over the Elgin Hills, known as an orchard area, almost down to the seaside at Hermanus. Tim Hamilton-Russell took Chardonnay and Pinot Noir to this extreme in the 1970s. The vines are sheltered from the ocean, three miles away, in the aptly named Hemel-en-Aarde (Heaven on Earth) Valley, and by the mid-1980s had proved that the Cape could truly move in international circles with both these grapes.

Tim Hamilton-Russell's winemaker, Peter Finlayson, has since joined forces with a Burgundian, Paul Bouchard, in a new venture almost next door which can only enhance the name of Hemel-en-Aarde, and with it Cape wines in general.

South America

Above: the vineyards of Chile and Argentina share a spectacular skyline: the 20,000-foot (6,000-metre) ridge of the Andes. To both it guarantees vital water supplies for irrigation. Without the melting snow most of Chile's vineyards, and all of Argentina's, would be barren scrub.

Right: the top three labels are from Bolivia, Uruguay and Brazil respectively. The Colon winery in San Juan, Argentina, will have to drop such names as Beaujolais on its labels if it plans to export.

--- International boundary

▨ Principal wine-producing regions

☐ Other regions producing wine

▨ Land above 3000 metres

1:74,000,000

Km. 0 — 1000 — 2000 Km.
Miles 0 — 500 — 1000 Miles

South America makes one bottle in twelve of the world's wine. Argentina is number five in the world's production table. Yet until the late 1980s the world heard little more of Argentine wine than it did of Russian, and for the same reason: the domestic market was apparently insatiable. Argentinians use wine almost like the French and Italians. Like them, though, they are drastically reducing their swallowing rate: from 76 to 52 litres a head in only a dozen years. But we can expect to hear more: Argentina needs exports, and more positively her wine is starting to challenge Chile's (pages 296–97) at a level of quality the world cannot ignore.

Overall the industry is organized on a mass-production basis. There are still few wines of individual interest. Of 1,800 wineries 40 at most are moving towards internationial quality, and perhaps half a dozen are moving fast. An endless stream of sound and easily enjoyable standard wines from ripe, healthy grapes satisfies local demand, which is decidedly traditional. The wine in the jug in Argentina can remind you of Italy or Spain a generation ago: the flavour of oxidation is still widely appreciated.

Seventy percent of Argentina's vineyards (or more than half those of South America) are in the state of Mendoza, under the Andes and on the same latitude as Morocco. San Juan to the north has the second largest acreage. Northernmost of all, Salta is on the equivalent latitude to Miami, while to the south Rio Negro (with 2.5% of the country's vines) is on the same latitude as Hawke's Bay in New Zealand.

In the rainshadow of the Andes the climate is arid and the massive flat vineyards are irrigated from the mountains by a network of canals begun by the native Indians centuries ago. The low latitudes are compensated by high altitudes, within a range from 2,000 to over 3,000 feet (600 to 950 metres). At this height night-time temperatures are regularly low enough to give well-flavoured grapes. With little or no disease in the dry air, usually on ungrafted roots and with abundant water, the crop can be huge. The national average is over 70 hectolitres per hectare, or three times that of Spain.

Apart from the traditional, now dwindling, Criolla (California's Mission grape), the most most widely planted variety is the Malbec, once dominant in Bordeaux and flourishing – as Auxerrois – in Cahors, but nowhere so important as it is in Argentina. Its best wine is rich and vigorous; overall the country's top red. Plantings of Cabernet and Pinot Noir are on the increase, and the best Cabernets contest for laurels with those from Chile as wines of serious merit. Red wines (which also include Barbera, Sangiovese, Bonarda and other Italians) are generally much better than white, which either tend towards the oxidized condition of sherry (the Spanish Pedro Ximénez is the main grape, and the name Jerez, like the name champagne, is freely used) or are just strong and dry, without the aromas of fruit. Torrontes is popular and can be very drinkable, both for old-style brownish wines and fruitier modern ones. Its origins are apparently in the

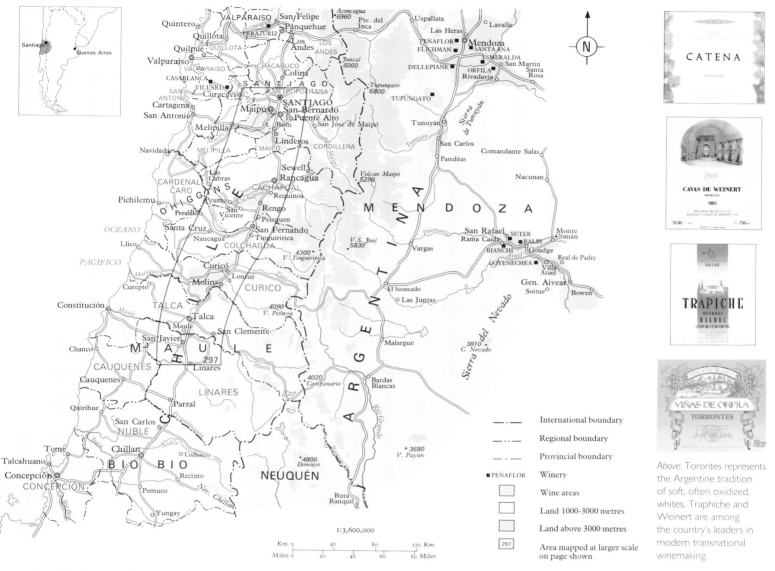

CATENA

CAVAS DE WEINERT
MENDOZA
1983

TRAPICHE
MENDOZA
MALBEC

VIÑAS DE ORFILA
TORRONTES

·—·—	International boundary
-·-·-	Regional boundary
--·--	Provincial boundary
■ PEÑAFLOR	Winery
▢	Wine areas
▢	Land 1000-3000 metres
▢	Land above 3000 metres
297	Area mapped at larger scale on page shown

1:3,600,000

Km. 0 ... 40 ... 80 ... 120 Km.
Miles 0 ... 20 ... 40 ... 60 ... 80 Miles

Above: Torrontes represents the Argentine tradition of soft, often oxidized, whites. Trapiche and Weinert are among the country's leaders in modern transnational winemaking.

north of Spain, in Galicia: could it perhaps be a form of the now rare Terrantez of Madeira?

The recent introduction of Chardonnay, Sauvignon, Sémillon, Chenin Blanc and even Riesling is demonstrating that Argentina will be able to handle these grapes too – given a little more practice.

Two companies dominate the industry in volume: Peñaflor (said to be second only to Gallo in the world) and Santa Ana. In 1973 Peñaflor bought the most prestigious quality bodega, Trapiche, and has used it to lead the modern movement. Trapiche entered the US market in the 1980s and was rapidly recognized as a good value-for-money supplier.

At the same time San Telmo was founded as Argentina's first California-style winery, dedicated to quality varieties only. Currently the Catena, Weinert and Norton bodegas in Mendoza, Etchart with its wines from Cafayete in Salta Province and Canale in Rio Negro are making some of the best Argentine wines from its enormous spread of vineyards. The point

has been reached where quality could and should rise rapidly.

Brazil and Uruguay both have flourishing wine industries for the home market. The centre of Brazilian viticulture, the province of Rio Grande do Sul, lies on the same latitude as Mendoza and Santiago, just north of Buenos Aires. Rainfall here is high and the climate mild and humid. *Vinifera* grapes have suffered in the past, and American vines have been grown. Nonetheless the University of California has encouraged new planting and such enterprises as National Distillers, Cinzano, Pedro Domecq and Moët & Chandon have taken an interest in a local supply for the huge Brazilian market. Cinzano has a vineyard near Recife only 10 degrees from the equator which produces two grape crops a year. The area is dry and the vines are forced to go dormant and make new buds by taking off the irrigation.

Uruguay is a considerable producer for a population almost as devoted to wine as the Argentinians. It has a tradition of growing

mostly French varieties (including the Tannat of Madiran), with most of the 50,000-odd acres (20,000 hectares) along the great estuary of the Rio de la Plata, west of Montevideo, in a humid warm-temperate climate very different from the Andes.

The premier-quality producer, however, is in the north of the country. Juan Carrau's vineyards are in Rivera, near the border with Brazil (and also over the border, in Caixas do Sul). Carrau's Castel Pujol label (on Cabernet, Merlot and Sauvignon) sometimes appears on the export market.

The greatest surprise in this roll-call of regions is wine of remarkable quality from Peru. The Tacama vineyards in Ica province benefit from the cold Pacific alongside in much the same way as those of the central California coast. Their Cabernet, Sauvignon Blanc and a *méthode champenoise*, started with the advice of Professor Peynaud from Bordeaux, are another revelation of what the least expected quarters of the globe can learn to do.

Chile

The Chilean capital, Santiago, fringed with its vineyards, is only 50 minutes by air from Mendoza – so close that shopping bags are a common sight on the crowded flights. Yet the plane climbs to clear the highest ridge of the Andes, a 20,000-foot (6,000-metre) serrated blade of rock and ice. The centres of Chilean and Argentine wine are cheek by jowl, yet poles apart.

Both lie in the low latitudes for wine-growing; on the equivalent to Beirut. Mendoza owes its ideal growing conditions to altitude; Chile to its isolation as the meat in a sandwich between the cold Andes and the cold Pacific. Chill drops from the glaciers on the one hand, and steals inland from the Humboldt Current on the other. To the north the Atacama Desert sees rain every few years; to the south the rain never stops. In this strange corridor of a country you can think of almost any degree of precipitation or temperature and find it in one of the gravelly valleys that cross the central plain, like gradations on a thermometer, to pierce the low coastal range and find the sea.

The founder of Santiago, Pedro de Valdivia, picked 14.5 inches (370 mm) of rain and an annual average temperature between 46° and 73°F (8° and 23°C) – somewhere between that of Lyon and Marseille. The summers are virtually rainless. Fortunately the Incas spotted this possible snag and planned an astonishing network of canals and gullies to flood the land, over 3 million acres (1.2 million hectares) of it, from the rivers. It is no wonder the words

Garden of Eden are heard so often here. If this is Eden it is the orchard section.

Winegrowing began in Chile early in the 16th century. Cortés gave the gruesome order that Spanish colonists should plant 1,000 vines for every 100 dead Indians. In 1578 'the pirate Drake' captured a Spanish ship carrying 1,770 wine-skins from Chile to Lima in Peru. The old viticulture was based on the País grape (Argentina's Criolla; California's Mission), which still accounts for over one-third of the total crop. Its other grapes, very much more interesting, are various moscatels for distillation into the national spirit, Pisco.

Modern winegrowing began in the 1850s, after Chile won independence from Spain, with the import of French vignerons and vinestocks by the (largely Basque) landowners around Santiago. In the temperate conditions and fertile soil growth was miraculous and fruit immaculate. A generation later the 2,470 acres (1,000 hectares) of the Errázuriz family, who settled at Panquehue in the Aconcagua Valley (see page 295) north of Santiago, were reputed the biggest single wine estate in the world.

With light but fertile soil and complete control of the water-supply – grapegrowing is absurdly easy. Phylloxera has still never reached

Below: horses may now be rare in Chile's vineyards, but the dominance of the Andes is omnipresent, isolating and air-conditioning. *Opposite*: quality Cabernet and Sauvignon from the Maipo Valley are established Chilean exports, but Casablanca is a new region to watch.

Chile. Vines can grow on their natural roots without grafting. A new vineyard is made simply by sticking canes of the desired vines in the ground at two-metre intervals. Within a year they are growing happily as new vines and within three years are bearing their first grapes.

Most of the new vines came from Bordeaux. Cabernet Sauvignon was, and is, the standard red, with Malbec, Merlot and Petit Verdot to back it up; Sémillon, and to a lesser extent Sauvignon, the standard white. Riesling and Pinot Noir were also introduced and can make good wine (however unfashionable their style today). Chardonnay, curiously, was not widely planted until very recently.

The industry based on these conditions rapidly grew rich. By the turn of the century its bodegas were enormous, filled with huge casks, some of Bosnian oak but most of *raulí*, the native 'beech'. It continued to supply the South American market from the same facilities until the 1980s, aware perhaps that its methods were hopelessly outdated and its standards sinking, but through political circumstances unable to modernize. Visitors had the frustration of seeing good wines tainted by ancient and unclean casks. The last edition of this Atlas reported that 'stainless steel and new oak are beyond the reach of most Chilean bodegas'. That was in 1986. By 1990 things were changing rapidly for the better.

The map shows the concentration of vineyards and wineries in the long broad central valley, or rather two concentrations: the original one around Santiago, watered by the River Maipo, and the more recent southerly one around Curicó, watered by the Tinguiricia, Teno, Mataquito and Claro rivers – although the province of Maule has over twice the rainfall of Santiago and irrigation this far south is not the complete imperative it is further north.

Beyond the scope of this detailed map to the north lies the Aconcagua Valley, named from the highest peak of the Andes, at 23,000 feet (7,000 metres), visible from Santiago. The warmth of this northern region, famous for Cabernet, is tempered by cooler sea air funnelling up from the river mouth. Off the map to the southwest, 60 miles (100 kilometres) from Talca in the coastal hills, the region of Cauquenes is currently being developed for white grapes. Californian experience sees Cauquenes, and also Casablanca, at the extreme northwest of the map, as comparable to parts of northern Sonoma where sea mists are critical to quality. The coastal cordillera is too arid here, however, to do without drip irrigation. (The Chilean word for unirrigated land is *secano*.)

Of the Maipo estates Cousiño Macul, in the eastern outskirts of the capital, remains the perfect example of a grand plantation of the 19th century, approached by a fine avenue of English oaks (the arboretum on the estate is also famous). Its Don Matías Cabernet (the old bodegas habitually call their better wines 'Don' X or Y) is a starting place for under-

standing the old Chilean style: dark, concentrated, and powerfully tannic.

In total contrast nearby is a symbol of the interest even Bordeaux is taking in Chile today: a partnership between Bruno Prats and Paul Pontallier, respectively of Cos d'Estournel and Château Margaux. There could hardly be a clearer message of confidence.

Chile's best-known bodega, Concha y Toro, has its headquarters at Pirque just to the south, overlooking the Maipo Valley. Concha y Toro is the biggest of the long-established 'big four' of Chilean winemaking which combine great estates with massive grape purchases to offer wines at all levels from everyday to some of the country's best: in Concha y Toro's case, Don Melchor Cabernet.

Santa Rita, the next biggest, with its excellent Casa Real label, is only a few miles away. San Pedro, for long the least interesting (but things change quickly these days), is based down at Lontué near Curicó. The fourth, Santa Carolina, always a prize winner, has been much talked about since its 1993 wines, made by a young winemaker, Ignacio Recabarren, who is fluttering dovecotes all over Chile. Recabarren sees the cool Casablanca region as Chile's answer to New Zealand for fresh fruity white wines.

One other estate with a long history of exporting which still commands respectful attention, not only for new ideas, is Undurraga, in the Maipo Valley just west of Santiago.

The most convincing signs of new ambition to capitalize on Chile's matchless fruit with modern technology came not from the giants but from José Canepa, an unromantic fruit-farming company of Italian origin with a bodega at Valparaíso, which even in Chile's darkest days exported strong clean Cabernet. Canepa's new plant in southwestern Santiago was the first to introduce large-scale stainless steel (with advice from E & J Gallo). The very first 'inox' had come with the arrival in 1975 in the south at Curicó of the Torres family from Catalonia. This more than any other event boosted the industry's morale.

Since then foreign investment has included the purchase of the Los Vascos estate in the western foothills of the Central Valley at Peralillo by the Rothschilds of Château Lafite, and a new Californian direction to the Errázuriz company under the name Caliterra, now among the technological leaders.

Home-grown talent has meanwhile founded Discover Wine, whose Montes Alpha from Curicó is regularly one of the best Cabernets of Chile in a lighter style than the traditional big Maipo wines.

The new generation of smaller estates and wineries in the manner of California is a very positive sign. The danger, in an industry that still needs instant profits, is the temptation to overuse the wonderful irrigation system that makes it all possible. So far, in its new age, Chile is a prolific source of fruity lightweights, and produces many wines of good Cru Bourgeois standard. The world awaits its Grands Crus.

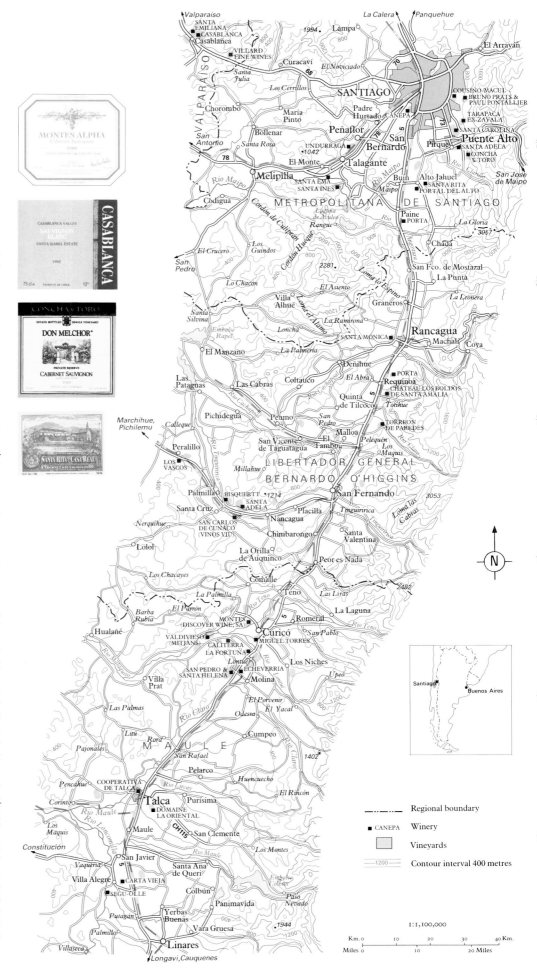

England and Wales

The past 15 years or so have seen the dawn of confidence in English wine. It used to be thought that England lies too far north for grapes to ripen – and besides, there is too much rain.

The fact remains, however, that in the early Middle Ages the monastic vineyards of England were extensive and by all accounts successful. Had it not been for England's acquisition (by the marriage of Henry II to Eleanor of Aquitaine in 1152) of Bordeaux they would probably have continued without a break. But they faded away in the later Middle Ages, and since then only spasmodic attempts at winegrowing in England and Wales were made until the 1950s, when the renaissance began at Hambledon in Hampshire.

Now England and Wales have some 2,000 acres (800 hectares) of vineyard, widely scattered over the southern half of the country, with the greatest concentration in Kent and Sussex, but large number so small plantings (there are some 440 in all) across the south to Somerset (further west rainfall is too high), along the Thames and Severn valleys and in East Anglia, the driest part of England.

The largest vineyard is Denbies, in Surrey, with 250 acres (100 hectares) – very much an exception in an industry where the average is two acres, or less than one hectare. Some 140 wineries now process the crop, which rose in 1992 to a total of 3.5 million bottles.

Until 1992 Table Wine status was the highest that English wine could claim in the EC. Since 1992 qualifying wines are classed as Quality Wines – an enormous boost to the morale of the young industry.

The great majority is white. Müller–Thurgau and Seyval Blanc are the two most popular vines, being early ripeners and disease resistant. German crosses are popular, particularly Reichensteiner, Bacchus and Schönburger, but also Kerner and Huxelrebe. The French table grape Madeleine Angevine is also successful in blends, which most wines are. A very little Pinot Noir is grown. The wine normally needs the help of sugar, as it does in Germany and often in Burgundy. But the quality has improved from a tentative start to steady and confident progress. England now has experienced winemakers who can make good white wines almost every year. Imports can (easily) be cheaper, but there is a brisk market (abroad, too) for the sort of aromatic and original light wines England and Wales are making today.

Almost all modern English wine is white, using German varieties, although a little red is also made.

Only one English vineyard is on an industrial scale: Denbies, with 250 acres, on the Surrey Downs.

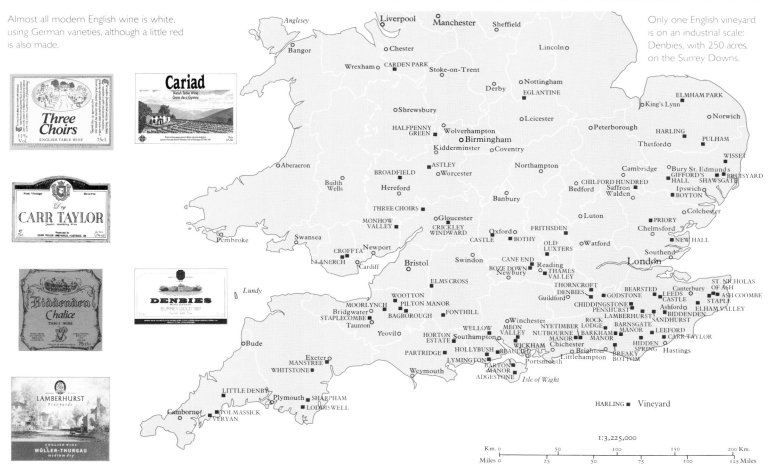

HARLING ■ Vineyard

1:3,225,000

Index, Gazetteer and Acknowledgments

General Index

Alphabetization is by word, ignoring au, de, les, etc. Châteaux, domaines, etc appear under their individual name. Asterisks indicate the main entry.

Ab Hummus 242
Abbaye, Clos de l' 117
Abîmes 137
Abruzzo 186
Abtsberg 148
Acacia 257
Achaia-Clauss 238
Aconcagua Valley 296
Adelaida 264
Adelaide 282, 284
Afames 244
Afghanistan 246
Africa 12; North 245; South 290-3
ageing 40-1
Agiorgitiko grape 238
Aglianico del Vulture 194
Aglianico grape 194
Ahera, Dom. d' 244
Ahr Valley 142
Ai-Danil 241
Aigle 220
Aïn-Bessem Bouira 245
Aïn-Merane 245
Airén grape 24, 198
Aisne 76
Ajaccio 140
Alba 172, 174
Alba Julia 237
Alban Hills 193
Albany 286
Albariño 196, 211
Albarola 172
Albenga 172
Albi 112
Alcamo 194
Alcobaça 209
Aldebrö 227
Aleatico 186, 194
Alella 205
Alenquer 209
Alentejo 209, 215★
Aleria 140
Alessandria 174
Alexander Valley 255
Alexandria 242
Alföld 226
Algarve 208
Algeria 245
Alghero 194
Aliança, Caves 210
Alicante Bouschet grape 215, 245
Aligoté grape: Bulgaria 234; Chablis 73; Côte Chalonnaise 68; Moldova 241; Romania 236
Alkoomi 287
Allegrini 183
Allegro 275
Allias family 118
almacenista 199
Almaden 262, 266
Almansa 198
Almeirin 209
Aloxe-Corton 62
Alsace 24, 120-3★
Alsheim 163
Altenberg 123
Altesse grape 137
Alto Adige 178, 184, 185★
Alupka 240, 241
Alushta 241
Alvarinho grape 24, 211
Alzey 162, 163
Alzinger 225
Amador County 267
Amador Foothill 267
Amandiers, Clos des 123
Amarante 211
Amarone 183
Amboise 114
America 12: North 250-1★; California 252-67, Eastern States 274-5, Pacific Northwest 270-3, Southwest States 268-9 and see Mexico, New York, Ontario: South 294-7 and see Argentina, Chile
American Wine Growers 272
Amindeo 238
amontillado 199, 207
Amoureuses, Les 67
ampelography 24
Ampuis 126
Ampurdan 205
Amselfelder 232
Anapa 241
Anatolia 242
Ancenis 114
Ancona 186
Andalucia 196, 207
Anderson Valley 256, 268
Andron Blanquet, Ch. 86
Angers 116

Anghelu Ruju 194
Angludet, Ch. d' 94
Añina 201
Ankialos 238
Annaberg 161
Annereaux, Ch. des 102
Anselmi 182
Ansonica 186
Antinori family 188, 191 192, 260
Aosta 172
Appellations 9; Bordeaux 81; communale 58; Côte d'Or 58; d'Origine Contrôlée (AOC) 52, 130, 138; d'Origine Garantie 245; Rhône 128; simple 138
Approved Viticultural Areas (AVA) 251, 252
Apremont 137
Aquileia 180
Aragón 198, 204
Aragonez grape 215
Aramon 134
Aranda 206
Aranda de Duero 206
Arbanats 96
Arbin 137
Arbois 137
Arcadia 238
Archambeau, Ch. d' 96
Arcins 93
Arcins, Ch. d' 92
Ardon 220
Arinto grape 24
Arizona 251, 268
Arkansas 251
Arlot, Clos 64
Armagnac 110, 111
Armailhac, Ch. d' 88
Armenia 241
Arnauld, Ch. 92
Arneis grape 174
Aroma Wheel 45
Arrabida 209
Arrosée, Ch. l' 104
Arrowfield 278
Arroyo Grande 264
Arroyo Seco 262
Arsac 94
Asenovgrad 234
Asia 246-8
Asprinio 194
Assmannshäusen 156
Associated Vintners 272
Asti 172, 255
Asti spumante 174
Asturias 196
Aszár-Neszmély 227
Ata Rangi 289
Ataturk, Kemal 242
Athens 238
Atlas Peak 260
Attica 238
Au Bon Climat 264
Aubance River 116
Aube 76
Auckland 288, 289
Audebert 117
Augusta 251
Ausbruch 223
Auslese 121
Ausone, Ch. 104
Australia 276-87★; South 282-4; Western 286-7 and see Coonawarra, New South Wales, Tasmania, Victoria, Yarra
Austria 222-5 and see Vienna, Wachau
Auxerre 73
Auxerrois grape 112, 274, 294
Auxey-Duresses 61
Avellino 194
Avelsbach 148
Avensan 92
Avignonesi 191
Avila 206
Avize 78
AXA 88, 94
Axarqua 207
Ay 78
Ayler Kupp 146
Ayse 137
Ayu-Dag 241
Azay-le-Rideau 114
Azerbaijan 241
Babcock 264
Babeasca grape 236
Babich 288
Bacalhoa, Qta de 209
Bacchus grape 26, 167, 298
Backsberg 292
Bad Dürkheim 161

Bad Kreuznach 154
Bad Münster 155
Bad Vöslau 224
Badacsony 227
Badacsonyi 227
Baden 224
Baden, Margrave of 164
Baden-Württemberg 164-5
Badischer Bergstrasse 164
Badischer Winzerkeller 164
Badstube 152
Baga grape 210
Baileys 280
Bairrada 208, 209, 210★
Baku 241
Balaton, Lake 226-7
Balatonboglár 227
Balatonfüred 227
Balatoni 227
Balbaina 201
Balgownie 281
Ballarat 281
Balti 241
Banat 237
Bandol 136
Banfi 274
Bannockburn 281
Banyuls 132
Barbaresco 174, 176★
Barbastro 198
Barbé, Ch. 108
Barbe, Ch. de 108
Barbeito 217
Barbera grape: California 266; Italy 174, 177; South America 294
Barboursville 275
Barca Velha 208-9
Barcelos 211
Bardolino 178, 183
Barjac, de 125
Barolo 174, 176★
Barossa Valley 282
Barracão 210
Barreyres, Ch. 92
Barry, Jim 283
Barsac 96, 100-1★
Barton family 36, 91
Bas-Armagnac 111
Bas-Médoc 84-5
Bas-Rhin 122
Basel 219
Basignani 275
Basilicata 194
Bass Charrington 94
Basserman-Jordan, von 160
Bastei 155
Basto 211
Bastor Lamontagne, Ch. 100
Batailley, Ch. 88
Bâtard-Montrachet 61
Batterieberg 153
Baudoin, Le Clos 118
Baume, Dom. de la 134
Baux-de-Provence, Les 128
Bay of Plenty 289
Béarn 112
Beau-Site, Ch. 86
Beaucastel, Ch. 128, 130, 264
Beaujolais 54, 55, 70-2★
Beaujolais-Villages 70
Beaulieu 116, 252, 260
Beaulieu Vyds 258
Beaume 127
Beaumont, Ch. 92
Beaunois grape 73
Beaune 58, 62-3★
Beblenheim 123
Bechtheim 163
Becker 123
Bedell 274
Beerenauslese 121
Bégadan 84
Béguey 96
Beiras 209
Bel Arbors 256
Bel Orme Tronquoy de Lalande, Ch. 86
Bel-Air, Ch. de 102
Belair, Ch. 104
Belgrave, Ch. 91
Bell Mountain 268
Bella Oaks 258
Bellapais 244
Belle Epoque 78
Bellefont-Belcier, Ch. 102
Bellegarde 128
Bellet, Ch. 136
Bellevue La Forêt, Ch. 112
Belvedere 191
Bendigo 281
Benede-Orange 290
Benedictine monks 14
Benmarl 274
Benton 273

Benziger-Glen Ellen 254
Bereich 142
Bereich Bernkastel 152
Bergamo 172
Bergerac 109
Bergheim 123
Bergkelder 292
Beringer 260
Berlou 134
Bern 218
Bernkastel 152-3★
Berri 277
Bertani 182, 183
Bessas 127
Best 281
Bévy 57
Bex 220
Beychevelle, Ch. 91
Béze, Clos de 16, 67
Béziers 134
Bianco della Lega 186
Bianco Vergine 191
Bianco Vergine Valdichiana 186
Biancolella 194
Bical grape 210
Bidwell 274
Bien Nacido 264
Bienne, Lake (Bielersee) 218
Bienvenues Bâtard Montrachet 61
Biferno 186
Bikavér 227
Bingen 162-3
Biondi-Santi 190, 191
Bischöfliches Konvikt 146
Bischöfliches Priesterseminar 146
Blaauwklippen 292
Black Spanish grape 217
Blagny 61
Blaignan 84
Blanc de Blancs 78
Blanc de la Salle 172
Blanc de Morgex 172
Blanchot 74
Blanck 123
Blandy 217
Blanquette de Limoux 112, 132
Blass, Wolf 280, 282
Blatina 232
Blauburgunder grape: Austria 223, 224; Switzerland 218, 219
Blaufränkisch grape 223, 226, 231
Blaye 108
Bleasdale 284
Blue Ridge Mountains 275
Blue-stalk (Kéknelyü) grape 226, 227
Böckelheim, Schloss 155
Bockenheim 161
Bodenheim 163
Bodensberg 163
Bogdanusa 232
Bogle 274
Bohemia 230
Bois 111
Bolgheri 191
Bolla 182
Bollinger 77
Bologna 178
Bonacossi, Count 186
Bonarda grape 24; Italy 172, 177; South America 294
Bonheur, Le 292
Bonifacio 140
Bonnes-Mares, Les 67
Bonnet, Ch. 72, 97
Bonnezeaux 116
Bonnievale 291
Bonny Doon 262
Boordy Vyds 251, 275
Borba 211
Bordeaux 13, 15, 16-17, 21, 24, 28-9, 80-108★, appellations 81; University of 17, 83
Borderies 110-11
Borges, H M 217
Bosco 172
Bosnia-Hercegovina 232
Botobolar 279
Botrytis cinerea 100, 228, 236 and see noble rot
Botticino 178
Bouchard 62
Bouchard, Paul 292
Bouchet grape 106
Boudriotte, La 59
Bougros 74
Bourdieu, Ch. 108
Bourdieu, Ch. Le 86
Bourg 108
Bourg, Clos de 118
Bourgogne 55, 58
Bourgogne Aligoté 55
Bourgogne Grand Ordinaire 55
Bourgogne Passe-Tout-Grains 55
Bourgogne Rouge 68

Bourgueil 117★
Bouscaut, Ch. 98
Bousquet, Ch. du 108
Bousse d'Or, La 61
Boutari 238
Bouvier grape 231
Bouzeron 68
Bouzy 78
Bowen's 285
Boyd-Cantenac, Ch. 94
Brachetto d'Acqui 174
Braga 211
Bramaterra 172
Branaire-Ducru, Ch. 91
Brand 123, 278
Brander Winery 264
Brand's 285
brandy 214, 241, 256 and see Cognac
Brandy de Jerez 198
Brane-Cantenac, Ch. 94
Branxton 278
Brasonyos-Csaszar 227
Bratislava 230
Braune Kupp 146
Brauneberg 150, 152
Brazil 295
Brédif, Marc 118
Breede River Valley 291
Breganze 178
Breisach 164
Bremmer Calmont 153
Brescia 172, 178
Bressandes 62
Breton grape 117
Breuil, Ch. du 86
Bricco Asili 176
Bricco Rocche 176
Bridgehampton 274
Bridgeview 270
Bridgewater Mill 284
Brights 274
British Columbia 251, 270
Broadbent, Michael 44
Brochon 67
Brokenwood 278
Brolio 188
Bronco 266
Brouilly 72
Brown Brothers 280
Brückstück 153
Bruderberg 148
Bruderschaft 150
Brûlesécaille, Ch. 108
Brun, Le 289
Brunate 176
Brundersberg 163
Brundlmayer 225
Brunello di Montalcino 190
Brunello grape 186, 190-1
Bual grape 217
Buçaco 210
Bucelas 209
Bué 119
Buena Vista 254, 257
Bugey 137
Buhl, von 160
Buitenverwachting 292
Bull's Blood 226, 227
Bundara Shiraz 280
Bundner Herrschaft 218
Burgenland 223
Burges 127
Burgos 206
Burgundy 13, 16, 21-2, 54-75★
Burgweg 155
Bürklin-Wolf 160
Bussia 176
Buttafuoco 177
Buxy 68
Buzbag 242
Buzet 112
Buzzetto 172
By 84
Byron 264
Bzenec 230

Cabernet Bosché 258
Cabernet Franc grape 24; Loire 114, 116-18; Midi 132; Pomerol 106; St-Emilion 104-5; 108, 109
Cabernet Sauvignon grape 21, 24, 25★; Australia 276, 278-87 passim; Austria 223, 224; Bordeaux 28, 84-107 passim; Bulgaria 234; California 255, 260, 261, 264; China 247; Cyprus 244; Greece 238; Hungary 226; Italy 171, 174, 178, 180-6 passim, 192; Japan 248; Lebanon 242; Mexico 269; Midi 132; Moldova 241; Morocco 245; New Zealand

23, 288-9; Ontario 274; Oregon 270; Portugal 209; Romania 236, 237; Serbia 232; South Africa 29-2; South America 294; Spain 198, 204-6 passim; Texas 268; Washington 270; Yakima 272
Cabrières 134
Cadarca grape 237
Ca'del Bosco 178
Cadillac 96, 97
Cádiz 200
Cafayete 295
Cahors 112
Cailleret, Le 61
Cairanne 130
Caixas do Sul 295
Calabria 194
Calamin 220
Calera 262
California 252-67★, 268; Baja California 269; Carneros 257; Central Valley 266-7; Lake County 256; Mendocino 256; Napa 258-61; Sonoma 254-5; South of the Bay 262-3; South Central Coast 264-5; University of (Davis) 26, 45, 252, 260, 266
Calistoga 258, 260
Caliterra 297
Callaghan 268
Callahan Ridge 270
Callaway, Ely 269
Calon-Ségur, Ch. 86, 94
Calvi 140
Camarate 209
Cambria 264
Camden 279
Camensac 91
Campania 194
Campbells 280
Campo Rotaliano 184
Campofiorin 183
Campomarino 186
Canada 251, 274-5
Canale 295
Canandaigua Wine Co. 266, 274
Canary Islands 207
Canberra 279
Canepa, José 297
Cannonau 194
Cannubi 176
Canoe Ridge Vyd 270
Canon, Ch. 104
Canon-Fronsac 102
Cantemerle, Ch. 94
Cantenac 94
Cantenac-Brown, Ch. 94
Canterayne 86
Canterbury 289
Cap Bon 245
Cap Corse 140
Caparede 209
Capbern Gasqueton, Ch. 86
Cape Clairault 287
Cape Mentelle 287, 289
Cape Province 290
Cape Riesling grape 291
Capel Vale 287
Capri 194
Caramany 132
carbonic maceration 34, 70
Carbonnieux, Ch. 98
Carcassonne 132
Carcavelos 209
Cardonne, Ch. La 84
Carema 172
Carey, J 264
Carignan grape 27★; California 266; Midi 132; Morocco 245; Spain 202
Cariñena grape 198, 202
Carmel Valley 242
Carmenet 254
Carmes Haut-Brion, Ch. Les 98
Carmignano 186
Carmignano grape 188
Carmo, Qta do 215
Carneros 254, 255, 257★
Carneros, Dom. 257
Carneros Creek 257
Carnuntum 223
Caronne Ste-Gemme, Ch. La 92
Carras, John 238
Carras, Ch. 238
Carras, Dom. 238
Carrascal 201
Carrau, Juan 295
Carrodus, Dr 281
Carruades 88
Carsin, Ch. 96
Cartaxo 209
Carvalhais, Qta dos 211
Cartizze 180
Caruel 108
Caruso 194
Carvalho 209

300

Casa Real 297
Casablanca (Chile) 296
Cassis 136
Casteggio 177
Castel del Monte 194
Castel Gandolfo 193
Castel Pujol 295
Casteldaccia 194
Castell 166
Casteller 184
Castelli Romani 193
Castello della Sala 192
Castello di Roncade 180
Castelvin 92
Castiglioncello 191
Castiglione Falletto 176
Castile 196
Castillo Ygay 202
Castres 96
Catalonia 196, 198, 204–5★
Catawba grape 27★, 250
Catena 295
Catoctin Valley 275
Catone 193
Cauquenes 296
cava 204
Cayuga, Lake 274
Cazes, Jean-Michel 88
Cazetiers 67
cellar-mould 229
Cellatica 178
Cembra Valley 184
Cencibel grape 198
Central Valley 266–7★
Cephalonia 238
Cerasuolo 186, 194
Cérons 96
Certan-de-May, Ch. 106
Cesanese 186
César grape 73
Cesare Mondavi Selection Cabernet 258
Cessnock 278
Cetto, L A 269
Ceves 266
Cevetto 176
Chablais 220
Chablis 54, 55, 73–5★
Chacolí 196
Chaddsford 275
Chagny 68
Chaintré 69
Chaize, Ch. de la 72
Chalk Hill 255
Chalone Vyd 262, 270
Chambers Rosewood 280
Chambert-Marbuzet, Ch. 86
Chambertin 58, 66, 67
Chambolle 66–7
Chambolle-Musigny 67
champagne 13, 16, 17, 24, 76–9★
Champagne Roederer 256
Champans 61
Champanski 241
Chandon, Dom. 38, 260, 281
Changyu 247
Chanson 62
Chante-Alouette 127
Chantebled, Ch. 245
Chantegrive, Ch. 96
Chapelle-Heulin, La 114
Chapitre, Clos du 67
Chapoutier 127
Chappellet 258, 260
Chardonnay grape 23, 25★; Australia 276, 278, 280, 284, 285, 286, 287; Austria 222–4; British Columbia 270; Bulgaria 234; California 255, 257, 260, 261, 264; Chablis 73; Champagne 78; China 247; Colorado 268; Côte de Beaune 59; Côte d'Or 57, 58; Cyprus 244; Germany 164; Hungary 226, 227; Idaho 270; Italy 174, 183, 186, 192; Japan 248; Michigan 274; New York 274; New Zealand 288, 289; Ontario 274; Oregon 270, 273; Romania 236; Slovenia 231; South Africa 290, 291, 292; South America 295, 296; Spain 204, 205; Switzerland 218; Texas 268; Washington 270; Yakima 272
Chardonne 220
Charente 110
Charlottesville 275
Charmes, Les 61, 67
Charmes, Ch. des 274
Charneco 209
Charta 159
Chasan grape 26
Chassagne 58
Chassagne-Montrachet 58, 59
Chasse-Spleen, Ch. 92
Chasselas grape 24, 26; Alsace 121; Germany 164; Savoie 137; Switzerland 218, 220
château, anatomy of 36–7
Château-Chalon 137
Châteauneuf-du-Pape 24, 124, 128, 130–1★
Châtillon-en-Diois 124
Chautauque 274
Chaves 209
Chavignol 119
Cheefoo (Yantai) 247
Cheilly 59
Chellah 245
Chénas 72
Chêne Marchand, Clos du 119
Chênes, Clos des 61
Chenin Blanc grape 25★; Anjou 116; Australia 286; California 266; Idaho 270; South Africa 291; South America 295; Texas 268; Vouvray 118
Cheurlin, Dom. 268
Cheval Blanc, Ch. 104
Chevalier, Dom. de 98
Chevalier d'Ars 92
Chevalier-Montrachet 58, 61
Chevalier de Rhodes 238
Cheverny 114
Chianti 24, 186, 188–9★
Chiaretto del Garda 178, 183
Chiavennasca grape 177
Chicane, Ch. 96
Chignin 137
Chile 296–7
China 246–7
Chinon 117
Chiroubles 72
Chisinau 241
Chitry-le-Fort 73
Christchurch 289
Church Road 289
Chusclan 128, 130
Chyorniye Glaza 241
Cigare Volant, Le 262, 263
Cincinnati 250
Cinque Terre 172
Cinsault/Cinsaut grape 132, 134, 242, 245, 291
Cinzano 295
Cirò 194
Cissac, Ch. 86
Cistercians 14, 22
Citran, Ch. 92
Clairette de Die 125
Clairette du Languedoc 134
Clape, La 125, 134
Clare Valley 283, 284
Clare, Ch. La 84
Clarke, Ch. 92
Clarksburg 267
Clear Lake 256
Clément V 98
Clerc Milon 88
Clerner grape 218
Clicquot, Veuve 77, 78
climate *see* weather
Climens, Ch. 100
Clinet, Ch. 106
Clinton 274
Clos L'Eglise Ch. 106
Clos, Les 74
Clos Fourtet, Ch. 104
Clos-René 106
Closerie Grand-Poujeaux, Ch. 92
Cloudy Bay 287, 289
Clover Hill 287
Cloverdale 255
Cocumont 112
Codorníu 204, 205, 257
Cognac 110–11
Colares 209
Coldstream Hills 281
Collards 288
Collavini 180
Colli Altotiberini 186
Colli Berici 178
Colli del Trasimeno 186
Colli Euganei 178
Colli Lanuvini 193
Colli Martani 192
Colli Orientali del Friuli 180, 183
Colli Perugini 192
Colli Piacentini 172
Colli Senesi 190
Collio 183★, 231
Collio Goriziano 183
collioure 132
Colmar 122, 123
Colombard grape 266, 291
Colony 266
Colorado 268
Columbia Winery 272
Combettes, Les 61
Comblanchien 57
Combottes 67
Commandaria 244
Commaraine, Clos de la 62
Comme, La 59
Completer grape 219
Comtes de Champagne 78
Conca de Barberá 205
Concha y Toro 297
Concord grape 250, 251
Conde de Santar 211
Condrieu 124, 126★
Conegliano 178, 180
Conestoga 275
Connétable 91
Conseillante, Ch. La 106
Constantia 17, 290, 292
Conthey 220
Contres 114
Contrie, Clos de la 117
Controliran 234
Cook, R & J 267
Cook's Champagne Cellars 266
Coonawarra 23, 278, 280, 281, 284, 285★
Copertino 194
Corban 288
Corbett Canyon 264
Corbières 132–3
Corbin, Ch. 104
Cordier, Dom. 96, 268
Corgoloin 57
Cornas 124
Corowa 280
Corsica 140
Cortaillod 218
Cortés, Hernando 269
Cortese di Gavi 174
Corton 16, 56, 57, 58, 62
Corton-Charlemagne 62
Corvina 183
Corvo 194
Cos d'Estournel, Ch. 86
Cos Labory, Ch. 86
Cossart 217
Coste, Pierre 96
Costières: de Nîmes 128; du Gard 128
Côte, La (Switzerland) 220
Côte de Beaune 54, 55, 56, 57, 58, 59–63★
Côte des Blancs 78
Côte Blonde 126
Côte Brune 126
Côte de Castillon 102
Côte Chalonnaise 55, 68★
Côte de Dijon 67
Côte des Francs 102
Côte de Nuits 16, 54, 55, 56, 57, 58, 64–7★
Côte d'Or 54, 55, 56–8★
Côte Rôtie 23, 124, 126★
Coteaux d'Aix en Provence 136
Coteaux d'Ardèche 128
Coteaux des Baux 136
Coteaux de Cap Corse 140
Coteaux de Carthage 245
Coteaux du Giennois 114
Coteaux du Languedoc 128, 134
Coteaux du Layon 116
Coteaux du Loir 114
Coteaux de Mascara 245
Coteaux de Pierrevert 136
Coteaux de Tlemcen 245
Coteaux du Tricastin 125, 128
Coteaux d'Utique 245
Coteaux Varois 136
Coteaux du Vendômois 114
Coteaux du Vernon 126
Coteaux du Zaccar 245
Côtes de Brouilly 72
Côtes de Cabardès 132
Côtes de Duras 112
Côtes du Frontonnais 112
Côtes de Gascogne 112
Côtes de Luberon 136
Côtes de la Malepère 132
Côtes du Marmandais 112
Côtes de Meliton 238
Côtes de Montravel 109
Côtes de Provence 136
Côtes du Rhône 124, 128, 130; -Villages 124, 130
Côtes de Roussillon 132; -Villages 132
Côtes du Ventoux 128
Côtes du Vivarais 128
Cotesti 236
Cotnari 236
Coufran, Ch. 86
Couhins, Ch. 98
Coulanges-la-Vineuse 73
Coulée de Serrant, La 22, 116
Couly 117
Couquèques 84
Courcel 62
Couronne, Ch. La 88, 89
Cousiño Macul 296
Coutet 100
Covey Run 272
Cowra 279
Craigmoor 279
Cramant 78
Crémant: d'Alsace 121; de Bourgogne 68, 73; de la Loire 114
Crépy 137
Cresta Blanca 266
Crete 238
Crianza de Castila la Vieja, Bodegas de 206
Cribari 266
Cricova 241
Crimea 240–1
Criolla grape 245, 294, 296
Criots, Les 61
Cristal 78
Croatia 232
Crock, Ch. Le 86
Croft 213
Croix-de-Gay, Ch. La 106
Croix-Millorit, Ch. La 108
Croizet-Bages 89
Croser, Brian 273, 284
Crouchen Blanc grape 290
Crozes-Hermitage 127
Cruzeau, Ch. 98
Csarfas 228
Csopak 227
Cucamonga 268
Culbertson 269
Cullens 287
Cumberland Valley 275
Curicó 296, 297
Cussac 92
Cuvaison 257
Cuvée du Président 245
Cuvée Napoléon 112
Cvicek 231
Cyprus 244
Czech Republic 230

Dafnes 238
Dahra 245
Dalmatia 232
Dalwhinnie 281
Dalwood 278
D'Ambra 194
Dames de la Charité 62
Daniel, John 258
Dão 208, 211★
D'Arenberg 284
Dauzac 94
de Wet, Danie 291
De Wetshof 291
Dealul Mare 236
Debrö 227
decanting 46
Deidesheim 160
Delaunay, Marc 117
Delaware 275
Delaware grape 248, 250
Delegat 288
Delheim 292
Delicato 262, 266
Demestika 238
Denbies 298
Denman 278
Denominación de Origen (Calificada) (DO(C)) 196, 204
Denominación Especifica (DE) 196
Denominazione di Origine Controllata (Garantita) (DOC(G)) 170–1, 178
Desertas 216
Desmirail 94
Deutz 264, 289
Dézaley 220
Dézize 59
Dhron 150
Dhroner Hofberger 150
Di Majo, Luigi 186
Di Rosa, Rene 257
Diamond Valley 281
Diano d'Alba 174, 176
Die 124
Dimiat grape 234
Dingac 232
Discover Wine Ltda 297
diseases 19 *and see* phylloxera
Dobrogea 236
Doctor 152
Dogliani 174
Doisy: -Däene; -Dubroca; -Védrines, Chx 100
Dolceacqua 172
Dolcetto grape 174, 176
Dôle 220
Doluca 242
Dom Pérignon 16, 77, 78
Domecq, Pedro 269
Domecq, Ch. 269
Dominique, Ch. La 104
Don Eugenio 269
Don Matas Cabernet 296
Don Melchor Cabernet 297
Donauland-Carnuntum 223
Donnafugata 194
Donnaz 172
Donnici 194
Doosberg 158
Dopff 123
Dopff & Irion 123
Dordogne 81, 97, 109
Dornfelder grape 161
Dorsheim 155
Doué-la-Fontaine 116
Douro 212–13
Dr Weil 159
Dragasani 237
Dragon Eye grape 247
Drava 231, 232
Draytons Bellevue 278
Dromana Estate 281
Drouhin, Maurice 62
Drouhin, Robert 273
Dry Creek Valley 255
Duboeuf, Georges 72
Duboscq, Henri 86
Duca Badoglio 180
Duca Enrico 194
Ducasse, Ch. 88–9
Ducq, Le 275
Ducru-Beaucaillou, Ch. 91
Ducs, Clos des 61
Duero 196, 198, 206★
Duhart-Milon, Ch. 88
Dumazet, Pierre 126
Dundee 273, 274
Durbach 164
Durfort-Vivens, Ch. 94
Dürkheimer 161
Dürnstein 225
Dutruch Grand Poujeaux, Ch. 92
Dynasty 247

Eaglehawk 283
Ebro River 196, 198
échelle des crus 78
Echevronne 57
Echézeaux 64
Echuca 281
Edelkeur 292
Edelzwicker 121
Eden Valley 282
Edes 229
Edmeades 256
Edna Valley Vyds 264
Eger 226, 227
Eglise-Clinet, Ch. L' 106
Eguisheim 123
Egypt 242
Ehrenfelser grape 26
Eichberg 123
Eileen Hardy Chardonnay 285
Einzellage 142
Eisenstadt 223
Eiswein 168 *and see* ice-wine
Eitelsbach 148
Ekigana grape 26
El Bierzo 196
El Dorado 267
Elba 186
Eltville 158–9
Elysium 267
Emerald Riesling grape 26
Emir grape 242
Enclos L' 106
Enfer d'Arvier 172
England 298
Enkirch 153
Enoteca 188
Ensenada 269
Entre-Deux-Mers 81, 96–7★
Epenots 62
Epernay 78
Epesses 220
Epirus 238
Erbach 144
Erbacher Siegelsberg 159
Erbaluce di Caluso 174
Erden 153
Erie-Chautauqua 274
Errázuriz 297
Escadre, Ch. l' 108
Escherndorf 167
Eshcol 38
Essencia 229, 267
Est! Est!! Est!!! 186
Estoril 209
Estrella River 264
Estremadura 209
Estremoz 215
estufas 217
Etchart 295
ETKO 244
Etna 194
Etoile, L' 137
Etschtaler 184
Etyek 227
Euboea 238
Evangile, Ch. L' 106
Evans & Tate 287
Evans, Len 278
Evans Vyd 285
Extremadura 198
Extrisimo Bach 205
Eyquem, Ch. 108
Eyrie Vyds 273
Ezerjó grape: Hungary 226, 227; Serbia 232; Slovak Republic 230

Faedo 184
Fairview 292
Faiveley 64, 68
Falanghina 186
Falfas, Ch. 108
Falkenstein 223
Falkensteiner Hofberg 146
Far Niente 38
Fargues, Ch. 100
Faugères 134
Favonio 194
Fayau, Ch. 97
Faye 116
Féchy 220
Federspiel 225
Feldebrö 227
Felsenkopf 150
Fendant grape 220
Feriani, Ch. 245
fermentation 32, 33–7
Fernández, Alejandro 206
Ferrand, Ch. de 102
Ferreira 208, 209
Ferrière 94
Fès 245
Feteasca grapes: Alba 226, 236, 237; Neagra 236, 237; Regala 236, 237
Fetzer 256
Feytit-Clinet, Ch. 106
Fiano 194
Ficklin 267
Fiddletown 267
Fieuzal, Ch. de 98
Figari 140
Figeac, Ch. 104
Finger Lakes 250, 274
Finlayson, Peter 292
Fino 199
Firestone 264
Fitou 132
Fixin 67
Flagey 64
Fleur du Cap 292
Fleur-Pétrus, Ch. La 106
Fleurie 72
Florence 188
Focsani 236
Foggia 194
Folatières, L' 61
Folle Blanche grape 24
Fombrauge, Ch. 102
Fonbadet 89
Fonpiqueyre 89
Fonréaud, Ch. 92
Fonsalette, Ch. de 130
Fonscolombe, Ch. 136
Fonseca 209, 211; J M da 209
Fontanafredda 176
Forastera 194
Forest Hill 287
Foris 270
Forst 160
Forster Mariengarten 160
Fort Stockton 268
Fortant de France 134
Fortia, Ch. 130
Forts de Latour, Les 88
Fourcas-Dupré, Ch. 92
Fourcas-Hosten, Ch. 92
Fourchaume 74
Foxen Canyon 264
foxiness 250–1, 274
France 9, 12, 52–140; *and see* Alsace, Anjou, Armagnac, Barsac, Beaujolais, Bergerac, Blaye, Bordeaux, Bourg, Bourgueil, Burgundy, Chablis, Champagne, Châteauneuf-du-Pape, Chinon, Cognac, Corbières, Corsica, Côte de Beaune, Côte Chalonnais, Côte de Nuits, Côte d'Or, Côte Rôtie, Entre-Deux-Mers, Gevrey-Chambertin, Graves, Jura, Languedoc, Libournais, Loire Valley, Mâconnais, Margaux, Médoc, Minervois, Muscadet, Pauillac, Pessac-Léognan, Pomerol, Pouilly, Provence, Rhône, Roussillon, St-Emilion, St-Estèphe, St-Julien, Sancerre, Sauternes, Savoie, Southwest 112–13, Vouvray
Franciacorta 172, 178
Franconia 73, 166–7★
Francusa grape 236
Frangy 137
Frank, Dr Konstantin 251, 274
Frank, Ch. 274
Frankland 286, 287
Frankova grape 230
Franschhoek 291, 292
Franzia 266
Frascati 186, 193
Frauenberg 153
Frecciarossa 177
Fredericksburg 268
Freemark Abbey 258, 260
Freie Weingärtner 225
Freinsheim 161
Freisa 174
Freixenet 204
Frescobaldi 186
Freslier, Dom. 118
Freundstck 160
Frickenhausen 167
Friedrich-Wilhelm-Gymnasium 146
Friuli 178, 180–1★
Fronsac 102
Frontignan 134
Fronton 112
Fruska Gora Hills 232
Fuissé, Ch. de 69
Fukushima 248
Furmint grape 24; Austria 223; Hungary 226, 227, 228; Slovenia 231
Furth 225

Gaensbronnel, Clos 123
Gaffelière, Ch. La 104
Gai, Ch. 274
Gaillac 112

Gaillat, Ch. 96
Gainey Winery 264
Gaja, Angelo 176
Galestro 186
Galicia 196
Galilee 242
Galitzine, Prince Lev 240–1
Gallais, Le 146
Gallais-Bellevue 84
Gallo, E & J 255, 266
Gamay 60
Gamay grape 24, 25★; Beaujolais 70; Bulgaria 234; Michigan 274; Ontario 274; Serbia 232; Switzerland 218, 220
Gambellara 178
Gamla 242
Gamza grape 226, 234
Gard 134
Garda, Lake 178, 183
Gardera, Ch. 96
Garganega grape 24, 178, 183
Garnacha grape 202, 204, 206; Tinta 26, 198 and see Grenache
Garrafeira 208
Gattinara 172
Gaunoux 62
Gauriac 108
Gavi 174
Gay, Ch. Le 106
Gazin, Ch. 106
Gebeit 142
Geelong 281
Geisenheim 156
Geneva 218, 220
Genevrières, Les 61
Genoa 172
Georges de Latour Private Reserve 258
Georgia 241
Germain-Robin 256
German Wine Academy 158
Germany 9, 142–68★; see Baden-Württemberg, Franconia, Mosel, Nahe, Pfalz, Rheingau, Rhein-hessen, Ruwer, Sachsen, Saale-Unstrut, Saar
Gerümpel 161
Gevrey-Chambertin 58, 66–7★
Gewürztraminer grape 27★; Alsace 120–1, 123; British Columbia 270; Bulgaria 234; California 25–6; Germany 163, 164; New Zealand 289; Ontario 274; Oregon 270, 273; Romania 236, 237; South Africa 291; Spain 204; Yakima 272
Geyserville 252
Ghemme 172
Ghisonaccia 140
Ghurdjaani 241
Gianaclis, Nestor 242
Gigondas 130
Gilbey 84, 86
Gilette, Ch. 100
Gimmeldingen 160
Girò 194
Gironde 81
Giscours 94
Givry 68
Glana, Ch. du 91
Glen Carlou 292
Glenrowan 280
Gloria, Ch. 90
Gloria Ferrer 257
Glun 125
Golan Heights 242
Goldbächel 161
Goldtröpfchen 150
Goldwater 288
gönci 228–9
Gonzales 262
Goria Law 171
Gorizia 183
Gornja-Radgona 231
Goron 220
Gottweig 225
Goulbourn River 281
Goumenissa 238
Goundrey Wines 287
Goutte d'Or 61
Graach 152
Graciano grape 202
Gräfenberg 159
Graham 213
Grahm, Randall 262
Grainhübel 160
Gramp's 282
Gran Coronas Mas la Plana 204
Gran Furore Divina Costiera 194
Gran Sangre de Toro 204
Grancey, Ch. 62
Grand Palais 238
Grand Poujeaux, Ch. 92
Grand-Puy, Ch. 88–9
Grand Roussillon 132
Grand Travers, Ch. 274
Grande Dame champagne, La 78
Grande Rue, La 64
Grands Echézeaux 64
Grange Hermitage 276, 282, 284
Grão Vasco 211

grapes 9, 24–7★ and see individual grape names
Grasa grape 236
Grasevina grape 232
Graubungunder grape 164
Grave del Fruili 180
Grave Trigant de Boisset, La 106
Graves 81, 96–7★
Gravières, Les 59
Graviera★
Great Plain 226
Great Wall 247
Great Western 281
Grechetto 192
Grechetto grape 186
Greco di Gerace 194
Greco di Tufo 194
Greece 9, 13, 238–9★
'Green grape' 291
Green Valley 255
Gréfieux 127
Grenache grape 25★, 26; Australia 282; California 266; Cyprus 244; Midi 132; Morocco 245; Rhône 124; Spain 198; Yakima 272; and see Garnacha
Grenouilles, Les 74
Gressier Grand Poujeaux, Ch. 92
Grèves 62
Greysac 84
Greystone 38
Grézillac 97
Grignolino grape 174
Grillet, Ch. 126
Griñon, Marqués de 206
Grinzing 224
Gris de Boulaouane 245
Gristina 274
Grk 232
Groot Constantia 292
Gros Plant 114
Grosseto 190
Grosskarlbach 161
Grosslage 142
Grosslangenfrei 167
Grottaferrata 193
Gruaud-Larose, Ch. 91
Gruet 268
Grumello 177
Grüner Veltliner grape 223, 224, 225, 230
Grünstadt 160
Guadalupe Valley 269
Guado al Tasso 191
Guebwiller 123
Guenoc 256
Guerneville 255
Guerrieri-Rizzardi 183
Guerry, Ch. 108
Guestier, Daniel 36
Guigal, Marcel 126
Guild 266, 274
Guiraud, Ch. 100
Gumpoldskirchen 224
Gumza grape 234
Gundlach-Bundschu 254
Guntersblum 163
Guoignière 127
Gutedel grape 164, 167
Gyöngyös 227

Hajós 226
Halkidiki 238
Hallgarten 158
Halliday, James 281
Halozan 231
Hambledon 298
Hamilton-Russell, Tim 291, 292
Hammelburg 167
Hammondsport 250
Hamptons 274
Hanepoot grape 291
Hanteillan, Ch. 86
Hanwood 279
Hanzell 252, 254
Haraszthy, Agoston 250, 254
Hardy, Thomas 284
Hardy's 134, 277, 284, 285
Hargrave, Alex and Louisa 274
Haro 202
Hárslevelü grape 226, 227, 228
Harsovo 234
Hasensprung 158
Haskovo 234
Hatschbourg 123
Hattenheim 158
Hauner, Carlo 194
Haut-Bages-Averous, Ch. 88, 89
Haut-Bages Libéral, Ch. 89
Haut-Bages Monpelou, Ch. 89
Haut-Bailly, Ch. 98
Haut-Batailley, Ch. 88
Haut-Benauge, Ch. 97
Haut-Brion, Ch. 16, 98
Haut-Comtat 128
Haut-Lieu, Clos Le 118
Haut-Marbuzet, Ch. 86
Haut-Médoc, Ch. 84, 86
Haut-Montravel 109
Haut-Rhin 122
Haut-Sarpe, Ch. 102
Haux, Ch. de 96
Hawke's Bay 288–9
He Ze 247

Healdsburg 255
Hecker Pass 262
Heemskerk 287
Heilbronn 164
Heitz 23, 252, 258
Hemel-en-Aarde Valley 292
Hendelberg 158
Hengst 123
Hennessy 110
Henriques & Henriques 217
Henschke 282
Hérault 134
Hermann J Wiemer Vyd 274
Hermannsberg 155
Hermannshöhle 155
Hermanus 291
Herrenberg 148, 161
Herrschaft 218
Hervelets 67
Heublien 266
Heurige★
Hickinbotham 281
Hilgard, Eugene, 251
Hill Country 268
Hill, William 273
Hillcrest 270
Hilltops, The 279
Hine 110
Hinzerling 272
Hipping 163
Hirtzberger 225
HJT Vyds 280
HMR (Hoffmann Mountain Ranch) 264
Hobart 287
Hochar, Serge 242
Hochheim 159
Hofstück 160
Hogue Cellars 272
Hohe Domkirche 146
Hoheburg 160
Hohenmorgen 160
Hohnen, David 289
Hollicks 285
Hong Kong 247
Honigberg 159
Honigsäckel 161
Horgan, Denis 287
Horney, Dr G 21
Hortevie 91
Horton 275
Hospices de Bearne 62
Hosten, Ch. 32
Houghton 287
Houghton's 'White Burgundy' 286
Hounza 246
Howell Mountain 260
Huadong 247
Huapai Valley 288
Hubert 230
Hudson River 274
Huet, Gaston 118
Hugel 123
Hügelland 223
Humbrecht 123
Hungary 223, 226–9★ and see Tokay
Hungerford Hill 278, 285
Hunter Valley 278
Hunter's 289
Huntington 279
Husch 256
Huxelrebe grape 298
Hvar 232
Hyams, Edward 246

Ialeveni 241
Ica 295
ice-wine 275 and see Eiswein
Idaho 251, 270
Idyll 281
Igé 69
il governo 188
Il Greppo 190
Ile de Beauté, L' 140
Ilios 238
Illats 96

irrigation 19, 296
Ischia 194
Iseo, Lake 178
Isonzo 180
Israel 242
Issan, Ch. d' 94
Issue, Ch. d' 94
Istituto Agrario Provinciale 184
Italian Swiss Colony 218, 255, 266
Italy 9, 12, 17, 170–95★; Central 186–7; Northeast 178–9; Northwest 172–3; Southern 194–5 and see Alto Adige, Barbaresco, Barolo, Bolgheri, Castelli Romani, Chianti, Collio, Friuli, Lombardy, Pavese, Piemonte, Trentino, Tuscany, Umbria, Veneto, Venezia Giulia, Verona

J P Vinhos 209
Jaboulet, Paul 127
Jaboulet 125
Jacob's Creek 282
Jacquère grape 137
Jacquet 117
Jadot 62
Jalle de Tiquetorte 92
Jamek 225
Jamet 117
Japan 247–8
Jarnac 111
Jasnières 114
Jefferson, Thomas, 250
Jekel 262
Jensen, Josh 262
Jeruzalem 231
Jesuitengarten 160
Jesuits 242
Ji Nan 247
Joching 225
Joguet 117
Johannisberg 156, 218
Johannisberg, Schloss 144, 158
Joly, Nicolas 22
Jordan 255
Juffer 160
Juhfark grape 226
Juliénas 72
Juliusspital 167
Jumilla 198
Jura 137
Jurançon 112
Jyonohira 248

Kadarka grape: Bulgaria 234; Hungary 226, 227; Romania 237; Serbia 232
Kahlenberg 154, 224
Kaiser Stuhl Cooperative 282
Kaiserstuhl 164
Kakhetian 241
Kakheti 241
Kalecik Karası grape 242
Kalimna Estate 282
Kalkofen 160
Kalkhorio 244
Kamptal (Kamptal-Donauland) 223
Kanon-kop 292
Karadoc 277
Karlovo 234
Karthäuserhofberg 148
Kasel 148
Katnook Estate 285
Katoyi 238
Kava Nemea 238
Kavaklidere 242
Kaysersberg 123
Kefraya, Ch. 242
Kékfrankos grape 226, 227
Kéknelyü grape 226, 227
Kendall-Jackson 256
Kennewick 272
Kenwood 254
KEO 244
Kerner grape 26, 27★; England and Wales 298; Germany 162, 167; Slovenia 231
Kesten 150
Keyneton 282
Khan Khrum 234
Kiedrich 144, 159
Kientzheim 123
Kikyogahara Merlot 248
Kimmeridge 73, 74
King City 262
Kinheim 153
Kirchberg 152
Kirchenstück 160
Kirwan, Ch. 94
Kistler 254
Kitterlé 123
Klein Constantia 292
Klevner grape 121
Klingelberger 164
Kloch 223
Kloster Eberbach 14, 158
Klosterneuberg 224
Klüsserath 150
Knappstein, Tim 283
Knight's Valley 255, 260
Knipperlé grape 121
Knudsen Erath 273

Knyphausen 158
Kobnert 161
Kofu 248
kokkineli 238
Konocti Cellars 256
Korbel 255
Korcula 232
Kosovo 232
Koshu grape 247
Kosuos 238
Kouros 238
Kourtakis 238
Kraichgau 164
Krems 225
Kremstal 223, 225
Kronenberg 155
Krötenpfuhl 154
Krug 77, 78
Krug, Charles 252, 258, 260
Kruzevac 232
Ksara 242
Kuehn 123
Kues 152
Kumeu River 288
Kupfergrube 155
Kurfürstlay 152
Kutjevo 232
kvevris 241
KWV 290, 292
Kyneton 281

Labarde 94, 108
Labégorce, Ch. 94
Labégorce-Zédé, Ch. 94
Lac des Roches 238
Lachryma Christi 194
Lacoste, Ch. 88–9
Ladoucette 118
Lafaurie-Peyraguey 100
Lafite, Ch. 16, 82, 86, 88, 297
Lafite-Rothschild, Ch. 84, 88
Lafleur, Ch. 106
Lafleur-Gazin, Ch. 106
Lafon-Rochet, Ch. 86
Lagarde-Paréol 130
Lago di Caldaro 178
Lagrange, Ch. 90, 91
Lagrein grape 184
Lagrima 207
Lagune, Ch. La 94
Laira 278, 285
Lake, Max 278
Lake County 256
Lalande 102
Lalande-Borie, Ch. 91
Lalande-de-Pomerol 102
Lamarque 92
Lamarque, Ch. de 92
Lamblot 245
Lambrays, Clos des 67
Lambrusco 178
Lamé-Delille-Boucard 117
Lamezia 194
Lancaster Valley 275
Lance, Dr 281
Lancers 208
Lände 142
Landiras, Ch. de 96
Landmark 254
La Landonne 126
Landwein 168
Langenlois 225
Langenmorgen 160
Langhorne Creek 284
Langoa Barton, Ch. 36, 91
Langoiran 96
Langon 96
Languedoc 13, 134–5★
Laona 244
Lar dos Barros 198
Larcis-Ducasse, Ch. 102
Larmat, Louis 8
Larose-Trintaudon, Ch. 91
Lascombes, Ch. 94
Laski Riesling grape 231, 232
Lassalle 84
Latisana 180
Latium 186
Latour, Louis 62, 68
Latour, Ch. 22–3,28, 82, 88
Latour à Pomerol, Ch. 106
Latour-de-France 132
Latricières 67
Lauds 127
Laudun 128, 130
Laujac 84
Launay, Ch. 97, 108
Laurel Glen 254
Laurensanne 108
Laurent-Perrier 98, 273
Laurentiuslay 150
Laurnersheim 161
Lavau 245
Lavaut 67
Lavaux 220
Laville Haut-Brion, Ch. 98
Lavillotte, Ch. 86
Le Roy, Baron 130
Leacock 217
Leasingham 283
Lebanon 242
Leconfield 285

Leeuwin Estate 287
Lehmann, Peter 282
Leibfraumilch 162
Leinhöhle 160
Leiste 166
Leiterchen 150
Leiwen 150
Lejon 266
Lemberger grape 164
Lemnos 238
Lemps 125
Lenchen 158
Lendava 231
Lenz 274
Lenz Moser 225
Leo Buring 282
Léognan 98
León, Jean 205
León 196, 206
Léoville 90
Léoville-Barton, Ch. 36, 91
Léoville-Las Cases, Ch. 84, 90–1
Léoville-Poyferré, Ch. 36, 91
Lérida 205
Les St-Georges 64
Lesparre 84
Lessini 183
Lessona 172
Lestage, Ch. 92
Lett, David 273
Leverano 194
Libournais 102–3
Libourne 106
Lichine, Alexis 94
Lider, James and Lloyd 260
Lieser 152
Ligré 117
Liguria 172
Lilian-Ladouys, Ch. 86
Lilydale 281
Lima 211
Limassol 244
Limberger grape 230
Limnio grape 238
Limoux 132
Lindemans 277, 278, 282, 285
Lingenfelder, Rainer 161
Linsenbusch 160
Lipari 194
Lirac 130
Lisbon 208, 209★
Lison 180
Listan grape 27
Listel 128
Listrac 92
Livadia 241
Livermore Valley 262
Liversan, Ch. 89
Livran, Ch. 84
Ljutomer-Ormoz 231
Llano Estacado 268
Locorotondo 194
Lodi 266
Loel 244
Logroño 202
Loire Valley 13, 114–15★
Lombardy 177★, 178 and see Oltrepò Pavese, Valtellina
Long Island 250, 274
Longworth, Nicholas 250
Lontué 297
López de Heredia 202
Los Gatos 262
Los Reyes 269
Los Vascos 297
Lösnich 153
Loubens, Ch. 96
Loudenne, Ch. 84, 86
Loupiac 96
Loupiac-Gaudiet, Ch. 96
Lousteau-Vieil, Ch. 96
Louvière, Ch. La 98
Lovedale 278
Lovico Suhindol 234
Lower Great Southern Region 286
Lubbock 251, 268
Lucca 186
Lugana 178
Lugny 69
Lumière, Ch. 248
Lump 167
Lunel 134
Lungarotti, Dr Giorgio 186, 192
Lungarotti 186
Lurton family 97, 98
Lussac 102
Lutry 220
Luxembourg 150
Luzern 219
Lynch-Bages, Ch. 86, 88
Lynch-Moussas, Ch. 89

Macabeo grape 202, 204
MacCarthy-Moula, Ch. 86
McCrea 254
McDonald, Tom 288
McDowell Valley 256
Macedonia 232, 238
McGuigan, Brian 278
Macharnudo 200, 201
McLaren Vale 278, 284
McMahon, Dr 281

McMinnville 273
Mâcon: -Prissé, -Clessé, -Lugny, -Villages, -Viré 69
Mâconnais, Le 54, 55, 69★
Maculan, Fausto 178
Macvin du Jura 137
McWilliam's 278, 279, 288
Mád 228
Madeira 17, 216–17★
Madeira Wine Company 217
Madeleine Angevine grape 298
Madera 266, 267
Madiran 112
Magarach 240
Magdelaine, Ch. 104
Magence, Ch. 96
Magny-les-Villers 57
Magon 245
Maier 225
Mailberg 223, 225
Maindreieck 167
Mainviereck 167
Maipo Valley 296, 297
Makhachkala 241
Málaga 17, 196, 198, 207★
Malartic-Lagravière, Ch. 98
Malat-Brundlmayer 225
Malbec grape 24; Australia 276; Bourg 108; Cahors 112; Midi 132; Moldova 241; South America 294, 296
Malescasse, Ch. 92
Malescot St-Exupéry, Ch. 94
Malmsey 216, 217, 238
Malvasia Bianco grape 186
Malvasia di Casorzo d'Asti 174
Malvasia grape: Greece 238; Italy 172, 183, 188, 193; Languedoc 134; Madeira 216 *and see* Malmsey
Malvasia Riojana grape 202
Malvaxia Reserve 275
Malvedos 213
Malvoisie de Corse 140
Mancha, La 198
Mandement 220
Manischewitz 274
Mannberg 158
Mann's 248
Manteca 266
Mantinia 238
manzanilla 199
Maranges 57, 59
Marastina 232
Marbuzet, Ch. de 82, 86
Marcobrunn 158
Maréchal, Clos de la 64
Marestel 137
Marey-les-Fussey 57
Margaret River 286–7
Margaux 83, 84, 88, 94–5★
Margaux, Ch. 52, 94
Maria Gomes grape 210
Maribor 231
Mariengarten 160
Marino 193
Markgräflerland 164
Markobrunn 144
Marlborough 288, 289★
Marne 76
Marquis d'Alesme 94
Marquis de St-Estèphe 86
Marquis de Terme, Ch. 94
Marsala 17, 194
Marsannay 67
Marsanne grape 125, 281
Marselan grape 26
Martell 110
Martha's Vyd 23, 258, 261
Martillac 98
Martin Brothers 264
Martinafranca 194
Martinborough 289
Martinenga 176
Martini, Louis 260
Martini 252, 254
Martinsthal 159
Maryland 251, 275
Marzemino 184
'mas' 127
Mas de Daumas Gassac 134
Mascarello 176
Masi 183
Masia Bach 205
Massandra 241
Masseria Di Majo Norante 186
Masson, Paul 262
Mastroberardino 194
Matanzas Creek Winery 254
Matawhero 289
Mateus 208, 209
Matrasa 241
Matua Valley 288
Maucaillou, Ch. 92
Maures 136
Maury 132
Mauves 125
Mauvezin, Ch. 92
Mauzac grape 112
Mavrodaphne 238
Mavron grape 244
Mavrud grape 234
Maximim Grünhaus 148
Mayacamas 258
Mazis 67
Mazouna 245
Mazuelo grape 202
Méal 127
Mecsek 226
Médéa Hills 245
Medjerdah Valley 245
Médoc 81, 82–5★; Central 92–3; Southern 94–5
Médoc Noir grape 226
Meerlust 292
Meersburg 164
Meknès 245
Melbourne 276
Melník 230
Melník grape 230, 234
Meloisey 57
Menaudat, Ch. Le 108
Mendoce 108
Mendocino 256
Mendoza 294, 295
Menetou-Salon 114
Ménétréol 119
Mercian 248
Mercurey 68
Meridian 264
Merler Fettgarten 153
Merlot grape 24, 27★; Arizona 268; Australia 276, 285, 287; Bas-Médoc 84; Bordeaux 82; Bourg 108; Bulgaria 234; California 260, 261, 264; Colorado 268; Hungary 226, 227; Italy 178, 180, 183; Japan 248; Michigan 274; Midi 132; Moldova 241; Morocco 245; Oregon 270; Pomerol 106; Portugal 209; Romania 236, 237; South Africa 290, 295; South America 296; St-Emilion 104; Switzerland 218; Texas 268; Washington 270; Yakima 272
Merrill, Geoff 284
Mertesdorf 148
Meseta 198
Mesilla Valley 268
Mesland 114
Mesnil, Le 78
Messeto 191
Messias 210
méthode champenoise 295
Metsovo 238
Metternich, Count Wolff 164
Meursault 56, 60–1★
Meursault-Villages 58
Mexico 250, 269★
Meyney, Ch. 86
Meynieu, Ch. Le 86
Mezesfeher grape 226
Mézesmály 228
Mezzalombardo 184
Mezzocorona 184
Michelmark 159
Michelsberg 150
Michigan 251, 274
Middle Rio Grande 268
Middleton, Dr 281
Midi 9, 132–5★
Mikulov 230
Milawa 280
Mildara 280, 285
Mildara-Wolf Blass 283
Mildura 280
Miles 217
Millbrook 274
millerandage 28
Mimbres Valley 268
Minervois 132–3★, 134
Minheim 150
Minho 208, 211★
Minis 237
Miraflores 201
Miralduolo 192
Mirassou 262
Mireval 134
Mission grape: America 250, 268; Morocco 245; South America 294, 296
Mission Haut-Brion, Ch. La 98
Missouri 251
Mitchell 283
Mitchelton 281
Mittelbergheim 123
Mittelhaardt 160–1
Mittleheim 158
Modena 178
Modesto 266
Modra 230
Modra Frankinja grape 231
Moët & Chandon 281, 295
Moldavia 236
Moldova 236, 240–1★
Molette grape 137
Molise 186
Mollina 207
Mommessin 67
Monbazillac, Ch. 109
Monção 211
Mondavi, Robert 252, 258, 260, 266, 287
Mondeuse grape 137, 180
Monfalletto 176
Monforte d'Alba 176
Monica 194
Moniga del Garda 178
Monprivato 176
Monsecco 172
Mont, Le 118
Mont-Jallon, Dom. 268
Mont de Milieu 74
Mont d'Or, Dom. du 220
Mont-sur-Rolle 220
Montagne 102
Montagne de Reims 78
Montagny 68
Montalcino 190, 191
Montana 288, 289
Montdomaine 275
Monte Rosso 254
Monte Xanic 269
Montebello 262
Montecarlo 186
Montée de Tonnerre 74
Montefalco 192
Montélimar 124
Montenegro 232
Monteporzio 193
Montepulciano 186, 190, 191
Montepulciano d'Abruzzo 186
Monterminod 137
Montes Alpha 297
Monthélie 61
Monthil 84
Monticello 275
Montilla 198, 207★
Montille, de 62
Montinore 273
Montlouis 118
Montmélian 137
Montpelier 26
Montpeyroux 134
Montrachet 16, 58, 59, 60–1
Montravel 109
Montrose 279
Montrose, Ch. 86
Monts Damnés, Les 119
Monts-Luisants 67
Monts du Tessala 245
Moondah Brook 287
Moorilla 287
Mór 227
Moravenka 230
Moravia 230
Mörbisch 223
Morey 66, 67
Morgeot 59
Morgon 72
Morillon grape 223
Morio-Muskat grape 167
Moristel grape 198
Mornag, Ch. 245
Mornington Peninsula 281
Morocco 245
Morra, La 174, 176
Morris 280
Morton Estate 289
Moscatel de Setúbal 208, 209
Moscatel grape 207
Moscato 177, 194
Moscato d'Asti 174
Mosel 150–3 *and see* Bernkastel, Piesport
Mosel Kabinett 142
Moselle 13
Moss Wood 286–7
Mostar 232
Motte, La 292
Mouchão 215
Mouches, Clos des 62
Moueix, Jean-Pierre 102, 106
Moulin à Vent 72
Moulin de la Rose 91
Moulin Touchais 116
Mouline, La 126
Moulinet, Ch. 106
Moulis 92
Mount Barker 287
Mount Harlan 262
Mount Helen 281
Mount Mary 281
Mount Pleasant 278
Mount Veeder 260
Mountadam 282
Mountarrow 278
Mourvèdre grape 132
Mouton Rothschild, Ch. 88
Mouton-Baronne, Ch. 88
Mudgee 278
Muga 202
Mukuzani 241
Müller, Egon 146
Müller-Thurgau grape 26, 27★; Austria 223, 224; Czech Republic 230; England and Wales 298; Germany 142, 162, 164, 167; Italy 177; New Zealand 288, 289; Slovenia 231; Switzerland 218, 219
Munson, Thomas V 268
Münsterer Dautenpflänzer 155
Münster-Sarmsheim 155
Muntenia 236, 237
Muré 123
Muret 127
Murfatlar 236
Murray River 277
Murrumbidgee Irrigation Area 278, 279
Musar, Ch. 242
Muscadelle grape 280, 286
Muscadet 114–15
muscat 130, 134, 240, 280
Muscat of Alexandria grape 244, 248, 291
Muscat Blanc à Petits Grains grape 228
Muscat de Frontignan 134, 280
Muscat de Kelibia 245
Muscat de la Pierre Rouge 241
Muscat de Rivesaltes 132
Muscat grape 25★, 26; Alsace 120–1, 123; Australia 280; Bulgaria 234; China 247; Greece 238; Tunisia 245
Muscat Ottonel grape 234, 236–7
Muscat-Silvaner grape 231
Musigny 58, 66–7
Muskat-Ottonel grape 223
Muswellbrook 278

Nackenheim 163
Nagambie 281
Nagano 248
Nagyburgundi grape 226
Nahe 154–5
Nahe State Domain 155
Nairac 100
Nantoux 57
Naoussa 238
Napa Valley 23, 38, 252, 257, 258–61★
Naparevli 241
Naples 194
Narince grape 242
Narvaux 61
National Distillers 295
Nava del Rey 206
Navarra 198, 204
Navarro 256
Naylor 275
Néac 102
Nebbiolo grape 27★; Austria 223; California 264; Italy 172, 174, 176, 177; Mexico 269
Nectar 238
Nederburg 292
Neef 153
Negro 244
Negroamaro grape 194
Negru de Purcar 241
Néive 176
Nelson 289
Nemea grape 238
Nerthe, Ch. La 130
Neuberger grape 224
Neuchâtel 218
Neumagen 150
Neusiedler See 223
Neustadt 160
Neustift 224
New Jersey 250
New Mexico 251, 268
New South Wales 278–9
New York 250, 251, 274–5★
New Zealand 288–9
Newberg 273
Newton Vyd 258
Nice 136
Nicoresti 236
Nieder-Walluf 159
Niederberg Helden 152
Niederhausen 155
Niedermennig 146
Niellucio grape 140
Nierstein 162, 163
Niersteiner Domtal 163
Niersteiner Gutes Domtal 163, 168
Nitra 230
Nizerand River 70
Nobilo 288
Noble, Dr Ann 45
noble rot 100, 228 *and see* botrytis
Nobling grape 164
Nobunaga, Oda 247
Noizay 118
Nordheim 167
Norheim 155
North Fork 274
North Yuba 267
Norton 295
Nosiola grape 184
Nostrano 218
Noto 194
Noval, Qta do 213
Novara 172
Nové Mesto 230
Nové Zámky 230
Novi Pazar 234
Novy Saldorf 230
Novy Svet 241
Nozet, Ch. du 119
Nuits-St-Georges 64–5
Nuragas 194
Nuriootpa 282
Nussbein 160
Nussdorf 224
Nuy 291
Nyon 220
oak, French, 41★, 252
Oak Knoll 273
Oakville 258, 260
Ober-Walluf 159
Oberloiben 225
Ockfener Bockstein 146
Odobesti 236
Oeste 209
Oestrich 158
Ohio 250, 251, 274
oidium 19, 217, 218
Oisly et Thésée 114, 118
Okanagan Valley 270
Oküzgözü grape 242
Olaszrizling 226, 227
Old Brookville 274
Oliena 194
Olivier, Ch. 98
Olmo, Dr H 26
Oloroso 199
Oltenia 237
Oltrepò Pavese 172, 177★
Omar Khayyám 246
ONIVIN 138
Ontario 251, 274–5★
Opimian 13
Opol 232
Oppenheim 163
Optima grape 26
Opus One 258, 260
Ordonnac 84
Oregon 251, 270
Oremus 228
Oriachovitza 234
Orlando 278
Orléans 114
Ormarins l' 292
Ormes de Pez, Ch. Les 86
Ormes Sorbet, Ch. Les 84
Ornellaia 191
Ortenau 164, 165
Orvieto 186, 192
Otago, Central 289
Othello 244
Ottoman Empire 242
Oudart, Louis 176
Ovada 174

Paarl 290, 291, 292–3★
Paceta 202
Padova 178
Padthaway 281, 285
País grape 245, 296
Palatinate 142, 160
Palava grape 230
Palette 136
Palliser Estate 289
Palmer 274
Palmer, Ch. 94
palo cortado 199
Palomino grape 24, 27★; Cyprus 244; South Africa 291; Spain 200
Pamid grape 234
Pancas, Qta das 209
Panciu 236
Panquehue 296
Pantelleria 194
Pape Clément, Ch. 98
Paradiso, Fattoria 178
Parducci 256
Parellada grape 204
Parker, Robert 45
Parrina 186
Parry, Michael 247
Paso Robles 264
Pasteur, Louis 40
Patras 238
Patriarche 62
Patrimonio 140
Pauillac 83, 84, 88–9★
Paulinshofberg 150
Paveil de Luze, Ch. 92
Pavie, Ch. 104
Pavlikeni 234
Pavlov 230
Pays Nantais 114
PDs (*producteurs directs*) 26
Pécharmant 109
Pedesclaux, Ch. 89
Pedro Domecq, 199, 295
Pedro Ximénez grape 24, 207, 294
Pedroncelli 255
Pegase, Clos 260
Pelee Island 274
Peljesac Peninsula 232
Peloponnese 238
Pelorus 289
Peñafiel 206
Penafiel 211
Peñaflor 295
Penedès 204, 205
Penfolds 241, 276, 278, 282, 284–5
Pennsylvania 275
Penola Fruit Colony 285
Perelada 205
Periquita grape 209, 215
Perlan 220
Perlé 112
Perle de la Moldavi 236
Perlillo 297
Pernand 62
Pernod-Ricard 247
Perrier-Jouët 78
Perrière, La (Fixin) 67
Perrière, La (Vougeot)64
Perrières, Les (Corton) 62
Perrières, Les (Meursault) 61
Perrin 264
Persia 246
Perth 286, 287
Peru 295
Perugia 186, 192
Pesos, Qta dos 209
Pesquena de Duero 206
Pesquera 206
Pessac-Léognan 96, 98–9★
pests 19 *and see* disease
Petaluma 279, 283, 284, 285
Peter Island 218
Petersons 278
Petit Chablis 74
Petit Mont, Le Clos du 118
Petit Rouge grape 172
Petit Verdot grape 24, 296
Petit-Village, Ch. 106
Petri 266
Pétrus, Ch. 106
Pettenthal 163
Pewsey Vale 282
Peynaud, Emile 206, 295
Peyrabon, Ch. 89
Pez, Ch. de 86
Peza 238
Pezinok 230
Pfalz 142, 160–1★
Pheasant Ridge 268
Phélan-Ségur, Ch. 86
Phelps Winery 260
Phillips, R H 267
Philo 256
Phoenicians 12
phylloxera 17–19★, 202, 217, 218, 250, 268, 280, 289
Piacines 262
Piave 180
Pibran, Ch. 88, 89
Pic St Loup 134
Piccadilly Valley 284
Pichler, F X 225
Pichon-Baron, Ch. 88
Pichon-Lalande, Ch. 88
Picolit 183
Picpoul de Pinet 134
Picutener grape 172
Piedmont 275
Piemonte 172, 174–5★
Pieropan 182
Pierreclos 69
Piesport 150–1
Piesporter Michelsberg 150
Piesporter Treppchen 150
Pietroasa 236
Pigato 172
Piketberg 291
Pindar 274
Pineau d'Aunis grape 114
Pineau de la Loire grape 116
Pinhão 212
Pinhão River 213
Pinot Auxerrois grape 121
Pinot Blanc grape 27★; Alsace 120, 121; Germany 164; Hungary 226; Italy 177, 178, 180, 183, 186; Slovenia 231
Pinot Gris grape: Alsace 120–1, 123; Germany 164; Hungary 226; Italy 177, 183; Oregon 270, 273; Romania 236, 237; Slovenia 231
Pinot Meunier grape 78, 164
Pinot Noir grape 24, 25★, 26; Alsace 121; Australia 276, 278, 281, 282, 284, 285, 287; Bulgaria 234; California 255, 264; Chablis 73; Champagne 78; Côte Chalonnaise 68; Côte d'Or 57, 58; England and Wales 298; Germany 142, 156, 164; Hungary 226; Italy 177, 178, 183; Mexico 269; New Zealand 289; Ontario 274; Oregon 270, 273; Romania 236, 237; Serbia 232; Slovak Republic 230; South Africa 290, 291, 292; South America 294, 296; Spain 204; Switzerland 218, 220; Yakima 272
Pinotage grape 26, 291, 292
Pinson, Bodegas 269
Piper-Heidsieck 255
Pipers Brook 287
Pirie, Andrew 287
Pirque 297
pisco 296
Pitesti 237
Pitigliano 186
Planalto 209
Planalto-Mirandès 209
Plantagenet 287
Plavac Mali grape 232
Plavina 232
Pleasant Valley Wine Co. 250
Pleven 234
Plovdina grape 232
Plovdiv 234
Plozner 180

Po Valley 178
Podensac 96
Podravje 231
Poggio alle Gazze 191
Pointe, Ch. La 106
Pojer & Sandri 184
Pokolbin 278
Pol Roger 77, 78
Polk 273
Pollino 194
Pomal 202
Pomerol 102, 106–7*
Pomino 186
Pommard 58, 62
Pommery 256
Pompadour 246
Poniatowski, Prince 118
Pontac 86
Pontallier, Paul 297
Pontet-Canet, Ch. 88
Ponzi 273
Poona 246
port 16, 17, 208, 212–13, 214–15*, 292
Porta dos Cavaleiros 211
Portets 96
Porto Santo 216
Porto Vecchio 140
Portugal 9, 208–17* *and see* Alentejo, Bairrada, Dão, Douro, Madeira, Minho, port
Portugieser grape 167, 224
Poruzot 61
Posip 232
Postup 232
Potensac, Ch. 84
Potter 256
Potts, Frank 284
Pouget 94
Pouilly 114, 119*; -Fuissé 69; -Fumé 119; -Loché 69; -Vinzelles 69
Pouilly-sur-Loire 119
Pourriture noble (noble rot) 100, 228 *and see* botrytis
Poverty Bay 289
Prager 225
Pramaggiore 180
Prats, Bruno 297
Preignac 100
Prémeaux 64
Preuses, Les 74
Prieuré, Ch. 94
Primitivo 194
Prince Michel 275
Priorato 205
Priorato Dulce 205
Procanico grape 186
Prokupac grape 232
Propriano 140
Prosecco grape 178, 180
Prosek 232
Protos 206
Provence 13, 136*
provignage 18
Provins coop 220
Prugnolo Gentile grape 190, 191
Ptolemées, Cru des 242
Ptuj 231
Pucelles, Les 61
Puerto de Santa Maria 201
Puglia 194
Puisseguin 102
Puligny 60
Puligny-Montrachet 61
Purcari 241
puttonyos 228–9
Puy-Blanquet, Ch. 102
Puygueraud, Ch. 102

Qindao (Tsingtao) 246–7
Quady 267
Qualitätswein bestimmter Anbaugebiete (QbA) 168
Qualitätswein mit Prädikat (QmP) 168
Quarts de Chaume 116
Quarts de Moncontour 118
Quelltaler 283
Queretaro 269
Quincy 114
Quintarelli 183
Qupé 264

Rabat 245
Rabelais (Aïn-Merane) 245
Rablay 116
Raboso grape 180
Raca 230
Racke 257
Radgona 231
Raffault 117
Rahoul, Ch. 96
Raimat 205
Rainbow Gap 268–9
Rákóczi 228
Ramage la Batisse, Ch. 89
Ramisco grape 209
Ramitello 186
Rancho California 268
Rancho Sisquoc 264
Rangen 123
Ranina grape 231
Rapidan River 275
Rapitalà 194
Rappu 140
Rapsani 238
Raucoule 127
Rauenthal 144, 159
Rauenthaler Berg 159
Rausan-Ségla, Ch. 94
Rauzan-Gassies, Ch. 94
Ravello 194
Ravenna 178
Raventos 205
Ray, Martin 262
rayas 199
Rayas, Ch. 130
Raymond-Lafon, Ch. 100
Rebula grape 231
Recabarren, Ignacio 297
Rechbächel 161
Recife 295
Recioto 177, 183
Red Misket grape 234
Redwood 256
Refosco grape: Italy 180, 183; Savoie 137; Slovenia 231
Regaleali 194
Réggio Emilia 178
Régnié 72
Regua 212
Reichensteiner grape 26, 298
Reine Cléopatre 242
Reiterpfad 160
Remy, Ch. 281
Rémy Martin 110, 247
Renaissance 267
Renardes, Les 62
Renault (Mazonna) 245
Renmano 277
Renmark 280
Respide, Ch. 96
retsina 238
Retz 223
Reuilly 114
Rêve, Le 274
Reynell, John 284
Reynella, Ch. 284
Reynolds 215
Reynon, Ch. 96
Rharb 245
Rheingau 21, 144, 156–9*
Rheinhartshausen, Schloss 158
Rheinhessen 142, 162–3*
Rhine 13
Rhodes 238
Rhoditis 238
Rhône 13; Central 130–1; North 124–5; South 128–9
Rías Baixas 196
Ribeiro 209
Ribera de Burgos 206
Ribera del Duero 206
Ribolla grape 183, 231
Ricasoli, Baron 188
Ricaud, Ch. 96
Richebourgs, Les 64
Riddoch, John 285
Ridge Vyds 255, 262
Rieslaner grape 167
Riesling grape 21, 24*, 26; Alsace 120–1, 123; Australia 276, 280, 282, 284, 285, 287; Austria 224, 225; British Columbia 270; Bulgaria 234; California 255, 256, 260, 264; China 247; Colorado 268; Czech Republic 230; Georgia 241; Germany 142, 146, 156, 160–4 *passim*; Idaho 270; Italy 177, 178, 183; Japan 248; New York 274; New Zealand 289; Ontario 274; Oregon 270, 273; Slovak Republic 230; Slovenia 231; South Africa 290–2 *passim*; South America 295, 296; Washington 270; Yakima 272
Rieussec, Ch. 100
Rijeka 232
Rio Grande do Sul 295
Rio Grande Valley 268
Rio Negro 294, 295
Rioja 196, 198, 202–3*, 204
ripasso 183
Ripon 266
Riquewihr 123
Riscal, Marqués de 206
Rishon-le-Zion 242
Riunite 178
Rivella, Ezio 191
Rivendell 274
Rivera 295
Riverland 276–7, 280
Rivesaltes 132
Rizvanec grape 231
Rkatsiteli grape 24, 234, 240, 241
Robert (Taughrite) 245
Robert Mondavi Reserve Cabernet 258
Robertson 291
Robola 238
Rocche di la Morra 176
Roche, Clos de la 67
Roche aux Moines, La 116
Rochecorbon 118
Rochefort 116
Rochegude 130
Rochemorin, Ch. 98
Rochepot, La 57
Rödelsee 166
Rodet 68
Roeda 213
Roederer 77, 78, 287
Rogliano 140
Rogue Valley 270
Rohrendorf 225
Roi, Le Clos du 62
Romagna 178
Roman wines 12–13
Romanée, La 64
Romanée-Conti 64
Romanée-Conti, Dom. de la 64, 68
Romanée-St-Vivant 64
Romanesti, Ch. 241
Romania 236–7
Romanovs 241
Rombola 238
Romorantin grape 114
Rosé d'Anjou 116
Rose Muscat 241
Rose-Pauillac, La 89
Rosehill 278
Rosemount Estate 278
Rosette 109
Rossese 172
Rosso Cònero 186
Rosso Piceno 186
Rotenfels 155
Rotgipfler grape 224
Rothbury 278, 279
Rothenberg 163
Rothschild, Baron Edmond de 92, 242
Rothschild, Baronne Philippine 88
Rothschild, Dom. 215
Rothschilds 297
Röttgen 153
Roudnice nad Labem 230
Rouge d'Alsace 121
Rouge de Guerrouane 245
Rouge Homme 285
Rouget, Ch. 106
Roupeiro grape 215
Roussanne grape 125
Roussette grape 137
Rousset, Ch. 108
Rousset-les-Vignes 128
Roussillon 132–3
Roxburgh 278
Rozay, Ch. du 126
Ruapehu 288
Ruban 230
Rubesco 186, 192
Rubino di Cantavenna 174
Rubired grape 266
Ruby Cabernet grape 26, 266
Rüdesheim 156–7
Rüdesheimer Berg 144, 156
Rueda 206
Rugiens, Les 62
Ruländer grape: Austria 223; Czech Republic 230; Germany 164; Slovak Republic 230 Rully 68
Ruppertsberg 160
Russe 234
Russia 240–1
Russian River 255
Rust 223
Rust-en-Vrede 292
Rustenberg 292
Ruster Ausbruch 223
Rutherford 252, 258, 260
Rutherglen 280
Ruwer 148–9
Ruzica 232

Saale-Unstrut 167
Saar 146–7
Sablet 130
Sachsen 167
Sadilly 241
Sag Pond 274
Sagrantino grape 192
Sahari, Dom. de 245
St-Amour 72
St-Aubin 116
St-Bris-le-Vineux 73
Ste Chapelle Winery 270
St-Chinian 134
St-Christoly 84
St-Christophe 102
Ste-Croix-du-Mont 96
St-Denis, Clos 67
St-Désirat 125
St-Emilion 16, 102, 104–5*
St-Estèphe 83, 84, 86–7*
St Esteve Sesrovires 205
St-Etienne 102
St-Fiacre 114
St Francis Xavier 247
St Gallen 219
Ste Genevieve 268
St-Georges, Ch. 102
St-Germain, Ch. 84
St-Germain-d'Esteuil 84
St-Gervais 130
St Hallett 282
St Helena 252, 258, 260
St-Hippolyte 102
St Huberts 281
Ste-Hune, Clos 123
St-Jacques, Clos 67
St Jean, Ch. 254, 255
St-Jean, Clos 59
St-Jean-de Minervois 134–5
St-Jean-de-Muzols 125
St-Jean-de-la-Porte 137
St-Joseph 125
St-Julien 83, 84, 90–1*
St-Lambert 89
St-Laurent 90, 91, 102
St Laurent grape 230
St Laurents 224
St Leonards 280
St Michael 150
Ste Michelle, Ch. 272
St-Nicolas-de-Bourgueil 117
St-Pantaléon-les-Vignes 128
St-Péray 125
St-Pierre, Ch. 91, 96
St-Pierre-de-Mons 96
St-Romain 61
St Sadurni d'Anoia 204
St-Saphorin 220
St-Saturnin 134
St-Saveur 89
St-Seurin 84
St-Seurin-de-Cadourne 86
St-Tropez 136
St-Urbain, Clos 123
St-Véran 69
St-Yzans 84
Saintsbury 257
Sakar 234
Salem, Schloss 164
Salento 194
Sales, Ch. de 106
Salice Salentino 194
Salinas Valley 262
Salo 178
Salon 78
Salta 294
Salta Province 295
Salvagnin 220
Samos 238
Samperi 194
Sampigny 59
San Diego 250
San Giorgio 192
San Guido 191
San Joaquin Valley 266–7
San Juan 294
San Juan del Río, Cavas de 269
San Luis Obispo 262, 264
San Michele 184
San Pedro 297
San Sebastián 196
San Telmo 295
Sancerre 73, 114, 119*
Sandalford 287
Sandgrub 159
Sandusky 274
Sanford & Benedict 264
Sangiovese dei Colli Pesaresi 186
Sangiovese di Romagna 186
Sangiovese grape 24, 27*; Austria 223; California 260; Corsica 140; Italy 178, 188; South America 294
Sangioveto grape 27
Sangioveto Grosso grape 190
Sangue di Giuda 177
Sanlúcar de Barrameda 199, 200–1
Santa Ana 295
Santa Barbera 264
Santa Carolina 297
Santa Cruz 268
Santa Lucia Highlands 262
Santa Maddalena 178
Santa Maria Valley 264
Santa Rita 297
Santa Rosa 255
Santa Tomas, Bodegas 269
Santa Ynez Valley 264
Sant'Angelo Scalo 191
Santenay 57, 59*
Santi, Clemente 190
Santiago 296
Santino 267
Santorini 238
Sanz 206
São João 210
Saône River 58
Saperavi grape 241
Saratoga 262
Sardinia 194
Sarget 91
Sárospatak 228
Sartènois 140
Sassella 177
Sassicaia 191
Satigny 220
Satov 230
Saumagen 161
Saumur 114
Saumur-Champigny 114, 117
Saussignac 109
Sauternes 81, 96, 100–1*
Sauvignon Blanc grape 21, 25*; Arizona 268; Australia 284, 285, 287; Austria 223; California 255, 261, 264; Chablis 73; Czech Republic 230; Greece 238; Hungary 226, 227; Israel 242; Italy 178, 183 186; New Zealand 289; Oregon 270; Pouilly 119; Romania 236; Sancerre 119; Serbia 232; Slovenia 231; South Africa 290; South America 295, 296; Texas 268; Washington 270; Yakima 272 291, 292, 295;
Sauvignon de St-Bris 73
Sava Valley 231
Savagnin grape 24, 137
Savatiano grape 238
Savennières 116
Savigny 16, 62
Savoie 137
Savuto 194
Saxonvale 278
Saxony *see* Sachsen
Scalabrone 191
Schaffhausen 219
Schafiser 218
Scharffenberger Cellars 256
Scharlachberg 163
Scharzhof 146
Scharzhofberg 146
Scheurebe 161
Schiava grape 24, 184
Schilcher 223
Schillerwein 164
Schlossberg 123
Schlossböckelheim 155
Schlosskapelle 155
Schlumberger 123
Schoenenbourg 123
Scholtz, Bodegas 207
Schönborn, Count 159
Schönborn, Schloss 158
Schönburger grape 298
Schönhell 158
Schoonmaker, Frank 251
Schorlemer estate, von 152
Schramsberg 258, 260
Schwarze Katz 153
Schwarzriesling grape 164
Sciacarello grape 140
Sciacchetrà 172
Scuppernong grape 251
Seagram 257, 260
Seaview Cabernet 284
'Seewein' 164
Segarcea 237
Segonzac 111
Segonzac, Ch. 108
Segovia 206
Seguin, Dr Gérard 83
Ségur, Marquis de 86
Seibel grape 26
Seifried Estate 289
sekt 146, 168
Selaks 288
Sélection des Grains Nobles 121
Sella & Mosca 194
Semeli 244
Sémillon grape 25*; Australia 276, 278, 280, 287; California 261; Japan 248; Oregon 270; South Africa 290; South America 295–6; Turkey 242; Washington 270; Yakima 272
Seppelt 281, 282, 285
Seppeltsfield 282
Serbia 232
Sercial grape 217
Sered 230
Sérine grape 27 *and see* Syrah
Serra, Junípero 250
Serralunga 174
Serralunga d'Alba 176
Serrig 146
Serriger Herrenberg 146
Sète 134
Setúbal 209
Seven Hills Vyd 270
Seville 200
Seville Estate 281
Sèvre-et-Maine 114
Seyssel 137
Seyval Blanc grape 27*, 298
Seyve-Villard grape 26
Sforzato 177
Sfursat 177
Shafer 260, 273
Shantung (Shandong) 246–7
Shenandoah Valley 267
sherry 17, 199, 200–1*, 241, 244, 292
Shiraz (Persia) 246
Shiraz grape: Australia 276, 278, 282, 284, 285, 287; Colorado 268; Cyprus 244; Rhône 124; South Africa 291 *and see* Syrah
Shumen 234
Siaurac, Ch. 102
Sichel, Peter 94
Sicily 12, 194*
Sidi Selem 245
Siebeldingen 160
Siegendorf 225
Siena 188, 190
Sierra Foothills 267
Sierre 220
Sievering 224
Sigalas-Rabaud, Ch. 100
Silvaner grape 27*; Germany 142, 162, 164, 166–7; Slovak Republic 230 *and see* Sylvaner
Silverado Trail 260
Silverado Vyds 260
Simburesti 237
Simi 255
Simmern, Baron Langwerth von 158, 159
Simone, Ch. 136
Simonsig 292
Sion 220
Sipon grape 231
Siran 94
Siskiyou 270
Sithonia 238
Sitia 238
Skalli 134
Slavonia 232
Sliven 234
Slovak Republic 230
Slovenia 231
Smaragd 225
Smart, Dr Richard 21
Smederevka grape 232
Smederevo 232
Smith Haut-Lafitte, Ch. 98
Smith-Madrone 260
Smith's 282
Smokvica 232
Snake River Valley 270
Soave 178, 182
Sociando-Mallet, Ch. 86
SODAP coop 244
SODEVI 245
Sogrape 209, 211
Solaia 188
solera wines 199
Solutré-Pouilly 69
Solvang 264
Somló 227
Somontano 198
Sonoita 268
Sonoma Valley 250, 252 254*, 257; Mountain 254; North 255
Sonoma Vyds 255
Sonoma-Cutrer 'Les Pierres' 254
Sophiste, Le 262
Sopron 223, 227
Sorbara 178
Sor Tildin 176
Sorni 184
Soussac 97
Soussans 92, 94
South Africa 290–3 *and see* Paarl, Stellenbosch
South African Winefarmers 292
South America 294–7 *and see* Chile
South Australia 282–4
South Fork 274
Southern Vales 284
Souverain, Ch. 252, 255
Soviet Union, former 240
Spain 9, 12, 196–207* *and see* Catalonia, Duero, Jerez, Málaga, Montilla, Rioja, Rueda, sherry
Spanna grape 172
Spätburgunder grape 142, 164
Spätlesen 142
Spielberg 161
Spiers 160
Spitz 225
Sporen 123
Spring Mountain 260
Springton 282
Squinzano 194
Staatliche Hofkellerei 167
Stag's Leap 260, 273
Stambolo 234
Stanton & Killeen 280
Starboard 267
Staton Hills 272
Stauceni 241
Staufenberg, Schloss 164
Steen grape 290, 291, 292
Stefanesti 237
Steigerwald 166, 167
Stein 166, 225
Steinberg 9, 14, 144, 158
Steiner Hund 225
Steinfeder 225
Steingarten 282
Steinmorgen 159
Steinwein 166
Stellenbosch 290, 292–3*
Sterling 257, 260
Stoniers Merricks 281
Stony Hill 252
Stony Ridge 288
Story 267
Strong, Rodney 255
Stuttgart 164
Styria (Steiermark) 223
Südbahn 224
Südliche Weinstrasse 160
Suduiraut, Ch. 100
Sultanine grape 242
Suntory 248
Svetozarevo 232
Svischtov 234
Swan Valley 286, 287
Swartland 291

Switzerland 218–21 and see Valais, Vaud
Sydney 276
Sylvaner grape 27★; Alsace 120, 121, 123; Italy 178; Switzerland 220 and see Silvaner
Symington 217
Symms 270
Syrah grape 27★; Australia 276; Mexico 269; Midi 132; Morocco 245; Rhône 124 and see Shiraz
Szamorodni 229
Szaraz 229
Szekszárd 226
Szepsi 228
Szürkebarát grape 226, 227

Tabilk 281
Tabor Hill 274
Tacama 295
Tâche, La 64
Tafelwein 168
Tahbilk Ch. 281,
Taille Pied 61
Taittinger 77, 78
Talbot, Ch. 91
Taltarni 281
Taluau 117
Tamaioasa grape 236
tanazukuri system 247–8
Tanca Farrà 194
Tanesse, Ch. 96
Tannat grape 112, 295
Taranto 194
Tarcal 228
Tardi 245
Tarik 245
Tarnave 237
Tarragona 205
Tart, Clos de 67
Tasmania 276, 287★
Tasso 191
Tastes, Ch. de 96
Taughrite 245
Taurasi 194
Tavel 130
Távora River 213
Tayac, Ch. 92
Taylor 213
Tchelistcheff, André 272
Te Mata 289
Tébourba 245
Tedeschi 183
Temecula 268–9
temperature 50
Templeton 264
Tempranillo grape 24; Portugal 215; Spain 198, 202, 204, 206
Ténarèze 111
Teran 231
terminology see wine, language of
Teroldego 184
Teroldego Rotaliano 184
Terra Alta 205
Terra Rossa 268
Terrey-Gros-Cailloux, Ch. 91
terroir 7, 9, 22–3★
Tertre, Ch. du 94
Tesseron 86
Texas 251, 268
Texas Hill Country 268
Thalabert, Dom. de 127
Thann 123
Thau, Ch. de 108
Thelema 292
Thermenregion 223, 224
Thesaly 238
Thésée 118
Thessalonki 238
Thibar, Ch. 245
Thivin, Ch. 72
Thompson Seedless grape 266

Thouarcé 116
Thrace 242
Tianjin 247
Ticino 218
Tierra Los Barros 198
Tiger's Milk 231
Tignanello 188
Tillets 61
Tinta Mole grape 217
Tintara 284
Tintas grape 24
Tinto del Pais grape 206
Tinto Fino grape 206
Tisdall 281
Tocai di Lison 180
Tocai grapes 178, 183; Friulano 183
Tokaj 226, 228
Tokay 9, 17, 228–9★, 230, 236
Tokay d'Alsace 121
Toledo 206
Tondonia 202
Tonnerre 73
Torbato 194
Torcolato 178
Torgiano 186, 192
Torrebianco 194
Torremilanos 206
Torres 204, 297
Torres Vedras 209
Torrontes 294
Torto River 213
Touchais 116
Toulouse 112
Toumilon, Ch. 96
Tour de By, Ch. La 84
Tour Carnet, Ch. La 91
Tour Figeac, Ch. La 104
Tour Haut-Brion, Ch. La 98
Tour du Haut-Moulin, Ch. 92
Tour-Martillac, Ch. La 98
Tour de Mons, Ch. La 92
Tour St-Bonnet, Ch. La 84
Touraine 114, 116
Tournon 125
Toutigeac, Ch. 97
Traben-Trarbach 153
Tracy, Ch. de 119
Traiser Bastei 155
Traiskirchen 224
Trakya 242
Traminac grape 232
Traminer grape: Austria 223; Czech Republic 230; Germany 167; Italy 183; Slovak Republic 230; Slovenia 231
Tramini grape 226
Transylvania 237
Trapiche 295
Trás os Montes 209
Trasimeno Lake 192
Trastavere 193
Trebbia Valley 172
Trebbiano grape 183, 186, 188, 193
Trefethen 38, 260
Treiso 176
Trentino 178, 184–5★
Trento 184
Treppchen 153
Tres Torres 204
Trévallon, Dom. de 128
Treviso 180
Trier 13, 146, 148
Trimbach 123
Trittenheim 150
trocken wines 142
Trockenbeerenauslesen 156
Trollinger grape 142, 164
Tronquoy-Lalande, Ch. 86
Trotanoy, Ch. 106
Tsantalis 238
Tsantalis Agiorgitiko 238
Tsimlyanskoye 241
Tsinandali 241

Tsingtao (Qindao) 246–7
Tua River 213
Tualatin 273
Tuart Sands 287
Tuilerie, Ch. de la 128
Tulloch 278
Tuniberg 164
Tunis 245
Tunisia 245
Turckheim 123
Turkey 242
Turque, La 126
Tuscany 12, 186, 190–1★
Twanner 218
Twin Brook 275
Tyrrell 278

Udine 180
Ugni Blanc grape 24, 110, 186
Ukiah 256
Ull de Llebre grape 204
Umbria 192
Umpqua Valley 270
Underhaardt 161
Underloiben 225
Undurraga 297
Ungeheuer 160
Ungstein 161
Unico 206
Union des Négociants en Vin du Valais 220
Untermosel 153
Uruguay 295
Utiel-Requena 198
Urzig 152–3

Vacqueyras 130
Val, Clos du 260
Val di Chiana 191
Valais 218, 220–1★
Valbuena 206
Valbuena de Duero 206
Valdadige 184
Valdeñas 198
Valdepeñas 198
Valdobbiadene 180
Valençay 114
Valencia 198
Valeyrac 84
Valgella 177
Valladolid 206
Vallagarina 184
Valle d'Aosta 172
Vallée de la Marne 78
Vallet 114
Valley View 270
Valmur 74
Valpaços 209
Valparaso 297
Valpolicella 178, 183
Valréas 130
Valtellina 172, 177★, 178
Valtice 230
Van der Stel 290
Van Loveren 291
Var 116
Vargellas 213
Varna 234
Varoilles, Les 67
Vasse Felix 286–7
Vat–47 278
Vaucrains 64
Vaud 218, 220–1★
Vaudésir 74
Vavasour 289
Vega Sicilia 206
Veldenz 152
Velké Pavlovice 230
Velletri 193
Vendage Tardive 121
Venegazzù 180
Veneto 180–1
Venezia Giulia 178, 180–1★
Verband Deutscher Prädikatsweingüter (VDP) 142

Vercelli 172
Verdea 238
Verdejo grape 206
Verdelho grape 216, 217
Verdicchio 186
Verdignan 86
Verdiso grape 178, 180
Verduzzo 180
Vereinigte Bischöfliches Weingut 146, 148
Vereinigte Hospitien 146
Vergisson 69
Vermentino grape 140, 172
Vernaccia 194
Vernaccia di San Gimignano 186
Vernatsch grape 184
Vernay, Georges 126
Verona 180, 182–3★
Verpelét 227
Vertheuil 86
Vertou 114
Vespolina grape 172
Vesuvio 194
Vétroz 220
Vicenza 178
Victoria 276, 280–1★
Vidal 289
Vieille Ferme, La 128
Vienna 223, 224★
Vieux-Château Landon 84
Vieux-Château-Certan 106
Vieux Télégraphe, Ch. Le 130
Vigne de l'Enfant Jésus 62
Vignelaure, Ch. 136
Vignes, Jean-Louis 250
Vila Nova da Gaia 214
Vilagrande, Barone 194
Villa Banfi 191
Villa Doluca 242
Villa Maria 288, 289
Villa Neva 242
Villafranca de Penedès 204
Villány 226
Villaudric 112
Villefranche 70
Villegeorge, Ch. 92
Villeneuve 220
Villers-Fontaine 57
Villette 220
Villeveyrac 134
Villiera 292
vin de: cépage 132, 138; garde 16, 40–1; paille 137; pays 52, 134, 138–9★; primeur 16; terroir 138
Vin de Constance 292
Vin Fou 137
vin gris 116, 121, 245
Vin Santo 184, 191
Vin-Union 220
Vinifera, La 108
vinho surdo 217
vinho verde 208, 211
vini da tavola 170–1
Vinifera, La 108
Vinifera Wine Cellars 274
Vino Nobile di Montepulciano 186, 191
Vins Délimités de Qualité Supèrieure (VDQS) 52, 138, 139
Vins Doux Naturels (VDN) 132, 140
Vintner's Quality Alliance 275
Viognier grape 126, 268
Vion 125
Viré 69
Virgin Hills 281
Virginia 250, 275
Vis 232
Visanto 238
Viseu 211
Visonta 227
Viti 218
Viticole des Salins du Midi, Dom. 128

Vitis: labrusca 250; rotundifolia 251; vinifera 24; vinifera orientalis 247
Vittoria 194
Viura grape 198, 202
Voegtlingshofen 123
Vojvodina 232
Vollrads, Schloss 144, 156, 158
Volnay 16, 58, 61
Volnay-Santenots 61
Vosne-Romanée 58, 64
Vougeot, Clos de 14, 54, 64
Vouvray 114, 118★
Vranac 232
Vrancea 236
Vraye-Croix-de-Gay, Ch. 106
Vredendal 291
Vriesenhof 292
Vugava 232

Wachau 223, 225★
Wachenheim 160–1
Wagner, Philip 251, 275
Wagner Vyds 274
Waiheke Island 288
Wairarapa 289
Waldrach 148
Wales 298
Walker, Hiram 247
Walla Walla 270
Wallachia 236
Wallhausen, Schloss 155
Wanaka Lake 289
Wangaratta 280
Warwick Estate 292
Washington 251, 270
Wasseros 159
Wawerner Herrenberger 146
weather 28–9★, 54, 82, 144, 253, 261, 276
Wehlen 152
Wei Fang 247
Weibel 256
Weinviertel 223
Weissburgunder grape: Austria 223, 224; Germany 164, 167
Weissenkirchen 225
Weissherbst grape 164
Welschriesling grape 27★; Austria 223; Bosnia-Hercegovina 232; Romania 236, 237
Weltvrede 291
Wendouree 283
Wente Bros 262
Western Australia 286–7
Westhalten 123
Whitlands 280
Widmers 274
Wienert 295
Willamette 270, 273★
Williams & Selyem 255
Willm 123
Wiltingen 146
wine: consumption 10; development 9, 10, 14–17, 298; history of 10, 12–13; language of 42–5; note taking 44–5; scoring 44–5; serving 48–50; storage 46; temperature 50; and time 40–1
wine laws 8–9; Austria 222; Bulgaria 234; France 52; Germany 142, 168; Italy 171, 188; Madeira 217; Morocco 245; Pacific Northwest 270; Portugal 208; South Africa 290–1; Spain 196
winemaking 16–17, 32–7★; Alsace 120, 121; America 270, 274; Australia 276–7; calendar 30–1; California 266; Chablis 74; Champagne 76–7; Cognac 111; Côte Rôtie 126; Georgia 241; Germany 142, 144, 160, 162, 164; Greece 238; Italy 176; Madeira 217; Madiran 112;

Midi 132; New Zealand 288; Pacific Northwest 270; port 214–15; Rhône 124, 130; Roman 12–13, 18; Sauternes 100; South Africa 290; Spain 196, 199, 202; Tokay 228–9
winery, anatomy of 38–9
Winery Lake 257
Winkel 158
Winningen 153
Wintrich 150, 152
Wintzenheim 123
Wirra Wirra 284
Wonnegau 162, 163
Woodbridge Cellars 266
Woodbury Vyds 274
Woodland 267
Woodstock 284
Woodward Canyon 270
Worcester 291
Worms 162
Woronzov, Count Mikhail 240
Württemberg 164
Würzburg 166, 167
Würzgarten 153, 158
Wyndham Estate 278
Wynns 285

Xarel-lo grape 204
Xinjan Urgur 247
Xynisteri grape 244
Xynomavro grape 238

Yakima 270, 272★
Yalumba 282
Yamanashi 248
Yamhill County 273
Yantai (Cheefoo) 247
Yantra Valley 234
Yarden 242
Yarra Valley 281
Yarra Yering 281
yeasts 34
Yecla 198
Yellowglen 281
Yerasa 244
Yeringberg 281
Yonne 73
York Creek 262
Young, Robert 254
Yountville 260
Yquem, Ch. d' 100
Yugoslavia (former) 232–3
Yvorne 220

Zaca Mesa 264
Zacatecas 269
Zaco 202
Zaer 201
Zakinthos 238
Zamorna 245
Zanella 178
Zell 153
Zellerbach, James D 251, 254
Zeltingen 152
Zemmour 245
Zenkoji grape 247
Zichron-Yaacov 242
Zierfändler grape 224
Zilavka grape 232
Zind-Humbrecht 123
Zinfandel grape 27★; Australia 287; California 255, 256, 260, 262, 264, 266; South Africa 292
Zinnkoepfle 123
Zitsa 238
Znojmo 230
Zonin 275
Zoopiyi 244
Zotzenberg 123
Zupa 232
Zupskocrno 232
Zürich 219
Zweigelt grape 223, 224

Gazetteer

This gazetteer includes place-name references of vineyards, châteaux, general wine areas and other information appearing on the maps in the Atlas, with the exception of minor place names and geographical features which appear as background information in italic type. All châteaux are listed under C (eg Château Yquem, d') in the gazetteer. Domaines, wineries, etc appear under their individual name. The alphanumeric after the page number refers to the grid reference system on the map pages. Vineyards, etc are indexed under their main name (eg Perrières, les). Identical names are distinguished by either the country or region being indicated in italic type. Alternative names are shown in brackets: Beijing (Peking), etc. Wine producers whose names appear on the maps are also listed.

Aarau 219 E3
Aargau 219 E3
Abacas 210 E2
Abalos 202 B5, 203 F3
Abaújszántó 229 E1
Abbaye de Morgeot 59 G5
Abbaye de Valmagne, L' 135 C3
Abbazia di Rosazzo 183 B4
Abbey d'Or 265 B4
Abbey Vale 287 C2
Aberdeen, *Australia* 279 E5
Aberdeen, *USA* 271 B2
Abergement-le-Grand 137 E5
Abermain 278 C6
Abilene 269 D5
Abîmes, les 137 D2
Abrantes 208 D4
Abtei 152 D5
Abtey 163 B4
Abtsberg, *Bernkastel* 153 E2
Abtsberg, *Ruwer* 149 E3
Abtsfronhof 161 C5
Abtswind 166 B6
Abú Hummus 243 F2
Acacia 257 F5
Acampo 267 B2
Acapulco 269 G5
Acciarella 193 G5
Achadas da Cruz 216 A5
Achem 165 D2
Achkarren 165 E1
Achleiten 224 F6
Acquasparta 192 E5
Acqui Terme 175 E6
Adams 273 B5
Adana 243 D4
Adapazari 243 B3
Adelaida 265 B2
Adelaida Cellars 265 B3
Adelaide 276 B6, 284 B2
Adelaide Metropolitan 276 B6
Adelberg 163 C4
Adelsheim 273 B4
Adgestone 298 G4
Adorigo 210 G4
Aetna Springs 259 A3
Afyonkarahisar 243 C3
Agde 135 D2, 138 D6
Agematsu 248 D2
Agenais 139 E4
Aglianico del Vulture 195 B4
Agrigento 195 G2
Agritiusberg 147 B5
Agua Alta, Qta da 210 F4
Agua Caliente 254 F5
Aguada de Baixo 214 E5
Agua de Pena 217 C5
Agualva-Cacém 209 F4
Aguascaltentes 269 F5
Águeda 214 E5
Aguiar da Beira 215 E6
Aguilar 207 B4
Agyag 229 E1
Ahlgren 263 C2
Ahr 143 A2
Ahtanum 272 E2
Aia Nuova 191 A4
Aigle 221 C1
Aignan 113 E2
Aigrefeuille-sur-Maine 114 C3, 115 G5
Aigrots, les 62 E3
Aiguamúrcia 205 F2
Aigues-Mortes 129 F2, 139 D2
Aiguillon 113 D3
Aïn-Bessem Bouira 245 B4
Aïn-Merane 245 B4
Aire-sur-l'Adour 113 E2
Airlie 273 D4
Aiud 237 C3
Aix-en-Provence 129 F6, 136 A1
Aix-les-Bains 137 C2
Ajaccio 140 F4
Akhisar 243 C2
Akron 275 C2
Aksaray 243 C4
Aksehir 243 C3
Ala 184 G4
Alaminos 244 G3
Alamo, El 201 C1
Alamos, Los 265 F4
Alandroal 213 E6
Alaric 133 C3
Alba, *Italy* 173 E3, 175 D3, 176 E3
Alba, *USA* 275 C4
Alba-Iulia 237 C3
Albana di Romagna 179 F3, 187 A5
Albano Laziale 193 E5
Albany, *Australia* 286 G4
Albany, *USA* 271 D2, 273 E4, 275 B5
Albarca 205 F1
Albersweiler 161 C1
Albertshofen 166 B5
Albi 113 D6
Albinyana 205 F3
Albosággia 177 B3
Al-Boulaida (Blida) 245 A4
Albrechtsburg 143 A4
Alburquerque 269 D4
Albury 277 C4, 280 C6
Alcácer do Sal 208 E4
Alcalde 201 C2
Alcobaça 208 C3
Alcover 205 F2
Aldeanueva 203 C3
Aldeno 184 D5
Alderbrook 255 C5
Alder Creek 273 B6
Aldinga 284 E1
Aldinga Beach 284 E1
Aleatico di Gradoli 187 D3
Aleatico di Puglia 195 B4
Alegria, Qta da 211 F2
Aleixar, l' 205 F1
Aleksinac 233 E5
Alella 197 B6, 205 E5
Alenquer 208 D3
Aléria 140 F5
Alès 129 D2, 139 B1
Alessándria 173 E4, 175 C6
Alexander Valley 255 B4
Alexandra 280 E4
Alexandria 275 D4
Alexandroupoli 239 B5
Alexandrovo 235 B3
Alezio 195 C6
Alf 143 B2
Alfaraz 201 D2
Alfaro 203 C4
Alforja 205 F1
Algarrobo 200 B4
Algés 209 F5
Alghero 195 C1
Algueirao Mem Martins 209 E4
Alicante 197 D5
Alijó 208 A5
Alió 205 F2
Aliquippa 275 C2
Al-Iskandariya (Alexandria) 243 F2
Aljarafe 197 D2
Al-Jazair (Algiers) 245 A4
Aljustrel 208 E4
Alkoomi 286 F3
Al-Ladhiqiya (Latakia) 243 D5
Allandale 278 B6
Allanmere 278 C5
Allan Scott 289 G4
Allegro 275 D4
Allemans-du-Dropt 97 F4
Allentown 275 C4
Allobrogie 139 F4
Allots, aux 65 F3
All Saints 280 C5
Almáchar 207 D5
Almada 209 F5
Almansa 197 C4
Almeirim 208 D4
Almocadén 201 B3
Almoçageme 209 E3
Almoster 205 F1
Aloha 273 B5
Aloxe-Corton 55 C5, 57 E4, 63 F3
Alpaugh 267 F5
Alpine 271 E2
Alsea 273 E3
Alsenz 155 D5
Alsheim 143 C4, 163 C5
Altafulla 205 F2
Altamura 259 F5
Altärchen 151 G2
Altdorf 219 F4
Alte Badstube am Doktorberg 153 F2
Altenbaumburg 155 C6
Altenberg, *Austria* 223 C4
Altenberg, *Ruwer* 149 E1
Altenberg, *Saar* 147 A5
Altenberg de Bergheim 123 D5
Altenburg, *Austria* 225 G3
Altenburg, *France* 123 C3
Altenburg, *Germany* 143 A5, 167 D4
Alto 293 G2
Alto Adige 179 B3, 184 G6
Alto Jahuel 297 B6
Alto Jiloca-Daroca 197 B4
Altona 282 C4
Altoona 275 C3
Alushta 240 C2
Aluze 68 C3
Alvaçes do Corgo 210 E1
Alvito 213 F4
Alzey 163 C4
Amadora 209 F5
Amarante 215 C6
Amarela, Qta 210 E5
Amares 215 B5
Amarillo 269 D5
Amarquillo 201 C2
Amasya 243 B5
Ambarès-et-Lagrave 80 E3
Amberley Estate 287 C2
Ambès 108 G4
Amboise 115 B2
Ambonnay 79 D5
Amelia 192 F5
Amélie-les-Bains-Palalda 133 G3
Amery 284 D2
Amfissa 239 C3
Amindeo 239 B2
Amity 273 C4
Amizetta 263 C4
Amman 243 F5
Ammerschwihr 123 C2
Amorgos 239 E5
Amorosa 201 C4
Amoureuses, les 66 F2
Ampuis 126 C4
Ampurdan Costa Brava 197 A6
Amtgarten 152 G5
Anadia 214 F5
Anaferas 201 E3
Anakie 280 F3
Anan 248 E3
Anapa 240 C3
Ancas 214 F5
Ancenis 114 B3
Ancienne Cure, Dom. de l' 109 D4
Ancona 187 C6
Andau 222 D4
Andel 153 G1
Andermatt 219 F4
Anderson 267 E5
Anderson, S 259 E5
Anderson Valley 256 C2
Anderson Valley Vyds 269 D4
Andes, Los 295 A3
Andlau 120 B4
Andosilla 203 B3
Andrew Garrett 284 E2
Andriano (Andrian) 185 C5
Andros 239 D4
Angad 245 B3
Angaston 282 B5
Angelo, D' 275 C1
Angers 114 B5
Anglesea 280 G3
Angles, les 61 F5
Anglisidhes 244 G3
Angwin 259 B3
Anières 220 C4
Animas 201 D1
Añina 201 C2
Añinas 201 D2
Ankara 243 B4
Ankeny 273 C4
Ankialos 239 C3
Annaba (Bône) 245 A5
Annaberg 161 A4
Annecy 137 B3
Annemasse 137 B3
Annonay 125 B3
Anoia 197 B6
Anse 71 F4
Anshan 246 A6
Antakya 243 D5
Antalya 243 D3
Antequera 207 C4
Antiene 279 F6
Antinori 189 C3
Antofagasta 294 F1
Antoniusberg 147 G3
Antonius-Brunnen 147 F2
Anzio 193 G4
Aosta 173 C2
Apetlon 222 D4, 223 C5
Apollo Bay 280 G2
Apotheke 151 F2
Appenzell 219 E5
Appiano (Eppan) 185 D5
Apples 220 A5
Apremont 137 C2
Aprica 177 B5
Aprilia 187 F3, 193 F4
Apt 129 E5
Aquila, L' 187 E5
Aquileia 179 C6, 181 C5
Arad 237 C2
Aradhippou 244 F4
Aranda de Duero 206 E5
Aranibal 201 E1
Aranyos 229 G4
Ararat 277 D2, 280 E1
Arbignieu 137 C2
Arbin 137 C2
Arboç, L' 205 F3
Arbois 137 E6
Arborea 195 D1
Arbresle, l' 71 G3
Arbues, les 60 G3
Arbus 113 F1
Arciero 265 B3
Arco 184 E3
Arco da Calheta 216 C6
Arco de São Jorge 217 A3
Arcos de Valdevez 215 A5
Arcs, les 136 B5
Ardailhou, L' 138 D6
Ardea 193 F4
Ardenno 177 B1
Ardila 201 C3
Ardillats, Les 71 C2
Ardoise, l' 130 E6
Ardon 221 C3
Arenberg, D' 284 D2
Arévalo 206 G2
Arezzo 187 B4
Arganil 215 G4
Argelès-sur-Mer 133 G5
Argens 136 A4, 139 G4
Argensol 131 D2
Argentario 187 D2
Arges 237 D3
Argillas, aux 65 F2
Argillières, les, *Chambolle-Musigny* 66 F2
Argillières, les, *Prémeaux-Prissey* 64 F4
Argyle 273 C4
Arhanes 239 F5
Aríccia 193 E5
Arizona Vyds 269 D3
Arlay 137 F4
Arles 129 F4, 139 C2
Arlewood 287 D2
Arlight 265 F3
Arlot, Clos 64 F4
Armagh 283 D5
Armagnac, Bas 113 E2
Armagnac, Haut 113 E3
Armavir 240 C4
Armida 255 C5
Armusères, les 118 B2
Arnas 71 E3
Arnedo 203 C2
Arnex-sur-Nyon 220 B4
Arnozelo, Qta do 211 G4
Arosa 215 B5
Arouca 215 D5
Árpád-Hegy 229 F1
Arrábida 208 E3
Arraiolos 213 E4
Arrançon 101 E5
Arrayán, El 297 A6
Arrecife 207 F6
Arrowood 254 F4
Arroyo Grande 265 D3
Arroyo Seco 263 F5
Arruda 208 D3
Arsac 95 E2
Arsos 244 F4
Arsures, les 137 E6
Arta 239 C2
Artena 193 E6
Arterberry 273 C4
Artés 197 B6
Artigues 89 D4
Artiguillon 85 G3
Artsyz 240 B1
Arve et Lac 219 F1
Arve et Rhône 219 G1
Arvelets, les, *Fixin* 67 E4
Arvelets, les, *Pommard* 61 E6, 62 E1
Arvin 267 G6
Arzier 220 B4
Aschaffenburg 143 B5
Ascó 204 F5
Ascoli Piceno 187 E5
Asenovgrad 235 D3
Ashbrook Estate 287 D2
Ashburton 288 E3
Ash Coombe 298 F6
Ashland 271 G3
Ashland Vyds 271 G3
Ashtarak 240 D5
Ashton, *Australia* 284 A4
Ashton, *S. Africa* 290 F3
Ashton Hills 284 A4
Ashue 272 F2
Assisi 192 C6
Assmannshausen 157 D1
Asti 173 E3, 175 C4
Astipalaia 239 E5
Astley 298 E4
Astoria 271 C2
Ászár-Neszmély 226 E2
Atacama 294 F1
Atalaya 200 B5
Atascadero 265 C3
Athées, aux 65 G2
Atherly 283 D5
Athets, les 66 F3
Athienou 244 F4
Athinai 239 D4
Atlantic City 275 D5
Atlas Peak 259 E6
Attilafelsen 165 E1
Atwater 267 C3
Aubenas 129 B3
Auberdière, l' 118 C3
Aubignan 131 E5
Au Bon Climat/Qupé 265 E4
Aubonne 220 A5
Aubuis, les 117 F3
Auburn, *Australia* 283 F6
Auburn, *USA* 271 A3
Auckland 288 B4
Audignac, Clos d' 61 F4
Auen 155 C3
Auersthal 222 B3
Auf der Heide 153 C3
Auf de Wiltingerkupp 147 B3
Auflangen 162 E4, 163 B5
Auggen 165 F1
Aumerade, Dom. de l' 136 C3
Aumsville 273 D5
Auriac-sur-Dropt 109 C4
Aurora 273 C5
Ausejo 203 C2
Aussy, les 61 F4
Austin 269 E5
Austin Cellars 265 F5
Autun 55 D4
Auxerre 55 A3, 73 E3
Auxey-Duresses 57 F3, 61 E1
Avallon 55 B3
Avaux, Clos des 62 F3
Avaux, les 62 F3
Aveiro 208 B4
Avellino 195 C3
Avelsbach 149 F2
Avenay-Val d'Or 79 D4
Avezzano 187 F4, 195 A2
Aviano 181 B3
Avignon 129 E4, 139 C3
Avila Beach 265 D3
Avinyonet 205 E4
Avio 184 G3
Avize 79 F3
Avoca 280 E2
Avoine 117 E2
Avusy 220 D3
Ay 79 D3
Aydie 113 F2
Ayent 221 C4
Ayios Efstratios 239 C5
Ayios-Nikolaos 239 F5
Ayl 147 D2
Ayse 137 B3
Aytos 235 C5
Azay-le-Rideau 115 B1
Azenhas do Mar 209 E3
Azov 240 B3
Azumi 248 C3
Az-Zarqa (Zarqua) 243 F5

Babcock 265 F4
Babillères, les 66 F2
Bacau 237 C5
Bacchus Marsh 280 F3
Backsberg 293 E3
Badacsony 226 F2
Bad Bergzabern 143 D3, 161 D1
Bad Cannstatt 165 D4
Bad Dürkheim 161 A2, C4
Bad Dürrenberg 167 C4
Baden, *Austria* 222 C3, 224 F2
Baden, *Germany* 143 F3
Baden, *Switzerland* 219 E4
Baden-Baden 165 D3
Badener Berg 224 F2
Badenweiler 165 F1
Badger Mountain 271 F4
Badia a Coltibuono 189 E5
Badische Bergstrasse Kraichgau 143 D5, 165 C3
Bad Kreuznach 143 B3, 155 C5, 163 B3
Bad Mergentheim 143 C6
Bad Münster a. S. 155 C6, F2
Bad Pirawarth 222 B3
Badstube 153 F2
Bad Vöslau 222 C3, 224 G1
Baena 207 B5
Bafra 243 B5
Bagat 113 C4
Bagauste, Qta de 210 G2
Bagborough 298 F4
Bagno a Ripoli 189 B4
Bagnols-sur-Cèze 129 D3, 139 B2
Baia-Mare 237 B3
Baião 215 C6
Baiken 159 E3
Bailén 197 D3
Baileys Bundarra 280 D5
Bainbridge Island 271 A3
Bairnsdale 277 D4
Bairrada 208 B4
Bairro 210 E1
Baja 226 G3
Bajo Aragón, Medio 197 B5
Bajo Aragón, Occidental 197 B5
Bajo Aragón, Oriental 197 B5
Bajo-Ebro Montsiá 197 B5
Bakersfield 267 G6
Bakers Gully 284 D3
Baki (Baku) 240 D6
Ba'labakk (Baalbek) 243 E5
Balatonboglár 226 F2
Balatonfüred 226 F2
Balatonfüred-Csopak 226 F2
Balatonmellék 226 F1
Balbaina Alta 201 D1
Balbaina Baja 201 D1
Balbi 295 C4
Balcon de l'Hermitage, le 127 A5
Baldivis Estate 286 D2
Baleira, Qta da 211 F3
Balgownie 280 D3
Balikesir 243 B2
Ballaison 137 A3
Ballan 280 F3
Ballarat 277 D2, 280 F2
Ballston 273 C4
Balmes Dauphinoises 139 D4
Balmoral Corner 279 F5
Balranald 277 B2
Balti 240 A1, 241 E5
Baltimore 275 D4
Banat, *Romania* 237 C2
Banat, *Yugoslavia* 233 C5
Banc, le 60 D1
Bandiera 255 A3
Bandol 136 C2
Bandon 271 F1
Banfi 275 C5
Banja Luka 233 C3
Bannay 119 E3
Bannockburn 277 D2, 280 F3
Baños de Ebro 203 G3
Banos, Los 267 D3
Banská Bystrica 230 G4
Banya 235 C3
Bányász 229 E2
Banyeres del Penedès 205 F3
Bányi-Hegy 229 C6
Banyuls 133 F5
Banyuls-sur-Mer 133 G5
Banzão 209 E3
Baodi 246 B4
Baoding 246 C3
Baraillot 99 A1
Baraques 67 F2
Baraques de Gevrey-Chambertin, les 67 F2
Baratas, Qta das 210 F5
Barbadillo 201 G2
Barbaresco 175 D3, 176 E3
Barbechat 115 E5
Barbera d'Alba 175 E3, 176 E3
Barbera d'Asti 175 B4
Barberà de la Conca 205 E2
Barbera del Monferrato 173 E4, 175 C4
Barbières, les 61 E3
Barboursville 275 E3
Barcelona 205 E5
Barcelos 208 A4, 215 B5
Barco, El 201 C2
Bardas Blancas 295 D3
Bardolino 179 D2, 182 E3
Bardolino Classico 179 C2, 182 F3
Bardonnex 220 D4
Bargetto 263 D3
Barguins, les 118 B3
Bari 195 B5
Barizey 68 D3
Barjols 136 A3
Barkham Manor 298 F5
Barletta 195 B4
Barnard Griffin 271 F4
Barnsgate Manor 298 F5
Baron 265 B3
Barone de Cles 185 F4
Barone Ricasoli 189 F5
Barossa Settlers 282 C4
Barossa Valley 276 B6
Barottes, les 66 F2
Barr 120 B4
Barrameda 200 A5
Barraud, chez 111 F2
Barraults, Clos des 68 C4
Barre Dessus, la 61 F2
Barre, en la 61 F2
Barre, la, *Montlouis-sur- Loire* 118 C4
Barre, la, *Volnay* 61 F4
Barre, la, *Vouvray* 118 B3
Barrières, aux 65 F3
Barrilário, Qta do 210 G2
Barrios, Los 201 F2
Barrô, *Portugal* 214 E5
Barro, *USA* 259 C3
Barrydale 290 F4
Barsac 80 G4, 96 F6, 101 A5
Bar-sur-Aube 76 E6
Bar-sur-Seine 76 E5
Bártfi 229 E2
Barton 273 B6
Barton Manor 298 G4
Basedows 282 B4
Basel 143 G3, 165 G1, 219 D3
Basignani 275 D4
Basket Range Wines 284 A4
Bassano del Grappa 179 C4
Bas Santenay 59 F3
Basse Goulaine 115 F4
Bassens 80 E3, 96 C4
Bastei 155 F1
Bastia 140 D5
Basto 215 C6
Bâtard Montrachet 60 G3
Bathurst 277 B5
Batiaz, La 221 D2
Battaudes, les 59 G5
Battenburg 161 A2
Batterieberg 153 C4
Bat'umi 240 D4
Baudes, les 66 F4
Baudines, les 59 F5
Baule 115 A3
Baulet, Clos 66 F4
Baume, Dom. de la 133 B6, 135 C1
Baumgarten 223 C4
Ba Xian 246 C3
Bayern (Main) 143 B5
Baynton 280 E3
Bay of Plenty 288 B5
Bayonne 112 F5
Bayon-sur-Gironde 108 F2
Bayrut (Beirut) 243 E4
Bayt Lahm (Bethlehem) 243 F4
Baywood Park 265 C3
Béarn 112 F6
Bearsted 298 F5
Beaucaire 129 E4, 139 C2
Beaucanon 259 D4
Beauder, Clos 61 E6
Beaufort 280 E2
Beaujeu 71 C2
Beaulieu, *UK* 298 G4
Beaulieu, *USA* 259 D4
Beaulieu-sur-Layon 114 B5, 116 C4
Beaumes 127 C5
Beaumes-de-Venise 129 D5, 131 D5
Beaumont-en-Véron 117 F3
Beaumonts, les 63 F2
Beaumont-sur-Vesle 79 B6
Beaune 55 D5, 57 E4, 62 G4
Beaupouyet 109 A4
Beau Puy 117 C2
Beauregard 59 F4
Beaurepaire 59 E3
Beauroy 75 C2
Beauvais 117 C3
Beaux Bruns, aux 66 F3
Beaux Fougets, les 62 F2
Beaux Monts Bas, les 65 F5
Beaux Monts Hauts Rougeots 65 E5
Beaux Monts, les Hauts 65 E5
Beaver Creek 273 C5
Beaverton 271 C3, 273 B5
Beblenheim 120 D4, 123 D3
Becamil, Dom. de 93 B4
Bechtheim 163 C5
Bechtolsheim 163 C4
Bédarieux 135 B1, 138 D5
Bedell 275 C5
Beechworth 280 D6
Be'er Sheva (Beersheba) 243 F4
Bégadan 85 C3
Bègles 80 F3, 96 D4
Begnins 220 B4
Begues 205 F4
Beijing (Peking) 246 B3
Beijing Winery 246 B4
Beilstein 143 B2, 165 C4
Beja, *Portugal* 208 E4, 213 G4
Beja, *Tunisia* 245 A6
Béjaia (Bougie) 245 A5
Bekaa 243 E5
Békéscsaba 226 F5
Bel Air 72 D4
Bel-Air, *Gevrey-Chambertin* 66 E6
Bel-Air, *Vouvray* 118 B3
Bélaye 113 C4

Belbourie 278 B5
Belcher 293 D4
Beleymas 109 A6
Belford 278 B4
Bélissand 62 F3
Bell Ana 191 A5
Bellbird 278 D5
Belle Croix 65 F1
Bellegarde 129 F3
Bellerose 255 C4
Belletins, les 119 F3
Belleville 71 D4, 72 F6
Bellevue 273 C4
Bellevue Cave Coop. 85 F4
Bellfountain 273 E4
Bellfountain Cellars 273 E4
Bellheim 161 C3
Bellingham 293 F5
Bellinzona 219 G4
Bell Mountain 269 E5
Bell Mountain Vyds 269 E5
Bellmunt del Priorat 204 F6
Bellota 267 B3
Belltall 205 E2
Belluno 179 B4, 181 B2
Bellvei del Penedès 205 F3
Bellville 290 F2
Belvedere, *Italy* 191 C3
Belvedere, *USA* 255 D5
Belvès-de-Castillon 103 D6
Belz 161 D5
Bemposta 209 D5
Benais 117 C3
Benalla 277 C3, 280 D5
Benavente 197 B2
Benbecula 285 B5
Bendigo 277 C3, 280 D3
Bend of Isles 281 C3
Benevento 195 B3
Benfeld 120 B5
Beniarrés 197 C5
Beni M'tir 245 B2
Beni Sadden 245 B2
Benissanet 204 G5
Benmarl 275 C5
Bennwihr 120 D4, 123 C3
Benoites, les 59 G5
Bénovie, La 139 C1
Bensheim 165 A3
Benton City 272 G5
Benziger-Glen Ellen 254 F4
Beograd (Belgrade) 233 D5
Bérange 139 C1
Berenda 267 D4
Beresford/Bosanquet 284 C2
Bergamo 173 C5
Bergbieten 120 A4
Berg-Bildstock 159 F6
Bergerac 109 B5
Bergères-les-Vertus 79 G3
Bergerie, la 60 G2
Bergfeld 259 B5
Bergheim 120 D4, 123 D5
Bergholtz 120 F3, 122 B1
Bergholtz-Zell 122 B2
Berg Kaisersteinfels 157 E2
Bergkirche 162 D5
Bergkloster 163 C4
Berg Roseneck 157 F3
Berg Rottland 157 F3
Berg Schlossberg 157 E2
Berg-Schlösschen 147 E2
Bergweingärten 223 B4
Beringer 259 D3
Berkane 245 B3
Bern 219 E3
Bernardine, La 131 F2
Berner Oberland 219 F3
Bernex 220 C3
Bernkastel, *Australia* 282 B4
Bernkastel (Mittelmosel), 143 B2, 151 B1, 153 B1
Bernkastel-Kues 143 B2, 153 F2
Bernot, Clos 59 G6, 60 G1
Bernouil 73 D6
Berre-l'Étang 129 G5
Berri 277 B1
Berson 108 D3
Bertaud, Dom. de 136 C5
Berthet, Clos 63 D4
Berthiers, les 119 F4
Bertineau 103 B3
Bertins, les 61 F5
Berzé-la-Ville 69 E3
Berzé-le-Châtel 69 D3
Besenello 184 D5
Besigheim 165 C4
Bessan 138 D6
Bessards, les 127 C4
Bessay 72 A5
Best's 280 E1
Betanzos 197 A2
Bethany 282 C4
Bethel Heights 273 C4
Betsek 229 F3
Bettelhaus 161 B5
Betteravia 265 E4
Beugnons 75 E2
Beung 147 F2
Beuttes, les 60 G2
Bevagna 192 D6
Bex 221 C2
Beychevelle 91 D5
Beyerskloof 293 E2
Bézannes 79 A3
Béziers 133 B5, 135 D1, 138 D6
Bianchet 281 C4
Bianchi, *Argentina* 295 C4
Bianchi, *USA* 267 D4
Bianco Capena 187 E4
Bianco dei Coloi Maceratesi 187 D6
Bianco della Valdinievole 187 A3
Bianco dell'Empolese 187 A3
Bianco del Metauro 187 C6
Bianco di Custoza 179 D2, 182 G3
Bianco di Pitigliano 187 D3
Bianco di Scandia 179 E2
Bianco Pisano di San Torpé 187 A2
Bianco Vergine Valdichiana 187 C4, 190 E6
Bianzone 177 B4
Biard 111 F2
Biarritz 112 F5
Biaune, la 72 C5
Bibbiano 189 F3
Bidarray 112 G5
Bidaude, la 66 E4
Bidaudières, les 118 B4
Biddenden 298 F5
Biebelhausen 147 D3
Biel 219 E2
Bielersee 219 E2
Biella 173 D3
Bienvenues Bâtard Montrachet 60 G3
Bierzo 197 A2
Bievaux 59 E3
Biferno 187 G6, 195 B3
Bigorre 139 D4
Biharia 237 B2
Bijeljina 233 C4
Bildstock 162 F3
Bilhorod Dnistrovs'kyy 241 F6
Billard 67 F2
Billaux, les 103 B1
Billy-le-Grand 79 C6
Bingen 143 B3, 155 A6, 157 F2, 163 B3
Bingerbrück 155 A6
Binghampton 275 C4
Binissalem 197 C6
Bin Xian 246 D4
Biola 267 D4
Birchfield 272 E2
Bisbal del Penedès, La 205 F3
Bischofsberg 157 E3
Bischofsgarten 161 D5
Bischofskreuz 161 C2
Bisquertt 297 D4
Bisseuil 79 D4
Bissey-sous-Cruchaud 68 F3
Bissy-la-Mâconnaise 69 B5
Bitola 233 G5
Bizarron, El 201 E2
Bizerte 245 A6
Blaauwklippen 293 G2
Blacé 71 E3
Black Mountain 255 C5
Blackwood Canyon 272 G5
Blagny 60 F4
Blagny, Sous 60 F5
Blagoevgrad 235 D1
Blaj 237 C3
Blancafort 205 E2
Blanc, Clos, *Pommard* 61 F6, 62 F1
Blanc, Clos, *Vougeot* 65 F6, 66 F2
Blanchards, les 66 F4
Blanche Barkly 280 D2
Blanches, ez 61 E4
Blanches Fleurs 62 F6
Blanches, les 61 F1
Blanchisserie, la 62 F4
Blanchot 75 D4
Blanchot Dessous 60 G2
Blanchot Dessus 60 G2
Blanquefort 80 E3, 96 C3
Blanquette de Limoux 133 E5
Blaye 80 D2, 108 D1
Bleinschwiller 120 C4
Blenheim, *New Zealand* 288 D4, 289 G5
Blenheim, *USA* 275 E3
Bléré 115 B2
Blewitt Springs 284 D2
Blodgett 273 E3
Blois 115 B3
Blonay 221 B1
Blottières, les 117 C4
Blütengrund 167 C3
Boada de Roa 206 E4
Boaventura 217 A2
Boa Vista, Qta da 210 F2
Boavista, Qta da 210 F4
Bobadilla, SA 201 G1
Boboshevo 235 D1
Boca 173 C4
Bockenau 155 C4
Bockenheim 161 A2
Bockfliess 222 B3
Bockstein 147 E4
Bodenheim 163 B5
Bodensee 143 G5, 165 F4
Bodegonera, La 201 E2
Bodrogkeresztúr 229 G3
Bodrogolaszi 229 D5
Bodrogzsegi 229 F3
Bogle 267 E3
Boglyoska 229 C6
Böhlig 161 D5
Böhlitz-Ehrenberg 167 C4
Bohorca 200 B4
Boiches, les 62 F5
Boichot, en 59 G3
Boirettes, les 59 G5
Bois de Blagny, le 60 E5
Bois de Chassagne 59 F5
Bois de Noel et Belles Filles, Sous le 63 D4
Bois-d'Oingt, le 71 F2
Bois Fleury 119 F4
Bois Gibault 119 F4
Bois-Rideau, le 118 B3
Boisse 109 C6
Bolandse 293 B4
Bolgheri 187 B2, 191 A5
Bolhrad 241 G5
Bollenar 297 A4
Bollène 129 D4
Bologna 179 E3
Bolzano (Bozen) 179 B3, 185 C6
Bomboly 229 F3
Bom Dia, Qta do 210 F4
Bomfim, Qta do 210 E6
Bommes 101 F3
Bompas 133 F4
Bom Retiro, Qta do 210 F5
Bonair 272 F3
Bondues, les 60 G2
Bonete, El 201 B4
Bonfoi 293 F1
Bonheur, Le 293 E2
Bonifacio 140 G4
Bonn 143 A2
Bonnes Mares, les 66 E3
Bonneville-et-St-Avit-de-Fumadières 109 B4
Bonnezeaux 114 B5, 116 D6
Bonnievale 290 F3
Bonny Doon 263 C2
Bonny-sur-Loire 115 B5
Bons Feuvres, les 62 F3
Boordy 275 D4
Boort 280 C2
Boppard 143 B3
Borba 208 D5, 213 D6
Bordeaux 80 E3, 96 D4, 99 A4
Borex 220 B4
Borgo Carso 193 F6
Borgo Conventi 183 D5
Borgo del Tiglio 183 C5
Borgo Flora 193 F6
Borgo Montello 193 G5
Borgo Podgora 193 F6
Borgo Priolo 177 F3
Borgoratto Mormorolo 177 G4
Borgo Santa Maria 193 G5
Borjas del Campo, Les 205 F1
Borkút 229 F3
Bormes-les-Mimosas 136 C4
Borna 167 C4
Borne, la Grande 59 G5
Bornheim 163 C4
Borniques, les 66 F2
Bornova 243 C2
Bortoli, De 281 A4
Bosc, Dom. de 133 B6, 135 D2
Boschendal 293 F4
Boschetto 193 E6
Boschis 176 F2
Bosenheim 155 C6
Bosnasco 177 E6
Bosquets, Les 131 D4
Bosset 109 A5
Bossey 137 B3
Bossière, la 67 D1
Bossières 65 G4
Boston 275 B6
Botarell 205 F1
Botaveau 59 E2
Botevgrad 235 C2
Bothy 298 F4
Botou 246 C3
Bottelary 293 E1
Botticino 179 C2
Bottière, la 72 A5
Bou 115 A4
Bouaye 114 C2
Bouchaine 257 F5
Boucharey 126 B3
Bouchassy 130 G6
Bouchère, la 61 E4
Bouchères, les 60 F6
Boucherottes, les 62 F2
Bouchot, le 119 F4
Bouchots, les 66 E4
Boudières, les 67 E4
Boudots, aux 65 F3
Boudrières, les 60 G4
Boudriottes 59 G6
Bouglon 113 C2
Bougros 75 D3
Bougy-Villars 220 A4
Bouillarges 129 E3
Boulaouane 245 B1
Boulay, Le 115 A2
Bouliac 96 D4
Boulmeau 63 F3
Boulotte, la 63 F3
Boulou, le 133 G4
Bouniagues 109 B6
Bourbonnais 139 B4
Bourdigny 220 C3
Bourg 80 D3, 108 G3
Bourg-Bassot 68 C4
Bourg-Charente 111 D2
Bourg-en-Bresse 55 F6
Bourgeots, les 63 E1
Bourges 115 C5
Bourgnac 109 A5
Bourgneuf-en-Retz 114 C2
Bourgneut-Vallée-d'Or 68 C3
Bourgogne, La 293 G6
Bourgueil 114 B6, 117 D2
Bouscat, le 80 E3, 96 C4
Bouscaut, le 99 E5
Bousse d'Or 61 F4
Bousselots, aux 65 F2
Boutenac 133 C4
Boutières, aux 63 E2
Boutières, les 63 F2
Boutiers-St-Trojan 110 C6
Boutoc 101 E4
Boutoillottes, aux 67 F4
Boutonniers, les 61 E2
Bouzeron 68 A4
Bouznika 245 B2
Bouzy 79 D5
Bovernier 221 D2
Bovlei 293 B6
Bowen 295 C5
Bowen Estate 285 D6
Boxing 246 D4
Boyes Hot Springs 254 F5
Boyton 298 E5
Boze Down 298 F4
Bra 175 D2
Branesti 241 F5
Brachetto d'Acqui 175 D5
Braga 208 A4, 215 B5
Bragança 208 A5
Bragão, Qta do 210 D5
Braidwood 277 C5
Brain-sur-Allonnes 114 B6
Bramaterra 173 C3
Bramois 221 C3
Brand 123 B1
Brander 265 F5
Brands Laira 285 B5
Branxton 278 B5
Bras 136 B3
Brasov 237 C4
Bratenhofchen 153 F2
Bratislava 230 G3
Brauneberg 151 B5, 152 G5
Braune Kupp 147 B3
Braunfels 147 C4
Braunweiler 155 B5
Brazey, les 66 F3
Brda 233 B1
Breaky Bottom 298 F5
Breclav 230 G3
Breganze 179 C3
Breisach 143 F3
Breisgau 143 F3, 165 E2
Breitl 225 G2
Brelance 60 G4
Bremblens 220 A5
Bremerton 271 A3
Brentonico 184 F4
Brentwood 267 B2
Bréry 137 F5
Bréscia 173 D6, 179 C1
Brescul, en 62 E2
Bressandes, les, *Aloxe-Corton* 63 F4
Bressandes, les, *Beaune* 62 E5
Brestnik 235 D3
Brétenins, les 61 D2
Bretzenheim 155 B6
Breuillards, les 119 E4
Brevau 59 E3
Breynets, le 72 C6
Brézé 114 C6
Brezovo 235 C3
Briar Ridge 278 D4
Bricco Asili 176 E4
Bricco Bussia 176 F2
Bricco di Nièvе 176 E4
Bricco Roche 176 F2
Bridgehampton 275 C5
Bridgeport 275 C5
Bridgetown 286 F2
Bridgeview 271 G2
Bridgewater 280 D2, 284 B4
Bridgewater Mill 284 B4
Brienz 219 F3
Brig 219 F3, 221 C6
Bright 280 D6
Brighton 284 B2
Brighton 298 G5
Brights 275 B3
Brignoles 136 B3
Bri, La 293 G6
Brinas 203 F1
Brindisi 195 C6
Brins, les Hauts 61 E4
Briones 203 F2
Brno 230 F3
Broad Crossing 279 D6
Broadfield 298 E4
Broadley 271 E2
Brochon 67 E3
Brockton 275 B6
Brokenwood 278 C4
Bronco, F J F 267 C3
Broni 177 E5
Bronzolo (Branzoll) 185 D6
Brookings 271 G1
Brouillards, les 61 F5
Brouilly 55 F5, 72 F4
Brouquet 101 G4
Brown Bros 280 D5
Brownstown 272 F2
Brownsville 273 E4
Broze 113 D6
Bruc, El 205 D4
Bruchsal 165 C3
Bruck am der Mur 222 E1
Brückchen 162 E4
Brückes 155 C2
Bruderberg 149 D4
Brudersberg 162 C4
Bruderschaft 150 E1
Brue-Auriac 136 A3
Bruges 80 E3, 96 C4
Brugg 219 D4
Bruisyard 298 E6
Brûlées, aux 65 F4
Brûlées, les 64 G6
Brunate 176 F2
Brunelle, la 67 F2
Brunello di Montalcino 187 C3, 190 F2
Brunettes et Planchots, les 63 F3
Brunn 222 C3
Bruno Prats & Paul Pontallier 297 A6
Brureaux, les 72 B5
Brussonnes, les 59 G5
Brutocao 256 C4
Bruyères, les, *Aloxe-Corton* 63 F4
Bruyères, les, *Beaujolais* 72 E4
Bruyères, les Petites 119 E4
Bucelas 208 D3, 209 D5
Bucherats, les 72 A5
Buchillon 220 B5
Buckingham Valley 275 D4
Bucuresti 237 D4
Budapest 226 E3
Büdesheim 155 A6
Bué 119 F2
Buehler 259 D4
Buell 273 C4
Buellton 265 F5
Buena 272 F3
Buena Vista, *Cameros* 257 F5
Buena Vista, *Sonoma* 254 G5
Buena Vista, *Willamette* 273 D4
Buenos Aires 294 F2
Buffalo 275 B3
Búglio in M. 177 A2
Bühl 165 D2
Bühlertal 165 D3
Buin 295 B3, 297 B5
Buisson Certaut, le 60 G6
Bükkalja 226 E5
Bulcy 119 G5
Bullas 197 D4
Bullay 143 B2
Buller 280 C5
Bully 71 G2
Bunbury 286 E1
Burdur 243 C3
Burg 222 E3
Burgas 235 C5
Burgberg 153 E3
Burge family 282 C3
Burgess 259 C3
Burggarten 225 G3
Burglay 151 C3, 153 B3
Burg Layen 155 A6
Burg Lichteneck 165 E2
Burg Neuenfels 165 F1
Burg Rodenstein 163 D5
Burgsponheim 155 C4
Burgstall 225 G2
Burgweg, *Franken* 166 C6
Burgweg, *Nahe* 154 F6, 155 C5
Burgweg, *Rheingau* 157 F5
Burgy 69 B5
Burg Zähringen 165 E2
Buring 282 B4
Burkheim 165 E1
Burleigh 289 G5
Burnie 287 F5
Burnside 284 A3
Burnt Woods 273 E3
Buronnes, les 119 E2
Burra 276 B6
Burrweiler 161 C2
Bursa 243 B2
Bur Sa'id (Port Said) 243 F3
Bursinel 220 B4
Bursins 220 B4
Buschenberg 224 F6
Busselton 286 F1
Bussia Soprana 176 G2
Bussière, la 66 F4
Bussières, *Beaujolais* 72 F4
Bussières, *Mâconnais* 69 E3
Bussières, les 66 F3
Busslay 152 C6
Bussolengo 182 G4
Bussy 220 A5
Busto Arsizio 173 D4
Buta Ranquil 295 E3
Butay, le 115 G4
Butteaux 75 F2
Buttes, les 61 F5
Buttonwillow 267 G5
Buttonwood Farm 265 F5
Búttrio 183 B3
Buvilly 137 E5
Buxton 273 A4
Buxy 68 F3
Buzau 237 D5
Buzet 113 D2
Byala 235 B4
Byala Slatina 235 B2
Byron, *California* 265 E5
Byron, *Washington* 272 G4
Bywater & Josse 281 B5
Bzenec 230 F3
Bzenec/Strážnice 230 F3

Caballo, El 201 E2
Cabana, Qta da 210 F2
Cabardès 139 G2
Cabassers 204 F6
Cabeceiras de Basto 215 B6
Cabestany 133 F4
Cabeza Gorda 200 A5
Cabeza Vaca 200 A4
Cabezudo 200 B4
Caborca 269 E3
Cabra 207 B4
Cabra del Camp 205 E2
Cabras, Las 295 B2, 297 C4
Cabrera de Igualada 205 E3
Cabrière, Clos 293 G6
Cabrières, *Châteauneuf-du-Pape* 131 E2
Cabrières, *Coteaux du Languedoc* 135 B2
Cabrils 205 E6
Cacak 233 D5
Cacc'e Mmitte di Lucera 195 B4
Cacchiano 189 F5
Cache 267 A1
Cadalen 113 D6
Caderousse 131 E1
Cadillac 80 F4, 96 F6
Cadima 214 G4
Cagliari 195 E2
Cagnina di Romagna 179 F4
Cahors 113 C4
Cahul 241 G5
Cahuzac-sur-Vère 113 D6
Cailleret 59 F6, 60 F1
Cailleret Dessus, les 61 F3
Cailleret, en 61 F4
Cailleret, le 60 F3
Caillerie, la 118 B2
Cailles, les 64 F5
Caillettes, les 63 F3
Cain Cellars 259 D2
Caiolo 177 B3
Cairanne 129 D4, 131 B4
Cakebread 259 E4
Calafell 205 F3
Calafia 259 F6
Calahorra 203 C3
Calais Estates 278 C5
Calamin 220 A6
Calatayud 197 B4
Calcinaia 189 D4
Caldaro (Kalterer) 184 G6, 185 A3
Caldaro (Kaltern) 185 D5
Caldas da Rainha 208 D3
Caldelas 215 B5
Calderin 201 E2
Caledon 290 G3
Calera 263 E4
Calero 201 C3
Calheta 216 C6
Calistoga 259 B2
Caliterra 297 E4
Calitzdorp 290 F5
Callaghan Vyds 269 D3
Callahan Ridge 271 F2
Callatoota Estate 279 F4
Callaway Winery 269 D2
Callezuela 200 A5
Calliano 184 E5
Calotta 275 B3
Calouère 66 E4
Caltagirone 195 G3
Caltanissetta 195 F3
Calulu Park 281 C6
Calvi 140 E4
Calvignano 177 F4
Camacha 217 C4
Câmara de Lobos 217 D2
Camaret-sur-Aigues 131 D3
Camas 271 C3, 273 B6
Cambrai 284 E3
Cambria 265 E4
Cambridge 275 B6
Cambrils de Mar 205 G1
Camden, *Australia* 277 B6
Camden, *USA* 275 D4
Caminha 215 A4
Campalli 189 F4
Campanário 217 C2
Campanhã, Qta de 210 F1
Campbells 280 C5
Camperdown 280 G1
Campidano di Terralba 195 D1
Campillos 207 C4
Campix 200 D6
Camp Meeker 255 E4
Campobasso 195 B3
Campo de Borja 197 B4
Campo de Cartagena 197 D5
Campo di Carne 193 F4
Campo lèmini 193 F4
Campoleone 193 E4
Campomaggio 189 E4
Campoverde 193 F5
Campsegret 109 A6
Camus 110 G5
Canais, Qta dos 211 F4
Canakkale 243 B1
Canal, Qta do 210 G2
Cañamero 197 C3
Canandaigua 275 B3
Canariera, La 201 C4
Canberra 277 C5
Canby 271 D3, 273 C5
Candia dei Colli Apuani 173 F6, 179 F1
Cane End 298 F4
Canéjean 96 D3
Canelones 294 F2
Canepa 297 A5
Canet, Champ 60 F4
Canet-en-Roussillon 133 F5
Canevino 177 G5
Cangas de Narcea 197 A2
Cangé 118 D5
Cangzhou 246 C3
Canhas 216 C6
Caniçal 217 B5
Caniço 217 D4
Canière, la 59 G6, 60 G1
Cannonau di Sardegna 195 D2
Cannubi 176 F2
Canon-Fronsac 102 C5
Canonja, La 205 F2
Cantanhede 214 G4
Cantarranas 201 D2
Canteloup 99 C4
Cantenac 95 C4
Canterayne Cave Coop. 89 C2
Canterbury 288 E3
Canton 275 C2
Cantonade 131 G1
Canyelles 205 F4
Canyonville 271 F2
Cáorle 181 D4
Caparone 265 B3
Capçanes 204 G6
Cap Corse 140 D5
Cape Barren Island 287 F6
Cape Clairault 287 C2
Cape Horn 273 B6
Capel Vale 286 E1
Cape Mentelle 287 E1
Cape Town (Kaapstad) 290 F1
Capirete 201 C4
Capitan 265 G5
Caplane 101 F3
Caplong 109 B4
Capo Rizzuto 195 E5
Capri 195 C3
Capriano del Colle 173 D6, 179 D1
Caprino Veronese 182 E3
Capriva del Friuli 183 C5
Cap Rock Winery 269 D5
Caradeux, en 63 D4
Carano 193 F5
Carbon-Blanc 96 C4
Carbonup Estate 287 C1
Carcassonne 133 C2, 138 E4
Carcassonne, Cité de 138 E4
Carcavelos 208 D3, 209 F4
Cardazzo 177 E6
Carden Park 298 E3
Cardeuse, la 59 G5
Carelles Dessous 61 F4
Carelle-sous la Chapelle 61 F4
Carema 173 D3
Carey 265 F5
Carignano del Sulcis 195 E1
Cariñena 197 B4
Carlton 273 C4
Carne 205 E3
Carmel 263 F3
Carmel Valley 263 F3
Carmen, El 201 C4
Carmenet 254 F5
Carmignano 187 A3
Carmo, Qta do 213 D5
Carmo, Snr do 210 F4
Carnaxide 209 F5
Cameros Creek 257 E5
Cameros, Dom. 257 E5
Cameros, Los 257 E5
Carnuntum 222 F4
Ca'ronesca-Ipplis 183 B4
Carougeot 67 F1
Carpentras 129 D5, 131 F5, 139 B3
Carquefou 114 B3
Carquelin, le 72 C5
Carrascal 200 C4, 201 C4
Carregal do Sal 215 F5
Carreña, La 201 B3
Carré Rougeaud, le 67 F2
Carrés, les 67 F3
Carretey, le Grand 101 A4
Carrières, les 66 F3
Carr Taylor 298 F5

Carruades de Lafite 89 B4
Cars 108 D2
Carso 179 C6
Cartagena 295 B2
Carta Vieja 297 G3
Cartaxo 208 D4
Carthage 245 A6
Carvalhas, Qta das 210 F5
Carvalheira, Qta da 210 F6
Casa Nuestra 259 B5
Casablanca, *Chile* 297 A4
Casablanca, *Morocco* 245 B2
Casabon 201 D2
Casale Monferrato 175 A5
Casalino 189 F4
Casape 193 C6
Cascadia 273 E5
Cascina Francia 176 G3
Cascina San Lorenzo 193 F4
Casenuove 189 D4
Caserio Tabajete 201 B2
Caserta 195 B3
Casmalia 265 E4
Cassan 138 D6
Cassereau, le 118 A3
Casse-Têtes, les 61 F1
Cassière, la 59 E3
Cassiers, les 119 F4
Cassis 136 C1
Castá 230 G3
Castanet 113 D6
Castedo 211 D1
Castéggio 177 F4
Castel del Monte 195 B4
Castèl Gandolfo 193 E4
Castèl Ginnetti 193 E6
Castelinho, Qta do 211 F2
Castell 166 B6
Castella, Le 193 F5
Castellammare 195 C3
Castellar del Vallès 205 E5
Castellbisba 205 E4
Castelldefels 205 F4
Casteller 179 C3, 184 G6
Castellet 205 F3
Castelli Grevepesa 189 C3
Castellina 189 E4
Castellina in Chianti 189 E4
Castell'in Villa 189 G5
Castello dell'Acqua 177 B4
Castello di Cerreto 189 G5
Castello di Montefioralle 189 D4
Castello di Nipozzano 189 A6
Castello di Rencine 189 F3
Castello di Uzzano 189 D4
Castello di Volpaia 189 E4
Castelloli 205 D3
Castellone, il 193 F6
Castellví de la Marca 205 F3
Castelnaudary 138 D3
Castelnau-d'Auzan 113 E2
Castelnau-le-Lez 135 B4
Castelnuovo Berardenga 189 G6
Castelnuovo di Verona 182 G3
Castelo Borges, Qta do 210 G4
Castelo Branco 208 C5
Castelo de Paiva 215 D5
Castelo Rodrigo 208 B5
Castel Oualou 130 F6
Castel Roubine 136 A4
Castelviel 97 E1
Castets 112 E6
Castets, les 60 D2
Castiglione 176 F2
Castiglione del Lago 192 C4
Castillo del Majuelo 201 C3
Castillo, El 201 C4
Castillon 110 G5
Castillon-la-Bataille 103 E6
Castione Andevenno 177 B2
Castle 298 F4
Castle Gap 279 E4
Castlemaine 277 D3, 280 E3
Castle Rock 279 E4
Castoro 265 B3
Castoro Cellars 265 C3
Castries 135 B4
Castro del Rio 207 A4
Caswell 255 E4
Catalan 138 F5
Catamarca 294 F1
Catánia 195 F4
Catanzaro 195 E5
Catignano 189 G4
Catllar, El 205 F2
Catoctin 275 D4
Catus 113 C4
Catusseau 103 C2, 107 E4
Caumette, Dom. de la 133 B6, 135 D1
Cauquenes 295 D2
Caussan 85 E3
Caux Pézenas 138 D6
Cavadinha, Qta da 210 E5
Cavaillon 129 E5, 139 C3
Cavaion Veronese 182 F3
Cave 193 D6
Cavédine 184 D4
Cave Junction 271 G2
Cave, la 61 E4
Cave Spring 275 B3
Cavriglia 189 E5
Caymus 259 D4
Cayucos 265 C2
Cazaiac 241 G5
Cazaubon 113 E2
Cazes, Dom. 133 F4
Cazetiers, les 67 E2
Cazetiers, Petits 67 E2
Cazouls-les-Béziers 133 B5, 135 C1
Cazzano di Tramigna 183 G1
Cebreros 197 C3
Cecchina 193 E4
Cedrasco 177 B2
Cèggia 181 D3
Cegléd 226 F4
Celeirós 210 D5
Celigny 220 B4
Cellatica 173 D6, 179 C1
Celle, la 136 B3
Cellier aux Moines 68 D4
Cellier des Templiers 133 G5
Cellier Le Brun 289 G3
Cellier, Sous le 61 E3
Celorico de Basto 215 C6
Cembra 184 B6, 185 G5
Cenon 80 E3, 96 C4
Centralia 271 B2
Central Otago 288 E3
Central Point 271 G2
Cents Vignes, les 62 E5
Cerasuolo di Vittoria 195 G3
Cerbère 133 G5
Cercié 71 D3, 72 F4
Cercot 68 E3
Cercueils, les 67 F1
Ceres, *S. Africa* 290 F2
Ceres, *USA* 267 C3
Céret 133 G3, 138 G5
Ceretta 176 F2
Cerhov 230 G6
Cerignola 195 B4
Cerna 189 F3
Cernay 120 G3
Cérons 80 F4, 96 F6
Cerro de Santiago 201 C3
Cerro Pelado 201 C2
Cerro Viejo, El 201 D3
Certaldo 189 D1
Cerveteri 187 E3
Cervignano 181 C5
Cesanese del Piglio 187 F4, 195 B2
Cesanese di Affile 187 F4, 195 A2
Cesanese di Olevano Romano 187 F4, 195 B2
Ceske Budejovice 230 F2
Cessenon 138 D5
Cessnock 277 A6, 278 D5
Cestas 80 F2, 96 E3
Cestayrols 113 D6
Cetto, L A 269 D2
Ceuta 245 B2
Cévennes 139 C2
Chabiots, les 66 F2
Chablais 219 F2, 221 B2
Chablis 55 A3, 73 E5, 75 D4
Chaboeufs, les 64 F6
Chacolí de Guetaria 197 A4
Chada 297 B6
Chaddsford 275 D4
Chaffee 272 G5
Chaffots, les 66 E4
Chagny 55 D5, 57 G3, 68 A4
Chaignots, aux 65 F3
Chailles 115 B2
Chaillots, les 63 F4
Chaînes Carteaux 64 F5
Chainey, le 59 D2
Chaintré 55 F5, 69 G4
Chalandins, les 65 G3
Chaliots, les 64 G6
Chalk Hill, *Australia* 284 D2
Chalk Hill, *USA* 255 D5
Chalone 263 F5
Chalonnes-sur-Loire 114 B4
Châlons-sur-Marne 76 C5
Chalon-sur-Saône 55 D5
Chalumeaux, les 60 F4
Chamard 275 C5
Chambers Rosewood 280 C5
Chambertin 66 E6
Chambertin Clos de Bèze 66 E6
Chambery, *Pessac Léognan* 99 D4
Chambéry, *Savoie* 137 C2
Chambolle-Musigny 55 C6, 57 C5, 66 E2
Chambost-Allières 71 E2
Chambraste 119 F3
Chambres, les 60 G2
Chamery 79 B3
Chamirey 68 C3
Chamisal 265 D3
Chamonix 293 G6
Chamoson 221 C3
Champagne de Savigny 62 F6
Champans, en 61 F4
Champeaux 67 E2
Champerrier du Bas 67 F2
Champerrier du Dessus 67 E2
Champéry 221 C1
Champigny 114 C6
Champillon 79 D3
Champlains, les 68 D4
Champlots, les 60 E3
Champonnet 67 E1
Champs, En 67 E2
Champs Fulliot, les 61 F3
Champs, les Grands 61 F5
Champs Pimonts 62 F4
Champ-sur-Layon, le 116 E4
Champtin 119 F2
Champtoceaux 114 B3
Chamusça 208 D4
Chanay 137 B2
Chançay 118 A5
Chanceleiros 210 F4
Chanco 295 D1
Chancy 220 D3
Chandler 272 G5
Chandlers Hill 284 C3
Chandon, Dom., *Australia* 281 B5
Chandon, Dom., *USA* 259 E4
Chânes 69 G4, 71 B4
Chanière, la 61 E6, 62 D1
Chaniot, au 60 F4
Chanlin 61 E5
Chanlins-Bas, les 61 E5
Chanlins-Hauts, les 61 E5
Channing Rudd 256 D6
Chanoriers, les 72 A4
Chantada 197 A2
Chante Alouette 127 C4
Chapel Hill 284 D2
Chapelle-Basse-Mer, la 115 E5
Chapelle Chambertin 66 F6
Chapelle-de-Guinchay, La- 71 B4
Chapelle des Bois 72 C4
Chapelle-Heulin, la 115 F5
Chapelle, la 127 B4
Chapelle, Petite 66 F6
Chapelle Reugne, la 61 E2
Chapelle-sur-Erdre, la 114 B3
Chapelle-sur-Loire, la 117 D3
Chapelle-Vaupelteigne, la 75 B2
Chapelot 75 D4
Chapître, Clos du 67 E2
Chapitre, le 118 C4
Chaponnières, les 61 F5
Chappellet 259 D5
Charbonnières 69 D5
Charbonnières, les 64 F4
Chardannes, les 66 F3
Chardonnay 69 A6
Chardonne 221 A1
Chardonnereux, les 62 G3
Chardons, aux Champs 63 E2
Chareau, Clos 59 G5
Charentais 139 B4
Charentay 71 D3, 72 G4
Charles Cimicky 282 C3
Charles F Shaw 259 C3
Charles Krug 259 C3
Charles Melton 282 C4
Charleston 275 E2
Charlottesville 275 E3
Charlton 280 D2
Charmes, aux 66 F5
Charmes Chambertin 66 F6
Charmes Dessous, les, *Santenay* 59 E2
Charmes-Dessous, les, *Meursault* 60 G5
Charmes-Dessus, les 60 G5
Charmes, les, *Chambolle* 66 F2
Charmes, les, *Puligny* 60 G5
Charmes, les Champs des 67 F3
Charmois, le 60 F2
Charmois, les 65 F1
Charmots, les 62 E1
Charmotte, la 65 F2
Charmotte, la Petite 65 F2
Charnay-lès-Mâcon 69 F4
Charneca 209 D6
Charnières, les 63 D2
Charolles 55 E4
Charondo, Qta do 210 F6
Charpignat 137 C2
Charrat 221 D2
Charreux 67 F2
Charrières, les, *Chassagne* 60 G2
Charrières, les, *Morey St-Denis* 66 F5
Charron, en 59 D3
Charrons, les Grands 61 F1
Charrons, les Petits 61 F1
Chassagne 59 F6, 60 F2
Chassagne du Clos St-Jean 60 F1
Chassagne-Montrachet 55 D5, 60 G2
Chasseignes, les 119 E3
Chasselas 69 F3
Chasselay 71 G4
Châtain 103 B3
Châtains 75 E2

Château

Abbaye-Skinner, de l' 87 E2
Abbé-Gorsse de Gorsse, L' 95 A2
Agassac, d' 95 G6
Aiguille, d' 103 C6
Alberts, les 108 B2
Alesme, d' 95 B2
Amon, le 280 E3
Andron-Blanquet 87 G4
Aney 93 C5
Angélus, l' 105 D3
Angludet, d' 95 D3
Annereaux, des 103A1, 107A2
Anseillan 87 G5, 89 A5

Château

Aquería, d' 130 G6
Arche, d', *Margaux* 95 F6
Arche, d', *Sauternes* 101 F3
Arche-Lafaurie, d' 101 F3
Arche-Pugneau, d' 101 E4
Arche-Vimeney, d' 101 F3
Armailhac, d' 89 B5
Arnauton 102 B6
Arrosée, l' 105 E4
Aubépin, l' 101 F3
Augey, d' 101 D4
Ausone 103 D3, 105 D4
Badon 103 D3
Balestard-la-Tonnelle 105 D5
Barbé 108 D2
Barbe Blanche, de 103 A5
Barbe, de 108 E2
Barbeyrolles 136 C5
Baret 99 C4
Barette 101 F4
Barker 286 G4
Barrails, les 103 B6
Barreyres 93 E6
Basque, le 103 B5
Bastienne, la 103 B3
Bastor Lamontagne 101 D5
Batailley 89 E4
Bayard 103 C4
Beaucastel, de 131 E2
Beaulac-Dodijos 101 C4
Beaulieu 108 F3
Beaumont, de 108 E2
Beauregard 107 E4
Beau-Séjour 103 C5
Beauséjour, *Montagne* 103 B4
Beauséjour, *St-Emilion* 103 D3
Beauséjour, *St-Estèphe* 87 E5
Beau Séjour Bécot 105 D4
Beauséjour Duffau-Lagarosse 105 D4
Beauséjour-Picard 87 E4
Beau-Site 87 D4
Beau-Site Haut-Vignoble 87 D4
Bécade, la 93 D2
Bédou, le 108 D2
Belair, *Blaye* 108 C2
Belair, *St-Emilion* 103 D3,105 D4
BelAir, *Bourg* 108 F3
Bel-Air, *Lussac* 103 A5
Bel-Air, *Puisseguin* 103 C5
Bel-Air, *Pomerol* 107 D3
Bel-Air, de 103 B1, 107 B3
Bel-Air-Marquis-d'Aligre 95 B1
Belgrave 91 D3
Belingard 109 D4
Bellefont-Belcier 103 D3, 105 E5
Bellegrave, *Bas-Médoc* 85 A2
Bellegrave, *Pauillac* 89 E5
Bellerive 85 A3
Bellerose 89 B5
Belles-Graves 103 B2, 107 C5
Bellevue, *Blaye* 108 E2
Bellevue, *Pomerol* 107 D3
Bellevue, *St-Emilion* 105 D3
Bellevue, de, *Beaujolais* 72 D4
Bellevue, de, *Montagne* 103 B4
Bel-Orme Tronquoy-de-Lalande 87 B4
Benoit 273 C4
Bergat 105 D5
Berliquet 105 D4
Berthou 108 F3
Bertineau de St-Vincent 103 B3
Beychevelle 91 D5
Beyzac 87 E3
Bianca 273 C4
Bidou 108 E2
Binet 103 C5
Biston-Brillette 93 G3
Blaignan 85 E4
Blanzac 103 E6
Blissa 108 F3
Bodet 102 C6
Boldos de Santa Amalia, Los 297 C5
Bonalgue 107 E2
Bondieu, le 109 D3
Bonneau 103 C4
Bonneau-Livran 87 C4
Bon Pasteur, le 107 D6
Boscq, le, *Bas-Médoc* 85 C5
Boscq, le, *St-Estèphe* 87 D4
Boswell 259 B5
Boulay, du 118 D6
Bourdieu 108 C2
Bourdieu, le, *Bas-Médoc* 85 B3
Bourdieu, le, *St-Estèphe* 87 F2
Bourgneuf-Vayron 107 D3
Bourgueneuf, de 107 D3
Bournac 85 D3
Bourseau 103 B1, 107 A4
Bouscaut 99 E5
Bousquet, du 108 F4
Bouyot, du 101 B4
Boyd-Cantenac 95 C4
Branaire-Ducru 91 D5
Brane-Cantenac 95 C3
Brégançon, de 136 C4
Brehot 103 D5
Breuil, du 87 G3

Château

Briante, de 72 F4
Bridane, la 91 C5
Brillette 93 F3
Brousseau 103 E4
Broustet 101 B4
Brown-Léognan 99 D3
Brûlesécailles 108 F4
By, de 85 C4
Cabanne, la 107 D4
Cadet-Bon 105 C5
Cadet-Piola 103 D3, 105 C4
Caillavel 109 D4
Caillou 101 B3
Caillou, le, *Bergerac* 109 D4
Caillou, le, *Bourg* 108 G4
Caillou, le, *Pomerol* 107 E4
Calon 103 B4
Calon-Ségur 87 D5
Cambon la-Pelouse 95 E4
Camensac 91 D3
Cameron 101 E3
Camperos 101 B4
Canon, *Canon-Fronsac* 102 C5
Canon, *St-Emilion* 103 D3, 105 D4
Canon-Chagneau 103 B3
Canon de Brem 102 C6
Canon-la-Gaffelière 105 E4
Cantegril 101 B4
Cantegrive 103 B6
Cantelaude 95 D4
Canteloup, *Bas-Médoc* 85 E4
Canteloup, *St-Estèphe* 87 E5
Cantemerle 95 E5
Cantenac-Brown 95 C2
Cantereau 107 D3
Cantin 103 D5
Canuet 95 B2
Capbern Gasqueton 87 D5
Cap de Faugères 103 D5
Cap de Haut 93 D6
Capdelong 91 C5
Cap-de-Mourlin 105 C5
Capet-Guillier 103 E4
Capitans, des 72 A5
Carbonnieux 99 E4
Cardonne, la 85 F3
Carelle, la 108 C2
Carles, de 102 A6
Carne 105 A4
Carte et le Chatelet, la 105 D4
Caruel 108 G3
Cassat 103 C5
Castelot, le 103 D3
Castel Viaud 103 B1, 107 A3
Castera, du 85 F4
Cause, le 103 D4
Cazals Viel 133 B5, 135 C1
Cazenove, de 133 F4
Certan de May 107 D5
Certan Giraud 107 D5
Certan, Vieux 107 D5
Chadène 102 B5
Chais, le 103 C5
Chaize, de la 72 G3
Chambert-Marbuzet 87 F5
Chantegrive 103 E3
Chapelle de Lescourts, la 103 D2
Chapelle-Madeleine 105 D4
Charmail 87 C4
Charmes, des 275 B3
Charron 108 C1
Chaumes, les 108 B2
Chauvin 103 C3, 105 B3
Chêne-Vieux 103 C5
Chesnaye, la 93 B4
Cheval Blanc 103 C2, 105 B2, 107 E5
Chevre 259 F5
Chevrol Bel Air 103 B2
Christoly 108 G5
Cissac 87 G2
Citadelle, de la 108 G3
Civrac 108 F3
Clare, la 85 C3
Clarière Laithwaite, la 103 D5
Clarke 93 F2
Clauzet 87 F4
Clerc-Milon 89 B5
Climens 101 C4
Clinet 107 D4
Cloquet, Vieux 107 C3
Clos de l'Oratoire 105 C5
Clos des Jacobins 103 C3
Clos Maisières 103 E6
Clotte Blanche, la 108 G3
Clotte, la 105 D5
Clusière, la 105 E5
Combrillac 109 D4
Commanderie, de la 103 A2
Commanderie, la, *Pomerol* 107 F3
Commanderie, la, *St-Estèphe* 87 F4
Condamine Bertrand, la 135 C2
Cones-Sebizeaux, les 108 D1
Conseillante, la 103 C2, 105 A2, 107 E5
Corbin 103 B3, 105 B3
Corbin-Michotte 105 B3
Cordeillan-Bages 89 D5

Château

Cos d'Estournel 87 G5, 89 A5
Cos Labory 87 G5, 89 A4
Côte Haut-Brion, la 99 A2
Coubet 108 E2
Coucheroy 99 E4
Coucy 103 C5
Coufran 87 B4
Couhins 99 D5
Couronne, la 89 E4, 91 B4
Court les Mûts 109 D3
Couspaude, la 105 D5
Coustolle 102 B6
Coutelin-Merville 87 F3
Coutet, *Barsac* 101 B4
Coutet, *St-Emilion* 105 D3
Couvent des Jacobins 105 D5
Crock, le 87 F5
Croix Bigorre 103 C6
Croix-de-Gay, la 107 D5
Croix-du-Casse, la 107 E3
Croix, la, *Fronsac* 102 B6
Croix, la, *Lalande-de-Pomerol* 103 B2
Croix, la, *Pomerol* 107 E4
Croix Landon, la 85 D3
Croix-Millorit, de la 108 F2
Croix St-Georges, la 107 E4
Croix Taillefer, la 107 F4
Croizet-Bages 89 D5
Croque Michotte 103 C2, 105 A3, 107 E6
Croûte Charlus 108 G4
Croûte Courpon 108 G4
Cruzeau 103 C1
Cruzelles, les 103 B2, 107 B5
Curebéasse, de 136 B5
Curé Bon la Madeleine 105 D4
Dalem 102 A6
Dassault 105 C5
Dauphine, de la 102 C6
Dauzac 95 D5
Dauzay, de 117 F3
Debaun 255 D5
Désert, le 99 E4
Desmirail 95 C3
Destieux 103 D4
Deyrem-Valentin 95 A2
Dian 93 C5
Doisy-Daëne 101 C4
Doisy-Dubroca 101 C3
Doisy-Védrines 101 C4
Dominique, la 105 B3, 107 E6
Dorrien 282 B4
Douglas 279 D6
Doumayne 103 C1
Ducru-Beaucaillou 91 D5
Dudon 101 B4
Duhart-Milon Rothschild 87 G4, 89 A4
Duplessis Fabre 93 G2
Durfort-Vivens 95 B3
Eglise-Clinet, l' 107 D4
Enclos, l' 107 C3
Escadre, l' 108 D2
Estang, de l' 103 C6
Evangile, l' 103 C2, 105 A2, 107 D5
Eyquem 108 F2
Eyquems, les 108 F5
Fabas 133 C2
Falfas 108 F3
Fargues, de 101 G6
Fatin 87 E5
Faures, des 103 B6
Faurie-de-Souchard 105 C5
Ferrade, la 99 B4
Ferran 99 G6
Ferrand 107 F3
Ferrand, de 103 D4
Ferrasse, *Castillon* 103 E6
Ferrasse, *St-Etienne* 103 E5
Ferrière 95 B2
Feytit-Clinet 107 C4
Fieuzal, de 99 G3
Figeac 103 C2, 105 B2
Filhot 101 G3
Fines Roches, des 131 F2
Fleur du Roy, la 103 C2, 107 F4
Fleurie, de 72 C5
Fleur-Milon, la 89 B5
Fleur-Pétrus, la 103 B2, 107 D5
Fleur-Pourret, la- 105 C4
Flojague, de 103 D6
Fombrauge 103 D4
Fonbadet 89 E5
Fongaban 103 B6
Fonplégade 105 E4
Fonroque 103 C3, 105 C4
Fontaine, la 102 B6
Font de Loup, de la 131 F3
Font-Petite 87 F5
Fortia 131 F2
Fougas 108 F4
Fourcas-Hosten 93 F2
Fournas Bernadotte, le 89 D3
Fournas, le 89 D2
Fourney 103 E4
France, de 99 G3
France, la 85 E3
Francois 278 C4
Franc-Maillet 107 D6

Château

Franc-Mayne 105 C3
Frank 275 B4
Gaby, du 102 C6
Gaffelière, la 103 D3, 105 E4
Gaillardet 103 E6
Gallant 271 C6
Galoupet, de 136 C4
Garcinières, des 136 C5
Garde, la, *Blaye* 108 C2
Garde, la, *Martillac* 99 G6
Gardine, de la 131 F2
Gardiole, la Grande 131 E2
Garëlle, la 103 E3
Garraud 103 B3
Gay, le 103 B2, 107 D5
Gazin, *Blaye* 108 E2
Gazin, *Fronsac* 102 B5
Gazin, *Léognan* 99 F2
Gazin, *Pomerol* 107 D6
Gilet Bayard 103 C4
Gilette 101 C6
Gironville 95 D5
Gironville, de 95 F5
Giscours 95 D4
Glana, du 91 D5
Gloria 91 D5
Gombaude-Guillot 107 D3
Gontet 103 C5
Gontier 108 D1
Gorce, la 85 E4
Goujon 103 B2
Gourgazaud, de 133 B3
Grand Barrail-Lamarzelle Figeac (Hôtel) 105 C2
Grand-Bigaroux 103 D3
Grand Corbin, de 105 B4
Grand Corbin Despagne 105 A3
Grand-Corbin-Manuel 105 A4
Grandes-Murailles 105 D4
Grandis 87 C4
Grand-Jour 108 G5
Grand-Mayne 103 D3, 105 C3
Grand Mazerolle, le 108 C2
Grand Moulin, *Bas-Médoc* 85 F5
Grand Moulin, *Corbières* 133 C4
Grand-Moulinet 107 C3
Grand Ormeau 107 B5
Grand Pontet 105 C4
Grand Poujeaux 93 E4
Grand-Puy-Ducasse 89 D6
Grand-Puy-Lacoste 89 D4
Grand Soussans, du 93 F6
Grand Tuillac 103 C6
Grange de Lescure, la 103 F2
Grange-Neuve, de 107 D3
Granges d'Or, les 85 D4
Grate-Cap 107 E4
Graulet 108 D2
Graulet, la 108 E2
Gravas 101 C4
Grave, de la 108 F3
Grave Figeac, la 105 A2
Gravet 103 D2
Grave Trigant de Boisset, la 107 C4
Greysac 85 B4
Grézan, de 133 A5, 135 C1
Grillet 126 D2
Grillon 101 C4
Grivière, la 85 E3
Gros Moulin 108 G4
Gruaud-Larose 91 D4
Guadet St-Julien 105 D5
Guerry 108 F4
Gueyrosse 103 D1
Guibeau 103 B6
Guillemot 103 D4
Guillotin 103 C5
Guillou 103 C3
Guionne 108 F4
Guiraud 101 G4
Guiraud, le 108 E2
Guitard 103 B4
Guiteronde 101 C3
Guitignan 93 F3
Hallet 101 B4
Hannetot, le 99 E4
Hanteillan 87 F3
Haut-Bages-Averous 89 D5
Haut-Bages-Libéral 89 E5
Haut-Bages-Monpelou 89 D4
Haut-Bailly 99 F4
Haut-Ballet 103 B3
Haut-Batailley 89 F4, 91 B3
Haut-Bergey 99 F3
Haut-Bernon 103 B5
Haut-Bommes 101 F3
Haut-Breton-Larigaudière 95 A1
Haut-Brion 99 A2
Haut-Corbin 105 A4
Haute-Fauchene 103 B3
Hauterive 85 G4
Haut-Gardère 99 G3
Haut Madère 99 C4
Haut-Madrac 89 D3
Haut-Maillet 107 D6
Haut-Marbuzet 87 F5
Haut-Nouchet 99 G6
Haut Piquat 103 B4
Haut-Sarpe 103 D4, 105 D5
Haye, la 87 F4

Château
Heaumes, les 108 E2
Hère, le 101 F3
Hontemieux 85 E4
Hortevie 91 D5
Houissant 87 F5
Hourbanon 85 F2
Hourtin-Ducasse 89 D3
Hourtou 108 F4
Hoyt Beauséjour 103 E5
Huchat, 102 B5
Issan, d' 95 B3
Jacobins, Clos des 105 C3
Jacques-Blanc 103 E4
Jappe-Loup 103 D5
Jarousse, la 103 C6
Jaubertie, de la 109 D4
Jau, de 133 E4
Jean-Blanc 103 E4
Jeandeman 102 B6
Jean-Faure 105 B3
Jean Loron, de 72 B6
Jouans, les 103 E2
Julien 263 F3
Juliénas, de 72 A5
Junayme 102 C6
Kefraya 243 E5
Kirwan 95 C3
Labarde 108 F4
Labégorce 95 A2
Labégorce-Zédé 95 A2
Laborde 103 A1
Labrède 108 F4
Labrousse 108 C1
Lacoste 103 B5
Lafaurie-Peyraguey 101 F3
Laffitte-Carcasset 87 E4
Lafite-Rothschild 87 G5, 89 A5
Lafitte Cante Loup 95 G5
Lafleur 103 B2, 107 D5
Lafleur-Gazin 107 D5
Lafon, *Bas-Médoc* 85 E3
Lafon, *Sauternes* 101 F4
Lafon-Rochet 87 G4, 89 A4
Lagrange, *Pomerol* 107 D5
Lagrange, *St-Julien* 91 D3
Lagüe 102 C6
Lagune, la 95 F5
Lagurgue 95 B2
Lalande-Borie 91 D4
Lalibarde 108 F3
Lamarque, de 93 D5
Lamarzelle 105 C2
Lamothe, *Bourg* 108 F4
Lamothe, *Sauternes* 101 G3
Lamothe Bouscaut 99 E5
Lamothe-Cissac 87 G2
Lamothe-Guignard 101 G3
Lamourette 101 F3
Lamouroux, de 95 B2
Landat 87 F2
Lanessan 91 E4
Langlade 103 C4
Langoa-Barton 91 C5
Laniote 105 C4
Lapelletrie 103 D4, 105 D6
Lapeyronie 103 E6
Larcis-Ducasse 103 D3, 105 E5
Larmande 105 C5
Larose-Trintaudon 91 C3
Laroze 105 C3
Larrivaux 87 G3
Larrivet Haut-Brion 99 F4
Lartigue 87 F5
Lascombes 95 B2
Lassègue 103 D4
Latour 89 F6, 91 B5
Latour à Pomerol 103 B2, 107 C4
Latour-Gayet 108 B2
Latour Haut-Brion 99 A3
Latour Martillac 99 G6
Laujac 85 C1
Launay 108 E3
Laurensanne 108 F3
Laurets, des 103 C5
Laussac 103 E6
Lavergnotte 103 E6
Laville Haut-Brion 99 A3
Lavillotte 87 E3
Lavinot-la-Chapelle 103 B3
Léoville-Barton 91 C5
Léoville-Las-Cases 91 C5
Léoville-Poyferré 91 C5
Lescaneaut, de 103 F6
Lescours 103 D2
Lestage 103 C5
Lestage-Simon 87 C4
Lieujan 89 D2
Ligondras 95 D2
Lilian Ladouys 87 G4
Lionnat 103 B5
Liot 101 C4
Liversan 89 C2
Livran 85 G3
Lorane 271 F2
Loudenne 85 E6, 87 A4
Loumède 108 D3
Louvière, la 99 E4
Lucas 103 B5
Ludon Pommiès-Agassac 95 G6
Lumière 248 D4

Château
Lussac 103 B5
Lynch-Bages 89 D6
Lynch-Moussas 89 D3
Macau 108 F5
MacCarthy Moula 87 F5
Magdelaine 103 D3, 105 D4
Maison Blanche 103 B3
Malangin 103 C5
Malartic-Lagravière 99 F3
Malescot St-Exupéry 95 B3
Malle, de 101 D6
Malleprat 99 F6
Malleret, de 95 G4
Manissy, de 130 G6
Marbuzet, de 87 F5
Marchand 103 B4
Marèchaude, la 103 B2, 107 B4
Margaux 95 B3
Marquis de Terme 95 B2
Marsac Séguineau 95 A2
Martinens 95 C2
Martinet 103 D1
Matras 105 D4
Maucaillou 93 E4
Maucamps 95 E6
Maucoil 131 E2
Mauras 101 E3
Maurens 103 D4
Mausse, le 102 B5
Mauvanne, de 136 C4
Mauvezin 105 C5
Mayne-Blanc 103 A5
Mayne, du, *Barsac* 101 B4
Mayne, du, *Preignac* 101 D4
Mayne, le 103 C5
Mayne-Vieil, le 102 A6
Mazeris 102 B5
Mazeyres 107 D2
Mazeyres, Clos 107 D1
Ménaudat, le 108 B1
Mendoce 108 E2
Menota, de 101 B4
Meyney 87 E5
Meynieu, le 87 E2
Miaudoux, les 109 D3
Michel-de-Montaigne 109 D3
Milhau-Lacugue 133 B5, 134 C6
Mille Secousses, de 108 G4
Minière 117 D3
Minuty 136 C5
Mission Haut-Brion, la 99 A3
Moines, des 103 A2
Monbadon, de 103 B6
Monbazillac, de 109 D4
Monbousquet 103 E3
Monbrison 95 E2
Moncets 103 A2
Monconseil 108 E2
Mondou 103 D3
Montaiguillon 103 C3
Montbrun 95 B3
Montelena 259 B1
Monthil 85 B2
Montlabert 105 B3
Montmarin, de 133 B6, 135 D2
Montmirail, de 131 D5
Montrose 87 F5
Morin 87 D4
Mouleyre, la 103 D5
Moulin-à-Vent, *Listrac-Médoc* 93 G1
Moulin à Vent, *Pomerol* 103 B2, 107 C5
Moulin-Blanc, *Néac* 103 B3
Moulin Blanc, *Lussac* 103 B5
Moulin-de-Cadet 105 C4
Moulin-de-Castillon 85 D5
Moulin de Courrech 103 B6
Moulin-de-la-Rose 91 D5, 93 A4
Moulin des Laurets 103 C5
Moulinet 107 B3
Moulin Pey-Labrie 102 B5
Moulin-Riche 91 C3
Moulin Rompu, le 108 G3
Moulin Rouge, du 93 B4
Moulin St-Georges 105 D4
Moulins de Calon 103 B4
Mouton-Rothschild 89 B5
Musar 243 E5
Musset, *Pomerol* 103 A2
Musset, *Montagne* 103 C4
Myrat 101 B4
Nairac 101 A4
Négrit 103 B3
Nenin 103 C2, 107 E3
Nerthe, de la 131 F2
Nervers, de 72 G4
Nodot 108 F3
Nodoz 108 F4
Notton-Baury 95 D3
Nouvelles, de, *Corbières* 133 E3
Nouvelles, de, *Fitou* 133 E4
Nozay, de 119 E3
Nozet, du 119 F4
Olivier 99 E3
Ormeau, Grand 103 B2
Ormes-de-Pez, Les- 87 E4
Ormes Sorbet, les 85 D4

Château
Pabeau 85 F5
Pailhas 103 E4
Palmer 95 B3
Panigon 85 D2
Panisseau, de 109 D3
Pape Clément 99 A1
Pape, le 99 F4
Papetene, la 103 C2
Paradis, du 103 F4
Pardaillan 108 D2
Parsac 103 C5
Partarieu 101 F6
Patâche 107 C4
Patâche d'Aux 85 C3
Pavie 103 D3, 105 E5
Pavie-Décesse 105 E5
Pavie-Macquin 105 D5, E5
Paynal, le 109 D3
Pech-Celeyran 133 C5, 135 D1
Pedesclaux 89 B5
Peillan, le 103 E3
Peillon-Claverie 101 G5
Perenne 108 C2
Pernaud 101 C4
Pernère, la 103 B5
Perron 103 B2, 107 A4
Perruchon 103 A5
Petit Bigaroux 103 E3
Petit Faurie de Soutard 105 C5
Petit Gravet 103 D3
Petits Arnauds, les 108 D2
Petit-Village 103 C2, 107 E4
Pétrus 103 B2, 107 D5
Peychaud 108 E3
Peyguilhem 102 A6
Peymartin 91 C3
Peyrabon 89 C2
Peyredoulle 108 E2
Peyre-Lebade 93 F3
Peyron 101 G6
Peyroutas 103 E3
Pez, de 87 E4
Phélan Ségur 87 E5
Piada 101 C4
Pibran 89 C5
Picard 87 E5
Pichon-Longueville (Baron) 89 E5, 91 B4
Pichon-Longueville-Comtesse-de-Lalande 89 E5, 91 B4
Pick, du 101 D4
Pierrière, la 103 D6
Pierreux, de 72 G3
Pinet 108 D3
Pin, le 107 F4
Piot 101 C5
Pipeau, *Fronsac* 102 B5
Pipeau, *St-Laurent* 103 E4
Pique-Segue 109 D3
Plagnac 85 D3
Plain Point 102 B5
Plaisance 103 C3
Plantes, les 101 A5
Plantey, le 85 E5
Plantier-Rose 87 E4
Platanes, des 103 E5
Pleytegeat 101 E5
Plince 107 E3
Pointe, la 107 E3
Pomys 87 F4
Poncier, de 72 C5
Pontac-Lynch 95 B3
Pontac-Monplaisir 99 D5
Pont de Langon, du 99 D5
Pont de Pierre 103 A4
Pontet-Canet 89 C5
Pontet-Clauzure 105 C4
Pontoise-Cabarrus 87 C4
Pontus 102 B6
Potelle 259 F3
Potensac 85 F4
Pouget 95 C4
Poujeaux 93 E4
Pourney 99 D2
Poupille 103 D6
Pres, les 72 D4
Pressac, de 103 D5
Preuillac 85 F3
Prieuré-Lichine 95 C3
Prost 101 A5
Puy Arnaud 103 D6
Puy-Blanquet Camille 103 D4
Puy-Castéra 87 G3
Puy, le 103 C5
Queyron 103 E3
Quinault 103 D1
Rabaud-Promis 101 E4
Raissac, de 133 B5, 135 D1
Ramage la Batisse 89 B2
Rasclet 103 E3
Raspail 131 C5
Rausan-Ségla 95 B2
Raux, du 93 C5
Rauzan-Gassies 95 B2
Rayas, du 131 F2
Raymond-Lafon 101 E4
Rayne-Vigneau 101 F3
Réal Martin 136 B3
Remparts, les 101 D4
Remy 280 E2

Château
Rétout, du 93 D4
Rêve d'Or 107 C3
Rey, de 133 F4
Reynella 284 C2
Reysson 87 E2
Rèze, la 133 C3
Richards, les 108 E4
Richelieu 102 C6
Rieussec 101 F5
Rigaillou 99 D4
Rigaud 103 C5
Ripeau 103 C3, 105 B3
Rivereau 108 F4
Rivière, de la 102 B5
Robin 103 C4
Roc de Boissac, du 103 B5
Roc de Joanin 103 C6
Rochemorin 99 F5
Rocher Bellevue 103 E5
Rocher-Corbin 103 B3
Rochers, des 101 C5
Rocheyron 103 D4
Roland 87 G5, 89 A5
Rolland 101 B5
Romefort 93 D5
Romer-du-Hayot 101 E5
Roques, de 103 B5
Roudier 103 C4
Rouet 102 B5
Rouget 107 C4
Roumieu 101 C4
Rousselle 108 E2
Rousset 108 F3
Roux, de 136 B4
Rozay, du 126 C2
Rozier 103 D4
Ruat Petit-Poujeaux 93 G2
St-Amand 101 B5
St-André 103 B3
St-André Corbin 103 C3
St-Bonnet 85 C5
Ste-Marguerite 136 C4
Ste Michelle, *Seattle* 271 A3
Ste Michelle, *Yakima* 272 G4
Ste-Roseline 136 B5
St-Estèphe 87 F4
St-Georges 103 C4
St-Georges Côte Pavie 105 E4
St-Georges Macquin 103 C3
St-Germain 108 D2
St Jean, *Green Valley* 255 E5
St Jean, *Sonoma* 254 D4
St-Jean de Baron 103 F5
St-Martin, de 136 B4
St Maur 136 C5
St-Paul 87 C4
St-Philippe, de 103 C6
St-Pierre 91 D5, 93 A4
St-Saturnin 85 C3
St-Vincent 102 B5
Sales, de 103 B1, 107 B2
Salle, la 108 B1
Sanctuaire, le 103 B6
Sansonnet 105 D5
Saransot-du-Pré 93 E2
Sassay, de 117 G3
Sassenage (Mont-Jallon) 269 D4
Segonzac 108 C1
Ségriers, de 130 F5
Selle, de 136 B4
Semeillan-Mazeau 93 F1
Serre, la 105 D5
Siaurac 103 B3
Sigalas-Rabaud 101 E4
Signat 102 B5
Sigognac 85 E5
Simon 101 B4
Simone 136 B1
Sipian 85 B2
Siran 95 C5
Smith Haut-Lafitte 99 E5
Sociando-Mallet 87 C5
Soucarde 108 F3
Soudars 87 B4
Soutard 103 C3, 105 C5
Souverain 255 B4
Suau 101 B5
Suduiraut 101 E4
Surbezy-Cartier 133 D4
Tahbilk 280 D4
Tailhas, du 105 C1, 107 F4
Taillefer 103 C2, 107 F3
Talbot 91 C4
Tayac, *Bourg* 108 G2
Tayac, *Soussans* 93 G5
Temple, le 85 B2
Terrefort 95 D5
Terrey-Gros-Cailloux 91 D4
Tertre-Daugay 105 E3
Tertre, du 95 D2
Tessendey 102 B6
Teynac 91 D4
Teyssier 103 E3
Teyssier, le 103 B5
Thau, de 108 F2
Thivin 72 F4
Tiregand, de 109 D4
Touilla 101 E6
Toumalin 102 B6
Tourans 103 D4
Tour Bigorre 103 D6
Tour Blanche, la, *Bas-Médoc* 85 D5

Château
Tour-Blanche, la, *Sauternes* 101 F3
Tour-Carnet, la 91 D2
Tour de By, la 85 B4
Tour de Grenet 103 A5
Tour de Marbuzet 87 F5
Tour-de-Pez, La 87 E3
Tour de Ségur, la 103 A5
Tour des Termes 87 D4
Tour d'Horable 103 E6
Tour du Mirail, la 87 G2
Tour du Pin Figeac, la 103 C2, 105 B2, 107 E5
Tour-du-Roc 93 F5
Tour-Figeac, la 105 B2, 107 F4
Tour Fonrazade 105 D2
Tour Haut-Caussan 85 E3
Tour Léognan, la 99 E4
Tournefeuille 103 B2, 107 C6
Tour Pibran, la 89 C5
Tour-Prignac, la 85 E2
Tour St-Bonnet, la 85 C4
Tour St-Joseph 87 G2
Tours, des 103 C4
Tour Seran, la 85 C4
Tourteran 89 C2
Tracy, de 119 F4
Trapaud 103 D5
Treille des Girondins, la 103 E5
Trimoulet 103 C3, 105 B5
Trinquevèdel, de 130 G6
Trois Moulins 105 D4
Tronquoy-Lalande 87 E5
Troplong-Mondot 105 D5
Trotanoy 103 C2, 107 D4
Trotte Vieille 103 D3, 105 D5
Tuilerie, la 108 E3
Tuilière, la 108 F4
Valade, la 102 B6
Valoux 99 E5
Vaudieu, de 131 F2
Verdet 103 D1
Verdignan 87 B4
Vernon 103 C6
Vernous 85 F2
Vésinerie 103 C5
Veyrac 103 D5
Viaud, de 103 B1, 107 A3
Victoria 87 F3
Videlot 103 D1
Vieux Certan 103 C2
Vieux-Château-Landon 85 D3
Vieux Chênes, des 103 B4
Vieux Chevrol 103 B2, 107 B6
Vignelaure 136 A2
Villars 102 A6
Villemaurine 105 D5
Vincent 95 B3
Violette, la 107 D4
Vrai-Canon-Bouché 102 C5
Vrai-Canon-Boyer 102 C5
Vray-Croix-de-Gay 107 D5
Woltner 259 C3
Xanadu 287 E1
Yaldara 282 C3
Yon 103 C4
Yon-Figeac 103 C2, 105 C3
Yquem, d' 101 F4
Châteaubernard 110 D6
Château-Chalon 137 F5
Châteaumeillant 53 D3, 139 F2
Châteauneuf-du-Pape 129 D4
Châteaurenard 129 E4
Châteauthébaud 115 F4
Château-Thierry 76 B3
Châteauvert 136 A3
Chatelots, les 66 F3
Chatenay 72 C3
Chatenière, la 60 E3
Châtenois 120 C4
Châtillon 71 G3
Chatsfield 286 G4
Chaudefonds-sur-Layon 116 C2
Chaume 116 C3
Chaume de Talvat 75 F2
Chaumées, les 60 F2
Chaumes de Narvaux, les 60 F6
Chaumes des Casse-Têtes 61 F1
Chaumes et la Voierosse, les 63 E3
Chaumes, les, *Aloxe-Corton* 63 E3
Chaumes, les, *Chassagne* 59 G6, 60 G1
Chaumes, les, *Côte Chalonnaise* 68 D3
Chaumes, les, *Meursault* 60 F5
Chaumes, les, *Vosne-Romanée* 65 F4
Chaux, les 127 B6
Chavanay 126 F1
Chaves 208 A5
Chavignol 119 F2
Chazay-d'Azergues 71 G4
Chazière 67 E2
Cheffes 114 A5
Chehalis 271 B2
Cheilly 55 D5
Cheleiros 209 E4
Chellah 245 B2
Chemarin, Grand 119 F3
Chemillé 114 C4
Cheminots, aux 67 F4

Chemnitz 143 A5
Chénas 55 F5, 72 B5
Chênelette 71 C1
Chêne Marchand, Clos du 119 F2
Chênes, Clos des 61 F4
Chênes, les, *Beaujolais* 72 D5
Chênes, les, *Chassagne* 60 G1
Chenevery, Bas 66 F4
Chenevery, les 66 F4
Chenevières, les 67 F4
Chenevières, les Basses 67 F4
Chenevottes, les 60 F2
Chengde 246 A4
Chenôve 57 B5
Chenys, Champs 66 F6
Cherasco 176 F1
Cherbaudes 67 F1
Chermont 275 E3
Chers, les 72 A6
Cheseaux, aux 66 F5
Chessy 71 G3
Chester 275 D4
Chétives Maisons, les 119 F5
Cheurlin, Dom. 269 D4
Cheusots, aux 67 E4
Chevagny-lès-Chevrières 69 E4
Chevalier, Dom. de 99 G2
Chevalier Montrachet 60 F3
Chevalière, La 126 B4
Chevalières, les 65 F1
Chevret, en 61 F3
Chevrette 117 C2
Chevrol 103 B2, 107 C6
Chexbres 221 A1
Chianciano 190 F5
Chianciano Terme 190 F5
Chianti 187 B4, 190 F4, G2
Chianti Classico 187 B3
Chianti Geografico, Agricoltori del 189 F5
Chicama 275 C6
Chichée 75 E5
Chicheng 246 B3
Chiddingstone 298 F5
Chienis 184 E4
Chieri 175 B2
Chieti 187 F6
Chignin 137 C2
Chigny-les-Roses 79 B4
Chihuahua 269 E4
Chilènes, les 62 F5
Chilford Hundred 298 E5
Chillan 295 D2
Chille 137 G4
Chillon 221 B1
Chimbarongo 297 D5
Chimney Rock 259 F5
Chindrieux 137 C2
Chino 248 C3
Chinon 114 C6, 117 F4
Chióggia 179 D4
Chiópris-Viscone 183 C4
Chiquet 99 B2
Chiripada Winery, La 269 D4
Chiroubles 55 F5, 72 C4
Chirpan 235 D3
Chisinau 240 B1, 241 F5
Chitry 73 E4
Chiuro 177 B4
Chiveau, en 61 E6
Chlmec 230 G6
Chlumcany 230 E2
Cholame 265 B4
Cholet 114 C4
Chorombo 297 A4
Chouacheux, les 62 F3
Chouillet, au 65 F2
Chouilly 79 E3
Chouinard 263 A3
Choully 220 C3
Chouzé-sur-Loire 117 E2
Chowchilla 267 D4
Christchurch 288 E4
Christian Bros 259 D3
Christiano, Qta do Dr. 210 F6
Christies Beach 284 C1
Christmas Hills 281 B4
Christopher Creek 255 C5
Chum Creek 281 A5
Chur 219 F5
Chusclan 129 D4
Ciadîr Lunga 241 G5
Ciampino 193 D4
Cibio, Qta do 211 E1
Cibonne, Clos 136 C3
Cienega 263 E4
Cigales 197 B3
Cigognola 177 E5
Cilento 195 C4
Cinfães 215 D6
Cinq Cantons, les 131 F5
Cinque Terre 173 F5
Cissac-Médoc 87 G2
Cisterna di Latina 193 F6
Citernes, les 63 F3
Citrusdal 290 D2
Città della Pieve 192 D4
Citta di Castello 192 B5
Ciuciuleni 241 E4
Ciudad de México 269 G5
Ciudad Juárez 269 D4
Ciudad Victoria 269 F5
Ciumai 241 G5
Civezzano 184 C5

Cividale del Friuli 181 B5, 183 A4
Civrac-en-Médoc 85 D3
Claiborne & Churchill 265 D3
Clairette du Languedoc 135 D5
Clanwilliam 290 D2
Clape, la 135 E1
Clapière, Dom. de la 136 C3
Clare 276 B6, 283 D5
Clare Estate, The 283 D6
Clarendon 284 C3
Clare-Watervale 276 B6
Clarksburg 267 A2
Claude, les Champs 59 G5
Claveries, les 101 G5
Clavoillon 60 G4
Clay 267 A2
Clear Lake 256 C5
Clearlake Highlands 256 C6
Clearlake Oaks 256 C5
Clearlake Park 256 C5
Cle Elum 271 A4
Clémenfert 67 E4
Clements 267 B2
Clermont-l'Hérault 135 B2
Clessé 55 E5, 69 C5
Cleveland 275 G2
Climat du Val 61 D2
Cline Cellars 257 F4
Clinton 275 C5
Clisson 114 C3, 115 G5
Clocher, Clos du 107 D4
Clomée, en 67 F4
Clos du Bois 255 B5
Clos, le 118 B4
Clos, Le 126 C3
Clos, les 66 E2
Clos, Les 75 D4
Clos, les Petits 59 F5
Closeau, au 67 F1
Closeaux, les 61 E1
Clou des Chênes, le 61 E3
Cloudy Bay 289 F4
Clous, aux 63 D1
Clous Dessous, les 61 F1
Clous Dessus, les 60 E6
Clous, les 61 E3
Cloux, les 68 A4
Cloverdale 255 A3, 256 D4
Clovis 267 D5
Cluj-Napoca 237 B3
Cobden 280 G1
Cobram 280 C4
Cochem 143 B2
Cochran 273 A4
Codevilla 177 F3
Codigua 297 B4
Codolet 130 E6
Codorníu Napa 257 E5
Codróipo 181 C4
Cognac 110 D5
Cognac et Vins Charentais, Coop. de 110 G6
Cogolin 136 C5
Cohn, B R 254 F4
Coihueco 295 D2
Coilsfield 281 C5
Coimbra 208 C4
Coin 207 D4
Coin, le 126 C2
Coinsins 220 B4
Coka 233 B5
Colac 277 D2, 280 G2
Colares 208 D3, 209 E3
Colbún 297 G4
Coldstream 280 F4, 281 C4
Coldstream Hills 281 C5
Coldstream West 281 C3
Cole Ranch 256 C3
Colima 269 G5
Colina 295 B3
Colinele Tutovei 237 C5
Collan 73 D6
Collavini 183 B4
Collbató 205 D4
Colldejou 204 G6
Colle di Val d'Elsa 189 F2
Colli Albani 187 F3, 193 E4
Colli Altotiberini 187 C5, 192 B4
Colli Amerini 187 D4, 192 F5
Colli Berici 179 D3
Colli Bolognesi 179 F3, 187 A4
Colli del Trasimeno 187 C4, 192 C4
Colli di Bolzano 179 B3, 185 B3
Colli di Luni 173 G6
Colli di Parma 173 E6, 179 E1
Colli Euganei 179 D3
Colli Fidrentini 189 B3
Colli Fiorentini 187 B4
Colli Lanuvini 193 E5
Colli Martani 187 D4, 192 D5
Colli Morenici Mantovani del Garda 179 D2
Colline Lucchesi 187 A3
Collines de la Moure 139 D1
Collines Rhodaniennes 139 C4
Collio Goriziano o Collio 179 B6, 181 C6, 183 C5, D5
Colli Orientali del Friuli 179 B6, 181 B5, 183 B4
Collioure 133 G5
Colli Perugini 187 C4, 192 D5

Colli Piacentini 173 E5
Colli Senesi 187 B3, 189 F2
Colli Tortonesi 173 E4
Collonges 221 D2
Colmar 120 E4, 123 C1
Colmenar 207 D5
Colognola ai Colli 183 G1
Cologny 220 C4
Colombette, Dom. de la 133 B5, 135 C1
Colombier 109 B6
Colombier, Le 131 C5
Colombière, la 65 G4
Colonia 294 F2
Colonna 193 D5
Colorina 177 B2
Coltanco 297 C5
Colton 273 C6
Columbia 271 A3
Columbia Crest (Ch. Ste Michelle) 271 C5
Columbia Valley 271 B5
Columbus 275 D1
Comalle 297 E4
Comandante Salas 295 B5
Combards, les 59 F6, 60 F1
Combe, au Bas de 65 F3
Combe au Moine 67 E2
Combe Brûlée 65 E4
Combe, Clos de la 107 C3
Combe Danay, la 61 D3
Combe de Lavaut 67 D1
Combe, Dom. de la 107 C3
Combe d'Orveau, la 66 E1
Combe Roy, En 67 E4
Combes Dessous, les 61 F5
Combes Dessus, les 61 F5
Combes du Bas 67 F2
Combes du Dessus 67 E2
Combes, les, *Aloxe-Corton* 63 F3
Combes, les, *Beaujolais* 72 G4
Combes, les, *St-Aubin* 60 F2
Combes, les, *Volnay* 61 F5
Combettes, les 60 G4
Combotte, la 61 E5
Combottes, aux, *Chambolle-Musigny* 66 F3
Combottes, aux, *Gevrey-Chambertin* 66 F5
Combottes, les 66 F3
Commaraine, Clos de la 61 F6, 62 E1
Comme Dessus 59 F4
Comme, la 59 F4
Communes, aux 65 G4
Como 173 C5
Compania, La 201 B3
Comps 108 F3
Comrat 241 F5
Comté de Grignan 139 C4
Comtés Rhodaniens 139 G3
Comté Tolosan 139 G2
Conca de Barberà 197 B5, 205 E2
Conca de Tremp 197 B5
Concannon 263 A3
Concepción, *Chile* 295 E1
Concepcion, *USA* 265 G4
Concha, La 201 D2
Concha y Toro 297 B6
Concord 275 B6
Condado de Huelva 197 D2
Condemennes, les 66 F2
Condobolin 277 A4
Condom 113 E3
Condorcet 131 G2
Condrieu 125 A4, 126 D3
Conegliano 181 C2
Conesa 205 E2
Connardises, es 63 E2
Conn Creek 259 D4
Conn Valley 259 C4
Conrotto 263 D4
Consorzio Agrario Provinciale di Siena 189 E3
Constanta 237 E5
Constanti 205 F2
Constantia 290 F1, G1
Constitución 295 C2
Conthey 221 C3
Conti 286 C2
Conti Bossi Fedrigotti-Foianeghe 184 E4
Conti Formentini 183 C6
Conti Martini 184 A5
Conti Sermston 189 B3
Contres 115 B3
Contrie, la 117 D2
Cook, R & J 267 E3
Coolalta 278 C4
Coolawin/Normans 284 C3
Cooma 277 C5
Coonawarra 277 D1, 285 B6
Coonawarra Station 285 B5
Cooper Mountain 273 B5
Coorara 284 C2
Coos Bay 271 F1
Cootamundra 277 B4
Copera, La 201 C4
Copertino 195 C6
Coppet 220 C4
Coquille 271 F1
Coquimbo 294 F1
Corbeaux, les 67 E1
Corbera d'Ebre 204 G5
Corbères-Abères 113 F2
Corbett 273 B6
Corbett Canyon 265 D3
Corbeyrier 221 B1
Corbières 133 E5, 135 D5
Corbins, les 61 F2
Corbonod 137 B2
Corcelles-en-Beaujolais 72 D5
Corchuelo, El 201 D2
Corcolle 193 C5
Corcoran 267 F5
Cordes 113 D6
Cordoba, *Argentina* 294 F2
Córdoba, *Spain* 207 A4
Cori 187 F3, 193 E6
Coriole 284 D2
Cormans 183 C5
Cormòns 181 C5
Cormontreuil 79 A4
Cornellà de Llobregat 205 E5
Cornesti 241 F5
Cornières, les 59 E2
Corno di Rosazzo 183 B4
Cornudella de Montsant 204 F6
Corowa 277 C3, 280 C5
Corowa-Rutherglen 277 C3, 280 D5
Corpus Christi 269 E6
Corregidor, El 201 C4
Corregidor Viejo, El 201 C4
Corsier 220 C4
Cortadedos 201 D2
Corte 140 E4
Cortese dell'Alto Monferrato 173 E3, 175 D5
Cortese di Gava 173 E4
Corti, Le 189 C3
Cortina d'Ampezzo 179 B4
Corton Charlemagne 63 E4
Corton, le 63 E4
Cortons, les 60 F3
Coruche 208 D4
Çorum 243 B4
Corvallis 271 E2, 273 E4
Corvées, aux, *Gevrey-Chambertin* 67 F1
Corvées, aux, *Prémeaux-Prissey* 64 F4
Corvino San Quirico 177 F4
Cosentino 259 E4
Cosenza 195 D4
Cosne-Cours-sur-Loire 115 B6
Costa-Albondón 197 E4
Costa de Bo, Qta da 210 F3
Costalunga 183 G2
Costa, Qta da 210 D5
Costello 259 F5
Costernano 182 E3
Costers del Segre 197 B5
Coswig 167 C6
Cotas 210 D6
Coteau des Bois, le 65 F1
Coteau de Vincy 220 B4
Coteaux Charitois 139 F4
Coteaux d'Ancenis 53 D1
Coteaux de Bessilles 138 D6
Coteaux de Cèze 139 B2
Coteaux de Coiffy 139 C4
Coteaux de Fenouillèdes 138 F4
Coteaux de Fontcaude 138 D5
Coteaux de Glanes 139 E4
Coteaux de la Cabrerisse 138 E5
Coteaux de Languedoc 134 D6
Coteaux de l'Ardèche 139 A4
Coteaux de l'Aubance 116 C4
Coteaux de Laurens 138 D5
Coteaux de Miramont 138 E4
Coteaux de Murviel 138 D5
Coteaux de Narbonne 138 E5
Coteaux d'Enserune 138 D5
Coteaux de Peyriac 138 D4
Coteaux de Pierrevert 53 F5, 139 G3
Coteaux de Salagou 138 C6
Coteaux des Baronnies 139 C4
Coteaux du Cher et de l'Arnon 139 B4
Coteaux du Grésivaudan 139 D4
Coteaux du Languedoc 133 B5
Coteaux du Libron 138 D6
Coteaux du Littoral Audois 138 E5
Coteaux du-Pont-du-Gard 139 C2
Coteaux du Quercy 139 F4
Coteaux du Termenès 138 E4
Coteaux du Vendômois 53 C2
Coteaux et Terrasses de Montauban 139 G4
Coteaux Flaviens 139 C2
Côte Blonde 126 B4
Côte Boudin 126 B4
Côte Brune 126 B4
Côte de Bréchain 75 D5
Côte de Brouilly 55 F5, 72 F4
Côte de Fontenay 75 C4
Côte des Prés Girots 75 D6
Côte, la 119 E2
Côte, La 219 F1
Côte Roannaise 53 D4, 139 F3
Côte Rôtie 126 B3
Côte Rôtie, *Beaujolais* 72 D4
Côte Rôtie, *Morey-St-Denis* 66 E4
Côtes Catalanes 138 F5
Côtes, Clos les 109 D4
Côtes d'Auvergne 53 E3, 139 F2
Côtes de Beaune, Hautes 57 F3
Côtes de Castillon 80 E5
Côtes de Duras 97 E3, 113 C2
Côtes de Francs 80 E5
Côtes de Gascogne 139 C4
Côtes de la Malepère 53 G3, 133 C1, 139 G2
Côtes de Lézignan 138 E5
Côtes de l'Orbe 219 F1
Côtes de Meliton 239 B4
Côtes de Montestruc 139 C4
Côtes de Nuits, Hautes 57 C4
Côtes de Pérignan 138 E5
Côtes de Prouille 138 E3
Côtes de St-Mont 113 E2
Côtes de Thau 138 D6
Côtes de Thongue 138 D6
Côtes de Toul 53 B4
Côtes du Brian 138 D5
Côtes du Brulhois 53 F2, 113 D4
Côtes du Cabardès et de l'Orbiel 53 G3, 133 B1
Côtes du Céressou 138 D6
Côtes du Condomois 139 C4
Côtes du Forez 53 E4, 139 F3
Côtes du Frontonnais 113 E5
Côtes du Lastours 138 D4
Côtes du Marmandais 53 F2, 113 C2
Côtes du Roussillon 133 E5
Côtes du Roussillon-Villages 133 F5
Côtes du Tarn 139 F4
Côtes du Vidourle 139 C1
Côtes du Vivarais 53 F4, 129 C3
Cotesti 237 C5
Côte Vermeille, La 138 G5
Cotnari 237 B4
Coton, en 67 E3
Cottage Grove 271 E2
Cotum & Sons Ltd, H 254 E3
Coucherias, aux 62 E4
Couëron 114 B2
Coufouleux 113 E5
Coulée de Serrant 116 A3
Couquèques 85 D4
Cour, Champ de 72 C5
Cour-Cheverny 115 B3
Courgis 75 F2
Courmayeur 173 C2
Courmonterral 135 B3
Couronne, La 293 G6
Courthil, Sous le 60 F4
Courts, les sous 61 E3
Courvoisier 110 F5
Cousiño-Macul 297 A6
Cousse, le Haut 118 A4
Coussergues, Dom. de 133 B6, 135 D2
Coutras 80 D4
Cova da Beira 208 C5
Covas do Douro 210 E4
Covelinhas 210 F3
Coventry 298 E4
Covey Run 272 F3
Covilhã 208 C5
Covurlui 237 C5
Cowaramup 287 D2
Cowra 277 B5
Coya 297 C5
Crabtree, *Australia* 283 E5
Crabtree, *USA* 273 D5
Crafers 284 B4
Craiova 237 D3
Craipillot 67 E1
Crais, les, *Fixin* 67 F4
Crais, les, *Santenay* 59 E2
Crais, les Petits 67 E4
Cramant 79 F3
Craneford 282 D5, E6
Crans 221 C4
Crans près Céligny 220 B4
Crapousuets, les 63 F3
Cras, aux, *Beaune* 62 F4
Cras, aux, *Nuits-St-Georges* 65 F3
Cras, les, *Aloxe-Corton* 63 F3
Cras, les, *Chambolle-Musigny* 66 E3
Cras, les, *Meursault* 61 F3
Cras, les, *Pommard* 61 F5
Crâs, les, *Vougeot* 65 F6, 66 F2
Cras, les Grands 72 E4
Crassier 220 B4
Crasto, Qta do 210 F3
Cravant 73 F4
Cravant-les-Coteaux 117 F5
Crawfordville 278 D4
Cray 118 C6
Crays, les 61 E2
Crechelins, en 67 F3
Crèches-sur-Saône 69 G4
Creixell 205 F3
Crema 173 D5
Crema, La 255 E4
Cremona 173 E6, 179 D1
Créole 67 E3
Créon 96 D5
Créot, le 67 E3
Créots, les 60 D3
Crépy 137 A3
Cres 233 C1
Crès, le 135 B4
Cressy 280 F2
Crest 125 F5
Creston 265 C4
Creston Manor 265 C4
Crètevent 67 F3
Crets, ez 60 G1
Creusot, le 55 D5
Creux Baissants, les 66 E2
Creux de la Net 63 D3
Creux de Tillet 61 D2
Creysse 109 B6
Crézancy-en-Sancerre 119 F2
Crichton Hall 263 F5
Crickley Windward 298 F4
Cricova 241 F5
Criots, les, *Chassagne* 60 G2
Criots, les, *Meursault* 61 F3
Crisana 237 C2
Crissier 220 A6
Crna Gora 233 F4
Croffta 298 F3
Croisettes, les 67 E3
Croix, aux 66 F3
Croix Blanche, la, *Fixin* 67 F4
Croix Blanche, la, *Pommard* 62 F1
Croix Blanche, la, *Vosne-Romanée* 65 G3
Croix, Dom. de la 136 C5
Croix, la 127 C5
Croix Noires, les 61 F5
Croix Planet, la 61 G5
Croix Rameau, la 65 F4
Croix Rouges, aux 65 G2
Croix Sorine 59 E3
Croix-Valmer, la 136 C5
Croix Viollette, la 67 E3
Croizet-Eymard 110 G5
Cromin, le 61 F2
Cronin 263 B2
Cros Martin 61 G4
Crosswoods 275 C6
Crotone 195 D5
Crotots, les 60 F6
Crots, aux 65 F1
Crottes, ez 59 G5
Crouin 110 D5
Croyen, Champ 60 G4
Crozes-Hermitage 127 A4
Cru Barjuneau 101 G3
Cru Caplane 101 F4
Cruces, Las 265 G5
Cru Commarque 101 G3
Cru de Bergeron 101 E3
Cruet 137 C2
Cru La Clotte 101 B5
Cru Lanère 101 G3
Cruots ou Vignes Blanches, les 65 F5
Cru Rousset 108 E3
Cru Thibaut 101 G5
Cruzille 69 A5
Csengöd 226 F3
Csongrád 226 G4
Csopak 226 F2
Cuadrados, Los 201 D1
Cuba 213 F4
Cubelles 205 F3
Cubuk 243 B4
Cuco, El 201 D1
Cucugnan 138 F4
Cuéllar 206 F3
Cuerno del Oro, El 201 B3
Cuers 136 C3
Cuevas de San Marcos 207 C5
Cuis 79 E3
Culiasán 269 F4
Cullens 287 D1
Cully 220 A6
Cumberland 275 D3
Cumières 79 D2
Cumpeo 297 F4
Cunèges 109 B5
Cúneo 173 F2
Cunit 205 F3
Curacavi 295 B3, 297 A5
Curepto 295 C2
Curicó 295 C2, 297 E4
Currais, Qta dos 210 F1
Curral das Freiras 217 C2
Cutler 267 E5
Cuvaison 259 B2
Cuzcurrita de Rió Tirón 202 B4
Cygnet 287 G6
Cziróka 229 D4

Dachsberg 158 E3
Dafnes 239 F4
Dahlenheim 120 A4
Dahra 245 B4
Daignac 96 D6
Dalboki 235 C4
Dalian (Lüda) 246 C5
Dallas, *Oregon* 271 D2, 273 D4
Dallas, *Texas* 269 D6
Dalla Valle 259 D5
Dalles, The 271 C4
Dalmatia 233 D2
Dalswinton 279 G4
Dalwhinnie 280 E1
Dalwood 278 A5
Damazan 113 D2
Dambach-la-Ville 120 C4
Damery 79 D2
Damianitza 235 D2
Damodes, aux 65 F3
Dancka 229 F2
Danguerrins, les 66 E2
Dannemoine 73 D6
Dannevirke 288 D5
Dão 208 B4
Darbonnay 137 F5
Dardagny 220 C3
Dargaville 288 B4
Darlington 284 B2
Darmstadt 143 B4
Dartbrook 279 D5
Darveniza Brothers 280 D4
Daubhaus 162 G5
Daubos 89 E5, 91 B4
Davayé 69 F4
David Bruce 263 C2
Davis 267 A1
Davis Bynum 255 D5
Davos 219 F5
Dawson Estate 278 C5
Daylesford 280 E3
Dayton 273 C4
Dazeshan 246 D5
Dázio 177 B1
Deák-Barát 229 G3
Dealu Bujorului 237 C5
Dealu Mare 237 D4
Dealurile Buzaului 237 D4
Dealurile Craiovei 237 D3
Debonné 275 C2
Debrecen 226 E5
Déduits, les 72 C5
Deer Park 259 C3
Dehesilla 200 B4
Dehlinger 255 E5
Deidesfeld 161 B2
Deidesheim 143 C4, 161 B2, F5
Delaire 293 F3
Delamain 110 G6
Delano 267 F5
Dél-Balaton 226 F2
Delgardo Zuleta 201 G1
Delheim 293 E3
Delicato 267 B2
Dellchen 154 F6
Dellepiane 295 B4
Denair 267 C3
Denbies 298 F5
Denicé 71 E3
Deñihue 297 C5
Deniliquin 277 C3
Denizli 243 C2
Denman 277 A6, 279 F3, F4
Denman Estate 279 F5
Dents de Chien 60 F3
Derbent 240 C6
Dérée, en 67 E2
Derrière, Champ 60 G2
Derrière chez Edouard 60 D2
Derrière la Grange 66 F3
Derrière la Tour 60 D3
Derrière le Four, *Auxey-Duresses* 61 D2
Derrière le Four, *Chambolle-Musigny* 66 E2
Derrière le Four, *Vosne-Romanée* 65 F4
Derrière les Crais 59 E2
Desenzano del Garda 182 G1
Desloch 155 D4
Dessewffy 229 G4
Detroit, *Michigan* 275 B1
Detroit, *Oregon* 273 D6
Dettelbach 166 B5
Deutelsberg 159 F1
Deutschherrenberg 152 C5
Deutschkreutz 222 D3
Deutschlandsberg 222 F1
Deutsch Schützen 222 E3
Deva 237 C2
Devesas 210 E1
Devil's Lair 287 F2
Devlin 263 D3
Devonport 287 F5
Devonvale 293 F1
Dezaley 220 A6
Dezhou 246 D3
Dezize 55 D5
Dezseffy 229 G4
Dhali 244 F3
Dhoros 244 G2
Dhron 151 D2
Diamond Creek 259 C2
Diamond Oaks 255 B4
Diamond Valley Vyds 281 A3
Diano d'Alba 176 F3
Didiers, les 64 F5
Dieli Donné 293 F6
Dienheim 143 B4, 162 G5, 163 B5
Dietlingen 165 C3
Dieulefit 129 C5
Digoine l'Hermitage, la 68 A4
Digrazia 275 C5
Dijon 55 C6, 57 A6
Dilley 273 B4
Dimashq (Damascus) 243 E5
Dimtcha 235 B3
Dinuba 267 E5
Diognières, les 127 C5
Diosig 237 B2
Diren 243 B5
Dirmstein 161 A2
Disznókö 229 F3
Dittelsheim 163 C5
Dixon 267 A1
Dixon's Creek 281 A4
Dizy-Magenta 79 D3
Djakovica 233 F5
Djidjelli 245 A5
Döbeln 167 C5
Dobrich (Tolbukhin) 235 B5
Dobrogea 237 D5
Doctor 153 F2
Doganella 193 F6
Doix, les Bas 66 F2
Doix, les Hauts 66 F2
Doktorberg 149 F5
Dolcetto d'Alba 173 E3, 175 E3, 176 G2
Dolcetto d'Asti 175 D5
Dolcetto delle Langhe Monregalesi 173 F3
Dolcetto di Acqui 173 E4, 175 E5
Dolcetto di Diano d'Alba 175 E3, 176 F3
Dolcetto di Dogliani 173 E3, 175 F2
Dolcetto di Ovada 173 E4
Dolegna del Collio 183 B5
Doluca 243 B2
Domane 147 E3
Domblans 137 F4
Domblick 163 D4
Domherr, *Piesport* 151 C2
Domherr, *Rheinhessen* 163 B4
Domherrenberg 149 D2
Domini-Kanerberg 149 E5
Dominode, la 63 E1
Dommartin 71 G4
Domodossola 173 C3
Domprobst 153 E1
Dona Elvira 200 B4
Donald, *Australia* 280 D1
Donald, *USA* 272 F2
Doña Mencia 207 B5
Donauland 222 F4
Dongying 246 C4
Donnafugata 195 F2
Donnerskirchen 222 D3, 223 B4
Donnici 195 D4
Donnybrook 283 D5
Donolga 284 E1
Don Valley 281 C6
Doonside Estate 281 C4
Dooms, De 290 F3
Doosberg 158 F5
Dorino Livon 183 C5
Dormans 78 D5
Dornava 231 B5
Doro Princic 183 C5
Dorsheim 155 B6
dos d'Ane, Sous le 60 F5
Dos Palos 267 D3
Douby 72 D4
Doué-la-Fontaine 114 C5
Doukkala 245 C1
Douvaine 137 A3
Douville 109 A6
Drachenstein 157 E3
Dragasani 237 D3
Dragon Seal Winery 246 B3
Draguignan 136 A5
Drake 265 G4
Drama 239 A4
Drayton's Bellevue 278 C4
Dresden 143 A4, 167 D6
Dressoles, les 61 G3
Drouhin, Dom. 273 C4
Drumborg 277 D1
Dry Creek 255 C4
Dry Creek Valley 255 B3
Dubasari 241 F5
Dubbo 277 A5
Dubois 118 B4
Dubrovnik 233 E3
Duckhorn 259 C3
Ducor 267 F6
Ducs, Clos de 61 E5
Duillier 220 B4
Dulce Nombre 201 C4
Dully 220 B4
Dunajská Streda 230 G4
Dunaújváros 226 F3
Duncan 283 D5
Duncan Peak 256 C3
Dunn 259 B3
Dunnewood Vyds 256 B3
Dunolly 280 E2
Dunsborough 287 B2
Duplek 231 B4
Durango 269 F4
Duras 97 F3, 109 C4, 113 C2
Durbach 165 D2
Durban 133 E4
Durbanville 290 F2
Duresses, Bas des 61 E2
Duresses, les 61 E2
Durney 263 F3
Dürnstein 222 B1, 225 G1
Durots, les 61 G3
Durtal 114 A5
Duxoup 255 B4
Dve Mogili 235 B4
Dyson 284 E1

Eagle Bay 287 B2
Eagle Creek 273 B6
Eaglehawk Estate 283 E6
Eagle Point 271 G3
Earlimart 267 F5
East 281 B4
East Side/Oak Ridge 267 F3
Eaton Hill 272 F3
Eauze 113 E2
Eberbach 143 C5
Eberle 265 B3
Ebernburg 155 C6
Ebersberg 162 E3
Echaillé 60 D2
Echandens 220 A5
Echanges, aux 66 F3
Echards, ez 61 F4
Echeverria 297 E4
Echézeaux, aux 66 F5
Echézeaux du Dessus 65 F5
Echézeaux, les 66 E2
Echézeaux, les Grands 65 F5
Echo, Clos de l' 117 F3
Echoppes, les 99 A2
Echo Vale 281 A4
Echuca 277 C3, 280 C3
Écija 207 B3
Eckelsheim 163 C4
Ecole No. 41, L' 271 G4
Ecu, à l' 62 E5
Ecublens 220 A6
Ecueil 79 B3
Ecusseaux, les 61 E2
Edelberg 153 B4
Edelmann 158 F4
Edenkoben 161 C2
Eden Valley 282 D6
Eden Valley Wines 282 D6
Edinglassie 279 F5
Edison 267 G6
Edmeades 256 C2
Edna 265 D3
Edna Valley 265 D3
Eerstenvier Valleise 293 G1
Egelsee 225 F3
Eger 226 E4
Eggenburg 222 B2
Eglantine 298 E4
Eglise, Clos l' 107 C4
Eglise, Dom. de l' 107 D5
Eglise-Neuve-d'Issac 109 A5
Egna 185 E5
Eguisheim 120 E4, 122 C5
Ehrenberg 149 G6
Ehrenhausen 222 G2
Ehrenstetten 165 F2
Eibelstadt 166 C4
Eibingen 157 E5
Eichberg 159 E1
Eichhoffen 120 B4
Eira Velha, Qta do 210 E5
Eisenstadt 222 D3, 223 C3
Eitelsbach 149 D4
Elâzig 243 C6, D6
Elbhänge 167 D6
Elchberg 122 C5
Elciego 202 B6, 203 G4
Elderslie 278 A5
Elderton 282 B4
Elena 235 C4
Elham Valley 298 F6
Elisenberg 152 G6
Elizabeth, *Australia* 276 B6
Elizabeth, *USA* 275 C5
Elk Cove 273 B4
Elk Grove 267 A2
Elkhovo 235 D4
Ellendale 273 D4
Ellensburg 271 B4
Ellergrub 153 C4
Elliston 263 A3
Elmham Park 298 E6
Elmira, *California* 267 A1
Elmira, *New York* 275 C4
Elmore 277 C3, 280 D3
Elms Cross 298 F4
Elne 133 F4
Előhegy 229 D4, G3
Elsewhere Vyd 287 G6
Elster 161 E5
Eltville am Rhein 143 B4, 159 G4
Elvas 208 D5
Embrazées, les 59 F5
Emerald 272 F3
Emeringes 71 B3, 72 B4
Emilio Lustau 201 G2
Emprunt, l' 131 G1
Encostas d'Aire 208 C4
Encostas da Nave 208 B5
Endingen 165 E2
Engelgrube 151 E1
Engelmannsberg 158 F6
Engelsberg, *Franken* 166 B5
Engelsberg, *Rheinhessen* 162 B5
Englefield 285 C6
Enkirch 153 B4
Enna 195 F3
Enseignères, les 60 G3
Ensenada 269 D2
Ensisheim 120 F4
Entraigues-sur-Sorgues 131 G4

Entre-Deux-Mers 80 F4, 97 E1
Entre Deux-Velles, les 67 E4
Enumclaw 271 A3
Enzan 248 D4
Epaisse, l' 117 C2
Epenotes, les 62 F2
Epenots, les Grands 62 F1
Epenots, les Petits 62 F2
Epernay 76 B4, 79 E3
Epesses 220 A6
Epinottes, les 75 E3
Epiré 116 A3
Episkopi 244 G2
Epointures, les 67 F1
Erbach 159 G2
Erbaluce di Caluso 173 D3
Erdek 243 B2
Erden 152 C6
Erdőhorváti 229 D4
Eregli 243 D4
Ergot, en 66 F6
Erie 275 C2
Erlenbach, *Baden-Württemberg* 165 C4
Erlenbach, *Franken* 166 B3
Ermite, l' 127 B4
Ermtebringer 158 E3
Eröbénye 229 E3
Errazuriz 295 A3
Ersingen 165 C3
Erstein 120 B5
Ervedosa do Douro 211 F1
Erzincan 243 C6
Eschau 120 B5
Eschbach 161 D1
Eschemdorf 166 B5
Escolives-Ste-Camille 73 F3
Eskisehir 243 B3
Esmeralda 295 B4
Esparreguera 205 E4
Espinho 210 F5
Espluga de Francolí, L' 205 E1
Esposende 215 B4
Essaouira 245 C1
Essarts, les 59 G6, 60 G1
Essertines 220 C3
Esslingen 165 D4
Estacada 273 C6
Est! Est!! Est!!! 187 D3
Esteves, Los 201 B4
Estoril 209 F4
Estoumelles 67 D2
Estreito da Calheta 216 B6
Estreito de Câmara de Lobos 217 C2
Estrella 265 B3
Estremoz 208 D5, 213 D5
Esvres 115 B1
Esztergom 226 E3
Etelois, aux 66 F6
Etna 195 F3
Etoile, l', *Jura* 137 G4
Etoile, l', *Vouvray* 118 B4
Etoy 220 A5
Etréchy 79 G3
Etroyes 68 C4
Etyek 226 F3
Eucharíusberg 147 A5
Eugene 271 E2
Euroa 280 D4
Euxinograd 235 B6
Evans & Tate 287 D1
Evans family 278 C5
Evensen 259 E4
Evêque, Clos l' 68 C4
Evesham 273 D4
Evionnaz 221 C2
Evocelles, les 67 E3
Evois, les 117 C3
Évora 208 E4, 213 E4
Evorilla 200 A5
Evouettes, les 221 B1
Evvoia (Euboea) 239 C3
Ewig Laben 166 B4
Exeter 267 E5
Extremo 215 A5
Eymet 109 C5
Eyrans 108 B2
Eyrenville 109 C6
Eyrie 273 C4
Eysines 80 E2, 96 C3
Eyton on Yarra 281 B5

Fabriano 187 C5
Facelli 271 A3
Faconnières, les 66 F5
Fadèze, Dom. de la 135 C3
Fafe 215 C5
Faial 217 B4
Fairendes, les 59 F6
Fairendes, les Petites 59 F5
Fairhall 289 G4
Fairview 293 D3
Fajã da Ovelha 216 B5
Falcognana 193 D4
Falerio dei Colli Ascolani 187 C5
Falerno del Massico 195 B2
Falkenberg 151 C2
Falkenstein 222 B3
Falklay 153 B4
Fall Creek Vyds 269 D5
Falletto 176 F2
Fall River 275 C6
Falls City 273 D3
Falset 204 F6
Famagusta 244 F5
Famines, les 61 G4
Famoso 267 G5
Fanhões 209 E5
Fara 173 D4
Faranda 286 C2
Fareham Estate 283 F6
Farfao, Qta do 211 G6
Farges, les 72 C4
Fargues 101 F6
Farmington 267 B3
Farnham 289 G5
Far Niente 259 E4
Faro, *Italy* 195 E4
Faro, *Portugal* 208 F4
Farra d'Isonzo 183 D5
Fatarella, La 204 F5
Fattoria Altomena 189 A5
Faubard, Clos 59 F4
Faubourg de Bouze 62 F4
Faugères 133 E5, 135 D5
Favaios 210 D6
Favray, Grand 119 E5
Favray, Petit 119 E5
Faye-d'Anjou 116 D5
Fayssac 113 D6
Fêchy 220 A5
Feguine, Clos de la 62 E4
Fehring 222 F2
Feilbingert 155 C5
Feilding 288 D5
Felanitx 197 C6
Feldebrö 226 E4
Felgueiras 215 C5
Fels, *Austria* 222 B2
Fels, *Germany* 147 B2
Felsenberg 154 G4
Felseneck 155 F2
Felsen, In den 154 G3
Felsenkopf 151 G1
Felsensteyer 154 F5
Felslay 149 E4
Fenestra 263 A3
Fengrun 246 B4
Feodosiya 240 C3
Fergusson 281 A4
Ferianes 200 C4
Fermoselle 197 B2
Fermoy 287 C1
Feman-Núñez 207 A4
Femhill 181 B5
Ferrad, Qta da 210 G3
Ferradosa, Qta da 211 F3
Ferrara 179 E3
Ferrari 184 C5
Ferrari-Carano 255 B4
Ferreija do Alentejo 213 G4
Ferres 151 C1
Ferrière, le 193 F5
Fès 245 B2
Fess Parker 265 F5
Fetters Hot Springs 254 F4
Fetzer 256 B3, C4
Feuerberg 161 A2, 161 B4
Feuersteige 223 C3
Feurer Kogl 223 B4
Feusselottes, les 66 F2
Fèves, les 62 E5
Feydieu 95 F4
Fiano d'Avellino 195 C3
Fichots, les 63 E3
Ficklin 267 D4
Fiefs-Vendéens 52 D6, 139 F1
Field Stone 255 C5
Fiésole 189 A4
Fiètres, les 63 F3
Figari 140 G4
Figline Valdamo 189 C5
Figuerola del Camp 205 E2
Filzen, *Piesport* 151 B4
Filzen, *Saar* 147 B2
Finagra 213 F5
Findling 162 D4
Finócchio 193 D5
Firebaugh 267 D3
Firelands 275 C1
Firenze 187 A4, 189 A3
Firestone 265 F5
Firvida 210 F1
Fitou 133 E5
Fiuggi 187 F4
Five Points 267 E4
Fixin 55 C6, 57 B5, 67 E4
Fläche 159 E1
Flaugeac 109 C5
Flaujagues 109 B3
Flèche, la 114 A6
Flein 165 C4
Fleix, le 109 B4
Fleurance 113 E3
Fleurie 55 F5, 72 C5
Fleurières, les 64 G6
Fleurieux-sur-l'Arbresle 71 G3
Fleurville 69 C6
Fleys 73 E5, 75 D6
Flichman 295 A4
Floirac 80 E3, 96 D4
Flora Springs 259 D3
Florimont 123 C1
Florina 239 B2
Flynn 273 D4, E4
Focsani 237 C5
Foggia 195 B4
Fogliano Redipuglia 183 D5
Fojo, Qta do 210 D5
Folatières, les 60 F4
Folgana 184 E5
Folgosa 210 F3
Folie à Deux 259 B5
Folie, la 118 A4
Foligno 187 D4, 192 D6
Follette, La 275 C4
Folligberg 223 C3
Fondemens, les 67 F4
Fondis, les 117 D1
Fonréaud 93 G1
Fonroque 109 C5
Fonsalade, Dom. de 133 A5, 135 C1
Fontaine de Vosne 65 G3
Fontaine de Vosne, la 65 G3
Fontaine Sot 60 G2
Fontainhas, Qta das 211 G6
Fontana di Papa 193 E4
Fontanafredda 176 F2
Fontanelas 209 E3
Fontelo 210 G2
Fonteny 67 E1
Fonterutoli 189 F4
Fontevraud-l'Abbaye 114 C6
Fontfroide 133 C4, 134 E6
Fonthill 298 F4
Fontmurée, Clos 103 B4
Font-Remeu 138 F3
Fontrubi 205 E3
Fontscaldes 205 E2
Foote, E B 271 A3
Foppiano 255 C5
Foradori 184 A5
Forbes 277 B4
Forcalqueiret 136 B3
Force, la 109 B5
Forcine, la 117 D1
Forest Grove 271 C2, 273 B4
Forest Hill 286 G3
Forest Hills 255 D4
Forestville 255 E4
Forêts, les, *Chablis* 75 E3
Forêts, les, *Prémeaux-Prissey* 64 F5
Forgeron 271 E2
Forges, les 61 F2
Foris 271 G2
Forjães 215 B4
Forli 179 F4, 187 A5
Forman 259 D3
Fomos de Algodres 215 F6
Forrás 229 G3
Forrest Estate 289 F3
Forst 155 C2
Forst an der Weinstrasse 161 B2, E5
Försterlay 153 C1
Forthof 225 G3
Fortino 263 D4
Fort Médoc 93 C6
Forts de Latour, Les 89 F5, 91 B4
Fortunago 177 G4
Fortuna, La 297 E4
Fortune, la 68 A4
Fosses, les 61 E2
Fossignano 193 F4
Fos-sur-Mer 129 G4
Fouchères, les 66 F2
Fougeray, le 118 B3
Fougueyrolles 109 B4
Foujouin 118 B4
Foulot, en 59 D2
Foulot, le 62 F4
Founex 220 B4
Fourchaume, la 75 C3
Fourches, aux 63 E2
Four Corners 259 C3
Fourneaux, aux 63 E2
Fourneaux, les, *Chablis* 75 D6
Fourneaux, les, *Santenay* 59 E2
Fournières, les 63 F3
Fours 108 B2
Fourtet, Clos 103 D3, 105 D4
Fowler 267 E5
Foxen Vineyard 265 E5
Foz de Temilobos, Qta da 210 G2
Foz, Qta da 210 E5, G2
Frades, Qta dos 210 G3
Fraisse 109 A5
Francemont 59 F5
Francesco Bertolli 189 F3
Franche-Comté 139 D4
Franciacorta 173 C6, 179 C1
Franciscan 259 D4
Frangy 137 B2
Franken 143 B6
Frankenberg 167 D5
Frankenberger Scholsstück 166 C6
Frankenthal 157 E2
Frankfurt 143 B4
Frankland Estate 286 F3
Franschhoek 290 F2, 293 G6
Franzia 267 B2
Frapin 110 G5
Frascati 187 F3, 193 D5
Fraser 278 C5
Frasinetti 267 A2
Fratenilli Ormanni 189 E3
Frauenfeld 219 D4
Frauengärten 224 F6
Frauenkirchen 223 C6
Frauenweingärten 225 G2
Frêche, le 113 E2
Fredericksburg 269 E5
Freemark Abbey 259 C3
Freiberg 143 A4, 167 C5
Freiburg 143 F3, 165 E2
Freimersheim 161 C2
Freinsheim 161 A2
Freisa d'Asti 173 E3, 175 C4
Freisa di Chieri 173 E3, 175 B2
Freital 167 D6
Freixial 209 D5
Fréjus 136 B5
Frelonnerie, la 118 D3
Fremantle 286 C2
Fremières, les, *Chambolle-Musigny* 66 F3
Fremières, les, *Morey-St-Denis* 66 F4
Fremiers, les 61 F5
Fremiets, les 61 F5
Fremont 263 A3
French Creek 271 A3
Fresno 267 D5
Frêterive 137 C3
Frétille, Sous 63 D5
Freundstück 161 E5
Frey 256 B3
Freyberg 143 A5
Freycinet 287 G6
Fribourg 219 F2
Frickenhausen 166 C5
Frionnes, les 60 D3
Frithsden 298 F5
Fritz 255 B4
Froehn 123 C3
Frog's Leap 259 C3
Froichots, les 66 F5
Fronhof 161 C5
Fronsac 80 E4, 102 C6
Frontera 207 G4
Frontignan 135 C3
Fronton 113 E5
Frosinone 187 F4, 195 B2
Fuchs 147 E2
Fuchsberg 157 F5
Fuchsen-Locherhöhe 223 C5
Fuchsmantel 161 C4
Fuées, les 66 E3
Fuencaliente 207 G4
Fuenmayor 202 B6
Fuentespina 206 E5
Fuerteventura 207 G5
Fuissé 55 F5, 69 F4
Fujimi 248 D3
Fuji-Yoshida 248 D4
Fulleda 205 E1
Fully 221 D2
Fulton 255 D5
Fumane 182 F4
Funchal 217 D3
Fundação Eugénio Almeida 213 E4
Fürsteneck 165 D2
Furstentum 123 C3
Fusine 177 B2
Fu Xian (Wafangdian) 246 B6
Fyé 75 C5

Gabbiano 189 C3
Gabiano 175 A4
Gabrielli 256 B3
Gabrovo 235 C3
Gageac-et-Rouillac 109 B5
Gaierhof 184 A5
Gaillac 113 D6
Gain, Champ 60 F4
Gainey Vineyard 265 F5
Gainfarn 224 G1
Gain, les Champs 59 F6, 60 G1
Gaisböhl 161 G5
Gaispfad 153 D4
Gai Xian 246 B6
Gaja 176 G2
Galafrey 286 G4
Galafura 210 F2
Galati 237 D5
Gales Creek 273 B4
Galienne, Dist. de 110 F6
Galippe, la 117 F6
Gallega Carrahola 201 E2
Gallicano nel Làzio 193 C6
Gallina 176 E4
Gallo, E & J 267 C3
Galt 267 A2
Galuches, les 117 D3
Gamaires, les 66 F3
Gamay 60 E3
Gamay à l'Est, le Bas de 60 E3
Gamay, Sur 60 E3
Gambellara 179 D3, 183 G2
Gamets, les 61 E2
Gamets, les Petits 61 G4
Gamlitz 222 G2
Gampel 221 C5
Gan 113 G2
Gäncä 240 D5
Gandesa 204 G5
Gan Eden 255 E5
Garanches 72 G4
Garancille 111 F3
Garcia 204 F6
Garcia, Qta do 210 G1
Garda 182 E3
Garde, la 136 C3
Gardière, la 117 C1
Gardone Riviera 182 E1
Gardonne 109 B5
Gárdony 229 F1
Garengue, la 101 C5
Garenne, Clos de la 60 F4
Garenne ou sur la Garenne, la 60 F4
Garéoult 136 B3
Garey 265 E4
Gargouillot, en 61 G3
Garidells, Els 205 F2
Garraf 205 F4
Garrants, les 72 C5
Garrigues, Les 130 G6
Gärtchen 151 C3
Garza Cellars, La 271 F2
Gaspar, Florido Cano 201 G1
Gassin 136 C5
Gaston 273 B4
Gates 273 D6
Gattinara 173 D4
Gau-Bickelheim 163 B4
Gau-Bischofsheim 163 B5
Gaudets, les 72 D4
Gaudichots, les 65 F4
Gaudichot/la Tache, les 65 F4
Gaudrelle, la 118 B3
Gauer Estate 255 C5
Gauriac 108 F2
Gauthey, le Clos 61 E3
Gavà 205 F4
Gaviota 265 G5
Gavoty, Dom. 136 B4
Gawler 276 B6
Gaziantep 243 D5
Gazzah 243 F4
Geaune 113 F1
Gedersdorf 222 B2
Geelong 277 D3, 280 F3
Gehm 159 E4
Geierslay 151 D3
Geisberg, *Austria* 225 G3
Geisberg, *France* 123 C4
Geisberg, *Germany* 147 E4
Geisenheim 157 F6, 158 G1
Geispolsheim 120 A5
Gela 195 G3
Gelida 205 E4
Gellibrand 280 G2
Gelos 113 F2
Genadendal 290 F3
Genaivrières, aux 65 G4
Genavrières, les 66 E5
General Alvear 295 C5
Genet, Clos 59 E3
Genêt, en 62 E6
Genève 137 A3, 219 G1, 220 C4
Genevrières Dessous, les 60 G5
Genevrières Dessus, les 60 F6
Genevrières et le Suchot, les 63 F3
Genheim 155 A5
Genova 173 F4
Gensac 97 D3, 109 B3
Gensac-la-Pallue 111 E1
Gensingen, *Nahe* 155 B6
Gensingen, *Rheinhessen* 163 B3
Genzano di Roma 193 E5
Geographe Estate 287 B2
George 290 F6
George Town 287 F6
Gera 143 A5
Geria, La 207 F6
Germolles 68 D4
Gerümpel 161 E5
Gevrey-Chambertin 55 C6, 57 B5, 67 E2
Geyser Peak 255 B4
Geyserville 255 B4
Ghemme 173 C4
Ghioroc 237 C2
Ghisonaccia 140 F5
Ghurdjaani 240 C5
Giacosa 176 E4
Gibassier, les 67 F4
Gibbon 272 G4
Gibson 267 A2
Gien 115 A5
Gifford's Hall 298 E5
Gigondas 129 D4, 131 C5
Gigotte, la 61 F4
Gilentown 283 E5
Gillespie Vyds 287 F2
Gilly 220 B4
Gilroy 263 D4
Gimarets, les 72 C6
Gimbsheim 163 C5
Gimileo 203 F2
Ginestar 204 G5
Ginestet 109 A5
Gioia del Colle 195 C5
Gippsland 277 D4
Girard 263 D4
Girardet 271 F2
Girardières, les 118 B3
Girarmes, les 119 F4
Girò di Cagliari 195 E2
Giroussens 113 E5
Gisborne 288 C6
Giulianello 193 E6
Giumarra 267 G6
Givry 55 D5, 68 D4
Gizeux 114 B6
Gland 220 B4
Glarus 219 E5
Gleiszellen-Gleishorbach 161 D1
Gleizé 71 E4
Glen Carlou 293 D3
Glenelg 284 B2
Glen Ellen 254 E4
Glenlea 281 A5
Glen Oak 278 C5
Glenora 275 B4
Glenouze 114 C6
Glenrowan-Milawa 277 C3, 280 D5
Glenwood 273 B4
Glöck 162 D5
Gloeckelberg 123 D5
Gloria Ferrer 257 F4
Gnadenfrei 282 B4
Godeaux, les 63 D2
Godeaux, Petits 63 D2
Godenano Secondo 189 E3
Godiasco 177 G3
Godramstein 161 C2
Godstone 298 F5
Goede Hoop 292 F6
Goedgeloof 292 F6
Goldatzel 158 E2
Goldbachel 161 D5
Gold Beach 271 G1
Goldberg, *Burgenland* 223 B4
Goldberg, *Kremstal* 225 F3
Goldberg, *Rheingau* 158 E4
Goldberg, *Saar* 147 C2
Goldendale 271 C4
Goldene Luft 162 C4
Golden Grape State 278 C4
Goldert 122 C4
Goldrube 153 C3
Goldschatz 152 G6
Gold-Tröpfchen 151 C1
Goldwingert 152 B5
Golferenzo 177 F5
Golop 229 E1
Gols 222 D4, 223 B6
Gomera 207 G4
Gomersal 282 C3
Gômez Palacio 269 E5
Gondeville 111 E4
Gondomar 215 C5
Gönnheim 161 B2
Gonzalez Byass 201 G2
Goosecross 259 E5
Gordon Brothers 271 B6
Gorges 115 G5
Gorges de l'Hérault 138 C6
Gorges de Narvaux, les 60 F6
Gorges et Côte de Millau 53 F3, 139 G2
Gorizia 179 C6, 181 C6, 183 C6
Goma 233 A3
Gornja Radgona 231 A5
Gomjeradgonske Gorice 231 B5
Goshen 267 E5
Göttersitz 167 C3
Gottesäcker, *Austria* 223 B4
Gottesacker, *Germany* 159 F5
Gottesfuss 147 B4
Gotteshilfe 163 C5
Gottesthal 158 F5
Gottesville 285 D5
Göttlesbrunn 222 C3
Götzenfels 155 F1
Goudge 295 C5
Goudins, Champs 65 G4
Gouin, en 60 D3
Goujonne, la 59 G6, 60 G1
Goulbum 277 B5
Goulbum Valley 277 C3, 280 D4
Goulots, les 67 E2
Goumenissa 239 B3
Goundrey 286 G3
Gouttes d'Or, les 61 F1
Gouveia 215 F6
Gouvinhas 210 F3
Goyenechea 295 C5
Graach a. d. Mosel 153 E1
Graacher Schäferei 153 E2
Graben 153 F2
Grace family 259 B5
Gracetown 287 D1
Gradignan 80 F3, 96 D4, 99 C2
Gradisca 181 C6
Gradisca d'Isonzo 183 D5
Grado 181 D5
Graeser 259 C1
Grafenberg, *Piesport* 151 D1
Gräfenberg, *Rheingau* 159 E2
Grafenstück 161 A2
Grafschafter Sonnenberg 152 G5
Grainhübel 161 F5
Gralyn 287 D1
Graminier 131 F5
Granada, La 205 E3
Gran Canaria 207 G5
Grand Boise, Dom. 136 B2
Grand Clos, les 59 F5
Grande Côte, la 119 F2
Grande Montagne, la 60 F1
Grande-Motte, la 135 B5
Grande Rue, la 65 F4
Grandes Bastes, les 118 A4
Grandes-Vignes, Clos des 101 C6
Grand, Le 267 C4
Grand-Maison, Dom. 99 E4
Grand Mont 117 C3
Grand River 275 C2
Grand Ronde 273 C3
Grands-Champs, les, *Auxey-Duresses* 61 E2
Grands Champs, les, *Puligny* 60 G4
Grandview 272 G4
Graneros 297 C5
Grange des Quatre-Sous, La 133 B4, 134 C6
Grange, La 267 C3
Granger 271 B5, 272 F3
Granit 235 C3
Granja-Amareleja 208 E5, 213 F6
Grant Burge 282 C4
Grants Pass 271 G2
Gratallops 204 F6
Graton 255 E5
Graubünden 219 F5
Grauves 79 F3
Gravains, aux 63 D2
Grave del Friuli 179 B5, 181 B4
Graves 80 F3, 96 E4
Graves de Vayres 80 A5, 96 G3
Gravières, les 59 F4
Gravina 195 C5
Gravner 183 C6
Graymoor 285 D5
Graz 222 F1
Greater Auckland 288 B4
Great Wall Winery 246 B3
Great Western 277 D2, 280 E1
Greco di Bianco 195 F5
Greco di Tufo 195 B3
Green & Red 259 C5
Greenberry 273 E4
Greenhill 287 C2
Greenock 282 A4
Greenock Creek 282 B4
Green Valley, *Australia* 287 F2
Green Valley, *USA* 255 E4
Greenwood Ridge 256 C2
Gréffieux, les 127 C4
Greiz 143 A5
Grenouilles 75 D4
Gresham 271 C3, 273 B6
Grésigny 68 B4
Greta 278 B5
Greve in Chianti 189 D4
Grèves, les, *Aloxe-Corton* 63 F4
Grèves, les, *Beaune* 62 F5
Grèves, sur les 62 E4
Grevilly 69 A5
Greymouth 288 E3
Grezzana 182 F5
Grgich Hills 259 D4
Griffith 277 B3
Grignolino d'Asti 175 C4
Grignolino del Monferrato Casalese 173 D3, 175 A4
Grigoriopol 241 F5
Grille, la 117 F3
Grillès, les Champs 72 A5
Grimisuat 221 C3
Grimma 167 C5
Grinzane Cavour 176 F2
Grinzing 222 C3, 224 B2
Griotte Chambertin 66 F6
Gristina 275 C5
Groendal 293 F6
Grombalia 245 B6
Gromore 272 E1
Groseilles, les 66 F3
Gros Plant du Pays Nantais 52 D6
Gross-Bottwar 165 C4
Grossenhain 167 C6
Grosser Hengelberg 151 D1
Grosser Herrgott 151 C3
Grosset 283 F6
Grosseto 187 C2
Grosshöflein 222 D3
Grosskarlbach 161 A2
Groth 259 E4
Grottaferrata 193 D5
Grove Hill Wines 284 A4
Grove Mill 289 G3
Grover City 265 D3
Grovetown 289 F5
Groznyy 240 C5
Grozon 137 E5
Grudovo 235 C5
Gruenchers, les, *Chambolle-Musigny* 66 F3
Gruenchers, les, *Morey-St-Denis* 66 F4
Gruet Winery 269 D4
Grumello 177 B3
Grund 158 G2
Grünstadt 161 A2
Gruyaches, les 60 G5
Gruyere 281 C5
Guadalajara 269 F5
Guadalupe, *Mexico* 269 D2
Guadalupe, *USA* 265 E3
Guado al Tasso 191 C4
Guanajuato 269 F5
Guarda 208 B5

Gueberschwihr 120 E3, 122 B4
Guebwiller 120 F3, 122 A1
Guelma 245 B5
Guenoc 256 D6
Guenoc Valley 256 D6
Guerchère 59 G5
Guérets, les 63 E3
Guéripes, les 66 E2
Guerneville 255 D4
Guernewood Park 255 D3
Guerrouane 245 B2
Guès d'Amant, les 118 B2
Guetottes 63 C1
Guettes, aux 63 D2
Gueulepines, les 67 F3
Guglielmo 263 C4
Guiães 210 E3
Guiamets, Els 204 G6
Guilherand 125 E4
Guillattes, les 72 C6
Guimarães 208 A4, 215 C5
Guinelay, En 72 B6
Güldenmorgen 162 G5, 163 C5
Guldental 155 B5
Gumiel del Mercado 206 E4
Gumpöldskirchen 222 C3, 224 E2
Gundelsheim 165 B4
Gundersheim 163 D5
Gundlach-Bundschu 254 G5, 257 E4
Guntersblum 143 B4, 163 C5
Gunterslay 151 D2
Guntramsdorf 222 C3, 224 E2
Gunyulgup 287 C1
Gustine 267 C3
Gutenberg 158 G3
Gutenhölle 154 F5
Gutental 155 C2
Gutes Domtal 163 B5
Gutleuthaus 162 G5
Guttenberg 161 D2
Gy 220 C4
Gyöngyös 226 E4
Gyopáros 229 D4
Györ 226 E2

Hacienda 255 D4
Hackham 284 D2
Hadres 222 B2
Hafner 255 B5
Hagafen 259 F5
Hagerstown 275 D3
Hahnheim 163 B5
Haie Martel, la 117 G5
Haillan, le 96 C3
Hainburg 222 C4
Hainfeld 161 C2
Hajós 226 F2
Hajós-Vaskút 226 G3
Hakuba 248 B3
Halab (Aleppo) 243 D5
Halbjoch 223 B4
Halbturn 222 D4
Halcyon Daze Vyd 281 C3
Halfpenny Green 298 E4
Hallcrest 263 D2
Halle 143 A5
Hallett Cove 284 C2
Hallgarten 158 E5
Haloze 231 C4, 233 B2
Halsey 273 E4
Haltingen 165 F1
Hamah 243 E5
Hambach 161 B2
Hameau de Blagny 60 F4
Hamilton, *Australia* 277 D2
Hamilton, *Canada* 275 B2
Hamilton, *New Zealand* 288 B4
Hamilton & Son, R 282 E6
Hamlet Hill 275 C6
Hamm 147 C2
Hammerstein 149 F2
Handley 256 C2
Hanford 267 E5
Hanging Rock 280 E3
Hanna 255 E5
Hannersdorf 222 E3
Hanns Kornell 259 C2
Hansenberg 158 F2
Hanzell 254 F5
Happ's 287 C2
Happy Valley 278 C4
Harbor 267 A2
Hardy 110 F5
Hargesheim 155 B5
Hargrave 275 C5
Harling 298 E6
Haro 202 B5, 203 F1
Harpersfield 275 C2
Harrah 272 F2
Harrisburg 275 D4
Harrison 259 D5
Harsovo 235 D2
Hartenberg 293 E1
Hartford 275 C5
Harvey 286 E2
Harwood 272 E2
Häschen 151 D1
Hasensprung 158 F3
Haslach 143 F4
Hassel 159 F1
Hastings 288 C5
Hastings 298 F5
Hatalos 229 F3
Hâtes, les 59 F3
Hato 200 B3
Hatschbourg 122 C4
Hattenheim 158 F6
Hattstatt 120 E4, 122 C4
Haugsdorf 222 B2
Haussatz 223 C3
Haut-Benauge, Entre-Deux-Mers 80 F4, 96 G3
Haut-Comtat 53 F4, 139 G3
Haute-Goulaine 115 F4
Hauterive en Pays d'Aude 138 E5
Hautés, les 61 E1
Haut-Langoiran 96 E5
Haut-Lieu, le 118 B3
Haut-Médoc 80 D2
Haut-Peyraguey, Clos 101 F4
Haut Santenay 59 E2
Hauts Champs, les 117 C3
Hauts-de-Badens 138 E4
Hautvillers 79 D3
Haux 96 E5
Havens 259 G6
Hawera 288 C4
Hawke's Bay 288 C5
Haye-Fouassière, la 115 F5
Hay Shed Hill 287 D2
Haza Pozo 200 A5
Healdsburg 255 C5
Healesville 280 F4, 281 B5
Heathcote 280 E3
Heathfield 284 B4
Hecker Pass 263 D3
Hedges 271 A3
Heemskerk 287 F6
Hefa (Haifa) 243 F4
Heggies Vineyard 282 C5
Heidelberg, *Germany* 143 C4, 165 B3
Heidelberg, *S. Africa* 290 F4
Heilbronn 143 D5, 165 C4
Heiligenbaum 162 E4
Heiligenberg 158 D6, 159 F1
Heiligenborn 147 G4
Heiligenstock 159 F2
Heimberg 154 F3
Heissenstein 122 A1
Heitz Wine Cellars 259 D4
Hejian 246 C3
Held 150 F6
Helenenkloster 152 G6
Helm 267 E4
Hendelberg 158 D6
Henderson 288 B4
Hengshui 246 C3
Hengst 122 C6
Henkell 281 A4
Hennessy 110 F5, F6, G6
Henry Estate 271 F2
Henschke 282 B6
Heppenheim 165 A3
Heras, Las 295 A4
Herbues, aux, *Fixin* 67 E4
Herbues, aux, *Nuits-St-Georges* 65 G2
Herbues, les 66 F3
Herbuottes, les 66 F5
Hercegkút 229 D5
Hercegovina 233 D3
Herdade de Madeira 213 E5
Herdade do Mouchão 213 E4
Heritage 282 B4
Hermance 220 C4
Hermannsberg 154 G4
Hermannshöhle 154 G4
Hermanus 290 G2
Hermigua 207 G4
Hermiston 271 C5
Hermosillo 269 E3
Hernals 224 B2
Herndon 267 D4
Herrenberg, *Bernkastel* 152 B6
Herrenberg, *Franken* 166 B6
Herrenberg, *Piesport* 151 B4
Herrenberg, *Rheinhessen* 162 F5
Herrenberg, *Pfalz* 161 B4
Herrenberg, *Ruwer* 149 E4
Herrenberg, *Saar* 147 A4
Herrenberger 147 D2
Herrengarten 162 F6, G6
Herrenmorgen 161 A4
Herrgottsacker 161 F5
Herrlich 161 D2
Herrnbaumgarten 222 B3
Herrschaft 219 E5
Hervelets, les 67 E4
Herxheim 161 D2
Hess Collection Winery 259 F4
Hessische Bergstrasse 143 C4
Hétszölö 229 G4
Heublein 267 D4
Heuchelberg 165 C4
Heywood 277 D1
Hidalgo del Parral 269 E4
Hidden Cellars 256 C3
Hidden Spring 298 F5
Hidden Springs 273 C4
Hierro 207 G4
Hietzing 224 C2
Highfield Estate 289 G4
High Wycombe 282 C4
Hillcrest, *Australia* 281 C6
Hillcrest, *USA* 271 F2
Hillebrand Estates 275 B3
Hillsboro 271 C2, 273 B4
Hill-Smith 282 C5
Himmelreich 152 C5, 153 E1
Hims (Homs) 243 E5
Hine 110 G5
Hinkelstein 155 C1
Hinman 271 E2
Hinter der Burg 224 G5
Hinterkirch 157 D2
Hinter-Kirchen 224 G6
Hinter-Seiber 224 G5
Hintós 229 F3
Hinzerling 272 G4
Hipping 162 D4
Hitzendorf 222 F1
Hitzlay 149 E5
H J T 280 D5
Hlohovec 230 G4
Hlohovec/Trnava 230 G4
H M R 265 B3
Hobart 287 G6
Hochbenn 161 B4
Hochmess 161 A2, B4
Hochstadt 161 C2
Hochstätten 155 D5
Hochstrasser 225 G2
Hódmezovásárhely 226 G4
Hodonín 230 G3
Hoeppslei 147 G4
Hofäcker 223 B5, C5
Hofberg, *Bernkastel* 152 D5
Hofberg, *Saar* 147 A4
Hofberger 151 D1
Hofgarten 155 D1
Höflein 222 C3
Hofrat 166 B5
Hofsatz 223 B4
Hofstatter, J 185 E5
Hofstück 161 B2, F6
Hogue 272 G4
Hoheburg 161 G5
Hohenberg 165 C3
Hohenmorgen 161 F5
Hohenneuffen 165 D4
Hohenrain 159 F2
Hohenwarth 222 B2
Höhereck 225 G2
Hohrodberg 120 E3
Hohwald, le 120 B4
Hokitika 288 E3
Holbrook 273 B5
Hold-Völgy 229 F2
Höll 155 F1
Hölle, *Austria* 223 C5
Hölle, *Rheingau* 158 F2
Hölle, *Pfalz* 162 E5
Hölle, *Saar* 147 B3
Höllenberg 157 D2
Höllenpfad 161 A2
Hollerin 225 G2
Hollick 285 D6
Hollister 263 D4
Hollybush 298 G4
Hollydene Estate 279 F4
Homburg 166 B3
Homme, L' 115 A1
Homme, l' 127 C5
Homme Mort, l' 75 B3
Honda 265 F3
Honeywood 273 D4
Honig 259 B6
Honigberg, *Bernkastel* 152 E5
Honigberg, *Franken* 166 B5
Honigberg, *Rheingau* 158 F2, 159 F2
Honigsäckel 161 A2, B5
Hood River 271 C3
Hoodsport 271 A2
Hope Farms 265 B3
Hop Kiln 255 D5
Hörecker 147 B3
Horizon's Edge 272 F3
Homillo, El 200 B5
Homstein 223 B3
Horowhenua 288 D4
Horra, La 206 E4
Horsham 277 C2
Horton 275 E3
Horton Estate 298 F4
Hossú-Hegy 229 D5
Hostalets, Els 205 E4
Hotaka 248 C3
Hotinja vas 231 B4
Houghton Wines 286 C1
Houillères, les 60 G3
Houston, *Oregon* 271 E2
Houston, *Texas* 269 E6
Houtz 265 F5
Howell Mountain 259 B3
Hradec Králové 230 E3
Huadong Winery 246 D5
Huailai 246 B3
Hualañé 297 E3
Huanghua 246 C4
Huasna 265 D4
Hubbard 273 C5
Hubertuslay 153 C1
Hughson 267 C3
Hugo 284 D3
Hühnerberg 153 E4
Huismes 117 E3
Hunawihr 120 D4, 123 C4
Hund 225 G3
Hundsheim 225 G3
Hungerford Hill, *Coonawarra* 285 C6
Hungerford Hill, *Hunter* 278 C4
Hungriger Wolf 155 C2
Hunter Estate 278 B4
Hunter's 289 F4
Hunter Valley 277 A6
Huntington 275 E1
Huntly 288 B4
Hurbanovo 230 G4
Husi 237 C5
Hurigny 69 E5
Huron 267 E4
Husch 256 C2
Husseau 118 C5
Husseren-les-Châteaux 122 C5
Hustopece 230 F3
Hustopece/Hodonín 230 F3
Hütte 147 B5
Hvar 233 D2
Hyatt Vyds 272 F3
Hyères 136 C3

Ialoveni 241 F5
Iasi 237 B5
Icod de los Vinos 207 G4
Idhra 239 D4
Idyll 280 F3
Igé 69 D4
Igualada 205 D3
Ihringen 165 E1
Iida 248 D3
Ikaria 239 D5
Ile-Bouchard, l' 117 G6
Ile de Beauté 139 B4
Ile Margaux, Dom. de l' 95 A4
Ile-Rousse, l' 140 E4
Illa, L' 205 E2
Illasi 183 G1
Illats 96 F5
Ille-sur-Têt 133 F3
Illkirch-Graffenstaden 120 A6
Illmitz 222 D4, 223 C5
Illzach 120 G4
Ilyama 248 B4
Imperia 173 G3
Imperial (State) Cellar 229 D4
Impruneta 189 C3
Ina 248 D3
Inca, Pte del 295 A3
Incisa in Val d'Arno 189 C5
Independence 273 D4
Inferno 177 B3
Ingelheim 143 B3, 163 B4
Ingenheim 161 D2
Ingersheim 120 E4, 123 C1
Inglenook 263 D4
Ingleses, Qta dos 211 G6
Ingleside Plantation 275 E4
Inglewood 280 D2
Ingoldby 284 D2
Inniskillin 275 B3
Interlaken 219 F3
Ioannina 239 C2
Ios 239 E5
Iphofen 166 C5
Iraklion 239 F5
Irancy 55 B3, 73 F4
Irbid 243 F5
Irlas, Las 205 F1
Ironbank 284 C3
Iron Horse 255 E4
Irouléguy 112 G6
Irsch 147 F4
Iscar 206 F3
Ischia 195 C2
Isera 184 E4
Iskenderun 243 D5
Isläcker 223 C4
Isle-sur-la-Sorgue, l' 129 E5
Isleton 267 B2
Isola Bella 193 F5
Isonzo 179 C6, 181 C6, 183 D5
Isparta 243 C3
Issan 95 B3
Issigeac 109 C6
Istanbul 243 B2
Isten-Hegy 229 F2
Istra 233 C1
Istres 129 F4
Istria-Babadag 237 D5
Ivanhoe 278 C4
Ivaylovgrad 235 D4
Izmayil 241 G5
Izmir 243 C1
Izmit 243 B3

Jachères, aux 65 G4
Jackson Estate 289 G4
Jacques, les 72 C6
Jacquines, les 65 G3
Jade Mountain 255 A3
Jadida, El 245 B1
Jaeger-Inglewood 259 A6
Jalama 265 G4
Jambles 68 E3
James Haselgrove 285 D6
Jamestown, *Australia* 276 A6
Jamestown, *USA* 275 C3
Jamieson 280 E5
Jara, La 200 B3
Jardim do Mar 216 B5
Jardin de la France 139 F2
Jardinito, El 201 C4
Jarnac 111 D4
Jarolières, les 61 F5
Jarrons, Hauts 63 E1
Jas d'Esclans, Dom. du 136 B5
Jasper Hill 280 E3
Jászberény 226 E4
Javernière 72 E4
Javrezac 110 C5
Jaxu 112 G6
Jefferson 273 D4
Jekel 263 F5
Jemciujina 241 F5
Jena 143 A5
Jendreau, Champs 59 G6
Jepson 256 C3
Jerez 197 E2
Jerez de la Frontera 201 D4
Jerrys Plains 279 G5
Jersey City 275 C5
Jesuitenberg 147 C2
Jesuitengarten, *Rheingau* 158 G3
Jesuitengarten, *Pfalz* 161 E5
Jesuitengarten, *Ruwer* 149 F5
Jeunelotte, la 60 F4
Jeunes Rois, les 67 E3
Jianchang 246 B5
Jiaonan 246 D5
Jiao Xian 246 D5
Jihlava 230 F3
Jim Barry 283 D5
Jimo 246 D5
Jinan 246 D3
Jingalla 286 G4
Jining 246 E3
Jinzhou 246 A5
Ji Xian 246 B4
Joching 224 G5
Johannisberg, *Rheingau* 143 B3, 157 D3, 158 F2, 159 G1
Johannisberg, *Ruwer* 149 D5
Johannisbrünnchen 153 F2
Johnson 275 B3
Johnson's Alexander Valley 255 C5
Johnson Turnbull 259 B6
Johnstown 275 D3
Jois 222 C3
Jolivet, Clos du 117 D3
Joncosa, La 205 F3
Jongieux 137 C2
Jonquières 131 E3
Jordan, *S. Africa* 292 F6
Jordan, *USA* 255 C5
Jory 263 C3
José de Soto 201 G1
Josef Brigl 185 D5
Jose Medina y Cia 201 G1
Joseph Phelps 259 D4
Josephshöfer 153 E1
Jota, La 259 C4
Jouènes, les 61 E2
Jouères, les 61 G4
Jouise 67 F1
Journaux, les 67 F3
Journoblot, en 60 G2
Jouy-lès-Reims 79 A2
Judd's Hill 259 C4
Jud's Hill 283 D5
Juffer 151 B4, 152 F5
Juffer Sonnenuhr 151 A5, 152 F5
Jujen Briag 235 C5
Jujuy 294 F2
Juliénas 55 F5, 72 A5
Jullié 71 B3, 72 A4
Jully-lès-Buxy 68 G3
Jumilla 197 D4
Junco, Qta do 210 E5
Junee 277 B4
Jungfer 158 E6
Juntas, Las 295 C4
Jurançon 113 F1
Jussy 220 C4
Justice, la 67 F2
Justin 265 B2
Jutruots, les 66 E2
Ju Xian 246 E4
Jyonohira 248 D4

Kabininge 282 C4
Kableshkovo 235 C5
Kadina 276 B5
Kaeffer-Kopf 123 C2
Kaesler's Farm 282 B4
Kafels 154 F6
Kahlenberg, *Austria* 224 B2
Kahlenberg, *Germany* 155 D2
Kaikohe 288 A4
Kaikoura 288 E4
Kaiserberg 224 F6
Kaisergarten 223 C5
Kaiserpfalz 163 B4
Kaiserstuhl-Tuniberg 143 F3, 165 E1
Kaitaia 288 A4
Kaituna 289 F3
Kalamata 239 E3
Kalbspflicht 159 F3
Kalecik 243 B4
Kalkofen 161 A4, F5
Kallstadt 161 A2, A5
Kalocsa 226 F3
Kalokhorio 244 G3
Kalorama 281 D4
Kaltenleutgeben 224 D1
Kambos 244 F2
Kamen Bryag 235 B6
Kammer 151 A4
Kamptal 222 E4
Kandel 161 D2
Kangarilla 284 D3
Kangaroo Island 276 C5
Kanonkop 293 E2
Kanzem 147 B3
Kanzlerberg 123 D5
Kapela 231 A5, 233 A3
Kapellchen 151 C3
Kapellenpfad 155 D2
Kapellenweg 224 E2
Kapfenberg 222 E1
Kapitel-Weingarten 223 C5
Kaposvár 226 G2
Kappelrodeck 165 D3
Kapuvar 226 E2
Karabük 243 B4
Karabunar 235 C3
Karaman 243 D4
Karcag 226 F5
Kardhitsa 239 C3
Kardinalsberg 153 F1
Karlovac 233 B2
Karlovo 235 C3
Karlovy Vary 230 E1
Karlsberg 147 B5
Karl Seppelt Grand Cru Estate 282 E5
Karlsruhe 143 D4, 165 C3
Karlstejn 230 F2
Karnobat 235 C5
Károlyfalva 229 C5
Karpathos 239 F6
Karthauserhofberg 149 D5
Karuizawa 248 C4
Kasel 143 C2, 149 E4
Kassaváros 229 E1
Kastoria 239 B2
Kathikas 244 F1
Kathryn Kennedy 263 C2
Katnook Estate 285 C5
Katoomba 277 B5
Katsunuma 248 D4
Kätzchen 151 A4
Katzenthal 120 D3, 123 C1
Kauzenberg in den Mauern 155 D2
Kauzenberg Oranienberg 155 E2
Kauzenberg-Rosenhügel 155 D2
Kavadarci 233 G5
Kavaklidere 243 B4
Kavalla 239 B4
Kavarna 235 B6
Kavuga 279 E5
Kawerau 288 C5
Kayseri 243 C5
Kaysersberg 120 D3, 123 B3
Kazanluk 235 C3
Kea 239 D4
Kecskemét 226 F4
Kefallinia (Cephalonia) 239 D2
Kehrnagel 149 E5
Keinbah 278 C5
Keith 277 C1
Keizer 273 C4
Kellerberg 225 G2
Kellereigenossenschaft Greis-Bozen 185 C6
Kellereigenossenschaft Terlan 185 C5
Kellermeister 282 C3
Kellybrook 281 C3
Kelokedhara 244 G2
Kelseyville 256 C5
Kelso 271 C2
Kendall-Jackson 256 C4
Kenitra 245 B2
Kennewick 271 C5, 272 G6
Kent 271 A3
Kent Rasmussen 257 E6
Kenwood 254 E4
Kerc' 240 B3
Kerkira (Corfu) 239 C1
Kerman 267 D4
Kertz 154 G5
Keskin 243 C4
Kessler 122 B1
Kesten 151 B3
Keszthely 226 F2
Kettleman City 267 F4
Kettmeir, G 185 D5
Keyes 267 C3
Keyneton 282 C6
Khalkis 239 C4
Khania 239 F4
Khan Krum 235 B4
Khaskovo 235 D4
Kherson 240 B2
Khios 239 D5
Khoulou 244 F1
Kickelskopf 155 F1
Kidricevo 231 C4
Kiedrich 159 E2
Kientzheim 120 D3, 123 C2
Kies 282 C3
Kieselberg 161 F5
Kikyogahara 248 C3
Kilani 244 G2
Kilis 243 D5
Kilmore 280 E3
Kilzberg 158 F2
Kincsem 229 E4
Kindenheim 161 A2
Kindred Lockleven 278 C4
King City 263 G5
Kingersheim 120 G4
Kingsburg 267 E5
Kings Valley 273 D4
Kinheim 153 C1
Kintzheim 120 C4
Kiona 272 G5
Király 229 F3
Király-Hegy 229 D5
Kirchberg, *Austria* 222 B2, 223 B5
Kirchberg, *Bernkastel* 152 G6
Kirchberg, *Franken* 166 B5
Kirchberg, *Saar* 147 B2
Kirchberg de Ribeauvillé 123 C5
Kirchenpfad 157 E5
Kirchensatz 223 B6
Kirchenstück 161 E5
Kirchenweinberg 165 C4
Kirchheim 161 A2
Kirchlay 153 C2
Kirchplatte 162 D3
Kirigin Cellars 263 C4
Kirklareli 243 A2
Kirrweiler 161 C2
Kirschheck 154 F6
Kirschroth 155 D3
Kirsehir 243 C4
Kiskörös 226 F3
Kiskunfélegyháza 226 F4
Kiskunhalas 226 G3
Kiskunság 226 F4
Kiso-Fukushima 248 D2
Kistler 254 D4
Kithira 239 E3
Kithnos 239 D4
Kitterle 122 A1
Kitzingen 166 B5
Klamm 154 G5
Klaus, *Austria* 224 F6
Klaus, *Germany* 158 G2
Kläuserweg 157 F6, 158 G2
Klavdhia 244 F4
Klein Karoo 290 F4
Klein Zalze 293 G1
Klettgau 219 D4
Klöch 222 F2
Klosterberg, *Bernkastel* 152 D5
Klosterberg, *Nahe* 154 F6
Klosterberg, *Rheingau* 157 E4, 158 E4, 159 E2
Klosterberg, *Saar* 147 E3
Klostergarten, *Piesport* 150 F6, 151 B4
Klostergarten, *Rheinhessen* 162 D4
Klostergarten, *Pfalz* 161 E6
Klosterkellerei Muri 185 C6
Klosterlay 157 E4
Kloster Liebfrauenberg 161 D2
Klosterneuburg 222 C3, 224 A2
Klostersatz 225 G2
Klüsserath 150 E5
Knapp 275 B4
Knappstein 283 D5
Knight Granite Hills 280 E3
Knights Valley 255 C6
Knudsen Erath 273 C4
Koblenz 143 A3
Kobnert (Kallstadt) 161 A2, A5
Kobuchizawa 248 D4
Kocher-Jagst-Tauber 143 C5
Koelenhof 293 D1
Kofu 248 D4
Kögel 225 F3
Kohfidisch 222 E3
Kollmitz 224 G5
Komagane 248 D3
Komarevo 235 B3
Komárno 230 G4
Kommlingen 147 A4
Komoro 248 C4
Königsbach 161 B2
Königsberg 153 C4
Königsfels 154 F3
Königsgarten 161 C2
Königswingert 161 D4
Konjic 233 D3
Konocti 256 C5
Konrad Estate 256 B3
Konstanz 143 G5, 165 G4
Kontinentalna Hrvatska 233 B3
Konya 243 C3
Konz 147 A3
Koolbury 279 E5
Koopmanskloof 292 E6
Kopf 165 D4
Kophinou 244 G3
Köporos 229 F2
Korbel 255 D4
Korcula 233 E2
Korinthos 239 D3
Korro 284 D2
Kos 239 E6
Koshoku 248 B3
Kosice 230 G6
Kosovo 233 F5
Kotor 233 E4
Kótsag 229 G4

Koumi 248 C4
Kővágó 229 F1, F3
Kövenig 153 C3
Köves 229 F1
Kövesd 229 G3
Köves-Hegy 229 C6
Köwerich 150 F6
Kozani 239 B2
Kralevo 235 B4
Královsky 230 G6
Kramer 273 B4
Kramolin 235 B3
Kranzberg 162 D4
Krasnodar 240 B3
Kräuterhaus 153 D3
Kreidkeller 161 A4
Krems 222 B1, 225 F4
Kremstal 222 E4, 224 F3
Krettnach 147 A5
Kreutles 225 G2
Kreuz 162 G5
Kreuzberg 153 E3
Kreuznach 143 B3, 155 E1
Kreuzweingarten 223 C3
Kreuzwingert 151 C2
Kriti (Crete) 239 F4
Kroemer 282 B4
Krondorf 282 C4
Krone 149 F5
Kronenberg, *Nahe* 155 B6, D1
Kronenberg, *Pfalz* 161 A5
Krötenbrunnen 162 F5, 163 C5
Krötenpfuhl 155 D2
Kröv 153 C2
Krupina 230 G4
Kruzevac 233 E5
Ksara 243 E5
Ktima 244 G1
Kurdzhali 235 D3
Kumeu/Huapai 288 B4
Kunde 254 E4
Kupfergrube 154 G4
Kupp, *Ruwer* 149 F2
Kupp, *Saar* 147 D2
Kurfürstenberg 149 F5
Kurfurstenstuck 163 B4
Kurfürstlay 151 B4, 152 G6
Kurzberg 223 B6
Kütahya 243 C3
K'ut'aisi 240 C4
Kutjevo 233 C4
Kútpatka 229 E4
KWV 293 D4
Kyabram 280 D4
Kyneton 277 D3, 280 E3
Kyrenia 244 E3
Kythrea 244 E4
Kyustendil 235 C1

Labarde 95 D4
Labastida 202 A5, 203 F2
Labastide d'Armagnac 113 E2
Labico 193 D6
Laborie 293 D4
Labrousse 89 C1
Lackawanna 275 B3
Lacomb 273 E5
Laconnex Soral 220 D3
Lacrima di Morro 187 C6
Ladbroke Grove 285 E5
Ladismith 290 F5
Ladoix-Serrigny 55 C5
Ladoschen 225 G3
Lafare 131 D6
Lafayette 273 C4
Lafões 208 B4
Lagares, Qta dos 210 D6
Laghetto 193 D5
Lagnieu 137 B1
Lagoa 208 F4
Lagos 208 F4
Lagrasse 133 C3
Laguardia 202 B6, 203 F4
Laguian 113 F2
Laguna de Duero 206 E2
Laguna, La 297 E5
Lahr 165 E2
Laives (Leifers) 185 D6
Laiwu 246 D4
Laixi 246 D5
Laiyang 246 D5
Laize 69 D5
Lajes, Qta das 210 F6
Lake Bolac 280 F1
Lake Oswego 271 C3, 273 B5
Lakeport 256 C4
Lakes Entrance 277 D4
Lakes Folly 278 C5
Lakespring 263 F5
Lakewood 275 C2
Lalande-de-Pomerol 80 E4, 103 B2, 107 A3
Lalden 221 C6
Lamagdelaine 113 C5
Lamberhurst 298 F5
Lambert Bridge 255 C4
Lambertuslay 152 F5
Lamborn family 259 B3
Lambots, les 61 E5
Lambrays, Clos des 66 F4
Lambrusco di Sorbara 179 E2
Lambrusco Grasparossa di Castelvetro 179 E2
Lambrusco Mantovano 179 D2
Lambrusco Reggiano 179 E2
Lambrusco Salamino di Santa Croce 179 E3
Lamego 208 B5
Lamezia 195 E5
Lamia 239 C3
Lamont, *Australia* 286 C2
Lamont, *USA* 267 G6
Lamonzie-Montastruc 109 B6
Lamonzie-St-Martin 109 B5
Lamoreaux Landing 275 B4
Lamothe 101 D4
Lamothe-Montravel 109 B3
Lampa 297 A5
Lana 185 B4
Lancaster 275 D4
Lancié 71 C4, 72 D5
Landau in der Pfalz 143 D4, 161 C2
Lande, la 117 C2
Landerrouat 109 C4
Landmark, *Chalk Hill* 255 D5
Landmark, *Sonoma* 254 D4
Landonne, La 126 B4
Landreau, le 115 F5
Landry, Clos 62 F3
Landskroon 293 C3
Langeais 115 B1
Langenberg 159 E5
Langenlois 222 B2
Langenlonsheim 143 B3, 155 B6
Langenmorgen 161 F4
Langenstück 159 F4
Langfang 246 B3
Langhorne Creek 276 C6
Langlade 129 E3
Langon 80 G4, 96 F6
Languettes, les 63 E4
Lania 244 G2
Lannepax 113 E3
Lanouais 109 B6
Lansac 108 F4
Lantignié 71 C3
Lanúvio 193 E5
Lanzarote 207 F6
Lanzerac 293 F2
Lapis 229 F3
Lapithos 244 E3
Lapuebla de Labarca 202 B6
Largillière, en 62 E1
Lariano 193 E6
Larisa 239 C3
Larkmead 259 C2
Larnaca 244 F4
Larrets, les 66 E4
Larsen 110 G5
Laruns 113 G2
Lasseube 113 G1
Lasseubetat 113 G1
Lastra a Signa 189 B2
Latina 187 F3, 195 B2
Latisana 179 C5, 181 C4
Latresne 96 D4
Latricières Chambertin 66 F5
Lattes 135 B4
Laubenheim, *Nahe* 155 B6
Laubenheim, *Rheinhessen* 163 B5
Laudamusberg 151 F1
Laudun 129 D4, 130 E5
Lauffen 165 C4
Laujar 197 D4
Laujuzan 113 E2
Laumersheim 161 A2
Launceston 287 F6
Launching Place 281 C6
Laurel Glen 254 E3
Laurel Ridge 273 B4
Laurentiusberg 149 G6
Laurentiuslay 151 F1
Laurier, Dom. 255 D4
Lausanne 219 F2, 220 A6
Lavalle 295 A4
Lavaut Saint Jacques 67 E1
Lavaux 219 F2, 221 A1
Lavey-Morcles 221 C2
Laveyssière 109 A5
Lavières, aux 65 F3
Lavières, les 63 E2
Lavigny 137 G5
Lavinio-Lido di Enea 193 G4
Lavis 184 B5, 185 G4
Lavrottes, les 66 F3
Lawndale 254 D3
Lawrence 275 B6
Lay 153 F2
Lazise 182 F3
Lazy Creek 256 C2
Leasingham 283 D5, F5
Lebanon 273 E5
Lecce 195 C6
Lecco 173 C5
Lèches, les 109 A5
Léchet, Côte de 75 D2
Lechinta 237 B3
Leconfield 285 D6
Leeds Castle 298 F5
Leeford 298 F5
Leeton 277 B4
Leeuwen Jagt, De 293 C3
Leeuwin Estate 287 E2
Lefka 244 F2
Lefkoniko 244 E4
Leftwich Vyds 269 E5
Legé 114 C3
Legyesbénye 229 G1
Lehmann 282 B4
Leibnitz 222 F1
Leimen 165 B3
Leinhöhle 161 F4
Leinsweiler 161 C1
Leipzig 143 A5, 167 C4
Leiria 208 C4
Leistadt 161 A4
Leiterchen 151 F2
Leiwen 150 G6
Leling 246 C4
Lelo, Qta do 210 F6
Lembeye 113 F2
Lembras 109 B6
Lemoore 267 E4
Lenart v Sl. goricah 231 B4
Lenchen 158 F5
Lengenfeld 222 B1
Lengfurt 166 B3
Lens 221 C4
Lenton Brae 287 D1
Lenz 275 C5
Léognan 80 F3, 96 E4, 99 F3
León 269 F5
Leonetti Cellar 271 G4
Leschenault 286 E1
Leskovac 233 E6
Lesnik 278 C5
Lesparre-Médoc 80 C1, 85 F1
Lessini Durello 179 C3, 183 F2
Lessona 173 D3
Lesvos 239 C5
Letten 161 E6
Letterlay 153 B3
Lettweiler 155 D5
Leuk 221 C4
Leurey, au 64 F4
Leutschach 222 G1
Leverano 195 C6
Lèves-et-Thoumeyragues, les 109 B4
Levice 230 G4
Levin 288 D4
Levkas 239 C2
Lèvrier, Champ 72 E4
Levrière, la 62 F1
Levrons, les 60 G4
Levski 235 B3
Lewisburg 273 E4
Lexton 280 E2
Leynes 69 G4, 71 B4
Leyssac 87 F4
Leytron 221 C2
Leza 203 F4
Lézignan 133 C4, 134 D5
Lézignan-Corbières 133 C3, 138 E5
Lhuis 137 C1
Liaocheng 246 D3
Liards, aux Grands 63 E2
Liards, aux Petits 63 D1
Liards, les Bas 63 E1
Liberec 230 E2
Liberty 272 F3
Libourne 103 C1, 107 E1
Lichtensteinerin 224 F6
Lichtgartl 224 G5
Lido de lésolo 181 E3
Lido dei Pini 193 F4
Liébana 197 A3
Liebenberg 224 F6
Liebfrauenberg 147 B2
Liebfrauenmorgen 163 D5
Lieser 152 F6
Liesing 224 D2
Lievland 293 E3
Ligist 222 F1
Lignano Sabbiadoro 181 D5
Ligné 114 B3
Lignes, les 117 E2
Lignorelles 75 A1
Ligny-le-Châtel 73 D5
Ligondras 95 D2
Ligré 117 G4
Ligueux 109 B4
Lilliano 189 F3
Lilydale 280 F4, 281 C4
Lilydale Vyds 281 C5
Lima, *Peru* 294 F1
Lima, *Portugal* 215 A5
Limas 71 E3
Limassol 244 G3
Limekiln Valley 263 E5
Limmattal 219 E4
Limnos 239 B4
Limoux 133 D1, 138 E4
Limozin, le 60 G6
Linares 295 D2, 297 G4
Lincoln 298 D5
Lincoln City 271 D2
Lindelberg 165 C5
Lindemans 285 B5
Lindemans Hunter River 278 C4
Linden 275 D3
Linderos 295 B3
Lindsay 267 E6
Lingolsheim 120 A5
Lingyuan 246 A4
Linqing 246 D3
Linsenbusch 161 G5
Linyi 246 D3
Lipanta Cellars 259 C4
Lipnita 237 E5
Lirac 129 E4, 130 F5
Lirralirra Estate 281 C3
Lisboa 208 D3, 209 F5
Lisle-sur-Tarn 113 D6
Lismore 280 F2
Lison-Pramaggiore 179 C5, 181 C4
Lissieu 71 G4
Listrac-Médoc 80 D2
Lithgow 277 B5
Litomerice 230 E2
Little Denby 298 G2
Little's 278 C5
Live Oaks 263 D4
Livermore 263 A3
Livermore Valley 263 A3
Livermore Valley Cellars 263 A3
Liverpool, *Australia* 277 B6
Liverpool, *USA* 275 C2
Livingston, *Merced* 267 C3
Livingston, *Napa* 259 B6
Livio Felluga 183 B4
Livorno 187 A2
Livron-sur-Drôme 125 F4
Lizzano 195 C5
Ljubljana 233 B2
Ljutomer 231 B6, 233 B3
Ljutomersko-Ormoske Gorice 231 B6
Llacuna, La 205 E3
Llana Estacado Winery 269 D5
Llanerch 298 F3
Llico 295 C2
Lloà 204 F6
Loachausses, les 65 F5
Loach, De 255 E5
Locarno 219 G4
Loché 69 F4
Locorotondo 195 C5
Löcse 229 E3
Loddiswell 298 G3
Lodève 138 C6
Lodi 267 A2, B2
Lodoline 189 F4
Loges, les 119 F4
Logroño 203 B1
Lohr, J 263 B3, 265 B3
Loiben 222 B1
Loibenberg 225 G2
Loja 207 C5
Lokoya 259 F4
Lola Hills 273 D4
Lolières, les 63 F5
Lolol 297 D4
Lolonis 256 B3
Lom 235 B2
Lombardes, les 59 G6, 60 G1
Lompoc 265 F4
Lonay 220 A5
Londe-les-Maures, la 136 C4
London 275 B2
London Wines 275 B2
Long 259 D5
Longecourts, les 64 F5
Longères, les 61 E3
Long Gully Estate 281 B5
Longhua 246 A4
Longkou 246 C5
Longvic 57 B6
Longview 271 C2
Longwood 284 C4
Lons le Saunier 137 G4
Lontué 295 C2
Lopera 197 D3
Lorch 143 B3
Loreley 143 A3
Lorettoberg 165 F1
Lorgues 136 B4
Lorimier, De 255 B5
Loriol-du-Comtat 131 F5
Lormont 80 E3, 96 C4
Lorne 280 G2
Loroil-sur-Drôme 125 F4
Loroux-Bottereau, le 114 B3, 115 E5
Lörrach 165 F1
Lösnich 152 C6
Lössnitz 167 C6
Lost Hills 267 F3, G5
Loubès-Bernac 109 C5
Louis Martini 259 D3
Louisvale 293 F1
Loumy 230 E2
Loupiac 80 F4, 96 F6
Lourdes 113 G2
Louroujina 244 F4
Lousa 209 E5
Lousada 215 C5
Louvazim, Qta do 211 F6
Louvois 79 C5
Lovech 235 B3
Lower Belford 278 A4
Lower Hutt 288 D4
Lozanne 71 G3
Lozitza 235 B3
Luan 246 B4
Lubbock 269 D5
Lucca 187 A3
Lucena 207 B4
Lucenay 71 F3
Lucerne 256 C5
Luchets, les 61 E1
Lucq-de-Béarn 113 G1
Ludes 79 B4
Ludon-Médoc 95 F6
Ludwigsburg 165 C4
Ludwigshöhe 163 C5
Lugana 179 D2, 182 G2
Lugano 219 G4
Luginsland 161 D5
Lugny 55 E5, 69 B5
Luins 220 B4
Lukovit 235 B2
Lully 220 A5, C3
Lunas 109 A5
Lunel 129 F2, 135 B5, 139 D1
Luraule, en 61 F1
Lurets, les 61 F4
Lüshun 246 C5
Luso 214 F6
Lussac 80 E5, 103 B5
Lussault-sur-Loire 118 C6
Lüsswiese 223 C5
Lussy 220 A5
Lutry 220 A6
Lutterbach 120 G3
Lutzmannsburg 222 E3
Luzech 113 C4
Luzern 219 E4
Luzin 126 F1
Lyaskovets 235 B4
Lymington 298 G4
Lynchburg 275 E3
Lyndoch 282 C3
Lyon 55 G5
Lyons 273 D5
Lys, les 75 D3
Lytton Springs 255 C5
Lyubimets 235 D4

Mabton 272 G3
Macabrée, la 61 E1
Ma Carrées, les 66 F2
Macau 95 D6
Macedon 277 D3, 280 E3
Macedon Rock 280 E3
Mácere 193 D6
Machali 297 C5
Machamudo Alto 201 B3
Machamudo Bajo 201 C3
Macherelles, les 60 F2
Machico 217 C5
Mâcon 55 F5, 69 F5, 71 A4
Macvale 285 B5
Mád 229 F2
Madalena do Mar 216 C6
Maddens Lane 281 C5
Madera 267 D4
Madères, les 118 B5
Madiran 113 F2
Madison Vineyard 269 D4
Magdalenen-Kreuz 157 E5
Maglieri 284 D3
Magnotta 275 B3
Magura 235 B1
Maia 215 C4
Mailberg 222 B2
Mailly 79 B5
Maina 200 B5
Maindreieck 143 B6, 166 B5
Mainviereck 143 B5
Mainxe 111 F3
Mainz 143 B4, 163 A5
Maipú 295 B3
Mairan, Dom. de 133 B5, 134 D6
Maisdon-sur-Sèvre 115 G5
Maison Blanche, la 127 C5
Maison Brûlée 66 F4
Maison Deutz 265 D4
Maitland 277 A6
Maizières Basses 65 F5
Maizières, Hautes 65 F5
Makhachkala 240 C5
Makioka 248 D4
Maladière, la, *Condrieu* 126 D2
Maladière, la, *Santenay* 59 E3
Maladières, les, *Chambolle-Musigny* 66 F3
Maladières, les, *Nuits-St-Georges* 64 G6
Málaga 197 E3, 207 D5
Malargue 295 D3
Malatya 243 C6
Malconsorts, au Dessus des 65 F4
Malconsorts, aux 65 F4
Maldon 280 E2
Maligny 73 D5, 75 A2
Mallemort 129 F5
Mallia 244 G2
Malloa 297 D5
Mallorca 197 D6
Malmesbury 290 F2
Malokarpatská 230 G3
Malpoiriers, les 61 G2
Maltroie, la 60 G1
Maluna 278 C4
Malvasia delle Lipari 195 E3
Malvasia di Bosa 195 D1
Malvasia di Cagliari 195 E2
Malvasia di Casorzo d'Asti 175 B4
Malvasia di Castelnuovo don Bosco 175 B3
Malvedos, Qta dos 211 E1
Malverne, Clos 293 F1
Malviera 209 F3
Mambourg 123 C3
Mancha, La 197 C4
Manchester 275 B6
Manchuela 197 C4
Mandelberg 123 C3
Mandelgarten 161 C5
Mandelgraben 151 B4, 152 G5
Mandelhöhe 161 C2
Mandement, Le 219 G1, 220 C3
Mándria, Cle. della 193 F5
Mandrolisai 195 D2
Mandurah 286 D2
Manfred Vierthaler 271 B3
Mango 176 E4
Mangoola 279 F4
Mangualde 215 F5
Maniago 181 B3
Manjimup 286 F2
Mann's 248 D4
Mannaberg 165 B3
Mannberg 159 F1
Mannheim 143 C4, 165 B3
Manning 273 B4
Manobalai 279 E4
Manoir de Gravoux 103 D6
Mansfield 280 E5
Manstree 298 G3
Manteca 267 B2
Mantinia 239 D3
Mantova 179 D2
Manuelas, Qta das 210 D5
Manuel de la Calle 201 G1
Manukau 288 B4
Manzanillos 201 C4
Manzano 183 C4
Manzano, El 297 C4
Maramures 237 B3
Marananga 282 B4
Marano di Valpolicella 182 E5
Maras 243 D5
Marbach 165 C4
Marbuzet 87 F5
Marça 204 F6
Marcamps 108 G5
Marcé 117 C2
Marchais, les 67 E1
Marchampt 71 D2
Marches de Bretagne 139 E4
Marches, les 137 D2
Marckolsheim 120 D5
Marckrain 123 C3
Marcobrunn 159 G2
Marco de Canaveses 215 C6
Marconnets, Bas 63 E1
Marconnets, Dessus de 62 E6
Marconnets, les 62 E6
Marconnets, les Hauts 62 E6
Marcorino 176 E4
Mardeuil 79 D2
Mardie 115 A4
Mareau, en 61 E6
Maréchale, Clos de la 64 F3
Maréchaudes, le Clos des 63 F5
Maréchaudes, les 63 F4
Marenca-Rivette 176 F2
Marestel 137 C2
Mareuil-le-Port 78 D6
Mareuil-sur-Ay 79 D4
Margaret River 287 E2
Margaux 80 D2, 95 B3
Margueron 109 B4
Mariages, les 62 F5
Mariano del Friuli 183 D4
María Pinto 297 A5
Mariazell 222 D1
Maribor 231 B4, 233 A2
Mariborski Vinorodni 231 B4
Marienberg 284 C3
Marienburg 166 B4
Mariengarten 161 B2, E5
Marienholz 149 D4
Marignane 129 G5
Marihernandez 201 D1
Marimacho 200 A5
Marimar Torres 255 E4
Marin 137 A3
Marina Danieli 183 B3
Marina di San Lorenzo 193 F4
Maring-Noviand 152 F5
Marino 187 F3, 193 D5
Marinot 60 D2
Marion, *Australia* 284 B2
Marion, *USA* 273 D5
Marion's 287 F6
Mario Schiopetto 183 C5
Marissou 68 B4
Markgraf Babenberg 166 C5
Markgräflerland 143 G3, 165 F1
Markham 259 C3
Markkleeberg 167 C4
Markko 275 C2
Markranstädt 167 C4
Markt Einersheim 166 C6
Marktheidenfeld 166 B3
Mark West 255 D5
Marlborough 288 D4
Marlengo (Marling) 185 A4
Marlenheim 120 A4
Marmande 113 C2
Marmella 205 E3
Marnoo 280 D1
Maroona 280 E1
Maroondah Province 281 B5
Marquam 273 C5
Marquam Hill 273 C5
Marquis de St-Estèphe Cave Coop. 87 E4
Marrakech 245 C1
Marsac 95 A2
Marsala 195 F2
Marsannay 55 C6
Marsannay-la-Côte 57 B5
Marsciano 192 D5
Marseille 129 G5, 136 B1
Marsh Estate 278 B4
Marshlands 289 F5
Marsillargues 129 F2
Marssac-sur-Tarn 113 D6
Marston 259 D3
Martell 110 F5, G6
Martellère, la 117 C2
Marten 223 C5
Martha's Vineyard 275 C6
Martignano 184 C5
Martigny 219 G2, 221 D2
Martigny-Bourg 221 D2
Martigny-Combe 221 D2
Martigues 129 G5
Martillac 99 G6
Martina 195 C5
Martinazo 201 B4
Martinborough 288 D5
Martin Bros 265 B3
Martinenga 176 E3
Martini & Prati 255 E5
Martin Miguel 200 A5
Martinsberg 223 B4
Martinstein 155 C3
Martinsthal 159 E4
Martorell 205 E4
Martorelles 205 E5
Maruko 248 C3
Maryborough 277 D2, 280 E2
Marysville 280 E4
Mas Amiel 133 E3
Mas Blanc, Dom. de 133 G5
Mascara 245 B4
Mas Crémat, Dom. du 133 E4
Mas de Daumas Gassac 135 B3
Mas Jullien 135 B2
Maslin 284 E1
Maslin Beach 284 E1
Masllorenç 205 F2
Masnou, El 205 E6
Masó, La 205 F2
Maspujols 205 F1
Masquefa 205 E4
Masroig, El 204 F6
Massa 173 G6
Massandra 240 C2
Masseto 191 B5
Massongy 137 A3
Masson Vyds 263 F4
Mastantuono 265 C3
Masterton 288 D5
Masures, les 59 F6, 60 G1
Matanzas Creek 254 E3
Matapozuelos 206 F2
Matera, *Italy* 195 C5
Matera, *USA* 259 B2
Matheisbildchen 153 F2
Mathéou 95 C2
Matino 195 C6
Matosinhos 215 C4
Mátraalja 226 E4
Matsukawa 248 D3
Matsumoto 248 C3
Mattersburg 222 D3
Matzen 222 B3
Maubourguet 113 F2
Mäuerchen, *Rheingau* 157 E5
Mäuerchen, *Ruwer* 149 E4
Mauguio 129 F2, 135 B4
Maulbronn 165 C3
Maule 295 C2, 297 F4
Maurens 109 A5
Maures 136 B5, 139 G4
Maurice Carrie Winery 269 D2
Maury 133 F5
Mäushöhle 161 F5
Mautern 225 G3
Mauvanne 136 C4
Maximiner 149 D3
Maxwell 284 E2
Mayacamas 259 F4
Mayat, Dom. de 109 D3
Maykop 240 C4
Mazatlán 269 F4
Mazeray, Clos de 61 F1
Mazière, la, *Fixin* 67 E4
Mazière, la, *Gevrey-Chambertin* 67 F3
Mazion 108 C2
Mazis Chambertin 67 E1
Mazo, El 207 G4
Mazotos 244 G4
Mazouna 245 B4
Mazoyères 66 E5
Mazoyères Chambertin 66 F5
McCoy 273 C4
McCullys Gap 279 E6
McDowell Valley 256 C4
McKinlay 273 C5
McLaren Vale 284 E2
McMinnville 271 D2, 273 C4
McWilliam's Mount Pleasant 278 C4
Mealhada 208 B4, 214 F5

Méal, le 127 C4
Meckenheim 161 B2
Mecsek 226 G3
Meda 208 B5
Meddersheim 155 C4
Médéa, *Algeria* 245 B4
Medea, *Italy* 183 D4
Medford 271 G3
Medgidia 237 D5
Medidora 200 B4
Medina del Campo 206 F2
Mediona 205 E3
Médoc 80 C1
Medoquine, la 99 A3
Meerlust 292 G6
Meersburg 165 F4
Meerspinne 161 B2
Meggyes 229 F1
Megyer 229 C5
Mehrholzchen 158 E5
Meinert 293 E1
Meinier 220 C4
Meisenberg 149 F6
Meisenheim 155 D4
Meissen 143 A4, 167 C6
Meix au Maire, le 67 F3
Meix-Bas Champ 67 E3
Meix Bas, le 67 E4
Meix Bataille, le 61 E3
Meix Chavaux, les 61 E2
Meix, Clos des 60 G3
Meix de Mypont, le 61 E3
Meix des Duches 67 E1
Meix-Fringuet 67 F3
Meix Gagnes, les 61 G1
Meix Garnier, le 61 E3
Meix Goudard, les 60 G2
Meix, les, *Aloxe-Corton* 63 F3
Meix, les, *Puligny* 60 G3
Meix Pelletier 60 G4
Meix Rentier 66 F4
Meix Tavaux, le 61 F2
Méjanelle, la 129 F2, 135 B4
Meknès 245 B2
Mel 181 B1
Melbourne 277 D3, 280 F4
Melegoldal 229 G3
Meleto 189 F5
Melgaço 215 A5
Melilla 245 B3
Melini 189 E2
Mélinots 75 E2
Melipilla 295 B2, 297 B4
Melissa 195 D5
Melk 222 C1
Mellecey 68 D4
Melnik, *Bulgaria* 235 D2
Mělník, *Czech Republic* 230 E2
Menama 273 D5
Mendavia 203 B2
Mendota 267 D4
Mendoza 294 F2, 295 A4
Menetou-Salon 115 B5
Ménétréol-sous-Sancerre 119 F3
Menétru-le-Vignoble 137 F5
Menoyia 244 G3
Mentrida 197 C3
Meon Valley 298 F4
Méounes-lès-Montrieux 136 B3
Meranese di Collina 179 A2, 185 A3
Merano (Meran) 179 A3, 185 A4
Merced 267 C3
Mercian 248 D4
Mercuès 113 C5
Mercurey 55 D5, 68 C4
Meredith 280 F2
Meredyth 275 D3
Meridian 265 B4
Mérignac 80 E2, 96 D3
Merlen 289 F4
Merlion 259 G5
Merouco, Qta do 211 E1
Merrill/Mount Hurtle 284 C2
Merryvale/Sunny St. Helena 259 B5
Merry Vintners 255 E5
Merseburg 167 C3
Mersin 243 D4
Mertesdorf 149 D5
Mértola 208 F5
Merton 280 E4
Mescoules 109 C5
Mesilla Valley 269 D4
Mesland 115 B2
Meslerie, la 118 A4
Mesnay 137 E6
Mesneux, Les 79 A3
Mesnil-sur-Oger, Le 79 F3
Messas 115 A3
Messina 195 E4
Messoirano 176 D4
Messzelátó 229 F3
Mestervölgy 229 G3
Mestre 179 D4, 181 E2
Mesves-sur-Loire 119 G5
Meszes-Major 229 E3
Métsovo 239 B2
Mettenheim 163 C5
Meung-sur-Loire 115 A3
Meursault 55 D5, 57 F3, 61 F2
Meuselwitz 167 D4
Mévelle 67 E1
Mézesmály 229 G3
Mézières 119 F5
Mezözombor 229 G2
Mezzane di sotto 182 F6
Mezzocorona 184 A5, 185 F4
Mezzocorona, C.S. Cooperative di 185 F4
Mezzolombardo 184 B5, 185 F4
Miamup 287 D2
Michelmark 159 F2
Michelons 72 B5
Michelsberg, *Piesport* 151 D2
Michelsberg, *Pfalz* 161 B5
Michurin 235 C6
Micot, Clos 61 F5
Middelvlei 293 F2
Middlebrook 284 E2
Middle Rio Grande Valley 269 D4
Middletown 256 D6
Miège 221 C4
Miery 137 F5
Mignotte, la 62 E4
Miguel Torres 297 E4
Miklavz 231 B4
Mikonos 239 D5
Mikulov 230 G3
Milano, *Italy* 173 D5
Milano, *USA* 256 C3
Milat 259 B5
Milawa 280 D5
Mildara 285 C6
Mildura 277 B2
Milesti 241 F5
Milieu, Qta 211 E2
Milikouri 244 F2
Millandes, les 66 F4
Millbrook 275 C5
Mill City 273 D5
Mill Creek 255 C4
Millers 281 A4
Milletière, la 118 D4
Millicent 277 D1
Milly 75 D3
Milly-Lamartine 69 E3
Milos 239 E4
Milton Freewater 271 C6
Milwaukie 273 B5
Mimbres Valley 269 D4
Minamimaki 248 C4
Minas Gerais 294 F2
Minerve 133 B3, 134 D5
Minervois 133 E5, 135 D5
Minheim 151 D3
Minimbah 278 B4
Minis 237 C2
Minobu 248 E4
Minowa 248 D3
Minzac 109 A3
Mirabell Heights 255 D5
Miraflores 200 C4
Miramas 129 F4
Mirambeau 108 G3
Mirande 113 F3
Mirassou 263 B3
Mirassou Champagne Cellars 263 C3
Miravet 204 G5
Mirebeau 99 G5
Mireille, Clos 136 C4
Misiones 294 F
Miskolc 226 E4
Mission View 265 B3
Mistelbach 222 B3
Misty Mountain 275 D3
Misty Valley 281 A4
Mitans, les 61 F5
Mitcham 284 B3
Mitchell 283 E5
Mitchellstown 280 E4
Mitchelton Vintners 280 E4
Mitiamo 280 D3
Mitomi 248 D4
Mitsero 244 F3
Mittelbergheim 120 B4
Mittelburgenland 222 F4
Mittelhaardt Deutsche Weinstrasse 143 C3, 161 D4
Mittelheim 158 G4
Mittelhölle 158 F2
Mittelrhein 143 A3
Mittelwihr 120 D4, 123 C3
Mittweida 167 D5
Miyun 246 B3
Mizil 237 D4
Miziya 235 B2
Mladina 233 B2
Mljet 233 E3
Moana 284 D1
Mocenni 189 F4
Mochamps, les 66 F5
Mochis, Los 269 E4
Moculta 282 B6
Módena 179 E2
Modesto 267 C3
Mödling 224 E2
Modra 230 G3
Modry Kamen 230 G5
Mogofores 214 F5
Mogyorósok 229 E3
Mohács 226 G3
Molalla 273 C5
Molar, El 204 F6
Moldava nad Bodvou 230 G5
Moldovia 237 B5
Molfetta 195 B5
Molina 295 C2, 297 E4
Molineuf 115 B2
Molins de Rei 205 E5
Mollenbrunnen 155 D1
Mollina 207 C4
Molly Morgan 278 B5
Molsheim 120 A4
Mombies, les 66 F3
Mombrier 108 E4
Monbadon 103 B6
Monbazillac 109 B5
Monbulk 281 D5
Monção 215 A5
Mönchberg 154 F5, 155 C2
Monchenevoy, Dessus de 63 C2
Mönchhof 222 D4
Monchique 208 F4
Mönchspfad 157 E6, 158 F1
Moncontour 118 B2
Mondéjar-Sacedón 197 B4
Mondim de Basto 215 C6
Monein 113 F1
Monemvasia 239 E3
Monestier 109 B5
Monéteau 73 D3
Monfalcone 181 C6
Monfalletto 176 F2
Monfaucon 109 A4
Monforte d'Alba 175 E3, 176 G2
Monnow Valley 298 F4
Monica di Cagliari 195 E2
Monica di Sardegna 195 D2
Monichino 280 C4
Moniga del Garda 182 F1
Monim, le Bas de 60 D2
Monistrol d'Anoia 205 E4
Monjos, Els 205 F3
Monmadales 109 B6
Monmouth 273 D4
Monnaz 220 A5
Monnet, J G 110 G5
Monnières 115 F5
Monok 229 F1
Monopoli 195 B5
Monprivato 176 F2
Monsaguel 109 C6
Monsanto 189 E3
Monségur 97 F3
Monsheim 143 C4
Montagliari 189 D4
Montagliari e Castellinuzza 189 D4
Montagnac-la-Crempse 109 A6
Montagna in V. 177 B3
Montagne 80 E4, 103 C4
Montagne, la Grande 59 F6
Montagne Saint Désiré 62 E2
Montagnieu 137 C1
Montagny 55 D5
Montagny-lès-Buxy 68 G3
Montaigu 290 F3
Montaigus, Clos des 68 C3
Montalcino 190 F2
Montalto Pavese 177 F4
Montana, *New Zealand* 289 G5
Montana, *Spain* 201 C1
Montana, *Switzerland* 221 C4
Montana (Mikhaylovgrad) 235 B2
Montanas, Las 254 E5
Montánchez 197 C2
Montans 113 D6
Montara 280 E1
Montarsino 176 F3
Montazeau 109 B4
Mont-Baudile 138 C6
Montbellet 69 B6
Montblanc 205 E2
Montblanquet 205 E1
Montbré 79 B4
Montbrió del Camp 205 F1
Montcada i Reixac 205 E5
Montcaret 109 B3
Mont Caume 136 C2, 139 G4
Montceau, en 60 E3
Mont-Chambord 115 B3
Montcuq 113 C4
Mont de la Grage 138 D5
Mont de Milieu 75 D5
Monte 217 C3
Monte Aribaldo 176 E4
Montebello d. Batt 177 F3
Montebelluna 181 C1
Montecalvo Versiggia 177 F5
Montecarlo 187 A3
Montecchia di Crosara 183 F1
Monte Comán 295 C5
Montecompatri 193 D5
Montecompatri Colonna 193 D5
Monte di Leva 193 E3
Montedor 215 B4
Montée de Tonnerre 75 D4
Monte, El 297 B5
Montée Rouge 62 E3
Montefalco 187 D4, 192 D6
Monteforte d'Alpone 183 G2
Montélimar 125 G4, 129 C4
Mont Elise 271 C3
Montello e Colli Asolani 179 C4
Montels 113 D6
Montemayor 207 A4
Montemor-o-Novo 208 D4, 213 E4
Monteneubel 153 B4
Montepaldi 189 C2
Monte Pórzio Catone 193 D5
Montepulciano 190 F4
Montepulciano d'Abruzzo 187 E6, F6
Monterey 263 E3
Monterey Peninsula 263 E3
Monterey Vineyard 263 F4
Monteriggioni 189 F3
Monte Rio 255 E3
Monte Rosso 254 F5
Monterrey 269 E5
Montes (Discover Wine, SA) 297 E4
Montesano 271 B2
Montescano 177 E5
Montescudaio 187 B3
Montespértoli 189 C2
Montestefano 176 E4
Monteux 131 G5
Montevarchi 189 E6
Monte Xanic 269 D2
Montfaucon 130 F6
Montferri 205 F2
Montgat 205 E6
Monthelie 55 D5, 61 E3
Monthey 221 C1
Monthoux 137 C2
Monticello Cellars 259 F5
Montigny 119 G1
Montigny-lès-Arsures 137 E6
Montilla 207 B4
Montilla-Moriles 197 D3, 207 B4
Montinore 273 B4
Mont, le 118 B3
Montlouis 115 B2
Montlouis-sur-Loire 118 C4
Montmains 75 E3
Montmelas-St-Sorlin 71 E3
Montmélian 137 C2
Montorio Veronese 182 G6
Montpellier 129 F2, 135 B4, 139 D1
Montpeyroux, *Bergerac* 109 A3
Montpeyroux, *Coteaux du Languedoc* 135 B2
Mont-Rachet 60 F3
Montrachet, le 60 G3
Mont-Redon 131 E2
Montrésor 115 C2
Montreuil-Bellay 114 C5
Montreux 219 F2, 221 B1
Montrevenots, les 62 E2
Montrichard 115 B2
Mont-roig del Camp 205 G1
Mont St John 257 E5
Monts Damnés, les 119 F2
Monts du Tessala 245 B3
Monts, les Petits 65 F4
Monts Luisants 66 E5
Mont-sur-Rolle 220 B5
Montu Becc. 177 E5
Montuni Del Reno 179 E3
Monza 173 D5
Monzel 151 B3
Monzingen 155 C3
Moonambel 277 C2, 280 E2
Moonta 276 B5
Moor, De 259 E4
Moorebank 278 C5
Moorilla Estate 287 G6
Moorlynch 298 F3
Mooroopna 280 D4
Moorreesburg 290 E2
Mopami 282 A6
Moquegua 294 F
Moques 119 E4
Mór 226 E3
Móra d'Ebro 204 G5
Móra la Nova 204 G5
Morais, les 63 F4
Morancé 71 F3
Morand, la 63 D4
Moraro 183 C5
Mörbisch am See 222 D3, 223 C4
Morein 75 D6
Moreira 215 C4
Morell, El 205 F2
Morellino di Scansano 187 C3
Morena 193 D4
Morera, La 204 F6
Moresco 267 B3
Môreson Blois 293 F5
Morey-St-Denis 55 C6, 66 F4
Morgan, *Australia* 276 B6
Morgan, *USA* 263 E4
Morgenhof 293 F2
Morgeot 59 F5
Morges 220 A5
Morgon 55 F5, 72 E4
Mori 184 E4
Morichots, les 59 G6, 60 G1
Moriers, les 72 C5
Moriles 207 B4
Morjot, Champs de 59 G5
Moroges 68 E3
Morphett Vale 284 D2
Morphou 244 F2
Morra, La 175 E2, 176 F2
Morris 280 C5
Morro Bay 265 C3
Morro Beach 265 C3
Mortágua 215 G4
Mortlake 280 F1
Morton 271 B3
Mós 211 G6
Mosby 265 F5
Moscadello di Montalcino 187 C3, 190 F1
Moscato d'Asti 175 D4, 176 E4
Moscato di Cagliari 195 E2
Moscato di Noto 195 G4
Moscato di Sardegna 195 E2
Moscato di Siracusa 195 G4
Moscato di Sorso Sennori 195 C2
Moscato di Trani 195 B5
Moscavide 209 E6
Mosconi 176 G2
Mosel 143 B2
Mosel-Saar-Ruwer 143 B2
Moseltor 143 C1
Mosny, Clos de 118 D5
Moson-magyaróvar 226 E2
Moss Brothers 287 C1
Mossel Bay 290 G6
Mossettes, les 119 E3
Moss Wood 287 C1
Most 230 E2
Mostaganem 245 B3
Mostar 233 D3
Motello e Colli Asolani 181 C1
Motrot, en 67 E2
Motta di Livenza 181 C3
Motte, la 136 B5
Motte, La 293 F5
Motueka 288 D4
Motz 137 B2
Mouchère, Clos de la 60 G4
Mouches, Clos des 59 F3
Mouches, le Clos des 62 E2
Mouchottes, les 60 G2
Mouille, la, *Fixin* 67 F4
Mouille, la, *Gevrey-Chambertin* 67 F3
Moulamein 277 B2
Mouleydier 109 B6
Moulin-à-Vent 55 F5, 72 C6
Moulin Cruottes Moyne, aux 63 D1
Moulin de Périès 133 C5, 134 D6
Moulin Landin, au 61 F1
Moulin, le 72 C4
Moulin Moine, le 61 E2
Mouline, la 95 E2
Mouline, La 126 C4
Moulineuf 110 F6
Moulis-en-Médoc 80 D2
Mounic 101 F6
Mountadam 282 D5
Mountain House 256 D4
Mount Angel 273 C5
Mountarrow 279 G5
Mount Avoca 280 E2
Mount Barker 286 G4
Mount Chalambar 280 E1
Mount Eden 263 C2
Mount Evelyn 281 C4
Mount Gambier 277 D1
Mount Harlan 263 E4
Mount Helen 280 E4
Mount Horrocks 283 F6
Mount McKenzie 282 C5
Mount Mary 281 C4
Mount Veeder 259 F4
Mount View 278 D4
Moura, *Alentejo* 208 E5, 213 F5
Moura, *Alto Douro* 210 F4
Mourão 208 E5, 213 F6
Mourenx 113 F1
Moussard 119 E4
Mousse, le Clos de la 62 F4
Moutier Amet 63 E1
Mouton-Excelsior 293 G6
Moutoullas 244 F2
Mouzillon 115 F5
Moxee City 272 E2
Moxheim 155 C3
Moyhu 280 D5
Mudgee 277 A5
Mues, Dessous les 60 G2
Mühlberg 154 F3
Mühlpoint 225 G2
Mulató 229 E3
Muldersbosch 293 E1
Mülheim 152 G5
Mulhouse 120 G4
Mulkirri 283 F5
Müllheim 165 F1
Mumm Napa Valley 259 D4
Mundelsheim 165 C4
Muniesa 197 B5
Münster-Sarmsheim 155 A6
Muntenia 237 D4
Münzlay 152 E6
Muratie 293 E2
Murchison 280 D4
Mure 248 B3
Murées, les 60 F1
Murets, les 127 C5
Murfatlar 237 D5
Murger de Monthélie, au 61 E2
Murgers, aux 65 F3
Murgers des dents de chien, les 60 F3
Murphy-Goode 255 B5
Murray Bridge 276 C6
Murray Robson 278 C4
Murrumbidgee Irrigation Area 277 B3
Murs, les Grands 66 F2
Mürzzuschlag 222 D2
Muscat de Frontignan 135 E5
Muscat de Lunel 135 E5
Muscat de Mireval 135 E5
Muscat de St-Jean de Minervois 133 F5, 135 E5
Muscle Creek 279 E6
Musenhang 161 E5
Musigny, les 65 F6, 66 F2
Musigny, les Petits 65 F6, 66 F1
Mussara, la 205 F1
Müstert 151 C2
Muswellbrook 277 A6, 279 E5
Mutigny 79 D4
Mutzig 120 A4
Muy, le 136 B5
Myambat 279 F4
Myans 137 C2
Myrtleford 280 D6

Nackenheim 162 B5, 163 B6
Nacktarsch 153 B2
Nacunan 295 B5
Nagambie 277 C3, 280 D4
Nagano 248 B3
Nagiso 248 D2
Nago 184 E3
Nagozelo do Douro 211 F2
Nagykanizsa 226 G2
Nahe 143 C3
Nájera 202 B5
Nakano 248 B4
Naked Mountain 275 D3
Nakotomi 248 E4
Nal'chik 240 C4
Nalles (Nals) 185 B5
Nalys 131 F2
Namiai 248 E2
Nancagua 295 C2, 297 D5
Nangong 246 D3
Nantes 114 B3, 115 F4
Naoussa 239 B3
Napa 257 E6, 259 G5
Napa Creek 259 D4
Napa, Dom. 259 D4
Napa Ridge 255 B4
Napa Valley 257 E5, 259 C4
Napier 288 C5
Napoléon, Clos 67 E4
Nápoles, Qta de 210 F3
Napoli 195 C3
Naracoorte 277 C1
Narbantons, les 63 E1
Narbonne 133 C4, 134 E6, 138 E5
Nardo 195 C6
Narni 192 F5
Narrandera 277 B4
Narrenkappe 155 C2
Narrikup 286 G4
Narvaux-Dessus, les 60 F5
Narveaux-Dessous, les 60 F6
Nasco di Cagliari 195 E2
Nastringues 109 B4
Natale, De 255 D5
Nathalia 280 C4
Natters 221 C6
Naumberg 143 A5, 167 C3
Nava de la Asunción 206 G3
Nava del Rey 206 F1
Nava de Roa 206 E4
Navaridas 202 B6, 203 F4
Navarra 197 A4
Navarrete 202 B6
Navarro 256 C2
Navidad 295 B2
Naxos 239 E5
Naylor 275 D4
Nazoires, les 66 F2
Néac 103 B2, 107 C6
Nebbiolo d'Alba 175 D3, 176 E2
Neckar 143 E5
Neckarsulm 165 C4
Neckenmarkt 222 D3
Nederburg 293 C5
Neethlingshof 293 F1
Negrar 182 F5
Neiderberghelden 152 F6
Neipperg 165 C4
Néive 176 E4
Nelas 215 F5
Nelson 288 D4
Nemea 239 D3
Nemi 193 E5
Néoules 136 B3
Nérac 113 D3
Neringah 285 B5
Nérolle, la 111 F3
Nervo 255 B4
Nesebur 235 C5
Neszmely 226 E3
Nettuno 193 G4
Neuchâtel 219 E2
Neufeld 223 C4, C5
Neuillé 114 B6
Neumagen 151 E1
Neunkirchen 222 D2
Neuquen 294 G
Neusiedl am See 222 C4, 223 B5
Neusiedlersee 222 F4
Neusiedlersee-Hügelland 222 F4
Neustadt an der Weinstrasse 143 C4, 161 B2
Neuweier 165 D3
Nevsehir 243 C4
Newark 275 C5
New Bedford 275 C6
Newberg 273 C4
New Brighton 288 E4
Newcastle 277 A6
New Hall 298 F5
New Haven 275 C5
Newlan 263 F5
Newman 267 C3
New Norfolk 287 G6
New Plymouth 288 C4
Newport 271 D2
Newton 259 D3
New York 275 C5
Niagara 273 D6
Niagara Falls 275 B3
Nicastro 195 E5
Nice 256 C5
Nichelini 259 D5
Niches, Los 297 E5
Nicoresti 237 C5
Nicosia 244 F3
Niculitel 237 D5
Niebaum-Coppola 259 E4
Niederemmel 151 C2
Niederhausen 154 G5, 155 C5
Niederkirchen 161 F6
Niederleuken 147 E2
Niedermennig 147 A5
Niedermorschwihr 120 E3, 123 B1
Niedermoschel 155 D5
Nieder-Olm 143 B4, 163 B5
Niederotterbach 161 D2
Nieder-Wiesen 163 C3
Nierstein 143 B4, 162 E4, 163 B5
Nies'chen 149 E4
Nigde 243 C4
Nikopol 235 B3
Niksie 233 E4
Nîmes 129 E3, 139 C2
Nimis 181 A5
Nipomo 265 E4
Nirasaki 248 D4
Nis 233 E6
Nisavsko-Juznomoravski 233 E6
Nisporeni 241 F5
Nissley 275 D4
Nitra 230 G4
Nizza Monferrato 175 D5
Noblaie, la 117 G3
Nogaro 113 E2
Nogent-sur-Seine 76 D3
Nogueira 210 E2
Noirets, les 63 D4
Noirots, les 66 F3
Noizay 118 B5
Noizons, les 62 E2
Noizons, les Petits 62 E1
Nolay 57 F2
Nolthalten 120 C4
Nomi 184 E5
Nonini, A 267 D4
Nonnenberg, *Bernkastel* 152 E6
Nonnenberg, *Rheingau* 159 E4
Nonnengarten, *Nahe* 154 F6
Nonnengarten, *Pfalz* 161 B5
Nonnenstück 161 E6
Noons 284 E2
Nordheim 166 B5
Norfolk 275 E4
Norheim 154 F6, 155 C5
Norieta, La 201 C4
Normas 281 A3
North Albany 273 D4
Northam 286 C3
North Bend 271 F1
Northland/Matakana 288 B4
North Plains 273 B4
North Rothbury 278 B5
Northwood 255 E4
Norton Summit 284 A4
Nort-sur-Erdre 114 B3
Norwood 284 A3
Nosroyes, les 60 G4
Nosroyes, les Petits 60 G4
Nou de Gaya, La 205 F2
Noue, Champ de la 119 E3
Nova do Roncão, Qta 210 E6
Nova Kakhovka 240 B2
Noval, Qta do 210 E5
Novara 173 D4
Nova Zagora 235 C4
Novello 176 G2
Nove Mesto 230 G6
Nové Zamky 230 G4
Novi Becej 233 C5
Novi Pazar 235 B5
Novi Sad 233 C5
Novorossiysk 240 C3
Novo Selo 235 A1
Novy Svet 240 C2

Novy Saldorf 230 G3
Nowra 277 B5
Noyer, Dom. du 136 C4
Nozzole 189 C4
Nuestra Señora de la Consolacion 201 E3
Nuestra Señora de la Esperanza 201 D4
Nuestra Señora del Valle 201 D1
Nueva Carteya 207 B4
Nuevo Laredo 269 E5
Nuits-St-Georges 55 C6, 57 D5, 65 F2
Nulkaba 278 C5
Nulles 205 F2
Numurkah 280 C4
Nuoro 195 D2
Nuovo di Presciano, Cle. 193 F5
Nuragus di Cagliari 195 E2
Nuriootpa 276 B6, 282 B4
Nuriootpa (Seppelt's) 282 B5
Nussberg 224 B3
Nussbien 161 G4
Nussbrunnen 159 F1
Nussriegel 161 A5, B5
Nusswingert 151 E1
Nutbourne Manor 298 F5
Nyetimber 298 F5
Nyíregyháza 226 E5
Nyon 220 B4
Nyulaszó 229 F2
Nyzhn'ohirskyy 240 B2

Oakdale 267 B3
Oak Grove 273 B5
Oak Knoll 273 B4
Oakley 267 B2
Oakmont 254 D3
Oakridge Estate 281 D5
Oakvale 278 C4
Oakville 259 E4
Oasis Vineyard 275 D3
Oaxaca 269 G6
Oberberg, *Nahe* 154 F6
Oberberg, *Rheingau* 159 E5
Oberemmel 147 C5
Obere Teilung 223 C5
Oberhausen 155 C5
Ober-Hilbersheim 163 B4
Oberkirch 165 D2
Oberland 219 E5
Oberleinach 166 B4
Oberloiben 225 G2
Obermorschwihr 122 C4
Obermosel 143 C1
Obernai 120 B4
Ober-Olm 163 B5
Oberrhein 143 D4, G3, G5
Obervolkach 166 B5
Obester 256 C2
Óbidos 208 D3
Obuse 248 B4
Oc, D' 139 G2
Oceano 265 D3
Ockenheim 163 B3
Ockfen 147 E3
Odemira 208 F4
Odenas 71 D3, 72 G4
Odernheim 155 D4
Oderzo 181 C3
Odesa 240 B2, 241 F6
Odinstal 161 E4
Odobesti 237 C5
Oeiras 209 F4
Oestrich 158 F5
Offenburg 143 E3, 165 D2
Offstein 163 D5
Ofir 215 B4
Oger 79 F3
Oggau 222 D3, 223 C4
Ohakune 288 C5
Ohligsberg 151 D3
Ohrid 233 G5
Oiã 214 E5
Oildale 267 G6
Oiry 79 E4
Óis do Bairro 214 F5
Oisly 115 B3
Okaya 248 C3
Olaszliszka 229 E4
Ölberg 161 G4, D4
Olbia 195 C2
Old Barn 282 B4
Old Clarendon 284 C3
Old Luxters 298 F5
Old Noarlunga 284 D2
Olerdola 205 F4
Olesa de Bonesvalls 205 E4
Olesa de Montserrat 205 E4
Oliena 195 D2
Olifantsrivier 290 D2
Olinda 281 D4
Oliva Gessi 177 F4
Olive Farm 286 C1
Oliveira do Bairro 214 E5
Oliveira do Hospital 215 G5
Olivella 205 F4
Oliverhill 284 D2
Olivier, l' 118 C1
Olivos, Los 265 F5
Ollauri 202 B5, 203 F1
Ollon 221 C2
Olomouc 230 F3
Ölspiel 166 C4
Olten 219 E3
Oltenia 237 D2
Oltrepò Pavese 173 E5, 177 F4
Olympia 271 B3
Omachi 248 B3
Omells de Na Gaïa, Els 205 E1
Omodhos 244 G2
Ond 229 F2
Onkelchen 154 F6
Onverwacht 293 A5
Oppenheim 143 B4, 162 F5, 163 B5
Optima 255 C5
Opus One 259 B6
Ora (Auer) 185 E6
Oradea 237 B2
Orange, *Australia* 277 B5
Orange, *France* 129 D4, 139 B3
Orange Cove 267 E5
Orbaneja 201 C2
Orbel 162 E4
Orbost 277 D4
Orchards 273 B5
Orcutt 265 E4
Ordensgut 161 C2
Ordonnac 85 F5
Ordu 243 B5
Oregon Cellars 271 E2
Oregon City 271 D3, 273 B5
Oremus 229 C6
Orfila 295 B4
Oriental, Dom. La 297 F4
Orilla de Auquinco, La 297 D5
Oristano 195 D1
Orlando 282 C4
Orléans 115 A4
Ormarins, L' 293 F4
Ormeau, en l', *Chassagne* 59 G6
Ormeau, en l', *Volnay* 61 F4
Orme, en l' 62 E6
Orme, les Clos de l' 66 F2
Ormes, aux 65 G4
Ormes, Clos des 66 F5
Ormesson, Dom. d' 133 C3, 135 C2
Ormoz 231 C6, 233 B3
Ornato 176 G3
Ornellaia 191 C3
Orotava-Los Realejos, La 207 G4
Orschwihr 120 F3, 122 B2
Orschwiller 120 C4
Orta Nova 195 B4
Ortenau 143 E4, 165 D2
Ortenberg 165 D2
Orthez 113 F1
Orveaux, En 65 F5
Orvieto 187 D4, 192 E4
Orvieto Classico 187 D4
Oryahovica 235 C4
Oryakhovo 235 B2
Osborne y Cia 201 G2
Oschatz 167 C5
Oschelskopf 161 A5
Oshawa 275 B3
Osicka 280 E3
Osijek 233 C4
Osos, Los 265 C3
Ossès 112 G6
Ost. dell'Osa 193 C5
Osterberg, *France* 123 C4
Osterberg, *Germany* 161 A5
Osterhöll 155 D1
Osthofen 163 C5
Ostrava 230 F4
Ostrov 237 E5
Ostuni 195 C5
Ostwald 120 A5
O'Sullivan Beach 284 C1
Osuna 207 C3
Otard-Dupuy 110 F5
Otsuki 248 D5
Ottakring 224 B2
Ouahran (Oran) 245 B3
Oude Nektar 293 G3
Oudtshoorn 290 F6
Ouintine, la 131 F5
Oujda 245 B3
Ourentã 214 F5
Outlook 272 F3
Ouvrées, Clos de 60 61 F3
Ouyen 277 B2
Overberg 290 G3
Overgaauw 293 F1
Oyon 203 B1
Ozenay 69 A6
Ozurget'i 240 C4

Paarl 290 F2, 293 C4
Paarl Valley 293 B5
Pachino Eloro 195 G3
Pachs 205 E3
Pacific Union College 259 C4
Paços de Ferreira 215 C5
Padova 179 D4
Padre Hurtado 297 A5
Padthaway/Keppoch 277 C1
Pag 233 C2
Pagadebit di Romagna 179 F4, 187 A5
Paganilla 200 C5
Page Mill 263 B2
Pagliaia, La 189 F5
Pagliarese 189 G5
Paglieri 176 E3
Paicines 263 E5
Paillère, la 99 B3
Paillot 119 E4
Paine 297 B5
Pajore 176 E3
Pajzos 229 E5
Pakhna 244 G2
Paks 226 F3
Palacios, Los 197 D2
Palavas-les-Flots 135 B4
Palazzo al Bosco 189 C3
Palermo 195 F2
Palestrina 193 D6
Palette 136 A1
Palhaça 214 E4
Pallet, le 115 F5
Pallud, en 67 F1
Palma, La 201 C2, 207 F4
Palmanova 181 C5
Palmas de Gran Canaria, Las 207 G5
Palmela 208 D4
Palmer 275 C5
Palmerston North 288 D5
Palmilla 297 D4
Palo Alto 263 B2
Palomino y Vergara 201 G2
Paloumey 95 F5
Pamhagen 222 D4
Pampa, La 294 G2
Panamena, La 201 C3
Panascal, Qta do 210 G5
Panciu 237 C5
Paneretta 189 E3
Panesa Baja, La 201 B4
Panimavida 297 G4
Panjas 113 E2
Pannonhalma-Sokoróalja 226 E2
Pano Lefkara 244 G3
Pano Panayia 244 F2
Pano Platres 244 F2
Panquehue 295 A3
Panshan 246 A6
Pantano Borghese 193 C5
Panther Creek 273 C4
Papagni 267 D4
Papakura 288 B4
Pape, Clos du 101 F5
Papes, Clos des 131 F2
Paphos 244 G1
Pápu 226 F2
Paquiers, aux 59 E2
Parada do Bispo 210 G1
Paradelinha 210 D5
Paradies 153 C2
Paradiesgarten, *Nahe* 155 D4
Paradiesgarten, *Pfalz* 161 F4
Paradis, le 119 F3
Paraiso, El 201 D2
Paraiso Springs 263 F5
Parana 294 F2
Parantoux, Clos 65 F4
Parc, Clos du 117 F3
Pardaillan 109 C4
Parducci 256 B3
Paredes 215 C5
Paredes de Coura 215 A5
Paredes do Bairro 214 F5
Pareditas 295 B4
Pargny-lès-Reims 79 A2
Parker 272 F2
Parkes 277 A4
Parlier 267 E5
Parma 173 E6, 179 D2
Parnac 113 C4
Paroisse Cave-Coop. La 87 C4
Paros 239 E4
Parpalana 201 F3
Parradero, El 201 C3
Parral 295 D2
Parramatta 277 B6
Parras 269 F5
Parrina 187 C2
Parsac 103 C5
Parterre, le 60 F1
Partridge 298 G4
Pasco 271 C6, 272 G6
Pas de Chat, les 66 F2
Pasignano 189 C2
Paso, El 269 D4
Paso Robles 265 B3
Pasquelles, les 60 F2
Pasquiers, les 61 G4
Passadoura, Qta da 210 D5
Passenans 137 F5
Passetemps 59 F3
Pastori 255 B4
Pastranilla, La 200 C5
Pastrengo 182 F3
Pataguas, Las 297 C4
Paterberg 162 F5
Paterhof 162 G5
Paterno 195 F3
Paterson, *New Jersey* 275 C5
Paterson, *Washington* 271 C5
Patócs 229 E2
Patrai (Patras) 239 D2
Patras 239 D3
Patrimonio 140 D5
Patritti 284 B2
Patterson 267 C2
Pâtureau, le Petit 119 E3
Pau 113 F2
Pauillac 80 C2, 89 D6
Paulands, les 63 F4
Paúl do Mar 216 B5
Paules, les 62 F3
Pauletts 283 E6
Paulinsberg, *Piesport* 151 B3
Paulinsberg, *Ruwer* 149 E4
Paulinshofberger 151 B4
Paulinslay 151 A4
Paul Thomas 271 A3
Paupillot, au 60 G4
Pave, le 72 F4
Pavia 173 D5
Pavillon Blanc 95 B1
Pavillon-Cadet 105 C4
Pavlikeni 235 B3
Pavlov 230 G3
Pavlovice 230 F3
Pavona 193 E4
Paxton 278 D4
Payneham 284 A3
Pays du Torgan 138 E4
Paz, La 294 F2
Pazardzhik 235 D3
Pcinsko-Osogovski 233 F6
Peachy Canyon 265 B3
Pec 233 E4
Pécharmant, Dom. du Haut 109 D4
Pechstein 161 E5
Pecs 226 G3
Pécsi 229 E3, G3
Pedee 273 D4
Pedrizzetti 263 C4
Pedro Domecq 269 F5
Pedro Domecq, SA 201 G1
Pedrogão, Qta do 210 F6
Pedroncelli 255 B4
Pedrosa de Duero 206 E4
Peel Estate 286 D2
Pegase, Clos 259 C2
Pego, Qta do 210 G5
Peissy 220 C3
Pekre 233 B2
Pélago 189 B5
Pelagonijsko-Poloski 233 G5
Pelarco 297 F4
Pelequen 295 C3
Peljesac 233 E3
Pellerin, le 114 B2
Pelles-Dessous, les 61 G1
Pelles Dessus, les 61 F1
Pemuco 295 E2
Peñafiel, *Spain* 206 E4
Penafiel, *Portugal* 208 B4, 215 C5
Peñaflor 295 A4, 297 A5
Penalva do Castelo 215 F5
Pendleton 271 C6
Penedès 197 B6, 205 F4
Peney 220 C3
Penfolds 278 C4, 285 B5
Penfolds/Tollana 282 B4
Penglai 246 C5
Penley Estate 285 B6
Pennes-Mirabeau, les 129 G5
Penola 277 D1, 285 E5
Penowarra 285 D5
Penrice 282 B5
Penrith 277 B6
Penshurst 298 F5
Pentro di Isernia 187 G5, 195 B3
Penwortham 283 E5
Penzing 224 C2
Peor es Nada 297 E5
Peoria 273 E4
Peppers Creek 278 C4
Pepperwood 256 C2
Perafort 205 F2
Peral, El 200 A5
Peralillo 295 C2, 297 D4
Perchots, les 61 F2
Perchtoldsdorf 222 C3, 224 D2
Perclos, les 60 G2
Perdrix, aux 64 F4
Perdrix, aux Champs 65 F3
Perelli-Minetti, M 259 A6
Pergine Valsugana 184 C6
Pernand-Vergelesses 55 C5, 63 D4
Pernik 235 C1
Pérolles, les 59 F2
Pérols 135 B4
Péronne 69 C5
Perpignan 133 F4, 138 F5
Perréon, Le 71 D2
Perrière, la, *Fixin* 67 E3
Perrière, la, *Gevrey-Chambertin* 67 F1
Perrière, la, *Sancerre* 119 E3
Perrière Noblot, en la 65 F3
Perrières, aux 60 F5
Perrières, Clos des 60 F5
Perrières Dessous, les 60 F5
Perrières Dessus, les 60 F5
Perrières, les, *Aloxe-Corton* 63 F4
Perrières, les, *Beaune* 62 E6
Perrières, les, *Meursault* 60 F5
Perrières, les, *Nuits-St-Georges* 64 F6
Perrières, les, *Pommard* 62 F2
Perrières, les, *Puligny* 60 G4
Perrières, les, *St-Aubin* 60 D2
Perriers, les Champs 67 F2
Perroy 220 B5
Pertaringa 284 E2
Perth 286 C2
Pertuis 129 F6
Pertuisots 62 F3
Perugia 187 C4, 192 C5
Perushtitsa 235 D3
Pesanella, La 189 E4
Pesaro 187 B6
Pescantina 182 F4
Pescara 187 F6
Peschiera del Garda 182 G2
Pesenti 265 B3
Peso da Regua 210 F1
Peso, Qta do 210 F1
Pesquera de Duero 206 E4
Pessac 80 F2, 96 D4, 99 A2
Pessac-sur-Dordogne 109 B4
Pessione 175 B2
Petaluma 283 D5, 284 B4
Petaluma/Evans Vyd 285 A5
Peterborough 276 A6
Petersberg 163 C4
Peterson S 278 D4
Petit Bois 99 A4
Petite Crau 139 C3
Petit Figeac 105 B2
Petit-Poujeaux, le 93 G3
Petits Grands Champs, les 60 G4
Petö 229 D4
Petone 288 D4
Petrich 235 E2
Pettenthal 162 C4, C5
Peuillets, les 63 E1
Peumo 295 C2, 297 D5
Peutes Vignes, les 61 F3
Peux Bois 60 F3
Pewsey Vale 282 D4
Peymilou 109 B5
Peyrassol, Com. de 136 B4
Pez 87 E4
Peza 239 F5
Pézenas 133 A6, 135 C2, 138 D6
Pézerolles, les 62 E2
Pezinok 230 G3
Pfaffenberg, *Austria* 225 G3
Pfaffenberg, *Germany* 158 G6
Pfaffengrund 161 D5
Pfaffenheim 120 E3, 122 C3
Pfaffenstein 154 G5
Pfaffental 225 F1
Pfaffstätten 224 F2
Pfalz 143 D3
Pfarrgarten 155 B5
Pfastatt 120 G4
Pfersigberg 122 C5
Pfeiffer 280 C5
Pfingstberg 122 B2
Pfingstweide 154 F5
Pforzheim 143 D4, 165 C3
Pheasant Ridge Winery 269 D5
Philadelphia 275 D4
Philip Togni 259 C2
Phillips, R H 267 A1
Philomath 273 E4
Phoenix 269 D3
Piacenza 173 E5
Pian d'Albola 189 E5
Pian-Médoc, le 95 G4
Piave 181 D2
Piazza Armerina 195 F3
Piazze, Le 189 F3
Picasses, les 117 E3
Piccadilly 284 B4
Piccadilly Fields 284 B4
Pichidegua 297 C4
Pichilemu 295 C2
Pichl Point 224 G5
Picotins, Grands 63 F1
Picotins, les Petits 63 F1
Picpoul de Pinet 135 C2
Pic St-Loup 135 A4
Picton 288 D4
Pièce Fitte, la 61 E3
Pièce sous le Bois, la 60 F5
Pied d'Aloue 75 D5
Piedmont 275 D3
Pienza 190 F4
Piera 205 E4
Pierelle, la 127 B5
Pierola 205 D4
Pierreclos 69 E3
Pierrefeu-du-Var 136 C3
Pierre, la 72 C6
Pierrelatte 129 C4
Pierres, les 60 G2
Pierres, Les 254 G4
Pierreux 72 G4
Pierre Virant 66 E4
Pierry 79 E2
Piesport 143 B2, 151 C2
Pietra de'Giorgi 177 F5
Pighin 183 C5
Pignans 136 B4
Pikes 283 E6
Piketberg 290 E2
Pikkara 284 E2
Pile e Lamole, Le 189 D4
Piles, Les 205 E2
Pilgerpfad 163 C5
Pillnitz 167 D6
Pilos 239 E2
Pilton Manor 298 F4
Pimentiers, les 63 F1
Pimont, Champs 62 E3
Pimont, En 60 F2
Pimpala 284 C2
Pina Cellars 259 D4
Pince-Vin 67 F2
Pinchons, les 72 B5
Pindar 275 C5
Pineaux, les 117 F3
Pinedale 267 D4
Pinell de Brai, El 204 G5
Pine Ridge 259 E5
Pinerolo 173 E2
Pinesse, la 101 C4
Pingdu 246 D5
Pinhao 210 E5
Pinhel 208 B5
Pinjarra 286 D2
Pin, le, *Chinon* 117 E4
Pin, le, *Jura* 137 G4
Pins, les 117 C2
Pinson 269 F5
Pintéus 209 E5
Pintray 118 D6
Piper Sonoma 255 D5
Pipers Brook 287 F6
Pira 205 E2
Pirgos 239 D2
Pirna 143 A4, 167 D6
Pirolette 72 A6
Pirque 297 B6
Pirramimma 284 E2
Pisa 187 A2
Pismo Beach 265 D3
Pissouri 244 G2
Pistoia 187 A3
Pitangeret 60 F2
Pitesti 237 D3
Pitois, Clos 59 F5
Pitschental 225 F3
Pittsburgh 275 D2
Pittsfield 275 B5
Pitures Dessus 61 E5
Pixley 267 F5
Pizay 72 E5
Places, les 60 G2
Plache 223 B6
Placilla 297 D5
Plá de Manlleu 205 E3
Plá del Penedès, El 205 E3
Plainoiseau 137 G4
Plainview, *Australia* 285 C5
Plainview, *USA* 273 E4
Plaisance 113 F2
Plaisir de Merle 293 E3
Plaiurile Drîncei 237 D2
Plam 259 F5
Planada 267 C4
Planalto-Mirandês 208 A6
Planches-près-Arbois, les 137 E6
Planchots de la Champagne, les 63 F1
Planchots du Nord, les 63 F1
Planes, Dom. des 136 B5
Planig 155 B6
Plantagenet 286 G4
Plante du Gaie 60 G2
Plantes au Baron 64 F5
Plantes, les, *Chambolle-Musigny* 66 F2
Plantes, les, *Monthelie* 61 E3
Plantes, les, *Sancerre* 119 E3
Plantes Momières, les 59 G5
Plantigone ou Issart 67 E1
Plassac 108 E1
Plateaux, les 65 F1
Platerie, la 117 C3
Platière, la, *Chassagne* 59 G6, 60 G1
Platière, la, *Pommard* 62 E1
Plâtre, le 72 D5
Pleasanton 263 A3
Pleven 235 B3
Plice, la 59 G4
Pljevlja 233 E4
Ploesti 237 D4
Plovdiv 235 D3
Pluchots, les 61 F4
Plume la Poule 99 B3
Plures, les 61 F3
Plush omer 282 B5
Plymouth Colony 275 B6
Plzen 230 F2
Poboleda 204 F6
Poca, Qta da 210 F4
Pocerina 233 D4
Podersdorf am See 222 D4, 223 B5
Podravje 233 A3
Podunajská 230 G4
Poggibonsi 189 E2
Poggio Reale 189 A5
Poggirindenti 177 B3
Poiares 210 F2
Poinchy 75 D3
Point du Jour, le 72 C5
Pointes, aux 63 D1
Pointes d'Angles 61 F5
Pointes de Tuvilains, les 62 F3
Poirets, les Hauts 64 F6
Poirets Saint-Georges, les 64 F6
Poirier du Clos, le 60 G1
Poisets, les 64 F5
Poisot, le 61 G5
Poisots, les Grands 61 G5
Poisots, les Petits 61 G5
Poissenot 67 D1
Pojer & Sandri 184 B5
Pokolbin 277 A6, 278 C4
Pokolbin Estate 278 C4
Polba de Claramunt, La 205 D3
Polesovice 230 F3
Poli 193 C6
Poligny 137 F5
Polis 244 F1
Pollero, El 200 D6
Pollino 195 D5
Polmassick 298 G2
Polski Trumbesh 235 B4
Pomerol 80 E4
Pomézia 193 E4
Pomino 187 B4, 189 A6
Pommard 55 D5, 57 E4, 61 F5, 62 E1
Pommeraye, la 114 B4
Pommière, La 126 B3
Pomone 235 C5
Pomport 109 B5
Ponce 201 C3
Poncey 68 E4
Pond 267 F5
Pontac 99 C5
Ponta Delgada 217 A2
Ponta do Pargo 216 A5
Ponta do Sol 217 C1
Pontaix, les 127 A4
Pontassieve 189 A5
Pontcharra-sur-Turdine 71 G1
Pontcirq 113 C4
Pont d'Armentera, El 205 E2
Pont de Crozes 127 A4
Pont de la Maye, le 99 B4
Ponte da Barca 215 B5
Ponte de Lima 215 B5
Ponte in V. 177 B4
Pont-Evêque 125 A5
Pontigny 73 D4
Pontils 205 E2
Pontin del Roza 272 G4
Pontons 205 E3
Pontremoli 173 F6
Pont-St-Esprit 129 D4
Ponzi 273 B5
Pope Valley 259 B3
Popovo 235 B4
Poprad 230 F5
Pordenone 179 C5, 181 B3
Porirua 288 D4
Porlottes, les 66 E2
Poros 239 D4
Porrera 204 F6
Porroux, les 66 F4
Porta 297 B5, C5
Port Adelaide 276 B6
Portal del Alto 297 B6
Portalegre 208 D5
Portarlington 280 F3
Port Augusta 276 A5
Port Campbell 280 G1
Port-de-Bouc 129 G4
Port de Fos 139 D3
Porte Feuilles ou Murailles du Clos 65 G5
Portel 213 F5
Portela, Qta da 210 G2
Porterville, *S. Africa* 290 E2
Porterville, *USA* 267 F6
Portes Feuilles, les 67 E3
Portes-lès-Valence 125 E4
Port Guyet 117 D1
Portimão 208 F4
Port Kembla 277 B6
Portland, *Australia* 277 D1
Portland, *USA* 271 C3, 273 B5
Port-la-Nouvelle 133 D5, 134 E6
Port Noarlunga 284 D1
Port Noarlunga South 284 D1
Porto 208 B4, 215 C4
Porto da Cruz 217 B4
Porto de Bois, Qta de 211 G5
Porto e Douro 208 B5
Portogruaro 181 C4
Porto Moniz 216 A6
Porto, Qta do 210 F5
Port Orford 271 G1
Porto Tolle 179 E4
Porto-Vecchio 140 G4, G5
Port Pirie 276 A6
Port-Ste-Foy-et-Ponchapt 109 B4
Port-St-Louis-du-Rhône 129 G4
Port San Luis 265 D3
Portteus 272 F3
Port Valais 221 B1
Port-Vendres 133 G5, 138 F5
Port Willunga 284 E1
Porusot Dessus, les 60 F6
Porusot, le 60 F6
Posavje 233 B2
Possonnière, la 116 B2
Postalésio 177 B2
Postaller 224 G5
Pot Bois 59 F6, 60 F1
Potenza 195 C4
Potets, les 59 E2
Pothana 278 B4
Pothana Vyds 278 B4

Potter Valley 256 A3
Pougets, les 63 E4
Pouilly 69 F4
Pouilly-Fuissé 69 F3
Pouilly-Loché 69 F4
Pouilly-sur-Loire 115 B6, 119 G4
Pouilly-Vinzelles 69 G4
Poulaillères, les 65 F5
Poulettes, les 64 F6
Poussie, la 119 F2
Poutures, les 61 F5
Pouvray 118 B4
Pouyalet, le 89 B5
Povardarski 233 F5
Poverty Bay 288 C6
Povoa de Lanhoso 215 B5
Póvoa de Varzim 215 C4
Powellhurst 273 B5
Poyebade, la 72 F3
Poysdorf 222 B3
Pozáldez 206 F2
Pozo 265 C4
Pradell de la Teixeto 204 F6
Prades 133 F2, 138 F4
Pradet, le 136 C3
Prado 215 B5
Prager 259 D3
Praha (Prague) 230 F2
Praia da Adraga 209 E3
Praia das Maçás 209 E3
Prälat 152 B6
Prangins 220 B4
Prarons-Dessus, les 59 G4
Prat de Llobregat, El 205 F5
Prática di Mare 193 E3
Prayssac 113 C4
Prazeres 216 B5
Préau 67 E3
Pré de la Folie, le 65 G4
Pré de Manche, le 61 F3
Preignac 101 C6
Preignes-le-Vieux 133 B6, 135 D2
Prellenkirchen 222 C4
Premariacco 183 B4
Premeaux-Prissey 64 F4
Premià de Mar 205 E6
Premières Côtes de Bordeaux 80 F3, 96 E5
Prepotto 183 B5
Presinge 220 C4
Preslav 235 B5
Presov 230 F5
Pressoir, le 117 F6
Preston 255 B4
Preston Cellars 271 F4
Preuses 75 C4
Prévaux, les 63 F1
Preverenges 220 A6
Prévoles, les 62 F3
Priego de Córdoba 207 B5
Prieur-Bas, Clos 67 F1
Prieur, Clos 67 F1
Prieuré d'Amilhac 133 B6, 135 C1
Prieuré de Ramejan 133 B5, 134 D6
Prieuré St-Jean-de Bebian 133 A6, 135 C2
Prievidza 230 G4
Prignac-en-Médoc 85 E2
Prignac-et-Marcamps 108 G4
Prigonrieux 109 B5
Prilep 233 G5
Primitivo di Manduria 195 C6
Primorska Hrvatska 233 D2
Primorska Slovenija 233 B1
Prince Albert 280 G3
Prince de Polignac 110 G5
Prince Michel 275 E3
Principauté d'Orange 139 B3, 139 G4
Priorato 197 B5, 204 F6
Priory 298 F5
Prissé 69 F4
Pristina 233 F5
Pritchard Hill 259 D5
Privas 125 F3
Prizren 233 F5
Procès, les 65 F1
Propiano 140 F4
Prosecco di Conegliano Valdobbiadene 179 C4, 181 C2
Prosser 272 G4
Provadiya 235 B5
Provence, Haute 293 F6
Provence, La 293 F6
Provesende 210 E5
Providence 275 C6
Provins 76 D3
Pruliers, les 64 F6
Pruliers, les Hauts 64 F6
Pruniers, aux Champs des 63 F2
Pruzilly 69 G3, 71 B3, 72 A5
Psara 239 C5
Ptuj 231 C5, 233 B3
Pucelles, les 60 G3
Puch, le 101 C5
Puebla 269 G6
Puente Alto 295 B3, 297 A6
Puente Genil 207 B4
Puerto del Rosario 207 G6
Puget-Ville 136 B3
Puiatti 183 D5
Puigpelat 205 F2
Puisac, le 119 F5
Puisieulx 79 B5
Puisseguin 80 E5, 103 C5
Puits, le 60 D2
Puits Merdreaux 60 G1
Puits, Sous le 60 F4
Pujaut 131 G1
Pujols 97 D2
Pulchen 147 B2
Pulham 298 E6
Puligny-Montrachet 55 D5, 57 F3, 60 G4
Pulkau 222 B2
Pully 220 A6
Punta, La 297 B6
Pupillin 137 E6
Purbach am Neusiedlersee 222 C3, 223 B4
Purcari 241 F6
Purísima 297 F4
Puyallup 271 A3
Puyguilhem 109 C5
Puy-l'Evêque 113 C4
Pyramid Hill 280 C2
Pyrenees 277 C2, 280 E2

Qacentina (Constantine) 245 B5
Qianxi 246 B4
Qingdao 246 D5
Qingdao Winery 246 D5
Qing Xian 246 C3
Qinhuangdao 246 B5
Quady 267 D4
Quai du Vin 275 B2
Quail Ridge 259 F6
Quarry Lake 271 F4
Quartier des Fleurs 123 C2
Quartiers de Nuits, les 65 F5
Quartiers, les 63 D5
Quarts-de-Chaume 116 C3
Quatourze 134 E6
Quatre Vents, les 72 C5
Queenscliffe 280 G3
Queenstown 287 G5
Quel 203 C3
Querceto e Santa Lucia 189 C3
Quercia, La 189 D4
Querétaro 269 F5
Quéribus 133 E3
Quéron, Clos 117 G6
Queue de Hareng 67 E3
Queyssac 109 B6
Quillan 133 E1, 138 F4
Quillota 295 A2
Quilpué 295 A2
Quincy 115 C4
Quindalup 287 B2
Quinta Grande 217 D2
Quintero 295 A2
Quintigny 137 G4
Quinhue 295 D2
Quivira 255 C4
Quorn 276 A6

Rabastens 113 E5
Rabat 245 B2
Rabbit Ridge 255 D5
Rablay-sur-Layon 116 D4
Raboatun 201 D4
Raca 230 G3
Race 231 B4
Racha, La 201 C2
Radda in Chianti 189 E4
Radebeul 143 A4, 167 C6
Radenci 231 A5
Radgona 231 A5, 233 A2
Radizelj 231 B4
Rafanelli, A 255 C4
Rafour, le 126 D3
Raguenières, les 117 C3
Ragusa 195 G3
Raiding 222 D3
Raignots, aux 65 F4
Rama Caida 295 C4
Ram Allah 243 F4
Rambla, La 207 B4
Rancagua 295 B3, 297 C5
Ranché, en la 60 D3
Rancho, El 201 D2
Rancho Sisquoc 265 E5
Randersacker 166 B4
Randogne 221 C4
Rangiora 288 E3
Rapaura 289 F4
Rapazzini 263 D4
Rapidan River 275 D3
Rapsani 239 B3
Rarangi 289 E5
Raron 221 C5
Râsiy 229 E4
Rasquera 204 G5
Rastatt 165 C3
Rasteau 129 D4, 131 B4
Ratausses, les 63 F1
Rátka 229 F2
Ratosses, les 63 F2
Rauenthal 159 D4
Raul 147 C5
Rausch 147 F2
Rauzan 97 D1
Ravelles, les 60 E4
Ravenna 179 F4, 187 A5
Ravensburg 166 B3
Ravenswood 254 F5
Raviolles, aux 65 G3
Raymond, *California* 259 D4
Raymond, *Washington* 271 B2
Razac-de-Saussignac 109 B4
Razac-d'Eymet 109 C5
Razgrad 235 B4
Razlog 235 D2
Reading 275 C4
Real de Padre 295 C5
Réas, aux 65 F3
Réas, le Clos des 65 G4
Rebeninha 210 E6
Rebichets, les 60 F2
Rebstöckel 161 B2
Recas 237 C2
Réchaux, la 67 D4
Rechbächel 161 D5
Rechnitz 222 E3
Recinto 295 E2
Redavalle 177 E4
Redbank 280 E2
Redgate 287 E1
Redhawk 273 C4
Redi Vazzoler 183 C5
Redman 285 B5
Redondo 208 E5, 213 E5
Redrescut 63 E1
Redwood City 263 B2
Redwoodtown 289 G5
Redwood Valley 256 B3
Reedley 267 E5
Reedsport 271 F1
Refène, la 61 F6, 62 E1
Referts, les 60 G4
Reggio di Calabria 195 F4
Réggio nell'Emilia 179 E2
Régnié 72 E3
Régnié-Durette 72 E3
Régrippière, la 115 F6
Régua 208 B5
Reguengos 208 E5, 213 F5
Reguengos de Monsaraz 208 E5, 213 F5
Rehbach 162 C5, 163 B5
Rehborn 155 D4
Reigny 119 F2
Reims 76 B4, 79 A4
Reinsport 151 D2
Reiterpfad 161 F5
Reland, le Clos 59 G6, 60 G1
Remanenzen 223 C5
Rémigny 59 G5
Remilly, en 60 F3
Remlingen 166 B3
Remstal-Stuttgart 143 E5, 165 D4
Rémy Martin 110 F5
Renardes, les 63 F5
Renault 275 D5
René, Clos 107 D2
Rengo 295 C3
Renmark 277 B1
Renqiu 246 C3
Renton 271 A3
Renwick 289 G4
Réole, la 80 G5, 97 F2
Requinoa 295 B3, 297 C5
Resende 215 D6
Restigné 117 D3
Retórbido 177 F3
Retz, *Austria* 222 A2
Retz, *France* 139 E4
Retzbach 166 A4
Retzstadt 166 A4
Reuilly 115 C4
Reulle-Vergy 57 C4
Reus 205 F1
Reverend, Dom. du 133 E3
Reversées, les 62 F4
Rex Hill 273 C4
Reynella 284 C2
Reynolds Yarraman Vyd 279 E4
Rezé 114 C3, 115 F4
Rharb 245 B2
Rhazir 243 E5
Rhebokskloof 293 B4
Rhein 143 A3, C4
Rheinberg 159 G5
Rheinblick 163 C5
Rheingarten 159 G1
Rheingau 143 B4
Rheingrafenstein 163 C3
Rheinhessen 143 C3
Rheintal 219 E5
Rias Baixas 197 B1
Riba, La 205 F2
Ribalonga 211 E2
Ribaudy 126 G1
Ribbon Yale 287 D1
Ribeauvillé 120 D4, 123 D4
Ribeira Brava 217 C1
Ribeira da Janela 216 A6
Ribeira de Pena 215 B6
Ribeira, Qta da 210 D5
Ribeiro 197 A2
Ribera del Arlanza, La 197 B3
Ribera del Cea, La 197 A3
Ribera del Duero 197 B3, 206 E4
Ribera del Sil 197 A2
Ribera de Salamanca, La 197 B2
Ribrita 241 E5
Ricard-Bisquit Dubouché 110 F5
Richarde, en la 60 F3
Richard Hamilton 284 E2
Richardson 257 E4
Richeaume, Dom. 136 A2
Richebourg, le 65 F4
Richemone, la 65 F3
Richgrove 267 F6
Richings 285 C5
Richland 271 B5, 272 F5
Richmond 275 E4
Richmond Grove 278 B4
Rickreall 273 D4
Riddes 221 D3
Riddle 271 F2
Ridge 263 B2
Riebeek-West 290 F2
Riefring 223 B4
Riegersburg 222 F2
Riera de Gaià, La 205 F2
Riesa 143 A4, 167 C5
Rieti 187 E4
Riex 220 A6
Rignano sull'Arno 189 B5
Rijeka 233 B2
Rilly-la-Montagne 79 B4
Rimauresq, Dom. de 136 B4
Rimavská Sobota 230 G5
Rimini 187 B5
Rimpar 166 B4
Riocaud 109 B4
Rio Dell 255 D4
Rio Grande do Sul 294 F2
Rioja 197 A4
Rioja Alavesa 202 B6
Rioja Alta 202 B6
Rioja Baja 203 C2
Rioja, La 294 F2
Rio Negro 294 G2
Rio Nido 255 D4
Rions 96 E5
Riotte, la 66 F4
Riottes, les, *Monthelie* 61 E3
Riottes, les, *Pommard* 62 F1
Rio Vista 267 B2
Ripaille 137 A3
Ripon 267 B2
Riquewihr 120 D3, 123 C3
Riscle 113 E2
Rishon-le-Zion 243 F4
Rising 281 B4
Ritchie Creek 259 C2
Ritsch 150 F5
Ritter Garten 161 B4
Ritterpfad 147 C2
Rittersberg 165 B4
Ritzling 224 G5
Riudecols 205 F1
Riudoms 205 F1
Rivadavia 295 B4
Riva del Garda 184 E3
Rivanazzano 177 G3
Rivaux, les 61 E3
Rivaz 220 B6
Rivendell 275 C5
Rivendell Vyd 287 C2
Riverbank 267 B3
Riverdale 267 E4
Riverland 277 B1, B2
Riverlands 289 G5
River Road 255 D5
River Run 263 D4
Riversdale 289 G5, 290 F5
Riverview 279 D6
Rivesaltes 133 F4
Riviera del Garda 182 E1
Riviera del Garda Bresciano 179 C2
Riviera Ligure di Ponente 173 F3
Rivière, au dessus de la 65 G3
Rivolet 71 E2
Rivoli Veronese 182 E3
Rixheim 120 G4
Rizhao 246 E5
Rizokarpaso 244 D6
Roa de Duero 206 E4
Rôaix 129 D4, 131 B5
Roanoke 275 E2
Robardelle 61 F4
Robert Keenan 259 C2
Robert Mondavi 259 E4
Robert Mondavi-Woodbridge 267 F3
Robert Pecota 259 B1
Robert Pepi 259 E4
Robert Sinksey 259 E5
Robertson 290 F3
Robert Stemmler 255 C4
Robertsvlei 293 G5
Robert Talbott 263 F4
Robinvale 277 B2
Rob Roy 281 B3
Rocafort de Querait 205 E2
Rocallaura 205 E1
Rocca di Papa 193 D5
Rocca Mássima 193 E6
Rocca Priora 193 D5
Rocca Susella 177 G3
Rocche di Castiglione 176 F2
Rocche di La Morra 176 F2
Roc de Puisseguin 103 C5
Rocfort 118 B5
Roche, *Switzerland* 221 B1
Roche, *USA* 257 G4
Roche aux Moines, la 116 A3
Roche, Clos de la 66 F5
Rochecorbon 118 B2
Rochefort-sur-Loire 114 B4, 116 B3
Rochegrès 72 B5
Rochegude 129 D4
Roche, la 126 B4
Rochelle, la, *Beaujolais* 72 B5
Rochelle, la, *Chinon* 117 F3
Rochepot, la 57 F3
Rochère, la 118 B5
Rocheservière 114 C3
Roches, les 118 B2
Roche, Sous la, *St-Aubin* 60 E3
Roche, Sous la, *Santenay* 59 E3
Roches, Sur 61 E5
Rochester, *Australia* 280 D3
Rochester, *USA* 275 B3
Rochette-St Jean 117 F4
Roche-Vineuse, La 69 E4
Rochioli 255 D5
Rockford 282 C4
Rock Lodge 298 F5
Rocoules, les 127 C5
Roda de Bera 205 F3
Rödchen 159 E5
Rodelsee 166 B5
Rodern 120 D4, 123 D5
Rodhos (Rhodes) 239 E6
Rodney Strong 255 D5
Rodonyà 205 F2
Roéda, Qta de 210 F6
Roederer 256 C2
Roero 173 E3, 175 D3
Rogaska Slatina 231 D4
Rogatec 231 D4
Rognac 129 F5
Rognet-Corton, le 63 F5
Rogue River 271 G2
Rogue Valley 271 G2
Rohrendorf 222 B2
Roi, Clos du, *Aloxe-Corton* 63 E4
Roi, Clos du, *Beaune* 62 E6
Roi, le Clos du 119 F2
Roichottes 63 D2
Roilette, la 72 C5
Rolle 220 B5
Roma 187 E3
Romagniens, les 61 E3
Romanèche-Thorins 71 C4, 72 C6
Romanée Conti, la 65 F4
Romanée, la 59 F5, 65 F4, 67 D1
Romanée St-Vivant 65 F4
Romaneira, Qta da 210 E6
Romanel-sur-Morges 220 A5
Romano, El 201 C4
Romans d'Isonzo 183 D4
Romarigo, Qta de 210 F1
Rombauer 259 A5
Romeral 297 E5
Römerhang 153 C1
Römerlay 149 F5
Romorantin-Lanthenay 115 B3
Ronca 183 G2
Roncé 117 G6
Ronceret, le 61 F4
Roncière 64 F6
Roncières 75 E2
Ronco del Gnemiz 183 C4
Ronds, les Champs 61 G5
Rongcheng 246 D6
Roquebrun 133 A5, 134 C6
Roquebrussanne, la 136 B3
Roquemaure 131 F1
Roquemaure, la 59 G5
Roriz, Qta do 211 E1
Rorschwihr 123 D5
Rosacker 123 C4
Rosaliakapelle 223 D3
Röschitz 222 B2
Roseburg 271 F2
Rosedale 282 C3
Rose family 255 D5
Roseglen 279 F3
Rosemount Estate 279 E3, F4, 285 D5
Rosenberg, *Bernkastel* 153 D1
Rosenberg, *Nahe* 154 F5
Rosenberg, *Piesport* 151 D2
Rosenberg, *Rheinhessen* 162 C4
Rosenberg, *Saar* 147 C5
Rosenberg Cellars 283 F5
Rosenbühl 161 A2
Rosengärtchen 151 E1
Rosengarten, *Bernkastel* 153 D4
Rosengarten, *Nahe* 154 F5, 155 B5
Rosengarten, *Rheingau* 157 F4
Rosenheck 154 G5
Rosenlay 152 F5
Rosental 223 B3
Rose-Pauillac, la 89 C5
Rosettes, les 117 G3
Rosey 68 F3
Rosheim 120 B4
Rossano 195 D5
Rossas 215 B6
Rossatz 225 G1
Rossese di Dolceacqua 173 G3
Ross McLaren 284 D1
Rosso Barletta 195 B4
Rosso Canosa 195 B4
Rosso Conero 187 C6
Rosso di Cerignola 195 B4
Rosso di Montalcino 187 C3, 190 G2
Rosso Piceno 187 D6
Rosso Piceno Superiore 187 E6
Rosstal 166 A4
Rosswein 167 D5
Rostov-na-Donu 240 B4
Rotenfels 154 F6
Rotenfelser im Winkel 155 F2
Roterd 151 D1
Rothbury 278 C5
Rothbury Estate 278 C4
Rothenberg, *Rheingau* 157 F6, 158 G1, 159 E4
Rothenberg, *Rheinhessen* 162 B5
Rothenhof 225 G2
Rothental 225 G2
Rotlei 149 F2
Rotorua 288 C5
Rott 165 A3
Rottendorf 166 B5
Roudnice nad Labem 230 E2
Roudon Smith 263 C2
Rouffach 120 F3, 122 C3
Rouffiac 113 D6
Rouffignac-de-Sigoulès 109 B5
Rouge Homme 285 B5
Rougeots, les 61 F1
Rougeotte, la 61 F5
Rouges du Bas, les 65 F5
Rouges du Dessus, les 65 E5
Round Hill 259 D4
Rourell, El 205 F2
Rousseau, Grand Clos 59 D2
Rousselle, la 60 G4
Roussenski Bnag 235 B4
Rousset-les-Vignes 129 C5
Roussillon 125 B4
Rouvrettes, les 63 E1
Rovalley 282 C4
Rovereto 179 C3, 184 E4
Rovescala 177 F6
Rovigo 179 D4
Rowland Flat 282 C4
Roxburgh 279 F5
Roxheim 155 B5
Royal Tokay Wine Co. 229 F2
Rozendal 293 F2
Rozova Dolina 235 C3
Rubino di Cantavenna 175 A4
Rubzi 235 A1
Ruche de Castagnole Monferrato 175 B5
Ruchots, les 66 F4
Ruchottes du Bas 67 E1
Ruchottes du Dessus 67 E1
Ruchottes, Grandes 59 F5
Rüdesheim 157 F4
Rudolf Carli Erben 185 B5
Rudolfsheim 224 C2
Rue au Porc 61 G6
Rue aux Vaches, la 60 G4
Rueda 197 B3, 206 F2
Rue de Chaux 65 F1
Rue de Vergy 66 E4
Rue de Vergy, en la 66 E4
Rue Rousseau 60 G3
Ruffey-sur-Seille 137 F4
Ruffieux 137 B2
Rufina 187 A4, 189 A5, B5
Rugiens-Bas, les 61 F5
Rugiens-Hauts, les 61 E5
Rührsdorf 224 G6
Rui Diaz 201 D3
Ruino 177 G5
Rully 55 D5, 57 G3, 68 B4
Ruppertsberg 161 B2, F5
Ruppertsburg 143 C4
Ruse, *Bulgaria* 235 B4
Ruse, *Slovenia* 231 B3
Rushan 246 D5
Rushworth 280 D4
Russian River 255 D4
Russilly 68 D3
Russin 220 C3
Rust 222 D3, 223 C4
Rustenberg 293 F3
Rust-en-Vrede 293 G2
Rute 207 B5
Rutherford 259 D3, D4
Rutherford Hill 263 D4
Rutherford Vintners 259 D3
Rutherglen 280 C5
Ruwer 149 C3
Ruyère 72 D4
Ryecroft 284 D2

Saarbrücken 143 D2
Saarburg 143 C1, 147 F3
Saarfeilser-Marienberg 147 D3
Saar-Ruwer 143 C1, 147 D4, 149 E5
Sabazan 113 E2
Sables-du-Golfe-du-Lion 139 D1
Sables, les 131 D2
Sablet 129 D4, 131 C5
Sablons, les 117 D2
Sabrosa 208 A5
Sabugo 209 E4
Sacile 181 C3
Sackträger 162 F5
Sacramento 267 A2
Sacy 73 F5, 79 B3
Saddlers Creek 278 D5
Sadillac 109 C5
Sadova 237 E3
Sadova-Corabia 237 E3
Saering 122 B1
Safi 245 C1
Sage 273 C6
Sagrado 183 D5
Sagrado, Qta do 210 F5
Sahel 245 B1
Sahy 230 G4
Saillans 102 A6
Saillon 221 D2
St-Aignan, *Fronsac* 102 B5
St-Aignan, *Touraine* 115 B3
St-Aigne 109 B6
St-Albain 69 C6
St-Amour 55 F5, 72 A6
St-Amour-Bellevue 72 A6
St-Andelain 119 F4
St-André-de-Cubzac 80 E3
St-André-et-Appelles 109 B4
St Andrews 259 F6
St Andrews North 281 A3
St-Androny 108 B1
St Anna 222 F2
St-Antoine-de-Breuilh 109 B4
St Amaud 280 D1
St-Aubin 55 D5, 60 D2
St-Aubin-de-Cadelech 109 C5
St-Aubin-de-Lanquais 109 B6
St-Aubin de Luigné 116 C2
St-Baillon, Dom. 136 B4
St-Barthélemy-d'Anjou 114 B5
St-Boi de Llobregat 205 E5
St-Bouize 119 F3
St-Brice 111 D1
St-Brice Cave Vinic. 85 E5
St-Bris, *Pessac* 99 B4
St-Bris, *Yonne* 55 A3
St-Bris-le-Vineux 73 F4
St-Capraise-d'Eymet 109 C6
St-Cernin-de-Labarde 109 B6
St-Chamas 129 F5
St-Chinian 133 E5, 135 D5
St-Christol 129 F2, 135 A5
St-Christoly-Médoc 85 C5
St-Christophe-des-Bardes 103 D4
St-Ciers-de-Canesse 108 E2
St Clement 259 C3
St-Clément-de-la-Place 114 B4
St-Corbian 87 D4
St-Crespin-sur-Moine 115 G6
St-Cugat del Vallès 205 E5
St-Cyprien 133 F5
St-Cyr-sur-le-Rhône 126 A5
St-Denis, Clos, *Morey-St-Denis* 66 F4
St Denis, Clos, *Vougeot* 65 F5
St-Denis-de-Vaux 68 D3
St-Désert 68 E3
St-Didier 137 G4
St-Dizier 76 D6
St-Drézéry 129 F2, 135 A4
Ste-Colombe 103 D5
Ste-Croix-du-Mont 80 G4, 96 F6
Ste-Eulalie-d'Eymet 109 C5
Ste-Foy 109 B5
Ste-Foy-Bordeaux 97 E3
Ste-Foy-la-Grande 80 E6, 109 B4
Ste-Gemme-en-Sancerrois 119 E3
Ste Genevieve Vyds (Cordier Estates) 269 E5
Ste-Innocence 109 C5
Ste-Marie-aux-Mines 120 C3
Ste-Marie d'Alloix 137 D2
Ste-Maure-de-Touraine 115 C1
Ste-Menehould 76 B6
St-Emilion 80 E4, 103 C3, D3, 105 D4
Ste-Radegonde 109 B3
Ste-Radegonde-de-Touraine 118 C1
St-Estèphe 80 C2, 87 D5
St-Esteve Sesrovires 205 E4
St-Etienne-de-Baïgorry 112 G6
St-Etienne-de-Lisse 103 D5
St-Etienne-des-Oullières 71 D3
St-Etienne-la-Varenne 71 D3
Ste-Vertu 73 F6
St-Feliu de Llobregat 205 E5
St-Félix de-Foncaude 97 E1
St-Fiacre-sur-Maine 115 F4
St-Florent-le-Vieil 114 B4
St-Forgeux 71 G1
St Francis, *Australia* 284 C2
St Francis, *USA* 254 D3
St Gallen 219 E5
St-Genès-de-Blaye 108 C1
St-Genès-de-Castillon 103 D5
St-Genès-de-Lombaud 96 E5
St-Gengoux-de-Scisse 69 B4
St-Geniès-de-Comolas 130 F6
St-Genis de Vilasar 205 E6
St Georgen 222 D3
St-Georges 80 E4, 103 C4
St-Georges-Blancaneix 109 A5
St-Georges-de-Reneins 71 D4

St-Georges-d'Orques 135 B3
St-Georges, les 64 F5
St-Georges-sur-Loire 114 B4
St-Géraud-de-Corps 109 A4
St-Germain-d'Esteuil 85 F4
St-Germain-les-Arlay 137 F4
St-Gervais 129 D3
St-Gervais-sur-Couches 57 G2
St-Géry 109 A5
St-Gilles 129 F3
St Goar 143 B3
St Goarshausen 143 B3
St Gregory, Dom. 256 C3
St Hallett 282 C4
St Helena 259 D3
St Helens 271 C3
St-Herblain 114 B2
St-Hilaire, Dom. de 135 C2
St-Hilaire-St-Florent 114 B6
St-Hippolyte, *Alsace* 120 D4, 123 D6
St-Hippolyte, *St-Emilion* 103 D4
St-Hippolyte, *Touraine* 115 C2
St Huberts 281 B4
St Innocent 273 D4
St-Jacques, le Clos 67 E2
St-Jaume dels Domenys 205 F3
St-Jean Cave Coop. 85 C3
St-Jean, Clos 60 F2
St-Jean-d'Ardières 72 F6
St-Jean-de-Braye 115 A4
St-Jean-de-la-Porte 137 C3
St-Jean-de Vaux 68 D3
St-Jean-d'Eyraud 109 A5
St-Jean-Pied-de-Port 112 G6
St Josef's Weinkeller 273 C5
St-Joseph 72 D3
St-Julien 71 E3
St-Julien-Beychevelle 80 D2, 91 C5
St-Julien-de-Concelles 115 E5
St-Julien-de-Crempse 109 A6
St-Julien-d'Eymet 109 C5
St Kereszt 229 G3
St-Lager 71 D3, 72 F4
St-Lamain 137 F5
St-Lambert 89 E5
St-Lambert-du-Lattay 116 D3
St-Laurent 119 E5
St-Laurent-de-la-Salanque 133 E4
St-Laurent-des-Arbres 130 F6
St-Laurent-des-Combes 103 D4
St-Laurent-des-Vignes 109 B5
St-Laurent-Médoc 91 D1
St-Léonard 221 C3
St Leonards 280 C5
St-Livres 220 A5
St-Llorenç d'Hortons 205 E4
St-Lothain 137 F5
St-Loubès 80 E3
St-Louis 131 F3
St-Lumine-de-Clisson 115 G5
St-Macaire 80 G4, 96 F6
St-Magne-de-Castillon 103 E5
St-Mamest 109 A6
St-Mard-de-Vaux 68 D3
St Margarethen i. Bgl. 222 D3, 223 C4
St Martin 155 C2
St-Martin-Belle-Roche 69 D6
St-Martin-d'Arrossa 112 G6
St-Martin-de-Crau 129 F4
St-Martin-de-Gurçon 109 A4
St-Martin-de-la-Garrigue 135 C2
St-Martin, Dist. de 110 F6
St-Martin-Lacaussade 108 C1
St-Martin-le-Beau 118 E6
St-Martin-sous-Montaigu 68 C4
St-Martin-sur-Nohain 119 E5
St-Matré 113 C4
St-Maurice 221 C2
St-Maurice-de-Satonnay 69 C5
St-Maurice-l'Exil 125 A4
St-Maurice-sur-Eygues 129 D4
St-Maximin-la-Ste-Baume 136 B3
St-Méard-de-Gurçon 109 A4
St-Médard-en-Jalles 96 C3
St-Même 111 F4
St Michael 150 E6
St-Michel-de-Fronsac 102 B5
St-Michel-de-Montaigne 109 B3
St-Michel-sur-Rhône 126 E2
St-Moritz 219 F5
St-Nazaire 114 B1
St-Nexans 109 B6
St Nicholas of Ash 298 F6
St-Nicolas-de-Bourgueil 114 B6, 117 C2
St Nikolaus 158 F4
St-Pantaléon-les-Vignes 129 C5
St-Paul, *Blaye* 108 C2
St-Paul, *Chinon* 117 G4
St-Pedro de Ribes 205 F4
St-Pedro de Riudebitlles 205 E3
St-Péray 125 D4
St-Perdoux 109 C6
St-Pey-d'Armens 103 E4
St-Philbert-de-Grand-Lieu 114 C2
St-Philippe-d'Aiguille 103 C6
St-Pierre-de-Clages 221 C3
St-Pierre-des-Corps 115 B1
St-Pierre-d'Eyraud 109 B5
St Pölten 222 C2
St Pons 138 D5
St-Pourçain 53 D3, 139 F2
St-Prex 220 A5
St-Quinti de Mediona 205 E3
St-Rémy 109 A4
St-Roman-de-Malegarde 131 A4
St-Sadurní d'Anoia 205 E4
St-Saphorin 220 B6
St-Sardos 139 G4
St-Satur 119 F3
St-Saturnin 135 B2
St-Sauveur 109 B6
St-Sauveur-Lalande 109 A4
Saintsbury 257 E5
St-Sébastien-sur-Loire 114 B3, 115 F4
St-Sernin 109 C4
St-Seurin-de-Bourg 108 F3
St-Seurin-de-Cadourne 87 C4
St-Seurin-de-Cursac 108 C2
St-Sigismond 114 B4
Saints Jacques, aux 65 F3
Saints Juliens, aux 65 F2
St Stefan 222 F1
St-Sulpice, *France* 113 E5
St-Sulpice, *Switzerland* 220 A5
St-Sulpice-de-Faleyrens 103 E2
St Supery 259 D4
St-Symphorien, *Nuits-St-Georges* 65 F1
St-Symphorien, *Touraine* 115 B1
St-Symphorien-d'Ancelles 71 B4
St Tamás 229 F2
St-Trélody 85 F2
St-Trojan, *Bourg* 108 E3
St-Trojan, *Cognac* 110 C6
St-Tropez 136 C5
St-Vérand 69 G3, 71 B4
St-Victor 133 D3
St-Vincenç dels Horts 205 E5
St-Vivien 109 B4
St-Yzans-de-Médoc 85 E5
Sais 245 B2
Sajgó 229 E3
Sakar 235 D4
Sakonnet 275 C6
Saku 248 C4
Salamandre 263 D3
Sale 277 D4
Salem 271 D2, 273 D4
Salernes 136 A4
Salerno 195 C3
Salgesch 221 C4
Salgótarjáno 226 E4
Salice Salentino 195 C6
Sálice Terme 177 G3
Salies-de-Béarn 112 F6
Salignac 110 G5
Salinas 263 E4
Salinillas de Buradon 203 E1
Salins 221 C3
Salins d'Hyères, les 136 C4
Salishan 271 C3
Salle, La 69 D6
Salles-Arbuissonas-en-Beaujolais 71 E3
Salò 182 E1
Salomó 205 F2
Salomon, Clos 68 D4
Salon-de-Provence 129 F5, 139 D3
Salou 205 G1
Salpetrière, la 117 C2
Salta 294 F
Saltillo 269 F5
Salto Grillo 200 A4
Saltram 282 B5
Salvador 259 F5
Salvador, El 201 B4
Salvagnac 113 D5
Salzberg 165 C4
Samaniego 202 A5, 203 F3
Samokov 235 C2
Samonac 108 F3
Samos 239 D5
Samothraki 239 B5
Sampigny 55 D5
Samsun 243 B5
Samtredia 240 C4
San Adrián 203 B3
San Antonio, *Chile* 295 B2
San Antonio, *Spain* 201 C3
San Antonio, *USA* 269 E5
San Bernardo 295 B3, 297 A5
San Bonifacio 183 G2
San Borondon 200 B4
San Carlos, *Argentina* 295 B4
San Carlos, *Chile* 295 D2
San Carlos de Cunaco (Vinos Viu) 297 D4
San Casciano in Val di Pesa 189 C3
San Cesáreo 193 D5
San Clemente 295 C2, 297 F4
San Colombano al Lambro 173 D5
San Cristovão do Douro 210 E5
San Daniele del Friuli 181 B4
San Diego 269 D2
San Dona di Piave 181 D3
San Esteban de Gormaz 206 E6
San Fausto de Campcentellas 205 E5
San Felice 189 F5
San Felice del Benaco 182 E1
San Felipe 295 A3
San Fernando 295 C3, 297 D5
San Floriano del Collio 183 C6
San Francisco de Mostazal 297 B5
San Gimignano 189 E1
San Giovanni al Natisone 183 C4
San Giovanni Ilarione 183 F1
San Giustino 192 B4
San Gregório da Sàssola 193 C6
San Isidro 201 C4
San Javier 295 D2, 297 G3
San Joaquin 267 E4
San Jose, *Uruguay* 294 F2
San Jose, *USA* 263 B3
San Jose de Maipo 295 B3
San Juan, *Argentina* 294 F2
San Juan, *Spain* 201 D2
San Juan del Rio 269 F5
San Julian 201 D2
San Lorenzo Isontino 183 D5
San Lucas 263 G5
San Luis 294 F2
San Luis Obispo 265 D3
San Luis Potosi 269 F5
San Mamede de Ribatua 211 D1
San Marino 187 B5
San Martin 295 B4
San Martino Buonalbergo 182 G6
San Martino della Battaglia 179 D2
San Martino di Castrozza 179 B4
San Martí Sarroca 205 E3
San Mateo 197 B5
San Michele all'Adige 185 G4
San Miguel, *Canary Islands* 207 G5
San Miguel, *Jerez* 201 C4
San Miguel, *USA* 265 B3
San Pedro & Santa Helena 297 E4
San Pedro de Premiá 205 E6
San Pietro in Cariano 182 F4
San Pietro Vara 259 B1
San Quírico d'Órcia 190 F3
San Rafael, *Argentina* 295 C4
San Rafael, *Spain* 201 C4
San Remo 173 G3
San Salvatore Monferrato 175 B6
San Severo 195 B4
San Vicente de Taguatagua 295 C3, 297 D5
San Vincente 202 B5
San Vincente de la Sonsierra 203 F2
San Vito al Tagliamento 181 C4
San Vito al Torre 183 D4
San Vito di Negrar 182 F5
San Vittorino 193 C5
San Ysidro 263 D4
Sance 69 E5
Sancerre 115 B5, 119 F3
Sanchez Romate 201 G2
Sandalford, *Margaret River* 287 D2
Sandalford, *Swan Valley* 286 C1
Sandanski 235 D2
Sandberg 147 B3
Sand Castle 275 C4
Sandeman 201 G2
Sandgrub 159 E3
Sandhurst 298 F5
Sandorini 239 E5
Sandy 273 B6
Sandy Hollow 279 F3
Sanford 265 F4
Sangalhos 214 E5
Sanger 267 D5
Sangiovese dei Colli Pesaresi 187 B6
Sangiovese di Romagna 179 F3, 187 B5
Sankt Alban 163 B5
Sankt Rochuskapelle 163 B3
Sanlúcar de Barrameda 200 A4
Santa Adela 297 B6, D4
Sant'Ambrogio di Valpolicella 182 F4
Santa Ana 295 A4
Santa Ana de Queri 297 G4
Sant'Anna di Isola 195 E5
Santa Barbara, Qta de 210 G1
Santa Brigida 207 G5
Santa Carolina 297 A6
Santa Catarina 294 F2
Santa Caterina 183 B5
Santa Clara 263 B2
Santa Clara Valley 263 C3
Santa-Coloma de Queralt 205 E2
Santa Comba Dão 215 G4
Santa Cruz, *Chile* 295 C2, 297 D4
Santa Cruz, *Spain* 201 E1
Santa Cruz, *Madeira* 217 C5
Santa Cruz, *USA* 263 D2
Santa Cruz de la Palma 207 G4
Santa Cruz de Tenerife 207 G5
Santa Cruz Mountain 263 C3
Santa Cruz Mountains 263 C2
Santa Cruz Winery 269 D3
Santa Ema 297 B5
Santa Emilia 201 C2
Santa Emiliana 297 A4
Santa Fe, *Argentina* 294 F2
Santa Fe, *USA* 269 D4
Santa Fe Vyds 269 D4
Santa Honorata 201 D2
Santa Ines 297 B5
Santa Isabel 201 B3
Santa Lucia Highlands 263 F4
Santa Maddalena 185 A3
Santa-Margarida de Montbui 205 D3
Santa Margarita 265 C3
Santa Maria 265 E4
Santa-Maria de Miralles 205 E3
Santa Maria di Cavamonte 193 D5
Santa Maria d. Versa 177 F5
Santa Maria Valley 265 E4
Santa Marta de Penaguião 210 E1
Santa Monica 297 C5
Santana 217 A3
Santa-Oliva 205 F3
Santa Palomba 193 E4
Santa-Perpètua 205 E2
Santa Prócula 193 E4
Santarém 208 D4
Santa Rita 297 B6
Santa Rosa, *Argentina* 295 B5
Santa Rosa, *USA* 255 E6
Santa Teresa 201 C2
Santa Teresa de Jesus 201 D2
Santa Valentina 297 D5
Santa Ynez 265 F5
Santa Ynez Valley 265 F5
Santedame 189 D5
Santenay 55 D5, 57 G3, 59 F3
Santenots Blancs, les 61 F3
Santenots Dessous, les 61 F3
Santenots du Milieu, les 61 F3
Santiago 295 B3, 297 A6
Santiago del Estero 294 F2
Santillana 200 A4
Santo Antonio 217 C3
Santo da Serra 217 C4
Santo Domingo 201 B2
Santo Stefano 189 C4
Santo Tirso 215 C5
Santo Tomas 269 D2
São Domingos de Rana 209 F4
São Gonçalo, *Alto Douro* 210 F1
São Gonçalo, *Madeira* 217 D4
São João da Pesqueira 211 F2
São Jorge 217 A3
São Lourenço do Bairro 214 F5
São Luis, Qta 210 F4
São Martinho 217 D3
São Martinho, Qta de 211 E2
São Paulo 294 F2
São Roque 217 C3
São Roque do Faial 217 B4
São Vicente 217 A1
Sapa de B., Qta da 210 F5
Sarah's Vineyard 263 D4
Sarajevo 233 D4
Sárazsadany 229 E5
Sarcignan 99 C4
Sardine 99 B2
Sarica-Niculitel 237 D5
Sárospatak 226 D5, 229 D5
Sarottes, les 67 F4
Sarral 205 E2
Sarrians 131 E4
Sarry, Dom. de 119 G2
Sartène 140 F4
Sarzedinho 210 F6
Sasalja 229 E2
Sassari 195 C1
Sassella 177 B2
Sassicaia 191 B4
Sátão 215 E5
Satiety 267 A2
Satigny 220 C3
Sátoraljaújhely 226 D5, 229 C6
Satov 230 G3
Sattui, V 259 D3
Satus 272 G3
Satz 223 C4
Sätzen 225 G2
Saucelito Canyon 265 D4
Saucours, les 63 D1
Saules, aux 65 G4
Saulieu 55 C4
Saumagen 161 A4
Saumur 114 B6
Saunieres, les 59 E2
Saussignac 109 B5
Saussilles, le Bas des 62 E2
Saussilles, les 62 E2
Saute aux Loups 117 G4
Sauternes 80 G4, 96 G6, 101 G3
Sauve, la 96 D6
Sauvetat-du-Dropt, la 109 C5
Sauveterre 131 G1
Sauveterre-de-Guyenne 80 F5, 97 E1
Sauvignon de St-Bris 53 C3, 139 F3
Sauzet 113 C4
Savennières 114 B4, 116 B3
Savièse 221 C3
Savignac-de-Duras 109 C4
Savigny 55 C5
Savigny-en-Véron 117 F2
Savigny-lès-Beaune 57 E4, 63 C1
Savogna d'Isonzo 183 D5
Savona 173 F4
Savuto 195 D5
Sawyer 272 F2
Sawyers Gully 278 C5
Saxon 221 D2
Scalabrone 191 C4
Scandicci 189 B3
Scappoose 273 A5
Scarborough 278 C4
Sceaux, les 62 F4
Schaffhausen 219 D4
Schalkstein 165 C4
Scharffenberger 256 C2
Scharzberg 147 C4
Scharzhofberg 147 C4
Schatzberg 224 E2
Schatzgarten 153 C3
Scheidterberg 147 D2
Schenectady 275 B5
Schenkenböhl 161 B2, C5
Schiesslay 150 F5
Schild 166 B6
Schiltigheim 120 A6
Schio 179 C3
Schivatschevo 235 C4
Schkeuditz 167 C4
Schlangengraben 147 C3
Schliengen 165 F1
Schloss 162 F5
Schlossberg, *Alsace* 123 B3
Schlossberg, *Baden-Württemberg* 165 B3
Schlossberg, *Bernkastel* 152 D6, 153 B4
Schlossberg, *Franken* 166 B6
Schlossberg, *Rheingau* 158 F3, 159 G2
Schlossberg, *Rheinhessen* 162 F5
Schlossberg, *Pfalz* 161 D4
Schlossberg, *Saar* 147 B3
Schlossböckelheim 143 C3, 154 G4, 155 C5
Schlossgarten 158 G2
Schlossheide 158 E2
Schloss Hohenreschen 162 E3
Schloss Johannisberg 158 F2
Schlosskapelle 155 B6, C1
Schlosskellerei Rametz 185 A5
Schloss Ludwigshöhe (Edenkoben) 161 C2
Schloss Neuenberg 143 A5
Schloss Reichartshausen 158 G5
Schloss Rodeck 165 D2
Schloss Saarfelser Schlossberg 147 G3
Schloss Saarsteiner 147 G3
Schloss Schwabsburg 162 E3
Schloss Staufenberg 165 D2
Schloss Vollrads 158 F3
Schlossweinberg 167 C6
Schnait 165 D4
Schneider 223 B4
Schnepfenflug an der Weinstrasse 161 B2, D5
Schoden 147 D3
Schoenenbourg 123 C4
Scholls 273 B5
Schönberg 222 B2
Schöneberg 155 B5
Schönhell 158 E5
Schomsheim 163 B4
Schozachtal 165 C4
Schrammel 223 C5
Schramsberg 259 C2
Schreck 225 F3
Schreiberberg 225 F1
Schriesheim 165 B4
Schubertslay 151 C1
Schug 257 F4
Schütt 225 G2
Schutter-Lindenberg 165 E2
Schützen 222 D3
Schutzenhaus 158 F6
Schützenhütte 162 F5
Schwabsburg 162 E3
Schwaigern 165 C4
Schwanfeld 166 A5
Schwarzenberg 273 D4
Schwarzenstein 158 F3
Schwarzerde 161 A2
Schwarzlay 153 D2
Schwechat 222 C3
Schwegenheim 161 C3
Schweich 143 B2
Schweigen 161 D1
Schweigenberg 167 C3
Schwenningen 143 F4, 165 E3
Schwyz 219 E4
Sciacca 195 F2
Sciez 137 A3
Scio 273 D5
Scott Creek 284 C3
Scotts Bottom 284 C3
Scranton 275 C4
Seacliff 284 B2
Seaford 284 D1
Seaside 271 C2
Seattle 271 A3
Seaview 284 D2
Sebastiani, *Lodi* 267 F3
Sebastiani, *Sonoma* 254 G5
Sebastopol 255 E5
Sebes-Apold 237 C3
Seca, La 206 F2
Séchet 75 E3
Secovce 230 G6
Secret House 271 E2
Secuita, La 205 F2
Seebach 161 C4
Seeweingarten 223 C5
Segarcea 237 E3
Segonzac 111 G2
Segonzac, Dist. de 110 F6
Segu-Olle 297 G3
Séguret 129 D4, 131 B5
Seia 215 F5
Seignelay 73 D3
Seigneurie de Peyrat 133 A6, 135 C2
Seillon-Source-d'Argens 136 B3
Seixal 217 A1
Seixo, Qta do 210 F5
Selah 271 B4
Sélestat 120 C4
Sellicks Beach 284 F1
Sellicks Hill 284 F1
Selma 267 E5
Selnica 231 A4
Selva del Camp, La 205 F1
Selvapiana 189 A5
Semblançay 115 B1
Sembrancher 221 D2
Semons 126 C3
Senan 205 E1
Sénas 129 F5
Senec 230 G4
Senhora da Ribeira, Qta da 211 F5
Señor, El 200 B4
Senouillac 113 D6
Senozan 69 D6
Sentier du Clou, Sur le 60 D2
Sentiers, les 66 F3
Sentilj 231 A4
Seppelt 282 B4
Seppelt Great Western 280 E1
Seppeltsfield 282 B4
Seppelt Wines 285 D5
Septèmes-les-Vallons 129 G5
Septemvri 235 D2
Sequoia Grove 259 E4
Sered 230 G4
Serédi 229 E4
Serendipity 273 D4
Serenella 279 F3
Serifos 239 D4
Sérignan 133 B6, 135 D1
Serpa 213 G5
Serpens, les 61 F5
Serpentières, aux 63 D2
Serraboella 176 E4
Serrada 206 F2
Serra de Agua 217 C2
Serrai 239 A3
Serra, La 176 F2
Serralunga d'Alba 175 E3, 176 G3
Serra, Qta da 210 F6
Serres-et-Montguyard 109 C5
Serrières-de-Briord 137 C1
Serrières-en-Chautagne 137 B2
Serrig 147 G3
Serta 208 C4
Serventy 287 F2
Serviès 133 C2
Sète 135 C3, 139 D1
Settlement, The 284 C2
Setúbal 208 E3
Seurey, les 62 F4
Sevastopol' 240 C2
Sevenhill 283 E5
Sevilen 243 C2
Seville 281 C5
Seville Estate 281 C5
Sevlievo 235 C3
Sewell 295 B3
Seyches 113 C2
Seymour 277 C3, 280 E4
Seyne, la 136 C3
Seyssel 137 B2
Shabla 235 B6
Shadow Brook 259 A6
Shafer, *California* 259 E5
Shafer, *Oregon* 273 B4
Shafter 267 G5
Shandon 265 B4
Shantell 281 A4
Sharpham 298 G3
Shawsgate 298 E6
Shedd 273 E4
Shell Beach 265 D3
Shellharbour 277 B6
Shelton 271 A2
Shepparton 277 C3, 280 D4
Sheridan 273 C4
Sheridan Wines 279 E5
Sherwood 273 B5
Shimobe 248 E4
Shinonoi 248 B3
Shinshushin-Machi 248 B3
Shiojiri 248 C3
Shouguang 246 D4
Shumen 235 B5
Sibenik 233 D2
Sicelle 189 D3
Sidi-bel-Abbes 245 B3
Sidi Slimane 245 B2
Siebeldingen 161 C1
Siebengebirge 143 A2
Siegelsberg 159 G2
Siegendorf i. Bgl. 222 D3, 223 C4
Siegersdorf (Hardys) 282 B4
Siena 187 B3, 189 G4
Sierra de Salamanca, La 197 B2
Sierra de San Cristobal 201 F3
Sierre 219 F3, 221 C4
Sifnos 239 E4
Sigean 133 D4, 134 E6
Signes 136 B3
Signorello 259 F5
Signy-Avenex 220 B4
Sigolsheim 120 D4, 123 C2
Sigoulès 109 B5
Siklós 226 G3
Silikou 244 G2
Silistra 235 A5
Sillery 79 B5
Silval, Qta do 210 D5
Silvan 281 D5
Silverado 259 E5
Silverado Hill 259 F6
Silver Falls 273 D5
Silver Falls City 273 D5
Silver Lake 271 A3
Silver Mountain 263 C3
Silver Oak 259 E4
Silverton 271 D3, 273 C5
Sima 229 D3
Sîmburesti 237 D3
Simferopol' 240 C2
Simi 255 C5
Simleul-Silvaniei 237 B3
Simondium 293 E4
Simonsig 293 E2
Simonstown 290 G1
Simonsvlei 293 D3
Sines 208 E3
Singen 165 F3
Singleyrac 109 C5
Sino-French Joint Venture Winery 246 B3
Sinop 243 B4
Sintra 208 D3, 209 E4
Sion 219 G2, 221 C3
Sionnières, les 66 F4
Siracusa 195 G4
Siscani 241 F5
Siria 237 C2
Sirmione 182 F2
Siros 239 D4
Siskiyou 271 G2
Sisquoc 265 E4
Sitges 205 F4
Sitia 239 F5
Sitzendorf 222 B2
Sivas 243 C5
Sizies, les 62 F3
Sizzano 173 D4
Skalica 230 G3
Skalice/Záhorská 230 G3
Skikda 245 A5
Skillogalee 283 E5
Skipton 280 F2
Skíros 239 C4
Skopje 233 F5
Sky 259 F4
Slaviantzi 235 C5
Slavonski Brod 233 C4
Sliboticko-Horgoska Pecara 233 B5
Sliven 235 C4
Slovenska Bistrica 231 C3
Slovenska Konjice 231 C3
Slovenské 230 G6
Smarje pri Jelsah 231 D3
Smederevo 233 D5
Smith & Hook 263 F4
Smith-Madrone 259 C2
Smiths Gully 281 A3
Smithton 287 F5
Smolenice 230 G4
Smolyan 235 D3
Smythesdale 280 F2
Snelling 267 C3
Snoqualmie 271 A3
Soave 179 C3, 183 F2, G2
Soave Classico 179 D3, 183 G2
Sobels 278 C5
Sobernheim 155 C4
Sochi 240 C4
Sofiya 235 C2
Soissons 76 A3
Soitue 295 C5
Soke 243 C2
Sokhumi 240 C4
Sokol Blosser 273 C4
Soledad 263 F5

Solis 263 D4
Solitude, Dom. de la 99 G5
Solitude, La 131 F2
Solivella 205 E2
Sologny 69 E3
Solon, Clos 66 F4
Solopaca 195 B3
Solothurn 219 E3
Sol, Qta do 210 G2
Soltvadkert 226 F3
Solutré-Pouilly 55 F5, 69 F4
Solvang 265 F5
Sombernon 55 C5
Sombor 233 C4
Somerset West 290 F2
Somló 226 F2
Somloire 114 C5
Sommerach 166 B5
Sommerberg 123 B1
Sommerhausen 166 C4
Sommières 129 E2
Somontano 197 B5
Sondrio 173 B6, 177 B3
Songe, en 67 E2
Sonnay 117 F5
Sonnenberg, *Austria* 223 C4
Sonnenberg, *Nahe* 154 F6
Sonnenberg, *Rheingau* 159 F4
Sonnenberg, *Ruwer* 149 G6
Sonnenberg, *Saar* 147 A5, C3
Sonnenborn 155 B6
Sonnenbühl 165 D4
Sonnenglanz 123 C3
Sonnenlay 152 G5, G6
Sonnenufer 165 F4
Sonnenuhr 151 F1, D6
Sonoita 269 D3
Sonoita Vyds 269 D3
Sonoma 254 G5, 257 E4
Sonoma Creek 257 F4
Sonoma-Cutrer 255 D5
Sonoma Mountain 254 F4
Sonoma Valley 254 E4, 257 E4, F4
Sooss 224 F1
Sopraceneri 219 G4
Sopron 226 E1
Soquel 263 D3
Sorbé, Clos 66 F4
Sorbés, les 66 F4
Sordes, les 66 F2
Sorgentière, la 67 F4
Sorgues 129 E4
Soriano 294 F2
Sori Tildin 176 E3
Sorni 184 G6, 185 F6
Sorocai 241 E5
Sosneado, El 295 C4
Sotillo de la Ribera 206 E4
Sottoceneri 219 G4
Soublecause 113 F2
Soultz-Haut-Rhin 120 F3
Soultzmatt 120 F3, 122 B3
Soumard 119 F5
Soumard, le Petit 119 F4
Soumensac 109 C5
Soussans 95 A1
Sousse 245 B6
Soutelo do Douro 211 E1
Southbrook Farms 275 B3
Southern Vales 276 C6
Southern Vales Co-op 284 E2
South Muswellbrook 279 F5
Spaargebirge 167 C6
Spabrücken 155 B4
Spannberg 222 B3
Sparkling Vale 278 C5
Sparti 239 E3
Sp.-Duplek 231 B4
Spello 192 D6
Speyerdorf Lachen 161 B2
Spezia, La 173 F5
Spiàggia di Rio Torto 193 F3
Spiegel 122 B1
Spiegelberg 162 E4, 163 B5
Spielberg 161 B4
Spielfeld 222 G2
Spier 293 G1
Spiess 161 F4
Spiessheim 163 C4
Spilimbergo 181 B4
Spitz 222 B1
Split 233 D2
Spodnje Hoce 231 B4
Spoleto 192 E6
Sporen 123 C3
Spottswoode 259 D3
Sprendlingen 163 B4
Spriana 177 A3
Spring Creek 289 F5
Springfield, *Australia* 285 B6
Springfield, *Mass.* 275 B5
Springfield, *Oregon* 271 E2
Springhill 273 D4
Springlands 289 G4
Spring Mountain 259 D2, D3
Springton 282 E5
Squinzano 195 C6
Sredisce 231 C6
Srednje Slov. Gorice 231 B5
Sremski Karlovci/Fruska Gora 233 C4
Stag's Leap 259 B6, E5
Stag's Leap Wine Cellars 259 E5
Staiger, P & M 263 C2
Stainz 222 F1
Stalden 221 C6
Stambolovo 235 D4
Stanhope, *New South Wales* 278 A5
Stanhope, *Victoria* 280 D4
Stanton & Killeen 280 C5
Staple 298 F6
Staplecombe 298 F3
Stara Zagora 235 C4
Starkenburg, *Hessische Bergstrasse* 143 C4
Starkenburg, *Bernkastel* 153 D4
Starkenburg, *Baden-Württemberg* 165 B3
Stary Plzenec 230 F1
Staton Hills 272 F2
Staŭceni 241 F5
Staudernheim 155 C4
Staufen 165 F1
Staufenberg 165 C4
Stawell 277 D2, 280 E1
Stayton 271 D3, 273 D5
Steele 256 D6
Steels Creek 281 A4
Stefanesti 237 D4
Stefanslay 151 B3
Steffensberg 153 B3
Steigerdell 155 F1
Steigerwald 166 C5
Steil 157 D2
Stein 225 F3
Steinacker 161 A4, A5
Stein am Rain 224 G5
Steinbach 165 D2
Steinberg, *Nahe* 154 G4, 155 C2
Steinberg, *Pfalz* 161 B4, C4
Steinberg (Ortsteil) 159 E1
Steinberger 147 B3
Steinert 122 C3
Steinertal 225 G2
Steingrubler 122 C6
Steinhardt 155 C4
Steinmächer 159 F4
Steinmorgen 159 F3
Steinmühle 223 B3
Steinriegl 224 G5
Steinwandl 224 G5
Steinwingert 154 G5
Steinzeiler 223 C3
Stellenbosch 290 F2, 293 F2
Stellenbosch Farmers' 293 F2
Stellenzicht 293 G2
Steltzner 259 B6
Stephanus-Rosengärtchen 153 G2
Sterling 259 A5
Stetten 165 D4
Steuk 275 C1
Stewart Vyds 272 F3
Steyer 154 F5
Stift 161 E5
Stiftsberg 165 C4
Stirling 284 B4
Stirn 147 E2
Stockerau 222 B2
Stockton 267 B2
Stockwell 282 A5
Stonegate 259 C2
Stoneleigh 289 F4
Stonestreet, J 255 C5
Stonington 275 C6
Stony Hill 259 C2
Stony Ridge 263 A3
Storrs 263 D2
Storybook Mountain 259 B1
Stradella 177 E5
Straden 222 F2
Straldzha 235 C5
Strand 290 G2
Strandja 235 D4
Strasbourg 120 A5
Strass 222 B2
Stratford, *Kings* 267 E4
Stratford, *Napa* 259 C3
Strathmerton 280 C4
Straznice 230 G3
Streda nad Bodrogom 230 G6
Strem 222 F3
Stromberg 165 C4
Stúrovo 230 G4
Stuttgart 143 E5, 165 D4
Subirats 205 E4
Sublimity 273 D5
Subotica 233 B5
Suceava 237 B4
Suchot, en 67 E3
Suchots, les 65 F4
Südburgenland 222 F4
Südliche Weinstrasse 143 D3
Süd-Oststeiermark 222 F4
Südsteiermark 222 F4
Sugarloaf Ridge 254 E4
Suizhong 246 B5
Sukhindol 235 B3
Sullivan 259 D4
Sulmona 187 F5, 195 A2
Sulzfeld 166 C5
Sumadijsko-Velikomoravski 233 D5
Summerfield 280 E2
Summerhome Park 255 D4
Summertown 284 B4
Summit Lake 259 B3
Sunbury 280 F3
Sungurlare 235 C5
Sunnyside 271 B5, 272 F3
Sunshine 278 B5
Suntory 248 D4
Superin 225 G1
Surf 265 F3
Sury-en-Vaux 119 E2
Susaka 248 B4
Süssenberg, *Austria* 225 G2
Sussenberg, *Germany* 152 F6
Suter 295 C4
Sutherland 278 B4
Sutherlin 271 F2
Sutter Home 259 D3
Suver 273 D4
Suwa 248 C3
Suzon 99 A4
Svetozarevo 233 D5
Svilengrad 235 D4
Svishtov 235 B3
Swan 255 D5
Swan Hill 277 C2
Swansea 287 G6
Swanson 259 E4
Swartland 290 E1
Swedish Hill 275 B4
Sweet Home 271 E3, 273 E5
Swellendam 290 F4, G3
Sybillenstein 163 C4
Sycamore Creek 263 C4
Sydney 277 B6
Sylvie 67 F2
Sympérieux 126 D1
Syracuse 275 B4
Szár-Hegy 229 D4
Szarvas 226 F4, 229 G3
Szeged 226 G4
Szegfü 229 D5
Szegi 229 F3
Szegilong 229 F4
Székesfehérvar 226 F3
Szekszárd 226 G3
Szentvér 229 E4
Szerelmi 229 G4
Szerencs 229 G1
Szolnok 226 F4
Szölö-Hegy 229 E1
Szombathely 226 F1

Tabilk 280 E4
Tábr 230 F2
Tábua, *Dão* 215 G5
Tabua, *Madeira* 217 C1
Taburno 195 B3
Tache, la 65 F4
Tacna 294 F1
Tacoma 271 A3
Taconera, La 201 E3
Taft Street 255 D4
Tai'an 246 D3
Taillan-Médoc, le 96 C3
Taille Pieds 61 F4
Tain-l'Hermitage 125 D4, 127 C4
Taissy 79 A4
Tajiguas 265 G5
Takato 248 D3
Talagante 297 B5
Talamona 177 B1
Talca 295 C2, 297 F4
Talca, Cooperativa de 297 F4
Talcahuano 295 D1
Talence 80 F3, 96 D4, 99 A3
Talent 271 G3
Talijancich Wines 286 C1
Tallawanta 278 C4
Talley Vyds 265 D4
Tállya 226 E5, 229 E2
Talmettes, les 63 D2
Taltami 280 E1
Tamalee 278 C5
Tamarit 205 F2
Tambo, El 297 D5
Tamburlaine 278 C4
Tamisot 67 F2
Tampico, *Mexico* 269 F6
Tampico, *USA* 272 E1
Tanami 284 E3
Tanger 245 B2
Tangshan 246 B4
Tanunda 282 B4
Tapogliano 183 D4
Tarabulus (Tripoli) 243 E5
Taraclia 241 G5
Taradeau 136 B4
Taranto 195 C5
Tarapaca 294 F1
Tarapaca ex-Zavala 297 A6
Tarare 71 F1
Tarascon 129 E4
Tarbes 113 G2
Tarcal 229 G3
Tarcento 181 A5
Tarchalice 282 B4
Tarcoola 280 F3
Tarczal, De 184 E4
Taree 277 B6
Targon 96 E6
Tarnave 237 C3
Tarragona 197 B5, 205 F1, G2
Tarrawarra/Tunnel Hill 281 B5
Tarres 205 E1
Tártano 177 B2
Tartaras 126 B3
Tart, Clos de 66 F4
Tartegnin 220 B4
Tasko 243 C4
Tatabánya 226 E3
Tatura 280 D4
Taubenberg 159 E4
Taubenhaus 153 E3
Tauberfranken 143 C5
Taughrite 245 B4
Taumarunui 288 C4
Taupe, la 66 E1
Taupine, la 61 E3
Taupo 288 C5
Tauranga 288 B5
Taurasi 195 B3
Tauriac 108 F5
Tauxières-Mutry 79 D5
Tavannes, Clos de 59 G4
Tavannes, les 62 F1
Tavel 129 E4, 130 G6
Tavernes 136 A3
Tavers 115 A3
Tavira 208 F5
Taylors 283 F6
T'bilisi 240 D5
Tecate 269 D2
Tedo, Qta do 210 F3
Tèglio 177 B4
Teià 205 E6
Teil, le 125 G3
Teixeira, Qta da 210 E6
Tekirdag 243 B2
Te Kuiti 288 C4
Tel Aviv-Yafo 243 F4
Telegrafo, El 201 C4
Telhada, Qta da 211 G6
Tellières, les 67 F3
Temecula 269 D2
Temora 277 B4
Tempier, Dom. 136 C2
Templeton 265 B3
Tenareze 113 E3
Tenerife 207 G5
Tenna 184 D6
Teno 297 E5
Tenuta 'Ricavo' (Hotel) 189 E3
Tequisquiapan 269 F5
Teramo 187 E5
Terang 280 G1
Terciona 189 C3
Tercios, Los 201 E2
Teremia Mare 237 C1
Terézia 229 G3
Terlago 184 C4
Terlano (Terlan) 185 B5, 185 B3
Termenès 133 D3
Termeno (Tramin) 185 E5
Términi Imerese 195 F2
Ternay 114 C6
Terni 187 D4, 192 E6
Teroldego Rotaliano 179 B2, 184 G6, 185 B3
Terra Alta 197 B5
Terra Bella 267 F6
Terrace Vale 278 B4
Terracina 187 G4, 195 B2
Terra Feita, Qta da 210 E5
Terras de Bouro 215 B5
Terre Ferme, La 131 F3
Terres 61 F1
Terres Blanches, les 64 F4
Terres, les Grandes 59 G5
Terroirs Landais 139 F4
Tesson, le 61 F1
Tête de Clos 59 F5
Teteven 235 C2
Têtière, la 60 G2
Tetouan 245 B2
Teufelstor 166 B5
Teuillac 108 E4
Teurons, le Bas des 62 F4
Teurons, les 62 F4
Te Whare Ra 289 G3
Texas High Plains 269 D5
Texas Hill Country 269 E5
Thalgara Estate 278 C4
Thames 288 B5
Thames Valley 298 F5
Thann 120 G3
Thasos 239 B4
Thauvenay 119 F3
Theilheim 166 B5
Thelema 293 F3
Thénac 109 C5
Theodorshalle 155 E2
Thermenregion 222 F4
Thesée 115 B2
Thessaloniki 239 B3
Thézac-Perricard 139 D4
Thiemère, la 118 B4
Thira (Santorini) 239 E5
Thivai 239 D3
Thomas 286 E1
Thomas Coyne 263 A3
Thomas Fernhill 284 D2
Thomas Fogarty 263 B2
Thomas Hardy 284 D2
Thomas Kruse 263 D4
Thomas Sellards 255 E5
Thonon-les-Bains 137 A3
Thorey, aux 65 F2
Thorins, les 72 B5
Thorncroft 298 F5
Thouarcé 114 B5, 116 E5
Thouars 114 C5
Three Choirs 298 F4
Three Rocks 267 E4
Thuir 133 F3
Thun 219 F3
Thüngersheim 166 B4
Thurgau 219 D5
Thüringen 143 A5
Thurston Wolfe 271 B4
Thurtal 219 D5
Tiana 205 E5
Tianjin 246 C4
Ticino 219 F4
Tiefenbrunner 185 E5
Tierra de Barros 197 C2
Tiffon 110 G5
Tigard 273 B5
Tighina 241 F5
Tijsseling 256 C3
Tijuana 269 D2
Tilcoco, Qta de 297 C5
Tillamook 271 C2
Tillets, les 60 F6
Tillières 115 F6
Tim Adams 283 D5
Timber 273 A4
Timisoara 237 C1
Timocki 233 D6
Timpert 149 E4
Tinglewood 286 G3
Tinguiririca 295 C3
Tinos 239 D4
Tinqueux 79 A3
Tions, les Champs 67 F4
Tipton 267 F5
Tirano 177 A5
Tirant, Champ 60 D1
Tiraspol' 240 B1, 241 F6
Tire 243 C2
Tirgu-Mures 237 C3
Tirnaveni 237 C3
Tisdall's 280 D3
Titograd 233 E4
Titov Veles 233 F5
Tivissa 204 G6
Tizon 201 C2
Tlemcen 245 B3
Todi 192 E5
Togura 248 B3
Toisières, les 61 E3
Tokaj 226 E5, 229 G4
Tokajhegyalja 226 E5
Tokájská 230 G6
Tokat 243 B5
Tokoroa 288 C5
Tolcsva 229 D4
Toledo, *Ohio* 275 C1
Toledo, *Oregon* 271 D2
Tolima 294 E1
Tolley Pedare 282 B4
Tolmezzo 179 B5
Tolochenaz 220 A5
Tomar 208 C4
Tome 295 D1
Tondela 215 F4
Tonnerre 73 D6
Toodyay 286 C2
Tophill 273 A4
Topolcany 230 G4
Topolos at Russian River Vyds 255 E5
Topons, les 64 F5
Toppe Marteneau, la 63 E3
Toppenish 271 B5, 272 F3
Törbole 184 E3
Tordesillas 206 F2
Torgiano 187 C4, 192 D5
Torino 173 D3, 175 A1
Toro 197 B3
Toro, El 201 E1
Toronto 275 B3
Torquay 280 G3
Torrão 215 D5
Torrazza Coste 177 F3
Torre Alta, La 200 D6
Torre de Fontaubella, La 204 F6
Torre de l'Espanyol, La 204 F5
Torredembarra 205 F2
Torre di Santa Maria 177 A3
Torre Gaia 193 C4
Torrelles de Foix 205 E3
Torremontalbo 202 B6, 203 G3
Torrenieri 190 F2
Torre Nova 193 C4
Torreón 269 F5
Torreon de Paredes 297 D5
Torreperogil 197 D3
Torre, Qta da 210 G1
Torre Rosazzo 183 B4
Torres 208 D3
Torricella Verzate 177 F4
Torri del Benaco 182 E2
Torrita di Siena 190 E4
Torroja del Priorat 204 F6
Torrox 201 F3
Torvaianica 193 F3
Toulifaut 118 B2
Toulon 136 C3
Toulouse 113 E5
Toulouse-le-Château 137 F4
Tour-de-Peilz, la 221 B1
Tour du Bief, la 72 B5
Tournon-sur-Rhône 125 D4, 127 C3
Tournus 55 E6
Tours 115 B1
Tours-sur-Marne 79 D5
Tourves 136 B3
Toussaints, les 62 E5
Touwsriver 290 E3
Touzac 113 C4
Toyoseto 248 C4
Toyoshima 248 C3
Toyotomi 248 D4
Traben-Trarbach 153 D3
Trabzon 243 B6
Tracy 267 B2
Tracy-sur-Loire 119 F3
Traisen 154 F6, 155 C5
Traiskirchen 224 F2
Traismauer 222 B2
Tranquillity 267 E4
Transilvania 237 C3
Trapani 195 F1
Trappenberg 161 B2
Traralgon 277 D4
Tras le Puy 130 F6
Traulsen 259 B2
Travaillan 131 C3
Travarnelle Val di Pesa 189 D2
Travers de chez Edouard, les 60 D2
Travers de Marinot, les 60 D2
Traversins, les Champs 65 F5
Trebbiano d'Abruzzo 187 F6
Trebbiano di Romagna 179 F4, 187 A5
Trèbes 133 C2
Tre Cancelli 193 G5
Trefethen 259 F5
Tregnago 183 F1
Trélazé 114 B5
Trencin 230 G4
Trentadue 255 B5
Trentino 179 C2, 184 G6, 185 B3
Trento 179 B3, 184 C5
Trenton 275 D5
Trépail 79 C5
Treppchen, *Bernkastel* 152 B6
Treppchen, *Piesport* 151 C2
Très Girard 66 F4
Tresivio 177 B3
Treux, les 65 F5
Treviso 179 C4, 181 D2
Trézin, le 60 F4
Tribourg 65 F1
Trier 143 C1
Trieste 179 C6
Trikkala 239 C2
Trinidad 201 C3
Trinidad, La 201 D2
Trittenheim 151 G1
Trnava 230 G4
Troësmes 75 C2
Trois Follots 61 E6
Trois-Puits 79 A4
Troyan 235 C3
Troyes 76 E4
Truchard 257 E5
Truel 131 G1
Truffière, la 60 F4
Tsadha 244 G1
Tsiandali 240 C5
Turgovishte 235 B4
Tualatin 273 B4
Tuamarina 289 F5
Tua, Qta do 211 E2
Tübingen 143 E5, 165 D4
Tucker Cellars 272 F4
Tucson 269 D3
Tudal 259 C3
Tudela de Duero 206 E3
Tudelilla 203 C2
Tuilerie, la 101 F5
Tula, La 201 E1
Tulare 267 E5
Tulbagh 290 E2
Tulloch 278 C4
Tulocay 259 G6
Tunis 245 A6
Tunuyán 295 B4
Tupin 126 C3
Tupungato 295 B4
Turckheim 120 E3, 123 B1
Turlock 267 C3
Turner 273 D4
Turque, La 126 B3
Tursan 113 E1
Tutrakan 235 A4
Tuvilains, les 62 F3
Tuyaux, aux 65 G2
Tuzla 233 C4
Twin Brook 275 D4
Twin Hills 265 B3
Twin Valley Estate 282 D3
Tyee Wine Cellars 273 E4
Tyland 256 C3
Tyrrells 278 C4

Überland 223 C5
Uberlingen 143 G5, 165 F4
Uchizy 69 A6
Údine 179 B6, 181 B5
Ueda 248 C3
Uenohara 248 D5
Uettingen 166 B3
Uiterwyk 292 F6
Uitkyk 293 E2
Ukiah 256 B3
Ullastrell 205 E4
Umbertide 192 C5
Umpqua Valley 271 F2
Umriss 223 C4
Undurraga 297 B5
Ungeheuer 161 E5
Ungheni 241 F4
Ungsberg 153 E3
Ungstein 161 A2, B5
Union Gap 271 B4, 272 E2
Union Wine (Douglas Green Wines) 293 A5
Unkenbach 155 D5
Unley 284 A3
Unterberg 147 B2
Untere Lüss 223 C5
Unterer Vogelsang 223 C4
Unterer Wald 223 C4
Untere Weissen 223 C5
Unterloiben 225 G2
Untersee 219 D4
Untertürkheim 165 D4
Upper Hunter Valley 277 A6
Upper Hutt 288 D4
Upper Lake 256 B4
Upper Sturt 284 B4
Urágya Birsalmas 229 F2
Uraidla 284 B4
Urbán 229 F2
Urbellt 147 B3
Urfé 139 E4
Ürgüp 243 C4
Ürzig 152 B5
Usak 243 C2
Uspallata 295 A4
Usuda 248 C4
Utica 275 B4
Utiel-Requena 197 C4
Uvrier 221 C3
Uzès 129 E3, 139 C2
Uzunköprü 243 B1

Vác 226 E3
Vacalar 210 G2
Vacaria, Qta da 210 F1
Vache, la 61 E6
Vacqueyras 129 D4, 131 D4
Vaillons 75 E2
Vaison-la-Romaine 129 D5
Valais 219 G3, 221 C4
Valbuena de Duero 206 E3
Valcalepio 173 C5
Valcargado 201 B2
Val, Clos du 259 F5
Valdadige (Etschtaler) 179 B2, 184 G6
Val d'Agly 138 F4
Val d'Arbia 187 B3
Val de Cesse 138 D5
Val de Dagne 138 E4
Valdejalón 197 B4
Val de Malhadas, Qta de 211 G5
Val de Montferrand 139 C1
Valdeorras 197 A2
Valdepeñas 197 C4
Valdespino, A R 201 G1
Valdevimbre-Los Oteros 197 A2
Valdivieso (Mitjans) 297 E4
Valdobbiádene 181 C1
Val d'Orbieu 138 E4
Valea Lui Mihai 237 B2
Valea Nucarilor 237 D6
Vale de Cambra 215 D5
Vale de Figueira 211 G3
Vale de Figueira, Qta do 210 F5
Valença 215 A4
Valenca do Douro 210 F5
Valençay 53 D2
Valence 125 E4
Valencia 197 C5
Valença do Minho 208 A4
Valette-du-Var, la 136 C3
Valeyrac 85 A3
Valgella 177 B4
Valladolid 206 E2
Vallclara 205 E1
Valldosera 205 E3
Val, le 136 B3
Valle d'Aosta 173 C2
Valle de Güimar 207 G5
Valle del Cauca 294 E1
Valle de Monterrey 197 B2
Vallée de l'Aude, La Haute 138 E4
Vallée de l'Orb, La Haute 138 D5
Vallée de Nouy, la 118 B3
Vallée du Paradis, La 138 E5
Vallée, la 119 E2
Valle Isarco 179 A3
Vallerots, les 64 F5
Vallet 114 C3, 115 F5
Valley Junction 273 C3
Valley of the Moon 254 F4
Valley View 271 G2
Vallmoll 205 F2
Vallromanas 205 E6
Valls 205 F2
Valmontone 193 D6
Valmur 75 D4

Valongo 215 C5
Valozières, les 63 F4
Valpaços 208 A5
Valpantena 179 C3, 182 F5
Valparaiso 295 A2
Valpolicella 179 C3, 183 F6
Valpolicella Classico 179 C3, 182 F4
Valréas 129 C4
Val St-Grégoire 123 B1
Valsetz 273 D3
Valtellina 173 B6, 179 B1
Valtice 230 G3
Vámosújfalu 229 E4
Vancouver 271 C3, 273 B5
Vandenburg Village 265 F4
Vár 229 E2
Varades 114 B4
Varages 136 A3
Vara Gruesa 297 G4
Varazdino 233 B3
Varen 221 C4
Varese 173 C4
Vargas 295 C4
Vargellas, Qta da 211 G4
Vár-Hegy 229 C6, E2, F3
Varna 235 B6
Varognes, les 127 C4
Varoilles, les 67 D1
Varosa 208 B5
Varot 68 B4
Vasa 244 G2
Vascos, Los 297 D4
Vasse Felix 287 D2
Vau Breton, le 117 G4
Vaucoupin 75 E5
Vaucrains, les 64 F5
Vaud 219 F1, 220 A5
Vaudemanges 79 D6
Vaudésir 75 C4
Vau de Vey 75 D1
Vaudois 221 C1
Vaufegé 118 B3
Vaufoynard 118 B1
Vaugiraut 75 E4
Vaugondy 118 A4
Vaulorent 75 C4
Vaumuriens-Bas, la 61 E5
Vaumuriens-Hauts, les 61 E5
Vaunage, La 139 C2
Vaupulent 75 C3
Vau, Qta do 211 E1
Vauvert 129 F3
Vaux Dessus, les 59 E2
Vaux, en 61 E5
Vaux-en-Beaujolais 71 D2
Vauxrenard 71 B3
Vavasour 289 G6
Vavatsinia 244 F3
Vayres 80 E4
Veaugues 119 G2
Végardo 229 D6
Vega Sicilia 206 E3
Veitsöchheim 166 B4
Velddrif 290 E1
Veldenz 152 G5
Velha, Qta 210 F1
Veliko Turnovo 235 C4
Vélines 109 B4
Velke 230 F3
Velké Zemoseky 230 E2
Velky Krtis 230 G5
Vellé, au 67 E2
Velle, Sous la 61 E2
Velle, Sous le 61 E2
Velle, Sur la 61 E3
Velletri 187 F3, 193 E5
Vendôme 115 A2
Vendrell, El 205 F3
Venézia 179 D4, 181 E2
Ventana 263 F5
Venthône 221 C4
Ventosa do Bairro 214 F5
Ventozelo, Qta de 210 F6
Vera Cruz 201 C2
Veracruz 269 G6
Verano, El 254 G4
Vérargues 129 F2, 135 A5
Vercelli 173 D4
Verchers-sur-Layon, les 114 C5
Vercots, les 63 E3
Vercots, les Petits 63 F3
Verdelais 96 F6
Verdicchio dei Castelli di Jesi 187 C5
Verdicchio di Matelica 187 C5
Verdigny 119 E2
Verdon, *Bergerac* 109 B6
Verdon, *Var* 139 G4
Verduno 176 F2
Vérenay 126 B5
Vergelesses, Basses 63 E2
Vergelesses, Ile des 63 E3
Vergelesses, les 63 E3
Vergelesses, les Basses 63 E3
Vergennes, les 63 F5
Verger, Clos de 61 F6, 62 E1
Vergers, les 60 F2
Vergisson 55 F5, 69 F3
Vérin 126 D2
Veritas, *Australia* 282 B4
Veritas, *USA* 273 C5
Verlieux 126 E2
Vermarain à l'Est, Bas de 60 D3
Vermarain à l'Ouest, Bas de 60 D3
Vermentino di Gallura 195 C2
Vermenton 73 G4
Vernaccia di Oristano 195 D1
Vernaccia di Serrapetrona 187 D5
Vernalis 267 C2
Vernois, le 137 G4
Vernonia 271 C2
Vernou-sur-Brenne 118 B4
Veroia 239 B3
Véroilles, les 66 E3
Verona, *Australia* 278 C4
Verona, *Italy* 179 D2, 182 G5
Vérottes, les 62 F3
Verpelét 226 E4
Verrazzano 189 D3
Verrillats, les 72 B5
Verroilles ou Richebourgs, les 65 F4
Verseuil, en 61 F4
Verthamon 99 A2
Vertheuil 87 E2
Vertou 114 C3, 115 F4
Vertus 79 G3
Veryan 298 G2
Verzé 55 E5, 69 D4
Verzenay 79 B5
Verzy 79 B5
Vésenaz 220 C4
Vesuvio 195 C3
Vesuvio, Qta do 211 G5
Veszprém 226 F2
Veteran Heights 259 C4
Vetioz 221 C3
Vetrun 235 C2
Vevey 219 F2, 221 B1
Veyras 221 C4
Vezzano 184 C4
Viana 203 B1
Viana do Alentejo 213 F4
Viana do Castelo 208 A4, 215 B4
Viansa 257 F4
Vibo Valéntia 195 E4
Vicairies 119 E3
Vicenza 179 C3
Vic-Fézensac 113 E3
Vich 220 B4
Vichon 259 E4
Vicomté d'Aumelas, La 138 D6
Victor Harbor 276 C6
Vide Bourse 60 G3
Vidigueira 208 E4, 213 F4
Vidin 235 A1
Vieille Montagne, La 259 A5
Vieira do Minho 215 B6
Vienne 125 A4
Vierzon 115 C4
Vieux Moulin, Le 130 G6
Vieux Télégraphe, Le 131 F3
Vieux-Thann 120 G3
Vigan, le 138 C6
Vignale 189 E4
Vignamaggio 189 D4
Vignavecchia 189 E5
Vigneau, Clos du 117 C1
Vigne au Saint, la 63 E3
Vigne Blanche 59 F5
Vigne dal Leon 183 B4
Vigne Derrière 59 F6, 60 F1
Vigne Rondes, aux 65 F3
Vignes aux Grands, les 67 E3
Vignes Belles 66 F6
Vignes Blanches, les 61 F3
Vignes Franches, les 62 F3
Vignes, les 119 E2
Vignes, les Grands, *Auxey-Duresses* 61 E1
Vignes, les Grands, *Prémeaux-Prissey* 64 F4
Vignes Rondes, les 61 E3
Vigness Moingeon 60 D3
Vigneux 65 F4
Vignobles Barde 109 D3
Vignobles de Pagnon 109 D3
Vignois 67 F3
Vignois, aux 67 F4
Vignonet 103 F3
Vignots, les 62 D1
Vignottes, les 64 F3
Vihiers 114 C5
Viladecans 205 F5
Vila do Conde 215 C4
Vila do Rei 209 E6
Vilaflor 207 G5
Vilanova 209 D5
Vila Nova de Cerveira 215 A4
Vila Nova de Famalicão 215 C5
Vila Nova de Gaia 208 B4
Vilanova de Prades 205 E1
Vilaplana del Camp 205 F1
Vila Real 208 A5
Vilarinho de Cotas 210 E5
Vilarinho dos Freires 210 F1
Vila-rodona 205 F2
Vila Seca 215 B4
Vila-seca de Soleina 205 G1
Vila Velha, Qta da 211 E1
Vilaverd 205 E2
Vila Verde 215 B5
Vila Viçosa 213 E6
Vilella Baixa, La 204 F6
Villa Alegre 297 G3
Villa Alhué 297 C5
Villa Arceno 189 G6
Villa Atuel 295 C5
Villabuena de Alava 202 B5, 203 F3
Villa Fornace 177 F5
Villafranca del Penedès 205 E3
Village, *Gevrey-Chambertin* 67 E2
Village, *Pommard* 62 F1
Village, *Vosne-Romanée* 65 G4
Village, au 61 F2
Village, le, *Aloxe-Corton* 63 F3
Village, le, *Chambolle-Musigny* 66 E2
Village, le, *Morey-St-Denis* 66 F4
Village, le, *Pernand-Vergelesses* 63 D4
Village, le, *Pommard* 61 F6
Village, le, *Puligny* 60 G3
Village, le, *Santenay* 59 F3
Village, le, *Savigny-lès-Beaune* 63 D1
Village, le, *St-Aubin* 60 D2
Village, le, *Volnay* 61 F4
Village, le, *Vougeot* 65 G6, 66 F2
Villa Grande 255 E3
Villa Helena 259 A6
Villamblard 109 A6
Villamediana de Iregua 203 B1
Villa Mount Eden 259 D4
Villanova i la Geltrú 205 F4
Villány 226 G3
Villány-Siklós 226 G2
Villa Prat 297 E4
Villar de Alava, El 202 A6
Villard 295 B2
Villard Fine Wines 297 A4
Villardeau 119 E5
Villarosa 189 F3
Villatte, la 117 D2
Villaudric 113 E5
Villaviciosa de Córdoba 197 D3
Villa Zapu 259 F4
Ville-Dommange 79 A2
Villefranche-de-Lonchat 109 A3
Villefranche-sur-Saône 55 G5, 71 E4
Villegouge 102 A5
Ville-la-Grand 137 B3
Villemajou, Dom. de 133 C4
Villenave-d'Ornon 80 F3, 96 D4, 99 D5
Villeneuve, *France* 108 E2
Villeneuve, *Switzerland* 221 B1
Villeneuve-de-Duras 109 C4
Villeneuve-de-Marsan 113 E1
Villeneuve-lès-Avignon 129 E4
Villeneuve-Renneville-Chevigny 79 G4
Villers-Allerand 79 B4
Villers-aux-Noeuds 79 B3
Villers-Marmery 79 C6
Villesse 183 E4
Villette 220 A6
Villette-lès-Arbois 137 E5
Villiera 293 D1
Villiers 119 E5
Villiersdorp 290 F2
Villié-Morgon 71 C3, 72 D4
Villingen 165 E3
Villy 75 A2
Vilobi del Penedès 205 E3
Vimbodi 205 E1
Vinag 231 B4
Vinas, Las 267 F3
Vina Vista 255 B4
Vin de l'Ouest 272 F3
Vinebre 204 F5
Vineburg 254 G5
Vineland Estates 275 B3
Vine Vale 282 B5
Vinhos Verdes 208 A4
Vini Affini, Societa Esportazione 189 D4
Vini del Piave 179 C4
Vinifera Wine Cellars 275 B3
Vinon 119 G3
Vino Nobile di Montepulciano 187 C3, 190 E6, F5
Vinos de Madrid 197 C3
Vinoteca 275 B3
Vins de Lavilledieu 53 F2, 113 D4
Vins de l'Orléanais 53 C2
Vins de Moselle 53 B5
Vins d'Entraygues et du Fel 53 F3, 139 G2
Vins des Coteaux du Giennois 53 C3
Vins d'Estaing 53 F3, 139 G2
Vins du Bugey 53 E5, 139 F3
Vins du Haut Poitou 53 D2, 139 F2
Vins du Thouarsais 53 D1, 139 F2
Vins du Tursan 53 G1
Vinsobres 129 C5
Vinyols i els Arcs 205 G1
Vinzel 220 B4
Vinzelles 55 F5, 69 G4
Violès 131 D4
Violettes, les 65 G5
Violet Town 280 D4
Vionnaz 221 C1
Vionne, la 67 F4
Vipava 233 B1
Viré 55 E5, 69 C5
Vireuils Dessous, les 61 E1
Vireuils Dessus, les 61 E1
Vireux, les 61 E1
Virgin Hills 280 E3
Virginie, Dom. 133 B5, 135 C1
Vina, La 126 B5
Virieu-le-Grand 137 C2
Virondot, en 59 F6
Vis 233 D2
Visalia 267 E5
Visan 129 D4
Viseu 208 B4, 215 F5
Visp 219 G3, 221 C6
Visperterminen 221 C6
Vistrenque, La 139 C2
Viterbo 187 D3
Viticulteurs Reunis 110 G6
Vitrolles 129 G5
Vitry-le-François 76 C6
Vittório Veneto 179 C4, 181 B2
Vitusberg 159 F5
Vivier, le 72 C5
Viviers 129 C4
Vlasotinci 233 E6
Vlottenburg 293 G1
Voegtlinshofen 120 E3, 122 C4
Vogelsang, *Austria* 223 C4
Vogelsang, *Nahe* 155 C2
Vogelsang, *Rheingau* 158 F3
Vogelsang, *Saar* 147 G4
Vogelsgärten 163 C5
Voghera 177 F3
Vogtei Rötteln 165 F1
Voillenot Dessous 60 G2
Voillenots Dessus, les 60 G2
Voipreux 79 G4
Voiteur 137 F5
Voitte 60 G4
Volano 184 E5
Volkach 166 B5
Volnay 55 D5, 61 E4
Volos 239 C3
Volpara 177 F5
Volta 267 D3
Volxheim 163 C3
Vongnes 137 C2
Vorbourg 122 C2
Vorder-Seiber 224 G5
Voriai Sporádhes 239 C4
Vösendorf 224 D2
Vosger, Champs de 67 F4
Vosgros 75 E4
Vöslauer Hauerberg 224 F1
Vosne, en 67 E2
Vosne-Romanée 55 C6, 57 C5, 65 G4
Vougeot 55 C6, 65 G6, 66 F2
Vougeot, Clos de 65 F5, 66 F1
Vougeots, les Petits 65 F6, 66 F2
Voulte-sur-Rhône, la 125 E4
Vouni 244 G2
Vouvray 115 B1, 118 C3
Vouvry 221 B1
Voyager Estate 287 E2
Vráble 230 G4
Vranje 233 F6
Vratsa 235 B2
Vredandal 290 C1
Vredenheim 293 G1
Vriesenhof 293 G2
Vufflens-le-Château 220 A5
Vukovar 233 C4
Vulcanesti 241 G5
Vulkanfelsen 165 E1
Vullierens 220 A5
Vully 219 E2
Vychodoslovenská 230 G6

Wachau 222 E4
Wachenheim 163 D4
Wachenheim an der Weinstrasse 143 C4, 161 B2, D4
Wachtberg 225 F4
Wagga Wagga 277 C4
Wagner 275 B4
Währing 224 B2
Waiau 288 E4
Waiheke Island 288 B4
Waikato 288 B4
Waipukurau 288 D5
Wairarapa 288 D4
Wairau Bar 289 G6
Wairau Pa 289 F5
Wairoa 288 C5
Waldäcker 223 B6
Waldböckelheim 143 B3, 155 C5
Waldheim 167 D5
Waldlaubersheim 155 A5
Waldrach 149 G5
Waldrue Heights 254 E3
Waldulm 165 D2
Walkenberg 159 F5
Wallaroo 276 B5
Walla Walla 271 C6
Wallhausen 155 B5
Walluf 159 G6
Walporzheim Ahrtal 143 A2
Wamakers-Vallei 293 A5
Wandin 281 C5
Wandin Park 281 C5
Wandin Valley 278 B5
Wanganui 288 C4
Wangaratta 277 C3, 280 D5
Wapato 272 F2
Wards Gateway Cellar 282 C3
Warpoo 282 C3
Warramate 281 C5
Warrenmang 280 E2
Warrnambool 277 D2, 280 G1
Wartbühl 165 D4
Warwick 293 E2
Wasco 267 G5
Washington 275 D4
Washington Hills Cellars 272 F3
Washougal 271 C3, 273 B6
Wasseros 159 E3
Wasson Bros 273 B6
Waterbrook 271 G4
Waterbury 275 C5
Waterloo 273 E5
Watervale 283 E5, F5
Water Wheel 280 D2
Watsons Creek 281 B3
Watzelsdorf 222 B2
Waurn Ponds 280 G3
Wawern 147 C2
Wedderburn 280 D2
Wehlen 143 B2, 152 E6
Weibel, *Mendocino* 256 B3
Weibel, *Santa Clara* 263 B3
Weiden 222 C4
Weifang 246 D4
Weihai 246 C6
Weikel 272 E2
Weilberg 161 A4
Weimar 143 A5
Weinböhla 167 C6
Weinheim 165 B3
Weinland 219 D4
Weinolsheim 163 C5
Weinsberg 165 C4
Weinsheim 155 C5
Weinsteige 165 D4
Weinviertel 222 E4
Weisenheim am Sand 161 A2
Weisenstein 153 G1
Weisinger's 271 G3
Weissenfels 143 A5, 167 C3
Weissenkirchen 222 B1, 224 G5
Weisser Stein 224 D2
Weitenberg 224 F5
Welgemeend 293 D3
Wellington, *Australia* 277 A5
Wellington, *New Zealand* 288 D4
Wellington, *S. Africa* 290 F2, 293 A5
Wellington, *USA* 254 E4
Wellington Wynboere 293 A5
Wellow 298 F4
Welmoed 292 G6
Wendelsheim 163 C4
Wendouree 283 D5
Wente Bros 263 A3
Wente Bros Sparkling Wine Cellars 263 A3
Wentworth 277 B2
Wermuth 259 A5
Werribee 280 F3
Wertheim 143 C6
Westfield 286 C2
Westhalten 120 F3, 122 B3
Westhofen 163 C5
West Linn 273 B5
Westport 288 D3
Westport Rivers 275 C6
West Richland 272 F5
West Slope 273 B5
West Stayton 273 D5
Weststeiermark 222 F4
Wettolsheim 120 E3, 122 C6
Whakatane 288 C5
Whaler 256 C3
Whangarei 288 A4
Wheeling 275 D2
Whitehall Lane 259 B6
White Oak 255 C5
White Rock 259 F5
White Salmon 271 C4
White Swan 272 F1
Whitfield 280 D5
Whitley Gardens 265 B4
Whitstone 298 G3
Whitstran 272 G4
Whyalla 276 A5
Wickham 298 F4
Widmer 275 B3
Wiemar 275 B4
Wien 222 C3, F4, 224 B3
Wiener Neustadt 222 D3
Wiesbaden 143 B4
Wiesloch 165 B3
Wignalls 286 G4
Wildcat 254 G5
Wildendürnbach 222 A3
Wild Horse 265 C3
Wildsau 159 E5
Wiley City 272 E2
Wilga 285 D5
Wilkes Barre 275 C4
Willamette Valley 271 D2
Willamette Valley Vyds 273 D4
Willamina 273 C3
Willespie 287 D2
William Hill 259 F6
Williams & Humbert 201 G1, G2
Williams & Selyem 255 D5
Williamsburg 275 E4
Williamstown 282 D3
William Wheeler 255 C4
Willows 282 A5
Willunga 276 C6, 284 E2
Wilmington 275 D4
Wilsford 282 C3
Wilson 283 E6
Wilson's 284 A4
Wilsonville 273 C5
Wiltingen 147 C3
Winchelsea 280 G2
Windesheim 155 B5
Windmeul 293 B4
Windsor, *Canada* 275 B1
Windsor, *USA* 255 D5
Wineck-Schlossberg 123 C2
Wine Group 267 B2
Winkel 158 G3
Winningen 143 A3
Winterhausen 166 C4
Winters 267 A1
Winterthur 219 D4
Wintrich 151 C3
Wintzenheim 120 E3, 122 C6
Winzenheim 155 B6, C2
Wipfeld 166 A5
Wirra Wirra 284 E2
Wisdom & Warter 201 G2
Wisselbrunnen 159 F1
Wissembourg 143 D3
Wisset 298 E6
Witchcliffe 287 F2
Witness Tree 273 C4
Wittelsheim 120 G3
Wittenheim 120 G4
Wittlich 143 B2
Wodonga 280 C6
Wolf 153 C3
Wolf Blass 282 A5
Wolf Creek 271 G2
Wolfsheim 163 B4
Wolfsmagen 165 A3
Wolfsworth 223 C5
Wolkersdorf 222 B3
Wollongong 277 B6
Wolxheim 120 A5
Wonga Park 281 C3
Wonnegau 143 C4
Wonthaggi 277 D3
Woodbourne 289 G4
Woodburn 271 D3, 273 C5
Woodbury 275 B3
Woodend 277 D3, 280 E3
Woodlake 267 E6
Woodland, *California* 267 A1
Woodland, *Washington* 271 C3
Woodlands 287 D1
Wood Orchard Heights 273 D4
Woodside 263 B2
Woodstock, *Australia* 284 D3
Woodstock, *USA* 275 C5
Woodward Canyon 271 G4
Woody 267 F6
Woody Nook Wines 287 C2
Woonsocket 275 B6
Woori Yallock 281 C6
Wootton 298 F4
Worcester, *S. Africa* 290 F2, F3
Worcester, *USA* 275 B6
Worms 143 C4, 163 D5
Wörrstadt 163 B4
Wren 273 E4
Wrexham 298 D3
Wrights 287 D2
Wuenheim 120 F3
Wülfen 159 E4
Wunnenstein 165 C4
Württemberg 143 D5
Württembergisch Unterland 143 D5, 165 C4
Würzberg 143 B6, 166 B4
Wurzen 167 C5
Würzgarten, *Bernkastel* 152 B5
Würzgarten, *Rheingau* 158 E5
Wybong 279 E3, E4
Wycheproof 280 C1
Wychwood 281 B4
Wyndham Estate 278 A6
Wynns 285 B5
Wynns High Eden 282 D5

Xanthi 239 A4
Xingcheng 246 B5
Xinji 246 C3
Xinjin 246 B6
Xintai 246 D4

Yakima 271 B4, 272 E2
Yakima River 272 G4
Yakima Valley 271 C5
Yallala 285 C6
Yallingup 287 B1
Yallourn 277 D3
Yalta 240 C2
Yalumba 282 B5
Yamanashi 248 D4
Yambol 235 C4
Yamhill 273 B4
Yamhill Valley 273 C4
Yanggu 246 D3
Yanqing 246 B3
Yanshan 246 C4
Yantai 246 C5
Yantai Chang Yu Pioneer Winery 246 C5
Yarra Burn 281 C6
Yarra Edge 281 C3
Yarra Glen 280 F4, 281 B4
Yarra Junction 281 C6
Yarra Ridge 281 B4
Yarra Valley 277 D3, 280 F4
Yarrawa 279 G3
Yarrawonga 280 C5
Yarra Yarra 281 A4
Yarra Yering 281 C5
Yass 277 B5
Yea 280 E4
Yecla 197 D4
Yellowglen 280 F2
Yens 220 A5
Yerasa 244 G2
Yerbas Buenas 297 G4
Yerevan 240 D5
Yering 281 B4
Yeringberg 281 B5
Yering Grange 281 B4
Yering Station 281 B4
Yerushalayim (Jerusalem) 243 F4
Yetto 284 D2
Ye Xian 246 D5
Yialousa 244 E5
Yingkou 246 B6
Ynocente 201 C3
Yonkers 275 C5
York 275 D4
York Mountain 265 C2, C3
Young 277 B4
Youngstown 275 C2
Yountville 259 E4
Yuncheng 246 E3
Yungarra Estate 287 B2
Yungay 295 E2
Yverdon, *Switzerland* 219 F2
Yverdon, *USA* 259 C2
Yvorne 219 F2, 221 B1

Zaca Mesa 265 F5
Zacatecas 269 F5
Zaccar 245 A4
Zadar 233 C2
Zaer 245 B2
Zagarolo 187 F4, 193 C5, D6
Zagreb 233 B3
Zahodnomoravski 233 E5
Zakinthos (Zante) 239 D2
Zalaegerszeg 226 F1
Zalhostice 230 E2
Zambelli Mount Anakie Estate 280 F3
Zambujal, Qta do 210 F2
Zandwijk 293 D4
Zarzuela 201 D2
Zarzuela, La 201 D2
Zayante 263 C2
Z-D 259 D4
Zehnmorgen 162 D5
Zeiskram 161 C2
Zeitz 143 A5, 167 D4
Zeletin 237 C5
Zell 143 B2
Zell (Untermosel) 143 A2
Zellenberg 120 D4, 123 C4
Zeltingen-Rachtig 152 D5
Zema Estate 285 C5
Zemmour 245 B2
Zenata 245 B2
Zeneggen 221 C5
Zenevredo 177 E5
Zeni 184 B5
Zeppwingert 153 C4
Zerhoun 245 B2
Zermatt 219 G3
Zernez 219 F6
Zemograd 240 B4
Zeutern 165 C3
Zg.-Duplek 231 B4
Zhanhua 246 C4
Zhucheng 246 D5
Zhuo Xian 246 B3
Zibo 246 D4
Zichron-Yaacov 243 F4
Ziem 275 D3
Ziersdorf 222 B2
Zilina 230 F4
Zillah 272 F3
Zillah Oakes 272 F3
Zimbro, Qta do 211 E2
Zinfandel 259 D4
Zingarini 193 E3
Zinnkoepfle 122 B3
Zistersdorf 222 B3
Zitsa 239 B2
Zlaté Moravce 230 G4
Z Moore 255 D5
Znojmo 230 G3
Znojmo/Mikulov 230 F3
Zoete Inval, De 293 D4
Zollturm 153 D4
Zonguldak 243 B3
Zoopiyi 244 G2
Zsadányi 229 E4
Zuckerberg 162 F5
Zug 219 E4
Zugdidi 240 C4
Zupa 233 D5
Zürich 219 E4
Zwenkau 167 C4
Zwickau 143 A5

Acknowledgments

France: F André (ONIVIN, Avignon); Anthony Barton (Bordeaux), Alain Berger and Agnès Payan (Institut National des Appellation d'Origine (INAO), Paris); Jean-Claude Berrouet (Château Pétrus); Paul Bonfils and Prof. Denis Boubals, (Montpellier); Stéphanie Bouachon (CIVCRVR, Avignon); Pierre Bouard (CIVA, Alsace); Yves Cariou (CIVAS, Angers); Cognac Information Centre (London) and Bureau National Interprofessionel du Cognac; Philippe Cottin (Château Mouton-Rothschild); Pascal Delbeck (Château Ausone); Jean Delmas (Château Haut Brion); M Duhaze (CIVRB, Bergerac); André Enders (Comité Interprofessionnel des Vins de Champagne); Eric Fournier (Syndicat Viticole de St-Emilion); Alain Fraty (INAO, Mâcon); Catherine Frugère (CIVCP, Provence); François Gaignet; Bill Hardy; Nicolas Joly (La Coulée de Serrant); Edouard Kabakian (INAO, Gaillac); Tony Laithwaite and Claudie Gomme (La Clarière, Castillon); C Lamoulie (BNIA, Armagnac); Jacques de Lamy (Conseil Interprofessionnel des Vins Fitou, Corbières et Minèrvois); Prof. Noël Leneuf (Dijon); Christian Le Sommer (Château Latour); Le Comte de Lur Saluces (Ch. Yquem); Alain Macaire (Office National des Forêts); Jean-Laurent Maillard (ANIVIT, Paris); Catherine Manac'h and Sylvie Vallejo (SOPEXA, London); Anne Marbot (CIVB, Bordeaux); Jean Miailhe (Syndicat des Crus Bourgeois du Médoc); Christine Ontivero (CIVDN (Vins Doux Naturels), Perpignan); Paul Pontallier (Château Margaux); Gérard Potel (Volnay); Bruno Prats and Claudine Izabelle (Syndicat des Grands Crus Classés du Médoc); Lucien Rateau (BIVB, Beaune); Gilbert Rokvam (Château Lafite); Philippe Roudié (University of Bordeaux); Peter A Sichel (Château d'Angludet, Cantenac); Société Civile du Cheval Blanc (St-Emilion); Robert Tinlot (Office International de la Vigne et du Vin (OIV), Paris); Georges Vernay (Condrieu); Claude Vialade-Salvagnac (Maison des Terroirs en Corbières); James E Wilson (Colorado)
Germany: Bernhard Breuer; Gary and Marlies Grosvenor; Tan Harrington, Martin Olheim and Barbara Tysome (German Wine Information Service, London); Fritz Haag; Dr Franz Werner Michel (German Wine Institute, Mainz); Stuart S Pigott; Michael Prinz zu Salm-Salm and Hilke Nagel (Verband Deutscher Prädikats und Qualitätsweingüter); Manfred Völpel (Deinhard's, Koblenz)
Italy: Marchese Lodovico Antinori, Christa Sutta and Claudia Stagi (Tenuta dell'Ornellaia); Marchese Piero and Albiera Antinori. Dr Gioacchino la Franca and Valeria Nebbio (Italian Trade Centre, London); Professor Mario Fregoni; Alois Laegeder (Alto Adige); Andreas März; Marchese Niccolò Incisa della Rocchetta (Tenuta san Guido);
Spain: Wines from Spain (London); John Radford; Jan Read; Bartolmé Vergara (Jerez)
Portugal: Dr José Leitão and Oliveira Silva (Portuguese Government Trade Office, London); David Orr; Baron Eric de Rothschild; Paul Symington (Silva & Cosens Ltd);
Madeira: Richard Blandy; John Cossart (Henriques & Henriques); Madeira Wine Company, Funchal; Paul Symington (Silva & Cosens Ltd)
Switzerland: Daniel Lehmann (Swiss Wine Growers Association, Lausanne), Anja Tschannen (Berne)
Austria: Fritz Ascher and Peter Schleimer (Osterreichische Weinmarketingserviceges MbH, Vienna); Geoffrey Kelly (Austrian Wine Information Service, London)
Hungary: Prof. Dr Á Ásvány (Országos Borminösitö Intézet); Dr Julius László; Istvan Müller (Tokaj Kereskedöház Rt); Samuel Tinon, Peter Vinding-Diers (Royal Tokaji Wine Company); Hungarian Wine Traders Association
Czech Republic and Slovakia: Vladimir Moskvan (Moravia)
Slovenia and former Yugoslavia: Ian Wraight, Pegasus Trade (Slovenia); Profs Kos and Sikovec, V Milat, B Stancl, Joco Znidarsic (Ljubljana)
Bulgaria: Ivan Zahariev (Bulgarian Vintners Co. Ltd); Margo Todorov (Domaine Boyar)
Romania: Dr Julius László; Dan Muntean (Halewood Vintners Ltd, Liversedge); Romanian Embassy (London)
Greece: Y Boutaris (J Boutari & Son, Thessaloniki); Maggie McNie and Colin Deane (Greek Wine Bureau, London); Maria Xanthopoulou (Tsantalis SA, Halkidiki)
Russia, Ukraine, Moldova: Dr sc. Günter R W Arnold; Martyn Assirati (Russian Wine Company); Prince Yuri Galitzine; David Molyneux-Berry MW; Anthony Taylor and Cécile Debroas; Serena Sutcliffe MW (Sotheby's, London)
The Eastern Mediterranean countries: Serge Hochar (Château Musar, Beirut); Mehmet A Masman (Kavaklidere Saraplari AS, Ankara); Adam Montefiore (Golan Heights Winery); Ephraim Sofer (Carmel, Rishon-le-Zion)
Cyprus: Stelios Damianou (KEO UK Ltd); Andreas Hambakis (Cyprus Trade Centre, London); Cleopatra Vrionides (ETKO Ltd, Limassol)
North Africa: Jean-Philippe Azais (Wm Pitters International); Comptoir des vins du Maroc (Brussels); Sincomar Parlier & Fermaud (Casablanca);
Asia: Jean-Marc Lieberherr, Nobuko Nishioka (Jardines Wine and Spirits KK); Gabriel Tam (Huadong Winery); Denis Degache (Dragon Seal Wines)
The United States: *California*: Bob and Harolyn Thompson; Donn and Molly Chappellet; James Lider (Napa); Andrew Montague and Fiona Leyland (Wine Institute of California, London); Stephanie Short (Wine Institute of California, San Francisco); Janet Trefethen and Jan Stuebing (Trefethen Winery)
Southwest States and Mexico: John J Baxevanis; Tim H. Dodd (Texas Wine Marketing Research Institute, Lubbock); Susan Dunn (Texas Dept of Agriculture, Austin); Sarah Jane English (Austin); Richard Jones (Sapello, New Mexico); Mexican Tourist Office (London); Francisco Mora-Figueroa (Domecq Internacional, SA); Ellen Veseth (New Mexico); Blanca Villarello (Mexican Embassy, London)
Pacific Northwest: David R Beaudry; Kenneth Christie MW; Marie Hardie (Washington Wine Commission); Kelly Olsen (Idaho Department of Agriculture); Roxanne Langer (Pacific Northwest Wine Coalition, Seattle); Doreen Waitt (Oregon Wine Advisory Board)
Northeast States: Howard Goldberg (*New York Times*); Jim Trezise (New York Wine & Grape Foundation);
Canada: British Columbia Wine Institute; Richard Feldkamp (Château des Charmes, Ontario); Michel Phaneuf
Australia: Australian High Commission (London); Len Evans; Sue Bussau (Margaret River Wine Industry Association); Graeme Haggart; James Halliday; Hazel Murphy and Cameron Hills (Austrade/Australian Wine Export Council, London/Magill, SA);
New Zealand: Vicky Bishop (New Zealand Trade Development Board, London); Bob Campbell (Auckland); Philip Gregan and Kate Kumarich (Wine Institute of New Zealand, Auckland); Kevin Judd (Marlborough)
South Africa: Tim Hamilton-Russell; Dr Julius László (Montestell Wines); John and Erica Platter; Rupert Ponsonby and Lucy Meager (Wines of South Africa, London); Nick Pryke (Bergvlei)
Argentina: Alejandro Castro (Asociacion Vitivinicola Argentina); Dereck Foster (Buenos Aires); Eduardo Rodolfo Garat (Bodegas y Vinedos Santa Ana)
Chile: Jorge Eyzaguirre; Douglas Murray, Aurelio Montes (Discover Wine Lda); Jan Read; F Hafemann and H Saez (Embassy of Chile, London); Wines of Chile (London)
England and Wales: Cdr G L Bond MBE (English Vineyards Association); Stephen Skelton

General: Berry Bros & Rudd (London); Michael Broadbent MW (Christie's, London); Caxton Tower Wines (Middlesex); Deinhard & Co. (London); Alison Franks; Hiram-Walker Group; Harvey's of Bristol; House of Hallgarten (Luton); O W Loeb (London); Mentzendorff (London); Mark Savage MW; Office International de la Vigne et du Vin (OIV), Paris; the regional Comités Interprofessionnels in France, Weinbauämter in Germany, Consorzi in Italy, Consejos Reguladores in Spain, the commercial counsellors of London Embassies of all winegrowing countries; university departments, and scores of growers, shippers, merchants and wine-lovers all over the world.

Photographs

Soprintendenza Archeologica delle Province di Napoli e Casserta 13 top; Ashmolean Museum, Oxford 12 below; Aspect Picture Library /Brian Seed 291; Bavaria Verlag /Rudolf Holtappel 164; Bayerische Landesanstalt fur Weinbau u. Gartenbau Wurzburg/Veitshochheim/Bildarchiv Kurt Furtner 166 below; Berry Bros & Rudd 16 below; Anthony Blake Photo Library /Gerrit Buntrock 156 top left; Bohnacker /F Prenzel 186; Boys Syndication /Michael Boys 171, 190; Bridgeman Art Library 246; Cephas Picture Library /Jerry Alexander 260, /Nigel Blythe 146, 148, 149, 247, /R & K Muschenetz 264, /Fred R Palmer 274, /Alain Proust 18 below right, /Mick Rock 23 below, 28 top, 34 below, 52, 65 left, 98, 121, 124 182 185, 188, 192 194, 196, 198 top, 202, 204 right, 204 left, 222, 227, 234, 236 left, 238, 252, 257, 262 left, 262 right 266, 272, 276 283 top, /Peter Stowell 230; Christie's London 44; Colorific 28 below, Crown Zellerbach Corp. 250–1; Sally Cushing 47 right; Denbies Wine Estate 298; Robert Dieth 150, 152 156 top right, 163 below left, 167; Patrick Eagar 63, 66, 74 left, 119, 127, 156 below, 279, 283 below, 285; Editions des Deux Coqs d'Or 92; Mary Evans Picture Library /I R & G Cruikshank 6; Explorer /F Jalain 54, 58, 60, 128, / Ly Loirat 232, /C Nardin 140, /P Thomas 23 top, /Rapa 220, 221; D J Flanagan /Buffalo 250–1; Werner Forman Archive 12 top; Konstantin Frank 250–1; Giraudon 15 top, 40 top; Guy Gravett 73, 102, 104 below; Susan Griggs Agency /Monique Jacot 218; Peter Hallgarten 157; Robert Harding Picture Library 46 top, /Fin Costello 198 below, /Nedra Westwater 267, /AdamWoolfit 81 below left, 81 below right, 81 top, 162; Historisches Museum der Pfalz Speyer/ Rhein 41; Michael Holford Photographs 14–15 below; Claude Huyghens 110; Tim Imrie 46–7 below, 47 top; By Courtesy of the Italian State Tourist Office (E.N.I.T.) London l78, 193; Hugh Johnson 209, 214 left, 214 right; Nicolas Joly 114; Kevin Judd 289; Fred Lyons 268 below, 268 top; Pierre Mackiewicz 18; Giles MacDonogh 236 right; Mauritius Bildagentur 225; James Merrell /Bibendum, 81 Fulham Rd, London SW3 51, /Pfälzer Weinprobierstube in der Residenz München, 80085 Munich 141, /La Famiglia, 7 Laughton St, London SW10 169 /Clarke's, 124 Kensington Church St, London W8 249; Bruno Murialdo 174; Musée des Arts et Traditions Populaires, Paris 34 top right; Picturepoint 216; Reading Museum 13 top right; Reed Consumer Books Picture Library /Kim Sayer 50, /Alan Williams 180; Réunion des Musées Nationaux /Philippe Mercier 16 top; Marc Riboud 104 top; David Ross 86; The John Rylands University Library of Manchester 14 top; Scope /Jean-Luc Barde 68–9, 200 right, /Frederic Hadengue 28 centre, /Jacques Guillard 65 right, 74 right, 116–17, 122, 130, 136, 200 left, 210, 211, 212–13, /Michel Guillard 22, 82, 84, 90 below, 90 top, 97, 100, 228 below, /Jacques Sierpinski 110, /Jean-Daniel Sudres 106; Sotheby's 240; Rodney Todd-White 166 top; Tokaj House of Commerce Co., 228 top; Viña Santa Ema 296; Visionbank /Colin Maher 9, 77, 163 below right, /Jon Wyand 154, 172; Philip Wagner 250–1; Alan Williams 109, 134. 138, Wines of South Africa /Schoongezicht, Rustenberg Estate 292–3; Zefa Picture Library 70, 112, /Allstock/David Barnes 258, /W Hasenberg 294, /John M Roberts 270, /Rossenbach 160; Joco Znidarsic 231.

Illustrations

Revisions and new illustrations and diagrams for this edition: Fiona Bell-Currie 25, 27; Bill Donohoe 32–3, 35; Paul Drayson 41; Paul Hogarth 2–3, 30–1; Lovell Johns 11; Radius 10, 17 right; Colin Rose 82, 144; Sue Sharples 20; Ed Stuart 56; Paul Tilby 50, 52, 54, 83, 111, 142, 170, 198, 211, 252, 277, 291; Keith Williams 45; Annabel Wilson 36–7, 38–9

Original illustrations: Norman Barber, Roger Bristow, Marilyn Bruce, Ray Burrows, David Cook, Diagram, Chris Forsey, David Fryer, Gilchrist Studios, Grundy & Northedge, Patrick Leeson, Michael McGuinness, Vernon Mills, Peter Morter, Shirley Parfitt, Charles Pickard, Quad, Rodney Shackell, Sue Sharples, Lesli Sternberg, Alan Suttie, and Peter Wrigley.

Picture Researcher: Anna Smith

Every effort has been made to trace the owners of copyright photographs and illustrations. Anyone who may have been inadvertently omitted from this list is invited to write to the publishers who will be pleased to make any necessary amendments to future printings of this publication.